Management and the Arts

Fourth Edition

William J. Byrnes

Foreword by Dan J. Martin

Focal Press
Taylor & Francis Group

NEW YORK AND LONDON

First published 1999 by Focal Press
This edition published 2008 by Focal Press
70 Blanchard Road, Suite 402, Burlington, MA 01803

Simultaneously published in the UK by Focal Press
2 Park Square, Milton Park, Abingdon, Oxon OX14 4RN

Focal Press is an imprint of the Taylor & Francis Group, an informa business

Library of Congress Cataloging-in-Publication Data
Byrnes, William J.
 Management and the arts / William J. Byrnes ; foreword by Dan J. Martin. -- 4th ed.
  p. cm.
 Includes bibliographical references and index.
 ISBN 978-0-240-81004-1 (pbk. : alk. paper) 1. Arts—United States—Management. I. Title.
 NX765.B87 2009
 700.68--dc22
                                                                        2008026268

ISBN: 978-0-240-81004-1 (pbk)

Contents

FOREWORD ix
PREFACE.. xiii
ACKNOWLEDGMENTS.. xix

CHAPTER 1 Management and the Arts.................................. 1
The business of arts and entertainment 2
Managers and organizations 6
The management process.. 15
Selecting a project organization.. 20
References.. 20

CHAPTER 2 Arts Organizations and Arts Management................... 23
The artist–manager 23
Arts institutions.. 24
A brief historical overview.. 25
The modern arts organization 34
Profile of the arts manager... 39
The growth of the arts manager role and the NEA 45
Goals 46
NEA.. 46
Conclusion... 52
Summary.. 52
Discussion article — managing the arts today 54
References.. 56

CHAPTER 3 Management History and Trends 59
Management as an art and a social science........................... 60
Evolution of management thought 62
Management trends to the present 66
Human relations management (1927 to present) 70
Modern management... 73 **v**

Conclusion...78
Summary...79
References...80

CHAPTER 4   The Adaptive Arts Organization...................................83
Competitive adaptation 84
Changing environments...86
Managing change...86
Growth and change...87
Content analysis 89
Assessing environments...91
Information sources...108
The impact of future trends on the arts.....................113
Summary..115
Suggested additional readings...................................117
References...119

CHAPTER 5   Planning and Decision Making.....................................121
Mission, vision, and values statement.....................122
The context of planning 122
Developing a planning process for the arts.............128
Strategy summary 137
Goals, objectives, action plans, and evaluation 138
Limits of planning..143
Decision making in planning 146
Decision theory 148
Conclusion...149
Summary..150
References..152
Additional Resources 153

CHAPTER 6   Organizing and Organizational Design 155
Life in organizations..156
The management function of organizing 156
Organizational design approaches 157
Organizational structure and charts.........................161
Informal organizational structure.............................169
Structure from an arts manager's perspective.........170
Coordination...176
Organizational growth 179
Corporate culture and the arts 180
Summary..182
References..185

CHAPTER 7   Human Resources and the Arts 187

Staffing the organization.. 188
The staffing process 188
The overall matrix of jobs 194
Constraints on staffing.. 195
Recruitment.. 197
Diversity in the arts workplace 199
Selection process 199
Orientation and training 202
Performance appraisals and firing 204
Volunteers in the arts.. 206
The board of directors 208
Unions and the arts 209
Maintaining and developing the staff.................................. 214
Summary... 216
Resource 217
Sample employee manual 218
References.. 219

CHAPTER 8   Leadership and Group Dynamics................................ 221

The central role of the leader.. 222
Leadership fundamentals 222
Formal and informal leadership modes 223
Power: a leadership resource... 225
Approaches to the study of leadership................................. 229
Leadership and the creative spirit 234
Future leadership?... 236
Motivation and the arts work setting 236
Theories of motivation 236
Theory integration... 244
Group dynamics... 245
Leadership and working with the board of directors........... 251
Communication basics and effective leadership 254
Conclusion.. 258
Summary... 258
Additional resource 261
Leadership books and resources.. 262
References.. 262

CHAPTER 9   Operations and Budgeting 265

Operational control as a management function................... 266
Elements of the operational control process 267

Management information systems 276
Budgets and the control system.. 284
From the budget to cash flow.. 294
Summary... 296
References.. 299

CHAPTER 10 Economics and Financial Management........................ 301
The economic big picture 302
The economic problems and issues facing the arts 302
The economic environment and the arts.............................. 308
The economics of spending more than you make 310
The multiplier effect and the arts 311
Applying basic economic principles to the arts................... 312
Elasticity change formula 319
Overview of financial management 324
Nonprofit financial management... 325
FMIS.. 326
Accounting and bookkeeping.. 329
Managing finances and the economic dilemma................... 339
Looking ahead... 340
Creating a financial report 341
Web source for financial statements..................................... 342
Other resources on arts economics and finance 342
References.. 343

CHAPTER 11 Marketing and the Arts 345
The marketing landscape 346
The search for the audience 347
Marketing principles and terms 348
Evolution of modern marketing... 352
Marketing Management 356
Strategic marketing plans.. 363
Conclusion... 372
Summary... 373
Additional Resources 376
References.. 377

CHAPTER 12 Fundraising... 379
Giving history and trends 380
Why do people give? 380
Fundraising and the arts.. 382
Management skills of the fundraiser 391

The case for support... 391

Data management 393

Fundraising costs and control 395

Fundraising techniques and tools................................. 396

The comprehensive campaign 397

Corporate giving.. 405

Foundations 407

Government funding 409

Conclusion.. 411

Summary... 412

Additional resources 413

References... 417

CHAPTER 13 Integrating Management Styles and Theories 419

Management styles 419

Management models.. 427

The organization as an open system 430

The contingency system: an integrating approach............. 430

Personnel management board, staff, labor, and relations.... 434

Fiscal management 436

Governmemt relations.. 437

Conclusion.. 438

Reference.. 441

CHAPTER 14 Career Options and Preparing for the Job Market 443

The evolving arts workplace 443

Where the jobs are and will be..................................... 444

Personal choices and selection criteria........................ 445

Develop a personal plan... 445

From the employer's perspective 446

Compensation issues 446

Career development options 450

Organizing Your Job Search 453

Building a career.. 460

Career development work plan 462

References... 463

INDEX... 465

Foreword

You are tired of hearing it. You roll your eyes and stifle your yawn every time you hear it. The adage has become a cliché.

"The only constant in life is change."

But you hear it again and again and again because it is a *truism*, clichéd or not.

The core challenge for us as arts managers is to deal with change: changing external environmental conditions, evolving styles and approaches to the arts by our artists, the advancements in how we present and distribute the art to our ever-changing audiences, and the shifting competition for resources and attention.

The only aspect of the process of creation, presentation, and preservation of art that has *not* changed since human life began is the inextinguishable impulse of artists to create. In spite of what naysayers have preached for years — that current economic or social conditions are not conducive to the creative process — artists continue to write, paint, sing, dance, sculpt, or act. As they always have. I'm convinced that the *second*-oldest profession on earth is that of artist. I also would suggest that the *third*-oldest profession is that of arts manager. I am sure that once early humans began sharing stories by the fire and creating drawings to illustrate their ideas or histories, there were arts managers helping promote the artists' events and conserve their creative products. Artists always will create new work, as they cannot help but respond to their inner creative passions and to the influences of the world around them. And we, as managers, need to facilitate both the creative process of our artists and provide venues for the appreciation of their work.

Our responsibilities as arts managers within the not-for-profit sector are daunting. Internally, we are charged with providing an atmosphere for artists to develop and realize their visions with resources that would otherwise be unavailable — or, at least, greatly diminished — if left to the pressures of the traditional free-market system. Externally, we must bring audiences to the work in as effective and efficient a manner as possible, and to do so with them eager and well-prepared for those experiences. Because of the reality of constant change, the management process never gets easier. With each passing day, as new situations and new realities confront us, some managers hunker down when these conditions are unfavorable and wait for life to "return to normal." Unfortunately, that never happens. As George Thorn, author and consultant, observed some years ago, "The current condition is the new 'normal.' There is no going 'back.'" We must adapt to the new realities and continue to serve our artistic missions to the best of our abilities.

As a result of the constantly changing environments, the key to being good managers is much more than simply knowing *what* to do; we also need to know *why* we do what we do — the theoretical foundations and fundamental principles that drive our actions. When *what* we are doing stops working for us, those basic concepts will help us understand *why*; they will inspire our creative thinking and help us modify our efforts to address the new conditions.

Being well-positioned to address and resolve challenges we face through this state of constant change requires an education, whether it is in the classroom, on the job, in professional development programs, or through informal inquiry. The most successful managers know that the best education is a combination of all four of those educational systems, or, simply put, lifelong learning.

Management and the Arts contributes to the life-long learning of today's arts managers, whether they are presently inquisitive students of the field or seasoned managers. In this book, William Byrnes does more than simply introduce the fundamentals of management as they are applied to the arts and entertainment fields. He provides us with a context for the management process and helps us understand the implications of our actions as managers — the ripple effect on our institutions, our partners, and our stakeholders. As we have learned from other industries and our ever more connected and interdependent world, actions have impact far beyond the visible landscape and with more than the expected collaborators. This is no less true in the arts. And in this book Mr. Byrnes provides a well-constructed map for navigating through the intersecting, interwoven, and sometimes conflicting issues, strategies, and opportunities. Those interested in beginning a career in arts management could not ask for a better introduction to the field. Working professionals will develop additional confidence in their skills as they come to understand more of the theoretical underpinnings of their work.

As the struggle intensifies to fulfill our artistic missions without weakening the institutional foundation, arts managers need every advantage they can get. *Management and the Arts* is a vital tool in confronting those challenges.

Dan J. Martin
Director, Institute for the Management of Creative Enterprises
Carnegie Mellon University
www.artsnet.org

Preface

It is hard to believe that what started as a personal project to help make teaching an interdisciplinary course in arts management a little easier fifteen years ago would have evolved into a textbook used around the world. When I first began teaching arts management, I had to use several textbooks to build the kind of interdisciplinary approach to the field I wanted. I set about writing this text with the goal of blending management theory and practice, economics, personnel management, marketing, and fundraising with the performing and visual arts. The focus of the book remains on the process of managing an arts organization through integrating many different disciplines.

There has been a great deal of change over the last fifteen years in the world that artists and arts organizations must survive every day. The process of operating an organization and producing productions or mounting an exhibition has been assisted in many ways by the improvements in technology. On the other hand, the way things get done in the arts is still very much the same as it has always been.

The performer might walk into the rehearsal hall listening to a set stage manager or director notes from yesterday's rehearsal downloaded from a Web site to their MP3 player. However, when it comes time for the rehearsal to start, the technology is set aside and a timeless process of engaging with a script, score, libretto, or the other members of the ensemble begins. Or, the museum or gallery director may finish recording the guided tour of the current exhibition for visitors to enjoy on their cell phone, but they still have to take a moment to walk over and straighten the artwork on the wall.

In many ways it is fascinating to ponder what the future will bring for the arts in our world. We all know that the struggle to make a life in the arts and arts management continues. Making a living in the arts can have a great many intrinsic rewards and in many cases those rewards are enough. However, we live in a world where the rewards for pursuing one's passion is not always rewarded.

Arts organizations, the majority of which are very small businesses, continue to face the challenges of paying the electric bill while contemplating reaching new audiences of all ages. All the challenges may be discouraging at times, but artists and arts managers also recognize the difference they can make in their community and in the world. Seeing the kind of transformative impact the arts can produce demonstrates the significance and value that far surpass the economic impact.

This book is intended for use in an arts administration or theater management course. However, it is also written for those working in the field who wish to expand their knowledge and understanding of many of the key management principles that underpin the business of running an arts organization. I have tried to provide examples and links to resources that arts managers can apply to their job today.

In the context of a college or university course, this book is designed to give the student an overview of the evolving field of arts management while introducing key concepts in management, marketing, and fundraising. I have assumed that the student has had some course work in the arts, even if only at the introductory level. Although every topic may not receive all of the attention it may deserve, it is hoped that the reader's interest in a specific topic will lead to an exploration of the other resources suggested in the sidebars or at the end of most chapters.

In the process of writing the fourth edition, I found it necessary to revise and update many of the news items and illustrations. In the time between the third and fourth edition an amazing array of resources have become available to arts managers via the World Wide Web. I have tried to select Web site links to allow readers to expand their involvement with the contents of the book. Of course, I cannot guarantee all these Web sites will serve your needs (or that all the links will be current), but my goal is to expand your search for information and increase your personal research tools.

Over the last 15-plus years, the phenomenal growth of access to information that is only seconds away has been nothing short of spectacular. Everything from online strategic planning software to donor tracking systems at a fraction of the cost they were just ten years ago is available to today's arts manager. At the same time, the ability of the arts manager to directly communicate with their audiences 24/7 is as exhilarating as it is daunting. It is truly an exciting time to be an arts manager.

This book continues to evolve but still has at its core the underlying belief that it is important to develop managers in the arts who have sensitivity, use common sense, and apply skills from disciplines such as business, technology, finance, economics, and psychology. Keeping the art in arts management may sound like a simplistic slogan. However, as anyone who has been in the field for a while will tell you, it is harder to do than one would think.

My central premise is that an arts manager's purpose is to help an organization and its artists realize its vision and fulfill the mission. Keeping the dream alive that started the organization and then continually advancing it is worth waking up for every morning. This lofty-sounding pursuit is grounded in the assumption that an effective arts manager helps bring to the public the unique benefits of the arts experience. There are different ways to describe this experience. For example, when a musical note is sung or played perfectly, or a dance movement seems to defy gravity or triggers an emotion or creates a realization, we experience something unique. Sometimes a painting, sculpture, or photograph provides an indescribable pleasure as we stand there viewing it. When we go to the theater and witness a scene that is acted with such power and conviction that it gives us chills, we are enriched. Working to bring these experiences to others is a supremely worthwhile endeavor to pursue.

Although this book makes no pretense of having all the answers about how best to go about maximizing the arts experience or operating the perfect organization, it is my hope that it will provide information and guidance about how an arts manager can be as effective as possible given the resources available. The information and ideas contained in this text are intended to be a springboard for developing your own schematic for leading and managing in the arts. Best wishes in your efforts.

ORGANIZATION OF THE TEXT

Here is a brief overview of the 4th edition of *Management and the Arts*.

Chapter 1 has a new title and provides an overview of types and levels of management found in arts organizations. The management process is also discussed and sample mission and vision statements are highlighted.

Chapter 2 has a new title and has also been updated. The chapter examines the historical origins of arts organizations as well as profiles the evolution of arts management. A sample business plan is included along with an updated section on the job of the arts manager today.

Chapter 3 introduces the reader to the evolution of management theory from ancient times to the present. This chapter is an overview of many of the key systems and people that contributed to what makes up the field of management. The basic concepts of systems and contingency management are introduced. Updates have been added to include some of the latest trends in the field of management.

Chapter 4 has a new title and has been revised to reflect the many changes that have taken place in the world in the last few years. However, the focus of the chapter is still on the relationship of the arts organization to the many external forces that shape how our society functions today. The section on content analysis has been revised and each of the external environments has been updated. The goal of this chapter remains to provoke your own pondering about what the future may bring.

Chapter 5 has been reorganized to better outline strategic planning and the decision-making process and a SWOT chart has been added.

Chapter 6 analyzes the principles of organizing and how organizations are designed. Organizational charts for several different types of arts organizations have been updated. The section on corporate culture has been rewritten.

Chapter 7 has a new title that reflects the integration of human resource management with strategic planning and organizational design. The goal is to show various methods for designing jobs, recruiting employees, selecting staff, and providing job enrichment.

Chapter 8 outlines the major concepts of leadership theory, including trait, behavior, and contingency leadership approaches, group dynamics, and behavior. I have also added more about working with boards and running meetings.

Chapter 9 has a new title and been revised to cover management information systems and the budgeting processes required to effectively operate an arts organization. The sections on control and resource allocation have been revised.

Chapter 10 has also been reorganized and updated. This chapter examines basic economic concepts and financial management techniques as applied to the arts. Concepts in the areas of supply and demand are related to arts organizations. Current and classic studies of the economics of the performing arts are also highlighted. Reading and understanding financial statements and the basics of financial planning are also discussed.

Chapter 11 has been updated to reflect many of the new marketing and audience development strategies explored via the Internet. A section on brand management has been added as well as new resource suggestions.

Chapter 12 has been updated to reflect many current practices in the field of development and fundraising. The basic focus of this chapter remains on ways that an organization can increase its revenues to meet its mission. The fundraising audit, strategic planning, working with different categories of funders, and the techniques of fundraising are discussed.

Chapter 13 has a new title and has been refreshed and revised in an effort to better integrate the revisions throughout the book. The chapter goal is still focused on developing an integrated system for applying the previous twelve chapters.

Chapter 14 has a new title and has been revised in this edition. Compensation and issues related to using technology to enhance the job search have been added.

OTHER HIGHLIGHTS OF THIS EDITION

Each chapter has several new sidebars and many of the chapters have all new case studies or discussion topics. I have kept the list of terms and concepts and discussion questions at the end of each chapter to promote in-class dialog opportunities. I have also updated many of the lists of references for further reading in related topics. Wherever possible I have tried to revise the illustrations to provide better visualizations of the concepts discussed in the chapter.

WEB SITE RESOURCE

Last, but certainly not least, this book now has a Web site that may be accessed at www.managementandthearts.com. I encourage instructors, students, and arts managers to explore further questions or ideas related to each chapter at the Web site. In addition, a sample course syllabus with additional project assignments and other suggested resources is available at the Web site. You may also participate in a blog at the site or e-mail me at byrnes@ managementandthearts.com. Over time, I plan to expand the Web site as an up-to-date complement to the book for general readers, instructors, and students.

I will also be happy to send instructors the answers to the dance company financial report used in Chapter 10. In addition, I welcome suggestions, corrections, or questions about this edition of the book. Thank you.

Acknowledgments

The fourth edition of *Management and the Arts* was a true team effort. I will try to do my best to thank all the people who have contributed to this effort. As always, I am deeply grateful for the assistance of my wife Christine over the eight months it took to research, revise, update, and write this edition.

I could not have completed this work without the support of Southern Utah University for my research and scholarship. The feedback and resources from the students in our arts administration graduate program at SUU has been invaluable. Our seminar classes have been a source of constant new ideas and perspectives about managing and leading in the arts. I'd specifically like to thank Anna Ables, Julie Harker Hall, Shannon Sundberg, and Elizabeth Van Vleck for source material used in this edition. Thanks to the many instructors who have used previous editions of *Management and the Arts*. Your questions and suggestions were very helpful in shaping this new edition.

I also want to thank my colleagues here in Cedar City at the Utah Shakespearean Festival for being part of an active and engaging dialog about how arts organizations can sustain, change, and thrive in these challenging times. Thanks to Fred C. Adams, R. Scott Phillips, Cameron Harvey, Douglas Cook, Kathleen Conlin, J.R. Sullivan, Todd Ross, Michael Bahr, and the dedicated staff of USF. Thank you for affording me the opportunity to be part of the Festival in my own small way.

I am also indebted to Patrick Overton and Jim Volz for sharing their observations and varied perspective about the challenges and triumphs of managing the arts in America. I would be remiss if I didn't also acknowledge the contribution to my ongoing education made possible by working with Donna Law of the Orlando Shakespeare Theater, Kerry McCarthy and Helene Bleiberg of McCarthy Arts Consulting, and Robert Bailey of AMS Planning and Research. I also appreciate the broader perspective I have gained about managing and leading arts and culture organizations from my colleagues at the Institut für Sprachen und Wirtschaft (ISW) in Freiburg, Germany. The opportunity to lecture at ISW annually since 2003 has been an honor. Hermann Ayen, Tenna

Jensen, Konrad Ayen, and all the students at ISW have helped expand my horizons.

All my colleagues at USITT continue to be a source of new opportunities that add to my knowledge about working with diverse points of view and perspectives in organizations. Sylvia Hillyard Pannell, Travis DeCastro, Carl Lefko, Michelle L. Smith, Barbara E. R. Lucas, Carol B. Carrigan, Monica L. Merritt, and many others, have been contributors to this book, whether they knew it or not. Their commitment to excellence is inspiring and their friendship is priceless.

I want to especially thank Will Maitland Weiss and Richard Maloney of Boston University for their valuable feedback on the manuscript. Their many suggestions were invaluable in the final stages of producing this edition. I also appreciate Dan Martin's thoughts on our evolving world of arts management in the forward to this edition.

Last, but not least, I'd like to thank my colleagues at Focal Press, especially Cara Anderson, Dawnmarie Simpson, Valerie Geary, and Alisa Andreola for their help and support over the many months it took to birth this edition.

April 2008
WJB — Cedar City, UT

CHAPTER 1

Management and the Arts

There's more to the arts than meets the eye. Yes, the performing and visual arts are supposed to be entertaining, but behind every creative endeavor exists a more profound concept without which a Community shrivels up and dies: the arts remind us of our power to innovate. The act of creation is the essence of our purpose and is essential to our progress as a humanity.

"The Importance of the Arts in a Community," Craig W. Johnson, April 2006

KEY TERMS

Review these terms from the chapter and begin to incorporate them into your day-to-day thinking about management and the arts.

Manager
Organization
Organizing
Open system model
Levels of management: operational, managerial, strategic
Types of managers: frontline, functional, general, administrative
Division of labor
Hierarchy of authority
Formal and informal structures
Corporate culture

Functions of management:
- planning, organizing, leading, and controlling

Functional areas of work for an arts manager:
- planning and development
- marketing and public relations
- personnel management
- fiscal management
- board relations
- labor relations
- government relations

In this introductory chapter we will engage in a quick overview of the field of arts and entertainment management. You will see there are numerous options for working in the field. The general process of management and the required skills to work in this area will be discussed. We will also introduce basic definitions of terms and concepts that will be applied throughout this book. Lastly, we will cover the basic management process and the key functional areas an arts manager will need to use if he or she is to be successful and effective in managing and leading in the arts.

THE BUSINESS OF ARTS AND ENTERTAINMENT

By a unique combination of historical circumstances and our consumer-driven economy, the United States has created a multibillion-dollar arts and entertainment industry that is a dynamic mix of professional for-profit and many smaller professional and nonprofessional not-for-profit, arts-related businesses. Unlike many other nations, the federal and state government provides minimal direct support to the arts and entertainment industry in the United States. However, the often maligned and complex income tax system in America does provide support that is a form of subsidy.

Museums and many performing arts centers are often owned by cities or states, but the vast majority of performing arts organizations, media companies, and sports teams are privately owned businesses, public companies with stockholders, or tax-exempt not-for-profit corporations. Figure 1.1 provides an overview of some of the various types of organizations where one may find employment in arts management.

Both for-profit and not-for-profit arts and entertainment organizations depend on the revenue from sales and other investments for income and special tax breaks to support day-to-day operations. For-profit organizations are able to take advantage of numerous tax laws that allow them legally to minimize their liabilities. Not-for-profit organizations enjoy the additional benefits of being exempt from paying many taxes and being permitted to raise money through the solicitation of tax-deductible contributions.

The roots of the current system of for-profit and not-for-profit arts businesses were established at the end of the nineteenth and beginning of the twentieth century as advances in technology began to change the way people experienced entertainment. The new technologies created the potential for establishing audiences on a mass scale never before possible. People tuned in to the radio, went to the movies, and eventually stayed home to watch television, videotapes, and DVDs, or to be entertained by any number of emerging personalized technology systems from MP3 players and online gaming. High Definition (HD) home entertainment systems costing thousands of dollars

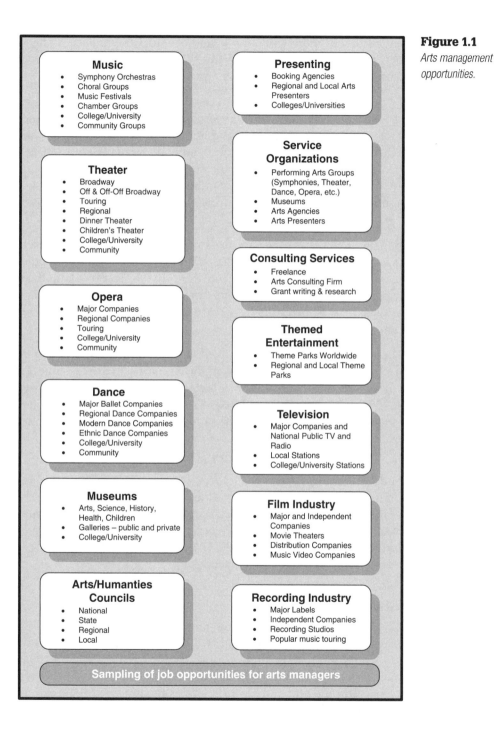

Figure 1.1
Arts management opportunities.

Music
- Symphony Orchestras
- Choral Groups
- Music Festivals
- Chamber Groups
- College/University
- Community Groups

Theater
- Broadway
- Off & Off-Off Broadway
- Touring
- Regional
- Dinner Theater
- Children's Theater
- College/University
- Community

Opera
- Major Companies
- Regional Companies
- Touring
- College/University
- Community

Dance
- Major Ballet Companies
- Regional Dance Companies
- Modern Dance Companies
- Ethnic Dance Companies
- College/University
- Community

Museums
- Arts, Science, History, Health, Children
- Galleries – public and private
- College/University

Arts/Humanties Councils
- National
- State
- Regional
- Local

Presenting
- Booking Agencies
- Regional and Local Arts Presenters
- Colleges/Universities

Service Organizations
- Performing Arts Groups (Symphonies, Theater, Dance, Opera, etc.)
- Museums
- Arts Agencies
- Arts Presenters

Consulting Services
- Freelance
- Arts Consulting Firm
- Grant writing & research

Themed Entertainment
- Theme Parks Worldwide
- Regional and Local Theme Parks

Television
- Major Companies and National Public TV and Radio
- Local Stations
- College/University Stations

Film Industry
- Major and Independent Companies
- Movie Theaters
- Distribution Companies
- Music Video Companies

Recording Industry
- Major Labels
- Independent Companies
- Recording Studios
- Popular music touring

Sampling of job opportunities for arts managers

are becoming more common in homes across the nation. Along with these new technologies, the evolving area of media arts has found its way into the landscape of for-profit and not-for-profit organizations.

By the latter part of the twentieth century, the concept of home entertainment centers built around ever-advancing computer technology allowed people even more entertainment options. In addition, family-oriented theme parks provide active entertainment experiences to millions annually with events and rides tied directly to film and television industry products. The profits attained by packaging and distributing entertainment to millions of people led to the creation of an industry based on appealing to the broadest possible audience.

Meanwhile, the live performing arts groups continued to face the inherent limitation of seating capacity, fixed schedules, and the rising costs of delivering the product. Fortunately, the rising levels of education, population, and income fed by economic growth after World War II, along with financial contributions by individuals, foundations, corporations, and state and federal arts agencies, helped support the art forms in the face of the continued migration to the mass media.

The media arts sector has also seen extraordinary growth tied to the rapidly declining cost of computing. Completely new design areas integrating film, video, and the Internet have come into existence in the last twenty years. A 2002 publication by the RAND Corporation[1] featured the important role media artists have in shaping the future of how people interact with organizations and the types of programmatic activity available to the public.

On paper, the future looks bright. For example, in 2005 the National Endowment for the Arts (NEA) reported that consumers spent $12.7 billion on live arts events.[2] The NEA reported 2.1 million Americans were employed in the arts in 2005.[3] And, in 2007, the National Center for Charitable Statistics at the Urban Institute reported there were approximately 1.4 million nonprofit organizations registered with the IRS. Of the total, 32,056 were classified as arts, culture, and humanities organizations.[4]

Opportunities

As you will see, there are a large number of organizations needing effective managers and leaders. As Figure 1.1 demonstrates, there are many different types of arts and entertainment organizations and companies seeking skilled managers. Popular music, theater, theme parks, television, other media companies, and the film and recording industry all need managers to help fulfill the primary purpose of the business. The entertainment industry is, of course, very concerned with maximizing revenue and creating a profit. In fact, we live in a world that delivers the majority of the entertainment we watch or attend through a for-profit business model. Although the risks of failure are very high, there is still a substantial number of people willing to take the chance of making a profit from the hit show, popular event, or artist.

Growing businesses

With the expansion of new ways to experience live and prerecorded entertainment and the increase in wealth among the general population came the proliferation of both profit and nonprofit businesses designed to meet the rising demand for entertainment. Thousands of new jobs were created for managers as companies expanded their operations. Each of these enterprises needed people with special skills and knowledge to ensure that the product was created and distributed in a way that realized the organization's goals, as stated by the owners or boards of directors.

For-profit theater, film, television, videos, nightclubs, popular music, radio, and spectator sports are big businesses employing highly visible stars and hundreds of thousands of support people. A report published by Rand Research noted that over 20,000 companies were in the broadcast, publishing, or wholesaling business of delivering entertainment product in the United States.[5] The total includes broadcasting and cable companies, film companies, and music stores.

Not-for-profit professional arts organizations in theater, music, dance, and opera and museums make up a great many of these businesses, providing year-round employment at all levels of management. There are also many smaller not-for-profit amateur community groups in music, theater, and dance that often hire a manager to help administer the organization. As noted earlier, these sectors of the entertainment market account for more than 2.1 million workers. People working in the arts in turn contribute to the national economic system with their purchases of goods and services. The arts help to foster economic growth in communities across America. Chapter 10, Economics and Financial Management, will elaborate on the economic impact of the arts.

Concerns about the future

Despite a history of growth, many people in the visual and live performing arts are anxious about the future. Some of these concerns stem from the changing demographics in America and the preference among young people for recorded or electronic media as their source for entertainment. The question about where future audiences will come from is very much on the mind of arts managers. Arts organizations are grappling with the future positive and negative implications of what has been termed the "digital divide."[6] Others see the political pressure at the state and federal level to limit or reduce taxes as only further increasing the demand on limited resources. Government policy has become more focused on delivering essential services at the expense of what is often perceived as more marginal activities, such as supporting arts and cultural groups.

The for-profit entertainment industry is also concerned about the plethora of entertainment opportunities available to consumers. As the capabilities of the Internet to deliver TV and movies on demand continue to improve, the multiplex movie theater owners are just as concerned about attracting customers as the managers of the many performing arts centers across America. The trend of flat or declining attendance numbers at movie theaters is a reality.[7] In addition, rising production and salary costs are driving ticket prices up for live and recorded arts products.

New technology has permitted entertainment to become more personalized and miniaturized. The change from mass media to more individualized entertainment systems, coupled with the often lagging resources for arts education in the schools, appears to many arts managers to be creating audiences with different attitudes about what they see and hear. Performers often note that audiences do not know how to "behave" any more at a concert, theater, dance, or opera event.

The often-predicted dramatic increase in leisure time seems to have vanished as people choose to do more in the day. With leisure time at a premium, consumers are making careful choices about how they spend their entertainment dollar.

Many arts leaders and their supporters also fear that too many groups are chasing too few patrons. Although many organizations agree that it is a sign of a thriving community to have many types of arts organizations existing side by side, they also recognize that their potential audiences only have so much time and money to spend on and to donate to the arts. These concerns have prompted several studies about the economic and cultural impact of the arts in communities across America.[8]

In Chapter 4, The Adaptive Arts Organization, we will delve into a more detailed examination of the forces and trends that affect arts organizations. The development of trend analysis skills can prove to be very useful in plotting the future of an arts organization.

MANAGERS AND ORGANIZATIONS

This book will examine how the arts manager can use the processes of *planning*, *organizing*, *leading*, and *controlling* to facilitate the operation of an organization and fulfill its mission in these uncertain times. These *four functions of management* are the basis for the working relationship between the artist and the manager. Because most of the activity associated with the performing arts and with museums occurs through some type of organization, this text concentrates on management in a group environment.

Let's look now at a brief overview of the manager, the organization, and the process of organizing.

The manager

In any organization, a *manager* is "a person who is responsible for the work performance of one or more people."[9] The manager's basic job is to organize human and material resources to help the organization achieve its stated goals and objectives. With this definition, a stage director or stage manager, a lighting designer, a conductor, a choreographer, and a curator are all managers. The details of their job descriptions may differ, but the responsibility of getting others to do something is the same. Leadership skills are needed to effectively direct others to accomplish the work that must be done.

The organization

Managers function within an *organization*, which has been defined as "a collection of people working together in a division of labor to achieve a common purpose."[10] This definition certainly describes the way we go about creating and delivering the artistic product in our world. Figure 1.2 shows how organizations interact with many external environments in a process of transforming their resources (inputs) to products or services. The output of an arts enterprise may be a performance or an exhibition. This *open system model*,[11] as it is called, is a graphic representation of how organizations interact with the world around them (see Figure 1.2).

The primary environments that affect all organizations are economic, political, cultural, demographic, and technological. Chapter 4, The Adaptive Arts Organization, examines the impact of each of these environments on organizations. As we will see, the survival and growth of an organization depend on its adaptability as these environments change. Managers of organizations must use all the skills and knowledge at their disposal, because these environments are always presenting new opportunities and threats.

The process of organizing

As we will see in Chapter 6, Organizing and Organizational Design, the process of achieving the organization's goals and objectives requires that the manager actively engage in the process of *organizing*, which has been defined as "dividing work into manageable components."[12] Typical examples of organizing in the arts include a director working with a stage manager to develop

Figure 1.2

Organizations as open systems.

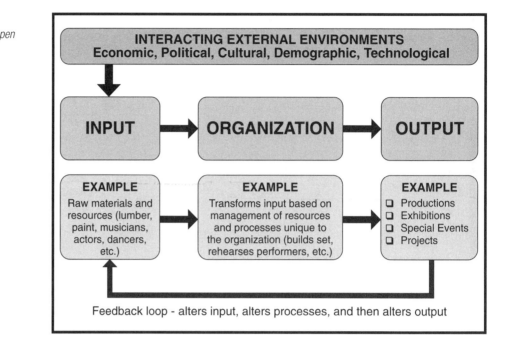

INTERACTING EXTERNAL ENVIRONMENTS
Economic, Political, Cultural, Demographic, Technological

INPUT → **ORGANIZATION** → **OUTPUT**

| EXAMPLE | EXAMPLE | EXAMPLE |
| Raw materials and resources (lumber, paint, musicians, actors, dancers, etc.) | Transforms input based on management of resources and processes unique to the organization (builds set, rehearses performers, etc.) | ❏ Productions
❏ Exhibitions
❏ Special Events
❏ Projects |

Feedback loop - alters input, alters processes, and then alters output

a rehearsal schedule for a production, or a box office manager designing a staff schedule to cover the upcoming performances.

Levels of management and types of managers

In any organization, there are different levels of management and different types of managers. Typically, organizations have operational, managerial, and strategic levels of management,[13] and line, staff, functional, and general managers or administrators.[14] (See Figure 1.3.)

Levels of management

The *operational level* of management is concerned with the day-to-day process of getting the work done. The sets must be built, the museum guards must assume their posts, the rehearsal schedule must be posted, the membership renewals must be mailed, and the box office must sell tickets. The operations level is central to the realization of the organization's goals and objectives. Without the efficient and productive management of its operations, the organization faces extinction.

The *managerial level* is often called *middle management*, because it coordinates the operations and acts as a bridge between the operational and strategic levels

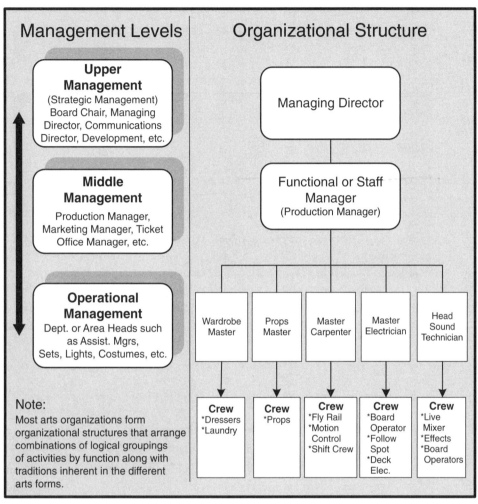

Figure 1.3
Management levels and organizational structure.

of management. For example, the board of directors and the artistic director of a theater or dance company ask the production manager to evaluate the impact of adding a touring season to the company's schedule. If the plan is feasible, the production manager will have the task of coordinating the schedules, materials, and people required to initiate this program of activity. The managerial level usually functions in a one- to two-year planning cycle in the organization.

The *strategic level* of management, on the other hand, watches the overall operation of the organization with an eye toward constantly adjusting and adapting to the changing environments that affect the future of the organization while staying true to the mission. The goals and objectives are typically assessed annually. Planning also may extend into the future as much as three to five years, or beyond. The artistic director, general manager, general director, managing director, marketing director, or other similar senior level personnel are associated with this role. In addition, strategic managers typically present these long-range plans to a board of directors. In most cases the board ultimately oversees the organization's mission and purpose.

Types of managers

The arts have evolved unique types of managers to make organizations work. The types of managers listed in this section are found in different combinations in arts organizations, depending on the purpose and design of the organization. Each art form has specialized job titles and responsibilities.

The first managerial role is the *frontline manager* and he typically "manages employees who themselves are not managers."[15] This person is directly responsible for getting the product or service completed. The head carpenter, who supervises a stage crew, is a good example of such a manager. The head carpenter's job is to get the set up on stage and ready for the performance in a venue that hosts touring productions. The assistant ticket office manager is another example of a frontline manager because they often directly supervise the window or phone sales employees.

Functional managers "lead a particular function or a subunit" and "they are responsible for a task, activity, or operation."[16] For example, the technical director in a performing arts group is usually given this responsibility. He coordinates the work of line managers such as the head carpenter or master electrician. Other examples of functional job areas could include production manager, ticket office, informational technology, membership, development, or accounting.

It is worth noting that because many arts organizations are understaffed, the roles played by the frontline and functional managers are often combined. As you will see in Chapter 7, Human Resources in the Arts, job titles are often doubled or tripled in arts organizations. For example, a manager may have the title of Marketing and Public Relations Director. These two functional areas are usually full-time jobs in themselves, but the lack of funds for managerial positions requires doubling up on work assignments. The lack of funding for staff may also mean that there are no frontline managers to work for the functional manager. For example, the Marketing Director and Public Relations Director may find themselves writing their own press releases and sending them to the media via e-mail.

General managers "are responsible for the overall performance of an organization or one of its major self-contained units."[17] For example, the general manager of an opera company oversees production, marketing, fundraising, and administration for the organization.

Another managerial title often found in arts or not-for-profit organizations is *administrator*. Although the administrator is typically playing the role of a general manager, the title is often used in nonprofit or academic organizations to refer to someone empowered to carry out goals and policies defined by others such as a board of directors. Depending on the bylaws or governing laws of the organization, the administrator may or may not be given the final authority to make plans or policies but is responsible for their implementation.

Common elements in an organization

A division of labor and some type of hierarchy exist in most organizations. The *division of labor* typically takes a form that matches the organization's function. A dance company has a different division of labor from an opera company for the simple reason that the processes and techniques used in creating the work and preparing a performance are different. For example, many regional opera companies have a small permanent staff. The singers, orchestra, director, stage crew, and designers are hired to do a single show. Ballet companies, on the other hand, often have 30 or 40 dancers contracted for up to 40 weeks a year, therefore requiring a different division of labor to meet the needs of a resident company of performers.

The *hierarchy of authority* in an organization is designed to ensure that the work efforts of the different members of the organization come together as a whole.[18] The typical hierarchy involves a vertical reporting, communication, and supervision system. Chapter 6, Organizing and Organizational Design, details various methods for organizing management systems.

In most arts organizations, which are small businesses with budgets under $2 million, the levels of management and the formality of the hierarchy are usually limited. However, as an organization grows in size and more staff is added, the levels of management increase, and the hierarchy tends to become more formal. Arts managers need to be watchful of this development, especially if overly complex divisions of labor or a burdensome hierarchy begin to impede the accomplishment of the organization's goals and objectives.

An *informal structure* also exists in all organizations. No organizational chart or detailed plan of staff responsibilities is able to take into account all of the ways people find to work with each other. Employees often find new combinations of people to accomplish tasks that do not fit into the existing hierarchy or organizational design. Some organizations thrive on this sort of internal innovation; others become chaotic.

Arts organizations often develop organizational designs aligned with functional areas. For example, the production staff, office staff, performers, and upper management develop structures to operate their own areas. The result can be four organizations instead of one. At the same time, organizations, like people, can lapse into habitual behavior patterns. Tradition becomes the norm, and innovation is resisted. Again, the arts manager must keep an eye on the organization's formal and informal structure. Careful intercession can correct unproductive structures that develop.

Organizations at their core are not neutral entities. They are microcosms of society. Organizations are collections of individuals with beliefs, biases, and values. Unique myths and rituals are part of what is called an organization's *corporate culture* (see Chapter 6). Simply described, the corporate culture is "how things are done" in the organization. For example, the culture of the organization usually establishes values for such things as the quality and quantity of work expected. Some organizations have a positive culture that is communicated to employees. For example, a manager might say, "Our stage crew is here to make things work, and their contribution is valued and recognized." In this situation, what is communicated is the overall culture of the organization that values the labor of its employees. Other organizations have weak or destructive cultures. Phrases such as "The crew around here is always looking for a way to get out of work, and they are not to be trusted," signal a culture based on distrust and possible conflict. The founder-directed organization, a model quite prevalent in the arts, can also help establish a strong culture imbued with the beliefs and values of one individual. Unfortunately, the departure of this person often leaves the organization adrift.

Any arts organization, no matter how small, is ultimately a complex mixture of behaviors, attitudes, and beliefs of the people who work or volunteer there. Because people are the major resource used in creating an arts product, an organization will continue to be influenced and changed in ways that no one can predict.

Interaction with external environments also affects the way people inside the organization think, feel, and behave. For example, changes in laws and the social system have led to the addition of multicultural programming and the hiring of more minorities in many arts organizations. (See Figure 1.4.)

Arts organizations as institutions

Arts organizations are learning to effectively integrate long-term strategic thinking while developing sensitivity to the changing environments that shape the beliefs and values of the entire culture. (See Figure 1.4.) Because the performing and visual arts are dependent on the creative explorations of individuals for the new material they present, the design and function of

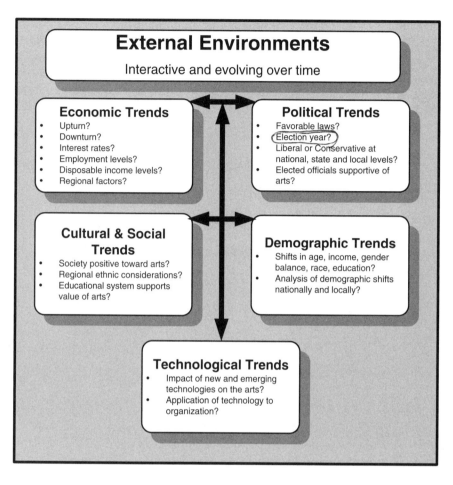

Figure 1.4
External environments.

these institutions should be focused on looking toward what will be and not at what was. However, many artists perceive arts organizations as institutions that are more comfortable with the past. The creation of organizations in the performing and visual arts that look like imitations of corporations with executive directors, vice presidents, and associate directors is not universally seen as a good sign.

Many artists are asking organizations to examine such fundamental questions as "What is our mission?" "Just what is it we are doing?" "What things are really essential to our mission?" "Whom do we serve?" "What do people think we do?" and "What are we really contributing to the community and our culture?" What are values and what do we deem important?" (See the following box containing the Oregon Shakespeare Festival Mission, Vision, and Values Statement as an example of how these questions are addressed.)

These question can also open a dialog in a community about the arts and what they can bring to the important questions about the quality of life in a community. The arts can offer communities opportunities to differentiate themselves from other regions in a state. Having clear and widely distributed mission, vision, and values statements can go a long way to actually building a type of community pride in its arts organizations.

The continual process of realizing a mission needs to be factored into the design and operation of the arts organization. The pursuit of an artistic vision and the successful presentation of that vision to the public needs as much attention and thought as any commercial business enterprise in the world.

Sample Mission, Vision, and Values Statement

The Oregon Shakespeare Festival articulates it mission, vision, and values in relation to its overall strategic plans.

Oregon Shakespeare Festival

Our Mission

The mission of the Oregon Shakespeare Festival is to create fresh and bold interpretations of classic and contemporary plays in repertory, shaped by the diversity of our American culture, using Shakespeare as our standard and inspiration.

Our Vision

We envision the Oregon Shakespeare Festival as a creative environment where artists and audiences from around the world know they can explore opportunities for transformational experiences through the power of theater.

Values

The following values support this vision and our overall mission. They are at the center of everything we do, and describe how we work together. While we recognize the need for balance among them, these values guide us in all our decisions:

Excellence

We believe in constantly seeking to present work of the highest quality, expecting excellence from all company members. We are committed to a bold, imaginative production style that illuminates our world in a fresh and insightful manner, producing theater that inspires profound understanding and hope for the human condition.

Learning

We believe in being an organization that offers company members, audiences and students the richest possible learning experiences.

Collaboration

We believe that the collaborative process is intrinsic to theater and is the bedrock of our working relationships.

Diversity

We believe the inclusion of diverse people, ideas, cultures, and traditions enriches both our insights into the work we present on stage and our relationships with each other. We are committed to diversity in all areas of our work and organization.

Company

We believe in sustaining a safe and flexible workplace where we rely on each other to work together with trust, respect, and compassion. We practice direct and honest communication. We encourage and support a balance between our lives inside and outside the Festival.

Financial Health

We believe in continuing our long history of financial stability, making wise and efficient use of all the resources entrusted to us.

Heritage

We believe that the Festival's history of more than seventy years gives us a heritage of thoughtful change and evolution to guide us as we face the future.

Source: http://www.osfashland.org/about/mission.aspx

THE MANAGEMENT PROCESS

The organization and systems described thus far are predicated on the assumption that there is an artistic product to manage. How does this product come into being? In many cases, an individual or a small group of people have the drive and energy to create something from nothing. For example, a playwright and director may team up to interest other people in a script. If people with money can be found to back the show, they hire performers and designers to bring the work to life. Sometimes, much less often than anyone cares to consider, the show is a hit.

A long-standing love for opera may drive someone to start a regional opera company or two dancers may decide that it is time to start their own company. The dancers may be tired of dancing someone else's choreography, and they have some ideas of their own that they would like to see performed. A group of visual artists may start a cooperative exhibition gallery and operate it themselves. A graphic designer or Web designer is weary of working for a large company and decides it is time to start his own business.

Whatever the circumstances, the success or failure of these ambitions will be related to how well the four functions of management are fulfilled. Without proper planning, good organization, creative leadership, and some control over the enterprise and its budgets, the chance of success is greatly diminished. Obviously many organizations exist in this world that do programs and projects that do not master these four functions. Poorly planned, badly organized, weakly led, and inadequately controlled events happen all the time. The events that suffer from various forms of dysfunctional management make for entertaining war stories, but the human toll taken by such examples of bad management is precisely why good managers are needed in the arts. There is no benefit to the art form or the community if the very people who love the arts are destroyed by it.

It is important to remember, however, that a bad play, opera, musical, ballet, symphony, or exhibition cannot be made good by excellent management. If people do not respond to a new theatrical work after rewrites and extra rehearsals, it does not matter how well the show was managed. Ultimately, if there is no artistic vision behind the enterprise, then the chances for long-term success are greatly diminished.

We will take more time to examine the evolution of the arts and how arts managers fit into the entire process in Chapter 2. For now, let's consider the four functions and relate each of them to an arts application.

Four Functions of Management
- *Planning* is deciding what is to be done.
- *Organizing* is deciding how it is to be done and who is to do it.
- *Leading* is deciding how other people are to get it done.
- *Controlling* is deciding if it is or isn't getting done, and what to do if it isn't.

Planning

This first function of management can be the hardest. Deciding exactly what we want to do, setting realistic goals (what the organization wants to accomplish), and then determining the objectives (the specific steps to take and the timetable for completing the tasks) to be used in meeting the goals is hard work.

There also are various sorts of plans. Some are short-range plans: What am I going to do tomorrow? Short-term plans usually don't present too much of a challenge for people. On the other hand, planning three to five years ahead can be an intimidating, if not impossible task.

Organizations and people must plan because the world is constantly changing. Audience tastes and values change over time. The arts manager's job is to recognize the elements in the world around the organization that may pose new opportunities or may be a threat. Then the manager must work with the board and the artistic leadership to chart a course of action designed to guide the organization into the future.

For example, the artistic director of the ABC Opera Company reads in the newspaper that state funds for arts organizations to visit schools will soon be increased. A goal is established to seek the funding and then implement a touring program in the next year because it relates directly to the organization's mission of bringing opera to the widest possible audience. The staff researches costs and benefits. A plan and the goals are drawn up and reviewed with the board. The board approves the idea and the company establishes a pilot program.

Organizing

Organizing is the process of converting plans into a course of action. Getting the people and resources together, defining the details, creating a schedule and budget, estimating the number of people needed, and assigning them their jobs is all part of organizing.

The ABC Opera Company, for example, sets up a special touring department. With the grant it obtains from the state the company hires a director of touring and puts into place the details of the plan. For the first year, the company will have a small group of 6 singers tour 10 schools to perform scenes and hold opera workshops. Detailed schedules, contracts, and evaluation methods are established.

Leading

The third function of management requires getting everyone in the organization to share a vision of what can be accomplished if everyone works together. Leadership skill and effectiveness are highly prized attributes in any situation. For the arts manager, working with the highly self-motivated, independent-minded people often found in the arts offers a unique leadership opportunity.

After the ABC Opera Company touring staff is hired, the artistic director meets with everyone to clarify the project's purposes and goals. The director provides an overall timetable and explains where this new operation fits into the organization. The company's mission is recalled, and a challenge is issued to make this a quality touring program. The leader of the tour group provides the day-to-day guidance needed to make the project a success.

Controlling

The fourth function of management is concerned with monitoring how the work is proceeding, checking the results against the objectives, and taking corrective action when required.

After six months, the artistic director reviews the activities of the ABC Opera touring company and finds that bookings are well below the number expected, singer turnover is high, and the budget for the year is almost gone. Meetings are held to pinpoint problems and consider solutions. Staffing changes are made, and the project is now monitored on a weekly basis. After a year, many of the problems have lessened, and the touring project is having a positive impact on the community.

Management in Practice

The typical production process for a performing arts event provides a good example of management in practice. For example, a director or choreographer working to prepare a production or concert draws on many of the same techniques and principles applied every day in the highly competitive world of business. Practices such as teamwork, project management, and performance appraisal are fundamental ingredients in a show. The leadership skills of a director or choreographer determine how well the entire production will go. Preparing a production or concert is a group management effort and therefore requires careful attention to the changing, complex dynamics of the performers, designers, and production staff. Motivation levels must be maintained, conflicts must be resolved, and effective time-management skills are required if the show is to open on time and be of a high quality. In other words, the skills required to successfully create a performance event are the same skills required to run a successful business.

Functional areas

When engaged in planning, organizing, leading, and controlling there are typically seven basic functions an arts manager fulfills:[19]

1. Planning and development
2. Marketing and public relations
3. Personnel management
4. Fiscal management
5. Board relations
6. Labor relations
7. Government relations

Planning and development are linked because arts organizations are always seeking ways to increase revenue to fund new programs and to pay for the inevitable increases in operating costs.

Marketing and public relations provide the organization's most visible link to the community. Without a strong connection to the community, the arts organization will find it difficult to attract audiences and donors.

Good personnel management and labor relations are essential if the organization is to be productive. Neglect or abuse of the human resources available to a manager can disrupt the entire enterprise.

Good fiscal management is critical if the planning, marketing, and fundraising efforts are to succeed. Generally, donors prefer to make contributions to organizations that show they know how to manage their financial resources.

As with personnel relations, an arts manager must effectively work with and report to a board of directors. The board and the management may sometimes have a different set of priorities. Until the differences are resolved, the organization will find it difficult to meet its goals and objectives.

Finally, government relations, which includes the local, state, and national levels, grow more complex each year. New laws are passed or court rulings are enforced that change the way an organization does business. These types of changes typically add to the expenses of the organization.

Throughout this text, we will examine how external environments and internal organizational dynamics make the task of managing in the arts a challenging and demanding job. The almost endless variety and changing circumstances in the world around the arts organization keep the manager's job from ever getting dull or routine.

For additional topics relating to an overview of arts and management, please go to www.managementandthearts.com.

Questions

1. Are you aware of any arts organizations that have been particularly successful or have faced difficulty in your community? Outline the situation, and explain why you think the organization did well or faltered.
2. Can you recall a work situation you have been in that was either positive or negative as a direct result of the manager in charge? What type of manager was this person (line, staff, functional)? What made this manager effective or ineffective?
3. List some examples of how you "manage" your life. Have you used any combinations of the management functions of planning, organizing, leading, or controlling to achieve objectives you have set for yourself?

SELECTING A PROJECT ORGANIZATION

Over the course of the semester select an arts organization and request (or download) a copy of its mission statement, bylaws, and other relevant planning documents (for example, a five-year plan) for a discussion in class. Based on the topics covered in this chapter, answer the following questions:

1. Does the organization seem to be fulfilling its stated mission? If yes, how? If not, why not? Does it have a vision statement? How does it articulate what it values?

2. Is the organization facing financial problems? Did it have a deficit or surplus in the last budget year? What is the deficit or surplus history of the organization?

3. Based on the information gathered, is it possible to ascertain if this is a well-managed organization? If yes, what evidence supports this finding? If no, what are the management areas that need improvement (e.g., planning and development, marketing and public relations, personnel management, fiscal management, board relations, labor relations, government relations)?

There are several sources for evaluating the general performance of an arts organization. Here are two links you may use to do more research about arts organizations:

1. http://www.guidestar.org/
2. http://www.charitynavigator.org/

REFERENCES

1. Kevin McCarthy, Elizabeth Heneghan Ondaatje, *From Celluloid to Cyberspace: The Media Arts and the Changing Arts World* (Santa Monica, CA: Rand, Inc., 2002).
2. NEA Research Division Note #91 (Washington, D.C., March 2006), p. 1.
3. NEA Research Division Note #90 (Washington, D.C., July 2006), p. 1.
4. "The Nonprofit Sector in Brief:" Facts and Figures from the *Nonprofit Almanac 2007* (The Urban Institute, Washington, D.C., 2007), pp. 1 and 3.
5. Kevin McCarthy, Arthur Brooks, Julia Lowell, and Laura Zakaras, *The Performing Arts in a New Era* (Santa Monica, CA: Rand, Inc., 2001), p. 68.
6. http://www.digitaldivide.org/dd/index.html, January 2008.
7. http://www.mpaa.org/researchstatistics.asp, January 2008.
8. An example of one such study can be found at The Boston Foundation Web site under a report entitled *Vital Signs: Metro Boston's Arts and Cultural Nonprofits, 1999 and 2004*. The link is: http://www.tbf.org/UtilityNavigation/MultimediaLibrary/ReportsDetail.aspx?id=7472&parentId=354

9. John R. Schermerhorn, Jr., *Management for Productivity*, 2nd ed. (New York: John Wiley & Sons, 1986), p. 7.

10. Ibid., p. 8.

11. Daniel A. Wren, *The History of Management Thought*, 5th edition. (New Jersey: John Wiley & Sons Inc., 2005), p. 448.

12. James H. Donnelly, Jr., James L. Gibson, and John M. Ivancevich, *Fundamentals of Management*, 7th ed. (Homewood, IL: BPI-Irwin, 1990), pp. 28–29.

13. Schermerhorn, *Management for Productivity*, pp. 13–15.

14. Ibid., p 13.

15. Charles W.L. Hill, Steven L. McShane, *Principles of Management* (McGraw-Hill Irwin, 2008), p. 7.

16. Ibid., p. 7.

17. Ibid., p. 7.

18. Schermerhorn, *Management for Productivity*, p. 12

19. Paul DiMaggio, *Managers of the Arts* (Washington, D.C.: Seven Locks Press, 1987), Research Division Report #20, NEA.

Arts Organizations and Arts Management

In this chapter, we review the evolution of arts organizations and the field of arts management. After examining the basic model used to establish a not-for-profit arts organization in America, we will study the evolution of the job of an arts manager. We explore how the responsibilities have changed to meet the increasingly complex demands placed on arts organizations and artists, and we also touch on the impact the National Endowment for the Arts has had on the arts scene in the United States.

THE ARTIST–MANAGER

For more than 2,000 years, the artist–manager has been the person who created and arranged the meeting of artist and public. Creative drive, leadership, and the ability to organize a group of people around a common goal remain the foundation on which all arts management is built. More recently, the traditional role of the artist-manager has been split into separate jobs to better cope with the increasingly complex demands placed on managers. However, this split does not mean that a division or barrier must be erected between these two roles. Instead, the separation should be viewed in much the same way as the human brain functions: the two hemispheres are linked and communicate with each other while each side continues to do what it does best.

ARTS INSTITUTIONS

One result of the political and social upheaval of the last 400 years has been the establishment of institutions designed to provide continuing support and recognition for the artist and the arts. In much of the world, the performing arts are part of a state-supported system and are operated by resident managers with administrative staffs. Performing and visual arts centers for opera, dance, theater, and music as well as museums reserved exclusively for art, history, and science are integral parts of many communities in the world.

In the United States, modest governmental backing for the arts is a recent phenomenon. Fund-matching grants, special project support, and a taxation system designed to promote deductible donations by individuals and corporations continue to be the extent of government involvement in the arts. More recently, in the last hundred years, the United States government opted for an alternative system that encouraged the creation of tax-exempt, not-for-profit corporations to supply and distribute the arts and culture in society.

The increasing complexity of an industrially and technologically based society hastened the shift from the artist-manager as the dominant approach to organizing and presenting the arts. As many communities began to establish arts institutions late in the nineteenth century (e.g., museums and symphony orchestras were the early leaders in this transition), year-round management experts began to emerge. Many arts institutions now appear to be organized along patterns similar to large business corporations.

Today, the role of the artist and the manager and the degree of control each has over her respective domains vary from art form to art form. Many small arts organizations are still created and managed by artist–managers. For example, a small theater company in New York City such as The Red Bull Theater (www.redbulltheater.com) is led by an artistic director who also functions as the manager. Like many small arts organizations, a business manager helps the artist–manager with day-to-day operations of the organization.

A BRIEF HISTORICAL OVERVIEW

Let's examine a few select points in Western history to trace the development of the management function in the arts. As has been noted, the artist–manager is a well-established pattern in the arts. Although this pattern of management has not changed much in the last 2,000 years, the demands placed on this individual have increased to the point where the artist–manager position is now only one of many ways to organize the presentation of arts events. Of course this brief overview is not intended to substitute for course work or readings in theater, dance, music, art, or media history.

Ancient times

As the centers of civilization grew, so did those functions we associate with the arts. The first examples of performance management were the public assemblies associated with religious rites in early societies. These performances were "managed" by the priest and were enmeshed in the fabric of a society. The theatrical trappings of costumes, dramatic settings, music, movement, and so on, all supported and heightened the impact of the event. Ultimately, though, these events were not an expression of the creative drive of a people, but rather a way of controlling and molding a culture. However, these staged events did provide a model for organizing large-scale public gatherings.

The beginnings of a system of state-sponsored play festivals can be traced to the Greeks around 534 BCE. These festivals required the management skills of planning, organizing, leading, and controlling, much as they do today. Typically, a principal magistrate, the *archon eponymous*, supervised the production of the play festivals sponsored in Athens. Financial support came from the richer citizens (*choregoi*), and the cities provided the facilities. The playwright functioned as the director and had something akin to total artistic control over the show.[1]

Museums were very much a part of the Greek culture. The word *museum*, in fact, comes from "the Greek *mouseion*, a temple of the muses."[2] Neil Kotler and Philip Kotler note that the early museums in places like Alexandria "functioned as a scholar's library, a research center, and a contemplative retreat."[3] Ancient Rome often displayed collections of items taken through military campaigns. The Catholic Church also amassed a considerable collection of art.[4]

The Romans produced state-sponsored arts festivals as part of an overall cycle of public events throughout the year. City magistrates were responsible for screening and coordinating the entertainment for their communities. The managers (*domini*) acted as producers, bringing the play and the performers to the festivals. These early managers arranged all the elements needed for the production with the financial support of the local magistrate. According to research in theater history, as many as 100 days a year[5] were committed to the various theater festivals of ancient Rome. If this schedule is indeed accurate, a great deal of managerial skill must have been required to coordinate and produce these events.

With the decline of Rome came the dissolution of the state-sponsored festivals. The breakup of the Empire did not mean that all artistic activity came to a halt. However, the transition into what is often called the Middle Ages left society without a developing dramatic literature to generate works for performance. The disappearance of organized financing and facilities also made it impossible to sustain an ongoing arts community. Performance groups therefore resorted to touring as a means of survival. Smaller scale community festivals helped provide opportunities for the itinerant artists to eke out a living. Overall, Western history has not provided much evidence of significant artistic activity in Europe during this time.

Other cultures were, of course, developing indigenous forms of music, dance, and theater. The arts were very much a part of Byzantium, India, and China. While Europe was struggling, other cultures were establishing forms of dance, theater, music, and visual arts that are with us today. Varying degrees of state and private sponsorship were involved. The role of the manager did not radically differ in these cultures because the functions required to organize and coordinate arts events were the same.

The Middle Ages

The Church was the producer of many sanctioned performances during the Middle Ages. The performance of liturgical drama, which served as a type of religious instruction, originally resided within the management structure of the Church. As communities developed and the overall economic environment improved, this drama moved outdoors and became part of public pageants and festivals, using stages mounted on portable wagons. Nonliturgical drama and various forms of popular entertainment, such as jugglers and mimes, were part of a rebirth of performance.

By the fourteenth century, the Church had little control over the proliferating performances. A system of patronage and sponsorship by the trade guilds led to an expanding role for the manager–director. Historians Oscar Brockett and Franklin Hildy note that during the fifteenth and sixteenth centuries:

> …complex productions required careful organization, for the handling of casts that sometimes included as many as 300 actors, of complex special effects, and large sums of money could not be left to chance. Consequently, the director (or stage manager, or pageant master) was of

considerable importance. …Often this position was given to a member of the guild, but in some instances a "pageant master" was put under contract for a number of years at an annual salary. For example, at Coventry in 1454 the Smiths contracted for a period of twelve years with Thomas Colclow, who was to supply everything needed except the wagons and costumes. The pageant master secured actors, arranged rehearsals, and took charge of every phase of production.[6]

There also are records of various productions making some kind of a profit. According to Brockett and Hildy there is the example "At Reims in 1490, 5616 persons paid admissions"[7] to a series of municipally sponsored performances. One might conjecture if admission was charged, then someone had to probably manage and coordinate the sales much as a ticket office manager would today.

The Renaissance

The continuing surge of the arts was dramatic throughout the Renaissance. The social, political, economic, and cultural environments were undergoing changes that fundamentally altered people's perceptions of the world. The rediscovery of the Greeks opened up the creative spirit of the times. During the fourteenth to sixteenth centuries, neoclassical theater began to flourish, opera and ballet were born, and the role of the arts manager burgeoned.

In opera, theater, and dance, the expansion of literature was accompanied by the construction of performance spaces that took advantage of the stage technology of the time. This in turn led to the rise of stage crew specialists in such areas as rigging, lighting, special effects, and costumes. The coordination required of the increasingly complex productions helped solidify many of the traditional roles in backstage operations and management.

In the late sixteenth century, opera was born in Italy out of the *intermezzi*, which was a form of entertainment that occurred between the five-act dramas of the time. In 1594, the first opera, *Dafne*, authored by Ottavio Rinuccini and Giulio Caccini, music by Jacopo Peri, premiered and laid the foundation for an entire art form. This work was born out of the Camerata of Florence, a group of scholars interested in "creating plays similar to ancient Greek tragedies."[8]

The court dance of the thirteenth and fourteenth centuries helped forge a path for the creation of ballet. One of the key developments in the seventeenth century was the development of schools of dance training. One of the more prominent academies was established in 1661. "Italian musician, composer, dancer, mime and musical administrator, Jean Basptiste Lully"[9] was appointed by Louis XIV to direct the Royale Academies of Dance and Music.[10] The first ballet, *Ballet Comique de la Reine*, was performed in 1581 in the French court at Fontainebleau.[11] As with opera, specialized production and management techniques evolved over the centuries to support the art form.

Private collections of art work and artifacts were also built during this time. However, access to the collections was very limited. Public museums did not become popular until the eighteenth century.[12]

Management challenges

As is the case today, finding financial support was an ongoing activity of the early artist–managers. Church support, royal patronage, and shareholder arrangements were the chief means of financing work. The shares sold to people helped provide the resources needed to pay for salaries and production support. Management functions were expanded to include overseeing the distribution of any profits to the shareholders.

The other major problem that managers and artists grappled with was censorship. Throughout history, the performing and visual arts have had to contend with varying degrees of control from both the church and the state. The selection of plays, the access to performance spaces, and sometimes even the selection of performers have been subject to severe constraints. The arts manager is often placed in the middle of the battle between an artist seeking an avenue of expression and a state or religious group attempting to suppress the work. We see the legacy of the uneasy relationship between the arts and society in the occasional controversies that arise when it comes to funding the arts at the local, state, or federal level.

The seventeenth through nineteenth centuries

In many European countries during this time, the arts continued to grow and flourish. Playwrights, directors, composers, musicians, dancers, and singers found work in newly created companies and institutions. In France, the theater, opera, and ballet companies were organized in state-run facilities, and the performers received salaries and pensions. Germany established a state theater by 1767. It became the foundation for a national network of subsidized arts institutions. England also had a thriving performing arts community. The Education Act of 1870 and the Local Governments Act of 1888 helped promote the growth of museums and performing arts facilities throughout Great Britain.[13] British support for museums was well-rooted in the nineteenth century. However, the first Arts Council in England was not created until 1946.[14] Throughout the seventeenth to nineteenth centuries, especially on the Continent, the formalization of management structures and systems to operate the state theaters solidified the role of the arts manager.

In the United States, theatrical presentations were made up of touring groups performing varied programs in cities across the nation. The development of the railroad system in America assisted with the spread of touring groups and artists in the eighteenth and nineteenth centuries. The local theater venue often contained stock sets that were used by the performers, who brought their own costumes. The expanding rail system of the mid-nineteenth century helped support an extensive touring network of performing groups. Companies were formed and disbanded almost constantly, and no permanent theater companies were established. The management structure was dominated by the producers and booking agents who arranged the tours. The control of most theaters eventually fell into the hands of these booking agents. A monopoly known as *The Syndicate* controlled what was available for viewing around the country. This monopoly was supplanted by another group of theater owners, the Shuberts. The Shubert brothers, who started out in Syracuse, New York, created a management dynasty that lasts to this day.[15]

Unlike the impermanent theater, symphony orchestras and opera companies began to secure a more stable place in the larger metropolitan areas in the United States. For example, the support of wealthy patrons made it possible to establish symphony orchestras in New York City (1842) and Boston (1881). Opera, which had been performed in the United States since early in the eighteenth century, found its first home in the Metropolitan Opera in 1883.[16] Dance was often included in touring theatrical productions in the eighteenth and nineteenth centuries. European dance stars also regularly toured the country. However, permanent resident dance companies were not a regular part of the arts scene until the twentieth century.

Museums developed in a uniquely American style according to Kotler and Kotler. As they point out, "The great majority of U.S. museums, by contrast, were created by individuals, families, and communities to celebrate and commemorate local and regional traditions and to enlighten and entertain people in the local communities."[17] They point to a city like Charleston, South Carolina, as a site of an early American museum (1773).

The twentieth century

The role of management increased as the continued growth of the arts accelerated. Despite two world wars, European arts institutions expanded into smaller communities, developing national networks of performing spaces and providing jobs for managers and artists. Seasons expanded, repertories grew, and new facilities were constructed — especially after World War II — in an overall environment of support from the government. As noted, England eventually established a state-supported system for the arts after the war.

In Europe and the United States, the new technologies of radio and film significantly changed attendance patterns at live performance events. The theater in the United States, for example, saw a rapid decline in attendance by the 1920s.[18] Because there were no resident theater companies, it was difficult to keep a loyal audience base such as existed for the few opera and symphony groups in the country.

Later in the twentieth century, the rise of the off-Broadway and regional theater system helped renew the theater and, at the same time, helped build a base for what were to become established organizations.

The more experimental, but still profit-driven, off-Broadway system was born in the early 1950s. The not-for-profit regional theater network was built from the Barter Theater in Virginia (1932), the Alley Theatre in Houston (1947), the Arena Stage in Washington, D.C. (1950), and the Actor's Workshop in San Francisco (1952). These theaters formed the nucleus of the new distribution system for theater in America.[19]

The need for good managers escalated in the professional world, and because of the unprecedented baby boom after the war, the educational system — especially colleges and universities — expanded offerings in the arts. Community and campus performing arts centers helped establish a new network for touring and provided local groups with venues to use. Managers were needed to operate the new multimillion-dollar complexes and to book events throughout the year.

Opera first spread beyond New York into the major metropolitan areas of Chicago, San Francisco, Philadelphia, St. Louis, and New Orleans. However, after the Great Depression, only New York and San Francisco were able to hold onto their companies.[20] The support in the 1950s from the Ford Foundation, among others, helped bring opera to the American arts scene. By the early 1970s, 27 opera companies were in operation.[21] As of July 2007 the Opera America Web site lists 118 major opera companies as members. Part of this growth was due to the NEA's matching grant programs, which enabled many companies to professionalize their management.

Until the early 1960s, dance companies were in limited supply in the United States. The American Ballet Theatre, the New York City Ballet, and the San Francisco Ballet topped the list of professional companies. Ballet West in Utah and Ruth Page's dancers, who were associated with the Chicago Lyric Opera, offered regular programs with their semiprofessional companies.[22] At the same time, modern dance companies were being operated on very tight budgets by such pioneers as Martha Graham, Alvin Ailey, Merce Cunningham, José Limon, and Paul Taylor. Their staff resources and their seasons were very limited.

The Ford Foundation in the 1960s and the NEA in the 1970s helped create a new national support system for ballet and later for modern dance. Although these groups still struggle, there are now more than 557 dance companies that operate, according to data collected by the NEA in 2002.[23]

Symphony orchestras have also grown in number over the last 30 years. According to the NEA, in 2002 there were 841 symphony orchestras and chamber music organizations in the United States.[24] It is also estimated that in 1992 there were 3,105 U.S. museums and art galleries, 2,749 of which were tax-exempt.[25]

In 1846 Congress accepted a bequest of the late James Smithson that led to the establishment of the Smithsonian, one of America's premier museums.[26] Business leaders and later philanthropists such as Andrew Carnegie, Marshall Field, and Julie Rosenwald helped found museums and libraries in the late nineteenth century in cities such as New York and Chicago. These museums continued to evolve and grow in the twentieth century to become the major cultural institutions we know today.[27]

The twenty-first century

The expansion period in the arts seems to be slowing now that most communities have established visual and performing arts institutions or centers. The continuing struggle for operating funds has been accelerated in recent years as the competition for support has increased. Significant increases in funding from the state and federal government appears to be an unrealistic expectation. Demand is increasing for resources to assist with social programs, medical research, and education. Foundation, corporate, and individual support is sought by increasingly sophisticated fundraising initiatives from all kinds of not-for-profit organizations. Within this complex mix of activities, the ever-advancing boundaries of technology are also having an impact on arts organizations. The ease with which information can be accessed through the Internet has also meant arts organizations have had to add or contract for skilled people to manage Web sites and the information flow to the public.

The expansion of the traditional relationships of the arts organization to its audiences is also evolving. Arts organizations are adapting to this new world of 24/7 access to better connect with their current and potential audiences. As has been noted, the expansion of the railroad system in the nineteenth century had a significant impact on the reach and impact of the arts. In many ways, an even faster technological change process is under way today that affects how arts organizations will meet the needs of future audiences.

International perspective

Meanwhile in Europe, the long-standing practice of government subsidies is being reevaluated. The model adopted is the American approach of a mix of private and public support for the arts. Many performing and visual arts organizations are scrambling to develop the expertise to become successful fundraisers to maintain their current levels of operation. The seeking of corporate or business sponsorships for arts organizations and festivals has now become a standard expectation of European arts organizations.

In England there have been significant struggles over the level of government support for the arts. For example, government support has shifted away from ongoing direct subsidies tapping revenue from lottery sales. In some cases this has proven to be a boon to arts organizations. Lottery funding has also gone to support projects that extend beyond the traditional scope of fine and performing arts funding. Australia is also undergoing similar shifts in government support. The expectation is now in place that less government support will motivate arts organizations to seek more support from corporations and individuals.

All of these worldwide changes make it imperative that the arts and culture managers and leaders adapt to the new demands and expand their skills and abilities to better serve their organizations.

In Practice: Writing a Business Plan

What steps do you need to take if you want to start up an arts organization? The following is a sample of an arts-focused business plan. The business section of your local bookstore will contain sources on writing a business plan. Potential financial backers or donors from the business community know what a business plan is and have expectations about how the document should be organized.

The area covering the financial plan is typically most important and is critical to developing the initial support to build your board of directors and to secure startup donations.

Business Plan for an Arts Organization
Outline of a Modified Business Plan

1. Title Page
2. Table of Contents
3. Executive Summary

Summarize the major points of the entire plan so that prospective board members, donors, and community or government members will be able to grasp what is contemplated (two pages maximum, if possible).

4. Vision/Mission/Goals Statement
   - Vision Statement.
   - Mission Statement.
   - Major goals and objectives for years 1 through 5 (3 to 5 goals maximum).

- How will the organization serve and enhance the quality of life in your community?

5. Organization Overview
   - Describe how you will be organized (a small business operated in a house, etc.).
   - Incorporation papers as per your state.
   - Bylaws – use standard bylaws customized for your organization.
   - Organizational chart.

6. Market Analysis and Marketing Plan
   - Present your research about how your organization is uniquely qualified to provide what is missing in your community.
   - Who are the "customers" for what you have to offer?
   - What is the demographic and psychographic profile of your potential audience?
   - Expectations you have about who and how many people will purchase tickets, subscriptions, or memberships.
   - How will you advertise (through expenditure) or publicize (for free) who you are and what you do? How will you develop your audience or membership base, attract customers, or develop new audiences for your organization?

7. Operations Plan
   - Overall description of how the organization will run on a daily basis.
   - Job descriptions of management and staff.
   - Employee Policy Handbook.

8. Financial Plan
   - Explanation of sources of revenue and description of expenses. How will you finance the startup of the organization? (For example, donations, grants, special local economic incentive supports, small business loans, and so forth.)
   - First-year operating. Your startup budget may have large capital outlays for equipment, or you may need to detail donations of equipment and space you anticipate receiving (see Chapter 9, Operations and Budgeting).
   - 12-month cash-flow statement for year 2.
   - Projected operating budget for years 2, 3, and 4.

9. Appendix (optional). You may need to supplement your plan with additional supporting materials or research that helps make the case that your organization is needed and that your organization is uniquely capable of solving the problems you have identified as needing solutions. Information (probably from the Internet) should be clearly organized for the reader to look up your sources.

THE MODERN ARTS ORGANIZATION

How organizations are formed

In the twentieth century, the development of arts organizations was fueled in part by changes in the tax laws. The requirements became more systematic and comprehensive in the process of establishing businesses that were designated to serve a public good. Let's take a brief look at the steps required for starting a nonprofit business, and then focus on what is required to establish an arts organization. The sidebar, In Practice: Writing a Business Plan, provides a practical example of how to go about starting an arts organization. Donald Farber's book *Producing Theatre: A Comprehensive and Legal Business Guide* (3rd revised edition) is also an excellent resource for how the process works for creating a theater company.

Legal status and financial statements

When a business starts up, it usually is owned and operated by one or two people. The founder–director often operates from home – or even from a car. However, once the operation grows to the point that a staff and office space are required, it is usually time to consider incorporating the enterprise. Individual artists may also incorporate to gain some specific tax advantages. In many parts of America the Volunteer Lawyers for the Arts helps individuals and organizations with the incorporation process. (For more information, go to www.vlany.org.)

Incorporation

The major reason why an individual or organization may decide legally to incorporate is to provide protection for the people who operate the business. Without the protection of incorporation, the owner is legally responsible for all debts incurred and may be sued personally. A legal settlement against an individual might mean that all personal assets would have to be sold to pay the organization's debts.

In the case of most arts organizations, filing for incorporation to become a for-profit or not-for-profit business is fairly straightforward. By incorporating the state bestows upon the organization the legal right to operate. However, filing for exemption from state and local taxes requires additional paperwork. Filing for incorporation is usually covered under the operational procedures established by the Secretary of State. Forms and detailed instructions on filing are typically available on the Web site for the Secretary of State. Typically, the following information is required to complete the filing:[28]

- Official name of the organization
- Purpose or purposes of the organization

- Scope of activities (if you are filing for tax exemption, it will limit what you can and cannot do with the profits or losses)
- Membership provisions (if any)
- Name of the person registering the incorporation and the place of business
- Names and addresses of the incorporators and the initial board of directors (if any)
- How any assets will be distributed when the corporation is dissolved

Additional legal regulations may affect nonprofit corporations, including business or occupation licenses and state or local charitable solicitation licenses. Incorporation and not-for-profit status, if accompanied by tax exemption, empowers the organization to raise funds and accurately report the sources of and value of the donations. Vending licenses may also be required if there is a plan to sell items through a gift shop.

Starting a for-profit business

When starting a small for-profit business it is not required to have a board of directors. For example, suppose an actor wants to start up a service company that provides training for corporate executives on how to be more effective public speakers. There would be no need for a board of directors to file with the Secretary of State if it was a for-profit enterprise. The legal types of for-profit small businesses most often used by someone trying to start a business, such as our actor and their public speaking training service, include the sole proprietorship, a partnership, or the limited liability corporation. The sole proprietorship business is, as has been noted, problematic when it comes to assuming personal legal and financial liability. A similar vulnerability exists with the partnership business. Many entrepreneurial individuals today create their business to meet the requirements of a limited liability corporation, or LLC. There are many distinct advantages to this corporation, not the least of which includes protection from personal liability.

There are numerous information resources available on the Internet about starting an LLC. For example, one such source is www.forminganllcguide. com. This Web site covers basic terminology for the LLC and contains links to information about starting an LLC in different states.

Creating a not-for-profit business

Creating a not-for-profit corporation is procedurally simple. However, underlying this process is the assumption that starting the business will be fulfilling a public good. The founder(s) of the arts organization, which may have been operating as a sole proprietorship or partnership at its inception, need to be ready to enter into a legal arrangement that requires relinquishing control of the organization. The legal understanding by the state and federal government is that by granting permission to incorporate, the individuals running the business are not going to personally profit from the operation. The "shareholder," in this case, is the public and the public should benefit in some way, no matter how indirectly, from the existence of this corporation. However, that does not mean an individual (e.g., an artistic director) cannot be paid a salary for their services from the not-for-profit business. The state expects that the business is incorporated by individuals who can be trusted to provide sufficient oversight to ensure the legal purpose of the organization is fulfilled and that the laws of the state are followed.

Typically, the not-for-profit incorporation process includes naming members of the board or specific officers of the corporation. In the beginning, the founding board may consist of a small group that would include a board chair, vice-chair, secretary, and treasurer. This core of people usually is made up of members of the community that the founder may know personally and who share his passion for the arts.

There is an expectation in most states that a set of bylaws (see sidebar, Outline of Bylaws, on the following page) will be filed at the time the business is incorporated. Bylaws are the rules by which the organization will be governed and operated. Bylaw wording templates are widely available and can be customized to the specific type of organization you are creating. The sidebar on "Outline of Bylaws" in this chapter provide an example of the typical structure of this document.

We will take a more in-depth look at the board of directors and board governance in Chapters 7 and 8. The broad topic of public policy pertaining to the subject of the purpose and place of the not-for-profit corporation in society is beyond the scope of this section. The subject will be covered in more depth in Chapter 10, Economics and Financial Management.

Tax exemption

Exemption from local, state, and federal taxes does not automatically come with not-for-profit incorporation. The Internal Revenue Service (IRS) Code, section 501(c)(3), exempts charitable organizations and public and private foundations from paying taxes on earnings. However, even a not-for-profit organization must still pay some taxes. In addition to payroll taxes, for example, a sales tax must be collected if the organization operates a gift shop. Some states have taxes on admission tickets too. The IRS has many tax-exempt categories that cover social welfare organizations such as the League of Women Voters (501,c,4), and even cemeteries (501,c,19).

When applying for tax-exempt status, financial data for the current fiscal year and the three preceding years is requested. If the organization is just getting started, the current year's budget and a proposal for the next two years will be accepted. A form that fixes the organization's fiscal year (e.g., July 1 to June 30) is also required.

To qualify for tax-exempt status, the organization must be operated for a purpose allowed by tax law. The exemption status is bestowed upon organizations that fulfill some of the following purposes: religious, charitable, scientific (research in the public interest), literary, educational, or testing for public safety.

The arts and education

Arts organizations typically are founded under the education category. The organization purpose is typically stated in terms such as "Increase appreciation and awareness of" chamber or symphony music, Shakespeare, ballet, and so forth. In addition, there are restrictions pertaining to making a profit from enterprises not directly related to the exempted purposes of the organization. These activities will be subject to the *unrelated business income tax* (UBIT). For example, if an arts organization starts acting as a travel agent and sells bookings for cultural cruises, the IRS might rule that this is unrelated to the organization's stated mission, and any surplus revenue from this activity would be subject to income taxes. There are laws also prohibiting certain lobbying and propaganda activities.

It is important to note that a 501(c)(3) organization is not restricted from making a profit. As long as the profit making relates to the stated purpose of the organization, net earnings (profit after deducting expenses for operations, programming, salaries, taxes, and benefits) may be accrued and retained. However, these earnings may not be distributed to members of the organization or the board of directors. Net earnings are usually placed in endowment funds or a restricted account and then put to use in a manner that helps fulfill the mission of the organization.

As should be expected, the rules and regulations pertaining to tax law contain a significant amount of fine print. Hiring a lawyer, using legal and accounting services donated by a board member, or contacting an organization such as the Volunteer Lawyers for the Arts can be helpful when applying for tax-exempt status.

Outline of Bylaws

Organizations typically develop a set of bylaws to help govern the operation. The following is an outline of the major sections of a bylaws document.

> Article I: Name — The entire name of the organization including the word Incorporated or Inc. Do a name search with the Secretary of State to make sure the name you have selected is not in use.

Article II: Purpose — State the purpose of the organization in one sentence.

Article III: Members — If there are members, outline what types there will be. For arts organizations membership is not recommended.

Article IV: Officers — Titles, how are they designated or elected, term of office, duties, how vacancies are filled.

Article V: Meetings — When you meet (once a month, first and third Tuesday), when is there an annual meeting, provisions for special meetings, quorum.

Article VI: Board of Directors — Number, how elected, are they also officers, term of office, responsibilities.

Article VII: Committees — Standing committees such as marketing/fundraising, finance, personnel, bylaws, and so forth.

Article VIII: Parliamentary Authority — Indication that you will run meetings using Robert's Rules of Order.

Article IX: Amendment of Bylaws — How you will make changes.

Source: Joyce L. Stephens, *Bylaws*, 2nd edition, Frederick Publishers. Largo. Florida, 2000. Used with permission.

For more information about bylaws go to: http://nonprofit.about.com/od/glossary/g/bylaws.htm.

Once an organization has attained the legal status to operate, it is obligated to provide reports and documentation to local, state, and federal agencies. The organization is also required to file forms related to Social Security taxes and withholding taxes, and to file tax forms with the IRS (IRS 990) that list revenues, expenses, and changes in net assets (the nonprofit organization's equivalency of worth is often called a fund balance or unrestricted net assets). The details of the organization's liabilities, assets, programmatic activities, revenues, donations, and expenses for the previous four years must be filed every year. We will review these business operation details in Chapter 9, Operations and Budgeting and Chapter 10, Economics and Financial Management.

A financial management information system (FMIS) and a person designated to oversee this important area become vital once the organization reaches the level of legal incorporation. The preparation of required reports — such as a balance sheet, a statement of account activity, and a financial statement of the worth of the organization — is also required (see Chapter 10). In addition, the organization's finances must be in order to the degree that an outside auditor can analyze the financial operation. A complete audit, which can be very costly, is often required.

PROFILE OF THE ARTS MANAGER

Now let's move on to the arts manager and the complex mix of responsibilities they must juggle. The growth in the arts in America since 1945 has created a tremendous demand for managers at all levels and in all arts disciplines. Unfortunately, arts managers are not clearly identified as a work group when counting the over 2.1 million people employed in all aspects of the arts. The Census Bureau counts performers, architects, composers, printmakers, and instructors in the arts but does not include people in arts management, sales, consulting, or promotion or public television employees.[29] Whether or not the people who do not directly create art are counted in the census data, they are obviously a central part of the culture industry in the United States.

One older source that provides information on the arts manager is Paul DiMaggio's 1987 book, *Managers of the Arts*. Originally created for the NEA under the official title *Research Division Report #20*, the book outlines the background, training, salaries, and attitudes of arts managers in theater, orchestra, and museum management and community arts associations.

Unfortunately, DiMaggio does not include data about opera or dance managers. In addition, the survey was conducted in 1981, which may make the data less relevant to today's market. DiMaggio's book only samples a limited number of people. With these limitations in mind, let's take a look at some of the highlights of this report (Figure 2.1).

DiMaggio's book reveals the following profile of arts managers: they are upper middle class, highly educated individuals who either majored in the subject they are managing or were humanities majors in English, history, or foreign languages. At the time of this study DiMaggio found that a limited number of managers had management or arts management degrees. The upper management jobs tended to be held by men in museums (85 percent), theater companies (66 percent), and orchestras (66 percent), but women held the majority of positions in community arts associations (55 percent).[30] The data also indicated that there were a variety of ways to enter the career path in arts management, thus making it a fairly open system.

The section of DiMaggio's report on training offers some interesting insights into the opinions of those surveyed regarding their preparation for their jobs in the early 1980s. Figure 2.1 shows the results of a survey that asked how well prepared participants felt to handle various aspects of the job, including fiscal and personnel management, planning, and board, labor, and government relations. These data indicate that "few managers felt they were well-prepared to assume many of [the] functions" required for their jobs.[31] Labor relations consistently stood out as an area for which respondents felt poorly prepared. The survey results show that in many areas, less than 40 percent felt

	Fiscal Mgt	Personnel Mgt	Board Relations	Planning & Develop.	Marketing & PR	Labor Relations	Govt. Relations
THEATERS							
Had good preparation	27.45%	42.57%	30.69%	37.62%	39.60%	20.00%	NA
Had poor preparation	25.49%	13.86%	29.70%	23.76%	16.83%	16.83%	
(Respondents)	(102)	(101)	(101)	(101)	(101)	(95)	
ART MUSEUMS							
Had good preparation	25.60%	30.40%	45.83%	32.52%	29.27%	15.25%	21.95%
Had poor preparation	40.80%	24.00%	14.17%	23.58%	30.89%	55.00%	43.09%
(Respondents)	(125)	(125)	(120)	(123)	(123)	(118)	(123)
ORCHESTRAS							
Had good preparation	26.42%	36.89%	43.14%	33.33%	47.06%	22.00%	NA
Had poor preparation	23.58%	15.53%	23.53%	19.61%	20.59%	49.00%	
(Respondents)	(106)	(103)	(102)	(102)	(102)	(100)	
ARTS ASSOCIATIONS							
Had good preparation	29.46%	39.84%	42.64%	52.71%	53.13%	11.02%	37.01%
Had poor preparation	20.16%	13.28%	17.83%	14.73%	11.72%	50.85%	25.20%
(Respondents)	(129)	(128)	(129)	(129)	(128)	(118)	(127)

NOTE: NA = Not asked/not applicable

Figure 2.1

Self-evaluation of preparedness at the time of first managership by function.

Source: *Paul DiMaggio, Manager of the Arts, Research Division Report #20, National Endowment for the Arts (Santa Ana, CA: Seven Locks Press, 1987). Used with permission.*

that they had "good preparation" for budgeting and finance, planning and development, personnel management, and government relations.

DiMaggio also asked arts managers how they learned to do their jobs. An overwhelming number of the respondents indicated that they learned how to manage while on the job. These managers included 95 percent in theater and orchestra management, 90 percent in museum management, and 86 percent in community arts agency (CAA) management.[32] Around 20 percent said they had learned through university arts administration courses.

Updating the profile

A 1997 survey of 641 professionally managed performing arts organizations, undertaken by J. Dennis Rich and Dan J. Martin, examined the role of education in arts administrative training.[33] The authors identified 26 management skills ranging from accounting to trustee and volunteer relations. Respondents provided their ratings of the skills needed to be an effective arts manager. (See Figure 2.2.) The top skills, not surprisingly, included leadership, fundraising,

Critical Value of Management Skills

NOTE: 10 being the highest	Median	Mean	High	Low
Leadership	10	9.12	10	1
Budgeting	9	8.82	10	4
Team Building	9	8.82	10	1
Fundraising	9	8.79	10	1
Communication Skills/Writing	9	8.76	10	3
Marketing/Audience Development	9	8.49	10	4
Financial Management	9	8.41	10	3
Aesthetics/Artistic Sense	9	8.23	10	1
Trustee/Volunteer Relations	9	8.12	10	1
Strategic Management	8	8.18	10	3
Grant writing	8	8.01	10	1
Public Relations/Press Relations	8	7.89	10	3
Organizational Behavior	8	7.69	10	1
Public Speaking	8	7.66	10	1
Etiquette/Social Grace	8	7.62	10	1
Information Management	8	7.52	10	1
Community Outreach/Education	8	7.41	10	1
Accounting	7	7.10	10	1
Expertise in One Arts Discipline	7	6.91	10	1
Political Understanding	7	6.50	10	1
Knowledge of Many Arts Disciplines	7	6.48	10	1
Personnel Relations/Unions	7	6.26	10	1
Contract Law	6	5.61	10	1
Statistical Analysis	6	5.38	10	1
Collective Bargaining	5	5.39	10	1
Computer Programming	5	5.08	10	1

Figure 2.2
Critical value of management skills.
Source: *Dennis Rich and Dan J. Martin, "The Role of Formal Education in Arts Administration Training,"* from The Guide to Arts Administration Training and Research 1997–1999 *(Washington, D.C.: Association of Arts Administration Educators [AAAE], 1997). Used with permission.*

communication and writing, marketing and audience development, and budgeting. The survey also identified skills employers thought best learned in the classroom versus those learned on the job. Interestingly, the respondents could not seem to agree about whether classroom or on-the-job training was better. For example, the authors noted:

- Arts managers want more training in marketing and fundraising (executive education).
- Arts managers prefer to hire marketing and development directors with formal arts administration training.
- They believe that marketing and fundraising is, by and large, best learned "on the job."[34]

In the 1990s, the diversification of arts institutions continued to increase the opportunities for women and minorities in the field of arts management.

As a result, today's arts manager profile is somewhat more representative of our society. With that said, the profile DiMaggio found of managers who were well-educated, upper middle class with a background in an arts discipline is still fairly accurate. Anecdotally, the retirement of the baby boom generation seems to be changing the arts manager profile. These individuals, many of whom have worked in the field of arts management for the last 30 years, are being replaced by a younger workforce that is made up of a higher percentage of women. A recent research study seems to offer evidence of what is anecdotally reported.

A study that shed some light on the changing arts manager profile was published in the *Journal of Arts Management, Law, and Society* in 1998. The National Study of Arts Managers conducted in 1996 found that "67 percent of the upper-level (management) positions are held by males, whereas 33 percent of upper-level positions are held by females."[35] The percentage of males to females was quite different at the middle-management level: 24 percent male and 76 percent female. The survey also found significant differences in salaries. "The average salary for a male arts manager is $56,936; however, the average salary for a female arts manager is $41,368."[36] Based on this survey, it seems logical to project that a significant percentage of females in middle-management jobs are likely to move up to the senior level positions in organizations and thus, the gender balance will undergo significant change in many arts and culture organizations over the next 10 to 20 years.

Today's arts manager has access to a wide array of information resources and skill building opportunities. There are numerous workshops and conferences sponsored by national organizations such as Americans for the Arts. Closer to home, many state and local arts agencies present information and training opportunities for the arts manager and the artist to develop their skills in leadership, marketing, fundraising, event planning, and utilizing computer technology.

The option of pursuing a formal education in arts management is also more widely available today. Master degree programs can be found at many universities across the United States and internationally. The Association of Arts Administration Educators (AAAE) Web site lists forty-four graduate programs (www.artsadministration.org). In addition, AAAE lists fourteen undergraduate programs as current members. The European Network of Cultural Administration Training Centres (ENCATC; www.encatc.org) was founded in 1992 and lists 127 members operating in 39 countries.

Jobs for arts managers today

Jobs in the private and public sector encompass an enormous range of possibilities. If one considers career opportunities in the broader scope of arts and entertainment, then the options available are extraordinary for an arts manager. Figure 1.1 is a snapshot of the range of options. However, sources such as arts employment newsletters or online arts employment services provide a more focused look at the jobs available for arts managers.

When scanning a publication like *ARTSEARCH*, an employment service bulletin that is published 23 times a year by the Theatre Communications Group (TCG),[37] it is possible to gain an overview of the job market for arts managers. TCG, as have many organizations, now posts job openings online. The typical job listings in *ARTSEARCH* and in other job listing services reveal the expectations of organizations about staff qualifications for an arts manager in today's workplace. For example, a typical issue of *ARTSEARCH* will list openings for artistic or executive directors, managing directors, administrative assistants, box office managers, development directors, education directors, general managers, public relations managers, and database managers.[38] The qualifications often noted for executive directors, for example, include skills in areas such as administration, communication, planning supervision, fundraising, and fiscal management. Obviously, executive director positions require previous experience or, as is often indicated in a job posting, "a proven track record."

The proliferation of online job postings and Web-based application processes has made the process of applying for a job easier. A few of these resources are discussed in Chapter 14, Career Options and Preparing for the Job Market. However, finding the information about the salary offered for these jobs can be a challenge. Most organizations now resort to wording such as "Salary and benefits commensurate with experience." There is general data available on salaries, but specific salary information is often only available in costly reports published by arts service organizations.

Salary ranges

Depending on what part of the United States the arts manager job is in and the overall operating budget of the organization, the full-time salaries for entry-level positions may range from as little as $15,000 to $30,000. Middle-management positions may start at $25,000 and range up to $60,000, and upper management salaries could start as low as $30,000 and go up to $75,000 and beyond. When it comes to the upper end of the pay scale, the salaries often reported in the media tend to focus on extraordinary compensation levels of CEOs or the five highest paid staff in an organization.

The benefits will also vary with the financial resources of the organization. Most offer health insurance through a group policy and may require the employee to pay a percentage of the benefit costs. Larger arts organizations and educational institutions (such as colleges and universities) offer more comprehensive benefit packages.

The NonProfit Times (www.nptimes.com) publishes an annual salary survey that offers survey information gathered from a few hundred not-for-profit organizations. Their 2007 salary survey report was based on 488 responses from organizations in America, of which only 8% were arts organizations.[39] The annual survey provided national salary averages by six organizational budget sizes (less than $500,000 all the way up to $50 million-plus) and for ten different job functions. It also reports geographical salary averages for seven different regions in the United States using ten job titles. For example, the overall average salary range for a development director (the person responsible for the fundraising in an organization) was $71,455 to $71,825. Organizations reporting budgets of less than $500,000 had salary averages for this position ranging from $33,493 to $33,890. On the other hand, the average for this job if you worked for an organization with a budget between $1 million to $9.9 million was between $61,539 and $64,650.[40] Salary averages were above the average in the Northeast and below average in the South and Midwest.

There are many employment opportunities in arts management, especially at the entry level. However, many of the smaller not-for-profit arts and culture organizations simply do not have the funding to offer salaries that are competitive with the private sector. Please refer to Chapter 14, Career Options and Preparing for the Job Market, for more information about career options and compensation in arts management.

The manager's personal mission

An essential ingredient in the mix of the knowledge, skills, and abilities that a person brings to any arts management job must include a passion for what he is doing and a strong sense of purpose. When it comes to compensation, as we have seen, the salary will very likely be lower if you opt to work in the arts and not-for-profit sector. However, salary might be only one of several criteria someone may have for selecting a career in arts management.

The rewards of working in this field can extend far beyond a paycheck. Having a strong personal mission and sense of purpose is an important part of the profile of an arts manager. In addition, although sometimes it is difficult to quantify what may be the intangible benefits of working in the arts, having a clear point of view about the value and contribution the arts make to a community is an important starting point. As you will see in Chapter 7, Human Resources and the Arts, and Chapter 8, Leadership and Group Dynamics, the successful arts manager must have skills that span many general management functions.

From the Bookshelf

Livingston Biddle's comprehensive personal history of the NEA, *Our Government and the Arts: A Perspective from the Inside* (New York: American Council for the Arts, 1988), is filled with hundreds of facts and anecdotes about the struggle to establish and maintain what may be one of the most cost-effective organizations in government. In addition to telling interesting stories, Biddle takes the reader inside the legislative system as well as the early management structure of the endowment.

For a more current insider's perspective on the NEA you would do well to read Jane Alexander's book, *Command Performance: An Actress in the Theater of Politics* (New York: Public Affairs, a Perseus Books Group publication, 2000). The book offers a fascinating look into the strategies used by Alexander to help ensure the survival of the NEA at a time when its very existence was threatened. In addition to offering a wealth of information about how the NEA met these challenges and survived, this book provides arts managers with valuable lessons on the fine art of working with the political system in the United States.

THE GROWTH OF THE ARTS MANAGER ROLE AND THE NEA

The role of arts managers in the United States was further defined and enhanced by the passage of legislation establishing the National Endowment for the Arts and Humanities on September 15, 1965.[41] The struggle to create a modest system for promoting growth and excellence in the arts took several years, numerous congressional hearings, and incredible dedication by a few people. Since its establishment, the NEA (www.nea.gov) has helped shape the arts scene in the United States by organizing an identifiable arts constituency, stimulating donations through matching grants, and providing guidance to arts groups on ways to manage their limited resources effectively. Although the NEA appropriation was only $121,314,072 in 2006, or roughly $0.41 per person in the United States,[42] the endowment regularly generates millions more through various matching grants programs.

However, the government support for the arts in the United States extends well beyond supporting the NEA. If agencies such as the Smithsonian, Corporation for Public Broadcasting, National Gallery of Art, the National Endowment for the Humanities, and dozens of other federally supported arts and culture organizations are added into the per person calculation the level of support for the arts increases to $6.00 based on 2006 data.[43] This per person figure would be even greater if the total amount of tax revenue that the IRS forgoes for charitable donations to the arts was included.

The NEA's vision and mission statements are worth noting, because they help shape the numerous grant categories created to support the arts. The following is from the NEA's Web site:

Mission: The National Endowment for the Arts is a public agency dedicated to supporting excellence in the arts, both new and established; bringing the arts to all Americans; and providing leadership in arts education.

Vision: A nation in which artistic excellence is celebrated, supported, and available to all Americans.[44]

The NEA also has a strategic plan for 2006–2011, which is structured as follows:

GOALS

1. Access to Artistic Excellence
   To encourage and support artistic excellence; preserve our cultural heritage; and provide access to the arts for all Americans.
2. Learning in the Arts
   To advance arts education for children and youth.
3. Partnerships for the Arts
   To develop and maintain partnerships that support excellence in the arts, both new and established; bring the arts to all Americans; and provide leadership in arts education.
4. Management
   To enable the Arts Endowment to achieve its mission through effective, efficient, and responsible management of resources.

NEA

Areas of Special Emphasis

1. National Initiatives
   A grants program that serves the American people by creating large model programs of indisputable artistic merit and broad public reach accompanied by substantive educational materials for schools, students, and teachers. The strategy embodies the agency's four-pronged commitment to artistic excellence, public accessibility, arts education, and partnership.
2. International Activities
   Programs that support the presentation of American arts and artists at international venues, encourage exchanges of U.S. artists with artists

of other nations, indemnify art objects from other countries for the purpose of exhibition in the U.S., and sponsor presentations of the work of foreign artists in the United States.[45]

The creation of the NEA has led to the development of a support system for performers, performing arts organizations, museums, and film, design, and humanities projects for over 40 years. Currently the NEA recognizes outstanding contributions to the arts through the National Medal of Arts, Jazz Masters Fellowships, and National Heritage Fellowships. Project grants are available to organizations in the areas of dance, design, folk and traditional arts, literature, local arts agencies, media arts, museums, music, music theater, opera, presenting organization, theater, and visual arts. Organizations are expected to have a three-year history of programming before they can apply. The NEA does not fund general operating expenses, the creation of new organizations, facilities construction, or elementary or secondary schools.[46]

The matching grant categories for organizations include, Access to Artistic Excellence ($5,000 to $100,000), Challenge America: Reaching Every Community Fast-Track Review Grants ($10,000), and Learning in the Arts for Children and Youth ($5,000 to $100,00). The NEA Literature Fellowships are non-matching grants for $25,000.[47] In addition to these awards and grants, the NEA is sponsoring a series of National Initiatives: American Masterpieces, The Big Read, Poetry Out Loud, Shakespeare in American Communities, NEA Jazz Masters, and the Arts Journalism Insititute.[48] The NEA also sponsors three Leadership Initiatives: The Arts on Radio and Television, The Mayors' Institute on City Design, and The Open World Cultural Leaders Program.[49] In addition, the NEA provides funds to regional arts agencies, who in turn distribute funds regionally and locally.

The typical application process moves through a system of staff screening, review by a committee of peers in the discipline, review of the peer group recommendation by the National Council on the Arts, and a final decision by the Chair of the NEA. Applications can take from six months to a year to work their way through the system. The chance of receiving funding is dependent to a large degree on how well the proposed project matches the criteria the NEA has set for the funding area. For example, in 2005 the NEA reported the Access to Artistic Excellence grants were awarded to 1,501 organizations. A total of 2,741 applications were received, which translates into about 54.7% of the requests being funded.[50]

Government support

The pros and cons of government support for the arts have not changed significantly since the inception of the NEA. The supporters of the legislation that led to the creation of the NEA saw it as an opportunity to make the arts more available to people throughout the United States and to enrich the nation's cultural life. Programs were designed to promote a type of cultural democracy through very modest grants to a wide range of projects and institutions. It was deemed important to support the creative spirit and at the same time promote new work. The preservation of a cultural heritage was a high priority, and the support of work that might not otherwise exist in a market-driven economic system was thought to benefit everyone.

The critics of the legislation believed that the establishment of a government subsidy system would eventually result in general mediocrity creeping into the arts. There was fear that centralizing the power of the subsidy in the hands of a few would lead to less, not more, creative work in the country. Others believed that it was wrong to give the taxpayers' money to projects and programs with no appeal beyond a limited number of people. Some people argued that a type of cultural dictatorship would result from the peer review system. Others argued that if the government started subsidizing the arts, private and corporate philanthropy would dry up.

Budget battles and censorship

In the end, the astute shepherding of the legislation through the House and Senate by Livingston Biddle (chairman of the NEA in 1977 to 1981) and others helped neutralize critics in the early days of the endowment. The NEA flourished and survived the annual congressional budget hearing process until 1981. Under the budget planning guidance of White House aide David Stockman, the new Reagan administration proposed a 50 percent cut in the NEA budget for 1982 and additional cuts in 1983–1986.[51] The new administration saw in the NEA an example of the government creating a disincentive for private support for the arts. When confronted with the increase in private giving that had been generated by the endowment, the Reagan administration backed away from massive budget cutting, and reductions of 6 percent were adopted by Congress. The political spotlight shifted off the endowment, and the budget actually continued to increase up until 1992 (see Figure 2.3).

The budget battles of the early 1980s were minor in comparison with the firestorm that erupted with reauthorization legislation in 1989 and 1990. The reauthorization of the NEA became the focal point for a political struggle over censorship and the whole concept of funding for the arts. In the fall of 1990, arts lobby groups pleaded with arts groups across the country to support the NEA's reauthorization. Telegrams and letters were sent to Washington to show members of Congress that there were constituents who supported the arts.

The compromise legislation eventually enacted required grant recipients to return their grant monies if the work they produced was found to be obscene by the courts. This compromise did not sit well with the artistic community.

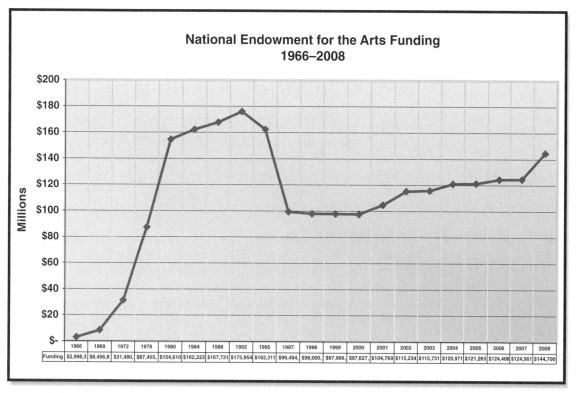

Figure 2.3

NEA funding 1966–2008. (Funding in millions.)

Source: *Summary of Appropriated Funds 1966–2008, National Endowment for the Arts, May 2008. Not adjusted for inflation.*

Controversy continued to follow the NEA as artists and organizations sued over the obscenity pledge. Several organizations, among them the Public Theater in New York City, turned down substantial grants rather than agree to the terms that the NEA established.

Censorship charges continued to be leveled at the NEA when grant recommendations by the National Council on the Arts were overturned by the acting director of the endowment in the spring of 1992. The resignations of peer review panels and key staff disrupted the operations of the endowment.

The remainder of the 1990s saw more trouble for the NEA as it went through further reauthorization hearings. The shift to a Republican controlled House and Senate in 1996 kept the NEA on the budget hot seat. Proposals to shut down the NEA found favor in the House, and the eventual budget compromise process led to the agency being funded for only $98 million in 1998.

There were layoffs and staff positions were eliminated to operate within the new budget constraints.

A casualty of the political struggles of the NEA has been funding for individual artists. In 1996 the NEA revised many of its grant categories and for the most part limited individual grants to fellowships. The hard work of Clinton appointee Jane Alexander, NEA Chair from 1993 to 1997, helped keep the agency alive. William Ivey was appointed Chair in 1998, and he was to be succeeded by Michael Hammond in 2002. However, Hammond, former Dean of the Shepherd School of Music at Rice University, passed away suddenly in January 2002, only a month into his administration. The agency appointed an interim chair soon thereafter.

New directions

In 2003 the current Chair, Dana Gioia (JOY-uh), was appointed by President Bush. Gioia is an award-winning internationally acclaimed poet with a background that includes an MBA from Stanford University and an MA in Comparative Literature from Harvard. Chairman Gioia has been an articulate spokesperson for the NEA and has initiated several new programs that have enhanced the impact of the Endowment.

Under the current Chair, the NEA has seen significant change and growth. The budget has increased and the mission focus seems to be clearer. Gioia has introduced several new initiatives while promoting a positive image of the NEA. In the "Chairman's Statement" in his 2003 Annual Report he noted:

> It was my conviction that the National Endowment for the Arts could best reestablish itself by focusing on its stated core mission to foster excellence in the arts — both new and established — and to make the best of the arts accessible to all Americans. ...The Arts Endowment needed to be confident and unapologetic about that mission as we communicated the value of our programming to the nation. It was my belief that by working in a positive, inclusive, and non-divisive manner with members of Congress, the Administration, arts and arts advocacy organizations, and artists, we could build a constructive new consensus in support of the Arts Endowment.[52]

The NEA and the arts manager

The granting process implemented by the NEA in the late 1960s helped to stimulate the growth of many careers in arts management and to hasten the professionalization of the field. The specialized skills required to seek out grants were in great demand. Because all organizational grants were at least a one-to-one match, meaning that for every federal grant dollar a matching dollar of other money must be found, fundraising staffs and development experts began to be hired. Typically, grants to large organizations required three dollars of private money for every dollar of federal money over a three-year period. This further necessitated establishing a staff support system to run the initial campaign and to continue bringing the money in after the grant expired.

The development of the now-common structure of a board of directors and management staff was a product of the new accountability that arts organizations faced. Organizations had to prove that they could responsibly manage the funds they were given. Annual reports, financial statements, and five-year plans became standard operating procedures for organizations that wanted to be considered by the federal, corporate, and foundation funders. The net result was an increase in staff openings, which provided jobs for the baby boomers graduating from the colleges and universities across America in the 1970s and 1980s.

The NEA offers career opportunities for arts managers interested in working in areas such as grants and awards, public relations, development, budget, finance, research, and human resources. There are also nonpaying internships at the NEA for undergraduate and graduate students.

State agencies

The original NEA legislation provided funds for the creation of state agencies to distribute 20 percent of the endowment's overall budget. The state and local arts agencies created another network of funding opportunities for artists and arts groups as well as staff positions for arts managers. The NEA is mandated to provide a percentage of its budget to the partnerships funding program with the states.[53]

The extensive reach of state and regional arts agencies makes it possible for an arts manager to interact with artists and other arts managers at multiple levels. The National Assembly of State Arts Agencies (NASAA) lists as its mission "to advance and promote a meaningful role for the arts in the lives of individuals, families, and communities throughout the United States."[54] The NASAA headquarters is in Washington, D.C. The NEA also funds the six regional arts organizations: Arts Midwest, Mid-America Arts Alliance, Mid-Atlantic Arts Foundation, New England Foundation for the Arts, Southern Arts Federation, and the Western States Arts Federation.[55]

These regional organizations "provide technical assistance to their member state arts agencies, support and promote artists and arts organizations, and develop and manage arts initiatives on local, regional, national and international levels."[56] The extensive network of regional arts agencies in turn supports over 56 state and district arts agencies. Last, but not least, there is a network of local arts agencies or arts councils within the states. These arts councils are often managed by volunteers, although some of the bigger councils have one or two staff. For example, the Web site for the Colorado Council on the Arts (www.coloarts.state.co.us) has a link to a spreadsheet with 49 local arts agencies or arts centers.

CONCLUSION

The evolution of the role of the arts manager continues as thousands of arts organizations undergo the arduous process of adapting to the changing cultural environment. As we will see in Chapter 4, The Adaptive Arts Organization, arts groups must constantly assess the opportunities and threats that present themselves in the world around them. In theory, at least, an arts manager should be trained to serve the needs of her particular discipline by effectively solving the problems of today and anticipating the significant changes of tomorrow. Unfortunately, the day-to-day struggle for financial survival that goes on in most organizations leaves little time for planning for the future.

Whatever changes take place in the next few years, arts managers working with artists, boards, and staffs will play a central role in the future of the arts in the United States. Dynamic vision and articulate leadership will be required if the arts are to build on the growth of the last 60 years.

SUMMARY

Over the last two thousand years, the basic functions of the artist–manager have remained the same: to bring art and the public together is the continuing objective.

In ancient times, simple religious ceremonies evolved into full-scale state-sponsored arts events that lasted from several days to a few weeks. The functions of management (planning, organizing, leading, and controlling) were distributed between artist–managers and the public officials who acted as arts managers. The rise of the Church and the decline of Rome created a shift away from state-sponsored events.

The late Middle Ages produced economic growth that allowed for the expansion of population centers. The rise of guilds and community-sponsored celebrations helped fuel changes in the overall arts climate. Complex pageants often needed people with management expertise to organize the large casts and the various sets associated with the productions.

Continued changes in society and the birth of more democratic forms of government eventually led to changes that became the foundation of many modern organizations. The Renaissance fostered the rebirth of drama and contributed to the development of the first operas and ballets. Problems with financing, patronage, and censorship also accompanied the growth in the arts, but the additional art forms created additional jobs for arts managers.

In the seventeenth and eighteenth centuries, some countries began to establish national dance, opera, music, and theater companies. Permanent staff members and performers received salaries and pension benefits.

By the nineteenth century in Europe and the United States, the arts had expanded into smaller population centers. However, there were no state-recognized arts institutions in the United States comparable to those of Europe. As communities became cities, orchestras, opera companies, and museums became permanent institutions. Most were supported by a small group of philanthropists.

The role of the arts manager in the United States expanded with the continued development of touring, which was made possible by an extensive rail system. Monopolistic enterprises took control of many of the theaters at the end of the nineteenth century. The invention of movies and radio contributed to a decline in attendance at arts events by the 1920s.

The last century has been shaped by major wars, improving economic conditions, the new technologies, and a population boom. At the same time, legislation and tax laws have helped artists and managers to establish nonprofit organizations to carry out their artistic vision. The process for establishing nonprofit, tax-exempt arts organizations is a well-established process widely used in America.

As a profession and a recognized field of work, arts management is a product of changes in U.S. national policy since the 1950s. Ford Foundation funding and, beginning in 1965, the National Endowment for the Arts helped make private and public support for the arts a priority. The expanding arts market resulting from the population increase and the education boom has also contributed to the creation of thousands of new jobs in the arts.

The typical arts manager profile in the 1980s was of a highly educated, upper-middle-class person with a background in the humanities. A limited number had done course work in management while in school. Survey results show that many arts managers had to learn the functions of their positions on the job. The growth in training programs in the 1980s and 1990s has created a more diversified group of arts managers.

The NEA was created in 1965 to promote excellence, broaden the availability of the arts, and preserve work identified as part of the United States' national heritage. The political environment has reshaped the NEA, and the resulting changes have reduced the budget by nearly 50 percent since 1992. The NEA has assisted many groups in organizing and professionalizing their staffs. In addition to promoting the growth of the arts at a national level, the NEA also supports numerous state and local arts agencies.

Questions

1. Summarize the major arts management activity associated with the following time periods:
   a. Ancient Greece
   b. Ancient Rome
   c. Middle Ages
   d. Renaissance
   e. Seventeenth through nineteenth centuries
   f. Twentieth century
2. What are the seven steps typically required to incorporate a nonprofit arts business?
3. What changes have taken place in the job market that might alter DiMaggio's profile of the arts manager?
4. How much control should management have over the artistic product of an organization? For example, how much input should management have when it comes time to select the season titles? Can you think of a situation in which too much or too little control was exercised by the management of an arts organization? What were the results?
5. Visit the NEA Web site and review its current funding programs. Have any of these programs had an impact on your state, region, or city? Discuss.

DISCUSSION ARTICLE — MANAGING THE ARTS TODAY

July 31, 2006

Act Like a Business? Why Aim So Low?

by Andrew Taylor

In his recent monograph, *Good to Great and the Social Sectors*, Jim Collins makes a rather bold statement: "We must reject the idea — well-intentioned, but dead wrong — that the primary path to greatness in the social sectors is to become "more like a business." His point is that most businesses are poorly run, and that many business practices correlate with mediocrity, not greatness. So, to him, telling nonprofit organizations to "run like a business" is like telling artists to lower their standards, or telling a visionary leader to "aim low."

For those of us who have been struggling to convince cultural leaders to work with more focus, more discipline, and more responsiveness, Collins' words come as a bit of a blow. But I have to admit he has a point. For the past decades, our industry has fundamentally misunderstood what it means to run "like a business." As a result, we've tended to become more rigid, less joyous, and increasingly disconnected from the communities and the creative spirit we were formed to serve.

In the Arts Administration MBA degree program I direct, we get to see both sides of the question — dwelling in a School of Business, and working every day with cultural nonprofits. From that perspective, I suggest a six-point alternative to "running like a business," to give ourselves more worthy targets:

1. Arts organizations must strive to be *better than* a business. Being responsible, accountable, transparent and responsive is the *lowest* standard we should set for ourselves. Let's be exceptional.

2. We must use business tools with an artist's hand. Business tools are merely ways to see the world, and ways to structure our interaction with it. Let's be like the artists around us and explore those tools with creative abandon.

3. We must embrace our roles as social engineers. So much of our work involves engineering compelling social experiences and catalytic community space. Let's learn the tools of those trades with the same energy and effort we commit to our more familiar tasks.

4. We must define our own goals, rather than having them assigned to us. We are continually lured by outside measures of success: economic impact, educational enhancement, social service. If these are our goals, let's embrace them. If not, let's clarify our purpose to our constituents and ourselves.

5. We must work with clarity and discipline. Nonprofit arts organizations don't have the luxury of elbowroom; *every* action must be taken with elegance, intent and an openness to learn and improve.

6. We must calculate our efforts in multiple currencies. There are a multitude of resources beyond money that drive what we do: joy, discovery, connection, sense of purpose, sense of place and on and on. Let's make room in our spreadsheets and strategic plans to ensure we're measuring what matters.

In the end, behaving "like a business" is a matter of semantics. Arts organizations *are* businesses, so their behavior is businesslike — just as good or just as bad. The deeper question is *what kind* of business do you want to be? And what skills and perspective do you need to get there? It's not about mimicry. It's about clarity, curiosity, and courage.

This opinion piece appeared in the July/August 2006 issue of Inside Arts, *the magazine of the Association of Performing Arts Presenters and is used with permission.*

Questions

1. The author raises the question of the role of arts managers as "social engineers." Discuss how arts organizations in your community engage in various forms of social engineering through the programs they create, sponsor, or present.
2. What are some of the goals that measure success for arts organizations in your community? The article mentions outside measures. Are these measures incorporated in arts organizations you are familiar with?
3. The article points out arts organizations are businesses. How would you assess the success of the arts organizations in your community as they behave or act like a business?

REFERENCES

1. Oscar G. Brockett, Franklin J. Hildy, *History of the Theatre*, 9th ed. (Boston: Allyn and Bacon, 2003), pp. 13–34.
2. Neil Kotler, Philip Kotler, *Museum Strategy and Marketing* (San Francisco: Jossey-Bass, Inc., 1998), p. 11.
3. Ibid., p. 11.
4. Ibid., p. 11.
5. Brockett, Hildy, *History of the Theatre*, pp. 43–69.
6. Ibid., p. 85.
7. Ibid., p. 95.
8. Ibid., p. 163.
9. Gayle Kassing, *History of Dance* (Champaign, IL: Human Kinetics, 2007), p. 98.
10. Ibid., p. 104.
11. Ibid., p. 104.
12. Kotler and Kotler, *Museum Strategy and Marketing*, p. 12.
13. John Pick, *Managing the Arts? The British Experience* (London: Rhinegold, 1986), p. 23.
14. Ibid., p. 45.
15. William J. Baumol, William G. Bowen, *Performing Arts: The Economic Dilemma* (Cambridge, MA: MIT Press, 1966), p. 20.

16. Ibid., p. 29.

17. Kotler and Kotler, *Museum Strategy and Marketing*, p. 12.

18. Baumol and Bowen, *Performing Arts*, p. 29.

19. Ibid., pp. 27–28.

20. Martin Mayer, "The Opera," in *The Performing Arts and American Society*, W. McNeil Lowry, ed. (Englewood Cliffs, NJ: Prentice-Hall, Spectrum Books, 1977), p. 45.

21. W. McNeil Lowry, ed. *The Performing Arts and American Society* (Englewood Cliffs, NJ: Prentice-Hall, Spectrum Books, 1977), p. 14.

22. Ibid., p. 11.

23. NEA Research Division Note #93, "State Counts of Performing Arts Companies," (Washington, D.C., November 2006), p. 2.

24. Ibid., p. 2.

25. NEA Research Division Note #64, "Museums, Arboreta, Botanical Gardens and Zoos Report 18% Growth, 1987–1992" (Washington, D.C., May 1998).

26. National Endowment for the Arts, "1965–1995: A Brief Chronology of Federal Involvement in the Arts," edited by Keith Donohue (Washington, D.C.: NEA, 2000), p. 4.

27. Kotler and Kotler, *Museum Strategy and Marketing*, p. 12.

28. From Anthony Mancuso's *How to Form a Nonprofit Corporation*, 4th ed. (San Francisco: Nolo Press, 2001), summary of chapters 1–3, pp. 1.2–3.14.

29. NEA Research Division Note #90 (Washington, D.C., March, 2006).

30. Paul DiMaggio, *Managers of the Arts*, NEA Research Division Report #20 (Santa Ana, CA: Seven Locks Press, 1987), p. 12.

31. Ibid., p. 42.

32. Ibid., p. 46.

33. J. Dennis Rich, Dan J. Martin, *The Guide to Arts Administration Training and Research 1997–1999* (Washington, D.C.: Association of Arts Administration Educators, 1997), pp. 69–73.

34. Ibid., p. 72.

35. Donna G. Herron, Tamara S. Hubbard, Amy E. Kirner, Lynn Newcomb, Michelle Reisner-Memmer, Michael E. Robertson II, Matthew W. Smith, Leslie A. Tullo, and Jennifer S. Young, "The Effect of Gender on the Career Advancement of Arts Managers," *Journal of Arts Management, Law, and Society.*, Vol. 28, No. 1, 1998, p. 30.

36. Ibid., p. 30.

37. *ARTSEARCH* is published by the Theatre Communications Group, Inc., 355 Lexington Ave., New York, NY 10017.

38. *ARTSEARCH* July 1, 2007, Vol. 27, #12, pp. 1–12.

39. Mark Hrywna, "NPT Salary Survey 2007," *The NonProfit Times*, February 1, 2007, p. 15.

40. Ibid., pp. 16–17.

41. Livingston Biddle, *Our Government and the Arts* (New York: American Council for the Arts, 1988), p. 180. After the passage of the bill, President Lyndon Johnson signed the legislation creating the NEA on September 29, 1965.

42. The per-person cost was arrived at by dividing the 2006 budget for the NEA by the total U.S. population of 299,398,484 according to the 2006 Census Bureau report.

43. *How the United States Funds the Arts*, 2nd edition, National Endowment for the Arts, January 2007, p. 10.

44. http://www.nea.gov/about/Facts/AtAGlance.html.

45. *NEA Strategic Plan 2006–2011*: http://www.nea.gov/about/Budget/index.html. pp. 1–2.

46. NEA 2007 Guide, p. 5.

47. Ibid., pp. 5–8.

48. Ibid., pp. 10–13.

49. Ibid., p. 14.

50. NEA 2005 Annual Report, p. 25.

51. Biddle, *Our Government and the Arts*, p. 492.

52. NEA 2003 Annual Report, p. 1.

53. http://www.arts.gov/partner/index.html.

54. http://www.nasaa-arts.org/aboutnasaa/about.shtml.

55. http://www.usregionalarts.org/.

56. Ibid.

CHAPTER 3

Management History and Trends

Management facilitates the efforts of people in organized groups and arises when people seek to cooperate to achieve goals.

Daniel Wren, "The History of Management Thought"

KEY WORDS

Robert Owen
Charles Babbage
Daniel Craig McCallum
Henry Varnum Poor
Frederick W. Taylor
Scientific management
Operations research
Critical path method (CPM)
Computer-aided design (CAD), computer-assisted manufacturing (CAM), and computer-implemented manufacturing (CIM)
Henri Fayol's Fourteen Principles
Human relations management
The Hawthorne Effect

Elton Mayo
Fritz Roethlisberger
Mary Parker Follett's integrative unity
Abraham Maslow's hierarchy of needs
Douglas McGregor's Theory X and Theory Y
Operations research (OR)
Systems theory
Contingency theory
Synergy
Paradigms
The Halo Effect

In this chapter, we scan the evolution of management thought. After a review of early management practices, we examine the management concepts that grew out of the shift to mass production during the Industrial Revolution. Finally, we will look at the impact of scientific management and the application of psychological theories to the workplace.

The primary objective of this chapter is to provide the reader with a general historical background on the field of management. Many of the terms and concepts noted in Chapters 1 and 2 have developed from classic and contemporary management theory and practice. If you have taken college courses in business or management, the terms, concepts, and people noted in this chapter should not be new to you. Before moving into the specific areas of external environments, planning, organizational design, and human resource management, it seems appropriate to explore the source of the current management systems used to operate all organizations.

MANAGEMENT AS AN ART AND A SOCIAL SCIENCE

A basic assumption of this text is that management is an art. In this case, an *art* is typically defined as *an ability or special skill that someone develops and applies.* Studying the theories of management, synthesizing the application of these theories to a practical work environment, and then creating a workable system for a specific organization require a tremendous amount of thought and effort. It is often a lifetime job.

Management can also be considered to be a social science. Although the idea of "science" in the workplace may not be very appealing to an aspiring arts manager, the reality is that applying some of the techniques noted in this chapter may help make a stronger arts organization.

As we will see, the general concept of *scientific management* is not universally welcomed in the workplace. The term describes a particular approach to maximizing productivity by applying research and quantitative analysis to the work process. The creation of general and specific management theories to explain and predict how organizations and people behave is also integral to thinking of management as a science.

At the center of any theory is the ability to predict an outcome if given a specific set of circumstances. A scientist develops a theory, conducts experiments, establishes an outcome that can be repeated by others, and provides proof of the theory. Management theory tries to achieve a similar goal: predictable outcomes given controlled inputs. Unfortunately, the science of management, as with any social science, is sometimes subject to unanticipated outcomes. In management science, numerous other variables, including the behavior of employees in the work environment, can quickly undermine a theory. Applying the techniques used by social scientists can assist a manager in the process of running an organization.

On-the-job management theory

When studying management theory and practice, which are often examined by using case studies, it becomes apparent that many managers enter into the practice of managing with virtually no theoretical background. Whether in the arts or business, not having formal training has never been a barrier to running an organization. For example, the late Katherine Graham, who once owned the *Washington Post*, had no formal training in business management. The sudden death of her husband thrust her into the role of chief executive officer. Nonetheless, she was able to successfully operate a major newspaper using her personal abilities and adaptability. She was able to learn on the job and to further develop her own operating theories and practices to maintain a successful business. For every Katherine Graham there are many other people in the workplace less successful at playing the role of manager. Your local bookstore is stocked with readings about how employees should deal with the boss or supervisor who does not seem to have mastered the art of managing. (For more information about Katherine Graham go to: http://womenshistory.about.com/od/journalists/p/katharinegraham.htm.)

In Chapter 2 we saw that Paul DiMaggio's 1987 study for the National Endowment for the Arts demonstrated more than 85 percent of the arts managers in theaters, art museums, orchestras, and arts associations said that they learned from on-the-job training.[1] The university-trained arts managers surveyed claimed that their schooling did not adequately prepare them for many of the demands of running an organization. The numbers of university-trained arts managers has increased in the last few years, but it is still safe to say that the experience of the workplace is required to complete the education of any arts manager.

The effective manager

Regardless of how an individual learns the art and science of management, an effective manager must eventually be able to analyze variables and predict outcomes based on experience. In other words, the manager must find a set of operating principles that can be used day to day. For example, an arts manager might have to say to the Board, "If we raise prices, ticket orders will decline based on discretionary spending patterns of our audiences. Or, if we change our subscription plans, fewer people will order because any change creates confusion. Or, if we perform nothing but concerts of modern music, a significant portion of our subscribers will stay home." These statements may all be true and based on good scientific research, but that does not mean the Board will follow the manager's recommendation. It may be perfectly appropriate, given the mission, for an organization to make a decision that will produce a negative outcome. An effective manager should be able to articulate her expectations of outcomes based on an understanding of the effects of variables on particular decisions. Obviously, experience is and always will be a great teacher.

To be an effective arts manager one should have an awareness and appreciation of the overall field of management. The rest of this chapter focuses on some of the major theories and principles that shape management today.

EVOLUTION OF MANAGEMENT THOUGHT

Preindustrialization

For the last several thousand years, organized social systems have managed the resources needed to feed, house, and protect people. The evolution of management is intertwined with the development of the social, religious, and economic systems needed to support cities, states, and countries. The church and state provided the first systems for planning, organizing, leading, and controlling. These management systems were predicated on philosophies that placed people within complex hierarchies.

History provides many examples of management systems established by the Egyptians, Romans, and Chinese. Many basic principles of supervision and control evolved from the projects undertaken by these societies. Building temples, pyramids, and other massive structures required extensive management and organizational skill. Organizing massive armies to go forth and conquer the known world required detailed organizational planning and logistical coordination. Many modern management concepts expanded on the skill needed to implement public works projects as the world shifted from an agrarian to an industrial base.

A change in philosophies

The decline in the control of the Catholic Church in the fourteenth and fifteenth centuries, and the subsequent religious struggles created by the rise of Protestantism, slowly changed the fundamental relationship of people to their governmental and religious systems. The seeds of the Protestant work ethic were planted in the new order. The expansion of trade and the creation of a permanent middle class grew out of the changes brought about by the national and international economic systems.

The effects of the Renaissance and the Reformation extended far beyond rediscovering the ideas and philosophies of antiquity. The development of new political and social theories of government and management by such theorists as Niccolo Machiavelli, Thomas Hobbes, John Locke, and Adam Smith led to crucial changes in thinking about the individual and the society. For example, Adam Smith's *Wealth of Nations*, published in 1776, moved economic theory beyond the mercantile system with Smith's now-famous economic principles. The "invisible hand" of the marketplace is the core concept of the system of economic self-regulation that survives today.

The Industrial Revolution and early pioneers of management

Four principal changes in the management of the workplace are often attributed to the Industrial Revolution:

1. Mechanization of work
2. Centralization of production
3. Creation of the labor class
4. Creation of the job of manager

The elements of science and technology, changes in government policies, population growth, improved health conditions, and the more productive use of farmland were all part of the changes that occurred during the seventeenth, eighteenth, and nineteenth centuries. The early entrepreneurs who established manufacturing businesses using the new technologies of the time (e.g., the steam engine) needed others to supervise the laborers hired to operate the equipment. Essentially, the industrial manager was created to watch over the laborers.

The problem of treating people as nothing more than extensions of machines and the subsequent abuses of labor — long hours, low pay, no job security, health and safety hazards, child labor, and so on — has left a legacy we still grapple with today. For example, the concept of "the carrot and the stick," which was used as a motivational management method in the factories, survives in the minds of many managers today. The positive inducement (the carrot) to earn more by working harder and faster was set off against a punishment (the stick), which included such things as a cut in wages or being assigned a more dangerous task, as a method of motivating people. However, not all owners and managers approached labor and production with the same attitude.

Management pioneers

One of the early pioneers of a more enlightened approach to management was Robert Owen (1771–1858). At age 18, Owen operated and supervised a cotton mill, where he observed problems occurring in the manufacturing process. He tried to improve overall working conditions and changed the equipment to reduce the hazards to workers. However, due to a shortage of labor, he too hired children to work 13 hours a day.[2]

Charles Babbage (1792–1871), often cited as the inventor of the world's first computer (a counting machine) in 1822, is also credited with creating the first research techniques to study labor.[3] His early research was the forerunner of what is now called *scientific management*. In *The History of Management Thought*, Daniel Wren notes that Babbage attempted to establish salary systems that reflected the mutual interest labor and management shared in the process of production: "Babbage's profit-sharing scheme had two facets: that a portion of wages would depend on factory profits; and two, that the worker 'should derive more advantage from applying any improvement he might discover,' that is, a bonus for suggestions."[4]

Figure 3.1 provides a visual depiction of the major movements and the people involved in the evolution of management theory.

Changes in America

The early stages of the Industrial Revolution in the United States depended on borrowing management and organizational techniques from England and Scotland. However, by the mid-nineteenth century, U.S. manufacturers began to show the world how to mass-produce interchangeable parts for a variety of equipment.[5] The development of late-nineteenth-century America's management system was due, in large part, to the engineer. The mechanical, industrial, and civil engineers were the primary force behind the development of "systems" for doing work.

The railroads and the new technology of the telegraph created a climate for rapid business expansion in America. Daniel Craig McCallum (1815–1878), a manager for the Erie Railroad, is credited with such things as creating a formal organization chart (it was shaped like a tree), matching authority with responsibility, and using the telegraph system to provide feedback about the location of trains.[6]

Henry Varnum Poor (1812–1905), the editor of the *American Railroad Journal*, wrote extensively about management organization and systems. Wren describes Poor's three-part philosophy as follows:

> [First,] organization was basic to all management; there must be a clear division of labor from the president down to the common laborer, each with specific duties and responsibilities. … [Second,] communication meant devising a method of reporting throughout the organization to give top management a continuous and accurate accounting of operations. Finally, information was 'recorded communication;' Poor saw the need for a set of operating reports to be compiled for costs, revenues, and rate making.[7]

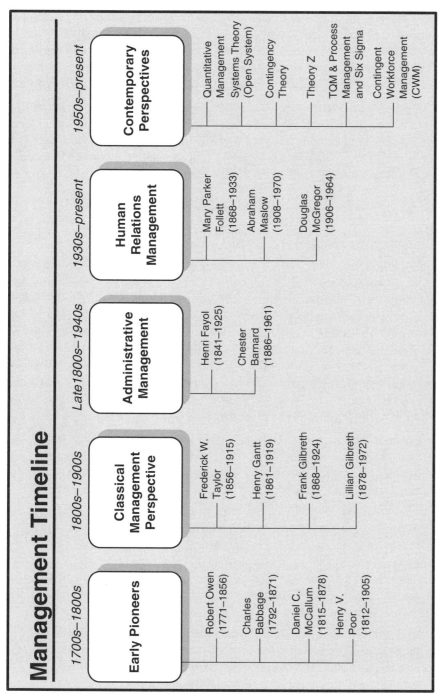

Figure 3.1
Management timeline.

As noted in Chapter 2, Arts Organizations and Arts Management, the railroads played an important part in changing how entertainment was distributed in the United States. As we saw, the railroad brought to the arts the need for a specialist to manage the logistics of moving the company from city to city. The complexity of railroad schedules (time zones as we know them today were not in place until the late 1880s) also demanded a large portion of a manager's time.

Although management concepts may have been growing in sophistication and depth during this period, the treatment of employees lagged behind. The safety and well-being of workers were not high priorities. Child labor, extremely low wages, and a lack of job security were catalysts for the creation of powerful labor unions later in the nineteenth and early twentieth century.

MANAGEMENT TRENDS TO THE PRESENT

Classical management perspectives

One of the founders of modern management is Frederick W. Taylor (1856–1915). Taylor is credited as the founder of scientific management. His efforts to change the workplace often faced bitter opposition. In 1912, Taylor stated his principles before a special congressional committee created to investigate the effects of scientific management on the worker. His words speak clearly of a management theory that is far different from the highly efficient assembly line many people imagine as the realization of his principles. Taylor's ultimate goal was to use his methods to achieve a "great mental revolution."[8] (For more information about Taylor go to: www.skymark.com/resources/leaders/taylor.asp.) His testimony makes a convincing case:

> Scientific Management is not any efficiency device, not a device of any kind for securing efficiency; nor is it any bunch or group of efficiency devices. It is not a new system of figuring costs;...it is not holding a stop watch on a man and writing things down about him; it is not time study; it is not motion study nor an analysis of the movement of men....

> Scientific management involves a complete mental revolution on the part of the working man engaged in any particular establishment or industry. And it involves the equally complete mental revolution on the part of those on the management's side — a complete mental revolution on their part as to the duties toward their fellow workers in the management, toward their workmen, and toward all of their daily problems.

> Frequently, when management has found the selling price going down they have turned toward a cut in wages...as a way of...preserving their profits intact. Thus it is over the division of the surplus [or profits] that most of the troubles have arisen; in the extreme cases this has been the cause of serious disagreements and strikes.[9]

The drive toward making the workplace and the work process as efficient as possible by careful analysis of all phases of manufacturing continues into the present. Taylor's early time and motion studies, for example, are now regular fixtures in examining how an organization is accomplishing its tasks, from building cars to making hamburgers.

Some of the other pioneers of the scientific management field were Henry L. Gantt (1861–1919), Frank Gilbreth (1868–1924), and Lillian Gilbreth (1878–1972).[10]

Application to the arts

Arts groups have limited use of the application of sophisticated scientific computer models in day-to-day operations. However, the fact is that whatever limited gains in organizational productivity are to be achieved will result from integrating specific quantitative techniques in the organization. As you will see in Chapter 10, Economics and Financial Management, the basic economics of the arts mitigates against significant productivity increases. It takes just about as long today to rehearse an orchestra for a concert as it did 75 years ago. Therefore, realizing cost savings and productivity gains associated with taking less time to produce the product does not often apply to the performing arts.

However, there are components of arts organizations that do lend themselves to quantitative applications rooted in scientific management. For example, inventory and accounting systems can easily be computerized and linked to a network of office computers. A graphic designer should be able to lay out a newsletter faster than the old cut-and-paste methods of 30 years ago. The process of assembling sets may be streamlined if time is spent analyzing how the work is done. Construction industry tools can speed up the process of building scenery.

In business and the arts the way a task is done is often based more on tradition than a detailed process analysis of the work. In fact, almost any routine procedure is worth examining. There is often a more efficient way to do almost any work, whether it is counting ticket stubs, building platforms, sorting color media, or hanging lights.

Administrative management (1916 to present)

Henri Fayol (1841–1925), a mine engineer, was a pioneer in the field of modern *administrative management*. The basic idea of this approach is that it focuses on principles that can be used to coordinate the work in an organization. Fayol's Fourteen Principles (Figure 3.2) helped to form the first comprehensive approach to management theory. Although many of Fayol's Fourteen Principles seem straightforward today, they broke new ground in 1917 by helping to establish a basis for administrative management.

Figure 3.2

Fayol's Fourteen Principles of Management.
Source: *Adapted from Henri Fayol, General and Industrial Management, trans., Constance Storrs, (London: Pitman and Sons, 1949), pp. 19–42. Used with permission.*

Fayol's Fourteen Principles of Management

1. **DIVISION OF LABOR -** Work specializations can result in efficiencies in both managerial and technical functions. However, there are limits to how much work specializations can be divided.

2. **AUTHORITY -** Managers have the right to give orders and exact obedience. With authority comes responsibility.

3. **DISCIPLINE -** Discipline is necessary to develop obedience, diligence, energy, and respect.

4. **UNITY OF COMMAND -** An employee should receive orders from one supervisor only.

5. **UNITY OF DIRECTION -** All operations with the same objective should have one manager and one plan.

6. **SUBORDINATION OF INDIVIDUAL INTERESTS TO GENERAL INTERESTS -** The interests of one employee or group of employees should not take precedence over the interests and goal of the organization.

7. **REMUNERATION -** Compensation should be fair for employee and employer.

8. **CENTRALIZATION -** The proper amount of centralization or decentralization should depend on the situation.

9. **SCALAR CHAIN (Hierarchical) -** A clear line of authority should extend from the highest to lowest levels in the organization. Horizontal communication is encouraged as long as the employees in the chain are informed.

10. **ORDER -** Materials should be kept in well-chosen places to facilitate activities.

11. **EQUITY -** Employees should be treated with kindness and justice.

12. **STABILITY OF PERSONNEL TENURE -** Because time is required to become effective in new jobs, high turnover should be prevented.

13. **INITIATIVE -** Managers should encourage and develop employee initiative to the fullest.

14. **ESPRIT DE CORPS -** Harmony and union build organization strength.

Fayol also postulated that an individual with more skill in management than in technical expertise would not necessarily be bad for a company. In fact, he believed that an engineer with no aptitude for management would do more harm than good in an organization.[11] He also saw that management could be studied separately from engineering, and he noted that every organization required management: "Be it a case of commerce, industry, politics, religion, war, or philanthropy, in every concern there is a management function to be performed."[12]

Chester Barnard (1886–1961) is also frequently cited as another contributor to the field of administrative management theory. In 1938 he published *The Functions of the Executive*, which brought forward the notion of *acceptance theory of authority*.[13] Acceptance theory postulates that authority is derived from the acceptance of authority by the people who are managed. The efficient day-to-day administration of an organization depends on the willingness of the employees to comply with directives given to them by managers. As long as these directives generally fit within the realm of the possible from the employees' perspective, they accept the control of the management structure. The successful Dilbert cartoon series often utilizes acceptance theory situations from the workplace. Humor is often found as the hapless employees receive directives from the manager that are often at odds with common sense. We will discuss the importance of acceptance theory in more detail in Chapter 8, Leadership and Group Dynamics.

Arts application

Many typical work situations in the arts can be identified by a quick review of Fayol's principles (Figure 3.2). For example, labor is divided on stage into specialized departments for carpentry, props, lighting, and sound. A gap between authority and responsibility (Principle 2) may be found in some arts settings. An example would be the university student stage manager with a great deal of responsibility but very little authority in the organization. Unity of command (Principle 4) can be applied to arts organizations in the supervisor and employee working relationship. For example, a ticket office employee may be instructed in how to sell a ticket by a fellow student supervisor. The ticket office manager, who is usually a full-time staff person, later instructs the student employee to sell the ticket differently. Suddenly the student employee has two supervisors giving contradictory instructions. Which supervisor should be listened to? Who is in command?

The idea of unity of direction (Principle 5) comes into play with the director, choreographer, conductor, or crew head leading the ensemble. For example, your event can quickly become disorganized if an assistant is providing contradictory information to the cast, ensemble, or crew. Principles 6 and 14 (subordination of individual interests and *esprit de corps*) describe what a choreographer, director, conductor, or crew chief is seeking to achieve with a group of dancers, actors, musicians, or staff: a group that works toward the greater good of the event over the personal interests of its members and, at the same time, achieves a unity or harmony as an ensemble. The idea of a clear hierarchy (Principle 9) is built into the structure of how many arts events are organized in the first place. The artistic leader assumes a place at the top of most arts organizations, and the basic structure of the organization includes people reporting to other people in a form that has evolved after hundreds of years of creating public performances.

Other principles such as order (10), equity (11), and stability of personnel (12) are easily connected to the behavior of people in arts organizations. For example, you need to be able to efficiently find the prop chair in storage; cast and crew want to be treated with respect for their efforts; and having a stable workforce is key to the success of an arts event. Given the choice, no arts organization would want to profess to be disorganized, treat people poorly, or have constant staff turnover. Of course, you may have had direct personal contact with arts organizations that could benefit from applying Fayol's principles.

A good example of Barnard's theory of *acceptance of authority* is often seen in the process of managing volunteers. Typically, the volunteers in an organization respond to the leadership of a manager based on the acceptance of the directives they are given. Since they do not have to be there, their willingness to work is based on their willingness to do what is asked of them. If "orders" exceed their usually unspoken sense of the scope of their volunteer effort, they will simply walk away. Anyone who has ever tried to work with an all-volunteer crew on a production understands the issue of acceptance of authority.

HUMAN RELATIONS MANAGEMENT (1927 TO PRESENT)

The behavioral approach

The major failure of the classic approaches to management mentioned thus far was the lack of understanding of the human factor in work. The most efficient way of accomplishing a task was often thwarted by what the scientific management theorists thought was employees' stubborn resistance to change. Researchers began to apply principles and concepts from what was then the new field of psychology in an effort to understand workers better and to make organizations and people more productive. The basic assumptions behind much of this research were that (1) people desire satisfying social relationships and derive satisfaction from accomplishing specific tasks; (2) they respond to group and peer pressure in their work output; and (3) they search for individual fulfillment in their work.

Mary Parker Follett (1868–1933), a Radcliffe graduate and social worker in the Boston area, articulated several ideas about group dynamics that still have a place in today's workplace. Follett noted that people working in organizations are continually influenced by each other and are very capable of accomplishing work in groups. In fact, her ideas are in use today as many organizations develop "teams" to accomplish tasks. Follett argued for a workplace in which management shared power with, not over, employees. She also developed the concept of *integrative unity* to describe how organizations could better reach their goals by coordinating group activities, which is at the heart of the whole notion of teamwork in a work setting.[14] (For more information about Follett go to: http://womenshistory.about.com/od/business/p/m_p_follett.htm.)

A valuable piece of research involving people in the workplace, and a classic example of an unintended consequence, can be found in a project undertaken at the Hawthorne Wire Works in Illinois in the 1920s.

The Hawthorne Effect

In 1924, Vannevar Bush of MIT undertook a study of worker productivity at the Hawthorne Wire Works. The employees wound wires on motor coils or inspected small parts. Bush and his colleagues experimented with different lighting conditions on the assumption that different intensities of light would affect worker output. They found that the lighting level had no effect. Worker output increased despite wide variations in brightness.

Elton Mayo and Fritz Roethlisberger, professors at Harvard, began the second phase of the study in 1927. A group of workers was carefully monitored for five years using a special test facility built for the experiment. The researchers gave the workers physicals every six weeks, monitored their blood pressure, recorded weather conditions, noted their eating and sleeping habits, and so forth. No matter what changes were instituted, worker productivity kept increasing.

It became clear to the researchers that other factors were influencing the employees' work behavior. Mayo and Roethlisberger surmised that the extra attention paid to the experimental group combined with such things as changes in the supervision system, the creation of a small social system in the work groups, and the creation of a type of *esprit de corps* among the workers contributed to the increased output.[15] The Hawthorne Effect, as it is now called, stresses the importance of human interaction in the workplace.

Maslow's hierarchy of needs

Another theory that helped shape the human relations approach to management was Abraham Maslow's hierarchy of needs. Maslow's 1943 paper, "A Theory of Human Motivation," was quickly incorporated into management theory and practice. Chapter 8, Leadership and Group Dynamics, discusses ways to apply his approach in the work setting from the leadership perspective.

In summary, the theory suggests that part of the manager's job is to provide avenues leading to employee satisfaction, and that managers must work to remove obstacles that prevent employees from accomplishing their jobs. According to Maslow, people have various needs, including (from lowest to highest) physiological, safety, belongingness, esteem, and self-actualization. These needs can neither be fully met by nor ignored in designing the workplace. The goal is for a person to become self-actualized so as to lead a full and productive life. (For more information about Maslow's work go to: www.businessballs.com/maslow.htm.)

Mcgregor's Theory X and Theory Y

Douglas McGregor gave a speech in 1957 at the Sloan School of Management called "The Human Side of Enterprise." His presentation included an idea about work that changed the relationship of manager to employee. McGregor's theory is based on the concept that managers develop "self-fulfilling prophecies" about people that affect all of their interactions with employees.[16]

He identified two major perspectives held by managers: Theory X and Theory Y. Theory X assumes that (1) people generally dislike work and avoid it when possible; (2) they must be coerced, controlled, and threatened with punishment to get them to work; and (3) they want to be directed and avoid taking responsibility. On the other hand, Theory Y assumes that (1) people are generally willing to work; (2) they are willing to accept responsibility; (3) they are capable of self-direction; and (4) they have creative and imaginative resources that are not effectively utilized in the work environment.

The Theory Y approach to management has become a part of current trend toward what is called *participative management*. Companies are now asking employees what they think, rather than treating them simply as labor. McGregor believed that any enterprise can flourish if there is a partnership between the workers and the managers.[17]

Arts application

The whole idea of work being a social activity is a common notion today. People working in arts organizations, like those in other professions, spend significant portions of their waking hours working with others. They develop complex patterns of interaction that are no different than any other business in our society. The very process of rehearsal in the arts is central to improving a person's eventual "performance." Therefore, the success of an arts manager is often tied to how well they can motivate the people around them to achieve their best performance. When we say the performance of a concert was "excellent," we are really responding to how well the people were managed and prepared for the performance. Follett's integrative unity, for example, can be seen in bringing together cast and crew in the group effort of producing a live performance, special event, or exhibition.

The Hawthorne Effect can be observed in a work call involving a crew on a production. The work to be done (e.g., a lighting instrument hanging session or cable sorting project) can be made a more positive and productive experience if the manager supervising the work creates a positive and enjoyable situation for the people doing the work.

Maslow's theories have found their way into many aspects of contemporary arts organizations. Achieving success by navigating the levels in Maslow's hierarchy may lead a person to being described as self-actualized. Artists are often seeking a level of enlightenment or connection through their art that also results in reaching a state of self-actualization. However, to accomplish that, artists must first have some basic needs met. For example, a performing ensemble that does not achieve a sense of belongingness may have a difficult time achieving the level of artistic excellence demanded of the art form. Individuals who do not feel a part of, or comfortable in, the ensemble may not be able to contribute their fullest to the enterprise.

McGregor's description of a Theory X manager might apply to directors, choreographers, conductors, designers, or crew heads who work with their cast, dancers, musicians, design assistants, or crew from a point of view assuming that people need to be coerced, controlled, and threatened to produce good work. The artistic director as a tyrant who must drive the talent to produce describes the Theory X manager to some degree. On the other hand, it is also possible to find artistic leaders who work with people from the Theory Y point of view. They see their job as carefully directing highly talented and self-motivated people to even higher levels of achievement.

MODERN MANAGEMENT

Scientific management today — quantitative approaches

The rise of research universities and graduate schools of business and management, and the increased application of scientific management to the workplace, have come together in the last 100 years to form a strong theoretical base for the study of management. Wharton was the first undergraduate school to offer a degree in business (1881), and Dartmouth (1900) and Harvard (1909) were the first universities to offer graduate programs in management.[18]

Scientific management techniques have undergone further refinement with the assistance of computer models to help design the most efficient and productive workplace. The worldwide application of these techniques is well documented. Terms such as *operations research* (OR), the application of quantitative analysis to all parts of a business operation, are now common.[19] OR can cover applying analytical processes from how work space is organized to how people are scheduled to work. For example, in an arts setting, OR could be applied to finding the most efficient way to process a ticket order. The critical path method (CPM) for scheduling and controlling work on projects is also part of standard operating procedures in many businesses. CPM is used in the industry as a method for planning how a project will move through its various steps to completion. For example, CPM may be applied to the process of building a stage set. Each step in the construction process is broken down into the smaller activities such as ordering the materials, cutting and framing the materials, and then assembling them. There is a series of dependencies between each step and each step has a duration which when totaled, provides the cumulative time it takes to complete a given task or a project.

Scientific management techniques have been applied by the Japanese, among others, in much of their manufacturing, and the resulting gains in productivity have advanced them to the forefront of world competition. Ironically, the processes to achieve this productivity were the result of the work of American quality expert W. Edwards Deming. Such concepts as "just-in-time inventory" (or Kanban), computer-aided design (CAD), computer-assisted manufacturing (CAM), and computer-integrated manufacturing (CIM) are natural extensions of the work started by Taylor nearly 100 years ago. The goal of applying these methods to the process of production has been to increase worker productivity and thereby lower costs to the firm. There will be more discussion of the topic of productivity in Chapter 10, Economics and Financial Management, and its impact on the costs of producing arts events.

Systems theory

Systems theory assumes that organizations are composed of inter-related parts and activities that are arranged by design to produce goods or services. The open system model (see Figures 1.3 and 6.1) is an example of a systems theory application to arts organizations. It assumes that an organization functions in a complex world influenced by multiple environments as it goes about gathering inputs and transforming them into outputs in the form of goods or services. The "inputs" are the people who work for the organization, and materials, equipment, and money required to produce the organization's goods or services. The "output," or performance of the organization, is not the sum of its parts, but rather the result of the interaction of the parts. The process of management transforms the inputs to the output. Ideally, an organizational *synergy* results from the process, and the whole becomes greater than the sum of its parts.[20]

Contingency approaches

The contingency approach to managing an organization works on the assumption that there is no one way that works best in all circumstances facing an organization. The management team must therefore be adaptable and capable of understanding the different mixes of management techniques that may be required at different times. This approach also recognizes that the people who make up the organization have differing styles of work and management. The top management must therefore expect that different work groups will have alternative ways of achieving the stated objectives. Rather than seeing this as a threat, diversity must be perceived as a strength. Synergy can once again be achieved if the management is capable of effectively coordinating the different work groups.[21]

Arts application

One assumption this text makes is that arts organizations are open systems subject to internal and external forces that shape and change how they operate. Chapter 4 specifically discusses the larger world in which the arts organization must function. The system model allows a manager to create, revise, or remove subsystems that are not effectively supporting the mission. For example, a subsystem within an arts organization might be volunteer support. As a subsystem it may have goals, specific objectives, a staff member assigned to coordinate work, and budget resources allocated. However, if there is poor turnout by volunteers, or low-quality work is done, then this subsystem is not effectively adding to the overall productivity of the organization. The arts manager then would step in, analyze the problems, and attempt to make changes that would help make the volunteer system work better.

Contingency theory assumes that the appropriate action to take by management should be driven by a careful analysis of the problem and situation. It is assumed that there is no one universal set of principles that works for all organizations. Situational factors should determine the best application of management solutions. For example, the solution to the volunteer problem may be a simple change in venues. Perhaps there is no problem with volunteer leadership, but rather it is too difficult to find a space big enough to have the group gather to work on their projects. So rather than delve into applying human relations theory solutions to the problem, a manager might apply a quantitative approach by studying the work processes of the volunteers and then improving the work space to facilitate what they do for the organization.

Emerging views

It remains to be seen if there will ever be one theory that can be applied to best establish and operate an organization. The basis for effectively managing most organizations in the world in which we live recognizes that a contingency approach makes the most sense. Flexibility and adjusting to pressures applied to the organization from the outside, while carefully monitoring the inside processes of the organization, is paramount. The theories will continue to evolve. For example, we have *Theory Z*, proposed by William G. Ouchi and Alfred M. Jaeger, which attempts to take the positive management techniques from American and Japanese manufacturing and integrate them into a system that is focused on increasing employee well-being and loyalty to the company.[22] *Total quality management* (TQM), embraced by companies producing goods and services, is based on the assumption that an organization can better satisfy its customers if it is dedicated to continuously improving its product or service. (TQM is also called *Kaizen* in Japan; see www.kaizen-institute.com for details.) The management and improvement of all of the processes an organization undertakes to accomplish its mission are very much a part of contemporary thinking about how to better manage organizations.

Another term added to the management vocabulary is *Six Sigma*. This phrase refers to a management system and philosophy that "focuses on eliminating defects through practices that emphasize understanding, measuring, and improving processes."[23] Six Sigma grew out of the need to improve the quality and reliability of microprocessor chip manufacturing. From its beginnings in the early 1980s, it became a way of life for many organizations as they worked to compete in the global marketplace.

Two other concepts have found their way into the business world: *flexible production technology* and *mass customization*. Flexible production technologies "are a set of methodologies that allow enterprises to produce a wider range of end products without incurring a cost penalty."[24] The worldwide automobile manufacturing process has adopted these methods to reduce the cost of producing a car. Toyota was a leader in applying new processes that increased productivity.

Mass customization is "the ability to customize the final output of a product to individual customer requirements without suffering a cost penalty."[25] One example of this process is a clothing company like Lands' End. If you go online and give them information about your clothing size needs they can then create a custom pattern for you.

Shifting paradigms

The management theorists often speak of major *paradigm shifts* and the *reengineering* of corporations today.[26] A current definition of a *paradigm* is a "set of rules and regulations (written and unwritten) that does two things: (1) establishes or defines boundaries, and (2) tells you how to behave inside the boundaries in order to be successful."[27] For example, we generally accept as a paradigm that a college education is best administered by gathering people together in large buildings, setting them down in neat rows of chairs, and imparting information from 9:00 to 9:50 a.m. Monday, Wednesday, and Friday for 15 weeks a year over a 4-year period. The emergence of distance learning and online instruction is a good example of a shift in that paradigm. In a larger sense, this shift is really about the way in which information is imparted to people and who controls the classroom. The nineteenth-century paradigm of the schoolroom, and all that it involves, is undergoing change.

Arts organizations face similar challenges from shifting paradigms, as you will see in Chapter 4, The Adaptive Arts Organization. One of the most obvious paradigm shifts facing the live performing arts involves the change brought about in how people interact with or experience what we do. The "digital age" is having an effect on how entertainment is delivered to and experienced by our audiences. The impact of this change appears to be profound, but as yet it is unclear what new "rules" or "boundaries" will require adaptation in the performance process.

What does the future hold for management theories? One place to look is the business section of any bookstore. There you will find the latest trends in management thinking. So many good books are published each year that it is difficult to keep up with the output.

Another good source is a book entitled *The Manager's Bookshelf* by Jon L. Pierce and John W. Newstrom. The sixth edition, published by HarperCollins College Publishers, covers a wide range of topics from management paradigms to ethics and management. The World Wide Web also offers a quick way to explore new ideas found in *The Manager's Bookshelf*. For example, if you search for information on the aforementioned Six Sigma concept, you will turn up dozens of Web sites on the topic. Be forewarned that there is a high degree of the "flavor of the week" syndrome to be found on the bookshelves. As Pierce and Newstrom point out, "These new terms feed the management world's preoccupation with quick fixes and the perpetuation of management fads."[28]

One of the more astute recent books on the whole subject of management theories is titled *The Halo Effect*, by Phil Rosenzweig. The subtitle of the book offers a preview of the contents and point of view of the author with "…and the Eight Other Business Delusions That Deceive Managers."

The nine business delusions are the Halo Effect, The Delusion of Correlation and Causality, The Delusion of the Single Explanations, The Delusion of Connecting the Winning Dots, The Delusion of Rigorous Research, The Delusion of Lasting Success, The Delusion of Absolute Performance, The Delusion of the Wrong End of the Stick, and finally, The Delusion of Organizational Physics.[29]

Rosenzweig offers a methodical look at some of the fundamental flaws in much of what passes for business research. He argues there is no one way or system that is the answer to how to run a successful business. He takes to task authors such as Tom Peters and Jim Collins for missing the halo effect in much of what they write about. The halo effect is defined as:

> The tendency to look at a company's overall performance and make attributions about its culture, leadership, values, and more. In fact, many things we commonly claim drive company performance are simply attributions based on prior performance.[30]

The Halo Effect in the arts

An arts example of the Halo Effect might be attributing excellent management processes and leadership to an arts organization that is known for producing high-quality and well-reviewed productions. In fact, the opposite may be true. The management and leadership of the organization could be severely lacking or even dysfunctional, but the success on stage creates a halo effect that shines on the organization's management team. Rosenzweig also faults the business press for often missing the problems of a poorly run company until long after the fact. For example, the widely held belief that the Enron Corporation was blazing a trail for a new way to do business proved to be false.

Other sources

University business schools are also a source for ideas about future directions in management. The major research universities support faculty in the development of refined and new theories of management and organizational design. Many of the journals found in college and university libraries also provide an academic view of all of the major fields of management. Specialty journals such as the *Harvard Business Review* are published regularly on such topics as operations, systems analysis, human resources, leadership, organizational psychology, and marketing.

CONCLUSION

Several thousand years of the evolution of management practice has helped inform modern management theory. During this time, societies have created organizations capable of accomplishing an incredible range of activities. Cities, roads, dams, hospitals, schools, and churches have been built by organized groups of individuals using the techniques of management. At the same time, it is important to remember that management techniques have been and continue to be used to organize and implement unimaginable amounts of destruction and suffering.

Organizations and systems of management are still evolving today. The nineteenth-century organizational model, with its rigid hierarchy and complex chains of command, has been proved to be incapable of responding quickly enough to change. Newer information-based organizational models with fewer levels of management are forming.

As we begin the twenty-first century, political and economic upheaval will continue in ways we cannot foresee. Change seems to be the only constant on which organizations and individuals can count. If change is managed wisely as part of the planning process, the resources needed to provide for the future of the organization will be available. However, it is also possible to envision a world that is overwhelmed by the problems of population, pollution, and hunger. The images of an unmanageable world that come to us from both science and fiction writers may provide the incentive people need to solve the problems around us.

Ultimately, it will be the people who make up the organizations who will determine the type of future we all share. Cooperation and collective action among these people and organizations hold the key to the future.

In Chapter 4, we will examine how all organizations are affected by the social and political systems within which they must function. These and other external environments shape how the organization defines its mission and what the people in the organization believe.

SUMMARY

Management is an integral part of all social systems, from a family to a multinational corporation. Whether the objective is gathering food or taking over another corporation, managers are required to coordinate the interactions of people carrying out designated tasks. Although many people have learned to manage while on the job, a body of knowledge accumulated over the last 2,000 years constitutes management theory and practice.

Preindustrial societies developed laws, rules, myths, and rituals to control and direct people. The Renaissance and the Reformation created many new dynamics in the Western world. The opening of trade, the expansion of city centers, the rise of the middle class, and the major changes in political and social philosophy led to the formation of more sophisticated concepts of managing.

The Industrial Revolution produced fundamental changes in the nature of work and production, thus transforming Western societies. The mechanization of work in factories created the need for managers to supervise the activities of the factory workers.

The railroads, telegraph communication, manufacture of precise interchangeable parts, and other new inventions and advances in technology radically altered the workplace in the nineteenth century. As new production methods were devised, techniques for managing employees and organizing work began to be documented. The early systems of organizational design, production supervision, and data recording that were used in the railroads and factories became the basis of modern systems of scientific management.

Frederick W. Taylor was the first to document techniques for improving work output and streamlining antiquated manufacturing techniques. Scientific research was quickly adopted by the business world. Computer models and simulations are now used regularly to improve productivity and output in factories.

Other major management practices focused on organizational design and optimal ways to structure the operation. The basic principles expressed by Henri Fayol and others about such things as chain of command, lines of authority, and rules and policies in business were thought to be applicable to any organization.

Another branch of management theory falls under the heading of human relations management. The premise underlying this research is that people want socially satisfying work situations. The Hawthorne studies verified that work output increases if employees are given more control over their jobs. Mary Parker Follett's integrative unity, Abraham Maslow's hierarchy of needs, and Douglas McGregor's Theory X and Theory Y articulated many of the complex needs and interpersonal relationships people bring to the workplace.

Contemporary management practices are based on integration models. One model assumes that organizations are open systems affected by external environments in the process of transforming inputs into outputs. The other model, the contingency approach, assumes that there is no best way to operate an organization; managers must therefore be flexible and find the best match between the resources available and the problems to be solved.

For additional topics relating to management history and management trends, please go to www.managementandthearts.com.

Questions

1. Describe examples from antiquity that demonstrate the use of the basic management functions of planning, organizing, leading, and controlling.
2. Describe some of the legacies of the Industrial Revolution in manufacturing today.
3. Which of Fayol's Fourteen Principles can be most easily applied in an arts organization? Which principles seem inappropriate?
4. Have you ever worked for a Theory X or Theory Y manager? To which theory do you subscribe?
5. How does a college or university fit into the open system model? What are the inputs? What happens in the transformation process? What are the typical outputs?
6. Do you think government, business, and social service organizations in the United States are capable of solving the problems facing society? If not, what changes must be made in these organizations to meet the demands?

REFERENCES

1. Paul DiMaggio, *Managers of the Arts*, NEA Research Division Report #20 (Washington, D.C.: Seven Locks Press, 1987), p. 46.
2. Daniel Wren, *The History of Management Thought*, 5th ed. (New York: John Wiley & Sons, 2005), p. 56.

3. Ibid., pp. 66–70.

4. Ibid., p. 70.

5. Ibid., pp. 81–82.

6. Ibid., pp. 85–88.

7. Ibid., p. 89.

8. Michael T. Matteson, John M. Ivancevich, eds., *Management and Organizational Behavior Classics*, 4th ed. (Homewood, IL: Richard D. Irwin, 1989), p. 4.

9. Ibid., pp. 3–5.

10. Wren, *The History of Management Thought*, p. 153.

11. Ibid., p. 212.

12. Henri Fayol, *General and Industrial Management*, trans. Constance Storrs (London: Sir Isaac Pitman and Sons, 1949), p. 15.

13. Chester Barnard, *The Functions of the Executive* (Cambridge, MA: Harvard University Press, 1938), pp. 165–166.

14. Kathryn M. Bartol, David C. Martin, *Management*, 3rd ed. (Boston: McGraw-Hill, 1998), pp. 47–48.

15. Wren, *The History of Management Thought*, pp. 279–296.

16. Warren Bemis, Foreword, *The Human Side of Management*, by Douglas McGregor (New York: McGraw-Hill, 1960), p. iv.

17. Douglas McGregor, *The Human Side of Management* (New York: McGraw-Hill, 1960), pp. 33–57.

18. Wren, *The History of Management Thought*, p. 231.

19. Ibid., p. 457.

20. Kathryn M. Bartol, David C. Martin, *Management*, 3rd ed., pp. 54–57.

21. Ibid., p. 58.

22. Ibid., pp. 58–60.

23. Greg Brue, *Six Sigma for Managers* (New York: Briefcase Books, McGraw-Hill, 2002), Comment: p. 2.

24. Charles W. L. Hill, Steven L. McShane, *Principles of Management*, (New York: McGraw-Hill Irwin, 2008), p. 162.

25. Ibid., p. 163.

26. Michael Hammer, James Champy, *Reengineering the Corporation* (New York: HarperBusiness, 1993).

27. Joel A. Barker, *Paradigms: The Business of Discovering the Future* (New York: HarperCollins, 1993), p. 32.

28. Jon L. Pierce, John W. Newstrom, *The Manager's Bookshelf: A Mosaic of Contemporary Views*, 6th ed. (New York: HarperCollins College Publishers, 2002).

29. Phil Rosenzweig, *The Halo Effect*, (New York: Free Press, Simon & Shuster, Inc, 2007), pp. xi–xii.

30. Ibid., p. xi.

CHAPTER 4

The Adaptive Arts Organization

The Royal Scottish National Orchestra has jumped on the digital download bandwagon and launched a subscription download site which links to nearly 60,000 recordings.

Playbill Arts, September, 27, 2006

KEY WORDS

Environments in the
  open system:
  economic
  political and legal
  cultural and social

demographic
technological
educational
Continual evaluation process
Content analysis

Demographic descriptor including sex, age, race, income level, occupation, education, birth and death rate, geographic distribution

Information sources:
  audiences
  other arts groups
  board and staff members
  the media

professional associations
consultants
SWOT Analysis
News aggregators

In this chapter we will begin the first steps in the journey of managing and leading in the arts. Before you develop and organize to execute your plans, you need to assess the larger issues facing an arts organization in the 21st century. To that end, we will work to develop your skills analyzing the potential impact of key environments that any business must consider when trying to realize its mission. We will also review the sources for information that can assist the arts manager in his quest for knowledge. Lastly, we will review a sampling of trends that may affect arts organizations over the next decade.

COMPETITIVE ADAPTATION

Arts organizations need to be adaptable to the changes in many areas of society if they are to continue to be successful in an increasingly competitive entertainment marketplace. Like any business, arts organizations must work within changing external and internal environments. The term *environment* is used throughout this text to denote forces that interact outside and within organizations. We examine six external environments: economic, political and legal, cultural and social, demographic, technological, and educational. We will assess the impact of each of these environments on arts organizations and, later in the chapter, examine some of the trends that may reshape the arts in the near future. In addition, we will examine how arts organizations interact with these environments based on the information received from six major sources: audiences, other arts groups, board and staff members, the media, professional associations, and consultants.

The quotation at the beginning of this chapter shows how organizations experiment with technological changes that effect their operations. This orchestra formed a partnership with an online retailer of classical music and the *Playbill Arts* article indicated the symphony was considering live streaming of concerts.

Over at the Metropolitan Opera during the 2006–07 season a new series of high-definition showings of the live performances in movie theaters was seen around the world. They claim to have had more than 325,000 viewers in their first season. The Met, like many other arts organizations, has a MySpace homepage as well.

The Royal Scottish National Orchestra and the Metropolitan Opera's adaptations of enhanced presentation technology illustrate the ways that an organization can exploit an opportunity made available by the changing world in which it functions. Podcasting of arts programming and art museum cell phone guided tours have become a standard part of many organizations' operations.

Figure 4.1 provides a graphic representation of the organization, the information sources (inputs), and the environments. An organization's relationship to information sources and to different environments vary. Some organizations are more responsive to audiences and patrons, and others are more responsive to their boards or staffs.

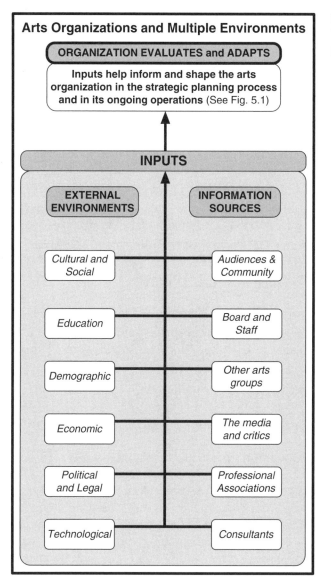

Figure 4.1

The arts organization and multiple environments.

The information provided by the external environments and other sources help organizations in the vital process of strategic and operational planning. The application of this information in the planning process is covered in more detail in Chapter 5, Planning and Decision Making. The inputs noted in Figure 4.1 are used collectively to develop what in the planning process is often called a *SWOT* (strengths, weaknesses, opportunities, threats) *Analysis.*

Nearly all of the activities that an arts organization undertakes are related to the interaction between these environments and information sources and the four functions of management: planning, organizing, leading, and controlling. Based on these relationships, a primary goal for an arts manager is to fulfill the stated mission of an organization by dynamically balancing all the various factors affecting it.

CHANGING ENVIRONMENTS

As depicted in Figures 1.3 and 6.1, organizations are open systems that receive inputs from various sources; the inputs are then processed and transformed to outputs. In the broadest sense, this process applies whether it is an arts organization or a company that manufactures automobiles. Although there are substantial differences in these "businesses," arts organizations would be better served by becoming more responsive to the public they serve.

It is a simple fact that if the enterprise does not adapt to changes in the world, it is likely to be less effective fulfilling its mission; and if it is too rigid or too slow to change, it will cease to exist. Ultimately, the abstract "organization" will not suffer if the business is shut down. It is the people who work for the organization who pay the price for its lack of adaptability.

MANAGING CHANGE

A manager of an arts organization is responsible for more than helping to get the show or exhibition opened. She must be aware of the world around the organization: locally, regionally, nationally, and internationally. How does one go about monitoring and managing change? One way is by developing a systematic process for monitoring key forces that may affect the organization. At the same time, the arts manager needs to appreciate that change will often happen in such a way that an organization has no choice but to be reactive. For example, if new legislation is enacted by the state government that affects fundraising activities or reporting, then the manager has no choice but to react to the change. On the other hand, if this same manager was more closely monitoring what was going on in a legislative session, she may be able to affect a change in the legislation before it becomes a law.

An effective arts manager also needs to keep a sense of perspective on the rate of growth and development inside the organization while watching the changing world around it for opportunities and threats. Change seldom happens overnight. In fact, change is more likely to come about from the accumulation of many small decisions a manager makes over time. These small adjustments can have a significant impact on the long-term operation of the organization. Unfortunately, change is often difficult to monitor accurately because, like the hands of a clock, you only notice the movement after the fact. It is a great deal easier to use hindsight when it comes to assessing change.

In addition to navigating the organization through uncertain circumstances and changing times, the manager must also attend to internal organizational needs. In most organizations, people feel comfortable with a certain degree of predictable routine. All organizations establish specific operating rules and detailed procedures for getting work done. Payroll procedures and basic work conditions are established as part of the fabric of an organization. People cannot function anywhere near their potential if they are worrying about whether they will be paid or about other conditions of their employment. Ironically, once conditions are stabilized, people have a tendency to become bored if their jobs assume routines that seldom vary. Subtle changes in work patterns can be just as important to the long-term health of an organization as major shifts to new programs. An important part of the manager's job is to remain aware of the overall direction and mood of the organization while helping people do their day-to-day jobs. The fine-tuning of operational activities never really ends.

GROWTH AND CHANGE

As we saw in Chapter 2, Arts Organizations and Arts Management, arts organizations are often created by a person or a small group of people willing to commit to the incredible effort it takes to bring a creative idea to life. Of course the same could be said for many of the major corporations in existence in the world today. It is possible to trace the founding of many businesses to one or two people with the drive, passion, and ambition to make it happen.

Many of today's arts organizations are the product of the generation that is part of the post–World War II boom coupled with increased access to education and financial support from individuals, foundations, and the government. An unplanned mix of circumstances after World War II supported the unprecedented growth in performing and visual arts organizations across the nation. New theater, dance, and opera companies were founded, symphony orchestras sprang up throughout the nation, new performing arts centers were built in communities, and many types of museums and galleries opened in large and small cities. The support and vision of the Ford Foundation, among others, helped support the establishment of many of these arts organizations in the 1950s and 1960s. Once established, the arduous task of sustaining what became arts institutions took center stage.

The example of the evolving opera company

Let's examine a hypothetical example. A founder-directed opera company with an annual budget of $35,000 in the early 1970s grows to become an arts "institution" in its community with a budget of $6.5 million in the early part of the twenty-first century. From a modest start of productions held in a 1000-seat suburban high school auditorium, the company has grown and flourished and now performs in a 3500 seat theater downtown. As the organization evolves, a board of directors representing the community is added and new staff members are hired to do what the original founder and one or two volunteers were doing. The tiny storefront office becomes a larger storefront office, and when that space is found to be too small, a suite of offices is leased in a high-rise office building near the performing arts center.

Slowly, but inevitably, the small opera company begins to function at a scale that requires longer term planning and careful analysis of future options. In other words, the company begins to move from hourly, daily, weekly, and monthly planning to year-to-year planning often spanning three to five years.

As any organization matures, it begins to take on characteristics that make it less responsive to change. After all, when a company finds something that works, it continues making more and more of that product. Our hypothetical opera company, for example, finds that a particular pattern of performances (two grand operas, two operettas, one musical) sells well, and so it repeats that cycle with different titles every year.

Now suppose that the same community also becomes home to a professional theater company, a ballet company, and a symphony orchestra. The creation of each new organization will have an impact on the opera company. It will find itself competing for arts revenues because audiences simply have more choices. The theater company, for example, may decide to do two musicals each season. The change in the cultural environment of the community requires that the opera company's decisions about programming now be made in the context of three other groups struggling for an arts audience.

To better adapt to its new circumstances, a process of *continual evaluation* should become the opera company's normal operating procedures. Asking questions about where the opera company stands with respect to the six environments and the other arts groups, and then sifting through the feedback from its information sources, should become as critical as mounting a season of high-quality productions.

It is important to remember that the process of continual evaluation is nothing more than a tool that will only be as effective as the manager and artist who use it. If the manager is unskilled at using the process, they may chart a course for the organization that leads to possible ruin. On the other hand, successful assessment and planning should lead the opera company to develop at a pace that fits well within the parameters of the community and the six environments.

Organizations discover that a process of monitoring their activities through ongoing assessment requires the development of techniques for gathering and analyzing information. Technique, as any performer will tell you, is acquired through long hours of rehearsal and disciplined practice. Just as painters, illustrators, dancers, singers, musicians, and actors learn to master their art and craft through developing techniques for approaching their work, so too can an arts manager master the art of organizational evaluation and adaptation. Once mastered, this technique can then be applied to the four functions of management. For example, to avoid programming duplication or conflicts the opera company could consult with the other arts organizations on upcoming titles and dates. Opportunities for collaborative projects may also be explored with the other producing groups.

Before discussing techniques for exploring individual environments, let's examine a general approach to organizational evaluation and assessment. As we will see, the biggest problem in assessing the opportunities and threats to an organization is the conflicting information facing a manager.

CONTENT ANALYSIS

An arts manager can start gathering vital information from books, newspapers, magazines, broadcast media, and the Web. The basic methodology, which is called *content analysis*, simply involves identifying key sources for clues about current practices and possible future trends. Gathering input from sources external to the organization is complicated by the cyclical patterns of the media. Topics come and go with incredible speed from the front page, TV news, and the Web. The key factor in an arts manager's quest for information through content analysis is to find enough trustworthy sources for facts and trends. This is not an easy task, as the sources for information have proliferated in recent years.

The manager must also differentiate between trends and fads. For example, shifts in population growth establish trends that ripple through a society for years: more people, more services, more houses, more apartments, and so forth. Fads, on the other hand, tend to die out more quickly. Arts organizations that react to fads sometimes find themselves scheduling programming that is out of step with what has become the current topical stories. In the time between the decision to produce a particular program and its actual production, a new hot issue may arise to take its place.

The arts manager must therefore use caution when trying to sort through their thinking about what the future may bring. For example, it is not unusual to find contradictory opinions expressed about a particular topic. One futurist Web blogger predicts a vision of a world where people will be able to use their hand-held computer to navigate through thousands of options for entertainment and information. Another pundit sees us becoming more isolated from each other as we spend our limited free time exploring these endless entertainment and information options in ways other than attending arts events. In this case, they may both be right and the manager is still left to contemplate the potential impact on his organization.

Where to look for arts content

If nothing else, the development of the World Wide Web has made it possible to access information much more quickly. Being selective about where you go for information is probably even more critical than it was before one could type in a few words and activate a search on to the Web. For example, online access to sources such as *The New York Times*, *The Wall Street Journal*, and *Business Week* should be an integral part of the information base that a manager can use to begin building a structure to hold the sources of their content analysis activities. These are not the only sources for general news of the world or the trends that are developing in our society, but having content delivered to you electronically every day has become a requirement for anyone trying to keep current.

The need to stay current in an arts discipline has also been aided by organizations better using their Web sites. Early Web sites often were simply electronic versions of the print content already generated by the organization. As arts organizations became more familiar with the Web they began to better exploit the differences and unique features only a Web site could offer. In fact, the development of the notion of Web 2.0 has become a common part of the vocabulary of organizations. Arts organizations now have Web sites that can be very interactive including video clips, podcasts, and blogs.

These Web sites provide managers with a great deal of information about what other arts organizations are doing when it comes to programming, pricing, or other activities. For example, finding out the names other organizations use for their various donor levels can be a helpful if you were considering new titles for your own giving levels.

Of course, the number of sources for information on the Internet is overwhelming. The words "arts organization trends" typed into an online search engine may return hundreds of thousands of potential links. Obviously, narrowing the Internet search is required, but narrowing it to what? Focusing on your discipline area as well as seeking information from organizations that specialize in research can help narrow your sources to a more manageable level. Wasting an inordinate amount of time doing online research can actually undermine the effectiveness of a manager. The research is not an end in itself.

Fortunately, an arts manager's Web research options have improved in recent years. For example, many arts managers review Web sites such as ArtsJournal. com on a daily basis for the latest worldwide arts news and ideas. In addition to dozens of links to stories in the media or even a YouTube video clip, the site contains Web logs or blogs on dozens of subjects (www.artsjournal.com). *The Arts Management Network*, a monthly newsletter service, also offers readers a worldwide perspective on arts and culture topics and publications (www. artsmanagement.net). The Americans for the Arts Web site is also an excellent resource for research (www.artsusa.org/NAPD/modules/resourceManager/ publicsearch.aspx).

Online research reports published by the NEA, Americans for the Arts, and sources such as the Pew Charitable Trust and the RAND Corporation can be of great assistance to a manager trying to stay informed about the possible trends affecting the arts. Many of these reports are free and easily download-able. In addition, major arts consulting firms publish online newsletters with content of interest to an arts manager. For example, firms such as AEA Consulting publish a quarterly newsletter called *Platform*, and AMS Research & Planning regularly publishes an electronic magazine titled *Insights*.

"The Performing Arts in a New Era" by the RAND Corporation is one of many reports that can be of assistance in the arts manger's search for information. The fact is no manager has the time to run their arts organization and keep up on everything published about arts and cultural trends. However, by exploring the RAND Web site (www.rand.org/research_areas/arts), the search for information may be narrowed.

Collecting and sorting through all of these sources has also been made a little easier through the Web technology known as *news aggregator*s. An arts manager can establish his own personalized news service by collecting information from key sources through either a Web system like Google or Yahoo, or the information can be gathered through application software such as Internet Explorer, Safari, or Firefox. There are applications that can function as "Podcatchers," which enable the capture of podcasts from organizations. There are other software applications available that will convert text to audio recordings that the arts manager may listen to later.

ASSESSING ENVIRONMENTS

To effectively manage organizational change, the arts manager must identify the environments that will have the most direct impact on his organization.

It is also helpful if the manager recognizes his biases and preconceptions and the readiness of the organization to change. Let's review the key environments that interact with arts organizations and explore some basic guidelines about what constitutes significant input.

Economic

Arts organizations, as part of the economic system, experience the effects of expansions and contractions in the local, regional, national, and world economy. Some of the factors that may have an impact on an arts organization include the federal banking system (raising and lowering interest rates), new tax increases or reductions, revisions in existing tax legislation (which may promote or hinder gifts and donations), international exchange rates (value of a currency such as the dollar), and inflation (general price increases). This last factor can be the most destructive to an arts organization. When the cost of doing business continues to escalate, the organization faces tremendous pressure to increase revenue from either more sales by raising prices or securing more donations. Chapter 10, Economics and Financial Management, reviews some basic principles of economics and explores the unique economic dilemma that increasing costs and limits on productivity impose on arts groups.

The Arts and the Economy

In 2007 Americans for the Arts published their latest national study about economic impact of the arts. Research such as this has helped strengthen the case to be made for the importance of the arts and has made the job of the arts manager easier. The full document contains over 160 pages of details about the economic impact at all levels in America. Below is a summary of the key findings.

Arts & Economic Prosperity III: The Economic Impact of Nonprofit Arts and Culture Organizations and Their Audiences documents the key role played by the nonprofit arts and culture industry in strengthening our nation's economy. This study demonstrates that the nonprofit arts and culture industry is an economic driver in communities — a growth industry that supports jobs, generates government revenue, and is the cornerstone of tourism.

Nationally, the nonprofit arts and culture industry generates $166.2 billion in economic activity every year — $63.1 billion in spending by organizations and an additional $103.1 billion in event-related spending by their audiences. This is the most comprehensive study of the nonprofit arts and culture industry ever conducted. It documents the economic impact of the nonprofit arts and culture industry in 156 communities and regions (116 cities and counties, 35 multicounty regions, and 5 states), and represents all 50 states and the District of Columbia.

The $166.2 billion in total economic activity has a significant national impact, generating the following:

- 5.7 million full-time equivalent jobs
- $104.2 billion in household income
- $7.9 billion in local government tax revenues
- $9.1 billion in state government tax revenues
- $12.6 billion in federal income tax revenues

Our Arts & Economic Prosperity studies continue to be among the most frequently cited statistics used to demonstrate the impact of the nation's non-profit arts industry on the local, state, and national economy.

Source: Americans for the Arts Web site, Research and Information link found at http://www.artsusa.org/. Used with permission.

The process of evaluating the economic environment is often subject to contradictory reports by experts in the field. One expert may issue a news release announcing that the recession is over, while another says it will continue for six more months. If a manager is trying to plan a budget based on projections of income and expenses in uncertain economic times, the most practical approach is to plan contingency budgets. In other words, the organization's budget would be subject to constant revision depending on whether the economy is growing, stable, or slowing down. Budgeting will be more comprehensively reviewed in Chapter 9.

Other changes in the economic environment are more straightforward and the impact may be more direct. For example, if you operate a destination arts event, such as an annual summer festival, fluctuations in the price of gasoline could have a positive or negative impact on attendance in a given year.

One of the enduring myths of the entertainment industry that can shape the thinking of an arts manager is that when times are tough, people seek escape by spending on entertainment. The facts indicate that when the economy goes into what is called a recession (a sustained slowdown in the economy), people in the middle income levels reduce what is called "discretionary spending." Meanwhile, people in the upper income levels do not radically change their spending patterns, and people in the lower income levels curtail what little spending they do on the arts.[1] Donation frequency seems to follow similar patterns.

If a recession extends beyond a year, arts organizations will generally also see a slowdown in ticket purchases and donations from upper-income patrons. In more severe economic conditions, such as a depression, all spending and donation activity will slow dramatically. Knowing this, arts organizations can plan for reduced revenues, plan to increase fundraising activity, or both. Again, the key to working with the economic environment is to have alternative budgets ready to implement should conditions change.

The impact of such extraordinary circumstances as the 9/11 terrorist attacks on the U.S. economy in general and arts organizations in particular, coupled with a recession already in place in the early 2000s, had a substantial negative effect on arts organizations. New York City arts organizations felt the economic impact first and hardest. The aftereffects of the attack on the World Trade Center were felt in many different external environments beyond the economy. Not only did people forego attending arts events in the period immediately after the attacks, but the loss in tax revenue to the city of New York reduced grant funding months later.[2]

Extraordinary events such as terrorist attacks or a devastating hurricane such as Katrina in 2005 and the impact on the economy are beyond prediction. However, such catastrophes demonstrate the need for every organization to have a disaster plan should a significant event curtail operations or severely reduce expected operating revenue.

Political and legal

Arts organizations in the United States are influenced a great deal by the political and legal environment. The arts manager's approach to assessing how best to gather information about the potential impact this environment may have on their organization is driven in part by the cycle of governmental activity. At the local level, the city or county government may meet weekly and the state legislation may meet for all or part of the year. The federal government is in session nearly year-round and the court systems are active at all levels for much of the year. Thousands of new laws are enacted every year and court case law is constantly under scrutiny in the normal course of business.

What are the kinds of issues an arts manager is likely to face in assessing this environment? Let's take the example of a local governmental decision that is pending about advertising signage for a business. In this example, the issue may be the allowable size of a sign promoting a business. After further investigation the arts manager may come to realize this pending change in the law may mean the sign in front of his museum will need to be changed if this ordinance passes. The impact might mean having to spend thousands of dollars to redo the museum's signage. Obviously, the museum director would want to make his concerns known to the city council. In effect, the museum director would need to lobby to revise the ordinance or alter it in a such a way that the law will not have a negative impact on the organization.

Lobbying for the Arts

The active presentation of information about the impact of government legal policy on arts organizations can be an important activity for an arts organization. In this example, Americans for the Arts is sharing updates about visa requests for foreign guest artists.

- **04–16–2007:** The U.S. Citizenship and Immigration Services (USCIS) has announced that it will change the visa processing rules to allow employers and agents more time to file visa requests for foreign guest artists. Extending the earliest filing date from 6 to 12 months will provide relief for those petitioners who are prepared to file far in advance of a performance. The arts community has asked for this rule change as part of its overall advocacy efforts to reduce the total processing times for O petitions (for individual foreign artists) and P petitions (for groups of foreign artists, reciprocal exchange programs, and culturally unique artists) filed by, or on behalf of, nonprofit arts-related organizations.

Source: Americans for the Arts — http://www.artsusa.org/. Used with permission.

With the heightened visibility of the arts comes the added responsibility of artists and arts organizations to advocate continually to protect the public support gained over the last 40 years. There are specific restrictions governing the extent to which a not-for-profit organization may engage in lobbying. However, that does not mean arts organizations are not able to influence policy and legislation. For example, while advocacy is allowed, the IRS will not grant federal tax-exempt status to an organization attempting to directly influence legislation. Your arts organization may suggest in its newsletter that readers should let their opinion be known about a specific issue that may be of importance to the organization. On the other hand, it cannot put an article in the newsletter telling its readers to vote yes or no on a specific issue that may have an effect on the arts organization.

Up until the creation of the NEA in 1965, the arts were minimally involved with the political system. One example of a time that the government and the arts joined forces in the United States was during the 1930s when work projects that employed actors, singers, dancers, painters, and others became part of the U.S. economic recovery plan. There were a significant number of successful projects accomplished through what was initially called the Works Progress Administration (WPA). The work included everything from employing famous artists to paint murals in public buildings to writer's projects. Theater was also funded by the WPA; however, there were some challenges when putting people to work ran into the politics of the times. For example, the Federal Theatre Project, part of the WPA from 1935 to 1939, was abruptly shut down in a maelstrom of political controversy after only four short years. The fear of Communist infiltration in theater groups sent the whole program into budgetary limbo. The productions produced by the Theatre Project often challenged the mainstream political environment at the time and ended up losing its base of support in Congress.[3]

Other input sources for the political environment

The input from such sources as professional associations, consultants, board members, and the media can also help shape how an organization will adjust to changes in the political and legal environment. The board and staff of an arts organization face scrutiny when they receive public funds to operate. It is unlikely that the pressure will subside on arts groups to justify their needs against the needs for the poor, the ill, and the homeless.

The recent trend to privatize some of the operations at the state and local government levels has affected many organizations. In addition, many states are pursuing the politically attractive path of downsizing — or to use a business term, "rightsizing" — state government payrolls. The theory is that more efficient and cost-effective private sector firms can do such jobs as run prisons, issue licenses, and so forth. The savings can then be passed along to the public in the form of either no tax increases or lowered tax rates. The goal of lowering taxes while delivering the same services typically can only be met by cutting funds for what are termed "nonessential" activities. The arts, unfortunately, in some legislators minds may fall under this category of activity.

Arts managers who are active in the community and who have clearly made the case for the place of the arts and culture in the quality of life of the region can often counteract the effects of this trend. State arts councils, for example, can be one of the first targets of the budget axe of the legislators. One reason for this may be the perception this voting constituency will not generate much vocal opposition. See the next section *In the News* for examples of the impact of the political and legal environment.

In the News

Congress Demands More Form 990 Changes
Less than a month before the Internal Revenue Service (IRS) is to release a new draft of Form 990, leaders of the Senate Finance Committee sent a letter to the U.S. Treasury Secretary Henry Paulson detailing changes they'd like to see to improve openness and transparency.

Source: *The NonProfit Times*, June 11, 2007. Used with permission.

Arts Funding Released with Severe Cuts

By Mark Stryker

The good news for Michigan arts and culture groups is that on Friday Gov. Jennifer Geanholm lifted the two-month moratorium on funding that threatened to take $7.5 million out of their pockets.

The bad news is the Legislature followed through on a $3.6 million cut in arts funding for this year. When the dust settles, arts groups will receive only about $6.5 million of the $10 million they were promised from the state arts council for 2007.

Source: Mark Stryker, *Detroit Free Press*, June 9, 2007. Used with permission.

Changes in the legal environment are carried out through a wide variety of federal, state, and local enforcement agencies and the courts. For example, the Occupational Safety and Health Administration (OSHA) and similar state agencies issue regulations that have a direct impact on the operation of the theater, dance, and opera production shops and museum preparatory facilities in the United States. Employees have sometimes reported unsafe work conditions and practices to these agencies as a way to force unresponsive arts managers to make the workplace safer.

The impact of laws that affect the design of public spaces and the workplace by mandating access for people with disabilities must also be taken into account. Issues relating to smoking (including no smoking on stage in a production), sexual harassment, medical insurance and retirement benefits, maternity leave, and other needs and concerns have had an impact on arts organizations over the last few decades. Although it is true that many arts organizations fall below the minimum size required for compliance with federal regulations (often 50 or more employees is a threshold), many state and local lawmakers have expanded the scope of the legal requirements to cover smaller businesses and organizations. In most cases, changes in the legal environment have a price tag attached, and the implementation of new laws translates into expense items that appear in the operating budget of arts organizations.

More arts organizations are adopting an active rather than a reactive approach to coping with changes in the political and legal environment. In fact, the word "proactive" has replaced "active" and has become a part of the arts managers' vocabulary. For example, arts organizations extend personal invitations to politicians to arts events. Trips to Washington, D.C., the state house, or city hall for one-on-one discussions with the legislators, a governor, or a mayor have become almost mandatory. In their regular communication with lawmakers, arts managers try to stress that the people who attend the arts are also voters.

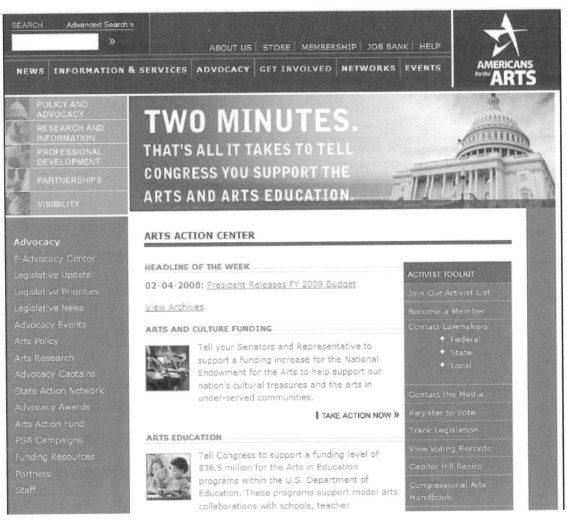

Figure 4.2

Americans for the Arts advocacy Web page. Used with permission.

The Americans for the Arts has made the process of getting messages to legislators about the concerns and interests of arts organizations and the public relatively simple. The Web page screen shot in Figure 4.2 shows how the Americans for the Arts have created a way to take action to tell a Senator or Representative your thoughts on a particular issue. This Web page is accessed from the Americans for the Arts homepage under "Policy & Advocacy." The option to send a template letter or to customize the content is available to the public before the e-mail is sent. Further information options such as how to track legislation, view voting records, or to learn "Capitol Hill Basics" is available in the "Activist Toolkit" on the right side of the Web page.

Each spring Americans for the Arts also sponsors an annual Arts Advocacy Day in Washington, D.C. The purpose of the day is

> to bring together a broad cross section of America's national cultural and civic organizations. These groups will join hundreds of grassroots advocates from across the country to underscore the importance of developing strong public policies and appropriating increased public funding for the arts.[4]

Cultural and social

The cultural and social environments represent a broad range of beliefs, attitudes, and behaviors that combine to make up our society. Cultural anthropologists study how groups of people interact with each other and create the common set of shared activities that helps form a community. From the studies of the anthropologists, we can begin to develop a vocabulary to help frame how the arts fit into this environment.

For the arts manager understanding the cultural and social environments of their community, region, and state is important for several key reasons. One important consideration an arts manager is always contemplating relates to the kind of programming the organization presents and its impact on the community. For example, the arts manager or a board of directors that allows an organization to move too far from the core values and beliefs of their community risk losing support. Arts managers often face complex and contradictory attitudes and beliefs in their community that can present opportunities to bring a people together, rather than divide them. Later in this section, we will look at the issue that has come to be known as the "Culture Wars" and its impact on arts organizations.

Traditional social structures (family, schools, and religious affiliations), though undergoing change, still play major roles in the transmission of social values and beliefs. Despite media stories about change, there still seems to be significant evidence that traditional structures are very much in place in society.

Some of the changes that are affecting the cultural and social environment include two-income households, single-parent households, changing attitudes about gender roles and race, affordable health care, and leisure time.

Another major force in the socialization processes is the broadcast media. Television and radio are still the major sources of information and entertainment for millions of people worldwide. Unfortunately, the broadcast media in America, other than public television and radio, do not focus much attention on the fine arts. An interest in opera, the symphony, or the fine arts is often the source of humor, if mentioned at all, in the TV shows watched by millions every night. An appreciation for the arts is often depicted as the act of a snob.

The arts manager must also recognize that alternative living arrangements have created new definitions of "families" and have led to different arts consumption patterns. In some cases, the high cost of housing has meant that many young people have not moved out of their family homes and established their own independent living arrangements. Single-parent families are also common today. In many communities, a greater number of people are living alone. In other situations, the number of households with couples not married but who are living together has increased. Career pursuits may also contribute to fewer leisure hours for a large segment of the highly educated population. For example, finding creative ways to reach these potential audiences with special discount ticket plans or through the types of programs offered will mean rethinking marketing and fundraising strategies for organizations.

Peer group influence is another social factor identified in research about potential audiences. A Ziff Marketing, Inc. survey undertaken for the Cleveland Foundation in mid-1980s found a strong correlation between arts attendance, education, and peer attendance. The survey found people will often try attending an arts event because a friend invites them. They may find they like the experience of attending the arts and become a regular consumer of the arts form they enjoy the most. Repeated surveys have confirmed that education and peer groups continue to play a significant role in the attendance habits of the public.

In contrast to these changing values and beliefs, much of the content of the traditional and, of course, popular titles in the repertories of symphony orchestras, theater, dance, and opera companies reflect gender roles or attitudes that were much different than they are today. Increasingly, the dominant culture is changing to reflect points of view that are more diverse. Women, African-American, Hispanic, and Asian-American artists are seeking to change cultural values to reflect a broader vision than that of the white Eurocentric worldview.

Arts organizations are attempting to respond to changes in their communities. For example, many arts organizations are proud of the programs they now do in February for Black History Month. However, for many African-Americans this special month of programming begs the question, "What about the other eleven months of the year?"

Contemporary marketing techniques and advertising campaigns attempt to segment the consumer with a degree of accuracy not possible in the past.

Sophisticated metrics are employed to track consumer behavior within ever-narrowing niches. However, arts organizations often do not possess the financial resources to purchase data about the specific market segments with the education and income profiles that correlate to regular arts consumption.

Other art organizations, especially in larger metropolitan areas, regularly sponsor events targeted to the under-30 crowd or other specific audience segments such as Gays, Lesbians, or Hispanics. Ultimately, arts organizations have to address the issue of the changing values and beliefs of the potential audiences in their community. Programming plays a big role in the organization's perceived relevance to its community.

It is also a fact that arts managers continue to grapple with the ongoing "culture wars" in some communities. In the early 1990s, James D. Hunter's book, *Culture Wars: The Struggle to Define America*, brought the debate into focus. Then presidential candidate Pat Buchanan added his perspective at the 1992 Republican National Convention, where he spoke of "a religious war going on in our country for the soul of America."[5]

The ebb and flow of the discussion about conservative or liberal views and values and how these are reflected in the arts continues. The constant media attention to Red States or Blue States hardly does justice to the complexity of this issue of values at the local level. Robert Lipsyte's opinion piece in the May 11, 2006, *USA Today* article titled "What Do Opera, Wine and Golf have in Common?" depicts one such skirmish. The substance of his story is that art forms like opera or pastimes such as playing golf or enjoying a glass of wine tend to become activities that separate us from each other as a society. The source of the arts-related controversy in this case was parental concern of exposing grade school children to the opera *Faust*. The opera was seen as unsuitable as a teaching tool in an elementary school outside Denver, Colorado, because of what were seen as themes of violence, Satanism, and suicide in the opera.

Of course, not all changes in the cultural and social environments may have negative implications for an arts organization. The excerpt in this chapter from Richard Florida's *The Rise of the Creative Class* and *The Flight of the Creative Class* speaks to complex mixes of economic, technological, and social changes that may bode well for the arts.

Book Sources for Trends

The Creative Class

In 2002 Richard Florida's book The Rise of the Creative Class: And How It's Transforming Work, Leisure, Community and Everyday Life *was received with much initial interest and favorable press. Richard Florida is on the faculty of the Rotman School of Management at the University of Toronto. His book, as its subtitle indicates, encompasses a wide range of topics. Professor Florida has done extensive research into the complex interaction of the rise of the creative class and its effect on America. Central to his premise is the recognition that creative activity isn't limited to artists and that expanding our understanding of how adaptable we are as a society is critical to our development as human. His book goes on to identify the geography of the creative class and its impact on the communities that foster and support its growth. That said, there are many critics of Florida's premise as the counterpoint notes.*

The New Class

The economic need for creativity has registered itself in the rise of a new class, which I call the Creative Class. Some 38 *million* Americans, 30 percent of all employed people, belong to this new class. I define the core of the Creative Class to include people in science and engineering, architecture and design, education, arts, music, and entertainment, whose economic function is to create new ideas, new technology, and/or new creative content. Around the core, the Creative Class also includes a broader group of *creative professionals* in business and finance, law, health care, and related fields. These people engage in complex problem solving that involves a great deal of independent judgment and requires high levels of education or human capital. In addition, all members of the Creative Class — whether they are artists or engineers, musicians or computer scientists, writers, or entrepreneurs — share a common ethos that values creativity, individuality, difference, and merit. For the members of the Creative Class, every aspect and every manifestation of creativity — technological, cultural and economic — is interlinked and inseparable.

Source: Richard Florida, *The Rise of the Creative Class* (New York: Basic Books, 2002), p. 8. Used with permission,

Counterpoint

There also have been critics of Florida's premise. For example, Harvard economist Edward Glaeser offered a generally favorable, but qualified, review of *The Rise of the Creative Class* in a journal article in "Regional Science and Urban Economics 35" in 2005. Glaesar notes:

> Florida makes the reasonable argument that as cities hinge on creative people, they need to attract creative people. So far, so good. Then he argues that this means attracting bohemian types who like funky, socially free areas with cool downtowns and lots of density. Wait a minute. Where does that come from? I know a lot of creative people. I've studied a lot of creative people. Most of them like what most well-off people like — big suburban lots with easy commutes by automobile and safe streets and good schools and low taxes. After all, there is plenty of evidence linking low taxes, sprawl, and safety with growth. Plano, Texas, was the most successful skilled city in the country in the 1990s (measured by population growth) — it is not exactly a Bohemian paradise. (p 594).

The Flight of the Creative Class

In 2005 Richard Florida published another book that looked at some of these same issues from a global perspective. From the perspective of pondering long-term trends his observations are well worth noting.

> ...the United States of America is now facing its greatest challenge since the dawn of the Industrial Revolution. This challenge has little to do with business costs and even less to do with manufacturing prowess. And, no, the main competitive threats are not China or India. Our country — for generations known around the world as a land of opportunity and innovation — may well be on the verge of losing its creative competitive edge.
>
> The core of this challenge is what I have come to see as the *new global competition for talent*, a phenomenon that promises to radically reshape the world in coming decades. ...Today, the terms of competition revolve around a central axis: a nation's ability to mobilize, attract, and retain human creative talent.

Source: Richard Florida, *The Flight of the Creative Class*, (New York: HarperCollins, 2005), p. 3. Used with permission.

As society and communities become more diverse, audience tastes and preferences will continue to change. Arts groups need to regularly reexamine their mission and fundamental choices in titles and programming options to ensure they stay in tune with the cultural and social environments. This does not necessarily mean not doing specific works from the repertory. Rather, arts organizations will need to assess the interpretation and adaptation of work to relate universal themes to the changing perspectives of audiences.

Demographic

The arts manager must closely monitor the demographic environment, which comprises the profile of the vital statistics of a society. Typical demographic measures that influence an organization include gender, age, race, income level, occupation, education, birth, and death rates, in and out migration, and geographic distribution. This information has been made relatively easy to access from the Census Bureau's Web site at www.census.gov. Selecting the menu item American FactFinder allows you to create your own reports by state and community. Another quick overview of demographic data may be found at www.zipskinny.com. Entering a zip code produces a profile with several social and economic indicators that an arts manager may find useful.

The broader questions this research on demographics raises are clearly longer term. If, for example, the population growth statics are negative in the community, the response an arts manager can take will probably have little influence. If there are decreasing opportunities to support a family in a community due to a significant economic decline, no amount of effort by an arts organization will solve the problem. Problem issues in the demographic environment are often rooted in the economic, cultural, and social environment. These larger issues may take changes in the legal or economic environment to address the problems.

The more that is known about a community and the surrounding region, the better the organization's ongoing assessment process will be in addressing community needs. For example, the baby boom generation will create a large number of elderly in the first quarter of the twenty-first century. Together, the boomers and the current elderly population account for a significant portion of today's arts consumers. Trying to anticipate the changing taste and attendance patterns of aging boomers will be a high priority for arts managers over the next 15 to 20 years. At the same time, attracting the next generation of arts audiences will take center stage.

Population shifts by region will also be a critical issue for arts managers to address. The Census data point to continued growth in the U.S. population. However, the demographic profiles indicate that where people live is changing. Data released in June 2007 indicated cities in the south and west are seeing significant growth while cities like Detroit, Cleveland, Buffalo, and Pittsburgh are shrinking. The report indicated that "Nearly a century ago, in 1910, each of the 10 most populous cities was within roughly 500 miles of the Canadian border. The 2006 estimates show that seven of the top 10 — and three of the top five — are in states that border Mexico."[6]

It is probably safe to assume that with an aging population health care costs will continue to take up a greater portion of the Gross Domestic Product (GDP). Age demographic trends are recognized by arts organizations as state funding comes under increasing pressure to finance health care support. In addition, artists and arts organizations have also had to face ever-increasing medical insurance costs. The escalating cost to offer benefits continues to be an issue for many arts organizations.

Demographic trends in the next 25 years also point to overall significant growth and increased ethnic diversity in America. The trend data all seem to point to the need for arts organizations to adapt to a more ethnically diverse audience that spans a greater age range.

Research Tool

A 1996 NEA report offers an in-depth study of demographic trends and arts participation (NEA Research Division Report #34, *Age and Arts Participation with a Focus on the Baby Boom Cohort*). The findings of this report raise questions about the attendance patterns of what is commonly called the baby boom generation. At issue is the lower attendance percentage of this generation at performing arts events. Despite being highly educated, many of the baby boomers seem to be seeking their entertainment from electronic and not live events. This report is published by Seven Locks Press of Santa Ana, California, and is worth adding to your management library.

Technological

As noted in Chapter 2, Arts Organizations and Arts Management, the invention and adaptation of film, radio, and television as a mass media entertainment option had a profound effect on the arts around the world. In the United States, the new technologies were quickly adopted for commercial profit-making purposes. The displacement of live performers with film, for example, put thousands of actors, dancers, singers, musicians, and technicians out of work in the 1920s and 1930s. New entertainment jobs were created, but many of the older performers in the larger metropolitan areas were permanently put out of work by the movie screen and the sound track. As the job market adjusted to the new technology, the live performing arts have adapted and grown since the end of World War II.

As we have seen, the arts boom was due in large part to the combination of the birth rate, economic growth, and increased levels of education. Through the 1960s and 1970s, arts centers and performing arts groups came into existence even though the number of television sets in households increased. The movie industry expanded the number of screens as the multiplex became the norm. Cable and satellite TV expanded the number of channel choices to a staggering level. By the 1980s, the home videocassette recorder (VCR), videodisc, and compact disc player created a new demand for program material. Home computers further expanded the market for entertainment in the 1990s. The ability to use the home computer as an entertainment center continued to expand.

In the twenty-first century, the VCR has lost its dominance to the ever-expanding DVD, DVR, and HD DVD and HD DVR formats, and the issues of control and the illegal distribution of media is a major problem facing distributors. Overall, the digital technology has provided more opportunities for viewers to rent or purchase programs of opera, theater, and dance performances or to see museum collections. Arts organizations have responded with more content in these evolving technologies. The Internet and increasingly sophisticated Web sites have further enhanced the opportunities for arts organizations to share who they are and what they do with wider audiences.

One example of the technology affecting distribution may be found in the music industry. The online access to thousands of classical music works has helped keep the limited classical music industry alive. At the same time, the costly economics of recording classical music is changing the dynamic of the industry. As the RAND study *The Performing Arts in a New Era* points out, the recording industry is clearly dominated by for-profit businesses.[7] Classical music recordings that often lose money, therefore, present a challenge to most music businesses owned by larger corporations. The degree to which a few classical "hit" recordings or artists subsidize the remainder of the music line has not gone unnoticed by these companies. The music industry has migrated toward online content delivery systems. The expanding capabilities of the Internet may provide opportunities to extend the reach of the classical musical niche if distribution, marketing, and packaging costs can be reduced. The sales of CDs is declining at a rapid rate and the quest is to make online delivery a profitable enterprise.

Some of the developments expected in the future offer further opportunities for the arts. For example, high-definition television (HDTV) is making the home entertainment center a reality for millions of consumers. Integrating advanced computer systems with these entertainment centers may make possible home versions of virtual reality technology. Gaming software and interactive computer technology allow the individual to enter into an electronic world that not only appears real to the viewer, but also allows direct interaction in an environment. As the current technology keeps improving and the cost of equipment continues to fall, the application of simulations and virtual reality will continue to expand. The technology is moving us toward the point where a person will be able to be part of a performance, rather than simply viewing it.

Although we may take comfort in the thought that people will want to continue to gather with other people and witness live performances, as they have done for thousands of years, we cannot assume that it will always be this way (See Shakespeare in the Metaverse later in this chapter).

New technologies seem to present opportunities rather than just threats to arts organizations. It remains to be seen, of course, how a product that is best delivered and experienced live will fare in an entertainment industry driven by a model that puts the choice of where and how to be entertained into the hands of end users. In fact, the birth rate may have more to say about the future than technological advancements. It is possible that there will be a continued decline in live arts attendance as the aging baby boomers and the digital generation stay home to be entertained by their own home theaters.

Educational

Studies show that education is one of the most significant factors in developing an arts consumer. Researcher Lynne Fitzhugh notes "The socio-economic variable most often and most perfectly associated with cultural attendance is, not surprisingly, education."[8] Many surveys have found that more than half of the people attending arts events have college or graduate degrees. The NEA 2002 "Survey of Public Participation in the Arts" pointed out that while only 26% of the U.S. population had college or graduate degrees, 58% of the classical music audience met that profile.[9] When considering the often limited focus given to arts education in the United States school systems, these attendance numbers are even more startling. One can only guess how much greater the attendance would be at cultural events if the arts were more consistently integrated into the educational experience of children.

As many arts organizations have discovered, there is great long-term benefit as a result of working in cooperation with local school systems. However, because the schools typically have limited resources to pay for the services of arts organizations, outside funding is required. Foundation and corporate grants to improve the quality of education provide opportunities for arts groups to establish good community relations and to build future audiences.

The most effective methods for making the arts a significant part of the educational environment usually combine visits to the schools with planned lessons throughout the year. The old notion that arts experiences consisted of transporting busloads of children to an auditorium to watch a show or listen to a concert has gone by the wayside. Those occasional enrichment activities typically offered a superficial connection to the arts, and, in many cases, only acted to alienate or bore young audiences.

The arts at the university and college level also have developed into a thriving sector in the last 50 years. In the 1970s and 1980s music, theater, dance, visual arts, and media arts programs became well-established on campuses large and small. Many artists found the relatively stable environment of higher education an attractive alternative to freelancing. In many instances, artists found it possible to continue to engage in their professional career while teaching or to become "artists-in-residence" at better funded schools. Higher education in the arts has evolved into a complex network of formalized training programs that produce — and some say over-produce — a steady supply of up and coming artists in all disciplines. Specialized undergraduate and graduate school programs continue to expand the scope of their course offerings and experiences for students.

Changes in the arts curriculum, as in most areas in a university, come slowly. Nevertheless, the process of constant institutional assessment has spurred the examination of how to most effectively educate and train future artists. One curricular trend that appears to be developing focuses on more interdisciplinary or cross-disciplinary work. The core education in each arts discipline continues to evolve too. At the same time, the opportunity to explore how the arts, technology, and human expression are connected seems to be an area higher education is continuing to develop.

Another by-product of the marriage of the arts and higher education is that America's universities and colleges have in effect become a patron of the arts through their funding of academic programs and by sponsoring performing arts series or the creative research and work of faculty and staff. Public performances and exhibitions have become an integral part of the arts programming in the communities where a college or university is located. (For an excellent example of campus arts and community initiatives go to the Web site for Imagining America: Artists and Scholars in Public Life at www.imaginingamerica.org.)

Many of the arts programs on campuses have also taken their role of developing future audiences as a serious charge. The attempt to interest students in enrolling at a particular school often includes recruitment materials that note the important part the arts will play in the quality of life on the campus.

As noted in Chapter 2, arts training programs have also encompassed arts management as part of the curriculum. On many campuses, this may only be one course offered in the subject area. The trend seems to be one that involves offering arts administration courses mixed with classes in business and communications. An article in the January 2007 issue of *American Theatre*[10] magazine offered an overview of graduate programs in arts or theater management and included a dialog about the future needs and trends for arts leadership with key managers and educators.

In the decades to come, education will also continue to be the focus of political attention. Performance standards, outcome assessment, national testing, accrediting, increasing budgetary pressures, home schooling, and parental choice in selecting schools will continue to face the 16,000-plus primary and secondary school districts across the United States. State government funding trends in higher education continue to decrease as a percentage of total government spending. The costs to sustain colleges and universities are constantly assessed relative to the benefit of a well-educated and trained workforce.

INFORMATION SOURCES

To effectively manage change and operate a continual self-evaluation system an arts manager needs to identify the sources they will use for gathering information. They should develop an ongoing process for evaluating the opportunities and threats facing the organization. Let's examine the type of information each source generates.

Audiences

Arts managers want to know as much as possible about the people who expend the effort to go to a show or an exhibition or who give the organization their financial support in exchange for a ticket, subscription, or a membership. The importance of volunteers and donors to help support the human resource and financial deficits faced by organizations also cannot be understated. Within the bounds of an ethical system of gathering data, an arts manager would want to know (1) why this person made the purchase, (2) what she liked about what was presented, (3) what she didn't like, and (4) what other arts-related "products" this person would be interested in purchasing. Members of the audience, patrons, donors, members — whatever the organization calls them — are tremendous resources usually receptive to questions about how they think and feel. For example, surveys asking about the museum experience, questionnaires inserted in programs, or contact by phone, online, or having discussion with small groups of randomly selected arts consumers are viable techniques for gathering information. Some techniques will be more effective than others, but regardless of the method, the arts organization that is able to provide detailed profiles of the consumers of its "products" will better predict how a planned change might affect the relationship that exists between the individual and the organization.

Does this data-gathering process imply pandering to the audience's tastes? Hardly. The primary purpose of asking people what they think about your organization is to learn how to communicate better with them. Arts organizations forget that their audiences do not use the same vocabulary to describe the product and the process of the arts. In the open system, the arts manager should be designing the communication devices (brochures, letters, posters, the Web site, and so on) to the outside world to reflect terms and concepts that effectively translate the organization's mission to the widest possible audience. Ineffective communication only raises barriers between the organization and repeat customers or future customers. (Chapter 11, Marketing and the Arts, and Chapter 12, Fundraising, will discuss this topic in more detail.)

In summary, establishing an ongoing communication process with your audiences or members is essential to the long-term health of an organization. The importance of knowing as much as possible about who is interested in what you do and why cannot be stressed enough. Feedback from the consumers of your arts service is a resource that will help shape the future of an organization.

Other arts groups

A community with several arts groups can achieve a synergistic boost from the combination of programs and activities. The term *synergy* is often used to describe a situation where two or more organizations working together can produce results greater than the sum of their individual efforts. The local arts scene can flourish when different arts groups recognize that they can benefit from communicating and collaborating with each other about their season or exhibition plans.

Strategic thinking and long-term planning should create a mutual understanding among arts groups that audiences are eager to participate in and experience that which makes their community unique. Research seems to indicate that a segment of the audience can be classified as users of different art forms, while other segments are loyal to one form and seldom go to see other events.[11] One strategy arts organizations explore is working together as a consortium. For example, many cities publish both print and online arts calendars covering different programs in a given period of time by the local arts groups and museums. These calendars give potential arts consumers an overview of all events happening in their area and can provide a type of one-stop shopping place. These calendars are often linked to an online ticketing system or to the Web site of the organization. Discount coupons and advertisements are often used to highlight special events in an effort to draw in new customers. Flyers can be widely distributed through a Sunday newspaper or a mass mailing. The net result of consortiums can be an enhanced awareness of the overall arts scene in a community and cooperation among the arts groups.

In addition to cooperative publications and shared Web sites, different arts groups can work together to present new programming combinations that benefit both organizations. The symphony and the ballet or the ballet and the opera can pool their resources on occasion to present larger scale productions than either could mount individually.

If nothing else, a regularly scheduled meeting among the different presenting groups in a community offers an opportunity to share ideas about trends in the different art forms. A regular "community arts summit" meeting designed to share information ultimately helps a manager better understand the total scope of activity.

Board and staff members

The board of directors and the staff of an arts organization are a vital component in the information-gathering process. One key part of this process includes ongoing input via staff meetings, suggestion boxes, retreats, informal social gatherings, and formal planning sessions. When a board member asks about presenting a particular type of program or a staff member suggests a new procedure, the organization should have mechanisms for effectively responding to the input.

Part of an arts manager's job is to actively sort through this input and try to adapt those suggestions and ideas that will more effectively support the mission and vision of the organization. The open system model depends on these suggestions and works from the assumption that there are always alternatives to current actions. An organization that does not listen to the input from the board or the staff will probably become stagnant and dysfunctional over time.

The media

The print and broadcast media and the Internet provide the arts manager with up-to-the-minute information about many of the external environments that have an impact on the organization. It is also possible to gain insight into the general mood of the country or region from polling or surveys conducted by the media. Granted, some of the published polling information can be superficially communicated. However, more often than not, Web links to the source material can provide a wealth of detailed information. Trade publications in the arts as well as national and regional news sources and selected Web sites should be part of the arts manager's regular reading list. Although contradictory information is often generated by these sources, this is to be expected in a diverse society.

Cultivating and sustaining a positive working relationship with the press and the broadcast media can be an obvious long-term benefit to arts organizations. However, arts and nonprofit groups are often naive about the realities of media coverage. Column space in the print media or airtime on TV is an issue of money. For the print media, advertising sales space and news articles are always in a complex struggle with each other. For the local commercial television or radio station, ratings determine advertising revenue. Therefore, coverage that will generate ratings is often the focus of attention. Getting a feature story in the arts section of a newspaper or getting 30 seconds of airtime at the end of the six o'clock news can be a struggle. The search for good news in a community, which an arts organization could provide, often is the best avenue to pursue with the local media.

Attaining a level of visibility is critical for an arts organization's interactions with these external environments. No matter how good and noble the programs or projects of an organization may be, it is hard to establish credibility in the community without publicity.

One example of the ebb and flow of media coverage was the NEA struggle described in Chapter 2, Arts Organizations and Arts Management. The media focused on the obscenity issue rather than on the larger questions of government support for the arts or artistic freedom because the struggle of Congress with the NEA was simply more interesting than a national policy issue. The net result was a great deal of publicity for the NEA, most of which, unfortunately, cast it in a negative light. Very few stories mentioned the thousands of grants made each year and the millions of people who benefit from grants and services of the NEA.

Arts organizations are in a very competitive situation when it comes to getting the attention of the media. However, a carefully designed public relations program can keep the arts organization in the news and help create a positive image. More discussion about the public relations function is seen in Chapter 11.

Professional associations

Each of the arts has a professional service organization or trade association that provides regular information about issues of importance to its constituency. Many of the organizations and associations publish newsletters or magazines, and almost all hold annual conferences. The information-exchange process among members often focuses on current operational problems or topics related to new methods for raising money. For the arts managers the benefit of belonging to these associations and attending these conferences lies in expanding their knowledge of how other organizations are adapting to external forces.

Consultants

Consultants are another source for information about methods of keeping an organization functioning effectively. In theory, a consultant should give the organization a needed outside and well-informed perspective. Of course, arts managers should never assume that consultants are always right any more than they would blindly trust any other source of information. However, because arts consultants usually deal with several organizations at one time and have a substantial list of clients, they can suggest new ideas and approaches that would not necessarily occur to the internal management staff. Consultants can also validate the staff's ideas about how best to manage change in the organization.

Other sources

Depending on the art form, other input sources may provide valuable information to the manager of an open system. As noted, the U.S. government regularly publishes statistical data from the Census Bureau and the Commerce Department that arts managers could apply to their analysis. The local or regional Chamber of Commerce Web site or the Convention and Visitors Bureau in a community are often very helpful sources of local economic and demographic information. States have active tourism bureaus that crave information about the kind of programming arts organizations routinely offer.

Another source of information can be found among the various suppliers of goods and services purchased by the organization. For example, the bank used by the organization could be an excellent source of local economic information. Printers or graphic arts firms could be a source of information about new trends and techniques in advertising. After all, the arts organization is a business in the community, and belonging to local groups that attract other businesses could prove helpful when seeking direct information about the economic health of the area.

THE IMPACT OF FUTURE TRENDS ON THE ARTS

Trying to anticipate how change will have an impact on an arts organization is a difficult task. As we have seen from this brief overview of the major environments affecting arts organizations, complex forces can interact to produce unforeseen results. Seeking additional points of view and analysis is critical to developing a better understanding of how to respond to change.

One of the more significant recent studies about trends in the arts in America was commissioned by the Pew Charitable Trusts in 2001. *The Performing Arts in a New Era*, published by the RAND Corporation, continues to be a source of a great deal of discussion by policy makers, arts leaders, and students. This publication offered a comprehensive overview and is required reading for anyone trying to develop a better understanding of the forces affecting the arts in America. The introduction of the report notes that:

> Our research offers evidence of a fundamental shift in the structure of live performing arts in the future. Specifically, we predict that the number of organizations supplying live performances of theater, music, opera, and dance will contract at the professional level and expand at the community level. Organizations that produce live professional performances face particular problems in many small and midsized cities across the country and could become increasingly concentrated in large metropolitan areas and important regional centers that can support high-budget nonprofit organizations with top-echelon performers and productions. For many Americans access to this level of performance arts will depend on touring productions. At the same time, Americans will have greater access to small, low-budget productions of greater cultural and artistic diversity performed largely by amateur artists (and professionals willing to perform for little or no pay) in their own communities. Also, as is true today, Americans will increasingly choose to experience the performing arts not through live performances but through recordings and broadcast media, the quality of which will continue to improve.[12]

This report offers a less-than-bright future for organizations situated between the large institutions and the small arts organization. High fixed costs and limited earned and unearned income (e.g., fundraising and grants) potential seem to be having the most negative effect on middle-sized arts organizations. Larger organizations have the income and gift earning power and a scale of operation that help sustain them. Smaller organizations are not burdened with as many fixed costs and are able to be more flexible in their operational decision making.

This study provides several recommendations for plans of action to meet the current and future problems facing arts organizations. Equally important, the report provides a forum for the kinds of policy discussions that seem to be lacking in all levels of government.

Another publication that helped frame the impact of the arts in America is *The Gifts of the Muse*, also published by RAND Corporation. This 2004 publication examines the extrinsic values (e.g., external factors such as the economic impact of the arts) and the intrinsic value, or the personal impact of the arts experience. This study helps balance the arguments for the importance of the arts in our society, which to the authors, seemed to have tilted too far toward extrinsic values.

A more recent discussion about trends may be found in a report by Andrew Taylor of the Bolz Center for Arts Administration at the University of Wisconsin-Madison. His summary report of a Getty Leadership Institute and National Arts Strategies conference on "Cultural Organizations and Changing Leisure Trends," held in May 2007, offers many intriguing perspectives from a diverse group of participants.[13] (For more information about the Getty Institute and its programming go to www.getty.edu/leadership.)

Some of the highlights of the report, including the perception that we have less leisure time, were not supported by personal time-diary studies. The studies indicate the average American has five to six more hours per week for leisure activities than in the 1960s. However, trends toward multi-tracking and multi-tasking have become part of the American lifestyle. Teenagers, while leading the multi-tasking way, are not alone by engaging in routine patterns of behavior that often include instant messaging and answering e-mail while watching television. The report notes the time we have to focus on a single task is made more difficult by these behavior patterns of constantly switching attention. The time-diary studies also pointed out that individual participation in conventional arts activities on average comes to a little less than nine hours per year.

The summary report shifted to examining some of the challenges facing the arts and culture world in what appears to be an increasingly fractured lifestyle of its audiences. Taylor offered what he identified as "three clusters of opportunity for cultural organizations in all sectors — nonprofit, public, commercial, and informal."[14]

The first cluster was the "culture as respite,"[15] which would focus on responding to how the arts can help mediate the fractured lifestyles people lead and stressing how this experience is different from daily life. The second opportunity was described as "culture as a connector."[16] In this instance the response would include recognizing "expression as a means to embrace complexity,"[17] and then attempt to "connect our individual experiences to a wider range of individuals."[18] The third cluster would focus on bringing a "connection between expression and daily life. In this world, art, science, humanities, and heritage would be integral to work and leisure, not unique and discernable endeavors."[19] The group gathered at this conference then shifted to developing scenarios for these ideas with different types of organizations.

For the arts manager steeped in the daily grind of running an organization, pondering the larger issues of leisure time and expression may seem a little abstract. However, it is precisely this kind of exercise in thinking that the often overextended manager needs to build into her work schedule. It is important to keep asking, "What is at the core of how people experience the programming offered by arts and culture organizations, and how does the organization's mission and the vision really serve to engage the community?"

What do these reports offer arts managers pondering the future of their organizations? If nothing else, the fact that the topic is even discussed shows how critical it is to step back from the daily grind and look around. Engaging the staff and board in regular future focused discussions can help keep an organization vital and aware. As we will see in Chapter 8, providing effective leadership for an arts organization involves a great deal more than events, exhibitions, or seasons of shows.

SUMMARY

All organizations in an open system interact with changing environments that shape the transformation and output of the product. The economic, political and legal, cultural and social, demographic, technological, and educational environments interact to form a complex set of conditions that influence how well an organization will be able to meet its objectives. The evaluation of the six environments is a function of information gathered from audiences, other arts groups, board and staff members, the media, professional meetings and associations, and consultants. Since environments are constantly changing, managers must develop a process for continually evaluating input.

The economic environment is the most influential external force. General conditions such as inflation, recession, interest rates, and the taxation system determine the financial health of the operation.

The impact of the political and legal environment on an arts organization extends from the international scene to the local level. Cultivating positive communication and stressing the important part the arts play in the lives of voters can help build support from within the political arena.

The cultural and social environment is a combination of the values and beliefs of the society, as communicated through the family, the educational system, religion, and increasingly, the broadcast media. The changing family profile, increased racial diversification, expanding career and work choices for women, and gender role differences in American society are creating a different profile of the potential audience member.

The distribution of the people in the United States is changing in terms of age, sex, race, income level, education, ethnicity, and location. The baby boom generation that fueled much of the growth in the arts is aging and is not being replaced in equally large numbers. The population is growing in numbers and diversity. The impact of these demographic changes will have a profound effect on the arts well into the next century.

Technology, once a major threat to the live performing arts, is now helping artists reach a wider audience than at any time in history. New technologies have helped increase the distribution of the arts in the United States, and may make the experience of the live performance available to consumers in their homes.

The U.S. education system is undergoing tremendous pressure to increase its effectiveness through accountability measures. Because education levels are a strong predictor of later attendance at arts events, arts managers would do well to become part of the education revolution by working to incorporate the arts into the changing educational environment.

For additional topics relating to the adaptive arts organization, please go to www.managementandthearts.com.

Questions

1. Do the six environments affect the various art forms in different ways? For example, are theater groups more or less influenced by changes in these environments than art museums? Explain.
2. This chapter focused on the influence of the environments on organizations. What influence do these environments have on the individual artist?
3. What combination of demographic descriptors would you use to outline why you and your family or friends are arts consumers?
4. What opportunities and threats will artists and arts organizations face over the next five to ten years?

SUGGESTED ADDITIONAL READINGS

Malcolm Gladwell, *The Tipping Point — How Little Things Can Make a Big Difference*, Back Bay Books, Little, Brown and Company, NY, 2002.

Malcolm Gladwell, *Blink — The Power of Thinking Without Thinking*, Little, Brown and Company, NY, 2005.

Henry Jenkins, *Convergence Culture — Where Old and New Media Collide*, New York University Press, NY, 2006.

Steven Johnson, *Everything Bad Is Good For You — How Today's Popular Culture Is Actually Making Us Smarter*, Riverhead Books published by the Penguin Group, NY, 2005.

Steven D. Levitt and Stephen J. Dubner, *Freaknomics — A Rogue Economist Explores the Hidden Side of Everything*, William Morrow, An Imprint of HarperCollins Publishers, NY, 2005.

DISCUSSION FOCUS — FUTURE TRENDS

The following article by Teresa Eyring, Executive Director of the Theatre Communications Group (TCG), an organization with the mission to strengthen, nurture and promote the professional not-for-profit American theater, offers some observations about the evolving nature of performance and technology.

Shakespeare in the Metaverse
By Teresa Eyring

O! for a Muse of Fire, that would ascend
The brightest heaven of invention;
A kingdom for a stage, princes to act
And monarchs to behold the swelling scene.

In Shakespeare's time, this prologue from *Henry V* summoned the space where a sweeping tale could be recounted for an enthusiastic audience. The performance might have taken place at the Globe Theatre, "a wooden O" that it was hoped could hold the "vasty fields of France" and "the very casques that did affright the air at Agincourt."

Today, the kingdom might be a community in Great Britain or the southern United States — or it may be a virtual social networking world such as "Second Life," where princes and monarchs are the virtual incarnations of individuals' real-world selves, also known as "avatars." And the stage might be the New Globe, a virtual 3-D representation of a theater space (which in real life is a theater designed for Governor's Island in New York). Yes, a theater scene is evolving in the metaverse, albeit gradually.

In Second Life, which was launched by San Francisco-based Linden Lab in 2003, "residents," now numbering more than 6.8 million, can purchase islands, build homes, travel and interact socially through their avatars. Recent estimates put its population growth at 15 percent per month and the average resident age at 32. Second Life describes itself as a 3-D virtual world built and owned by residents, who can create their own digital items (art, clothing, tools, etc.) for sale or trade, retaining all rights to their work. As much as $1.5 million is spent "in-world" each day. The currency of the land is the Linden dollar, which can be converted to U.S. dollars at online exchange booths.

Last summer, the virtual New Globe Theatre was the site of the premiere of a play called *From the Shadows*, written by SL resident Enjah Mysterio and instigated by an Internet 3-D company called Millions of Us. Bloggers were generally positive about the experience, while acknowledging that the real essence of the theater experience doesn't translate well into the metaverse. Giff Constable of the software design firm Electric Sheep Company commented in his blog: "Putting on a play using Second Life is a bit like trying to crack a walnut with a refrigerator. Emotions are really hard to convey."

DISCUSSION FOCUS — (CONTINUED)

But this challenge has not stopped performing artists from attempting to create a presence in an online world. The Second Life ballet company performs regularly, with a piece called Olmannen, an original three-act love story written, choreographed, and narrated by Inarra Saarinen. In April, Ohio-based Red (an orchestra) premiered the first-ever live digital-simulcast of an American orchestra into the 3-D virtual Web. The concert celebrated the opening of Case Western Reserve University's virtual campus in what is known in SL as OneCleveland. Red (an orchestra) used the event to explore ways of introducing new audiences to classical music.

In discussions about theater in this century, the speed of technological advancement is on everyone's mind, and its attractiveness to younger generations offers up a challenge for the future. Theater leaders and practitioners are attempting to articulate what our industry's relationship is and should be to the rapidly developing interactive forms that allow individuals to participate in international communities that socialize, compete, create new stories, and solve problems together.

Even more populous than online social networking worlds are MMORPGs, or Massively Multiplayer Online Role Playing Games such as World of Warcraft, EverQuest, Ultima Online, and RuneScape. They've also become economies of their own, originally leading to the term Real Money Trading (RMT), in which virtual items are traded for dollars or other real-world currency. In April of this year, a new online alternate reality game, World Without Oil, was launched, dubbing itself "a serious game for the public good." It envisions a world where oil supplies are completely depleted. The

players imagine how they will navigate and function within such a world, using blogs, videos and online chat to grapple with ideas such as how to get groceries during an oil shortage. Sounds like what we hope theater inspires in its participants.

We know that theater is difficult if not impossible to translate into other media forms with the same impact. There's the irreplaceable nature of the connection between live actor and live audience. Still, the ability to build community in a virtual world around the creation of artistic work is becoming more available. In the same way that a theater designer uses a model to show how a play might unfold on the proposed set, a virtual 3-D theater space can be used to connect artists from all over the globe in creating and workshopping certain aspects of a production. Existing residents of that virtual world can be invited to participate. Or a theater's own real-life audience can be invited to create a personal avatar in order to participate in the proceedings and give feedback or help with the creative process. In a sense, this is an out-of-town tryout in the metaverse before premiering in real life.

While hours at a computer producing theater in a virtual world seems counter to the mystery and magic that live theater represents, these technologies may provide great opportunities to test ideas and build awareness of what we do across a broad audience. Who knows: If virtual worlds such as Second Life become more heavily utilized by our members, TCG may just have to set up offices in the metaverse.

Source: *American Theatre*, July/August 2007, p. 8. Used with Permission.

Questions

1. The author noted the New Globe Theatre premiere of *From the Shadows* was generally positive, "…while acknowledging that the real essence of the theatre experience doesn't translate well into the metaverse." Based on this observation, do you think younger audiences share the same value of the essence of the live theatrical event?

2. What do you think should be the relationship between "the rapidly developing interactive forms" and the live performing arts? If you think it should be a closer

relationship, explain how. Should theater leaders even be worrying about this relationship?

3. What do you think might be some helpful ways to use the metaverse to develop new work or new ways of interacting with potential audiences?

REFERENCES

1. Lynne Fitzhugh, "An Analysis of Audience Studies for the Performing Arts in America," Part 2, *Journal of Arts Management and Law* 13 (Fall 1983), p. 7.

2. Robin Pogreen, "Arts Groups in New York Brace for Cuts in City Funds," *New York Times* (Monday, May 20, 2002), pp. B-1.

3. John O'Connor, Lorraine Brown, eds., *Free, Adult, Uncensored: The Living History of the Federal Theatre Project* (Washington, D.C.: New Republic, 1978).

4. Americans for the Arts Web page: http://www.artsusa.org/events/2007/aad/default.asp.

5. James Davidson Hunter, Alan Wolfe, *Is There a Culture War?*, (Washington, D.C.: Brookings Institution Press, 2006), p. 1.

6. Press release, June 28, 2007: *Census Bureau Announces Most Populous Cities*, U.S. Census Bureau, Washington, D.C.

7. Kevin McCarthy, Arthur Brooks, Julia Lowell, and Laura Zakaras, *The Performing Arts in a New Era* (Santa Monica, CA: RAND Institute, 2001), p. 10. http://www.rand.org./ARTS_area.

8. Lynne Fitzhugh, "An Analysis of Audience Studies for the Performing Arts in America," Part 1, *Journal of Arts Management and Law* 13 (Summer 1983).

9. *2002 Survey of Public Participation in the Arts*, National Endowment for the Arts, p. 14.

10. *The Management Puzzle*, and *Where Do Managers Come From?* Joan Chanick, Jim Volz, *American Theatre*, January, 2007.

11. McCarthy, Brooks, Lowell, and Zakaras, *The Performing Arts in a New Era*, p. 56.

12. Ibid., p. 3.

13. Andrew Taylor, *Cultural Organizations and Changing Leisure Trends Post-Convening Summary Report*, (J. Paul Getty Leadership Trust, 2007), summary of pages 2–6.

14. Ibid., p. 5.

15. Ibid., p. 5.

16. Ibid., p. 5.

17. Ibid., p. 5.

18. Ibid., p. 6.

19. Ibid., p. 6.

CHAPTER 5

Planning and Decision Making

Decision makers need to factor into their present decisions the "future that has already happened."[1]

Peter Drucker

KEY WORDS

Planning	Top-down and bottom-up plans
Goals	Contingency and crisis plans
Objectives	Mission statement
Short-, intermediate-, and	Vision statement
long-range plans	Values statement
Strategic plans	SWOT analysis
Operational plans	Decision-making
Single-use and standing-use plans	Inventory of alternatives

As noted in Chapter 1, Management and the Arts, planning is one of the primary functions of management. However, as the above quote also notes, the decisions made in planning for an organization are often a product of changes that have already taken place in the world. Thus, we have the interesting challenge of planning for future changes by becoming acutely aware of our current circumstances. For the arts manager this translates into developing a planning process that is both flexible and systematic.

In this chapter, we define planning and look at strategic and operational planning. We will also discuss the decision-making process, which is an important tool you will need to assist you with the planning process.

Before we can delve into the topic of planning, we need to step back for a moment and consider an important question: Why are we doing this concert, play, or exhibition? Are we trying to introduce our audiences to a new work or artist? Are we trying to raise money for a cause? Are we trying to make a profit or generate a surplus in our depleted operating budget? The planning we do must be driven by the answer to this important "why."

MISSION, VISION, AND VALUES STATEMENT

The "why" should be answered by the organization developing a carefully crafted *mission, vision, and values statement*. Later in the chapter we will provide more detailed examples of these statements. Concisely, the *mission* is *the purpose* the organization exists (e.g., to bring high quality new plays about contemporary issues facing the world we live in). The *vision* is what the organization sees will be the outcome of pursuing this mission (e.g., we will gain a better understanding of how we can work together to make our world and community a better place to live). Finally, the *values* articulate what the organization *holds most important* in the process of pursuing its mission and vision (e.g., we value the input of our creative team, staff, board members, and our community in shaping our choice of the issues we focus on in the creation of new plays).

Ultimately, the mission, vision, and values statement should inspire your board, staff, and volunteers and be a call to action. The mission statement should be able to stand alone and offer anyone who reads it a clear sense of the reason your organizations exists. As you will see later in this chapter, the mission statement should be concise enough that anyone associated with your organization can communicate it when the occasion demands.

THE CONTEXT OF PLANNING

As we discovered in Chapter 4, The Adaptive Arts Organization, there are complex forces at work in the various environments in which arts organizations must function. Artists and organizations have to adapt to the pressures of the external environments that are an integral part of our society. For example, a solo artist unencumbered by a board of directors and an administrative staff may be able to achieve the goal of performing a new work through the sheer force of her energy and drive. However, solo artists still face very practical issues related to the political and legal environments in the process of trying to present their work. The board of a well-established orchestra, on the other hand, may debate for months over the conductor's desire to do a new series of modern music concerts. In this case, the differing attitudes of the members of the board and the management team enter into determining why an organization selects a new direction.

Relationship of planning to the arts

The creation and use of a planning process can be an excellent way to provide the overall framework needed to keep an organization and its board headed in the same general direction. For plans to be effective, they should be integrated into the daily operation of the organization. Does this ensure that the organization will be a success? No. In fact, many founder-driven arts organizations came to life and struggled to national prominence without any planning documents. However, it is difficult today for an arts organization to attain support from foundations, corporations, or government agencies without a published mission statement and a strategic planning document.

The necessity of planning

Over the last 50 years, arts organizations and artists have had to deal with ever-increasing accountability, especially when dealing with individual donations or gifts, public money, corporate donations, and foundation support. It is typical for arts organizations to provide three- to five-year plans in their funding applications. However, the need for arts organizations to remain flexible and open to change is also important. Planning that locks an arts organization into rigid thinking and action can be deadly to the whole enterprise.

The management of any arts organization must assume that change is a given. Opportunities and threats to the organization will constantly present themselves. Therefore, there is no choice other than to draw up plans detailing how the organization will respond to change. The key is to develop a planning process and planning implementation system that fits with the scope and scale of the organization.

The organization's map and leadership

Most of us have had to read a map at some point in our lives. In effect, the planning document for an organization is the map to help it get to its desired destination. Although most of us have read maps, few of us create them. Arts organizations need the skilled assistance of managers who are in essence mapmakers. These maps are translated into a workable planning process for the organization.

Ultimately, planning cannot ensure success. Without dynamic and articulate leadership, an organization will probably be less likely to succeed. Board and management leadership that is not trained in developing and implementing plans must learn these skills if the organization is to remain healthy over the long run.

Planning Proverb #1

"Planning is 80% thinking and 20% writing. Then 100% doing!"
Harold McAlindon, *Management Magic*

Planning terminology

Let's begin our overview of planning by defining some of the basic terms used in the process. First, *planning* is a process of stating what you want to do and how you want to do it. Planning involves thinking about the future — even if that is only tomorrow. It requires imagination, careful thought, and, most important, time. This text uses the term *plan* to mean *a statement of intended means for accomplishing stated results*. A plan should answer at least these six questions:

1. Why?
2. What?
3. When?
4. Where?
5. Who?
6. How?

Here is an example of how one might use this six questions approach:

> To fulfill our mission of bringing new music to the community, we have set a goal of attracting more patrons to our events. To achieve that goal we have set a specific objective for our marketing and sales staff to expand our subscription audience by 7 percent for next year's concert series in New Hall. To meet this objective the marketing and sales staff will increase its contact with corporate personnel departments and offer group discounts. The methods they will use will include personal contacts to the corporate personnel departments and a flyer and e-mail to businesses promoting group sale discount plans.

As you can see, this simple plan answers all six questions: *why* — the organization's mission to bring new music to the area; *what* — meet our goal and objective to expand concert subscriptions by 7 percent through group sales; *when* — for next season; *where* — New Hall; *who* — the marketing and sales staff; and *how* — by making personal contacts and stepping up the group sales offer.

In this text, a *goal* is defined as *a desired outcome* and an *objective* is the *specific means to achieve the desired outcome*. In our example, the goal is to attract more patrons (a desired outcome), and the specific objective is to increase the subscription audience by 7 percent next season by corporate group sales (specific means). The result of this process should be goals that are feasible to achieve and objectives that are realistic given the financial and human resources available. Clear, simple, direct language should be used to make it easy to understand what is attempted and why.

Short-, intermediate-, and long-range plans

There are many different types of plans typically used by people and organizations. When we refer to short-range plans, we mean one that is a year or less. Intermediate-range plans are usually one to four years, and long-range plans cover five or more years. Generally, long-range plans that exceed five years are of limited value because there are too many unforeseen intervening variables. However, that does not mean an arts organization shouldn't plan that far ahead. For example, raising funds for a major building project often has five or more years associated with the entire process. As you will see in Chapter 12, Fundraising, fundraisers may deal with gifts that will not come to the organization until far in the future; therefore, their planning horizon may extend well beyond 10 years.

Why planning is difficult

It is important to consider how people within the organization perceive time as you start the planning process. Research on planning points out that most people are comfortable with thinking three to six months ahead. Once you get past one year, most people are only able to think in the most general terms. Therefore, it is not advisable to develop overly detailed planning objectives and documents that extend too far into the future. The age of an organization also determines perceptions of time. When you first establish an organization, four months can seem like a long time. However, if you are part of a long-standing arts organization, three- to five-year plans might not be so difficult to comprehend.

As noted, the perception of time has a profound impact on the planning process. As human beings, we also have the ability to use our imagination to project what we think our future might look like. If you are currently in college, you are very likely to have considered the age-old question of "What's next?" If you are working in an arts organization you may have a moment to look up from your desk and wonder "What important issues are shunted aside to deal with urgent everyday demands?" Daniel Gilbert's fascinating book *Stumbling on Happiness* observes: "When people daydream about the future, they tend to imagine themselves achieving and succeeding rather than fumbling or failing."[2] Organizations and the people who make plans operate in much the same way. However, Gilbert observes, "Because most of us get so much more practice imagining good than bad events, we tend to overestimate the likelihood that good events will actually happen to us, which leads us to be unrealistically optimistic about our futures."[3]

This same pattern of behavior is often carried out in a group setting when a management team and a board sit down to create planning documents. In a sense, the planning process is a product of how our brains are wired. Part of that wiring includes our tendency to base future outcomes on past experience. It is difficult work to engage in planning because there are many unspoken assumptions about how we perceive the future of our organization. Getting everyone to agree on a mission, vision, and values statement for an organization can be a daunting experience.

Reading Gilbert's book before starting a planning process might be an excellent exercise for the staff and the board. It could prove a healthy exercise to make everyone aware of the psychological processes at work when trying to imagine a future for an organization.

At the root of much of the forward thinking we do in planning is a need to feel in control. Keeping this in mind Gilbert notes, "one of the fundamental needs with which human brains seem to be naturally endowed, and much of our behavior from infancy onward is simply an expression of this penchant for control."[4]

We make plans for our lives and our organizations in a much more complex psychological environment than we realize. With these complexities in mind, let's look at the process of planning, but let's remember mapmaking is much more difficult than map reading.

Strategic and operational plans

For our purposes, a *strategic plan* is a set of comprehensive plans designed to marshal all of the resources available to the arts organization for the purpose of meeting defined goals and objectives derived from the mission, vision, and value statements. Within this set of strategic plans, the organization could have several specific strategies. For example, the strategic plan for the organization may be focused on growing the organization. Within the overall strategic growth plan, there could be a specific strategy to expand the number of shows and performances in the season. In theory, this strategy should result in the organization fulfilling its overall strategic plan of growth. The strategy to add more shows and performances in turn drives other plans that effect the operation of the organization.

One impact of the strategy to add more shows directly affects another important component in the planning process: formulating *operational plans*. Operational plans are usually limited to activities designed to support the day-to-day operations of the organization. For example, adding more shows has an impact on the production manager of a performing arts organization. Their day-to-day plans would reflect the change in the schedule, which in turn is supporting the strategic plan to grow the organization. In addition, areas such as marketing and public relations would need to design operational plans to help achieve that strategy. Therefore, your operational plan identifies and develops the resources you need to support components of the strategic plan.

Implied in the relationship between the strategic plan, the strategy, and the operational plans is a process that involves all levels of the organization providing input and suggestions as plans are developed. Unfortunately, organizations do not always develop fully integrated planning processes and systems. It is not unusual to hear war stories from staff working in arts organizations about "after the fact planning." In this example of expanding the season schedule, the executive level leadership and the board may all agree it is a wonderful idea and the organization should go forth with the growth plan. However, no one actually brings the production manager or the marketing and PR department in on the decision. The result is those who must implement the plan end up scrambling to try to make the strategy work without the resources they need.

Single-use and standing-use plans

Single-use and standing-use plans are the most common in arts organizations. *Single-use plans* "address unique events that do not recur."[5] Examples of single-use plans could include relocating the office of the organization, or purchasing a building and converting it to a scenery or costume shop. *Standing-use plans* are designed to "handle events that recur frequently."[6] For example, an opera company rents a performing arts center for its season of four productions. Plans are made for the scheduling of rehearsals, load-ins, and technical rehearsals. The same basic schedule plan is carried out for each opera.

A *budget* can also be thought of as a standing-use plan. It is designed for the purpose of clarifying the organization's decisions about the distribution of resources. A budget that allocates more money for costumes than for scenery says something about the ideas driving the production. An exhibition may allocate 80 percent of the budget for a full-color book and only 20 percent for mounting the exhibition. A symphony may decide to focus on national touring and reduce its home schedule by 20 percent. These choices ideally represent a plan agreed to by all of the people involved in putting on the show or concert or setting up the exhibition.

A *production schedule* for an arts organization might combine single- and standing-use plans. We are all familiar with a schedule as a list of deadlines for completing specific tasks designed to meet an overall objective. Most arts managers work with either weekly or monthly calendar formats. For example, when an opera company sits down to plan a season, it works from a standing-use plan: the season production schedule. However, if the company knows it will perform *Aida* next season, it can create a single-use plan for accommodating the animals for the triumphal march scene. The logistics related to this part of the plan can be arranged far in advance. (Budgeting is discussed in more depth in Chapter 9.)

Since a standing-use plan is designed to be used repeatedly, it can be helpful in dealing specifically with how the administrative offices will operate. For example, the office operations plan would include such things as how the phones are to be answered, messages taken, mail opened, filing systems managed, and so forth. A ticket office should have a standing-use plan detailing the day-to-day operational procedures for processing orders and accounting for all revenue. Standing-use plans are also typically found in policy books, employee handbooks, or posted rules.

On the surface, these two planning components may seem less weighty than the grand strategic plans, but they are often critical for the success of an organization. As we will see in Chapter 7, Human Resources and the Arts, employees depend on well-designed, single-use and standing-use plans to do their jobs.

DEVELOPING A PLANNING PROCESS FOR THE ARTS

Let's now examine in more detail how to develop a planning process for an arts organization. Most of us use a planning process of one sort or another to get through the day: "After class or work I have to go to the bank, then have dinner with Fred, and then head over to the library or the store this evening." When people make the transition to a formal planning process they can become bogged down in a level of detail that makes the idea of planning daunting. Planning should be approached as a practical and enjoyable journey, not a set of abstract tasks.

The mission statement

As you see in Figure 5.1, the first step in the planning process is to create or analyze your mission statement. A clear mission statement, which defines the organization's "purpose or reason to be," is the source from which all plans should spring. The basic elements of any mission statement typically includes wording to help the reader understand what the organization does and why it does what it does. For example, a theater company might be dedicated to presenting new works, or a ballet company might be committed to performing classical works. Groups of all sizes need a concise statement that communicates

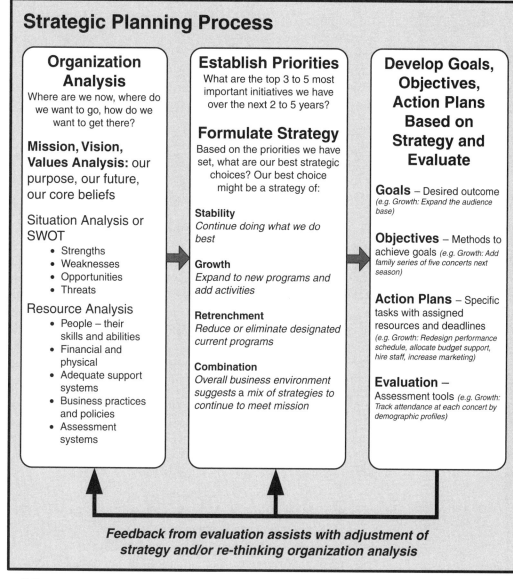

Figure 5.1
Strategic planning process.

to the world who they are and why they exist. However, when looking at the mission statement of arts organizations you will usually find a great deal of variety when it comes to length and clarity.

The following seven arts organization mission statements offer a sample of the kind of variety to be found among arts organizations.

1. Seattle Opera strives to produce musically extraordinary, theatrically compelling operas, employing uniformly high-quality casts, dramatically aware conductors, and innovative yet textually concerned directors and designers. By continuing our emphasis on the work of Richard Wagner and by achieving national and international recognition for the quality of all of our performances, Seattle Opera commits itself to advancing the cultural life of the Pacific Northwest.[7]

2. The Mission of The Actors Guild of Lexington is to produce quality live professional theater that stimulates, engages, and entertains; elevates the quality of life for citizens of the Bluegrass region of Kentucky; and affirms the commonality of human experience through sustained production excellence and educational outreach." Vision Statement: The Actors Guild of Lexington aspires to be the leader in the cultural community of Central Kentucky by producing quality professional theater that illuminates and examines the common humanity in all of us. We affirm that theater can and should entertain, enlighten, stimulate, inspire, provoke, question, elevate, transform, uplift, challenge, and awaken. We believe that theater can and should generate meaningful public discourse and be truly public: responsive to the evolution of our community and accessible to a wide cross-section of our populace. The Actors Guild of Lexington will share and celebrate stories from across the spectrum of time and place while consistently reminding our community of timeless themes and universal interconnectedness.[8]

3. Our Mission: The Guthrie Theater, founded in 1963, is an American center for theater performance, production, education, and professional training. By presenting both classical literature and new work from diverse cultures, the Guthrie illuminates the common humanity connecting Minnesota to the peoples of the world.[9]

4. The Red Mountain Chamber Orchestra exists to educate and give pleasure to the public by performing a repertoire of classical music composed especially for chamber orchestra, music not otherwise heard in Birmingham. One of the few such orchestras in the Southeast, it was founded to provide a musical outlet for skilled players, conductors, and soloists in the community.[10]

5. The Museum of Fine Arts houses and preserves preeminent collections and aspires to serve a wide variety of people through direct encounters with works of art. The Museum aims for the highest standards of quality in all its endeavors. It serves as a resource for both those who are already familiar with art and those for whom art is a new experience. Through exhibitions, programs, research, and publications, the Museum documents and interprets its own collections. It provides information and perspective on art through time and throughout the world.[11]

6. The San Francisco Museum of Modern Art is a dynamic center for modern and contemporary art. The Museum strives to engage and inspire a diverse range of audiences by pursuing an innovative program of exhibitions, education, publications, and collections activities. International in scope, while reflecting the distinctive character of our region, the Museum explores compelling expressions of visual culture.[12]

7. The central mission of the Chicago Symphony Orchestra Association is to present classical music through the Chicago Symphony Orchestra to Chicago and national, and international audiences. The mission is supported by four mutually reinforcing elements:
   - Artistic excellence: continued international preeminence in the field of orchestral excellence
   - Audience development: leading audience development initiatives
   - Education: superior education and community programs
   - Financial stability: fiscal responsibility for long-term stability[13]

Mission analysis

The Seattle Opera mission sends a strong message about what it aspires to be with the selection of words such as "extraordinary," "compelling," "high-quality casts," and "innovative." There is also a clear commitment to the work of Wagner and to serving the region of the Pacific Northwest. This seems a clear statement of what the opera company intends. The phrase "textually concerned" probably could be worded to be more reader friendly. It comes across as what might be called "arts speak." Arts speak in this case means using a type of organizational jargon that does not necessarily communicate well to the general public.

The Actors Guild of Lexington, Kentucky, is a multi-part mission statement separated by semicolons. The first part clearly establishes the organizations purpose of producing "quality live theater." The remainder of the statement addresses goals and methods they will use to fulfill the mission. It is not unusual to find arts organizations that mix mission statements with outcomes or goals. However, it can leave the reader to wonder just where the mission statement ends.

The statement of the Actors Guild's goals are "elevating the quality of life," and affirming "the commonality of human experiences." The statement ends with two methods of fulfilling the goals: "sustained production excellence and educational outreach."

Of the seven examples of mission statements, this was the only organization with a vision statement on its Web site. The vision statement includes a mix of "We believe" statements along with a list of what the company also values about the impact it wants to have by doing live theater. This vision statement offers ways it can measure and assess its effectiveness as an organization. The statement also clearly indicates the theater "aspires to be a leader in the cultural community."

The Guthrie Theater mission statement begins by interrupting the flow of the first sentence with the insertion of its founding date. To the casual reader this may be a point of interest, but it delays getting to the point. However, in this statement the point of the first sentence seems to be the organization describing itself as "an American center for theater performance, production, education, and professional training." The list of items seems to focus on what it does rather than stating its purpose as a theater company. The next sentence seems more focused on the organization's purpose: illuminating "the common humanity connecting Minnesota to the peoples of the world." The word order to the sentence again delays getting to the point. The statement starts by describing how the mission will be accomplished which will be by "presenting both classical literature and new works from diverse cultures."

The Red Mountain Chamber Orchestra Web site does not actually indicate that this statement is the organization's mission. However, the first two sentences seem to be trying to offer a statement of purpose. The two key purposes of the chamber orchestra are "to educate" and to "give pleasure to the public" through its choice of music. The statement further clarifies its commitment to "classical music composed especially for chamber orchestra." It also lists as a secondary mission or purpose to "provide a musical outlet for skilled players, conductors, and soloists in the community."

The Boston Museum of Fine Arts has a compact and direct mission statement. The only thing preventing it from being 100 percent effective is its omission of the word "Boston." This museum mission statement could describe any number of organizations anywhere in the world. The statement indicates the MFA aspires to high standards and how it will go about achieving its mission through becoming a resource for people.

The San Francisco Museum of Modern Art starts its mission statement by saying what it does, not its purpose. The second sentence articulates what it "strives" to do, what it does, and for whom. The sentence ends with what seems to actually be the core purpose or mission of the SFMMA: "explore compelling expressions of visual culture." This final phrase is also an example of arts speak. One wonders if readers will know how to define the term "visual culture" as they scan the statement.

As you can see from this sampling, there are as many different ways to state a mission as there are organizations. Some missions are composed of one sentence, and others take a paragraph. A mission statement is your main tool for describing the organization to the world. Some of the mission statements cited achieve that outcome, but others are less successful.

Perhaps the best advice about formulating a mission statement is to remember that this is *an introduction of the organization to people who do not know what it is and have no idea what it does.* A mission statement is directed at audiences, donors, funding sources, and other public agencies. For example, think about how easy it would be to introduce yourself at a reception or public function by saying, "I am with the Seattle Opera, and we strive to produce musically extraordinary, theatrically compelling operas, employing uniformly high-quality casts, dramatically aware conductors, and innovative yet textually concerned directors and designers." It is likely (assuming you can remember all of this statement) the person you are talking to will stop listening after a few words. Most staff members of arts organizations would probably shorten the mission statement to "we produce musically extraordinary and theatrically compelling operas." Try this exercise with the some of the other mission statements we examined, and you will see why staff often make up variations on the published mission statement to actually communicate about their organization when meeting the public.

Reading these sample mission statements may lead you to question the admonition that planning should be driven by the mission and vision, since some well-known organizations publish mission statements that do not clearly present the primary purpose of the organization or articulate its vision. Yet many of these same organizations still do quite well. The real world of how arts organizations function and the textbook models for how to accomplish certain activities — such as developing mission and vision statements and planning — do not always match. Nevertheless, it is easier to plan and set priorities as an arts manager if the mission and vision is clear and is widely communicated inside and outside the arts organization. In fact, many arts organizations have vision statements; they just do not publish them on their Web sites.

Vision statement and planning resources

There are many resources available for developing vision statements and engaging in the planning process. The Alliance for NonProfit Management Web site has a FAQ section on strategic planning that is of value to anyone getting started with this process (www.allianceonline.org/). Another company in the non-profit sector offering examples of planning tools is mystrategicplan.com. The nonprofit planning process has been greatly facilitated by this Web site, which allows for developing a strategic plan collaboratively. Alternatively, simply doing a Web search for "Creating a Vision Statement," will yield a large number of links to explore. What is common to all these various resources is the reinforcement of the idea that a vision statement is an important tool in helping the organization describe successful future outcomes that will result from accomplishing its goals and fulfilling its mission.

Situation analysis

The process of looking at oneself and frankly assessing one's good points and shortcomings is as difficult for an organization as it is for an individual. Arts consultants thrive on bringing the outsider's viewpoint into what too often becomes a self-congratulatory process. Organizations, like people, have a hard time seeing their flaws.

The first key step in the planning process typically involves undertaking of what is often referred to as a *SWOT analysis* (strengths, weaknesses, opportunities, and threats — see Figure 5.2). One creates a detailed inventory list of items under each area to develop an overview of the organization in relationship to factors that may help or hinder the organization realize its mission. To be open and honest about the organization's current status is critical, as is

Figure 5.2

Sample of SWOT analysis.

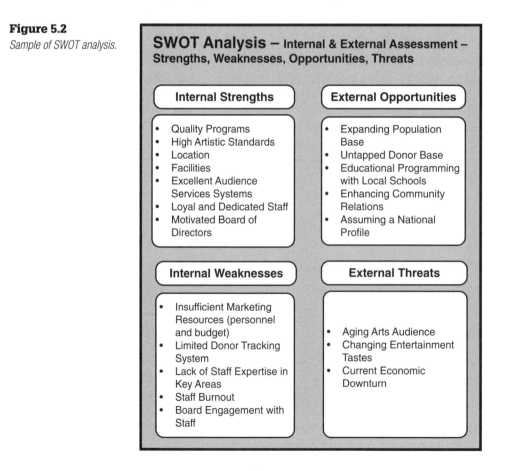

SWOT Analysis – Internal & External Assessment –
Strengths, Weaknesses, Opportunities, Threats

Internal Strengths

- Quality Programs
- High Artistic Standards
- Location
- Facilities
- Excellent Audience Services Systems
- Loyal and Dedicated Staff
- Motivated Board of Directors

External Opportunities

- Expanding Population Base
- Untapped Donor Base
- Educational Programming with Local Schools
- Enhancing Community Relations
- Assuming a National Profile

Internal Weaknesses

- Insufficient Marketing Resources (personnel and budget)
- Limited Donor Tracking System
- Lack of Staff Expertise in Key Areas
- Staff Burnout
- Board Engagement with Staff

External Threats

- Aging Arts Audience
- Changing Entertainment Tastes
- Current Economic Downturn

recognizing that at times a strength can be a weakness and an opportunity may also be a threat.

For example, an experimental theater company, with a mission of presenting *only* new works, may have the strength of very talented writers and an outstanding acting company. The company's weakness may also be its newness. It lacks experience working within the existing arts community in the area. It may also have an opportunity in the newness of its work, and thus may be able to capture more attention than one more production of *Hello, Dolly!* or *A Streetcar Named Desire*. Lastly, it may face the threat of censorship in the community if the work is considered controversial.

How do all of these factors shape planning for our experimental theater company? First, in doing a rigorous analysis of the situation the company may discover that it might never thrive in this community and that relocation to a more tolerant city would be advantageous. Alternatively, the company may decide that the challenge of presenting new works in this community is worth the effort, even if it never achieves widespread public and financial support. On the other hand, based on its SWOT analysis, it could decide to change its artistic mission and produce a season of more accessible works along with new plays.

As you can see, a planning process can be directed at creating goals, objectives, and plans of action for the purpose of fulfilling a mission statement. This may seem like an obvious starting point for planning, but I have spent many hours in meetings where conflicting views of an organization's mission statement were never resolved. The planning went ahead, but conflicts always arose when the process led to the stage of deciding what was most important to the organization — what is the top priority? A weak or contradictory mission statement is a bit like an out-of-focus photograph. When people view the picture, they often see different things. They reach conclusions and make assumptions based on imprecise information. Actions are taken, and then questions are raised: "How does this project or program serve our mission?" Often it does not, but resources are allocated anyway.

Resource analysis

The next step of an organizational analysis, as shown in Figure 5.1, involves a resource assessment. An important aspect of organizational self-analysis is to evaluate the organization's internal human, material, technological resources, and operating systems. Questions such as the following must be answered:

1. Do we have the people with the skills we need to realize our plans?
2. Do we have the facilities, money, equipment, and other resources needed to make our plans work?
3. Do we have the ability to monitor progress and make corrections as we proceed?

These questions raise critical issues facing an arts organization. Many plans are never realized because the first question on this list cannot be answered in the affirmative. You may want to expand your Web site as a marketing and sales tool for your season, but if you do not have the staff you cannot engage in this activity. You may wish to have your museum staff engaged in more educational activities with the community, but not if the staff is already strapped for time to accomplish their existing task list. Even if you have the human resources available to support the plan, lack of space, equipment, or budget support can thwart those trying to achieve the goals you have all agreed need to be addressed. Lastly, plans that are made and then executed need to be monitored and often adjusted as they unfold. Having the time and energy it takes to keep your plans moving through to completion is also a critical part of the planning process.

Formulating strategies

The next step in the planning process is to take the organizational analysis and shape a strategic direction for the organization (see Figure 5.1). Strategy defines the *direction in which the whole organization intends to move*. It implies the priorities and it establishes the framework for the action to be taken to achieve the goals outlined in the strategy. We have noted that the strategy should relate to the environment in which the organization must function. In Chapter 4, The Adaptive Arts Organization, six environments were outlined: economic, political and legal, cultural and social, demographic, technological, and educational. Depending on any number of conditions, one or more of these environments could be stable, undergoing change, or even be uncertain.

Strategic planning usually draws on one or more of the following approaches: stability, growth, or retrenchment. It is also possible to use some combination of all three of these strategies.

Stability strategy

The basic thinking behind this strategy is "We are doing pretty well with our current operation, and there is no reason to make any big changes." This does not mean that the organization is doing nothing about meeting its stated goals and objectives or improving its effectiveness. It simply implies there is no reason to move off in new directions. Many arts organizations would probably feel comfortable adopting this strategy because so much of an arts organization's programming is set into an annual pattern. The major arts organizations in a community are often seen as institutions that are part of the basic fabric of the area. People cannot imagine not having the museum, the symphony, and so on.

Growth strategy

This approach makes sense when expanding operations into new markets or if the organization is considering starting new programs. With this strategy, a company may diversify its product line or actively seek a bigger share of the market. Arts organizations may adopt growth as an overall strategy by doing such things as increasing the numbers and types of events that it produces. Another example of a growth strategy is to deliberately push for greater community involvement by adding a ballet school or an art school to the dance company or museum. With growth comes increased costs and, one hopes, increased income. Expanding without offsetting increases in revenue or staff can create a level of organizational stress that reduces its effectiveness.

Retrenchment strategy

The third strategy describes a slowdown, cutback, or elimination of some portion of the organization's activity. Because this process is often viewed as retreating, many organizations will go to great lengths to describe it as something else. For example, a music group might say "We are engaged in a planned phase-out of our Tuesday night concert series." In other words, the group is retrenching and cutting back on its programming, probably to save money. Like the early 1990s, the 2000s have been marked by a great deal of cutting back and retrenching among many arts organizations. Retrenching can also be an effective strategy if the organization expanded beyond its resource capacity. Arts organizations, like people, can over-commit themselves. Saying "no" can also be an effective tool for keeping the organization stable.

Combination strategy

An organization might use all three of these strategies at any given time. Again, the influence of the external environments we have talked about in Chapter 4 will determine to what degree various strategies must be adopted. If the community is experiencing an economic slump combined with an uncertain political environment, the organization might need to retrench in some areas and expand in others.

STRATEGY SUMMARY

To formulate an overall strategy, an honest appraisal of the organization's mission statement and the organization's strengths, weaknesses, threats, and opportunities must be made. Here again, the services of an outside consultant can help the board of directors and staff to keep a sense of perspective about what the organization will really be able to accomplish through its strategic plan.

GOALS, OBJECTIVES, ACTION PLANS, AND EVALUATION

The final phase of the planning process results in developing goals, objectives, action plans, and evaluation systems. The goals are shaped by the choice of strategy, and the objectives address fulfilling the goals with specific methods. The action plans develop concrete steps in the allocation of human, financial, and equipment resources to meet the objective. Lastly, a measurement or assessment process monitors how well the organization is achieving the goals and objectives it has set for itself.

In Figure 5.1, the example of a growth strategy goal of expanding the audience base is outlined. One objective is to add a series of concerts to the season. Some of the specific action plans required to achieve the objective and fulfill the goal include changing the performance schedule, establishing a budget to support the new series, hiring more staff to run the series, and devoting support for marketing the new series. Last, but not least, the example notes methods that will be used to evaluate how the new series did. This could include tracking sales, attendance, and developing demographic profiles of the audiences.

A more detailed depiction of this type of planning process is shown in Figure 5.3. In the sample planning document a dance company is seeking to expand its audience base. From that overall goal, the more specific objective is stated to increase the percentages of buyers and ticket revenue. From this objective a series of more specific action plans are developed. There could be many more action plans created for this objective. Figure 5.3 is intended to provide just a small sampling of the planning options the dance company could explore.

Please feel free to use this sample form to organize your planning documents. It really does not matter if you use a word processing, spreadsheet, or database application to assemble and track your planning effort; the key is to write it down.

Figure 5.4 demonstrates that within the overall strategic plan of an organization there are many component parts. It is not unusual to find plans for marketing, fundraising, programs, or facilities driven by the overall strategic plan. The dynamic nature of planning, implementation, and assessment is difficult to impart in a single diagram. As the diagram depicts, the flow of the process leads back to analysis and assessment. To have an effectively managed planning process it must be clear to the board, staff, artists, and potential supporters what you are trying to achieve. In general, plans that are expressed through diagrams are often easier for everyone to comprehend and implement.

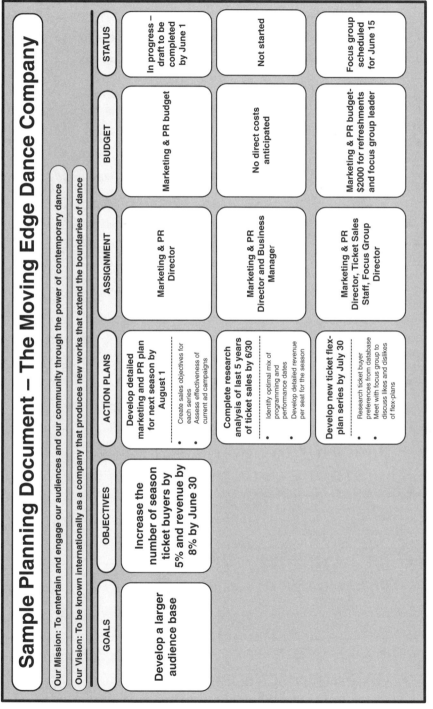

Sample Planning Document – The Moving Edge Dance Company

Our Mission: To entertain and engage our audiences and our community through the power of contemporary dance

Our Vision: To be known internationally as a company that produces new works that extend the boundaries of dance

GOALS	OBJECTIVES	ACTION PLANS	ASSIGNMENT	BUDGET	STATUS
Develop a larger audience base	Increase the number of season ticket buyers by 5% and revenue by 8% by June 30	**Develop detailed marketing and PR plan for next season by August 1** • Create sales objectives for each series • Assess effectiveness of current ad campaigns	Marketing & PR Director	Marketing & PR budget	In progress – draft to be completed by June 1
		Complete research analysis of last 5 years of ticket sales by 6/30 • Identify optimal mix of programming and performance dates • Develop detailed revenue per seat for the season	Marketing & PR Director and Business Manager	No direct costs anticipated	Not started
		Develop new ticket flex-plan series by July 30 • Research ticket buyer preferences from database • Meet with focus group to discuss likes and dislikes of flex-plans	Marketing & PR Director, Ticket Sales Staff, Focus Group Director	Marketing & PR budget- $2000 for refreshments and focus group leader	Focus group scheduled for June 15

Figure 5.3
Sample planning document.

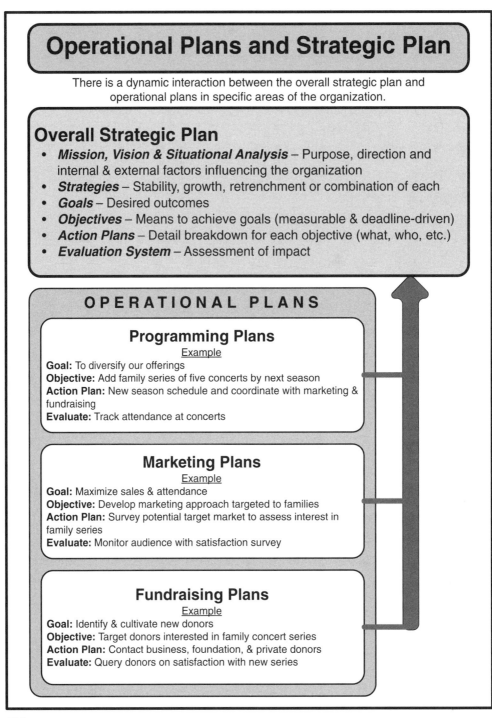

Operational Plans and Strategic Plan

There is a dynamic interaction between the overall strategic plan and operational plans in specific areas of the organization.

Overall Strategic Plan
- *Mission, Vision & Situational Analysis* – Purpose, direction and internal & external factors influencing the organization
- *Strategies* – Stability, growth, retrenchment or combination of each
- *Goals* – Desired outcomes
- *Objectives* – Means to achieve goals (measurable & deadline-driven)
- *Action Plans* – Detail breakdown for each objective (what, who, etc.)
- *Evaluation System* – Assessment of impact

OPERATIONAL PLANS

Programming Plans
Example
Goal: To diversify our offerings
Objective: Add family series of five concerts by next season
Action Plan: New season schedule and coordinate with marketing & fundraising
Evaluate: Track attendance at concerts

Marketing Plans
Example
Goal: Maximize sales & attendance
Objective: Develop marketing approach targeted to families
Action Plan: Survey potential target market to assess interest in family series
Evaluate: Monitor audience with satisfaction survey

Fundraising Plans
Example
Goal: Identify & cultivate new donors
Objective: Target donors interested in family concert series
Action Plan: Contact business, foundation, & private donors
Evaluate: Query donors on satisfaction with new series

Figure 5.4
Operational plans related to strategic plans.

Other planning approaches

The business world is filled with different approaches or combinations of approaches to take when planning. Arts organizations are usually not as bureaucratic in the planning process as businesses or governmental agencies. However, care must be taken not to fall into the trap of spending more time planning than actually doing the work that needs to be done.

Developing a formal business plan

One of the fundamental approaches used when starting up an enterprise is to create a business plan. Chapter 2, "Arts Organizations and Arts Management" provides an outline for a business plan that can be adapted to an arts organization. As you will see, engaging in creating mission statements, setting goals, and developing objectives closely parallels the format we have discussed in this chapter. Answering the questions of why, who you are, and how you are going to accomplish what you say you are going to do is just as important when writing a business plan.

Top-down and bottom-up planning

Top-down planning simply refers to a process where upper level management sets the broad objectives, then middle- and lower level management work out detailed plans within a limited structure. *Bottom-up planning* begins with lower and middle management setting the objectives; upper management responds with final planning documents that reflect the input. A mixture of these approaches make sense for most organizations.[14]

Top-down planning can fail if upper management does not consult with middle and lower management and labor when setting objectives. For example, suppose the board and artistic director of an opera company plan to expand the season of the company from 8 to 16 weeks. Before trying to implement this plan, they should ask the people in the other levels of management (production manager, marketing and fundraising directors) to evaluate the impact of this change. Middle- and lower level management will be asked to prepare reports showing the increased costs and increased revenue anticipated as a result of this plan. Upper management will then have the information it needs to assess the consequences of expanding the season. Modifications can be made in the plan before final implementation. (Given the number of anecdotal stories by staff about never being consulted when sweeping changes are made in their arts organizations, I surmise that an effective top-down planning process is only an ideal in many settings.)

Pure bottom-up planning is fairly rare because it is usually a very cumbersome process. Too much staff time is spent meeting and reviewing every detail of the planning documents. More typically, the process might begin with upper management requesting that middle and lower management draw up planning documents for their areas or departments. Difficulties may arise when middle and lower management are not well-informed about the overall organizational financial resources, goals, and objectives. The fact is, if everyone in the organization does not understand the mission and the goals of the organization, this bottom-up planning process may actually be counterproductive.

Contingency planning

As the name implies, *contingency planning* sets alternative courses of action that depend on different conditions. Contingency planning is most effective when trigger points are built into the process. For example, suppose that your season subscription campaign began in March. You expected to have a 70 percent renewal rate by July, but the box office reports only a 40 percent renewal by July 15. You would now activate your contingency plan for another mailing and a media blitz.

Crisis planning

Crisis planning is an offshoot of contingency planning. Plans for dealing with a crisis do have a place in arts organizations. This is especially true when the organization must deal with the media, supporters, subscribers, or the general public. For example, an arts organization should have a plan ready to activate in the event of the death of a key person like a founder–director. It is also a good idea to plan for crisis if an organization decides to tackle a controversial project or programming choice. Arts organizations all too often go through months and years of chaos because no one took the time to map out a plan before a crisis struck. In fact, lacking a crisis plan can ironically lead to operating the organization by crisis planning. In fact, some organizational leadership is so inept at planning that the standard mode of operation is from one crisis to another. This high stress operating environment usually burns out staff quickly and leads to high personnel turnover.

FYI — Other Resources for Planning

A source for highly systematized information about planning may be found in John M. Byron's *Strategic Planning for Public and Nonprofit Organizations*, 3rd edition. Byron sets a benchmark for organizational planning. His approach is particularly helpful because it recognizes the unique elements of the nonprofit organization in a planning process. He also articulates a useful perspective about strategic thinking and acting as it informs strategic planning. Lastly, he provides concrete examples of successful and unsuccessful planning practices.

LIMITS OF PLANNING

One of the by-products of the growth and development of the arts in the 1960s and 1970s has been the steady increase in organizations developing strategic plans. The NEA helped foster the process of organized planning as part of its funding mechanisms. In the 1980s and 1990s the word "visioning" became a verb and was added to our planning vocabulary. To secure funding arts organizations had to demonstrate that they had a vision and a planning process in place for the funds they were requesting. Although the level of resources allocated to arts planning never reached the intensity that it did in the corporate world, many arts organizations generated thick tomes of strategic plans that took considerable time and effort to assemble. Unfortunately, many of these plans gathered dust on a shelf in an office because they lacked an operational relevance to the organization. The systematic application of these plans often failed to materialize for the simple reason that they were never fully integrated into the day-to-day operation of the organization.

In *Management for Productivity*, John Schermerhorn cites seven general reasons why organizational plans fail:[15]

1. The upper management fails to build a formal planning process into the general operating routine.
2. The people involved in planning are not very skilled in the planning process.
3. The data used in making the plans are incorrect [or incomplete].
4. The resources needed are not made available to execute the plans.
5. Circumstances change due to unforeseen events.
6. Staff members do not want to change, and they hold to plans that do not work.
7. Staff members become bogged down in the details and fail to reach the broader objective of the plan.

For many arts organizations a combination of these reasons may limit the success of the planning process. For example, months might be spent developing detailed planning documents with the help of outside consultants, only to have them become irrelevant because of a change in board or artistic leadership. In many cases, the planning documents are too complex to implement given the limited staffing resources of the organization. Nello McDaniel and George Thorn pointed out in *Towards a New Arts Order* that planning often "places one more burden and distraction on an already overburdened organization."[16] Another writer in the field of management, Richard Farson, points out in his book *Management of the Absurd* that "By and large, organizations are simply not good at changing themselves. They change more often as a result of invasions from the outside or rebellion from the inside, less so as a result of planning."[17]

Another point of view about planning was raised by Henry Mintzberg, a respected management author, in his book *The Rise and Fall of Strategic Planning*. It is Mintzberg's opinion that the term "strategic planning" is an oxymoron, and that strategy and planning are two different processes that do not work well together. He states:

> An organization can plan (consider its future) without engaging in planning (formal procedure) even if it produces plans (explicit intentions); alternately, an organization can engage in planning (formalized procedure) yet not plan (consider its future).[18]

At the heart of Mintzberg's challenge to some aspects of the strategic planning process is the assumption that one can predict the future. On the positive side, Mintzberg challenges many planning assumptions and offers good suggestions to all managers on how to develop a realistic planning process that will be more responsive to change.

When we sit down to "plan," do we really know what unforeseen events will occur and shape how an arts organization behaves? As noted earlier in the chapter, we are not particularly psychologically well-equipped to create accurate future scenarios. For example, would anyone have predicted the impact that an arts manager's decision to cancel Robert Mapplethorpe's exhibit would have on the arts in America? Canceling this exhibit of photographs in a gallery in Washington, D.C., in 1990 nearly led to the demise of the NEA a few years later. Politicians focused on what kind of work was receiving public funding and artists rallied against censorship. One of the results of this chain of events was a significant funding cut to the NEA in 1997 (see Figure 2.3). In fact, at one time in 1996, the House and Senate were considering motions to shut the NEA down.

Sample Decision Making and Planning Process

Let's assume that you manage a small professional chamber music group. You have decided that your mission is "To broaden the appreciation and understanding of chamber music in the tri-state area" and your overall goal is "To present quality concerts that will reach geographically diverse audiences." To fulfill your mission and realize your goal you are going to have to develop strategic growth plans to carry out specific activities. Let's walk through the process.

1. Define your objectives.
   This key first step defines what you want to achieve. For example, "I want to have 40 bookings for my touring concert group by November 1, two weeks before we start our seven-month season." You must be specific in this first step. Specifying a quantitative achievement by a fixed date is one way to define your objectives.

2. Assess the current situation in relation to your objectives.
   You must clearly assess where you are and just how far you have to go. "I have 15 bookings, and it is September 1. I still have 25 to go in two months. It took me 4 months to book the first 15. I'd better be more aggressive in seeking out bookings, or I'll never make my target."

3. Formulate your options regarding future outcomes.
   Now you must design specific options to choose from to reach your objective. "I will need three to four bookings per week over the next eight weeks. I can only devote two more hours per day to this project after I adjust my schedule. I could hire someone to help me, but I'll have to pay him or her. I could lower my target figure to 30 bookings, but our booking income will go down and we will not meet our revenue budget. I could extend the deadline to January 30 in the hope of reaching my original target figure."

4. Identify and choose among the options.
   After creating and reviewing your options, you must select the option you assess as the most effective. For example, you might decide to hire a temporary assistant to help you secure bookings. Your reason might be driven by financial need or by the fact that your musicians have other commitments and they need to know the final tour schedule by November 1st.

5. Implement your decision and evaluate the outcome.
   If this plan is to work, it will be critical for you to set up short-term measuring points to mark how well you are doing. You may find that you need to implement other options if the outcome still seems questionable. You may establish a weekly review of the bookings totals and further adjust the plans as needed.

These five steps may seem simple and straightforward, but more often than not, people and organizations fail to even make a detailed plan. It takes work and self-discipline to keep on top of this process. One of the most important skills you can develop as a manager is to master the planning process and effectively put it to use.

DECISION MAKING IN PLANNING

For any planning process to succeed, the organization must have a well-defined decision-making process in place. A good arts manager (or any manager, for that matter) identifies problems to be solved, makes decisions about appropriate solutions, and uses organizational resources to implement the solutions. Our discussion of planning was based on the assumption that the ability to make decisions was an integral part of the manager's background. Let's take a closer look at this key part of the entire planning process.

Choices, decisions, and problem solving

You make hundreds of decisions every day. For example, you make a choice to wear a coat after (1) identifying a problem (it's cold); (2) generating alternatives (wear no coat, wear two sweaters, wear lightweight coat); and (3) evaluating the alternatives (wear no coat and freeze, or two sweaters and look too bulky). This process leads to solving a problem (keeping warm). *Problem solving*, then, is "the process of identifying a discrepancy between an actual and desired state of affairs and then taking action to resolve this discrepancy."[19]

There are typically three styles of problem solving: problem avoiders, problem solvers, and problem seekers.[20] The first two styles need little explanation. The third style describes the rare person who actively goes out and looks for problems to solve. At any given time, all of us have probably exhibited a little of each of these styles. Give some thought to whether or not one of these styles dominates your problem-solving approach.

When approaching problems, it is helpful to define whether you are dealing with *expected* or *unexpected problems*. For example, you should expect that from time to time an audience member will appear on Saturday night with a ticket for Friday's show. You should have a solution to this problem ready to be activated when the situation arises. An unexpected problem might be smoke pouring into the lobby from an overheated motor in the air circulation system. In this case, you must quickly assess your alternatives without creating a panic.

Steps in problem solving

The following example illustrates one way of proceeding through the problem-solving process:

1. Identify the problem
   What is the actual situation? What is the desired situation? What is causing the difference? For example, suppose that your interns are always late and you obviously want them to be on time. You must

first try to determine why they are late. Is it inadequate transportation, inappropriate work schedules, an unsafe workplace, the workload and expectations, or their supervisor?

2. Generate alternative solutions
   This step is critical and often requires some imaginative thinking. Continuing the example, your investigation of the situation should allow you to gather as much information as possible to evaluate various courses of action. For example, you may discover that the interns are late because they do not like their supervisor. They feel the supervisor is disorganized and sometimes verbally abusive. Further investigation reveals that one of the interns also has an attitude problem. He has been rallying others to stage a work slowdown by showing up late every day.

3. Evaluate alternatives and select a solution
   You consider replacing the supervisor, the interns, or both. You also assess the workload expectations and any other relevant information you gathered about the situation. Your solution may be to dispense with the assistance of the intern and reassign the supervisor. You may also enroll the supervisor in a two-day workshop on human relations skills.

4. Implement the solution
   After consulting others within the organization (there could be some legal or interpersonal problems you had not foreseen), you implement your solution.

5. Evaluate the results and make adjustments as needed
   You monitor the new supervisor and interns on a regular basis, conduct formal and informal talks with all concerned, and monitor the former intern supervisor. (See Sample Decision Making and Planning Process for another example of how to approach the process.)

Problem-solving techniques

If problem solving were as easy as these five steps imply, then managing would be a much simpler task. In reality, problem solving is a difficult and demanding part of the manager's job.

Defining problems, making hasty decisions, and accepting risk

One of the many difficulties in problem solving is accurately defining the problem. People often incorrectly identify the symptom as the cause of the problem. For example, the lateness of the interns was the symptom for which causes were later identified. In the planning process, you may create many extra difficulties if you formulate objectives based on incorrectly identified problems. For example, a drop in subscription sales is a warning symptom of a whole host of possible problems. The ultimate cause may be show titles, prices, schedule, or even sales staff, among other things. (See Calibrating Success)

Another difficulty in problem solving is jumping to a solution too quickly. The first solution is not always the best solution. This is where trying out ideas on others can be helpful. A group brainstorming session may give you the added dimension you need to solve the problem.

Management texts frequently note that problem solving can take place in environments that are uncertain and risky.[21] The way you go about implementing the five-step, problem-solving process depends a great deal on factors that you may have little control over. For example, if the intern supervisor happened to be the spouse of the artistic director of the theater company, there would be an added element of risk in your decision.

Analyzing alternatives

Probably the best approach to analyzing your alternatives is to write them down. You can make an *inventory of alternatives* by simply listing all of the alternatives you have and writing out the good and bad points of each choice.[22] By forcing yourself to write your choices down, you may see other alternatives or ramifications of a decision.

Making a final choice

After you have written out all of the alternatives, you have reached the stage of making a decision. After all is said and done, you need to ask yourself, "Is a decision really necessary?" The intern may quit out of frustration, or the supervisor may ask for a transfer to some other part of the operation before you have finished gathering all of the evidence you need for a decision.

DECISION THEORY

In reality, the classic decision theory situation (clear problem, knowledge of possible outcomes, and optimum alternative) seldom exists.[23] Arts managers more often find themselves operating in the realm of *behavioral decision theory*. This theory assumes that "people only act in terms of what they perceive about a given situation. Because such perceptions are frequently imperfect, the behavioral decision maker acts with limited information."[24] According to this theory, people reach decisions based on finding a solution they feel comfortable with given their limited knowledge about the outcome. For example, when faced with the problem of the difficult intern, you may opt to dismiss the intern and tolerate the obnoxious supervisor. You may assess the risk of transferring the supervisor and in turn alienating the artistic director and find that it is too high.

Calibrating Success

In Jim Collins' monograph *Good to Great and the Social Sectors*, he raises the important distinction in not-for-profit management about how success can be mis-measured. Let's assume you have what you feel is a solid plan and a good decision-making process in place, how are you going to measure your success as you move forward with your plan? To this end, Collins makes an excellent point by using the example of how organizational inputs and outputs can be inappropriately measured.

> For example, one measure of a successful arts organization may be the low cost it incurs in its fundraising. This is, in fact, a common measure of organizational effectiveness. However, the purpose of the fundraising activity is not really addressed with this measure. Let's say a fundraising program of a museum made it possible for 5,000 more schoolchildren to visit an exhibit in a year. Achieving this objective of increasing school attendance helped fulfill what might be a mission of "reaching people of all ages through dynamic presentations of art across the ages." Shouldn't that be the output that is the measure of success then? If the cost to raise the funds to do this were 10% more than last year's budget, does that mean the museum was less successful, efficient, or effective? In this example you see that by focusing on the cost efficiency of fundraising, the measure of success missed the very purpose of the organization.

CONCLUSION

Planning, as described in this chapter, is a series of logical steps that can lead to creative solutions to problems. One of the manager's most important functions is to solve problems. An excellent way of solving problems is to ensure that planning is integrated into all phases of an organization. For an arts manager, the organization's mission and vision statement is a fundamental element in the planning process. The mission and vision statement is not some historical relic to be taken off the shelf once a year and dusted off for a board meeting. Rather, it is a statement of the purpose and aspirations of the organization, and, therefore, the force behind all decision making. The distribution of resources to performance, production, marketing, fundraising, and administration should be traceable back to the mission statement. When this link is broken, an organization finds itself in a struggle to make sense of why it is doing what it is doing.

Planning is a tool that any organization can put to good use. Michael Allison and Jude Kaye's book *Strategic Planning for Nonprofit Organizations* makes an excellent point about planning when they note:

> Leadership guru Warren Bennis writes in his book, *On Becoming a Leader*: "Managers are people who do things right, and leaders are

people who do the right things." Strategic planning is both a leadership tool and a management tool. As a leadership tool, a successful planning process encourages the organization to look at the question: "Are we doing the right thing? As a management tool, an effective planning process focuses on whether the organization is "doing things right."

Planning alone does not produce results; it is a means, not an end. The plans have to be implemented to produce results. However, well-developed plans increase the chances that the day-to-day activities of the organization will lead to the desired results. Planning does this in two ways: It helps the members of an organization bring into focus its priorities, and it improves the process of people working together as they pursue these priorities.[25]

Later in this text, we will focus on planning as it relates to the areas of finance (Chapter 9), marketing (Chapter 11), and fundraising (Chapter 12). All three areas rely on and should come from the work done in the strategic planning process.

SUMMARY

Planning is a primary function of management. For arts organizations, creating a mission, vision, and values statement that defines their reason to be, their aspirations, and core values held is an important first step in the planning process. A plan is a statement of means to accomplish results. The entire process of planning should clearly state the organization's objectives and help determine what should be done to achieve those objectives. Short-range plans (under one year), intermediate-range plans (one to four years), and long-range plans (five to ten years) are used to reach the stated objectives.

The overall master plan, which is typically called a strategic or long-range plan, supports the mission and vision of the organization. Strategic plans may stress stability, growth, retrenchment, or some combination of these. The strategic planning process analyzes the organization's mission, vision, reviews external environments, and examines the organization's strengths and weaknesses. Within the strategic plan, various operational plans are designed to achieve specific objectives. Strategic plans imply priorities have been established to focus on the most important action to take. Operational plans include single- and standing-use plans.

There are five steps in formal planning: defining objectives, assessing the current situation, formulating options, identifying and choosing options, and implementing the decision and evaluating the outcome. Planning approaches include top-down and bottom-up planning, contingency planning, and crisis planning. Organizations can benefit by formulating plans in case a crisis occurs.

For the planning process to be effective, an organization must have a decision-making system in place. Problem solving is the process of identifying a discrepancy between an actual and a desired state of affairs and then acting to resolve this discrepancy. There are five steps to the process: identifying the problem, generating alternative solutions, evaluating the alternatives and selecting a solution, implementing the solution, and evaluating the results. You must assess the risks involved in your decision and carefully analyze alternatives.

For additional topics relating to planning and the arts, please go to www.managementandthearts.com.

Questions

1. Analyze the mission/vision/values statement of an arts organization you are familiar with. Is it clear and to the point? What changes would you make to the mission/vision statement to improve its clarity?

2. What would be a good strategy for an arts organization to adopt if the national economy is in a recession and it is affecting the community?

3. Use the five steps of the formal planning process to plot out your own personal short-range plans (for the next year) and intermediate-range plans (for the next two to three years).

CASE STUDY — MISSION, VALUES, GOALS, AND VISION

Seacoast Repertory Theatre (SRT)

Seacoast Repertory Theatre, located in Portsmouth, New Hampshire, was founded in 1988. It is a professional theater (non-AEA) presenting a summer and fall season of musical and plays. Thanks go to Artistic Director John McCluggae for agreeing to share this document and to Jim Volz for suggesting this as a case study.

In 2005 SRT reported total revenues of $1,332,913 and total expenses of $1,340,638. Their 2005 990 tax report indicates the total revenue from contributions, gifts, grants, and indirect public support was $245,251. The information below was provided by Mr. McCluggae in July of 2007.

To check for updates on Seacoast Repertory Theatre, please link to the organization's Web site: www.seacoastrep.org/about.

Here's the Rep's Mission Statement. It's what we do and just as important, why we do it!

Mission

Seacoast Repertory Theatre will reflect and enhance our community through the shared experience of live theater. Our productions and outreach programs will be inclusive and accessible and will empower and inspire the imaginations of both audience and artist.

"reflect and enhance our community" We want to be active listeners to our stakeholders; we seek to become a part of the social/artistic fabric of the seacoast and help it thrive.

"shared experience" Not only between actor and audience, but audience and audience. Think of our space—no matter where you sit, you see other audience members and their reactions...our post show discussions are a direct result of increasing this sharing.

"live theater" Not PBS (though we think that's great too!) Our theater needs to be for this audience at this moment, with each and every performance. Live theater is ultimately like

CASE STUDY — (CONTINUED)

life—it exists for a specific time, i.e. a given night, a given show and then it is gone.

"inclusive and accessible" Our programming should have variety and we will structure our policies to afford as many people the opportunity to join us as a patron or participant.

"imaginations of both audience and artist" Creativity is the thing human beings do best. And we want to be known as a company that nurtures not only its patrons, but the people who work there.

Vision

Seacoast Repertory Theatre is a community gathering place, a resource where our community comes together to share entertainment and stories; it is a place for reflection on life, and a place for celebrating the essence and hope of humanity. Locally and regionally, people plan their summers around our productions and travel to the Seacoast to experience our work. In the winter our year-round subscribers engage in a dialog around compelling and high quality work including packed pre-show symposiums and post-show discussions. The local community has ownership of the theater as a vital component of its social fabric and the transient community supports the theater for the dynamic, provocative and yet entertaining element to their summers and weekends.

We create memorable moments for audience members and build bridges between people by the shared experience of our productions. We provide significant opportunities for youth in our area to explore the power of theater and use that power to improve their lives and prepare them to be successful, contributing members of our community. We do this through presenting a season of plays and a program of theater education which is entertaining, provocative and creative with the highest artistic quality. Our investment in early career artists results in established artists returning to the Rep to share their experience and reconnect with the theater that gave them their start. Our Senior Moments program provides our community's seniors the artistic platform to create new work of and about their generation.

We will expand our audience and donor pool and increase our financial resources to ensure our service to our community for many decades to come. We will hire exceptional, visionary, and exciting artists. We will serve our local community and continue to attract new audiences from surrounding areas and offer visitors to the area an artistic destination worth the trip.

Questions

1. What is your assessment of the organization mission statement? Does it clearly state its purpose? Are there changes or additions you feel would make the statement more effective?

2. How would you go about assessing whether the organization was living up to the key phrases enumerated in the five paragraphs starting with "reflect and enhance our community"? What would be indicators of success in these areas?

3. How much of the "Vision" statement is about vision? How would you characterize the vision statements clarity as a document?

4. Does the inclusion of a specific program title such as "Senior Moments" add or detract from the scope of the Vision?

REFERENCES

1. Peter F. Drucker with Joseph A. Marciariello, *The Daily Drucker*, (New York: HarperBusiness, Harper Collins, 2004), p. 14.

2. Daniel Gilbert, *Stumbling on Happiness* (New York: Vantage Books, Random House, 2007), p. 8.

3. Ibid., p. 9.

4. Ibid., p. 22.

5. Charles W.L. Hill, Steven L. McShane, *Principles of Management* (New York: McGraw-Hill Irwin, 2008), p. 109.

6. Ibid., p. 109.

7. http://www.seattleopera.org/about/company/mission.aspx, August 2007.

8. http://www.actorsguildoflexington.org/about_agl.htm, August 2007.

9. http://www.guthrietheater.org/about_the_guthrie, August 2007.

10. http://www.rmco.org/index.jsp, August 2007.

11. http://www.mfa.org/about/index.asp?key=53, August 2007.

12. http://www.sfmoma.org/info/mushist_overview.asp, August 2007.

13. http://www.cso.org/main.taf?p=7,9,2, August 2007.

14. John R. Schermerhorn, Jr., *Management for Productivity*, 2nd edition. (New York: John Wiley & Sons, 1986), p. 105.

15. Schermerhorn, *Management for Productivity*, p. 114.

16. Nello McDaniel, George Thorn, *Toward a New Arts Order* (New York: ARTS Action Issues, 1993), p. 44.

17. Richard Farson, *Management of the Absurd* (New York: Touchstone, 1996), p. 122.

18. Henry Mintzberg, *The Rise and Fall of Strategic Planning* (New York: The Free Press, Simon & Schuster, 1994), p. 32.

19. Schermerhorn, *Management for Productivity*, p. 64.

20. Ibid., p. 65.

21. Ibid., p. 76.

22. Ibid., p. 77.

23. Ibid., p. 79.

24. Ibid., p. 80.

25. Michael Allison, Jude Kaye, *Strategic Planning for Nonprofit Organizations*, 2nd edition. (Hoboken, NJ: John Wiley & Sons, Inc., 2005), p. 3.

ADDITIONAL RESOURCES

The following sources were also used in developing this chapter.

Kathryn M. Bartol and David C. Martin. *Management*, 3rd ed. Boston: Irwin, McGraw-Hill, 1998.

Arthur G. Bedeian. *Management*. New York: Dryden Press, 1986.

John M. Bryson. *Strategic Planning for Public and Nonprofit Organizations*, Rev. ed. San Francisco: Jossey-Bass, 1995.

James H. Donnelly, Jr., James L. Gibson, and John M. Ivancevich. *Fundamentals of Management*, 8th ed. Homewood, IL: BPI/Irwin, 1992.

Richard Farson. *Management of the Absurd*. New York: Touchstone Books, 1996.

Henry Mintzberg. *The Rise and Fall of Strategic Planning*. New York: The Free Press, 1994.

CHAPTER 6

Organizing and Organizational Design

The art of organization is not to create organizations but to multiply our effectiveness.

Rob Reiner, *Improving the Economy, Efficiency, and Effectiveness of Not-for-Profits*

KEY WORDS

Organization

Organizing

Organizational structure

Mechanistic versus organic organizations

Organizational chart

Division of work

Informal organizational structure

Agency form of management

Functional department management

Departmentalization

Organization by division

Organization by matrix

Vertical coordination

Chain of command, or the scalar principle

Span of control

Delegation

Centralization versus decentralization

Horizontal coordination

Open system model of organizational design

Bureaucracy

In this chapter we take the next step in the management process: organizing. To implement your plan you must have the organizational framework established that will allow you to lead and control your arts organization. First, we will discuss the benefit of organizing. Then we will review concepts of applying the appropriate organizational design and structure to an arts organization. We will look at how organizations function through their informal systems of getting goals achieved and work done. We will also review the concepts of vertical and horizontal coordination in organizations. Lastly, we will

155

cover the concept of corporate culture and the part it plays in managing and leading in the arts.

LIFE IN ORGANIZATIONS

Whether we like it not, we spend the greater part of our lives in organizations. Our contact with organizations may start with a day care center, then move to a series of educational institutions, then on to a place of work, and finally, we may live out our retirement years in an elder care system.

Our ability to relate to the numerous complex organizations in our society may determine how successful we are in achieving our personal goals and objectives. The powerful myth of the individual going it alone in society is offset by the reality that we need the support of people to achieve maximum results. One person can make a difference, but many people working together can create permanent change.

THE MANAGEMENT FUNCTION OF ORGANIZING

In the study of management, organizing usually follows planning as the second basic function. If you are to implement effectively the strategic plans formulated in Chapter 5, Planning and Decision Making, you need a way to organize your resources to realize your goals and objectives. And, as the epigraph for this chapter points out, we need to stay focused on organizing to produce effective organizations.

A good starting point is to return to our earlier definition of an *organization* as "a collection of people in a division of labor working together to achieve a common purpose."[1] The term *organizing* was defined as "a process of dividing work into manageable components and coordinating results to serve a specific purpose."[2] We previously defined a *manager* as a person in an organization who is responsible for the work performance of one or more people, and we defined *management* as a process of planning, organizing, leading, and controlling.

Four benefits of organizing

No matter what project or production you undertake, four benefits can be derived from organizing:[3]

1. Making clear who is supposed to do what
2. Establishing who is in charge of whom
3. Defining the appropriate channels of communication
4. Applying the resources to defined objectives

It is part of the arts manager's job as an organizer to decide how to divide the workload into manageable tasks, assign people to get these tasks done, give them the resources they need, and coordinate the entire effort to meet the planning objectives.[4]

Organizing for the arts

The task of organizing to achieve results should always be the arts manager's objective. It is the underlying assumption of this text that an effective arts manager is functioning in a collaborative and cooperative relationship with the artist. People outside the arts sometimes erroneously assume that artists and arts organizations, by their very nature, are less structured than other organizations or that they function best by operating in a disorganized manner. Nothing could be further from the truth.

Although there are different ways to approach the process of putting on an exhibition or presenting a theater, dance, opera, or concert performance, each art form shares an inherent organizational structure that best suits its function.

Each art form typically faces the pressure of being ready for an audience by a specific date and time. For example, theater is rooted in developing a performance based on many hours of text study, blocking and line rehearsals, technical and dress rehearsals, and eventually opening night. The organizational support required to prepare, rehearse, design, produce, and find an audience for the play need not be discovered each time a new show is put before the public. There are standard ways of moving from auditions to opening night. When the support system is in place and functioning correctly, it is almost invisible. However, when something goes wrong with this system, it becomes the hot topic of discussion.

As we will see in this chapter, there are various ways to go about organizing any enterprise. It is not an issue of a right or wrong way. As previously noted, organizational design and organizing should be aimed at achieving the desired results. Before exploring the structural details of various arts organizations, let us look at the overall concept of the organization as an open system.

ORGANIZATIONAL DESIGN APPROACHES

Management theory approaches organizational design by using concepts such as mechanistic versus organic organizations, the relationship to external environments, and the degree of bureaucracy within an organization.[5] The mixture of these concepts can be outlined in a model of an open system.

Figure 6.1 depicts how an organization transforms inputs to outputs. Within the overall environment, a constant feedback loop exists back to the input

Figure 6.1

Open systems model for organizations.

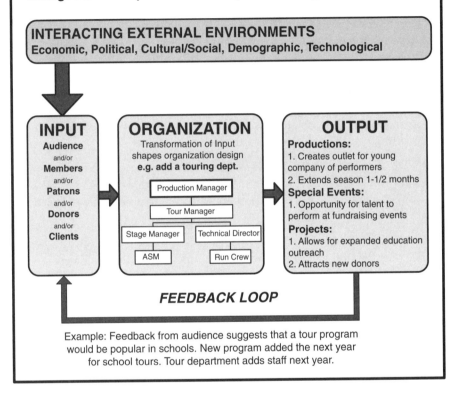

Open System Model

Structural changes in an organization chart respond to changes in the input and the output of an organization

INTERACTING EXTERNAL ENVIRONMENTS
Economic, Political, Cultural/Social, Demographic, Technological

INPUT
Audience
and/or
Members
and/or
Patrons
and/or
Donors
and/or
Clients

ORGANIZATION
Transformation of Input shapes organization design
e.g. add a touring dept.

Production Manager

Tour Manager

Stage Manager | Technical Director

ASM | Run Crew

OUTPUT
Productions:
1. Creates outlet for young company of performers
2. Extends season 1-1/2 months
Special Events:
1. Opportunity for talent to perform at fundraising events
Projects:
1. Allows for expanded education outreach
2. Attracts new donors

FEEDBACK LOOP

Example: Feedback from audience suggests that a tour program would be popular in schools. New program added the next year for school tours. Tour department adds staff next year.

stage. For example, if the output or product is an exhibition and the stated mission is education, you will want to monitor the input from the people using your "product" to see if you are fulfilling your mission. You would want to design the organization so that it had the ability to respond to the input from the public. This may translate into a department that gathers survey data, tabulates the results, and publishes reports informing management of how effectively the mission is being met.

Organic and mechanistic organizational design

Arts organizations tend to be found at the organic end of the continuum of mechanistic versus organic organizational structure. The distinguishing features of an *organic organization* are a less centralized structure, fewer detailed rules and regulations, often ambiguous divisions of labor, wide spans of control or multiple job titles, and more informal and personal forms of coordination. A *mechanistic organization* tends to have a great deal of centralization, many rules, very precise divisions of labor, narrow spans of control, and formal and impersonal coordination procedures.[6] Of course, organizations vary in degree when it comes to classifying them on this continuum. Some arts organizations may adopt aspects of a mechanistic organization.

The size and complexity of the operation usually dictate these attributes. For example, the Metropolitan Opera is more likely to adopt aspects of a mechanistic organization than a smaller organization like the Opera Theatre of St. Louis. Why? The size and scale of the operation both play a role in determining the placement of an organization along this continuum. Figure 6.2 shows the administrative structure of the Philadelphia Orchestra, which like the Metropolitan Opera, has a complex and varied staff structure. There are over 75 designated staff titles plus the added organizational complexity of sharing the human resources and technology departments with the Kimmel Center.

Bureaucracy

When an organization adopts a mechanistic organizational structure, we often refer to it as a bureaucracy. Ideally, a bureaucratic organization has clear lines of authority, well-trained staff assigned to their areas of specialization, and a systematic application of rules and regulations in a fair and impersonal manner.[7] This form of organization, originally found in governments administered by bureaus or civil servants, was created to overcome the excesses of nepotistic hiring methods found so often in history.

Today, we tend not to associate bureaucracy with democratic principles. Instead, we have very negative perceptions of bureaucracy. Anecdotes abound regarding bureaucratic structures bringing out the worst in an organization. We have all seen a rigid and unwieldy organization where, like a black hole in space, things are sucked in and never seen again. Governmental agencies are often cited as prime examples of bureaucracy at its most entrenched. However, James Q. Wilson's insightful book, *Bureaucracy: What Government Agencies Do and Why They Do It*, argues that bureaucracies are not black boxes into which input is impersonally converted to output, but rather changing complex cultures.[8] Wilson also argues that the perceived mission of and the people within the government bureaucracies are significant forces in shaping interactions with the society at large.

Modern views of bureaucratic organizational structure suggest that it would be best to adopt a contingency approach in organizational design in the arts. In other words, the organization adopts only the amount of bureaucratic structure necessary to accomplish its objectives. Does this mean that an arts organization needs to have some bureaucratic structures? Yes, to some degree.

Figure 6.2

Administrative staff titles and organization for the Philadelphia Orchestra.

Administrative Staff Titles & Organization
Symphony Orchestra *

EXECUTIVE LEADERSHIP
- Executive Director
- VP Marketing & PR
- VP Development & Board Relations
- VP for Artistic Planning
- VP and Chief Financial Officer

ARTISTIC PLANNING
- Artistic Administrator – Pops Series
- Artistic Administrator
- Artistic Assistant

ORCHESTRA MANAGEMENT
- Director, Orchestra Personnel and Production
- Orchestra Personnel Manager
- Production Manager
- Assistant Personnel and Production Manager

PUBLIC RELATIONS
- Director, Public/Media Relations
- Public Relations Coordinator

EDUCATION & COMMUNITY PARTNERSHIPS
- Director
- Assistant Director

MARKETING
- Director, Communications ad Publications
- Director, Marketing
- Publications Editor
- Design Manager
- Group Sales Manager
- Assistant Marketing Manager
- Graphic Designer
- Web Designer
- Marketing Coordinator
- Marketing Assistant

FINANCE
- Controller
- Accounting Manager
- Accountant/Payroll Mgr
- Staff Accountant
- Accounting Coordinator

HUMAN RESOURCES
- Human Resources and Benefits Coordinator

DEVELOPMENT
- Director

ANNUAL GIVING
- Director
- Assistant Director
- Annual Fund Coordinator
- Development Coordinator and Managerial Assist. Pops Series

CORPORATE & FOUNDATION RELATIONS
- Corporate Sponsorships
- Foundations Officer

DEVELOPMENT SERVICES
- Director
- Development Services Coordinator
- Development Information Coordinator
- Development Information Assistant

ACADEMY OF MUSIC FUNDRAISING
- Director, Principal Gifts
- Academy Program Book Manager
- Academy Ball Coordinator

MAJOR GIFTS AND PLANNED GIVING
- Director, Planned Giving
- Director Major Gifts
- Campaign Manager
- Major Gifts and Stewardship Manager
- Prospect Research and Reports Coordinator
- Development Coordinator

VOLUNTEER PROGRAMS
- Director, Volunteer Programs and Centennial Campaign

INFORMATION TECHNOLOGY
- Director
- Systems Manager
- Database Manager
- Assistant Database Manager
- Database Analyst
- Help Desk Technician

* SOURCE: The Philadelphia Orchestra Association program, 2005, p. 73.

For example, an arts organization must establish ticket or admission refund, crediting, and billing policies and procedures. It needs a consistent process that handles most, if not all, transactions in the same manner. You cannot operate a ticket office with every employee setting his or her own rules or procedures for routine tasks. The patron who comes to the ticket office to request a refund or exchange should be given fast and efficient service. Staff members should not have to consult one another on the proper procedure.

Another area in which arts organizations need a great deal of structure is the payroll department. Employees may complain about the bureaucracy, but because the payroll department must interface with local, state, and federal agencies, there is no choice in the matter. Because of the complexity of local and state payroll rules and IRS regulations, you cannot make it up as you go along.

The idea of a flexible framework of policies, rules, and regulations makes a great deal of sense for an arts organization when it comes to adopting bureaucratic structure. As we have just seen, different areas within the organization need more rigid structure than others. The ticket office and payroll both need a clearly defined framework with rules, regulations, and policies. However, a resident scenic artist in a regional theater will not find a highly structured framework very helpful if he has to fill out a purchase requisition every time a can of paint is opened. Likewise, a curator at a museum should be expending his creative effort on activities that will enhance the public's enjoyment and understanding of an exhibition rather than be mired in restrictive paper shuffling within the organization.

Probably the most useful tool for an arts manager to use in managing the degree of bureaucracy in the organization is *testing*; that is, go through the procedures that are in place step by step. The manager may discover policies, procedures, or rules that are confusing, contradictory, or nonessential to the mission of the organization.

ORGANIZATIONAL STRUCTURE AND CHARTS

Let's delve into a more detailed examination of how to go about structuring an arts organization. When we talk about *organizational structure*, we are referring to the "formal system of working relationships among people and the tasks they must do to meet the defined objectives."[9] These relationships and tasks are usually shown in an *organizational chart*, which is "an arrangement of work positions in an organization."[10]

In the business or arts world, rigid adherence to the organizational chart must be tempered with a healthy dose of reality. It is important to establish the organizational chart to help clarify how reporting lines are set up and whom to contact about getting something done. The organizational chart should help, not hinder, operations. If an organization finds itself unable to accomplish its goals and objectives because the organizational structure frustrates action, it is time to reexamine how it is organized.

A typical organizational chart should clearly show six key elements about the organization: divisions of work, types of work, working relationships, departments or work groups, levels of management, and lines of communication.[11]

Divisions of work

Each box (or whatever shape you prefer) in an organizational chart represents a work area. Each area should designate an individual or group assigned to complete the organization's objectives. Figures 6.3, 6.4, 6.5, and 6.6, show divisions of work in a hypothetical regional theater, symphony, a dance company, and an art museum.

Let's look at Figure 6.7, which shows the staff organization of the National Museum of Wildlife Art in Jackson Hole, Wyoming, as of April 2007 (www.wildlifeart.org). The Wildlife Art museum has an operating budget of around $4 million. The organization's Web site notes the museum "strives to enrich and inspire public appreciation of fine art and humanity's relationship with nature by focusing its exhibitions and programs on wildlife." The organizational chart shows eight direct reports to the President and CEO. Based on the job titles in each box, you can begin to see the logic of the groupings of jobs that report to the various curator, director, or manager positions. There are twenty-six named positions and in some cases, the number of staff hired in the area is indicated (security, admissions, and shop sales).

Type of work performed

The title you use for the work area (e.g., finance, marketing and public relations, development, as shown in Figure 6.4) helps describe the kind of work the person or group will do. Care should be taken to avoid obscure work area titles. Vague or misleading titles often indicate that an organization is carrying staff positions that serve marginal functions.

Working relationships

The organizational chart shows who reports to whom in the company. The solid line in Figure 6.3 between the production manager and the technical director indicates a supervisor–subordinate relationship. The production manager and the sales, marketing, and publicity director are on the same level, and they report to either the producing artistic director or the managing director.

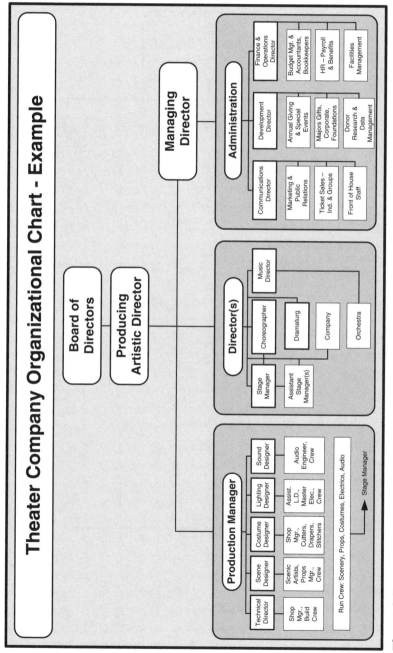

Figure 6.3
Theater company organizational chart.

Figure 6.4

Symphony orchestra organizational chart.

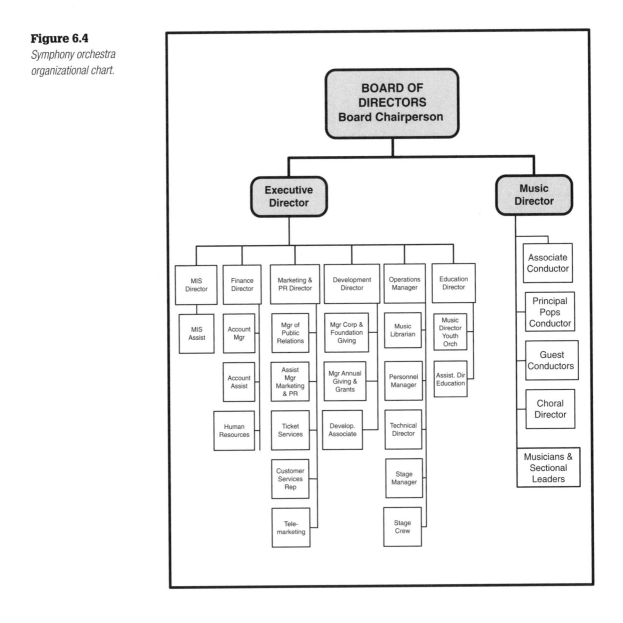

Departments or work groups

The grouping of job titles under a work group or area should be communicated by your organizational chart. A performing arts organization may be large enough to warrant separate departments for work areas. For example, Figure 6.6 shows the grouping of the curators under a Chief Curator of Collections, while the associate director responsible for Exhibitions, Programs, and Development

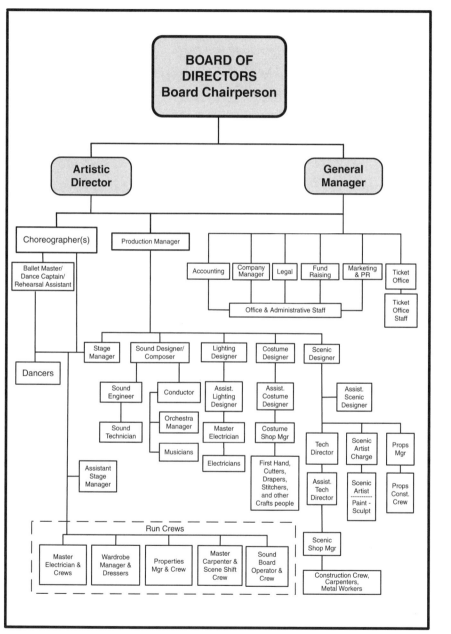

Figure 6.5
Dance company organizational chart.

has four workgroups with a supervisor for each. In Figure 6.7 there are separate curators for different functional areas: art and education.

In Figure 6.4 the ticket services area might include all single and subscription sales. Group sales and telemarketing might also be included in this

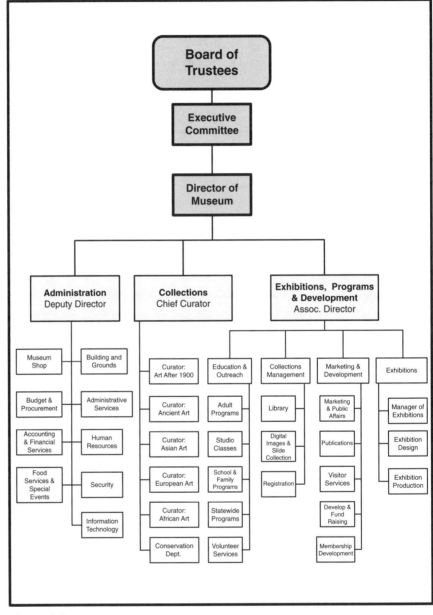

Figure 6.6

Art museum organizational chart.

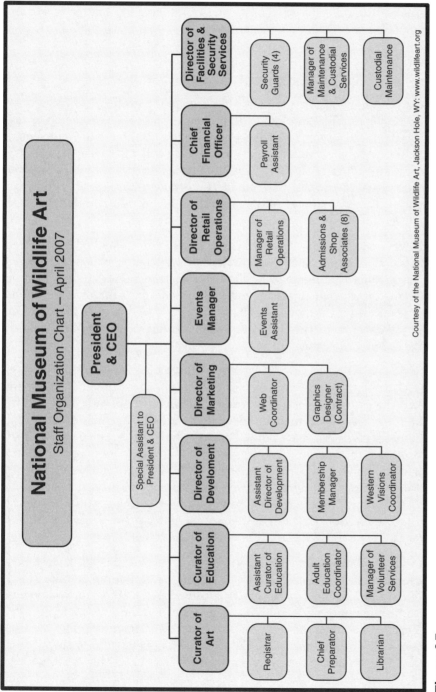

National Museum of Wildlife Art
Staff Organization Chart – April 2007

President & CEO

Special Assistant to President & CEO

Curator of Art
- Registrar
- Chief Preparator
- Librarian

Curator of Education
- Assistant Curator of Education
- Adult Education Coordinator
- Manager of Volunteer Services

Director of Develoment
- Assistant Director of Development
- Membership Manager
- Western Visions Coordinator

Director of Marketing
- Web Coordinator
- Graphics Designer (Contract)

Events Manager
- Events Assistant

Director of Retail Operations
- Manager of Retail Operations
- Admissions & Shop Associates (8)

Chief Financial Officer
- Payroll Assistant

Director of Facilities & Security Services
- Security Guards (4)
- Manager of Maintenance & Custodial Services
- Custodial Maintenance

Courtesy of the National Museum of Wildlife Art, Jackson Hole, WY: www.wildlifeart.org

Figure 6.7
National Museum of Wildlife Art.

department. It is not unusual in a small operation to find one person heading up four or five different sub-departments. As an organization grows, the creation of separate departments usually follows.

The levels of management

The organizational chart should act like a map in depicting all management levels (upper, middle, and lower). In the organizational charts the upper levels for the theater, symphony, dance company, and museum are represented, respectively, by the producing artistic director and the managing director, the executive director and the music director, the artistic director and the general manager, and the museum director. In the theater organization chart (Figure 6.3), the technical director could be identified as middle management, and the shop manager as lower level management.

This hierarchy theoretically reflects how information flows and work objectives are carried out in the organization. For example, one would expect the marketing/PR director to be the person passing along the information about the shows to the press and ticket office staff in the theater organization (Figure 6.3). In the symphony orchestra (Figure 6.4), the stage manager and technical director are listed under the operations manager who in turn reports to the executive director.

As an organization grows, the layers of management also tend to increase. When an arts organization first begins to operate, each level is minimally staffed and each person fulfills several major job functions. Arts organizations tend to have flat rather than tall hierarchies. A flat hierarchy is distinguished by fewer layers of management and typically has what is called a wider span of control.[12] Each person tends to supervise a greater number of staff simply because not enough supervisors are on staff. For example, if you call the artistic director of a small new dance company, the phone may be answered by her. Or, at most, there may be one administrative assistant who will connect you to the director. This administrative assistant probably provides support for most, if not all, of the artistic and management staff.

Now let's assume our dance company is successful and expands its operation. It adds an associate artistic director, establishes a central receptionist to take all calls, and hires an assistant to the artistic director. Your call may now be taken by a receptionist, who in turn transfers you to the assistant to the artistic director, who then connects you to the associate artistic director. The associate artistic director screens the call to see if you really need to speak to the artistic director. By the way, when this type of scenario actually exists, it might be time to reexamine how many levels of management the organization really needs.

Lines of communication

Finally, the organizational chart should represent the lines of communication throughout the hierarchy. For example, in a theater organization the scene shop manager tells the technical director that he will have to go over budget to complete the set as designed. The technical director informs the production manager of the situation. The production manager informs the artistic director, who in turn communicates to the managing director. In theory, the upper managers decide what they want to do, and that decision is passed back down through the hierarchy. The phrase "in theory" is not used to be facetious, but to remind the reader that the way things are supposed to work and the way they actually work in an organization do not always match up. This is partly due to the shadow of informal structures that develop as people work together over time.

INFORMAL ORGANIZATIONAL STRUCTURE

Every organization has an informal organizational structure. Good managers remain aware of this underlying framework and use it to their advantage. At the same time, they must discern when this informal structure is damaging the organization and hindering the achievement of its overall goals and objectives.

One of the reasons why an informal structure exists is to fill in the gaps in the formal structure. Interactions in an organization involve people, and that translates into a complexity no chart can capture. Inventive employees will always find a way to get things done in an organization with or without using the formal structure. For example, suppose that the scene shop manager wants a new table saw, but the technical director has refused to act on the request for months. At a cast party, the shop manager casually lets the production manager know that the shop could speed up the set construction process if only it had that new saw. If the crafty shop manager uses this informal communication system properly, he or she may end up with a new saw before the technical director knows what has happened. This will also enhance the shop manager's status with the shop staff because of his ability to get what is needed despite the system. In so doing, the shop manager may unwittingly send a message to the staff that it is all right to bypass your supervisor to get things done.

Problems inherent in the informal system

This example points out some of the problems with the informal structure. One major fault is that the informal structure diverts efforts from the important objectives of the organization. This shadow organization may be more concerned with personal status.

Another difficulty with the informal organization is its resistance to change. You may define new objectives and marshal your resources to put a new procedure in place, but if the informal organization rallies around the "old way," your efforts may be in vain.

As in the example of the table saw, an alternative communication system usually accompanies an informal structure. One key element of this informal system is the rumor-spreading mechanism. The rumor mill is usually a prime source of informal communication in any organization. Good managers will determine how the informal communication system works in their organizations to track what employees are really saying about the workplace and their jobs. From time to time, a manager may find it can be useful to feed information into the rumor mill. For example, you might let it leak that upper management is not happy with the lax compliance with the new no-smoking policy. If carefully leaked, the rumor might create greater adherence to the new rule if staff members think there will be consequences if they continue their current behavior.

STRUCTURE FROM AN ARTS MANAGER'S PERSPECTIVE

General considerations

The complexity of the organizational structure should be directly related to the size and scope of the operation. However, it is a good practice to keep the structure to a minimum. If an arts organization's mission is to further its art form and serve the public, creating elaborate organizational systems may be diverting time and energy from its core purpose. To help keep organizational design in perspective, consider the five elements that are often listed as influences on the final design: strategy, people, size, technology, and environment.[13] Of these five influences, strategy, people, and size have the most direct applications to the arts.

Strategy

The organizational structure needs to support the organization's overall strategy. For example, if you are starting a new regional opera company, your objective might be to build a subscription base as quickly as possible. Your strategy in building that base might be to select your season around well-known titles with famous guest artists. Your organizational design would therefore stress more staff to take care of the artists and to carry out the organization's marketing, public relations, and ticket sales activities. To maximize resources, your strategy would also include keeping your operating costs as low as possible. One way to do that might be to rent all of the sets and costumes for the season. You would therefore need only a relatively small production department and no resident design staff.

A few years later, you might develop a strategy focused on expanding your audiences by adding a community outreach or engagement program. Now your objective is to hire a tour director and staff to promote and support bringing an opera scenes program into schools. You might consider reorganizing another area within your existing organization to save on the expense of adding staff. Either way, you must make changes in the organization's design.

One of the reasons why new programs of activity sometimes suffer in an organization is that no one has thought about what is going to be done by whom. Without careful thought about job design, an organization can quickly overload an employee with too many tasks.

People

The most important element in any organization is the people who work within the overall structure. Realistically, there must be flexibility between the structure and the people in an arts organization. The military is a prime example of a rigid organizational structure designed to mold its "employees" to the specific jobs at hand. A strict hierarchy and adherence to numerous rules and regulations are all focused toward a set of specific objectives. People usually do not join the staff of an arts organization because they want a rigid and highly controlled work environment. In fact, people who work in arts organizations are often highly self-motivated and vigorously resist regimentation.

Care must be taken when applying organizational theory to real organizations. In an arts organization, for example, the degree of structure varies with the type of job. For example, the director of a museum would probably be wise to allow for a high degree of creative independence among the department heads of the curatorial staff. The security guards, on the other hand, would have a rigid work schedule with limited independence to set their hours.

Size

When an arts organization is first established, there may be no more than three or four people doing all of the jobs in the organization. The artistic director may direct the operas, write the brochure copy, hire all of the singers and the artistic staff, and do all of the fundraising. As the organization grows — a board of directors is added, staff specialists are hired to do the marketing, scheduling, advertising, and so on — the simple organizational chart and lines of communication suddenly become much more complicated. In management theory, the organization would be said to be moving from an "agency form" to a "functional department form."[14] An *agency organization* refers to a structure in which everyone reports to one boss, and this boss provides all of the coordination. Each staff member is in effect an extension of the boss. When an arts organization decides to hire a marketing director, it may be because the artistic director can no longer supervise all of these activities. In this scenario, a new department with a specific function and the support staff to do the marketing would be established. Problems and conflicts will arise if the artistic director attempts to give direct orders to the staff of the marketing director instead of going through the new structure.

Technology and environment

The other elements that influence organizational design are technology and environment. When speaking of the influence of technology in the business world, it is easier to see how new systems and methods can affect how products are produced. There is usually a direct connection between how an organization is structured and how technology may help it become more productive. For example, a large company may add a whole department to do nothing but assess new technologies and advise about their application to that business. Arts organizations, on the other hand, have used new technologies in office and information management and, in limited ways, applied new approaches to the technical production aspects of their operations.

In recent years, it has become more common to find staff positions designated in the information technology (IT) area in many arts organizations. As organizations have expanded their capabilities through their Web sites, staff support has become an important issue. Arts organizations may provide staff support for their Web site as part of the marketing and publications function. Data management of ticketing systems as well as coordinating the in-house computer network in the organization are two more areas now common in many arts organizations. Many organizations also outsource by contracting this support function as a way of controlling staff costs.

Technology tends not to be at the core of how most performing arts organizations operate; therefore, the organizational structures tend to be more static. However, other arts organizations, such as museums, may dedicate significant technological resources to analyzing and preserving works of art.

External environments

The political and legal environments may legislate new laws that affect hiring or training in the organization. For example, there were very few if any affirmative action or health and safety programs in arts organizations 40 years ago. Today, we find staff members designated to administer and monitor these areas of activities in the organization. In addition, the ever-increasing complexity of tax laws and compliance with proliferating local, state, and federal regulations has no doubt added to the workload of the finance and accounting departments of many arts organizations.

Departmentalization

Let's move on to looking at other components in the process of establishing organizational structure. One of the central parts in most organizations is found in a designated department. To *departmentalize*, or to set up departments in an organization, simply means "grouping people and activities together under the supervision of a manager."[15] Departments may be structured in three ways: by function, by division, and by matrix.

Function

Most arts organizations use a structure defined by functional departments. It makes sense to group people by the specialized functions they perform within the organization. Figures 6.3 to 6.7 show how various managers supervise the functional departments within the organization. For example, the symphony (Figure 6.4) has a marketing and public relations area with a director, a public relations manager, an assistant manager, and various related support areas such as telemarketing and patrons services.

Divisions

Departments can be organized around a product or a territory. An example on a small scale is a major arts center that not only hosts touring productions but also produces its own shows, runs a gift shop and an art gallery, and operates a restaurant. An organization may decide to establish a divisional structure that keeps booking, production, exhibition, and food services separate. The logic behind this choice is that each of these activities involves very different operating conditions with specialized supervision and staff needs. The division in charge of production might include a marketing person to supervise the subscription series for the regular events. The division in charge of touring might employ another person to market the shows to other arts centers and producers. Both employees are marketing specialists, but they market their products from very different perspectives.

Another divisional structure is by territory. A dance company decides to pursue a strategy of dual-city operations. One of the first steps would be to establish an organizational structure to staff two different geographical sites. There would need to be some staff duplication. You cannot expect the city A marketing staff to do the marketing for city B without local staff designated for each campaign.

Matrix organization

One the more interesting organizational structures found in many businesses combines both horizontal and vertical reporting and communication. This evolution is often called a matrix organization structure and has very practical application to the project-drive focus in many arts organizations.

The matrix system was developed in the late 1950s by the cofounder of TRW Inc., Simon Ramo.[16] The department structure proved to be inadequate when TRW tried to manage several technologically complex projects for the defense industry. His scheme was to use a department structure for important activities like research and development (R&D) and place the department under the control of a department head. However, within the R&D department were smaller groups of people working on different projects under the supervision of a project manager. The vertical matrix in the structure is thus the department head working with the various R&D groups. The horizontal matrix consists of the individual project managers working with the separate R&D groups.

In an arts organization, a matrix structure often evolves as an optimal way to work. At its most basic level the matrix structure in an arts organization means an employee may have two or more bosses, depending on the project. For example, suppose that a museum is organized around a department structure. The six departments are responsible for various sections of the collection, and there are other departments for marketing, fundraising, operations, maintenance, accounting, and payroll.

The museum's centennial is coming up in three years. Typically, a staff member is designated as the director of the "centennial project." If this project director is to achieve the objective of creating a successful celebration of all the things the museum has done in the last 100 years, a matrix structure could be created to assist with the project. The project director will request that each department head designate a person to be the centennial coordinator for that department. In addition to their regular duties, the marketing staff will also have to work on this special project with the project manager. The project manager, in effect, becomes their temporary supervisor.

Arts organizations also often find themselves involved in special projects. However, without recognition of the need to shift to a matrix organizational structure, trouble may occur. For example, if the staff required to make a special project work are not hired, the project coordinator will have to work horizontally through the organizational structure. He will discover that the overworked staff in the various departments do not have time to give to the project, or worse, the staff will find the time at the expense of their regular responsibilities, and the effectiveness of the entire organization will suffer.

There are other examples of the matrix organizational structure in arts organizations (see Figure 6.8). There is often a matrix working relationship between a resident design staff and the guest directors or choreographers that may come into a regional arts organization. The staff are hired by the organization and may work within separate departments. When a guest director or choreographer arrives, this staff now have a new "boss" specifically for a particular show.

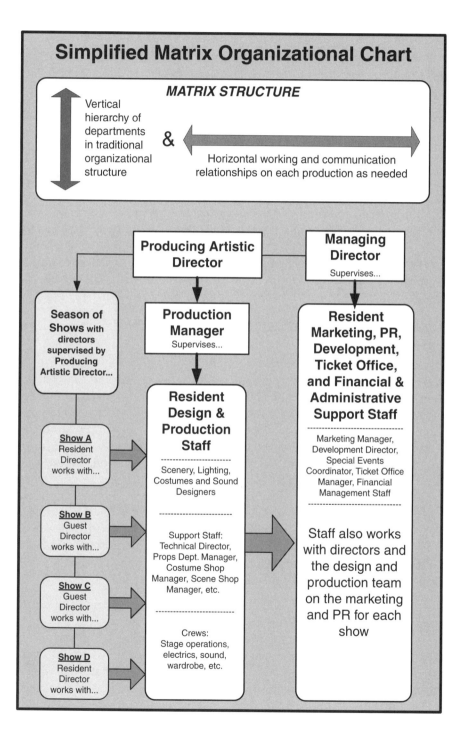

Figure 6.8
Simplified matrix organizational chart for a theater company.

A good production manager will recognize this matrix structure and establish the needed lines of communication to keep all of these overlapping projects on track.

COORDINATION

Another principal concept in organizing any enterprise is coordination. Coordination can be divided into vertical and horizontal components. The first area of concern, *vertical coordination*, is defined as "the process of using a hierarchy of authority to integrate the activities of various departments and projects within an organization."[17] *Vertical coordination* is split into four areas: chain of command, span of control, delegation, and centralization–decentralization. Each of these has applications to arts groups. *Horizontal coordination* simply refers to the process of integrating activities across the organization. Many arts organizations use this structure to promote interdepartmental cooperation.

Vertical coordination
Chain of command
Classic management theory, as exemplified by Fayol's Fourteen Principles (see Chapter 3), states that "there should be a clear and unbroken chain of command linking every person in the organization with successively higher levels of authority."[18] This is known as the *scalar principle*. The military is a good example of a thoroughgoing application of such a chain of command. Common sense should tell you that problems will develop in an organization that lacks clear authority and clear lines of communication. On the other hand, not all situations allow for a clear "unbroken chain of command" within an organization. A small arts organization may hire an administrative assistant to work for several people and departments. On paper, the job description says that the "administrative assistant is supervised by the managing director." However, as the organization grows, the assistant is asked to complete work for the artistic director, the new marketing director, the newly formed fundraising department, and others.

Unless the staff member is extremely good at time management and setting priorities, work may become backed up or simply not get done. In this example, too many people have authority to ask the administrative assistant to work for them. Ironically, what often happens is that to survive in the job, the administrative assistant becomes the person determining what work is done for whom and when. The administrative assistant becomes a de facto manager of the supervisors. This phenomenon is often seen in academic departments in colleges and universities. The "department secretary" often has many faculty and staff requesting administrative support. To cope with the workload the assistant determines when work gets done through self-management. The administrative assistant often becomes the "boss" of the department since she actually determines what work will get accomplished.

Span of control

The span of control describes how many people report to one person. There are no fixed rules about how much or how little span of control one person should have in an organization. However, common sense tells you at some point you will not be able to keep track of who is doing what if you have too many people reporting to you. The factors often cited in determining span of control are "(1) Similarity of functions supervised, (2) physical proximity of functions supervised, (3) complexity of functions supervised, and (4) the required coordination among functions supervised."[19]

Let's look at span of control in an arts setting. For example, if the marketing director is asked to take over the supervision of the fundraising and ticket service operation, there is a reasonable match between functional areas and a limited span of control. However, if the marketing director tries to take over the management of the acting company and becomes, in effect, the company manager — there may be problems. The needs of the acting company are not similar to the needs of the marketing department. It is also possible to exceed the marketing director's expertise. The marketing director could possibly supervise the company manager — the person responsible for seeing to all of the needs of the acting company. However, the marketing director may not have enough understanding of the job to know if it is done properly.

An example of physical proximity in span of control occurs when the production manager is asked to supervise the activities in performance spaces in three different locations in the city. The production manager soon discovers that it is impossible to be in three places at once. Three staff assistants may be needed, one for each theater.

Similarly, if the functional areas become complex, as in the data-management system for an organization, you may need to reduce the span of control. The staff member in the accounting area, who became the "systems administrator" in the finance department by virtue of his knowledge, can no longer keep control of the expanded computer systems used in the marketing department, the box office, and fundraising. Either someone must be hired to coordinate the organization's computer needs, or the accounting work of the existing staff member must be reduced.

Delegation

As a manager, you must decide how much day-to-day work you should do yourself and how much should be assigned to others. *Delegation* is "a distribution of work to others."[20] The process involves three steps: assigning duties, granting authority, and establishing an obligation.

When you assign duties, you must have a solid understanding of the work to be done, and you must spend time analyzing what you expect the employee to do. Problems sometimes arise with the second step: granting authority. If the delegation process is to be effective, you must give up some of your authority and transfer it to the employee. If you do not grant that authority, it is difficult to establish an obligation on the part of the employee to assume the responsibility. For example, suppose that you delegate the responsibility of providing daily sales summaries for the organization to your ticket office manager, but you go down to the office the next day and run the numbers yourself. The ticket office manager will wonder what happened to this delegated responsibility if you duplicate her work. She will assume that you do not trust that the work will get done.

A key principle to remember in delegation is that the "authority should equal the responsibility when you delegate work."[21] If you give a staff member responsibility for a budget but then take away the authority to expend the funds, you have undermined the delegation process.

Unfortunately, no area creates more bad feelings in an organization than delegation. Overprotective or micromanaging supervisors tend to create employees who are bored with their jobs and not particularly committed to meeting the organization's objectives. Because they have not been given any real responsibility, they develop the attitude that is expressed in the phrase "Don't ask me; I just work here." Meanwhile, the whole organization suffers because the supervisor is spending time doing work that would be more effectively done by others.

Centralization–decentralization

This last area of vertical coordination simply refers to how the organization will concentrate or disperse authority. Colleges or universities are often cited as examples of decentralized organizations. The individual departments (history, government, physics, and so on) often have autonomy over personnel and course offerings. They report to a central authority; that is, the dean, but the faculty members of the department exercise a great deal of control over their own day-to-day activities. On the other hand, a large corporation may have a rigidly organized authority structure in which only designated managers have the authority to make decisions.

In an arts organization, the degree of centralization or decentralization depends on the functional area. For example, the process of running a subscription or membership campaign requires a centralized authority structure. One cannot have several people making key decisions about the campaign autonomously. To control the look and language of the campaign, one person must make the final decisions.

In other areas, it may be more efficient to decentralize the authority. For example, the production manager delegates the purchasing of production supplies (lumber, fabric, steel, paint, and so on) to the technical director. The technical director then delegates the purchasing to the individual department heads or shop managers.

Horizontal coordination

Horizontal coordination is a key function in any organizational structure. In the business world, the function of horizontal coordination is most often identified with such areas as personnel and accounting. All of the departments in the organization use the personnel department as a resource for hiring, firing, and evaluating employees. Payroll is a good example of another department that has a horizontal relationship to a vertical structure. Everyone in the organization is affected by the payroll department. Organizations could not function effectively if every department handled its own payroll.

In an arts organization, similar personnel and payroll functions may cut across departmental lines. As already noted, the project orientation of many arts organizations creates the need for horizontal coordination. A successful production, concert, or exhibition often requires that different departments cooperate and communicate over an extended period of time. For example, a stage manager must be able to coordinate with what is called *functional authority*. This authority allows the stage manager to cut across the formal chain of command. When a problem backstage needs to be solved instantly, the stage manager can issue orders that bypass the traditional crew head hierarchy.

When an event is presented, horizontal coordination is typically shown through the formation of a production team. The heavy emphasis on team management as an innovative approach to solving problems in the business world over the last 30 years is, in fact, standard operating procedure in the arts. Without effective horizontal coordination a theater, dance, or concert event or an exhibition opening suffers.

ORGANIZATIONAL GROWTH

Organizations seem to have a way of growing beyond anyone's original expectations. As one sage wit once noted, "The number of people in any working group tends to increase regardless of the amount of work to be done."[22]

Almost constant attention must be paid to the proliferation of staff with each new cycle of strategic planning. As new plans are implemented, the workload seems to increase, so new staff members are hired, and more levels of management may be put into place. The production manager now has three production assistants. The secretary is now the office manager and has three administrative assistants working for him. This growth carries with it increased costs to the organization. The cycle of overloading the current staff, hiring new staff to help reduce the overload, overloading the budget, laying off the new staff, thus overloading the original staff, and so on, can be avoided if the manager retains control of the planning function.

As we have seen, one of the key elements of planning is keeping accurate records of where you have been. Tracking the growth of a department over a period of time can be a helpful way to monitor growth. In my comparisons of staff growth in arts organizations over the last 30 years, I found that increases of 25 to 125 percent were not uncommon. This is all the more significant since many of these organizations were only doing 5 to 10 percent more programming.

Managers must think of the design of the organization as a creative challenge and not a burden. As we have seen, the manager's job is to anticipate and solve problems. Lack of attention to problems with organizational design can lead to fundamental flaws in the operation of the enterprise, and these flaws could lead to the demise of the organization.

CORPORATE CULTURE AND THE ARTS

In the last 30 years, management experts have found organizations function in ways that theories cannot always explain. As you would expect, no theory of organizational design can take into account all of the variables that affect businesses. One of the more interesting approaches to analyzing how organizations function beyond the charts and reporting diagrams uses principles of anthropology to look at what is referred to as the *corporate culture* of the organization. In fact, this concept has become so popular that a Goggle search using the term "corporate culture" will result in millions of links to sources on the topic area.

The basic premise of this application of anthropology to organizations is that businesses create their own social systems. Typically these social systems evolve around the shared values, beliefs, myths, rituals, language, and behavioral patterns of the leadership and employees. All of these aspects of the social system are carried on from year to year over the life of the organization. A manager may find comfort in the structure, policies, and procedures of the company, but in reality, these things are not necessarily why people choose to work in the organization. Even the most casual observer of workplace behavior would notice how much time is spent socially interacting while at work.

These seemingly casual interactions help form the social system that becomes the corporate culture of an organization.

Levels in corporate culture

Edgar Schein's book, *The Corporate Culture Survival Guide,*[23] is one resource for arts managers that is both immediately accessible and applicable. Schein outlines what he sees as three levels of culture in organizations: *artifacts, espoused values,* and *shared tacit assumptions.*[24]

Artifacts are found in the top layer of an organization's culture and are manifest in "what you see, hear, and feel as you hang around"[25] an organization. For example, in an arts organization you may observe the kind of office space occupied and the kind of furniture used by the staff as clues to the culture of the organization. You may find the organization is in an older building that may have office furniture that looks dated and well used. The staff may be casually dressed, there may be a common work area, desks are piled high with papers and folders, and if there are offices, the office doors may mostly be opened. At first glance, these outward appearances represent your first evidence of the organization's culture. These artifacts help you create your initial impressions of the organization and how the people interact as they work together.

At the next level, Schein notes you will find the espoused values of an organization. He suggests we often find this information in combinations of sources such as published strategies, goals, mission, and values statements. In addition, Schein points out you can seek out "insiders who can explain their organization to you. Anthropologists call them 'informants' and depend heavily on such conversations to decipher what is going on."[26] In an arts setting this level of culture will be evidenced in the passion about the art form. There are usually the powerful statements made by the organization about how important music, opera, theater, and art are in shaping and changing the world.

The third level of an organization's culture is found in the "shared tacit assumptions."[27] In this level you find "the unconscious, taken-for-granted beliefs"[28] that are unspoken. In an arts organization that level of culture may reside in the strong historical beliefs of the founder or artistic director of the organization. For example, you might find the organization grew and thrived based on unspoken assumptions of the founder that to be in the arts it is assumed that the sacrifice of personal time and the lack of resources were good things. These were sacrifices to be made and challenges to be risen to, and that doing whatever it takes to get the show or exhibit opened is expected in the normal course of doing your job. In this culture, someone who might value a life outside the organization would soon discover they did not fit in.

Corporate cultures and the real world

When you start a new job, you are brought into an organization's cultural system. It may be a very strong culture that stresses maximum performance at all times, or it may be a very relaxed culture that stresses slow and steady progress. No matter where the culture fits along this continuum, it will exist. The sooner you recognize it, the sooner you can adapt to it as needed. For example, if you go to work for a marketing director in an arts organization that prides itself on huge leaps each season in its subscriber base, you better be ready to adopt the attitudes and beliefs that go along with the job, or you will find yourself outside the system and eventually out of a job. On the other hand, once you have established yourself as a manager in the organization and have come to know the culture, you can begin to alter it to better achieve the overall goals and objectives established in your strategic plans. Remember, the culture of an organization is not static. It adapts to changes in the internal and external forces that affect the organization.

SUMMARY

Organizations are collections of people in a division of labor who work together for a common purpose. Organizing makes clear what everyone is to do, who is in charge, the channels of communication, and resource allocation. Managers should organize for results. Organizational structure and charts provide an operational map. All organizations have informal structures, which managers should monitor. Organizations can be designed to use functional, divisional, or matrix structures, or a combination of these. Organizations use vertical and horizontal structures and coordination to operate effectively. They may take on organic or mechanistic structures, depending on what they do. All organizations have social systems that define a distinctive culture. Strong leadership helps define the culture. Organizational design is affected by the culture and social systems.

For additional topics relating to organizing and organizational design, please go to www.managementandthearts.com.

Questions

1. What are the formal and informal organizational structures of the theater, dance, music, art, or arts administration department at your college or university? Do these structures effectively support the mission of the department? Explain. How would you reorganize the department to make it more effectively support the mission of the university?
2. Can you cite examples of breakdowns in the vertical or horizontal coordination on a project or production with which you were recently involved? How would you improve the coordination systems to minimize these problems in the future?

3. Based on your own work experience, identify as many of the values, behavior patterns, language, rites, and rituals that formed the corporate culture of the organization.

CASE STUDY

The practice of arts organizations merging as part of a strategy for organizing resources more effectively is not widely seen in the United States. The 2002 merger of the Utah Symphony Orchestra and Utah Opera was driven in part by financial necessity. The following newspaper story offers a progress report as of the spring of 2006. For more recent developments, please go to the online archives of the Salt Lake Tribune at www.sltrib.com.

Symphony-opera works to restore fiscal harmony

*By Jennifer Barrett, The Salt Lake Tribune, 3/26/06.
Used with permission.*

The Utah Symphony & Opera seemed on the verge of financial disaster a year ago. Ticket sales had been sliding, donations were down, and cash reserves were quickly running out. Headlines proclaimed the dire news, and patrons began to fear that their beloved symphony and opera could be lost.

But Utah Symphony CEO Anne Ewers and music director Keith Lockhart say all that was a good thing.

"Whatever doesn't kill you makes you stronger," said Lockhart.

The outlook for the US&O is now "cautiously optimistic," words recited like a mantra by management, musicians, and patrons alike. Indeed, there is reason for hope: Ticket sales are up and donations are rising. But the institution isn't in the clear yet. Administrators need to keep the numbers moving upward and grapple with ongoing challenges, such as ensuring the viability of the Deer Valley Music Festival.

In February 2005, orchestra members went to the media with news that US&O was in trouble. In the two years after the symphony and opera merged in 2002 — a marriage proposed to save money — the organization had run up deficits totaling $3.4 million, and was surviving on donations.

The situation was alarming, but administrators now say there was no need to panic. They were finalizing a plan to fix the problems, said Sean Toomey, US&O director of marketing and communications.

But some orchestra members are convinced that had they not gone to the media, the situation today would be different.

"There would be 86 musicians looking for a job right now," said principal flutist Erich Graf.

In the past year, the US&O has made progress in several areas outlined by Tom Morris, a consultant hired to find problems and solutions. He concluded the US&O was in "peril," suffering from declining audiences, a drop in donations, burgeoning expenses, and structural problems. Here are some of the successes:

Ticket sales: Ewers said all the publicity helped light a fire under the community. "One guy was so ticked off, he marched into the box office and said, 'I may not even be able to attend, but damn it, I'm buying eight tickets because I'm sick of this.'" After dropping 27 percent in two years, Utah Opera sales gained ground in the 2004–05 season. The Utah Symphony last year managed to stop its downward slide — nearly 18 percent in three years — ending with relatively flat sales.

As of last week, ticket sales for both groups were about 4 percent ahead of projections, and in line with plans to balance the budget.

Donations: Gifts to the US&O took a one-two punch when the economy stumbled and disgruntled fans pulled funds to protest the merger.

Some patrons have come back, said Ewers. "Everybody had to get used to this merged organization and see if they still wanted to support it," she said. However, some patrons "may never come back," she said. A report given to board members

CASE STUDY (CONTINUED)

last week shows that with five months left in the fiscal year, the US&O has raised $3.5 million, slightly more than half of its $6.2 million target for this year.

"We think we're on track to hit the goal," said Toomey.

Stronger board: Consultant Morris said if US&O wanted real change, it needed new blood, including a "committed chair — a champion." The organization found that person in Patricia Richards, a senior vice president with Wells Fargo and chairwoman of the US&O board. She has been given high marks by most everyone involved.

"Pat Richards has been incredible in implementing a lot of these issues," said bass player Claudia Norton. "I'm very thankful to her and the board for taking on [the Morris] report."

Under Richards' leadership, board members agreed to make personal contributions of $10,000 to the organization each year. Attendance at meetings is up, and members are more "engaged," said Richards. In fact, she said, the board is reviewing the US&O's very direction and purpose.

"There is absolutely nothing in it for the board, except the pure love of the art," said Richards. "We all have to pull together to make this work."

The board is also exerting more control over the CEO, redefining the job description and conducting annual reviews.

Changes for Ewers: No one took more heat than Ewers last year. "The tallest statue in the park gets the most pigeon jazz," she said recently. But Ewers — an ever-perky pitchwoman who greets reporters with a hug — admits she made mistakes.

"Let me tell you," she said, "Pollyanna is gone." Morris stated point blank that the CEO needed to show "improved performance," and took her to task for trying to do too much — she was not only the CEO, but also the driving force behind the Deer Valley Music Festival and the general director for the opera. She responded by giving up day-to-day control of the opera.

She also came under fire for program changes and unpopular concert "enhancements," which have all been reversed.

Ewers said she's modified her approach to potential donors. "I always talk about the challenges now," she said. In the past, she was so busy sharing "the vision" that she didn't always talk about realities. "I needed to bring balance to it." Despite criticism aimed at Ewers, Richards said "the board itself feels it has the right leadership in place."

Challenges ahead: The mountain of graphs and pie charts the US&O churned out over the past year suggests the organization is on track to meet its goals, but challenges remain. Relations between the musicians and administrators hit a low point last year. Both sides are trying to mend the rift, partly with bimonthly "fireside" chats where any musician can sit down with Ewers to discuss anything. "It takes time to build trust," said bassoonist Christine Osborne.

US&O will also have to find ways to fund inevitable growth in orchestra salaries, the institution's single biggest expenditure — $8 million of its $17 million budget. Compensation climbed 80 percent between 1994 and 2004. Last year, the musicians agreed to a two-year wage freeze, though they have the option of reopening negotiations this spring. Base pay is $57,000, the lowest among the nation's 17 orchestras that work year-round. The US&O must still attract more patrons and will again tinker with programming, offering a "casual" concert next fall to see if it can entice audiences who usually shy away from starchy, formal affairs. They may also drop a few concerts in the future, said Toomey.

"The symphony is just unrelenting," he said, referring to the orchestra's regular-season schedule of concerts nearly every weekend. "It's hard to stop people in their tracks and say, 'This is the concert you want to go to,' and then say the next week, 'This is the one you want to go to.'"

Despite criticism from Morris, the US&O still gives away thousands of tickets every year. "We can't stop giving away free tickets," said Toomey. The US&O uses them instead of cash to make the marketing budget go further, and they help attract prospective future buyers, he said.

Morris and the community would like to see more of conductor Keith Lockhart, but that is unlikely to change much. Lockhart will continue to split his time between Salt Lake City and Boston, where he heads up the Boston Pops.

Lockhart said his living here year-round wouldn't guarantee a better orchestra. "What matters is what you do when you're here. My commitment to this place is real," he said.

CASE STUDY (CONTINUED)

The biggest challenge may be ensuring the success of the US&O's summertime offering, the Deer Valley Music Festival. A second consultant, Stephen Basili, last fall pointed out a number of troubling issues with the festival, including the fact that it relies precariously upon the largesse of just a few donors. It also has trouble attracting a consistent audience. US&O gave away more tickets than it sold for three concerts last summer, and Basili called the number of returning ticket buyers "atrocious."

Despite the remaining challenges — and the fact that US&O must continue to cut the budget and drum up support — most people involved feel the US&O will be returned to fiscal health in the near future.

What about the long term?

"Once in a while, you wonder: Will the world be the same 20 years from now, and will we still have an orchestra?" said Richards. "Everyone in the country is asking those questions."

Note: In January 2008 the Utah Symphony and Opera named Melia Tourangeau as the new CEO.

Questions

1. Offer a brief summary of the article and its major points regarding the status of the symphony and opera mergers.

2. What do you think would be some of the advantages and disadvantages of merging designated arts organizations in your community?

3. Do you think the merger of a theater company and a dance company would be more or less likely to succeed than the merger of an orchestra and opera company? Why or why not?

4. What might be a few differences in the corporate cultures of arts organizations that might be considering a merge? What are your perceptions about the culture of an opera company and a symphony orchestra?

REFERENCES

1. John R. Schermerhorn, Jr., *Management for Productivity*, 2nd ed. (New York: John Wiley & Sons, 1986), p. 161.

2. Ibid., p. 161.

3. Ibid., p. 162.

4. Ibid., p. 163.

5. Ibid., p. 190.

6. Ibid., p. 191.

7. Ibid., p. 188.

8. James Q. Wilson, *Bureaucracy: What Government Agencies Do and Why They Do It* (New York: Basic Books, 1989).

9. Schermerhorn, *Management for Productivity*, p. 163.

10. Ibid., p. 164.

11. Ibid., p. 164.

12. Charles W.L. Hill, Stevene L. McShane, *Principles of Management*, (New York: McGraw-Hill Irwin, 2008), p. 189.

13. Schermerhorn, *Management for Productivity*, p. 167.

14. Arthur G. Bedeian, *Management* (New York: Dryden Press, 1986), p. 258.

15. Schermerhorn, *Management for Productivity*, p. 169.

16. Bedeian, *Management*, p. 265.

17. Schermerhorn, *Management for Productivity*, p. 173.

18. Ibid., p. 174.

19. Ibid., p. 174.

20. Ibid., p. 176.

21. Ibid., p. 177.

22. Arthur Bloch, *The Complete Murphy's Law* (Los Angeles: Price-Stern-Sloan, 1990), p. 62.

23. Edgar H. Schein, *The Corporate Culture Survival Guide,* (San Francisco, CA: Jossey-Bass, 1999.)

24. Ibid., pp. 15–20.

25. Ibid., p. 15.

26. Ibid., p. 17.

27. Ibid., p. 19.

28. Ibid., p. 16.

CHAPTER 7

Human Resources and the Arts

Attracting, hiring, and ultimately retaining productive employees are obvious needs if firms are to achieve organizational excellence. While the level of rewards may have a direct impact on the number of individuals wanting to work in an organization, it is of the utmost importance that the right people apply.

Edward E. Lawler III, *Rewarding Excellence:*
Pay Strategies for the New Economy

KEY WORDS

Human resources planning

Job description

KSAs

Job matrix

Equal Employment Opportunity
   Commission (EEOC)

On-the-job training (OJT)

Wrongful discharge

Employment-at-will

National Labor Relations Board
   (NLRB)

The last two chapters covered the areas of planning and organizational design. We saw how the mission of an organization becomes the foundation on which the strategic and operational plans are built. Specific goals and objectives are then established. The plans also indicate how human and financial resources are to be used to meet the organization's goals and objectives. The organizing process is designed to move plans from an idea to a reality. The manager designs the organization to fulfill the plans. The structure of the organization, the lines of communication, and the combinations of vertical, horizontal, and matrix relationships are established among the departments and projects. Departments and other subunits are created to support the plan effectively.

STAFFING THE ORGANIZATION

The next stage in the process of creating an organization is staffing it. This chapter looks at the human resources required to fulfill the mission and to support the strategic and operational plans of the organization—the key to the success or failure of the enterprise. The organization's strategic and operational plans must also provide staffing objectives. Descriptions of jobs and the complex working relationships among employees must be carefully factored into the organization.

Arts organizations face numerous challenges when it comes to staffing their organizations. As the epigraph to this chapter notes, having the right people is a key to organizational success. Unfortunately, the arts and not-for-profit job marketplace do not always provide the level of compensation and benefits many people are seeking, especially in the managerial or administrative area. The lack of competitive compensation can make finding the right person problematic. The employment marketplace is even more challenging for performers, designers, and technicians. Steady employment in the arts can be rare and holding second or third jobs is the norm for many people.

An arts manager must also be aware of the laws regulating employment and must be versed in the art of negotiation. Several unions may represent employee groups throughout the organization, and they may have different contract periods. The task of finding the right people for the jobs, keeping them, and developing them is a never-ending process.

THE STAFFING PROCESS

Any organization wants to fill its jobs with the best people available. Finding the most talented, qualified, and motivated people to work with you is much harder than it sounds. To make the overall system clear, we will break the staffing process into six parts: planning, recruiting, selecting, orienting, training, and replacing.[1] We also will look at how this process varies across the fields of theater, dance, opera, music, and museums. Figure 7.1 provides an overview of the entire human resource management system. As you would expect, there are variations among and within various art forms.

In the business world, the somewhat imposing phrase *human resources planning* simply translates into analyzing your staffing needs and then identifying the various activities you need to make the organization function effectively. In many large corporations, a manager identifies specific staffing needs to determine where the staffing resources are required. The manager then works with the human resources or personnel department to find the required staff. Because most arts organizations do not have separate human resources

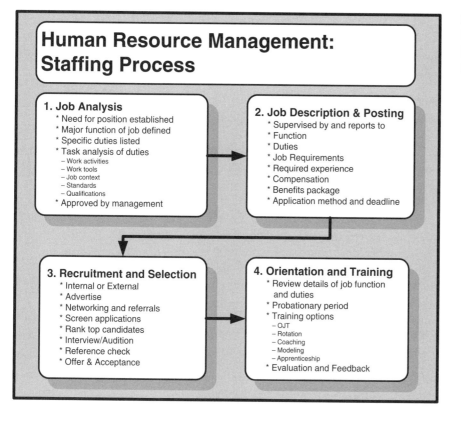

Figure 7.1

Human Resource Management Staffing Process.

departments, it becomes all the more important for the manager to have an excellent grasp of the rules and regulations controlling the hiring and firing of employees. Mistakes in personnel management can be very costly. More and more organizations face lawsuits because of badly handled personnel decisions. Given the often informal circumstances surrounding the hiring of many people in the arts, it is surprising that there are not more lawsuits. Let's take a look at the steps involved in planning to hire the people needed to make a performance or exhibition possible.

Job analysis

Everyone would agree that an arts organization wants to hire the most talented artists and support staff. What will be the screening process that ensures you have the best your organization can afford?

Your organization may also have larger goals about the composition of the total staff for the organization. Do you have a commitment to achieving diversity in your workplace? How will you even ensure that minority applicants apply for the openings you advertise? Will your workplace accommodate individuals with disabilities? Whatever the circumstances, the planning phase requires that you review five key areas for all of the jobs in the organization: work activities, work tools, job context, standards, and personnel qualifications.

Work activities

What is to be done? A performing arts organization will obviously need actors, singers, dancers, or musicians. Plans for the season often dictate the range of performer needs the organization will have. A dance company regularly performing *The Nutcracker* needs the correct mix of dancers to reach a desired level of quality. Acting companies seek to cast their shows with actors of the right age range if they are going to achieve a level of believability in various roles. An opera company must hire singers with the vocal talents necessary to perform their specific repertory. A season with Wagnerian opera requires different types of singers than a season with an Offenbach operetta. When considering the design staffing for a season, a producer works from the assumption that some designers are better than others at doing specific kinds of shows. Likewise, an organization considers how to market a season and wants a staff person fully capable of meeting the demands of promoting the season.

Based on your organization's design (as illustrated in Chapter 6, Organizing and Organizational Design), you should be able to create a clear distribution for the rest of the staff you need. In arts organizations, where staff resources are usually very limited, it is critical that the manager carefully analyzes how to combine the work activities to get the most productivity from each person.

Work tools

Some employees need specific tools to do their jobs. For example, a regional ballet company that decides to set up its own scenery and costume shop will need thousands of dollars for equipment and space rental. An organization that hires a marketing director had better be ready to provide the computer equipment and software needed to do the job.

Job context

Each employee has an overall context in which he functions. Performers have a set rehearsal and performance schedule; office personnel work within a daily schedule; and all employees work within an overall package that includes contracts, compensation, and benefits.

Standards

The manager of an organization must set clear standards for work output and quality. The manager of an arts organization may have various degrees of control of the workforce, depending on contracts and agreements in place. For example, the music director of the symphony and possibly a select group from the ensemble may be responsible for maintaining the performance standards at the highest level. On the other hand, complex negotiated agreements may limit the actions that the management may take to dismiss a musician who is not performing up to that standard.

Personnel qualifications

The level of education and experience required for each position may vary widely in an organization. The process used to select performers requires different personnel qualifications than those used to hire ticket office salespeople.

One obvious problem that arts organizations face in hiring support staff with the right qualifications is the funding available for salaries. The low pay often associated with working for an arts organization leads to the practice of hiring or relying on unemployed artists to fill staff positions. A passion for the arts may lead artists to decide to work for an arts organization, even if it isn't in their specific talent area. However, some artists are better than others when it comes to fulfilling the specialized administrative staff functions in an arts organization. As in all industries, the most qualified person does not always fill the job. The net effect of this hiring practice is that the arts organization may find itself unable to achieve its goals and objectives because the staff do not have the skills required to do the job.

Job description for staff openings

From this analysis of the basic requirements for the work to be done, the manager is able to create a job description for a staff position. The description, which is usually distributed to the labor market, usually covers six areas: general description of the job, responsibilities, specific duties, requirements for employment, compensation, and application method.[2]

Sample Job Posting

Here is a sample job posting for a hypothetical arts organization in a community with a performing arts center. Often this type of posting is derived from the job description for the specific position. (For more information about ticket service job opportunities go to www.intix.org/index.php. This Web site offers a glimpse into the wider world of event ticketing.)

The Harper Performing Arts

Center invites applications for the position of Ticket Services Manager. This is a full-time, 12-month, administrative staff position supervised by and reporting to the Managing Director.

Responsibilities

The incumbent will have general responsibility for the sales and accounting of individual tickets and subscriptions for productions by the Performing Arts Center. The Ticket Service Manager will perform the following duties:

1. Provide daily operation of a ticket service in a courteous and efficient manner through telephone sales, exchanges, and reservations. In addition, he will process Internet orders, mail-orders, e-mail, and voice-mail messages related to sales.

2. Using a computerized ticketing system, account for daily income and issue timely sales and deposit reports. In cooperation with other staff, maintain a ledger file of revenue from cash sales, credit card charges, money orders, and open accounts.

3. Provide general information in response to inquiries about the Performing Arts Center and various performing arts events.

4. Update information on the Ticket Service Web site on a regular basis.

5. Train, supervise, and schedule a staff of three and five volunteer assistants in customer relations, subscription and single ticket sales, and general daily ticket office transactions.

6. Assist with marketing projects as needed and specifically with the following: (1) manage the ticket service and supervise the concession operations the night of performances and (2) train and supervise a house manager and ushers.

7. Assist with the maintenance and development of mailing and e-mail lists for arts events.

8. Provide statistical reports on sales, subscriptions, and attendance at arts events during the year.

9. Perform other related duties as required.

Requirements

Three or more years of experience in ticket office and house management and sales required. A proven record of accomplishment of positive interactions with customers and staff required. Other desired qualifications include a performing arts background, excellent computer skills, and familiarity with office equipment.

Compensation

Salary commensurate with experience. Full benefits package available.

Applications

Send cover letter, current résumé, and three letters of reference to the Human Resources Dept., Harper Performing Arts Center. EOE/AA.

This "Sample Job Posting" shows how a staff opening might be worded. A shortened version of this description normally appears in a newspaper or job placement listing service. Let's look briefly at each section of this description.

General description

The opening paragraph describes who is looking for what position and for what length of employment. The opening also clarifies to whom the employee reports and by whom the employee is supervised. Regardless of the exact wording chosen, these basic ingredients can be used in any job description.

Responsibilities

The next section of the description lists the employee's general responsibilities in the job. This example clarifies the scope of the job, the types of shows done, and the departments producing the events.

Specific duties

Here you have the opportunity to list the tasks you expect the employee to carry out on a regular basis. In the example, the duties are ranked in order of frequency. Items 1, 2, and 3 are daily and weekly tasks, and items 4 through 7 occur on a monthly or semiannual basis. You can extrapolate this section to almost any job in the organization. The wording will be different, but performers, shop staff, ushers, museum guards, curators, and so on, all have lists of specific duties.

Requirements for employment

The education, experience, and specific knowledge, skills, and abilities (KSAs) required are listed in this section. The KSAs are important indicators in the screening process. Do the applicants have the knowledge of the area you are trying to fill? Do they have proven skills in specific tasks you need done? Do they have the general abilities to succeed in the job as defined? You can further clarify your KSAs by indicating which are required and which are desired. You may require applicants to have skills in specific software applications, but desire that they speak a second language. This specification does not mean that the employee must have these skills. In fact, she may bring unanticipated skills to the job that will benefit your organization.

Compensation

There are differing opinions about what to list for salary information. In some cases, unions may require that the salary be stated in the advertisement. In other cases, you may use a range to suggest some latitude in the salary to be offered. For example, "in the mid-20s" may mean as little as $23,000 to as much as $27,000. Other listings will simply say "compensation commensurate with experience." This lack of salary information could create budget problems for a manager when it comes time to negotiate a salary offer. For example, you might be wasting your time by talking to an applicant who is making $40,000 when all you can offer is $30,000.

One way to cover not posting the salary is to be sure that you clearly state the experience level required for the job in the requirements section. If you require a MA or MFA (Master of Arts or Master of Fine Arts) or equivalent experience, the applicant should take that to mean at least one to three years of work. This equivalent experience idea is based on the fact that most MA or MFA programs require two to three years to earn the degree. In the end, you may save yourself and the applicant a great deal of confusion if you are clear about the compensation levels at the beginning.

Benefits

The term *full benefits* usually means the following:

- Health insurance
- Life insurance
- Disability insurance
- Retirement benefits

The benefits package an arts organization can offer is a budget decision in many cases. The cost of benefits can run as much as 40 percent of an employee's salary. Remember, as an employer the organization must pay part of the Social Security and other taxes as part of the benefits cost of an employee. In addition, many arts organizations expect employees to pay a portion of the health insurance. The employee's share may be as high as 50%.

Application method

The final section of the job posting explains what is required for the application, when it is due, and to whom it should be sent. This section of the description is the appropriate place to state your concerns about seeking applications from special constituencies. You also want to include your participation in an equal-opportunity employment process.

THE OVERALL MATRIX OF JOBS

In the initial stages of forming an arts organization, time must be spent analyzing the minimum number of people required to operate the enterprise. This task is best done by identifying the key functions the organization must perform to present its mission-driven programming. For example, if you present concerts of chamber music, a series of major activities have to be done if you want to sell tickets for a performance on a specific night in a specific place. At the very least, you will need someone to assume the function of promoting and publicizing the concerts. If the budget for the organization does not permit hiring someone to do this work, you still must fulfill these job functions. In small organizations a board volunteer may take on the job function of promoting the series or the one staff person on the payroll will take on these duties as the concert performance schedule demands. Regardless who is doing the work, having a job description with a set of clear responsibilities and duties allows the essential work to be done.

As you begin to get a clearer picture of the overall scope of the jobs required to make the organization function, your job descriptions should reflect how you are going to achieve your objectives determined in your planning process. The number of full- and part-time employees and contractors and how they all relate to the performance season or exhibition schedule becomes the foundation of your operating budget. When salary and benefits often account for up to 80 percent of an arts organization's budget, it is critical that the manager keep the overall picture of the staffing as clear as possible. For example, when it comes time to initiate a new program or project, the ability to look at the overall organizational structure can prove helpful. Seeing where you can make adjustments and predicting the possible impact of staffing changes should make the planning process less difficult.

CONSTRAINTS ON STAFFING

The costs related to staffing a position play a key part in the constraints placed on managers. For example, if you hire an administrative assistant for $20,000, your first-year costs need to include at least another $8,000 for benefits and taxes. If you consider a $28,000 staff position over a five-year period, assuming an inflation rate of 3 percent, your salary and benefits cost for this position will be in excess of $32,000 by the fifth year. Over five years, you will have paid out more than $153,000 in salary and benefits. This cost does not include equipment or extra training the employee may require. Assuming you are able to justify the expense for the staff addition, you must still face the ever-increasing complexity of laws and regulations that control hiring in the United States.

Government regulations

Arts organizations are not necessarily exempted from the rules and regulations on hiring. The Equal Employment Opportunity Commission (EEOC; www.eeoc.gov) rules generally apply to all private and public organizations that employ 15 or more people. In addition, some state laws supplement various federal laws. In Chapter 4, The Adaptive Arts Organization, we discussed the impact of the political and legal environment on arts organizations. Here are examples of some of the major pieces of federal legislation that affect the hiring process:

- The Title VII Civil Rights Act (1964) and the Equal Employment Opportunity Act (1972) prohibit employment discrimination based on race, color, religion, sex, or national origin.

- The Equal Pay Act (1963) prohibits wage discrimination based on sex. The law requires equal pay for equal work regardless of sex.

- The Age Discrimination Act (1967; amended 1973) protects people from 40 to 70 years old against discriminatory hiring.

- The Rehabilitation Act (1973) provides for affirmative action programs for hiring, placing, and advancing people with disabilities.

- The Mandatory Retirement Act; Employment Retirement Income Security Act (1974) was designed to prohibit mandatory retirement before age 70. The law also provides for some pension rights for employees.

- The Privacy Act (1974) gives employees the right to examine letters of reference in their personnel files.

- The Pregnancy Discrimination Act (1978) requires pregnancy and maternity to be treated as a legal disability.

- The Immigration Reform and Control Act of 1986 requires employers to check the identities and work authorization papers of all employees.

- The Americans with Disabilities Act (1990) requires businesses and public services to open up jobs and facilities to disabled people.

- The Older Workers Benefit Protection Act (1990) prohibits age discrimination in employee benefits.

- The Civil Rights Act of 1991 strengthens Title VII of the 1964 Civil Rights Act, granting the opportunity for compensatory damages and clarifying the obligations of employers and employees in unintentional discrimination cases.

- The Family and Medical Leave Act (1993) allows up to 12 weeks of unpaid leave during a year for the birth or adoption of a child, family health needs, or the employee's own health needs.

Each state and local government also has various employment rules and regulations in place. Licenses, fees, and annual reporting and tax filing are just a few of the many requirements that must be complied with. State and local government Web sites routinely list various laws, regulations, and procedures for running a not-for-profit business.

Organized labor

An organization required to employ people working under a union contract must adopt rules and policies for employment that fulfill specific legal procedures agreed to by the union and the management. Although union membership has been dropping steadily since 1956,[3] a variety of unions represent various employment groups in the arts and entertainment industries. Unions represent artists and craftspeople such as actors, singers, musicians, writers, directors, choreographers, and technicians. In addition, specific contracts with unions like the Teamsters (who may control the loading and unloading of trucks at the performance space) might be required in larger metropolitan areas. Some states are designated as "Right to Work States," which means unions have less control in hiring and employment. With that said, a performing arts center in a Right to Work State (there are twenty-two such states) may have a contract with various unions. However, in a Right to Work State you cannot be compelled to join a specific union to keep your job.

The human resource function of an arts organization must take into account the myriad rules and regulations that typically accompany a union contract. We discuss this later in the chapter in the section Unions and the Arts.

RECRUITMENT

Depending on the situation, you may face many or few choices in filling a staff position. The range involves the limits placed on the overall contractual relationship between the employees and the employer. If you need an extra electrician for a lighting setup in a union theater, the local sends over whomever it has on call. If, on the other hand, you need to fill the position of head electrician for the theater complex, you may take steps similar to filling a salaried staff opening.

The three steps in recruiting for a standard administrative staff position are advertising the opening, screening possible candidates, and critically evaluating possible candidates for a list of finalists.

Internal

As you may know, many jobs are filled before anyone hears about the openings. The internal recruitment process is common in companies that have a promote-from-within policy. For example, if you are hired as the assistant to the marketing director for the museum and you are aware that the promotion policy favors internal candidates, you may have an additional motivation to do your best work. In fact, many organizations lose good employees because there is no room for advancement within the organization.

External

Many arts organizations use a dual policy of internal promotions and external recruitment. As organizations seek to create multicultural staffs, active external recruitment has become a regular procedure. When doing external recruiting, there are various avenues to pursue, depending on what you seek. Some organizations may arrange auditions just to build files of possible performers for the future.

Specialized publications like *ARTSEARCH*[4] can be used to seek out executive and administrative staff, designers, technicians, and craftspeople. *Variety* and other trade newspapers covering the arts and entertainment industry offer job postings online. In fact, the wealth of online opportunities can be overwhelming. Simply posting your job openings on the organization's Web site may be sufficient to attract a good applicant pool.

Finally, a professional recruitment service can be hired to find candidates for higher level executive positions in the organization. Although "head-hunter" services may be an extra expense, they may also generate the most likely candidates for executive level positions, such as a museum director or artistic director. A designated subcommittee of the board may also carry out searches for executive-level personnel.

Recruitment philosophy

There are two fairly common philosophies about recruiting.[5] One approach assumes a traditional "selling" of the organization, and the other takes the "realistic," or real-time, approach. In the selling approach, you stress the most positive features of the job and the work environment. Essentially, you try to present an upbeat picture of the organization. The real-time approach tries to depict accurately what day-to-day life is like in the organization. Try to present an objective view of the work situation and be forthright about answering questions about the less positive aspects of working in the organization. Organizations often blend these two approaches in their recruitment activities, but the tendency is to sell the organization. After all, who wants to paint a picture that might scare off the applicants?

People involved in the recruitment process have been known to use the realistic approach to discourage candidates that they perceive as not "right" for the company. Obviously, care must be taken when selling the organization in the recruitment process. If an interviewer frames the wrong picture of the organization, an applicant could be very unhappy once she gets the job.

Recruitment difficulties

Arts and other nonprofit organizations have complex personnel needs like any other business. Arts organizations hire people for vastly different kinds of jobs to fulfill their mission. Recruiting a soprano for an opera, hiring a marketing director, filling an administrative assistant position, or negotiating a union contract with the musicians or stagehands requires different priorities and screening strategies. As noted, recruiting staff for salaried positions is often difficult because many arts organizations do not offer competitive pay rates. Artists, on the other hand, often negotiate contracts through their agents that exceed union scale minimums. Employees who work for wages that are negotiated by union representation often receive pay at rates comparable to those of private industry. This difference may lead to pay disparities that have a negative impact on recruitment strategies.

Trying to attract quality candidates to staff positions with no advancement possibilities, low salary, minimal (if any) benefits, and an overwhelming workload is a difficult task. It is not surprising that there is a high turnover rate in lower level staff positions. Ironically, the people in these positions often do the basic work that keeps the organization going, such as payroll taxes, ticket office sales, or scenery or costume shop work. Competent, skilled administrative staff members are needed to ensure that the organization complies with all of the federal, state, and local laws pertaining to collecting and reporting taxes.

DIVERSITY IN THE ARTS WORKPLACE

Arts organizations should also consider workforce diversity in the process of staffing the organization. Having a staff that mirrors the organization's community speaks volumes about the values of that organization. A starting point begins with the simple process of researching the demographics of the community. That research can lead to adopting hiring goals to be better aligned with the ethnic and racial diversity of the region.

The same diversity issue applies to the composition of the board of directors of the organization. Again, a goal of representing the community through the board membership and developing a recruiting strategy can benefit the organization.

SELECTION PROCESS

Auditions

Different selection processes are used for different employee groups in the arts. The performers may all be selected by audition, depending on how the schedule is organized. For example, most regional theater companies now hold auditions in New York and a few other selected cities at various times during the year. It is rare to find a theater company with actors in residence for a full season. Ballet companies, on the other hand, have yearly auditions for a resident group of dancers. Smaller dance companies try to provide at least 26-week contracts for their dancers. Lead dancers for special performances in the repertory may be contracted as the need arises.

The larger regional opera companies, which have lengthy seasons, tend to audition resident choruses, dancers, and musicians and to hire the principal singers and conductors on a show-by-show basis. Smaller regional opera companies often work with a minimal staff and contract for all singers, dancers, and musicians on a show-by-show basis. Larger orchestras usually have a blind audition process in which the musician plays behind a screen so the judgment about their musicianship is based on their sound. The competition for places in the major orchestras is very stiff. Regional and smaller orchestras also have some type of audition process. However, the limited performance schedule may mean the players hold other full-time jobs as music teachers in schools and universities.

The audition process requires a great deal of data management. Records, which may include photos, lists of special skills, and so on, must be organized so that they can be easily retrieved. An audition space with a piano, tape player, dressing room, and warm up areas must be secured. If union contracts are in force, restrictions may apply to a variety of actions taken by management. For example, the Actors' Equity Association (AEA) contract with the League of Resident Theaters (LORT) contains dozens of stipulations about auditions.[6]

Ultimately, the organization's survival depends on its ability to select the right talent for the positions available. Since the performer is the product that the audience "purchases," it is critical that the artistic management establish criteria that match the company's desired quality level. A poor casting choice or a weak player can bring down the overall quality of the artistic product.

Traditional application process

The typical pattern for filling many administrative staff positions in an arts organization follows these six steps: formal application, screening, interviewing, testing, reference check, and hiring. Let's take a brief look at each stage.

Formal application

Standard forms are typically used to take applications for job openings in writing or online. Arts organizations often invite applications and request a cover letter, a résumé, and three or four references. In some cases, organizations actively seek out specific individuals and ask them to apply for the opening. The advantage of the application form becomes clear when you begin reviewing the candidates for the job. By using a similar format for gathering data, it may be easier to see which candidates have the qualifications you seek. When no formal application form exists, the person responsible for reviewing the files must develop a checklist of qualifications and require-ments for the job. This checklist should be easily gathered from the written job description you wrote.

Screening

The next step requires narrowing the list of applicants by eliminating those who do not match your search criteria. Further fine-tuning of the applicant pool usually reveals a short list of qualified candidates for the job. This work may be done by an individual or by a committee. For example, if the board is trying to hire a new artistic director, a search committee will be established and chaired by one of the board members. The screening process may become a very difficult stage in the hiring process because of strife within the organi-zation. For example, the search committee may be divided about the kind of person wanted, or the committee may arrive at a set of finalists that the rest of the board finds unacceptable. A significant number of variables can add to the complexity of the screening process.

Interviewing

The interview is equivalent to the audition for an administrative staff posi-tion. If the search is conducted by a staff member (not a search committee), the usual procedure is to interview several of the top candidates and to sched-ule second interviews for the best candidates. The committee approach may involve interviews with the top two or three candidates over a day or two by a wide range of people. Because the costs of conducting staff searches can run into the thousands of dollars, it is important to take the time to narrow the list of finalists before beginning the interview process. When pressed, some of the finalists may withdraw their candidacy, leaving you to fall back on other candidates on the list.

During the scheduled interviews, care must be taken to deal fairly with the candidates. Questions about age, marital status, family, national origin, dis-abilities, or religion are not legal. The same questions should be asked of each candidate, and they may be structured in such a way that you can legally dis-cover whether the prospective employee can meet your work schedule, can communicate and write effectively, and can perform the specific tasks you require. Requesting writing samples, reviewing a detailed production sched-ule, or testing may help you assess the potential employee's ability to do the job.

Prospective employees should not leave the interview process with the impression that you were engaged in discriminatory activities. Your organi-zation may have to answer to a lawsuit if you do not manage your interview process carefully.

Testing, reference check, and hiring

The decision to hire the candidate who is best suited for the job sometimes rests on intangible emotional responses by those doing the hiring. After you evaluate and compare the composite skills of the people most likely to fill the staffing needs of the organization, you may still be left with a high degree of uncertainty. Further background checks and additional on-site interviews may help. Ultimately, a degree of chance is always involved in hiring.

Many large corporations use detailed screening tests for applicants in an attempt to narrow down the variables involved in hiring. Psychological, medical, or specific skills tests are often administered to applicants. Organizations also use behavioral interview techniques for screening applicants. In the interview the applicant is asked to problem-solve or interact through role playing in a specific situation (e.g., "You need to discipline one of your staff. Talk us through how you would approach this situation?") Because of the high cost of hiring the wrong employee, corporations are not shy about spending several thousand dollars to hire the right person. On the other hand, the company's needs must be balanced against the individual's right to privacy.

Arts organizations typically work with very limited recruitment budgets. High staff turnover creates an even greater burden on the budget because too much time is spent seeking replacements for people who quit. Few arts organizations have the time to conduct an extensive background check on a prospective employee. As a result, the organization may find itself on a hiring treadmill.

Legal issues also enter into the hiring process. If you narrow your candidates down to two or three finalists, the potential for sending misleading signals to the candidates is very high. You will need sufficient documentation to stand up in court about why you did not hire candidate B or C — should your decision be challenged. When you make any hiring decision, you face some risk that the rejected finalists will take legal action. This potential outcome may sound pessimistic, but more organizations face lawsuits over hiring practices each year.

ORIENTATION AND TRAINING

The fourth stage in the process begins once the hiring has been completed. There are countless variations on the employee orientation process. Some organizations have fixed probationary periods (three or six months) in which very specific activities are planned to acquaint the employee with the organization. In other cases, a new person is hired and told to direct any questions to a specific individual or mentor.

The most important element in the orientation process is the socialization of the new employee into the organization. New employees are often anxious about their jobs. They want questions to be answered and clarifications made about where they fit into the entire operation. The informal interactions new employees encounter will help shape their perceptions of the entire organization. To avoid problems later, it is best to schedule a review of the overall policies with new employees when they first start and then again near the end of their probationary period. It is also important to note the date that you reviewed all of the relevant material with the new employee. You may later incur a problem with an employee who claims to have never been told about a specific policy. It may prove helpful to document when you reviewed a specific problem area with the employee.

Training and development

In corporate America, millions of dollars are spent each year on employee training and development. Due to their limited resources, arts organizations do not usually have intensive training programs. Training often takes place only after costly errors have been made by a new employee. Although employee training is recognized as a real cost to organizations, few take into account the financial impact of not having a training program.

On-the-job training

Most arts organizations use some variation of on-the-job training (OJT). The formal OJT approach includes very specific work abilities that are tested by the supervisor at specific time intervals. The less formal approach usually includes quick demonstration sessions, after which the new employee is expected to get on with the task at hand. More rigorous OJT structures include some combination of job rotation, coaching, apprenticeships, and modeling.

Job rotation and cross-training

In this approach, employees move around to different areas in the organization to receive training in specific activities. This training is helpful when an employee later has to fill in for someone who may be out of the office. Organizations also often engage in cross-training their staff. The idea is to always have two people who can accomplish a set of tasks in the event that someone is out of the office or leaves for another job. For example, having only one person who knows how to process subscription orders could prove harmful to an organization dependent on daily sales revenue.

Coaching

With coaching, as the term implies, a new employee receives very specific help with a skill related to the job. For example, an experienced stagehand may guide a new crew member through the operation of a follow spot. The stagehand watches the employee's performance and offers suggestions on improving her technique as he or she runs the spot. This same technique may be applied at all levels of the organization. In fact, the whole field of executive coaching is now a booming industry world-wide.

Apprenticeships and internships

The apprentice system is used extensively for training in the arts. Ideally, the apprentice works alongside a more experienced employee. If the system is to function effectively, apprentices should be given specific tasks that allow them to assume substantial responsibility. For the apprentice system to work best, the person doing the training should set clear deadlines and milestones for the apprentice to achieve job competency.

The opportunity to serve as an intern in an organization is another valuable method for screening and assessing a good personnel fit for an arts organization. An intern position should have a job description just as any employee in the organization. By organizing specific skill level tasks for the intern to execute, the management of the organization has the opportunity to assess ability and observe on-the-job behavior. Internships also serve as a valuable learning opportunity for students trying to gain more "real-world" experience. Many a career in arts management has been launched from a successful internship experience. Likewise, an internship may be a great opportunity for a person to re-think their career options.

Modeling

In modeling, a new employee watches the performance of the supervisor or trainer. Personal demonstrations of what is expected help form a consistent presentation of the organization. This technique is especially important for employees who come into contact with the public. For example, people who sell subscriptions or museum memberships are involved in using performance-related skills. They must be able to act out the script with which they have been provided to make the correct sales presentation. Watching and listening to a more experienced staff member go through the "scene" is a useful way to train a person.

PERFORMANCE APPRAISALS AND FIRING

There may be a number of reasons to replace an employee. You may have made a selection error that resulted in a poor match between the individual and the organization, or the person you hired may have outgrown the job. In this case, you may decide to move someone to a new job and create a vacancy due to reorganization. Alternatively, the person you hired may have violated the rules and procedures of the organization, leaving you no choice but to fire him or her. You may experience a slowdown or a budget cut that requires you to lay someone off, or an employee may develop an illness and be unable to work for an extended period. You may need to replace someone due to a retirement, military service, or death, or the employee may quit.

Performance appraisals

Most organizations have probationary periods for new administrative or professional staff (See Chapter 9, Operations and Budgeting, for more on appraisal systems). The probationary period may be for three or more months. During this period, the supervisor should be closely monitoring the new hire's job performance. Regular feedback sessions mixed with specific training opportunities are typically used to assess the new hire. Ideally, this person has a clear job description, detailed expectations, and specific objectives to meet so he can progress beyond the probationary period. The purpose of this type of probationary hiring process is to afford the organization a way to terminate the employment of someone who is not meeting the employer's expectations.

The range from formal to informal appraisals or evaluations can be wide in arts organizations. Many small arts organizations have no formal appraisal systems in place given the limited resources available. The result of this lack of an evaluation process can become problematic if the new hire proves to be less than anticipated. Should the new hire not meet the organization's needs, then firing them may be the only option.

Firing

No part of the staffing process is more challenging than firing an employee. Obviously, care must be taken when firing someone because of the legal ramifications. A poorly handled employment termination can cost an organization a great deal of money. *Wrongful-discharge* legal suits, as they are called, are becoming more common in the not-for-profit sector. Assessing the risks of firing an employee has led to better evaluation and documentation procedures. A verbal and up to two written warnings typically precede a termination action. Although a union contract may stipulate very precise steps that must be taken, it should not be assumed that it is impossible to fire a union employee. Clauses that provide for the rights of management usually address this issue.

On the other hand, many people work with no contracts whatsoever. Most arts organizations hire administrative staff under what is called *employment-at-will*. Simply stated, you can be fired at any time with no or limited notice, but you may also quit with the same limited notice. If some indication has been provided to an employee that her job performance is unsatisfactory, and an employment-at-will environment is in place, firing is best done swiftly.

Typically, when someone resigns from a staff position the notification period is 7 to 14 days. However, employment-at-will means that you may be fired at 9:00 a.m. and then be told to clear out of your office immediately. However, abrupt employee terminations typically create a negative atmosphere in the workplace, especially if they seldom happen.

Upper level management staff in larger arts organizations may have very detailed contracts developed by their lawyers and the organization's legal advisers. Precise language is often used to cover all aspects of compensation, evaluation, retirement, and termination.

Volunteer Contracts

It may be helpful to develop a contract form to use with your volunteers. Some of the obvious advantages of a contract are clear expectations about the work schedule, responsibilities, and duties and what support you will be providing to cover the expenses incurred by the volunteers. One good source for an example of such a contract may be found in Emily Kittle Morrison's book *Leadership Skills: Developing Volunteers for Organization Success*. This 1994 publication by Fisher Books offers some excellent guidance on selecting volunteers for service in the organization, as well as listing comprehensive criteria for selecting board membership.

VOLUNTEERS IN THE ARTS

In addition to the paid staff, volunteers may constitute a significant portion of the workforce in an arts organization. There is a long history of volunteerism in a variety of nonprofit organizations in America and, in fact, the IRS provides the opportunity for a tax deduction for volunteers who assist nonprofit organizations with out of pocket expenses.

The management of volunteers is often a separate functional work area in an arts organization. The staff volunteer coordinator serves the important role of managing a resource that may save the organization thousands of dollars in staff salaries. However, the time and energy required to recruit, train, supervise, and evaluate volunteers can be considerable. Volunteers also have a different relationship to the organization and therefore must be evaluated with criteria that are relevant. Most active volunteers come to the organization with a commitment that is refreshing. In other cases, the volunteer may possess special skills the organization can use in areas such as advertising, marketing, legal, or accounting.

To effectively operate the usually understaffed arts organization, volunteers may be needed in many areas. They can help realize the mission of the organization and help fulfill its goals and objectives by covering key areas where staff resources are limited. However, for the volunteers to be effective, as much attention must be paid to their job descriptions, recruitment, and training as for paid staff.

One obvious consideration in the use of volunteers is the risk factor. Management must assess the risk of using volunteers based on the work to be done. For example, it would probably be unwise to use a volunteer accountant or bookkeeper to manage the day-to-day financial activity of the organization. On the other hand, volunteers could be effective in seeking renewals by calling lapsed subscribers or members. Their personal commitment to the organization may make them ideal salespeople. Assisting with specific group projects such as stuffing envelopes for a big renewal campaign can be a good affiliation building experience.

Many organizations have guilds that sponsor annual fundraising events. The social element of the volunteer's participation in the organization can be a very positive way to strengthen ties to the organization. Ultimately, a well-managed arts organization needs a volunteer staffing system that is an integral part of the overall operating plan.

The volunteer staffing system also has its disadvantages. For example, it is difficult to manage volunteers in the same manner as staff since they are not paid. The working relationship between volunteers and staff may become strained, as can any working relationship. However, in this case, if your volunteer is also a major donor to the organization, how do you say that his "job" performance is inadequate? Philip Kotler and Joanne Scheff, in their book *Standing Room Only*, point out that organizations often do not anticipate full output from their volunteers:

> One manager of a large volunteer force has developed what he calls his "rule of thirds." One-third of his volunteer workforce works avidly with very little direction and encouragement, one-third will work only with considerable motivation and are only effective with careful supervision, and one-third will not work at all under any circumstances.[7]

Regardless of how productive the volunteers may be, there is enormous benefit to a well-managed volunteer system. Since the model of so many arts organizations includes a volunteer board of directors and general volunteers working with a paid staff, the necessity of developing and maintaining a healthy organization requires a staffing plan that allows for and uses volunteers.

Board of Directors Responsibilities and Duties

What exactly are the responsibilities and duties of a board of directors? In a not-for-profit arts organization this group constitutes the legally empowered group that has the ultimate responsibility and financial responsibility for the corporation.

Typically, this group is empowered to serve a public purpose (see Chapter 2, Arts Organizations and Arts Management as well as the section Legal Status and Financial Statements) and is sanctioned by the laws of the state in which the organization operates. At a bare minimum, a board must file annual reports with the state, and it is the entity that hires the executive director or other staff leadership to run the arts organization on a day-to-day basis. The general duties of a board includes:

- Hire, evaluate, and replace, if necessary, the executive leader.
- Provide oversight of the staff and generally make sure the management of the organization is doing what it should to fulfill the mission.
- Approve the annual budget.
- Accept and approve the annual financial report.
- Help raise funds to support the organization as it fulfills its mission.
- Set and monitor policies that provide guidance to the board and staff on how the organization will operate.

An excellent resource about boards and board governance for students and arts managers may be found in Nancy Roche and Jaan Whitehead's book *The Art of Governance — Boards in the Performing Arts*, published by the Theatre Communications Group. There are also numerous resources available on the Internet. For example, John Carver, a well-known writer and consultant on boards, has books, training, and a Web site devoted to this topic. For more information go to www.carvergovernance.com.

THE BOARD OF DIRECTORS

As seen in Chapter 6, Organizing and Organizational Design, one of the distinctive elements of many arts organizations is the volunteer board of directors. This group represents a very potent element in the overall personnel mix of a typical not-for-profit arts organization. The dynamic between the executive leadership, staff, and volunteer board can be challenging for even the most experienced arts manager. The board–staff working relationship will be discussed in more detail in Chapter 8, Leadership and Group Dynamics.

The process of putting together a functional and productive board of directors follows many of the same guidelines used for staffing the organization. The general scope and responsibilities of the board are usually defined in the bylaws of the organization. A typical board of directors includes a core executive committee usually composed of key people in areas such as finance, marketing, and fundraising, as well as the secretary, vice chair, and chair of the board. The general board members usually have committee assignments as part of their responsibility.

An effective board should make use of the same tools used to organize the staff. Creating position descriptions, establishing clear functions and purposes for committees, and defining a system for evaluating the "job" performance of volunteers is critical to the long-term success of the organization. However, while the executive leadership of staff has control over the scope of the staff duties and their job performance, the same cannot be said of the board. It is up to the board leadership to establish the benchmarks for performance that determine if a volunteer remains on the board.

Ideally, an organization has a board and board leadership that is fully functioning and meeting the responsibilities set down in the bylaws and in the board policies and procedures manual. In practice, the effectiveness of not-for-profit boards (or for-profit boards, for that matter) runs along a continuum from highly effective all the way to highly ineffective. Having clear job descriptions and leadership committed to professionally operating the board will make the manager's job significantly easier.

In the News

(Dec 06, 2007) — NEW YORK: Actors and assistant stage managers at American Girls Place theater in New York voted 9–6 on Saturday to unionize, a second attempt to have Actors' Equity Association negotiate their contracts.

The first attempt was held November 2006 after a tumultuous summer where 14 of the toy store's 18 actors went on a two-day strike. Although the actors voted 7–5 for Equity representation, *Backstage* reports that American Girls Place officials disputed the deal, believing voters had been persuaded to become members prior to the election.

"After 18 months of campaigning; two petitions — one verified by an independent arbitrator; one Unfair Labor Practice strike; one letter from the Actors signed by name, and two elections, the Actors and Assistant Stage Managers have chosen Equity again," said Flora Stamatiades, national director of Equity's Organizing & Special Projects. "We are looking forward to sitting down at the bargaining table and swiftly completing our negotiations."

American Girls Place officials have seven days to contest the election's results. Once the National Labor Relations Board verifies the election, negotiations could commence.

Source: *Stage Directions*, Industry News, December 2007.

UNIONS AND THE ARTS

Some of the unions involved in the arts include:

- Actors' Equity Association (AEA) for actors and stage managers
- American Federation of Musicians (AFM)

- American Guild of Musical Artists (AGMA)
- American Guild of Variety Artists (AGVA)
- American Federation of Television and Radio Artists (AFTRA) for performers
- United Scenic Artists (USA) for scenery, costume, and lighting designers
- International Alliance of Theatrical Stage Employees (IATSE), and Motion Picture Machine Operators of the United States and Canada representing stagehands.

The opportunity to review actual contracts is now possible by going to the Web sites for many of these unions. For example, you may look at the detailed contract with AGMA and several opera companies. Many of these contracts include pay rates and per diem information as well as detailed explanations of working conditions and work rules. The AEA Web site includes downloadable files for the many different contracts used with theaters.

Large arts organizations like the Metropolitan Opera in New York City must negotiate with multiple unions. The Met management must negotiate contracts with everyone from the musicians to the people who hang the posters in the marquees. Museums located in the larger cities must also work with unions who represent employees from many different groups, such as security guards.

Sample Wording from a Contract

The following is from the Actors' Equity Association (AEA) contract with The Broadway League, formerly the League of American Theatres and Producers, for the time period of June 28, 2004 to June 29, 2008. Page 35.

17   Costume calls

(A) Once a contract has been issued by the Producer, the Actor shall be available for costume measuring (one costume measuring for Chorus) prior to the rehearsal period at mutually convenient times. If given his notice prior to the third week of rehearsal, Actor shall receive one-sixth of Rehearsal Salary, for each such day or part thereof applied to costume measuring in addition to other sums provided for in the Contract of Employment.

(1) Principals and Chorus may be called for up to four hours of costume calls in addition to the rehearsal period herein prescribed. In no event may a costume call be less than one hour.

(2) Said costume calls shall be permitted in addition to the rehearsal period herein described, provided they are consecutive with the eight and one half-hour period specified in Rule 58(D)(1)(a)58D1.

(3) After the Actor's first paid public performance, costume calls shall be considered part of the rehearsal hours and span of day.

(B) When a costume call occurs at a place other than the place of rehearsal, the Producer shall provide, or reimburse the Actor for, transportation to and from such costume call. The manner of transportation shall be determined by the Producer.

Used with permission from the Actors' Equity Association.

Definition and purpose

The classic definition of a trade union is a "continuous association of wage-earners for the purpose of maintaining or improving the conditions of their working lives."[8] Unions arose to fight the exploitation of employees, which was, more often than not, the norm. Although it might be argued that the unionization of the arts has created a division between salaried artists and employees who are paid a wage, the reality is that unions are very much a part of the arts.

The union's primary responsibility to the workers is to derive benefits from the working relationship with the employer through a written contract. This contract is carefully negotiated by individuals elected by union members to represent them and designated representatives from management. The life of the contract is generally limited to two or three years. Although there are thousands of variations on the terms in a contract, the six key areas are

1. Compensation and benefits: pay increases and extent of benefits
2. Job specifications: what exact duties will be proscribed for the employee
3. Grievance procedures: in the event labor or management has a grievance, how will it be resolved
4. Work rules: start and stop times, overtime, number of people required for various tasks (e.g., load-ins, load-outs, and so forth) and break.
5. Seniority rules: often affects internal promotions and sets criteria
6. Working conditions: health and safety, equipment provided, training

Disputes

The agency most often involved in labor and management disputes is the National Labor Relations Board (NLRB; www.nlrb.gov). This governmental organization investigates unfair labor practices by employers and unions. An NLRB representative listens to both sides of a dispute and renders a decision aimed at resolving the conflict. If either party is unhappy with the ruling, the court system is the next step. The high cost of litigation motivates both sides to try to reach an out-of-court agreement.

Many companies are now making use of mediation services to avoid a prolonged NLRB process or the courts. Specialized firms now offer this service on a contract basis, thereby helping companies keep their legal costs down. However, since the results of a mediation are final, employees do not necessarily do as well as they would if they went to court. In fact, some critics have noted that since the company hires the mediation firm, there is a tendency to seek out firms that side with management more than labor.

Because the corporate culture of many nonprofit arts organizations stresses "giving to the cause," nonunion staff tend to repeat stories that have been heard about union abuses. The most common complaint is *featherbedding*, which involves adding employees who are not really essential to the project. The unions are often blamed for creating a very high overhead for professional productions. However, since the union's mandate is to achieve the best wages and working conditions for its membership, equally compelling arguments for the number of employees working an event can be made. From the union's perspective, having the correct number of workers at the event could be an important safety issue. This is especially true if the event has dangerous scenery changes or special effects or complex costume changes. The producer's goal is, of course, to keep the number of staff as low as safely possible, since over the run of a show one extra person will add thousands of dollars to the operating costs. This issue of how many stagehands would be required during the performances was at the center of the Local One IATSE strike in the fall of 2007 on Broadway.

FYI — Actor Salaries

Based on the Actors' Equity Association (AEA) contract with the League of American Theatres and Producers the minimum salaries for actors and stage managers in many Broadway theaters effective June 28, 2004 to June 24, 2007. For the current contract go to www.actorsequity.org.

	6/28/04	6/27/05	6/26/06	6/25/07
Actor	$1,381	$1,422	$1,465	$1,509
SM (Musical)	$2,270	$2,338	$2,408	$2,480
SM (Dramatic)	$1,951	$2,010	$2,070	$2,132
1st ASM (Musical)	$1,795	$1,849	$1,904	$1,961
1st ASM (Dramatic)	$1,594	$1,642	$1,691	$1,742
2nd ASM (Musical)	$1,499	$1,544	$1,590	$1,638

Source: *http://www.actorsequity.org/library/library.asp?cat=3. Used with permission.*

FYI — Designer's Contract

Local 829 of IATSE publishes the contract rates (minimums) for the League of Resident Theatres (LORT) on its Web site at www.usa829.org.

If you then go to Contracts, Collective Bargining Agreements, and then Theatre, Dance and Opera CBAs you will find up-to-date information on contract rates.

Scenery and Costume Design:

Stage Category	July 1, 2005	July 1, 2006	July 1, 2007	July 1, 2008
A	$6,851	$7,125	$7,410	$7,744
B+	$5,601	$5,825	$6,058	$6,330
B	$4,567	$4,750	$4,940	$5,162
C-1	$3,426	$3,563	$3,705	$3,872
C-2	$2,664	$2,771	$2,881	$3,011
D	As negotiated	As negotiated	As negotiated	As negotiated

Lighting:

Stage Category	July 1, 2005	July 1, 2006	July 1, 2007	July 1, 2008
A	$5,111	$5,315	$5,528	$5,776
B+	$4,350	$4,524	$4,705	$4,917
B	$3,615	$3,760	$3,910	$4,086
C-1	$2,609	$2,714	$2,823	$2,950
C-2	$2,175	$2,262	$2,353	$2,458
D	As negotiated	As negotiated	As negotiated	As negotiated

Sound:

Stage Category	July 1, 2005	July 1, 2006	July 1, 2007	July 1, 2008
A	$4,855	$5,049	$5,528	$5,776
B+	$4,132	$4,298	$4,705	$4,917
B	$3,434	$3,572	$3,910	$4,086
C-1	$2,479	$2,578	$2,823	$2,950
C-2	$2,066	$2,149	$2,353	$2,458
D	As negotiated	As negotiated	As negotiated	As negotiated

*D to A LORT classifications are determined by weekly box office sales. A is the highest ticket sales range.
Source: Union Local 829 Web site: http://www.usa829.org. Used with permission.

The 1980s saw a major shift in the way in which the business community dealt with unions. Led by President Ronald Reagan's dissolution of the Air Traffic Controllers Association, company after company simply let unions call strikes and then went out and hired replacement workers. Management became much bolder in demanding concessions from the unions. Unions continued to fight a losing battle in the 1990s as more companies shifted work overseas. Well-paid union workers were seen by many companies as a liability, not an asset, in a competitive world economy. It was argued that the cost of labor in the United States was simply too high, so many companies took the work elsewhere. Congress passed legislation requiring advance notice of plant closings, but this law had little effect on the trend.

For companies that stayed in America the strategy became to work in a more cooperative association with labor. Many union contracts began to include differential pay scales for new hires, reduced benefits, early retirement buy-outs, and a modification of restrictive work rules. Many of these changes trickled down into negotiations between arts organizations, performing arts centers, producers, and the unions. These changes were not met with enthusiasm, and suspicion about the motives of management remained high. Unfortunately, an attitude of "us versus them" is still very much a part of the day-to-day relationship of labor and management. The negotiation process often tends to set up a win–lose mentality that can lead to internal strife.

The corporate culture of the arts organization can play a big part in forming the overall attitude about employees and the perceived value of their contribution to the organization's goals and objectives. If the organization's values express the attitude "We are here to do quality work as creatively and efficiently as possible, and we appreciate and reward people who have these work ethics," the odds are that the relations with the union will be positive. However, if management's attitude is "You can't trust them, they always goof off, and they are slow to get work done," a work environment filled with suspicion and mistrust is reinforced.

The union members and their leadership will be more likely to respond favorably if the culture of the organization is cooperative, not confrontational. However, if the union members, from the stagehand to the first violinist, feel that management is out to get them, the entire artistic product may suffer. Cultivating good labor-management relationships in an arts organization must be a high priority from the board president on down.

MAINTAINING AND DEVELOPING THE STAFF

If an arts organization is to be successful over the long run, it must have a dedicated and experienced staff. The only way to build such a staff is to monitor the work environment constantly. A good manager should be aware of the staff's changing needs. The degree of intervention exercised by the manager depends on whether problems have arisen that require correction.

The psychological atmosphere of the workplace changes almost every day. One of the most important parts of the manager's job is staying attuned to the mood of the workplace. You can employ several strategies to help you stay in touch with your employees. Organizations must develop ongoing systems to assess regularly the concerns of employees in the workplace. Annual or ongoing evaluations, scheduled project assessments, production meetings, informal lunch or dinner meetings, and awards for outstanding performance or achievement all form a menu of choices that an organization must have available. (See the section Performance Appraisal Systems in Chapter 9, Operations and Budgeting.)

Career management

If an organization places a high value on employee retention, a career management system should be established. Employees need to believe that they are learning and growing in their jobs. Some of the ways to help employees develop a long-term commitment to the organization is to offer financial support for additional training, provide leaves of absence for outside study, and solicit employee input about job and work expectations. Obviously, there are limits to the amount of career enrichment available for every level within an organization, but the creative application of these ideas can help promote an organizational culture that places a high value on people. For example, it would be a mistake to assume that someone functioning as a receptionist is only capable of answering the phone and directing inquiries. It is true that this job is not a staff position with a great deal of potential for career development. However, by carefully designing the job to provide additional duties, such as assisting with gala event planning or conducting donor research, you may be able to make the job more challenging for an employee.

The "Right Staff"

The importance of staffing the organization cannot be stressed enough. All of the neat and tidy organizational charts, beautifully detailed strategic plans, forceful mission statements, and carefully designed marketing and fundraising campaigns will be of no use without the people to make it all happen. To function effectively as an organization you must have the personnel with the skills and dedication suited to the mission.

As you will see in Chapter 8, the success or failure of an organization is directly related to the effectiveness of its leadership. Finding the right people for the jobs you have and building a team of productive staff members is one of the most difficult tasks a manager faces. In situation after situation, the failure to assemble the right combination of people on the workforce leads to the failure of organizations to achieve their aims. A symphony with a brilliant conductor is only as good as the musicians in the orchestra. The finest collection in a museum will fail to live up to its potential without an effective curatorial staff. A dynamic choreographer or director needs equally dynamic dancers, actors, or singers to grab the audience's interest and support.

SUMMARY

The staffing process can be broken down into four major steps: job analysis, job description, recruitment and selection, and orientation and training. The process of analysis assumes that you are staffing the organization to realize strategic and operational objectives. Job design helps integrate the staffing plan with specific job responsibilities and duties.

Organizations must function within the laws that affect hiring personnel. Union contracts and stipulations are a fact of life in the arts. Arts managers must be well-versed in negotiating contracts and structuring their organizations to work effectively with unions.

The two major recruitment methods are internal and external recruitment. Recruitment options include auditions and traditional application and screening processes. When interviewing candidates for jobs, managers must carefully follow legal guidelines. The hiring and orientation of new staff can be assisted through formal procedures to ensure that consistent information is presented. Job training and long-term staff development are a key component in building an experienced and productive staff. Firing and replacing staff can be legally risky if handled improperly.

For additional topics relating to human resources in the arts, please go to www.managementandthearts.com.

Questions

1. Based on your own employment experiences, give an example of how the job requirements differed from the official job description. Relate the problems or benefits of the situation.
2. Discuss the impact of unions in the arts. Make a case for the positive or negative effect of a unionized workforce.
3. Write a job description for a position in an arts organization using the outline provided in the box titled Sample Job Posting.

4. What does a Web search return when you ask about diversity in the arts? Discuss some of the sites you found and relate them to how to better address workplace diversity among arts staffs and board.

5. Have you ever gone through a formal job orientation? Was it an effective tool for bringing you into the work environment?

RESOURCE

A good resource for your own use as an employee in an organization may be found in the Nolo Press book entitled *Your Rights in the Workplace* by Barbara Kate Repa, 8th edition, 2007. The Web site link to Nolo Press is www.nolo.com/index.cfm.

CLASS DISCUSSION TOPIC

The Arts Workplace and the Working Artist

In recent years, studies have been made of the employment patterns of artists. For example, in 2000 a report issued by the NEA noted that, "Over the past several decades artists have experienced unemployment rates roughly twice those of other professionals and have had annual earnings ranging from 77 to 88 percent of the average earnings of other professionals." The report also noted, "artists moonlight more frequently than all workers in the labor force." Moonlighting is the practice of holding a second job usually with the goal to bring in sufficient income to achieve an acceptable standard of living. There often is no choice but to moonlight, given the often seasonal or short-term nature of employment for the performing artist.

For many artists the potential of a steady income may lead them to pursue a career shift to the field of arts management. Many arts organizations hire staff who were or continue to be performing or visual artists. The arts organization workplace is often populated with dedicated and passionate people with administrative and managerial skills learned on the job.

Those who seek to pursue a career in the performing or visual arts pay a stiff economic penalty for doing so. It has also been observed that the growth of administrative positions in arts organizations seems to be a given. Meanwhile, the artists still must struggle with chronic under-employment as a way of life. While this may be the case in some circumstances, the financial stress related to the low compensation levels in arts management jobs also takes its toll on people. It is not unusual to find individuals who formerly worked as managers for arts organizations to have migrated to the for-profit sector as a way to improve their standard of living.

Source: *More Than Once in a Bluemoon: Multiple Job Holdings by American Artists,* Neil O. Alper, and Gregory H. Wassail, Research Division Report #40, National Endowment for the Arts, Seven Locks Press, 2000, Santa Ana, California. The free PDF of this report is available at www.nea.gov/research/ResearchReports_chrono.html.

Discussion points:

Are you aware of artists in your community who moonlight? Are they visual or performing artists? What are some of the circumstances that would have to change in your community to provide more steady employment for artists? Are you aware of the background of some of the staff who work in arts organizations in your community? Are the administrative staff former performing or visual artists? What is your opinion about the perception that the group benefitting the most from the growth in the number of arts organizations in communities is the managers and administrators? Are you aware of arts managers who moonlight?

SAMPLE EMPLOYEE MANUAL

Listed below is the Table of Contents from a typical employee manual for an organization. This sample is from USITT (United States Institute for Theatre Technology) and it is used in the operation of a seven-person office. Whenever you have four or more people in an office, it is a good idea to develop a manual to answer typical employee questions or clarify important policy issues decided by the board of directors. The section on hiring is printed in full to give the reader an idea of the kind of issues that need to be covered in a manual of this type.

General information

I-A. Equal Opportunity
I-B. Hiring Procedures [detailed]

1. Selection of candidates for all positions follows USITT Equal Opportunity policies.

2. USITT provides an opportunity for employees to take initiative toward their career development and to enhance their possibilities for advancement within USITT. Current employees are considered for filling a vacant position prior to hiring from the outside based on their qualifications and work history.

3. Qualifications matching existing position descriptions provide the basis for initial screening of applications.

4. Verification of employment information provided by the applicant is part of candidate selection. Generally, the only information to be verified from prior employers is the following, unless the applicant agrees, in deference to the applicant's privacy:
   a. Dates of employment
   b. Positions held and duties for each

5. Applicants must be advised that this information will be verified. Verified information shall be documented and maintained in successful candidates' personnel files.

6. New employees must confirm their acceptance for employment within three business days after being offered a position. At that point, new employees complete all pre-employment forms, benefit applications, and enrollment forms; and are provided basic information regarding pay policy, leave policy, benefits, and working hours.

7. Each new employee shall receive a complete copy of the current Employee Manual prior to beginning work.

Other sections in the handbook include:

I-C. Employment Classifications
I-D. Performance Review
II-A. Workday and Payroll
II-B. Overtime Compensation
II-C. Meal Break and Rest Period
II-D. Compensatory Time
II-E. Flextime
III-A. Insurance
III-B. Retirement Annuity Program
III-C. Vacation/Personal Leave
III-D. Holidays
III-E. Personal Time Off
III-F. Leave of Absence
III-G. Compassionate Leave
III-H. Jury Duty
IV-A. Employee Incurred Expenses and Reimbursement
IV-B. Conferences and Meetings
IV-C. Professional Memberships
V-A. Sexual Harassment
V-B. Substance Abuse
V-C. Smoking
V-D. Grievances

REFERENCES

1. John R. Schermerhorn, Jr., *Management for Productivity*, 2nd ed. (New York: John Wiley & Sons, 1986), p. 241.

2. Ibid., p. 243.

3. Howard M. Wachtel, *Labor and the Economy*, 2nd ed. (New York: Harcourt Brace Jovanovich, 1988), p. 373.

4. *ARTSEARCH* is published by the TCG, New York. Yearly paper and online subscriptions are available.

5. Schermerhorn, *Management for Productivity*, p. 249.

6. Actors' Equity Association, *Agreement and Rules Governing Employment in Resident Theatres*. Effective February 25, 2005; terminates February 24, 2008.

7. Philip Kotler, Joanne Scheff, *Standing Room Only* (Boston: Harvard University Press, 1997), p. 427.

8. Sidney Webb, Beatrice Webb, *The History of Trade Unionism* (London: Longmans, Green and Co., 1894), p. 1.

CHAPTER 8

Leadership and Group Dynamics

The domain of leaders is the future. The leader's unique legacy is the creation of valued institutions that survive over time. The most significant contribution leaders make is not simply to today's bottom line; it is to the long-term development of people and institutions so they can adapt, change, prosper, and grow.

James M. Kouzes and Barry Z. Posner, *The Leadership Challenge*, 4th edition.

KEY WORDS

Leadership and power

Formal and informal leadership

Theory X and Theory Y

Position power: reward power, coercive power, legitimate power

Personal power: expert power, reference power

Acceptance theory

Zone of indifference

Approaches to leadership: trait, behavioral, contingency and situational, transactional and transformational

Motivation and theories of motivation

Need theories: hierarchy of needs (Maslow), ERG (Alderfer), two-factor theory (Herzberg and Syndermann), acquired-need (McClelland)

Cognitive theories: equity theory (Adams), expectancy theory (Vroom)

Reinforcement theory: organizational behavior modification (OBM)

ABC — Antecedent, Behavior, Consequence

Social learning theory

Group dynamics: formal and informal groups; command, task, interest, and committee groups; group development stages; group norms and cohesiveness; groupthink

Distributed leadership

Communication process: stereotypes, Halo Effect, selective perception, and projection

We are now ready to examine the complex areas of leadership, the management communication process, and group dynamics in arts organizations. In this chapter we discuss the use of power in leadership and briefly review trait, behavioral, contingency, and situational approaches to leadership. We take a look at what motivates people, as well as the key factors required to successfully work with and lead groups. Lastly, we review the important issues related to communication in the workplace. I also suggest you explore the list of leadership books at the end of this chapter.

THE CENTRAL ROLE OF THE LEADER

Up to this point, we have created an organization, given it an overall structural framework, established strategies and plans to realize its mission, and begun staffing the enterprise with the best people we can find. Before we move into the specific operational areas of finance, budgeting, scheduling, marketing, and fundraising, we need to examine the talent and tools needed to realize the vision, fulfill the mission, and develop and sustain the values of the organization. Every day, arts organizations face the changing dynamics of people working together. With sensitive and adaptive leadership, the organization will go far. As you will see in this chapter, developing an organization with effective leadership is a continually challenging process.

LEADERSHIP FUNDAMENTALS

The subject of leadership is explored in numerous books each year. It seems to be a topic that is constantly revisited and explored. Stop by your local bookstore and go to the section on business books, you will find dozens of titles on this topic. The search for the best way to develop leadership skills and how to use those skills to create an organization that flourishes is a popular topic in today's business literature. A few books are listed at the end of this chapter that may prove helpful in expanding your leadership studies. There are also numerous Web sites that provide a wealth of information about how to effectively lead and manage all types of organizations. Again, a few of these Web sites are noted at the end of this chapter.

As you see from the epigraph to this chapter, leadership is about the future and creating sustainable organizations through working with people. For that to happen the person in the leadership role must first be able to influence others. Simply put, *leadership* is the manager's use of power to influence the behavior of others.[1] *Power*, as we will use the term, is defined as the ability to get someone else to do something you want done. The effective use of power in a leadership situation is also influenced by respect for the person who is doing the leading. Someone may have power over you, but you may have little respect for that person. This ultimately does not make for an effective leadership situation.

In all of our discussions of leadership, keep in mind that leadership success is a necessary, but not the sole, condition for managerial success. It is also important to remember that although a good manager should be a good leader, a good leader is not necessarily a good manager. People have ranges of skills, some of which are more developed than others. For example, someone identified as an excellent leader may not be particularly good at planning and organizing. Some managers may be wonderfully organized with detailed plans but lack leadership abilities to inspire others. Engaging in your own assessment of the leadership and management skills and abilities you possess can be a worthwhile activity.

Let's start our look at this topic by examining two basic leadership modes found in many work place settings: formal and informal leadership.

FORMAL AND INFORMAL LEADERSHIP MODES

Formal leadership is leadership by a manager who has been granted the formal authority or right to command.[2] The director of the play, the conductor of the orchestra, the executive director of the arts council, and the chair of the board of directors have been given formal authority by the organization to act on behalf of the organization. *Informal leadership* exists when a person without authority is able to influence the behavior of others.[3] Often informal leadership grows out of specific situations where an individual steps in and takes over. For example, suppose that an inexperienced student stage manager (formal leadership role) is unable to control the large cast of a Shakespeare play. A cast member with some stage managing experience steps in and starts giving orders (informal leadership). Because other students have respect for her, they listen to this informal leader and ignore the formal leader.

Was this the best way for the cast member to help the inexperienced stage manager? No; in fact, by engaging in this informal leadership role the cast member undermined the power base of the stage manager. Power is a relatively fragile tool at the disposal of a leader. In this little scenario our student stage manager will have to re-establish the formal leadership authority and power base quickly, or risk losing control of the cast. How can power be used in an arts organization?

Figure 8.1

Four leadership styles.

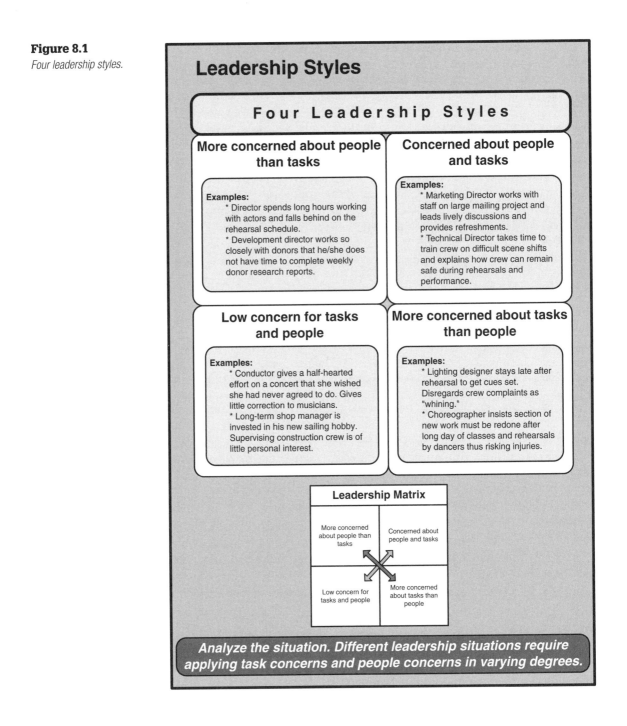

Leadership Styles

Four Leadership Styles

More concerned about people than tasks

Examples:
* Director spends long hours working with actors and falls behind on the rehearsal schedule.
* Development director works so closely with donors that he/she does not have time to complete weekly donor research reports.

Concerned about people and tasks

Examples:
* Marketing Director works with staff on large mailing project and leads lively discussions and provides refreshments.
* Technical Director takes time to train crew on difficult scene shifts and explains how crew can remain safe during rehearsals and performance.

Low concern for tasks and people

Examples:
* Conductor gives a half-hearted effort on a concert that she wished she had never agreed to do. Gives little correction to musicians.
* Long-term shop manager is invested in his new sailing hobby. Supervising construction crew is of little personal interest.

More concerned about tasks than people

Examples:
* Lighting designer stays late after rehearsal to get cues set. Disregards crew complaints as "whining."
* Choreographer insists section of new work must be redone after long day of classes and rehearsals by dancers thus risking injuries.

Leadership Matrix

More concerned about people than tasks	Concerned about people and tasks
Low concern for tasks and people	More concerned about tasks than people

Analyze the situation. Different leadership situations require applying task concerns and people concerns in varying degrees.

Revisiting Theory X and Theory Y Approaches to People

Consider a topic we touched on in Chapter 3, Management History and Trends. Douglas McGregor argued that Theory X and Theory Y represented the contrasting fundamental beliefs that managers have about the people who work for and with them. A Theory X manager assumes that people dislike work, lack ambition, are irresponsible, resist change, and prefer to be led rather than to lead. A Theory Y manager works with people from the opposite perspective; he assumes that people like to work, are willing to accept responsibility, are capable of self-direction and self-control, and can be imaginative, ingenious, and creative.[4]

McGregor's theory raises the issue of the *self-fulfilling prophecy*. This psychological term applied to the management of people simply means people will perform in their jobs at the level you establish for them. In other words, if you treat your staff, cast, and crew like idiots, they will tend to fulfill your expectations.

This topic of self-fulfilling prophecies, for example, is fundamental to the underlying attitude a manager has about the people she works with and supervises. An aware manager realizes that the psychological landscape of the workplace is rugged terrain. If you assume a leadership position without having developed an overview about the people you work with, you will probably run into a series of personnel problems that will limit your effectiveness.

Before you can develop your leadership skills, you must seriously evaluate your attitudes about work and people. In many arts organizations, both X and Y attitudes operate. These conflicting approaches usually lead to varying degrees of employee satisfaction. In addition, some arts organizations function with leadership that borders on the tyrannical, while other organizations appear to be without leaders and the staff feels adrift. Establishing a consistent balance of approaches to working with people helps provide a stable and productive work environment.

As we saw in Chapter 6, Organizing and Organizational Design, the corporate culture of an arts organization is established and reinforced by its leaders. The communication style of the leaders (open or closed), the trust level given to employees (great or little), and the core values of the organization (followed or ignored) all combine to create a great or terrible place to work.

POWER: A LEADERSHIP RESOURCE

The word *power* often has negative connotations. Yet without power, it would be impossible to operate most organizations. As we defined it, power is *the ability to get someone to do what you want*. However, in most arts organizations (or any organization), you have only as much power as your coworkers are willing to give you.

We begin our investigation of leadership power by posing three questions:

1. What sources of power are available to the leader?
2. What are the limits to the leader's power?
3. What guidelines exist for acquiring and using power?

Sources of power

Two sources of power are available to the leader: *position power* and *personal power*.[5] The first comes with the job you occupy, and the second is directly attributable to you.

As we saw in Chapter 6, the organizational design process should establish the working relationship between and among employees in the organization. No matter how little vertical or hierarchical structure exists in the organization, leaders and managers are given *position power* by their designated place in the organization's supervisory system. For example, a production manager has more power than a technical director, a technical director has more power than a stage carpenter, and so forth. Management texts identify three types of position power: reward, coercive, and legitimate.

Reward power is the capability to offer something of value as a means of controlling others.[6] For example, a position may carry with it the power to grant raises, promotions, special assignments, or special recognition.

Coercive power is defined as the ability to punish or withhold positive outcomes as a way of controlling others.[7] For example, if you have ever received a verbal reprimand or a demotion or been fired from a job, you have been subjected to coercive power. Control over the work schedule may be used as a form of coercive power. Scheduling could also be used as a reward power in some cases. For example, the ticket office manager may reward a productive staff member by giving them first right of refusal when it comes to working the evening performances.

Legitimate power is the ability to control others by virtue of the rights of the office.[8] It is asserted in the phrase, "I am the boss, and therefore you must do what I ask."

Personal power

Along with the position you hold, you bring your unique attributes and talents to the situation.[9] The two types of personal power are expert power and reference power.

Expert power is simply the ability to control others because of your specialized knowledge.[10] This could include special technical information or experience that others in the organization do not possess. For example, a stage manager with production experience could have expert power when it comes to planning a scenery shift on stage. This would allow the stage manager to exercise more power in a production meeting when alternative ways of doing a set shift are being discussed.

Reference power is derived from a more personal level of interaction with employees. Reference power is the ability to control others because of their desire to identify personally with the power source.[11] This use of power is often found among strong founder–directors of arts organizations. Their charismatic personality and forceful approach to managing the organization are used as a way of controlling others. Staff may feel personally compelled to work extra hours because they want to emulate the leader's work ethic.

It is fairly easy to apply the five types of power — reward, coercive, legitimate, personal, and reference — to such familiar roles as conductor, director, production manager, technical director, stage manager, or choreographer. Each of these leadership positions requires the use of some combination of these powers. After this brief introduction to the use of this topic, you have probably realized that some individuals are better than others at using the power they have been given.

Limits to power

Now that we have looked at the sources of power, let's examine some of the limits of power. In the organizational setting of the arts, the power to control others is more often a potential than an absolute. Although history provides many sad examples of individuals abusing the power they have had over others, there are limits to power.

In arts organizations several different groups of employees work to support the organization's mission, stated goals, and objectives. Within each employee group, differing degrees of power are exercised. The union stage crew has a different relationship to the power structure of the organization than the senior administrative staff. However, whatever the differences may be within each work group, there are limits to how effectively power can be used to control work output. For example, the union crew is most likely operating under a contract with very specific work rules that control supervision. If a stage manager begins giving orders to the fly crew without going through the fly crew chief first, not much is likely to happen. The stage manager may have the power to give commands, but the contract may stipulate who really has power over the fly crew. On the other hand, the lowly marketing assistant, not protected by a union contract, may find himself with little recourse when he finds out his boss "volunteered" him to work the fundraising gala on Saturday night.

Acceptance theory

As noted in Chapter 3, Management History and Trends, Chester Barnard's 1938 book titled *The Functions of the Executive* articulated what is known as *acceptance theory*. Simply stated, power is only realized when others respond as desired — that is, when they accept the directive.[12] Acceptance theory states that people are most likely to accept orders or requests when one or more of these four conditions are met:

1. They truly understand the directive.
2. They feel capable of carrying out the directive.
3. They believe that the directive is in the best interests of the organization.
4. They believe that the directive is consistent with their personal values.

Of course, each of these four conditions are not absolutes, nor do they need to be 100% clear and unequivocal for the leader to use their power. For example, you may have had a supervisor or instructor who through their position of authority gave you a directive that you were not certain about. Many of us have gone forth in a class or in our jobs by doing something without really understanding the directive. We may have felt unsure of our capabilities to carry out the directive, we also may have felt the directive might not be mission-related, and we may have found ourselves concerned the directive conflicted with our values. Yet, we went ahead and followed the directive anyway. Why? More than likely, we did what we were asked because we wanted to keep our jobs or pass the course. From the perspective of Barnard's theory we only partially responded to the use of power in this leadership situation.

Zone of indifference

Another part of Barnard's leadership theory focuses on what is called the employee's *zone of indifference*. This theory states that power in organizations is limited to the range of requests and directives that people consider appropriate to their basic employment or the psychological contracts they make with the organization.[13]

A directive that falls within the zone of indifference tends to be accepted and followed automatically. For example, if a marketing research assistant in an art museum is asked to check the membership list for zip code distribution in comparison to census data reports, he would not react negatively. However, if his supervisor asks him to pick up her dry cleaning on the way to work, the odds are good that the supervisor has crossed the zone of indifference of the employee. The assistant will probably react by thinking "That's an inappropriate request to make. What does this have to do with the research job?" He may still pick up the dry cleaning, but resentment and negative feelings about the leader will no doubt affect the employee's attitude and work behavior.

Both of these theories can be easily applied to an arts organizational setting. Trying to ignore these theories may make the leadership role very difficult. Put yourself in the position of a cast member, intern, or crew member, and think about how the acceptance theory may affect your interaction with your supervisor.

Guidelines for using power

Consider using the guidelines that follow when you find yourself exercising formal or informal power. These very practical applications of Barnard's acceptance theory are summarized from an article by John R. Kotter in the *Harvard Business Review*.[14]

1. Do not deny your formal authority. It is acceptable to act like the boss if you keep your perspective and remember that you are dependent on the goodwill and cooperation of the people who work for you.

2. Do not be afraid to create a sense of obligation. Doing a few favors or clearing the path so that employees can get their jobs done will help establish their obligation to follow your direction.

3. Create a feeling of dependence. Although care must be taken not to create a negative dependence (employees cannot make a decision without you), it can be helpful to establish a situation in which people depend on your help to make their job easier. This will make it easier to gain their cooperation later.

4. Build and believe in expertise. A few solid examples of your having accomplished something will help build a belief by others in your expertise. No one likes working for know-nothing bosses who do not seem qualified to hold the positions they do. (Many good examples of negative employee behavior in such situations may be found in the Dilbert cartoon series.)

5. Allow others the opportunity to identify with you as a person. When you create an environment in which the people you work with know and respect you as a person, they are more likely to follow your direction and supervision.

APPROACHES TO THE STUDY OF LEADERSHIP

Management researchers have developed several theories that attempt to predict why some people are better leaders than others. An excellent summary of all the various leadership theories may be found in Stephen R. Covey's

Figure 8.2

Leadership, motivation, and group dynamics.

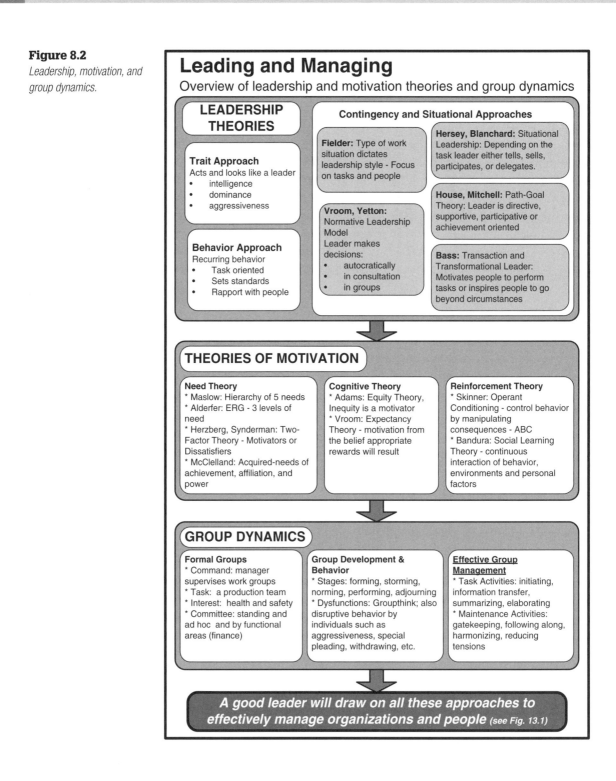

Leading and Managing
Overview of leadership and motivation theories and group dynamics

LEADERSHIP THEORIES

Contingency and Situational Approaches

Fielder: Type of work situation dictates leadership style - Focus on tasks and people

Hersey, Blanchard: Situational Leadership: Depending on the task leader either tells, sells, participates, or delegates.

Vroom, Yetton: Normative Leadership Model
Leader makes decisions:
- autocratically
- in consultation
- in groups

House, Mitchell: Path-Goal Theory: Leader is directive, supportive, participative or achievement oriented

Bass: Transaction and Transformational Leader: Motivates people to perform tasks or inspires people to go beyond circumstances

Trait Approach
Acts and looks like a leader
- intelligence
- dominance
- aggressiveness

Behavior Approach
Recurring behavior
- Task oriented
- Sets standards
- Rapport with people

THEORIES OF MOTIVATION

Need Theory
* Maslow: Hierarchy of 5 needs
* Alderfer: ERG - 3 levels of need
* Herzberg, Synderman: Two-Factor Theory - Motivators or Dissatisfiers
* McClelland: Acquired-needs of achievement, affiliation, and power

Cognitive Theory
* Adams: Equity Theory, Inequity is a motivator
* Vroom: Expectancy Theory - motivation from the belief appropriate rewards will result

Reinforcement Theory
* Skinner: Operant Conditioning - control behavior by manipulating consequences - ABC
* Bandura: Social Learning Theory - continuous interaction of behavior, environments and personal factors

GROUP DYNAMICS

Formal Groups
* Command: manager supervises work groups
* Task: a production team
* Interest: health and safety
* Committee: standing and ad hoc and by functional areas (finance)

Group Development & Behavior
* Stages: forming, storming, norming, performing, adjourning
* Dysfunctions: Groupthink; also disruptive behavior by individuals such as aggressiveness, special pleading, withdrawing, etc.

Effective Group Management
* Task Activities: initiating, information transfer, summarizing, elaborating
* Maintenance Activities: gatekeeping, following along, harmonizing, reducing tensions

A good leader will draw on all these approaches to effectively manage organizations and people (see Fig. 13.1)

The 8th Habit. Covey notes "five broad approaches in leadership theories have emerged on the twentieth century; approaches include trait, behavioral, power-influence, situational and integrative."[15]

The first studies of leadership examined the personal traits and psychological characteristics of people in leadership roles.

Trait approaches to leadership

The earliest research was based on the assumption that a person with particular traits has leadership potential. The idea was to establish an inventory of traits and to match them to people. This early research focused on physical and psychological attributes. However, there proved to be a limited correlation between these traits and leadership. Recent studies have shown, however, that the specific traits of intelligence, dominance, aggressiveness, and decisiveness do tend to be associated with people identified as leaders.[16] However, the focus on traits is still secondary to most research on leadership. The actual behavior of leaders is the current focus.

Behavioral approaches to leadership

Other researchers have tried to formulate a leadership model by studying recurring patterns of behavior by people in leadership positions. This research has focused on the leader's orientation toward tasks and people. Leaders who were highly concerned about the tasks to be done exhibited certain behaviors: planning and defining the work to be done, making clear assignments of task responsibility, setting work standards, following up on task completion, and monitoring. The people-oriented leaders tended to emphasize other behaviors: developing social rapport with employees, respecting the feelings of others, and developing a work environment of mutual trust. These styles of leadership are diagrammed in Figure 8.1. A practical application of this matrix is the relationship between a stage director and the cast. Consider your own experience, and try to place an arts leader you have worked with somewhere within this matrix.

Contingency and situational approaches to leadership

Circumstances in the workplace change and these changes may require different leadership approaches. Researchers questioned the idea that any one particular leadership style is effective in all situations. Out of their studies came *contingency* or *situational leadership theories*. The source for these theories is Fred E. Fielder's 1967 book *A Theory of Leadership Effectiveness*.[17] Fielder's study indicated that leaders differ in how oriented they are to tasks and people. Some situations require more focus on tasks and some toward people. (See Figure 8.2.) Here are two examples of contingency leadership required in a typical arts setting.

A membership manager for a museum must coordinate a renewal and new members drive each year. Once it is planned, the entire operation is very task-oriented, specific, and deadline driven. The leadership requirements in this situation would be directed toward ensuring that employees were accurate and timely in completing routine tasks. At the same time, because this project requires repetitive work on the part of the staff, the manager's leadership challenge is to keep people motivated and productive. Therefore, the manager might structure the day with frequent breaks or some other form of stress relief for the staff.

After finishing the big renewal campaign, the membership manager is appointed to chair an ad hoc committee to study and improve management and employee relations. Different leadership skills will be required. The goal is articulated, but the specific tasks are not indicated. Other committee members will be volunteers, and the manager will have little direct control over them. This situation requires strong group leadership skills. The manager must also develop clear objectives for all phases of the study. Deadlines will have to be set, objectives defined, and committee procedures established.

Another leadership theory aligned with the situational approach is called the *normative leadership model*. This model, from Victor Vroom and Phillip Yetton, bases its approach on the idea that a leader acts from either an autocratic, consultative, or group decision-making style.[18] As an autocratic leader you either solve the problem or make the decision yourself with the available information or after consulting a subordinate. If you engage in consultative leadership behavior, you may gather ideas from your subordinates individually or in groups, and then make the decision yourself. Alternatively, if the situation warrants, you may decide that a group approach to solving the problem works best, in which case you accept and implement the group decision.

Yet another model was developed by Paul Hersey and Ken Blanchard: It is "based on the premise that leaders need to alter their behaviors depending on one major situational factor — the readiness of followers.[19] *Situational leadership theory* focuses on two leader behaviors: *task* and *relationship*. The task behavior refers to how much the leader tells people what, how, when, where, and who is to do something. Relationship behavior describes the communication processes used by the leader: listening and facilitating.[20] This model is based on the assumption that, depending on the task and the employee's readiness, the leader may need to use some combination of telling, selling, participating, or delegating to accomplish a task. For example, telling may be used as the leadership approach if the employee is "unable or also unwilling or too insecure to take responsibility for a given task."[21]

Let's put this approach in the context of an arts organization. A ticket office manager would be wise to use a *telling* style of situational leadership when training a new employee to process a credit card phone order. Given the fact that errors can be very costly, this type of leadership is appropriate. Once the task is mastered by the employee, the manager no longer needs to use a telling style when supervising the employee. This same manager would probably want to use a *participating* style when establishing the work schedule during a particularly heavy part of the season. Working with employees and gaining their investment in developing a schedule in which the workload is perceived as equally distributed will probably have a positive effect.

Management researchers Robert J. House and Terence R. Mitchell developed the *Path-Goal Theory* as another approach to the study of situational leadership. This approach focuses on how leaders affect the "way subordinates perceive work goals and possible paths to reach work and personal goals."[22] The situational behaviors of the leader include *directive, supportive, participative,* and *achievement-oriented*. The leader needs to assess which combination of these four behaviors will work best depending on the subordinates' current situation and the anticipated result. The challenge in this leadership model is that the leader must understand that what worked in one situation may not work in another. For example, using a directive approach to explain to an intern the process for putting labels on season brochures when, in fact, they have already done this task before, can only lead to the intern thinking, "this person must really think I am dumb." In this case, the directive approach places a barrier for the intern whose goal may be to be recognized as someone employable by the organization, not a lowly intern.

Transactional and transformational leadership

Leadership expert Bernard M. Bass distinguished between the *transactional leader*, people who motivate people to perform tasks and achieve stated objectives, and the *transformational leader*, someone who motivates and inspires people to go beyond their normal work behavior.[23] In Bass's model, managers are people who "do things right" over and over, while a leader is someone who innovates, inspires, and changes by getting people to "do the right things."[24] A good leader should be able to perform both leadership behaviors.

The leader's analysis of the situation should help clarify how much of each approach to apply. For example, an opera director communicating her concept for a production of *The Magic Flute* could outline for the design team her ideas in either a more directive or transformational leadership approach. She might begin by being very directive and talk about when the show must be completed, where she sees it being set in time and place, and how it should look. Or, she could take a more transformational approach by focusing on larger philosophical or thematic issues of the piece and discuss what the music evokes in each of the designers' imaginations. In other words, she could work from a more transformational style by using a participative process to inspire the group to move beyond a standard vision of a work of art.

Applications of theories to the arts

Management theory tries to be scientific about creating "experiments" and "controls" in an attempt to "test" the theories. In reading the literature, it becomes apparent that no one theory can explain why some people are dynamic, productive leaders and others are not. While there is no single test that will identify you as a good leader, that does not mean you should not try to better understand how you can lead.

One such leadership self-assessment tool is available through author and leadership expert John C. Maxwell's book and Web site. His book, *The 360° Leader* offers a comprehensive "Leader Survey Report" online. Using an access code that comes with the book, the reader can access a nearly 100-question survey.[25] (For more information go to the Web site www.maximumimpact.com.)

After taking the survey, a report is produced that details how you lead up (to your boss), lead across (with your colleagues), and how you lead down (to your followers). The basic premise of *The 360° Leader* is that no matter where you fit in the organization, you will be exercising forms of leadership.[26] The survey and the Web site offer a good resource for any manager aspiring to improve their leadership effectiveness.

As you have seen from the myriad theories we have touched on, a great deal of individual effort must be taken by an arts manager to identify and cultivate leadership skills that are appropriate to the situation and that can inspire people to do better.

LEADERSHIP AND THE CREATIVE SPIRIT

In an arts organization, keeping the creative spirit alive and promoting a positive work environment is a full-time job for a manager. It is extraordinarily easy to become bogged down in the day-to-day operation of the organization. For example, leadership directed at trying to run an arts organization "just like any other business" could be a formula for disaster. Although it is true that an arts organization must function in a businesslike way, arts managers must address the larger issues of the relationship of their organization to the larger society and culture. For example, authors like Warren Bennis (see the section Additional Resources at the end of this chapter) point out that the trend toward two- and three-part leadership — distributed leadership — of organizations only tends to dilute the effectiveness of each leader. Instead of leadership, the result is more bureaucracy.[27] Instead of looking to the future, managers spend their time dealing with the routine of supporting the bureaucracy.

Arts Leader Profile

This excerpt from the September 2007 issue of *Opera News* provides evidence of the positive effect a legacy of strong leaders can have on an arts organization. The reader must also keep in mind that what may have worked well for the Lyric Opera of Chicago may not work for other arts organizations in different circumstances.

Company Man

By Megan Mckinney

In late May, at Lyric Opera of Chicago's annual board meeting in the ballroom of the city's Four Seasons Hotel, Lyric general director William Mason stepped up to the podium and announced the company had concluded the 2006–07 season with an estimated $143,000 surplus. His audience applauded with enthusiasm but without surprise. At a time when arts organizations worldwide face major financial challenges and other leading opera companies are hemorrhaging cash, Lyric has been in the black for nineteen of the past twenty years, with 2006–07 ticket sales in excess of 95 percent of seating capacity and half its performances sold out.

Lyric's amiable general director, who has led the company through roughly half this extraordinary era, literally grew up with the Lyric, absorbing its evolving style from its first season in 1954…. At twenty, Mason began working as an assistant to Lyrics' co-artistic director Pino Donati, while studying voice at nearby Roosevelt University's Chicago Musical College, and has been associated with the company for all but three seasons since. In 1981, during a potentially devastating financial crisis, the board ousted [cofounder Carol] Fox and replaced her with her assistant, Ardis Krainik, who almost immediately brought solvency to the Lyric…. When the much-loved Krainik died, in 1997, she was succeeded by Mason, who has zealously adhered to her fiscal policies.

He has built on the Krainik legacy of fiscal caution within the context of artistic excellence but is alert to the possibility of erosion of the subscription base if productions veer too far from what Chicago expects…. "My goal for the company is for it to continue to remain healthy and prosperous, producing excellent and varied work. When I took the job, my only thought was to leave the company in as good a shape as it was when I found it. Personally, that's still my goal."

Source: Originally published in *Opera News*, Volume 72, No. 3 (September 2007). Reprinted with permission.

FUTURE LEADERSHIP?

As more arts organizations move away from the founder–director leadership structure, the trend seems to be toward adopting the multiple-manager leadership model. The older, intuitive leaders with great charismatic appeal seem to be fading from the scene. Corporate structures and distributed leadership may be the only way that arts organizations can gain the required fundraising credibility in the community, but it seems doubtful that this is a formula for artistic leadership that goes beyond a safe, conventional approach. There are many examples of arts organizations founded in the 1970s that are now cornerstones in regional arts consortiums. Obviously, artistic leadership need not succumb to conventionality just because it is accepted in the community. However, since so much money for the operation of arts organizations comes from ticket sales and regional fundraising, there is a point at which controversial leadership becomes a detriment to the organization.

MOTIVATION AND THE ARTS WORK SETTING

No discussion of leadership would be complete without examining the area of individual and group motivation and the communication process. To lead effectively, you must understand basic concepts about what motivates individuals to make them want to work and create. At the same time, most of the activity that occurs in an arts organization revolves around groups. As we have seen, organizations are divided into work groups that ideally should match the operational and planning objectives that the organization has established. Creating, maintaining, and keeping these work groups productive is one of the manager's major leadership responsibilities. To work with individuals and groups, you must communicate your expectations and objectives, and the people you work with also must effectively communicate their progress and problems to you.

Let's look at the area of motivation first. The people who make up a large segment of an arts organization are usually highly self-motivated. The discipline and motivation required to become a singer, dancer, actor, designer, or musician are not universally found in society. Ideally, professional performers need not be told to learn their lines, practice the music, or rehearse the movements. However, we do not live in an ideal world. People respond in often unpredictable ways to various challenges they face in work and in life. Therefore, even the most gifted and motivated may benefit from carefully structured communications that help them achieve their goals.

THEORIES OF MOTIVATION

Motivation theories and applications arise from research in psychology. These applications are directed toward the workplace and making workers more productive. Researchers have identified four broad theory areas: need, cognitive, reinforcement, and social learning. *Need theories* "argue that we behave the way we do because of internal needs we are attempting to fulfill."[28] *Cognitive theories* attempt to isolate the thinking patterns we use in deciding whether or not to behave in a certain way."[29] *Reinforcement theory* relies heavily on the *law of effect*, which states that "behaviors having pleasant or positive consequences are more likely to be repeated and behaviors having unpleasant or negative consequences are less likely to be repeated."[30] Lastly, *social learning theory* "argues that learning occurs through the continuous interaction of our behaviors, various personal factors, and environmental forces.[31] (See Figure 8.2.)

Need theories

Abraham H. Maslow's 1954 book *Motivation and Personality*[32] created a foundation on which many business psychologists have built. Maslow proposed that humans have five levels of needs arranged in a hierarchy of importance. These fall into lower order needs (physiology, safety, and society) and higher order needs (esteem and self-actualization). The system is based on the assumption that *only unmet needs act as motivators*. The other key principle is that these *needs are arranged in a strict hierarchy*. The implication is that an individual can move to the next level only after satisfying the needs in the next lower level.

Maslow's theory has been embraced by much of the business world, but that does not mean that it can explain all facets of human behavior. Cultural differences, the reality that strict hierarchy does not always describe how people behave in a work environment, and the fact that people's needs change over time are not easily accommodated by Maslow's theory.

Researcher Clayton Alderfer proposed an alternative to Maslow's hierarchy known as *ERG Theory*. His approach took the five need levels and compressed them to three: *existence, relatedness,* and *growth* (ERG). Existence needs cover things such as food, water, shelter, and work-related desires such as pay, benefits, and the actual working conditions. Relatedness needs encompass things such as relationships with friends and families, work groups, and professional associations. Our desire to be accepted by others and to have some control over our lives also falls under this classification. Growth needs cover things such as creativity and innovation. Alderfer argues that we could be concerned with more than one level at a time and that if we are continually frustrated from reaching a level such as growth, we may cease to be concerned about that need. This concept was expressed in what he called the *frustration-regression principle*.[33]

In an arts organization, Maslow's theory may be applied by the leader providing a job in a comfortable work environment (physiological need) that does not endanger health (safety need), has a degree of group stability (social needs), recognizes good performance (esteem need), and offers opportunities for creativity (self-actualization need). For example, if the actors fear for their lives whenever they go out on the stage because the overhead stage rigging system is dangerous, their safety and physiological needs are not being met. In this situation the actor is not likely to give as good a performance given their anxiety about the rigging system.

Alderfer's frustration–regression principle might be exhibited by a qualified employee who is working for a supervisor who is not particularly effective at their job. The museum research assistant may have skills and abilities to be much more effective than her boss, but they are held back because the leadership of the organization does not want to fire the supervisor. The research assistant may then throttle back suggesting improvements in the museum operation because she knows no one will listen.

Two-factor theory

Frederick Herzberg and B. Syndermann's 1959 book *The Motivation to Work*[34] became the cornerstone for another need theory of motivation. This study focused on what the authors called the *two-factor theory* of motivation. The *hygiene factors* were items that seemed to make individuals dissatisfied with their jobs. For example, people may become less motivated if they think their pay, benefits, company policies, or the working conditions are not as they perceive they should be. *Motivators* were identified as things such as achievement, responsibility, the work itself, recognition, growth, and personal achievement.

The limited scope of the study on which the two-factor theory is based (only about 200 engineers and accountants) invalidates the theory for some critics. For example, by only studying professionals, Herzberg and Syndermann do not address the fact that hygiene and motivational factors might differ for hourly employees. In other words, the staff members in the marketing department of a performing arts center will probably have different perceptions about motivators than the stagehands who unload the trucks at the loading dock.

However, the limited nature of the study does not necessarily totally invalidate the two-factor concept. Managers may obviously adjust the range of hygiene and motivational factors for particular work groups. For example, most employees like recognition. Prominently displayed "employee-of-the-month" plaques with photographs and accompanying praise for some accomplishment can boost morale. Unfortunately, the two-factor theory does not provide much guidance on how the motivational factors can be translated into measurable increases in productivity.

Acquired-needs theory

The last needs-related motivational theory is a product of psychologist David C. McClelland's research. His studies focused on three needs: achievement, affiliation, and power.[35] The need for achievement, in McClelland's view, was a "desire to accomplish challenging tasks and achieve a standard of excellence in one's work."[36] Affiliation was seen as "the desire to maintain warm, friendly relationships with others,"[37] and power was "the desire to influence and control one's environment."[38] He further broke power down to *personal power* and *institutional power*.[39] Some individuals enjoy using power over others, and others are able to work in organizational settings to express their power needs.

McClelland developed the Thematic Apperception Test as a measurement tool to assess the degree to which individuals were motivated by these varying needs. In this theory, one could posit that an individual with a strong need for affiliation would probably not be successful in a high-level leadership position because his primary motivation would interfere with the requirements of exercising power and control over people and organizations. A good director, conductor, and choreographer will probably exhibit strong needs to achieve. Their success in different institutional settings will depend to some degree on how strong their needs for power and affiliation are. For example, high-powered and driven guest artists brought into an academic environment may find that they lack the affiliation needs required to successfully relate to students and to carry on positive work relationships with others.

Cognitive theories

We now turn to two of the cognitive theories of motivation. Essentially, these theories look at how people think about their jobs and their work. The theories attempt to isolate the patterns of thought people use in deciding which behaviors to choose. It is assumed that people find their own sources of motivation and dissatisfaction in the workplace.

Equity theory

The equity theory of motivation is based on J. Stacy Adams' work in the 1960s.[40] The theory states that *a perceived inequity functions as a motivator*. When employees believe that they are not treated equitably, they are motivated to try to change the source of the perceived inequity. Employees perceive inequities whenever they feel that they are not rewarded for their work at the same level as someone else who works equally hard. To resolve the equity conflicts, Adams predicts that employees will change how much work they do, try to get their salary increased, rationalize the inequity, or quit.[41]

Equity issues most often arise with highly separated work groups. For example, an arts organization might have union stage employees with a high school education who receive $30 per hour for their labor, and a market-ing assistant with a master's degree who receives the equivalent of $8.50 per hour. Based on a forty-hour work week, the stagehand could gross $62,400 a year while the marketing person might earn $17,680 (assume 52 weeks at 40 hours per week). It will not take long for the research assistant to pick up on these wage differences, thanks to the informal communication system in most organizations. According to Adams' equity theory, the research assistant will probably create some rationalization to minimize the inequity, or she will quit. If she approaches the head of the marketing area for a pay increase and is told that the budget is too tight, she may go back to work, but she will probably temporarily reduce her work output. The inequity will not go away. In fact, the problem may grow as the unhappy employee lets other employees know that they are receiving a lot less money for their hard work than others in the organization. The employee may also think, "If that's all you think I'm worth, then that's all the work you are going to get from me." The net result is dissatisfied employees with low motivation levels and less work output. Of course, our marketing assistant may also have long-term goals based on the assumption that a job that pays $8.50 an hour is not a reflection of her true skill and, in the short-term, she can accommodate the inequity. In a few years, she believes she will be the marketing manager or even the marketing direc-tor. Once she moves up the ladder she will be paid better and the perceived inequity will fade away.

Arts managers would do well to read up on equity theory. (For more informa-tion go to www.mindtools.com/pages/main/newMN_LDR.htm.) They must anticipate these equity issues and formulate some strategies to help employees. The employee's perspective is important here. For example, when it is time for contract negotiation with union employees, typically nonunion employ-ees will start talking about wage inequities. Managers might explain that the stagehands typically do not work year-round, so they do not make as much as other employees imagine. In fact, they may make less on average per year than salaried employees.

Expectancy theory

Another motivation theory often cited in management textbooks is the *expec-tancy theory*. Simply stated, Victor Vroom's theory postulates that people will be motivated to work if they expect that they will be adequately rewarded for their effort.[42] Expectancy theory has three major components: effort, perfor-mance, and outcome.

The first component is *effort-performance expectancy*.[43] The employee may ask how probable it is that he can actually perform at the required level. For example, if you are given a task such as updating a 20,000-name mailing list in two days, or building an entire set of stage platforms without any assistance in three days, your expectancy will be zero. On the other hand, your expectancy will probably be higher if you are given six weeks for the mailing list and three weeks for the construction project.

Next we assess the *performance-outcome expectancy*, or the belief that "our successful performance will lead to certain outcomes."[44] If you are told that you will receive an extra vacation day if you finish the mailing list or the construction project early, you must decide whether the value of the reward is worth the extra effort. In this example, since the value of your performance expectancy is so low ("I can't do all that work in that short a time!"), the outcome expectancy of getting a day off is equally low.

Outcome is also affected by the types of rewards the employee perceives are available. Vroom identifies *extrinsic rewards* as things such as a day off, a bonus or merit pay, awards, and promotions. *Intrinsic rewards* include things such as feelings of achievement, being challenged, or being given the opportunity to grow.[45]

The last component in Vroom's motivation theory is *valence*, or our assessment of the anticipated value of the various outcomes or rewards.[46] The motivational strength of rewards for the work effort is determined by the value we assign to these rewards. If, for example, you have not had a day off in weeks, that promised day may be a strong motivator despite the low expectancy that you can complete the task.

For the arts manager this expectancy theory suggests that you need to be aware of the performance-outcome when you are planning projects and creating tasks to accomplish. For example, suppose you assign four people to the mailing list project and you divide the task into four parts, 5,000 names each. You give an equal pay bonus to all four employees, even though only two of the four actually did the work on time. Have you not sent a mixed signal about your performance-outcome expectancy to the two employees who actually did the work on time? In this case, the motivational strength of the pay bonus is weakened for the high-achieving employees by the fact that the underachievers were paid the same.

Probably the most important element of this theory centers on the extrinsic and intrinsic rewards system you establish in your arts organization. The limited budget resources of arts organizations will probably curtail the use of monetary rewards as a motivator. A good source for ideas for non-monetary rewards may be found in Bob Nelson's book *1001 Ways to Reward Employees*.[47] He offers a comprehensive list of informal and formal awards as well as awards for specific achievement and activity awards.

Does this theory of motivation offer any help to arts managers? Yes. For example, you can influence expectancy by establishing a general attitude in your work group that the work is important and does make a difference. You can also hire and train people in the work group who are willing to accept the attitude you desire. You can influence preferences by developing an ongoing system of listening to employees' needs and guiding them toward results.[48]

Never underestimate the power of perception, and never assume that the people who work for you or who you work with have the same values and assign the same priority to the work to be done. Your effectiveness in a leadership role is dependent on your ability to motivate the people with whom you work. Understanding what motives them, what they perceive as a reward, and what they value in the workplace is a key element to your success.

Reinforcement theory

The third area of motivation falls under the broad heading of *reinforcement theory*. The motivational theories we have discussed up to now approach behavior from the perspective of how people perceive the value of work, how they satisfy needs, or how they try to resolve inequities. Reinforcement theory focuses on the behavior or the output of the person and does not concern itself with what may be behind or motivating the behavior. The use of *positive and negative reinforcement is the motivating force* that managers use in their leadership roles. As a manager, you cannot possibly know the psychological issues all of your employees bring to work with them. Your job is not to be their psychologist but their supervisor or leader. Reinforcement theory requires observing behavior and modifying it to support the mission of the organization. Let's take a quick look at this topic. (See Figure 8.2.)

Organizational behavior modification

Organizational behavior modification (OBM) is an approach that uses the principles of B. F. Skinner's research on human behavior.[49] *Operant conditioning*, a key element in the research, assumes that you can control behavior by manipulating its consequences. By using positive and negative reinforcement, you can increase desired behaviors or eliminate undesired behaviors.

Another key concept in the system is the *law of contingent reinforcement*, which states that for a reward to have maximum impact, it must be delivered only if the desired behavior is exhibited. Equally important is the *law of immediate reinforcement*, which states that the quicker the delivery of the reward after the desired behavior, the greater the reinforcement value.

This theory is often summarized as *antecedent, behavior, consequence* (ABC).[50] The antecedent is what precedes the actual behavior, and the consequence is the result of the behavior. For example, a policy about lateness to rehearsals establishes an antecedent; showing up on time is the desired behavior, and the consequence is starting on time. If a performer is late (the behavior) and there is no consequence (a fine?), reinforcement theory predicts that this person will continue to engage in this behavior. You may modify the behavior if you enforce a consequence that causes the person to change the behavior.

Does behaviorist theory have a place in an arts organization's leadership system? Yes, if carefully applied. For example, something as subtle as nodding in agreement occasionally during a meeting as your assistant makes a presentation about a new marketing plan can have a positive reinforcing effect.

As an example of behavior modification through *negative reinforcement*, suppose that you always make a point of saying, "I thought we had a no-smoking rule on stage in this theater," whenever you find the crew head smoking. Then one day you see that the employee is not smoking, and you walk by without saying anything. You stop nagging the employee when he stops the undesired behavior. Negative reinforcement, by the way, is not necessarily the best way to approach behavior modification. Unfortunately, for most of their lives, people hear only about the behaviors that they are not supposed to engage in. In some organizations, negative reinforcement is the main operating mode. It is often summarized by employees who say "The only time I get noticed around here is when I do something wrong."

As an approach to organizational leadership, behavior modification has been criticized because it focuses solely on extrinsic reinforcers. The complex reasons behind a particular behavior pattern are of little interest to the leader who relies on behavior modification. Critics argue that self-motivated and highly educated artists, who are independent and creative, will laugh at attempts to influence their behavior through simplistic, positive-reinforcement techniques. However, praise is a powerful leadership tool, and as a positive reinforcer, most people do not seem upset when it is used sincerely.

An aware arts manager who carefully and thoughtfully uses some components of operant conditioning usually cannot go wrong. A director, choreographer, or manager of any type will usually get better results with positive reinforcement than with negative reinforcement. Berating and belittling people usually instills hostility and resentment among employees or volunteers. Managers who believe that the only way to get top performance from their employees or volunteers through terror tactics are sadly out of touch with reality.

Social learning theory

The final motivational theory we will discuss is based on integrating cognitive and reinforcement theory. Albert Bandura's *social learning theory* posits that "learning occurs through the continuous interaction of our behaviors, various personal factors, and environmental forces."[51] The learning that in turn affects our behavior includes three cognitive processes: *symbolic processes*, *vicarious learning*, and *self-control*.[52] Let's look at how this theory may be applied in motivating employees.

The *symbolic processes* include how we use verbal and imagined symbols to process and store experiences in words and images. We also use *self-efficacy* to imagine and project goals and outcomes that we desire.[53] We would be motivated, for example, if we imagine the outcome of our completion of the labeling or platform construction project as leading to more significant or weighty tasks or a promotion.

Social learning theory also includes the concept that "*vicarious learning*, or observational learning, is our ability to learn new behaviors and/or assess their probable consequences by observing others."[54] For example, as a new employee, you observe a particular staff member who seems to be respected and rewarded for the way he does his job. You in turn model your behavior along the lines of this person and find reinforcement and rewards for doing so.

Lastly, we engage in forms of *self-control* in the workplace. We control our behavior and provide for our own self-rewards.[55] You may congratulate yourself for completing a project ahead of schedule by going out to dinner or simply giving yourself a break. In other words, social learning theory recognizes self-reinforcement as part of a behavioral response that motivates people.

In an arts organization the social learning theory can be applied as a motivational tool by establishing clear and visible rewards for learning and developing new skills. Encouraging and rewarding employees who acquire new skills or who provide models for interns should have a positive outcome. Establishing and supporting a corporate culture of learning makes a great deal of sense in a workplace that tends to attract highly educated people in the first place.

THEORY INTEGRATION

Figure 8.2 summarizes the various theories about leadership, motivation, and group dynamics discussed in this chapter. An arts manager would benefit from adopting a mix of these theories to create a system for leading the organization. The manager's objective is to be as effective as possible in getting people in the organization to achieve the results that support the organization's goals and objectives. It is not by chance or through the efforts of one person that an organization reaches and exceeds its goals. The motivational theories are tools to be used by the manager. Within an arts organization, some employee groups are motivated by extrinsic rewards, others by how they perceive their role and status, and still others by the need to achieve some degree of self-actualization.

It will take time and experimentation to find the best mix of motivators in any work situation. The investment of time by the leadership of an arts organization in establishing a coherent and effective motivational system will help maintain a positive work environment. The fact that so many organizations, arts and business, operate with motivationally and psychologically dysfunctional cultures speaks directly to the lack of training in working with people by the leadership and managers. It is safe to say that employees, no matter how highly educated or self-motivated, are not maintenance-free entities.

GROUP DYNAMICS

A fact of organizational life is that managers must work effectively with many different groups. Whether the group is formal or informal, when you put several people together, a collective behavior pattern emerges that is usually different from an individual acting singly. Therefore, someone in a leadership role should understand group dynamics, which is the actual behavioral output exhibited when the various standing groups interact on a daily basis within an organization.

Arts organizations are made up of several groups: a cast, corps de ballet, an ensemble, a crew, board of directors, committees, subcommittees, a task force, and so on. The effective leadership of all of these various groups can result in a dynamic, creative organization that has a positive impact on the community. Similarly, ineffective group leadership can result in low-quality events and productions, poor use of resources, high turnover of staff and board members, labor problems, and marginal community support. Let's look at some of the basic terms and concepts of group management and leadership. (See Figure 8.2.)

Group management activities and forms

A *group* is a collection of people who regularly interact with one another in the pursuit of one or more common objectives.[56] A *formal group* is created by the authority structure within an organization to transform inputs into product or service outputs.[57] For example, a theater company sets up a formal group (e.g., a cast) by deciding to do a play and present it to the public. A board of directors creates a formal group when it selects a personnel search committee to find a new museum director.

Organizations may establish permanent work groups to carry on specific operational activities. For example, the production staff in an opera company or the curatorial staff in a museum may meet regularly as a group to make plans, assign work, and evaluate progress. Temporary groups, such as a personnel search committee, may be established to accomplish a particular task. The group is disbanded after it completes the job.

An *informal group* is "one that emerges in an organization without any designated purpose."[58] These informal groups can satisfy employee needs for socialization, security, and identification.[59] Informal groups can also help people get their jobs done by establishing a network within an organization. For example, a production manager in an arts organization may establish a formal working relationship with the crew heads through regular staff meetings. However, various informal groups may form within the crews that can help or hinder the overall operation, such as a group (usually with an informal leader) centered on the belief that the production manager is incompetent. This informal group may try to influence others in the formal work group about the manager's incompetence. Soon, the production manager finds that things are not getting done or are done in the way that the informal group decides is best. Direct intervention by the formal leader of the group may be the only way to disrupt the influence of the informal group.

Types of groups

Various types of groups are formed in organizations, including command, task, interest, and committee groups.[60]

Command groups are established in an organizational chart by defining the working relationship between supervisors and subordinates. In Chapter 6, the Theater Company Organizational Chart (Figure 6.3) depicts the command group relationship between the managing director and the marketing, finance, and fundraising directors.

Task groups are groups of employees who work together to complete a project or job. A major portion of the activity in arts organizations is accomplished by task groups. Figure 6.8 depicts that "Show A" is a task group.

Interest groups form when employees unite around a particular issue. The members of this group could be from different work groups who are brought together to resolve a short-term problem. For example, when a symphony orchestra announces that, due to a shortfall in fundraising, all medical benefits for the regular staff will cease, an interest group forms to deal specifically with this issue.

Finally, we have the *committee*, which has been humorously defined as "the only life form with twelve stomachs and no brain."[61] The seasoned manager in an organization might see the operations of a committee falling under Old and Kahn's law: "The efficiency of a committee meeting is inversely proportional to the number of participants and the time spent on deliberations."[62] A more formal definition of a committee is "a group of two or more people created to perform a specific task."[63] A board of directors of an arts organization may establish standing committees to fulfill ongoing needs (e.g., a finance committee) or ad hoc committees to fulfill specific needs (e.g., the search committee).

Numerous books offer suggestions for making committees function effectively in organizations. Such issues as committee composition, size, clarity of purpose, and ability to bring resources to bear on a problem are covered in a variety of texts and business books. The disadvantages of compromised decisions, long deliberation periods, and expense are often cited in the literature. However, committees do tend to proliferate in organizations. Care must be taken to avoid using the committee approach to avoid taking individual responsibility for decisions.

Stages of group development

The study of groups shows that when a new group is formed, it typically undergoes five stages: forming, storming, norming, performing, and adjourning.[64]

In the *forming stage*, the group tries to establish its purpose, define its operational rules, establish the identity of members of the group and what they have to offer, and define how people will interact with each other. Any committee chair needs to recognize this list of organizing activities must be addressed to help successfully support the group in fulfilling its purpose.

The *storming stage* may be very emotional or relatively calm, depending on the personalities of the group members. For example, an ad hoc committee to examine employee benefits that is made up of staff and hourly workers could experience substantial personal style differences that take some time to work out. It could take several heated discussions to move everyone to a common agenda.

The *norming stage* is characterized by building group cohesiveness, developing consensus, and clarifying roles. It is typically at this stage that the group leader will emerge if one was not designated initially. Constructive ways of handling disagreement are eventually found, and group discussions allow differences to be expressed. Group members will feel more confident about their specific responsibilities and will help keep the group focused on the problems that must be solved.

As a group reaches the *performing stage* it begins to actively address its purpose. If the group leader is able to effectively engage everyone, the entire group should be contributing to the committee's work. Unfortunately, many groups do not reach this stage. More often than not there are a few members of the committee who actually work and a few who are marginal. The group still performs, just not as effectively as it could if everyone were contributing.

In the final stage, *adjourning*, the committee wraps up its work and disbands. For example, the board search committee completes its job and no longer needs to meet.

A group such as a cast of a play will go through some variation of this process as it moves from auditions to rehearsals. Other ensemble efforts share similar patterns of development in arts organizations.

An arts manager must watch vigilantly for committees that become dysfunctional. For example, some committees never achieve norming and performing. The committee output is often slow in coming or is marked by minority reports by differing subgroups that form within the larger committee.

Group norms and cohesiveness

Group norms is a familiar phrase related to leading and managing groups. Norms are the rules that guide group behavior.[65] The leader of a group must establish behavior norms ("One person talking at a time, please") as well as performance norms ("We must finish deliberations and report to the board by March 1.").

At the same time, a leader must develop cohesiveness among the group if it is to be effective. *Cohesiveness*, in this case, refers to the degree of motivation of members to stay in the group. For example, a running crew for a production is a task-specific group that often requires a high degree of cohesiveness. You can use specific circumstances, such as having to do a complex scene change in a limited time, as a way of building cohesiveness among a group. For example, if the performance norm is to complete the scene change in one minute, the group may be challenged to beat that norm and do the shift in 45 seconds. When this new norm is established, the group usually feels some sense of collective accomplishment, which is a way of building cohesiveness.

Successfully managing groups in an arts organization requires careful thought about establishing norms, performance expectations, and building cohesiveness. In arts organizations, group performance extends from the board through the construction shops. Let's look now at some of the problems that can arise with groups.

Dysfunctional group activities

One of the well-noted problems with groups that are too cohesive has been termed *groupthink*. In an article in 1971, Irving Janis defined the groupthink phenomenon as "a tendency for highly cohesive groups to lose their critical evaluative abilities."[66] Unless a member of the committee or work group is designated to be the devil's advocate, there is the danger that groupthink will establish itself in an organization. The peer pressure to appear to agree is enormous. A group leader should make it a point to have conflicting points of view aired before the group.

Some of the symptoms of groupthink are rationalizing data that contradict the expectation; self-censorship by group members; and creating an illusion of unanimity by stopping the discussion of a topic prematurely. As an example of groupthink, imagine a design-development discussion that includes a director, the designers, and key technical staff. The production manager, who is running the meeting, knows that the proposed set design is too big and expensive to produce, but the designer and director do not want to hear that. In fact, the director has said on several occasions, "Don't tell me what you can't do, tell me what you can do." The technical director has tried to tell everyone that this design is more than the shop can handle. Every time the technical director tries to bring up the subject of time, money, and personnel constraints, the production manager cuts off the conversation. The schedule dictates that construction start immediately. The group "decision" is really nothing more than a groupthink trap. The technical director knows it can't be done, but goes along with the group decision anyway. The shop proceeds to construct the set as designed. Later, when the show is over budget and behind schedule, the technical director may be asked, "Why didn't you say something before we started building the set?"

Strategies for making groups more effective

There are many predictable common problems that occur when people get together to function as a group. An aware manager leading a group must act immediately to stop these dysfunctional activities. Here are some behaviors you may find disrupting a meeting:[67]

- *Aggressiveness* — One or more members of the group uses an aggressive tone of voice to dominate the discussion. "Well that's a stupid idea. I think we should do this."

- *Blocking* — Committee members who go off on tangents or bring unrelated personal experiences in to the meeting can sidetrack discussion. For example, a season selection committee is trying to pick programming and one member chimes in with, "I remember several years ago when we performed a piece by Philip Glass, people walked out of the concert."

- *Self-confessing* — Sometimes committee members interject their personal non-group feeling into a meeting. In a budget planning discussion a committee member chimes in with, "I am uncomfortable with this investment plan, and it just seems to me we should be rethinking this whole approach."

- Competing — Some committee members think they must have the final idea on how something should be done. After a lengthy discussion about a change in the season schedule and as the group starts to approach consensus, a committee member offers, "Yes, well, that's all well and good, but I think my idea is best, and in fact, this current idea lacks merit."

- Seeking sympathy — Some committee members feel compelled to share their ideas for purposes that do not advance the agenda. For example, a ticket office manager uses the meeting as a chance to whine about how out of date his computers are. "If the budget committee would only pay attention to my pleas, this equipment is so slow and I just can't do my job with this junk."

- Special pleading — Our ticket office manager above not only seeks sympathy, but is also providing an example of someone trying to get a special need or pet project addressed by the committee.

- Horsing around — Some members of the committee may find that clowning, joking, or mimicking someone is enjoyable. While a little humor is always useful to move a group along, these types of behaviors are usually disruptive.

- Seeking recognition — On occasion you may have a committee member who feels it is necessary to propose extreme ideas or to try to dominate discussion. "I think we should do away with the concerts in the park. It is usually too hot outside in the summer, and I don't like sitting on the ground."

- Withdrawing — When a committee member becomes passive, doesn't engage in discussions, daydreams, doodles, or starts whispering to others, he is disrupting the meeting by withdrawing or acting preoccupied.

To counteract some of these behavioral problems in a meeting it would be wise to build in some simple behavior patterns as norms from the very beginning. The first set of behavior patterns falls under the heading of *task activities*, and the second group is called *maintenance activities*. Both support a set of healthy group interactions.

Edgar H. Schein, in his book *Organizational Psychology*, lists these *task activities* as:

1. Initiating: Setting agendas, giving ideas, defining problems, and suggesting solutions.
2. Giving and seeking information: Offering information directly related to the problem, asking others for ideas, and seeking facts.
3. Summarizing: Restating the highlights of the discussion can help keep everyone on track.

4. Elaborating: Clarifying ideas by citing relevant examples can help keep the group working effectively.

The *maintenance activities* include the following:

1. Gatekeeping: Allowing various members of the group to talk. Sometimes one person will try to dominate the discussion and direct the group to her opinion by monopolizing the discussion.
2. Following: Going along with the group and agreeing to try out an idea.
3. Harmonizing: When appropriate, reconciling differences and promoting compromise can help keep the group going.
4. Reducing tensions: Using humor as an antidote when the situation becomes emotional. This can help shift the energy of the group long enough to put the conflict in perspective.[68]

LEADERSHIP AND WORKING WITH THE BOARD OF DIRECTORS

Leaders in arts organizations will find people engaging in combinations of these group behaviors on a regular basis. Someone in the role of executive director or managing director would do well to actively engage in the strategies suggested by Schein to head off problems in the board and staff working relationship. Keeping board committees and subcommittees productive is hard work.

The dynamic between a board and the staff can be very fragile. Given the unfortunate tendency of humans to misunderstand or misinterpret the motives of others, an arts manager and leader must work very closely with the board president to address group dynamics problems when they arise. A smoothly run meeting is part of the art of being a leader. Sensing when a group is getting off track and bringing the discussion back to the issue at hand without heavy-handedness is a highly prized skill. Realizing that there are very practical methods you may use to keep a group on task and productive will help further the mission and goals of the organization.

An excellent resource for the arts manager working with a board chair may be found in the September–October 1996 *Harvard Business Review* article titled "The New Work of the Nonprofit Board" by Barbara Taylor, Richard P. Chait, and Thomas P. Holland. This article also appears in the Theatre Communications Group book titled, *The Art of Governance*. The article offers practical suggestions for shifting the focus of the board to issues that matter from being process driven.

Applying rules of order

It is also helpful for the arts manager to be familiar with a few of the basic concepts of Robert's Rules of Order.[69] Following Robert's Rules of Order would be a cumbersome way of doing business when you are running a weekly staff meeting. However, when it comes to the formal business meetings of the board or board committees, applying the principles and procedures specified by Robert's Rules can be helpful in keeping the meetings on track and ensuring the organization is operating in a legally responsible way.

The executive director, or whatever title applies to the CEO of the arts organization, works closely with the board chair to ensure the business meetings are run in an efficient and effective manner. One of the first assumptions should be that not everyone is familiar with the rules of running meetings. Developing a summary sheet of the basics of Robert's Rules for the board chair can be a helpful tool.

The typical key items about running a business meeting include how to establish the agenda, call the meeting to order, propose motions, accept motions, engage in discussion on a motion, take votes, and then adjourn the meeting. One of the underlying principles of Robert's Rules is meetings are to be democratically run and allow for the members of the board or committee to express their thoughts on the subject of the specific motion under consideration.

Running a meeting

For the meeting to be run democratically the person chairing the meeting, typically the board chair or board president, needs to allow for discussion on the topic before a vote is taken. For example, the typical process for approving or amending the budget of an arts organization first would be for the finance committee to hold a formal meeting to review it. In their meeting they may accept it or amend the budget as proposed by the staff business manager or finance director. Before taking a vote there normally would be discussion about the budget details with the staff, and then a vote would be taken by the committee to recommend the budget be brought to the board for approval.

Following Robert's Rules, the meeting would start with the finance committee chair calling the meeting to order and then making a motion to approve the yearly budget and then to seek a second from another committee member. Once seconded, the chair would open the meeting for discussion about the budget. (The assumption is the committee members would have been provided with copies of the budget in advance.) Committee members would ask questions and seek clarification and explanations about the budget until they felt all the relevant issues were resolved. The committee chair would then close the discussion and ask for a vote. If a committee member still had questions, the discussion would continue. When the group had reached a satisfactory resolution to any concerns about the budget, a vote would be taken to recommend the budget be brought to the board for action at the next meeting.

At the board meeting, depending on where in the agenda the finance committee was scheduled, the committee chair would make a motion requesting the board approve the annual budget. The motion would need a second and then discussion by the whole board would take place. Of course, for the discussion to be meaningful, the finance committee, working with the staff and the board chair, should have distributed the budget to the board in advance of the meeting based on procedures stipulated in the organization bylaws.

If an amendment is made to the budget as presented, then that amendment needs to be approved first. Once the amendment is approved, the board then can vote on the "budget as amended." Assuming a majority of the board votes to approve the budget, then the organization staff can go forth and expend funds. Since one of the principle responsibilities of a board is to approve the budget for the organization, it behooves the CEO and the board to make sure the approval process is carried out in an orderly and professional manner.

In an ideal world this scenario of budget adoption and the application of Robert's Rules of Order would be the norm. Alas, the leadership of boards is just as susceptible to the same dysfunctions noted earlier in this chapter. Recognizing that some of the disruptive behaviors by board or committee members are bound to come up is a good starting place for the arts manager. Likewise, applying many of the tools to keep a meeting and committee members on track should offer some remedy for problems when they arise.

Typical Agenda for a Business Meeting

Here is a typical agenda for a business meeting of an arts organization. Please note that there are variations on this order of business. For example, many arts organizations may place various reports at the end of the meeting so action items or specific topics of concern to the group may be addressed earlier. One thing that can happen with the traditional agenda order proscribed by Robert's Rules is the important unfinished or new business items are at the end of the meeting. This often means the most interesting and engaging part of the meeting is occurring when board members are often eager to conclude what may have already been a two hour meeting. One thing to keep in mind is that with the approval of the board, the chair can reorder the agenda if it makes sense.

Agenda (simplified)

I. Call the meeting to order
II. Approval of the minutes of the previous meeting

III. Reports by the officers and standing committees (e.g., finance, marketing, development, planning, and so forth.)

IV. Reports by special committees, ad hoc committees or task force groups

V. Unfinished business (items left from the previous meeting that may require action)

VI. New Business

VII. Adjournment

Distributed leadership

For any organization to function effectively as a group, there must be a healthy interchange among its members. Arts organizations, especially performing arts organizations, spend a lot of time engaged in group activities. The management of these various group efforts calls for the recognition of the concept of *distributed leadership*. Simply put, it means that the group members share the leadership responsibility. As a member of a committee, a work group, or a cast, you share a responsibility to keep the group from becoming dysfunctional. Leaders who point out effective strategies and dangerous behaviors have the best chance of bringing distributed leadership to life for the group. As noted earlier, distributed leadership can create another layer of management and can add more bureaucracy in an arts organization. However, if all members of the group adopt the attitude that being a leader means making decisions, the organization does not have to become mired in inaction.

Good to Great in the Social Sectors

Jim Collin's monograph titled *Good to Great and the Social Sectors* offers some excellent insights into the whole issue of leadership as it applied to the not-for-profit business. His good to great principles include achieving what he calls "Level 5 Leadership." This level of leadership is subtitled "getting things done within a diffuse power structure." He goes on to note that "Legislative leadership relies more upon persuasion, political currency, and shared interests to create the conditions right for the decisions to happen."[70] There is a strong element of truth to this as it applies to the arts. Collins' monograph offers several excellent insights about leadership and management that an arts leader could capitalize on.

COMMUNICATION BASICS AND EFFECTIVE LEADERSHIP

Underlying the entire area of leadership is the assumption that good communication and listening skills are used daily in the workplace. Success as a manager in a leadership role directly relates to your ability to send, receive, interpret, monitor, and disseminate information. However, because the process of communication is so simple and at the same time so complex and subtle, we often overlook the obvious when we hunt for the source of a problem.

The consequences of miscommunication — ranging from the simple "go" on a cue by the stage manager that is misunderstood by the crew to the complex report by the director of finance that the board does not understand — can be devastating. A missed special effects cue may be life-threatening to a performer, and a misunderstood financial report may lead to bankruptcy for the enterprise.

Unfortunately, it is not hard to find the staff in an arts organization saying, "We have a communication problem around here." Whether this is true or not is irrelevant. If the phrase is repeated often enough, the perception that a communication problem exists will be created.

We next examine some of the basic terms and definitions in communications, and then explore some strategies to minimize the problems.

The communication process

We use the following definitions as a starting point.

Communication is the creation of meaning through the use of signals and symbols. Furthermore, meaning is defined as the perception that takes place when we formulate the relationship between two statements or images. Lastly, signals and symbols are key components in a message. Signals mean the messages which a communicator feels are beaming from a source, and they suggest very limited but concise meanings. Symbols suggest broader and more complex meanings assigned to the verbal and nonverbal language of the communicators.[71]

Let's take something as simple as coming into work in the morning to make a point about communication. Suppose that a museum director walks into work on Monday morning, scowls at everyone, goes into her office, and slams the door. This nonverbal symbolic behavior communicates a wealth of information to the office staff. People in the office speak more quietly and become anxious — "What's wrong?" Or, imagine that the director of a play watches a scene and says to the cast in a monotone, "Very good." The message is mixed. The verbal tone communicating a half-hearted endorsement contradicts the meaning of the words: "Very good" might mean "You did fine, but I really was not impressed."

As you can see from these examples, the communication process carries many nuances that have different meanings to people. Figure 8.3 depicts a graphic overview of the communication process. Let's briefly review what takes place in a typical interchange between two people.

Figure 8.3

Communication process.

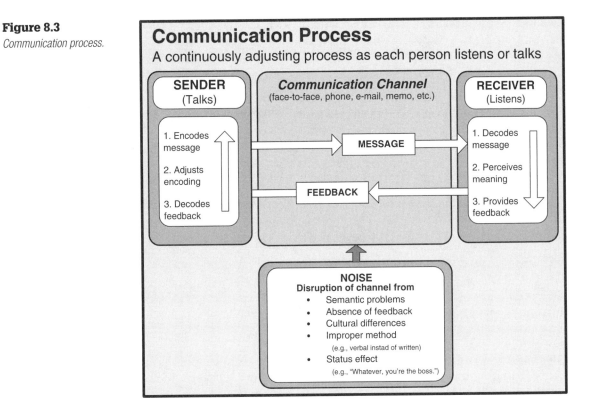

The communication process includes a *sender*, who *encodes* and delivers a message through a *communication channel*, and a *receiver*, who *decodes* the message and perceives *meaning*. The sender receives some *feedback* or an acknowledgment that the message has been received. At the same time, the communication channel is directly affected by *noise* that interferes with the message. Noise, in this case, means anything that disrupts the message or the feedback.

Perception

For the communication process to be effective, both the sender and the receiver should be aware of four key elements that modify the perception of the communication by each party. These four elements are stereotypes, the Halo Effect, selective perception, and projection.[72]

Stereotypes

When you speak of "dumb dancers," "techie types," or "musicians!" you are using *stereotypes*. When you refer to the board of directors as the "board," you are implying that they are all of one mind, and are classifying individual members as if they all acted and thought the same way. If you are to become a credible leader, you must abandon stereotypical thinking and the classifying of people.

Halo Effect

The *Halo Effect* is the perception of an individual based on one strong attribute. For example, a person who shows up late for a rehearsal or a meeting more than once will suddenly be known throughout the organization for "always being late." The Halo Effect can also be used positively. For example, a recent report on the long-term funding prospects for the organization may make a staff member a star just in time for the annual board meeting when, in fact, this individual has been coasting all year and does not deserve the praise.

Selective perception

Selective perception refers to noticing only those incidents or behaviors that reinforce what you already strongly believe about a situation or a person. You may choose not to see problems that particular employees are having because it is inconsistent with your perception of them.

Projection

When you project, you assign your personal attributes to someone else. The classic example of *projection* is when you assume that everyone who works for you shares your attitudes and beliefs about their job and the organization.

Formal and informal communication

Within an arts organization, formal and informal networks exist to communicate with and among employees. Managers must give constant attention to how well both systems are serving the organization's communication needs. Letters, memos, e-mail, text messages, small group meetings, forums, newsletters, the Web site, and annual meetings make up a part of the organization's formal communication system. At the same time, the informal communication system exists at every level in the organization. Phone conversations, waiting in line to use the copy machine, coffee breaks, and rehearsal breaks may all be touch points for informal communication. The informal system may seem impossible to manage, but by simply recognizing its existence and monitoring the information (or misinformation) communicated, a manager can creatively intervene when required.

A manager needs to assume there will be misunderstandings generated by the formal and informal communication systems in the organization. Keeping the communication system within the organization requires constant vigilance.

CONCLUSION

This chapter provided background on one of the most important areas in operating an arts organization: leadership. One question remains, "What makes a good leader?" As you have seen, it takes a great deal of hard work to be an effective leader. Having a vision of where you want to go, and being skilled in such areas as communication, interpersonal relations, and situation analysis are equally important.

In fact, being a leader means playing a role to some degree. Some people are very comfortable performing on a stage, making a presentation in front of a group, arguing a point, or carrying on an intensive negotiation. People you work with perceive your performance as a leader in much the same way that an audience perceives a performer and develops an impression of a character during the course of the show. A complex combination of body language, tone of voice, and ultimately the conviction with which you deliver your lines forms your coworkers' overall perception of and opinion about your leadership. If you are unsure and do not act committed to the idea or project, it will be hard to convince your "audience" that you have the leadership needed to see something through to the end.

Is there a lack of good leadership in many organizations? Sadly, yes. Coping with ineffective leadership is the topic of Muriel Solomon's *Working with Difficult People*.[73] Chapters such as "When Your Boss Is Belligerent," "When Your Boss Is Arrogant," and "When Your Boss Is Exploitative" depict real-world examples of less than effective leadership in the workplace. Good management and good leadership do exist. Although there are few studies of arts organizations, authors like Jim Collins (*Good to Great*) are reporting on companies that meet their goals and keep their people happy and productive. For arts organizations, with their never-ending struggle against limited resources, it is especially critical for the leadership to recognize and reward the hard work and sacrifices of its employees.

SUMMARY

Leadership is the use of power to influence the behavior of others. Power means getting others to do what you want. Formal leadership is granted to a manager by the organization. Informal leadership arises from special situations. A manager can draw on position power and personal power. Power is limited by acceptance theory and the zone of indifference.

Leadership theories have developed from trait studies that tried to identify leadership qualities by evaluating personal attributes. Behavioral theories are based on the study of a leader's attitudes about tasks and people. Contingency and situational theories work from the concept that leadership approaches must be adjusted based on the particular situation. Transactional leaders work to motivate people to perform tasks and achieve objectives and transformational leaders work to inspire people to exceed their capabilities.

An effective leader must understand the four main motivation theories and how they apply in the workplace. Need theories argue that we behave the way we do because of internal needs we are trying to fulfill. Maslow, Alderfer, the two-factor theory, and McClelland's acquired-needs theory all offer variations on the concept that we seek to meet needs such as recognition, self-esteem, responsibility, and growth, and to become self-actualized.

Various factors such as working conditions, pay benefits, and polices may act to reduce motivation.

Cognitive theories are based on isolating and studying the thought processes used to select work behavior; the idea is that people find their own sources of motivation in the workplace. Adams' equity theory argues that people use perceived inequities to motivate them to action. Vroom's expectancy theory states that we work most effectively when we believe the effort we put in will produce a desired outcome; if the probability of success is believed to be low, then we are less motivated to attempt the task or project. Reinforcement theory assumes that through operant conditioning and controlling rewards people are motivated to repeat behaviors that are productive to them and the organization.

Lastly, social learning theory integrates cognitive and reinforcement theories to create a model in which the continuous interaction of the behaviors of processing words and images, vicarious learning, and self-control motivates a person to action. Real-life situations require that managers recognize that different work groups are motivated by different things. Theory integration is a possible model.

Managers must lead and effectively work with groups. Both formal and informal groups are a part of every organization. Group dynamics include understanding what happens when people are brought together to achieve certain objectives. Norms of behavior and cohesiveness are key elements of group development. Like people, groups can become dysfunctional over time. Groupthink is one symptom of ineffective group management.

An effective leader understands and uses the communication process between people and among groups. Elements of the process include the sender, the receiver, the channel, and the effects of noise on communication.

For additional topics relating to leadership and group dynamics, please go to www.managementandthearts.com.

Questions

1. The use of power is a key component in leadership. Discuss examples from your work experience in which power was used effectively or ineffectively.

2. What are some additional examples of acceptance theory and the zone of indifference in the psychological contract people have in an arts organization?

3. Can trait theory be effectively applied in evaluating arts leadership? Explain.

4. A directive or autocratic leadership style is often exhibited in an arts setting. Is it possible to have a strong artistic vision for a project and a participative leadership style? Explain.

5. Cite examples in which situational leadership worked or failed in an arts setting.

6. Discuss the quote from the *Arts Leader Profile*. Mr. Krainik is quoted as saying, "When I took the job, my only thought was to leave the company in as good a shape as it was when I found it." What is your assessment of this statement within the context of all the leadership models covered in this chapter?

7. Analyze a recent motivation problem you encountered in your work or educational setting. What steps would you have taken to motivate the individual or group involved?

8. Can you cite a recent example from your own experience of a dysfunctional group? How would you have solved the problem knowing what you do now about group behavior?

CASE STUDY

The article below provides a glimpse into the circumstances surrounding the departure of an executive in an arts organization. As you will see, the board took an action that falls under the category of forcing a leadership change. As we have seen in this chapter, a positive working relationship between the board and the executive director is critical and clearly fragile.

Philharmonic director resigns
November 29, 2007

The executive director of the Rhode Island Philharmonic has resigned after he was told he was being let go. David Wax, who joined the orchestra in 2001 after more than a dozen years at the helm of the Houston Symphony, submitted his resignation to the board last week.

Board president Almon C. Hall was tight-lipped yesterday about Wax's resignation, saying only that the board is looking for a change of leadership to take the organization to a "totally new level." He would not discuss what, if any, shortcomings the orchestra found in Wax's performance.

But in a letter dated Nov. 16, Wax wrote, "you recently informed me of your decision reached after your consultation with other members of the board that a change in executive leadership is required." He added that he was resigning.

The letter was sent to the board and read to a reporter by a board member who asked not to be identified.

"Wax submitted his resignation to the full board at the Nov. 21 meeting," said Hall, during which a vote was taken. He would not discuss the outcome of the vote.

As executive director, Wax handles all the business dealings of the orchestra, including establishing budgets and negotiating contracts. Hall would not say how much the job pays. [Author's

CASE STUDY (CONTINUED)

note: According to the Rhode Island Philharmonic's 990 report in 2005 the executive director's salary was $154,202.]

Wax was no more forthcoming than Hall, saying he was not comfortable discussing the content of his letter. He said he agreed Hall should speak on behalf of the orchestra and he wasn't "interested in stirring anything up."

Meanwhile, Philharmonic conductor Larry Rachleff was not consulted about the move to oust Wax and was taken by surprise when Wax told him after the Philharmonic's Nov. 17 concert that he had resigned.

"I really thought with David Wax we had a consummate professional, said Rachleff from his home in Houston.

Rachleff called Wax, 66, one of the profession's most experienced and talented managers. We have been lucky to have his leadership." He said his relationship with Wax was "wonderful."

The departure of Wax, who has a doctorate in political science from Harvard University, comes at a crucial time for the 63-year-old orchestra, which is in the middle of a $12-million fund drive. The money will be used to bolster the orchestra's endowment and fix up its new home in East Providence, a 50,000-square-foot complex that once housed the Meeting Street School. The orchestra, with a $4.6-million budget, also runs a music school, which will use much of that space for classrooms and rehearsal space.

This is also the time when Wax and Rachleff are planning next year's season.

Wax won't be leaving for a while, though. He said he is willing to stay on to help with the transition to a successor. But he said he probably won't stay past February.

"There is only a certain amount of time you can spend as a lame duck and be effective," he said.

Source: "Philharmonic Director Resigns," by Channing Gray, *The Providence Journal*, November 29, 2007. Used with permission.

Discussion Questions

1. The article points out the orchestra is in the middle of major fundraising campaign. By taking this action to "let go" the executive director what might be some of the ramifications on the fundraising of the orchestra?

2. When the board president indicates they were "looking for a change in the leadership to take the organization to a 'totally new level,'" what do you imagine that means? What might a "totally new level" mean to an arts organization or to this orchestra?

3. The executive director indicated a willingness to stay on "to help with the transition to a successor." If you were the board president would you take him up on the offer? If yes, why? If no, why not?

ADDITIONAL RESOURCE

Another self-assessment tool that can prove helpful may be found in Tom Rath's book *Strength Finder 2.0* (see #15 in the list on the next page). Rath takes the approach that we are better off identifying our strengths and talents rather than trying to overcome weaknesses. He argues that focusing on our weaknesses takes time and energy away from doing what we are good at. His book includes an access code to an online test you can take to identify your strengths. For more information go to www.strengthsfinder.com.

LEADERSHIP BOOKS AND RESOURCES

1. Judith M. Bardwick. *Danger in the Comfort Zone.* New York: American Management Association, 1995.

2. Robert C. Benfari. *Understanding and Changing Your Management Style.* San Francisco: Jossey-Bass Inc., 1999.

3. Warren Bennis. *Why Leaders Can't Lead.* San Francisco: Jossey-Bass Inc., 1997.

4. Warren Bennis. *On Becoming a Leader.* Cambridge, MA: Perseus Publishing, 1989 and 2003.

5. Kenneth H. Blanchard, Paul Hersey, and Dewey E. Johnson. *Management of Organizational Behavior*, 8th ed. Englewood Cliffs, NJ: Prentice Hall, 2001.

6. Stephen R. Covey. *The 8th Habit.* New York: Fress Press, Simon & Shuster, Inc., 2004.

7. Peter Drucker. *The Effective Executive: The Definitive Guide to Getting the Right Things Done.* New York: Harper Business Essentials, 2006.

8. Richard L. Hughes, Katherine Colarelli Beatty. *Becoming a Strategic Leader.* San Francisco: John Wiley & Sons, Inc., 2005.

9. Phillip L. Hunsaker, Anthony J. Alessandra, *The Art of Managing People.* New York: Touchstone Books, Simon and Schuster, Inc., 1986.

10. Barbara Kellerman. *Bad Leadership.* Boston: Harvard Business School Press, 2004.

11. James M. Kouzes, Barry Z. Posner. *The Leadership Challenge*, 4th ed. San Francisco: Jossey-Bass Inc., 2007.

12. John C. Maxwell. *The 360° Leader.* Nashville, TN: Thomas Nelson Publishers, 2005.

13. Henry Mintzberg. "The Manager's Job: Folklore and Fact." *Harvard Business Review* (July–August 1975).

14. Emily Kittle Morrison. *Leadership Skils: Developing Volunteers for Organizational Sucess.* Tucson, AZ: Fisher Books, 1994.

15. Tom Rath. *Strengths Finder 2.0.* New York: Gallup Press, 2007.

16. *Leadership in Organizations: Current Issues and Key Trends*, edited by John Storey, New York: Routledge, 2004.

17. Marilyn Taft Thomas. *Leadership in the Arts: An Inside View.* Bloomington, IN: AuthorHouse, 2008.

REFERENCES

1. John R. Schermerhorn, Jr., *Management for Productivity*, 2nd ed. (New York: John Wiley & Sons, 1986), p. 275.

2. Ibid., p. 276.

3. Ibid., p. 276.

4. Ibid., p. 46.

5. Ibid., p. 279.

6. Ibid., p. 279.

7. Ibid., p. 279.

8. Ibid., p. 279.

9. Ibid., p. 280.

10. Ibid., p. 280.

11. Ibid., p. 280.

12. Chester Barnard, *The Functions of the Executive* (Cambridge, MA: Harvard University Press, 1938), pp. 165–166.

13. Schermerhorn, *Management for Productivity*, pp. 280–281.

14. John R. Kotter, "Acquiring and Using Power," *Harvard Business Review* 55, July–August 1977, pp. 130–132.

15. Stephen R. Covey, *The 8th Habit* (New York: Free Press, A division of Simon & Shuster, 2004), p. 352.

16. Kathryn M. Bartol, David C. Martin, *Management*, 3rd edition (Boston: Irwin McGraw-Hill, 1998), p. 417.

17. Fred E. Fielder, *A Theory of Leadership Effectiveness* (New York: McGraw-Hill, 1967).

18. Victor H. Vroom, Phillip W. Yetton, *Leadership and Decision Making* (Pittsburgh: University of Pittsburgh Press, 1973).

19. Bartol and Martin, *Management*, p. 429.

20. Ibid., p. 429.

21. Ibid., p. 430.

22. Ibid., p. 431.

23. Ibid., p. 434.

24. Ibid., p. 434.

25. John C. Maxwell, *The 360° Leader* (Nashville, TN: Thomas Nelson, Inc., 2005).

26. Ibid., p. 6.

27. Warren Bennis, *Why Leaders Can't Lead* (San Francisco: Jossey-Bass, Inc., 1989).

28. Bartol and Martin, *Management*, p. 385.

29. Ibid., p. 392.

30. Ibid., p. 400.

31. Ibid., p. 405.

32. Abraham H. Maslow, *Motivation and Personality* (New York: Harper and Row, 1954).

33. Bartol and Martin, *Management*, p. 388.

34. Frederick Herzberg, B. Syndermann, *The Motivation to Work* (New York: John Wiley & Sons, 1959).

35. Bartol and Martin, *Management*, p. 389.

36. Ibid., p. 390.

37. Ibid., p. 390.

38. Ibid., p. 391.

39. Ibid., p. 391.

40. J. Adams Stacy, "Toward an Understanding of Inequity," *Journal of Abnormal Psychology* 67, 1963, pp. 422–436.

41. Schermerhorn, *Management for Productivity*, pp. 338–340.

42. Victor Vroom, *Work and Motivation* (New York: John Wiley & Sons, 1964).

43. Bartol and Martin, *Management*, p. 392.

44. Ibid., p. 393.

45. Ibid., p. 393.

46. Ibid., p. 394.

47. Bob Nelson, *1001 Ways to Reward Employees* (New York: Workman Publishing, 2005).

48. James H. Donnelly, James L. Gibson, and John M. Ivancevich, *Fundamentals of Management*, 7th ed. (Homewood, IL: BPI-Irwin, 1990), pp. 313–316.

49. B. F. Skinner, *Science and Human Behavior* (New York: Macmillan, 1953); B. F. Skinner, *Contingencies of Reinforcement* (New York: Appleton-Century-Crofts, 1969).

50. John N. Marr, Richard T. Roessler, *Supervision and Management* (Fayetteville, AK.: University of Arkansas Press, 1994), pp. 9–12.

51. Bartol and Martin, *Management*, p. 405.

52. Ibid., p. 405.

53. Ibid., p. 405.

54. Ibid., p. 405.

55. Ibid., p. 406.

56. Schermerhorn, *Management for Productivity*, p. 359.

57. Ibid., p. 359.

58. Ibid., p. 361.

59. Ibid., p. 361.

60. Donnelly, Gibson, and Ivancevich, *Fundamentals of Management*, pp. 346–347.

61. Arthur Bloch, *The Complete Murphy's Law* (Los Angeles: Price-Stern-Sloan, 1990), p. 48.

62. Ibid., p. 71.

63. Arthur G. Bedeian, *Management* (New York: Dryden Press, 1986), p. 508.

64. Bartol and Martin, *Management*, p. 490.

65. Schermerhorn, *Management for Productivity*, pp. 370–371.

66. Ibid., p. 374.

67. J. William Pfeiffer, John E. Jones, eds., *Annual Handbook for Group Facilitators* (San Diego: Pfeiffer and Co., 1976).

68. Edgar H. Schein, *Organizational Psychology*, 2nd ed. (Englewood Cliffs, NJ: Prentice-Hall, 1970), p. 81.

69. Robert McConnell Productions, *Robert's Rules of Order: Simplified and Applied*, 2nd ed. (Indianapolis, IN: John Wiley Publishing, 2001), pp. 14–16.

70. Jim Collins, *Good to Great and the Social Sectors*, A monograph to accompany *Good to Great*, 2005, Jim Collins, p 11.

71. John J. Makay, Ronald C. Fetzer, *Business Communication Skills: Principles and Practice*, 2nd ed. (Englewood Cliffs, N.J.: Prentice-Hall, 1984), pp. 5–6.

72. Schermerhorn, *Management for Productivity*, pp. 310–315.

73. Muriel Solomon, *Working with Difficult People* (Englewood Cliffs, NJ: Prentice-Hall, 2002).

CHAPTER 9

Operations and Budgeting

KEY WORDS

Operational control system
Output and input standards
Internal and external controls
Management by exception (MBE)
Management by objectives (MBO)
Performance appraisal system
Management information
   system (MIS)
Budgets

Fixed and flexible budgets
Zero-based budgets
Short- and long-term budgets
Budgetary process
Budget control system
Summary budget
Detailed budget
Project budget
Cash flow projections

Before we move on to the topics of finance, economics, marketing, and fundraising, we need to examine the areas of operational control, management information systems, and budgets. We have seen how planning helps set the organization's direction and establish financial resource needs. We have studied the organizing process to see how best to bring together people and resources. Our discussion of the leadership part of the process focused on effectively directing people in the utilization of resources. We now look at operational control, the part of the management process that ensures that the right things happen, in the right way, and at the right time.[1] We will also study how organizations need to establish internal communication systems and budgets as part of the overall control system in an organization.

In an arts organization, the very word *control* carries connotations that often make people uncomfortable. People generally do not like to think of themselves as being controlled by others. At the same time, however, they are not comfortable in situations that could be described as being "out of control."

If an arts manager is to lead an organization successfully, systems of control in the operation must be in place and must function effectively. Far too often we hear of the results of a faulty control process in an arts organization, particularly as it pertains to budget. When you read about an arts organization that incurred an unanticipated deficit of $200,000 in one season, you have to ask yourself how this could happen. The assumption is that the budgetary and financial control systems must have broken down. After all, a $200,000 deficit does not just appear in a budget report one day. Or, as this chapter case study demonstrates, you may have an employee who steals from the organization (See Ex-official of Orchestra Tells Court He's a Thief).

OPERATIONAL CONTROL AS A MANAGEMENT FUNCTION

We will use the term *operational control* to mean "a process of monitoring performance and taking action when needed to ensure that the desired results are achieved."[2]

The factors that affect the design of any operational control system are the *clarity of the objectives, uncertainty, complexity, human limitations,* and the *degree of centralization* in the organization. Let's briefly examine each of these factors.

First, *clarity* is needed if the staff and board are to help achieve the objectives. For example, setting an objective of increasing ticket sales by 20 percent when the data indicate the organization's ticket sales growth pattern has been 3 to 4 percent is probably not very realistic. Unless the detailed action plans supporting the objective offer new sales approaches, there is little likelihood the organization will achieve the objective. Therefore, establishing a control to measure progress (e.g., weekly sales reports) will probably show how unrealistic the objective was.

Secondly, as noted in Chapter 5, Planning and Decision Making, *uncertainty* exists in all planning. Every organization must assume there will always be a level of uncertainty as the season progresses, and the control system must take this into account. One useful way of accommodating uncertainty is to create "What if" scenarios. For example, what if the critical reaction to the new play is largely negative and audiences stay away in droves? Or, what if the critics love the show and ticket demand necessitates extending the number of performances? Does the production schedule allow for capitalizing on a success? If it does not, how can the organization build more flexibility into its schedule to permit extending the runs of specific shows?

If there is no system in place for addressing uncertainty, the organization, in this example, could lose thousands of extra dollars in much needed sales revenue.

A situation such as this becomes a control point at which you may make adjustments in the activities performed. The whole notion of self-assessment and measuring the outcome of the events the organization sponsors assumes an effective control system is in place.

Over time, *complexity* tends to be a by-product of organizational growth. The controls required to monitor increasingly complex activity in an organization often lag behind growth. For example, if you shift from processing all of your ticket and subscription revenue through your own box office to a new performing arts center, your old control system for tracking revenue will probably be inadequate for the new system. At the same time, you are still going to need accurate, up-to-date reports. New processes and procedures will be put in place and the level of complexity will most likely increase.

All operational control systems also must take into account *human limitations*. Errors will be made. An incorrect amount will be entered in the computer, an order form will be misplaced, a costume or set piece will be constructed incorrectly, or a purchase order or invoice will be lost. Errors carry with them varying risks. If the data entry error makes it appear the organization has thousands more in revenue than it actually has, the entire budget could be thrown off track. The costumes must be rebuilt and the overtime costs to do so puts the costume budget in the negative. The control system must recognize that these things (and many more) will happen.

The basic design of your organization may require different control processes because of the *degree of centralization* or *decentralization*. If you operate a decentralized organization, authority will normally be delegated to more people in middle- and lower level management positions. Control systems that ensure accountability will be required. For example, if the scenery construction shop is ten miles from the administrative offices, you do not want to make a staff member drive over to the office every time a purchase order needs a signature. Instead, you will probably delegate the authority to approve purchases up to a designated amount to a staff member at the shop. An operational control system would include a weekly review by one of the accounting staff of purchase orders and invoices from the shop. Why? Because purchases could be made that were inappropriate. For example, why is the shop manager purchasing food supplies for the shop from a grocery store? The accounting staff provides some oversight through their review of the weekly spending activities.

ELEMENTS OF THE OPERATIONAL CONTROL PROCESS

There are four steps in the operational control process: establishing performance objectives, measuring results, comparing the actual outcome with the

Figure 9.1

The operational control process.

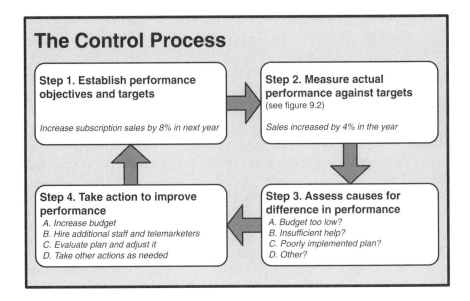

objectives, and implementing corrective procedures.[3] Figure 9.1 is a diagram of this process using an example of a missed sales target.

The first area to examine in the control system is that of the *performance objectives*. What were the expectations about how much, how good, how expensive, or how timely the work performed was? How many membership or subscription orders do you want to process in a day, in a week, in a month, in a year? How was the audience reaction to the concert, or play? What do the comment cards say about what the gallery visitors thought of the exhibit? How many costumes were supposed to be built in a two-week period? How far along should the painting of the set be after two weeks?

The second step in the control process is to *measure and compare* what was achieved. How much did sales increase? Is the audience still giving the performances standing ovations after two weeks? How long did it take to build the scenery or make the costumes? For the measurement system to work you must have the mechanisms in place to track the responses or data and compare it to reasonable time frame.

The third step requires an *assessment of what caused the difference* between your objective and the actual results. Was there a lack of resources, poorly trained staff, high turnover, or weak management? Why have the performances stopped getting standing ovations? Has one or more of the performers lowered the intensity of their performance energy? Were the fabrics ordered on time? Were the fabric patterns made in time? Was the gel ordered soon enough?

The fourth step culminates in taking *action to correct the problem*. Assuming that your control system is providing feedback in a timely manner, you may increase staff, institute new training programs, or replace the manager leading the work group. You may call a special brush up rehearsal with the cast. In the production example, you may need to intervene immediately if a deadline has been missed.

The operational control system extends into areas that may not be as easily quantified. For example, what is the appropriate output standard for the rehearsal process of a play, opera, dance, or concert, or for the preparation of an exhibition or special event? Assuming that all of these events have a deadline for an "opening night," the person in the leadership role (director, choreographer, and others) must make it clear through the schedule what will be expected during the preparation stage for the event. However, if no one monitors the process, the control system breaks down. For example, if the artistic director is directing a play and spends the first five weeks of a six-week rehearsal period on the first act, who is in a control position to take corrective action? The stage manager may point out that the play is behind schedule, but if the person in charge of the whole operation does not stick to the schedule as written, there isn't much to be done.

For some arts organizations, there may be very limited solutions available for an ineffective or dysfunctional control system. For example, the manager in a position of authority may hold others to the established output standard while personally ignoring it. The net result is an organization in a constant state of panic about getting an event ready for opening.

This is a circumstance where strong board leadership could influence the operational control systems. For example, the board president and the personnel committee could mandate that a different working relationship between an artistic director and a managing director be established. The board would have to grant the managing director authority to monitor the schedule and take corrective action when required. Under this scheme, the managing director would point out at the appropriate times that the published rehearsal schedule is not being followed. She would request adjustments in the schedule be made, and it is hoped, the show gets back on schedule.

In the real world, of course, it is much harder to get people to accept intervention in their projects. It is often the case in arts organizations that people occupy multiple positions of control. The artistic director may be very effective at setting the output standards for a guest director and others in the organization, yet react negatively to criticism for falling behind schedule themselves.

Ultimately, the ability of the organization to realize its mission depends on how well the operational control systems function. There are countless ways things can go wrong in an organization. The working assumption should be that there are many factors that could positively or negatively affect the overall quality of what we are trying to do and we need to anticipate them.

Input standards

Another component of the control process is to set *input standards*. This process involves evaluating the effort that goes into a task. One way to evaluate the work is to look at how well the person used the available resources. For example, a staff member might ask for two extra helpers to complete the subscription orders within the six weeks allotted for the task. If the orders actually take nine weeks to complete and, halfway through the schedule, two more people had to be hired, the supervisor might wonder about the staff member's ability to estimate the resources needed to complete a project.

Once you have put in place the input standards you need to establish objectives for output. There are many ways of measuring performance in an arts setting. In some cases, a manager can define clearly the quantitative measures and communicate them to the employees. For example, a manager expects at least 25 subscription orders to be processed each day. The actual number of orders filled in one day gives the manager a specific piece of information. A lower output would lead to an investigation of the work process, and it may be found that by changing the order in which the work is completed, the average number of orders filled daily exceeds 25.

Alternatively, a director can indicate when she expects the cast to be off book (to have memorized their lines). The critical work of establishing the output objectives for the cast can begin in earnest when they are not carrying a script. The director or choreographer knows the cast or ensemble can't move the work along as long as they are still learning the lines or the movement phrases.

Since many areas in an arts organization deal with specialized craftwork and custom construction techniques, it is much harder to make accurate projections about the performance level of a staff member. Suppose that eight chairs must be built for a dining room scene in a production. The shop supervisor asks the properties master how long it will take to build the chairs, and they agree on five days as the output standard. At the end of that period, only three chairs have been completed. The shop supervisor notes that the expected output level was not met and intercedes to change the input standard. Two extra people are assigned to assist the properties master to complete the remaining chairs.

The previous examples demonstrate how a manager will compare the actual performance with the standards they have established and make adjustments to correct any problems. The success of any of the projects cited in these examples depends on active and involved management of the control process.

In an arts setting, the critical work of all of the creative artists must also undergo a similarly active interaction with management. For performers, the roles they act or sing and the music they play represent a complex mix of talent, ego, and ensemble interaction. How do you set standards, evaluate performance, and take corrective action when a performer does not measure up to expectations? One tool at your disposal is to develop the ability to tactfully communicate that the problem exists, suggest alternatives, and ultimately, if the work does not meet the expected standards, replace the performer. Circumstances may prevent taking such direct action, however. For example, a union contract may prevent or hinder abrupt changes in casting.

In some situations, you may have no recourse. For example, suppose that the scene designer you hired to do the sets for your opening production misses the deadline for submitting the plans. Your shop staff cannot start building the set, and the entire construction process begins behind schedule. Your only recourse would be to refuse to hire that designer for your next show. By the time you confront the problem of failing to meet an output standard, it is too late to take much corrective action. You may also incur significant cost increases to make up the lost time by the missed design deadline. Overhires may be needed or overtime will need to be paid to complete the show in time for opening night.

The deadline of an "opening night" is one of the operational control factors arts managers face every day. If the stage production or performance is not ready in time for the advertised date, the postponement is typically the option of last resort. The negative consequences of not being ready to open or perform can be profound. Likewise, opening a show or performing a concert that is not ready yet can also damage the reputation of a quality professional arts organizations.

Management by Exception

One way of creating a operational control system is to establish a *management by exception* (MBE) process within the organization.[4] Essentially, the MBE process (shown in Figure 9.2) works as a part of the comparative element outlined in the control system. Once you establish clear performance standards and communicate them throughout the organization, you can focus your energies on the exceptions to the norm. In this approach, you spend time on the less-than-standard performance. However, you can also boost morale and productivity if your management team recognizes and rewards people who meet or exceed the standards.

Figure 9.2

Management by exception — control system at work.

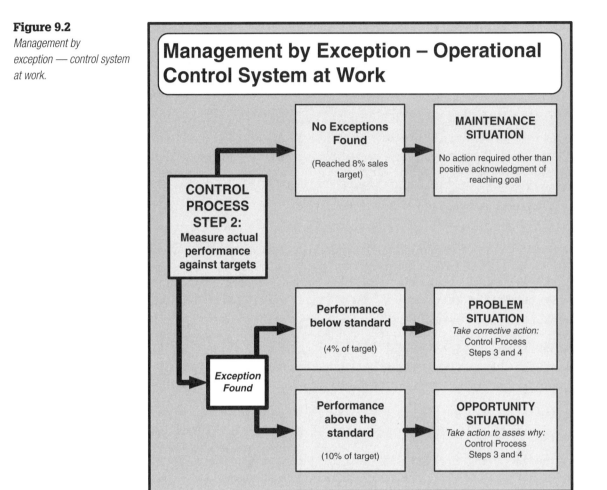

For MBE to work, internal control must be at a high level in the organization. High standards for performance must be central to the culture and value system of the organization. From this strong culture should come attitudes among your staff that support them in setting high goals for their own work output. An arts manager who approaches the staff from McGregor's Theory Y perspective, as noted in Chapters 3 and 8, will assume that staff members want to do a good job. Of course, if clear standards are not communicated to employees, you cannot expect even the most highly self-motivated people to meet your expectations.

Another element in the MBE process is a system of *external controls*. Every organization needs some ongoing policies and procedures to guide work behavior and to state expected standards clearly. When the organization sets these standards (smoking policy, break periods, vacations, sick days, and so forth), it frees the manager from expending energy on routine expectations. The manager need only be concerned with the exceptions to the external controls.

Management by objectives

In the late 1960s, the concept of *management by objectives* (MBO) began to be applied widely in the business world. Simply put, MBO is an integrated planning and control system that involves a formal agreement between a supervisor and subordinate concerning:[5]

1. Employee's performance objectives for a specific period of time
2. Plan(s) to be used to accomplish the objectives
3. Agreed upon standards for measuring the work accomplished
4. Procedures for reviewing results

When properly applied, MBO is integrated into the overall strategic plan for the organization. For example, if one of an organization's goals is to increase the level of gift income from corporations, and the objective is to increase corporate giving by 10 percent this year, then the development staff can specifically create quantitative objectives for the year. Specific methods would be developed to meet the objectives (phone, mail, and direct contact campaigns), and standards of achievement would be set for each employee (each staff member is given a specific dollar amount as the goal for a specific time period). During regular meetings, the employee and the supervisor would evaluate the employee's progress in meeting the objective.

As you can see, the MBO process can take a lot of time. When you begin to account for all of the time spent drawing up objectives, meeting regularly to review and revise objectives, and documenting the MBO of each employee, you can begin to see one problem with this approach. You may also encounter problems if the objectives you set are too easily reached. In a sense, you begin to establish lowered performance expectations.

In an arts organization, different employee groups have different time frames in their work. As a system, MBO does not make much sense for performers. Elements of MBO may make sense in administrative and production areas in the organization, provided that the time and commitment to support the extensive demands of MBO really exist.

Performance appraisal systems

When an arts organization grows big enough to keep a staff employed on a year-round basis, a *performance appraisal system* should be established. Performance appraisal simply means formally evaluating work performance and providing feedback so that performance adjustments can be made.[6] Performance appraisal is part of the overall operational control system for the organization. If the system is working well, it should provide employees with constructive feedback about their strengths and areas for improvement and concrete suggestions for developing their potential. The objective of the appraisal system should be to benefit the employee and the supervisors and to help the organization reach its goals.

Personnel appraisal methods

The business of evaluating people should be tailored to the organization's overall design and structure. For example, people who work in arts organizations would probably be put off by the various numerical rating scales devised by business specialists. For example, there is dubious value in giving an employee a rating of 7 on a scale of 1 to 10. However, a rating of "unsatisfactory" on a behavioral scale in a specific job area ("relates well to others") might draw more attention.

Arts organizations typically find the *critical incident appraisal* technique to be more acceptable for monitoring job performance. The supervisor keeps a running log of positive and negative work performance over a given time period and reviews it with the employee at specific intervals. Arts organizations also could use a *free-form narrative* to evaluate employees. This essay format usually notes overall job performance, specific accomplishments, strengths, and weaknesses.

Timely feedback

The annual evaluation is a key part of an organization's overall control system, but it does not provide feedback on work performance on a day-to-day basis. An effective control system must give employees regular feedback about their work output. Some organizations tend not to comment about the good work someone is doing until the annual evaluation. The net result is that the employee spends a year working in a vacuum. Even worse, a serious problem in an employee's work habits will be left unattended for a year.

A good manager realizes that each employee has a different need for feedback. Some people need constant monitoring, and others are happy when left alone. An appraisal system must be flexible enough to accommodate a range of employee needs.

One additional point to consider: even organizations with a seasonal workforce or interns can benefit from developing a system for giving feedback about job performance. From a management point of view, it can be problematic if seasonal employees are not performing up to the expected standards. Tight timetables or production schedules may not allow for replacing someone

quickly. Therefore, having a system in place that allows for immediately identifying employees who are having problems meeting the work standards can
be a significant asset. Correcting problems and helping an employee or intern
get back on track will be less stressful for all parties.

Summary of operational control systems

The operational control process extends into all areas of an organization.
The planning, organizing, and leading functions of management interact
with the control systems in a way that should provide an effectively managed
organization.

As noted earlier in this chapter, the word *control* is a source of discomfort to
many people. How can you have a dynamic, creative arts organization and
still have effective control systems? The two elements do not need to cancel
each other out.

In an arts organization there will ideally always be an element of creative
chaos. The creation of an evening of theater, dance, opera, or music, or the
creation and installation of an exhibit, will develop a life of its own. Your
plans may be in place, but then circumstances dictate sudden changes in your
course of action. The whole process may be very messy. The artistic process
could very well be filled with conflict, tension, and passion.

It has been my experience that no two events will ever come together in
exactly the same way, and therefore one must be careful not to over-control a
production or a project. The ability to be an adaptable manager is a requirement for survival and effective monitoring in an arts organization.

What, then, is an effective way to establish an operational control system in
the arts environment? One simple approach is to recognize that producing art
is not the same as producing large quantities of a product or rendering a service. The unique event presented needs a set of mutually agreed upon rules,
regulations, and guidelines specific to that project. Recognizing that the event
may interface with an ongoing organizational structure, the challenge to the
arts manager is to find a way to create bridges between the inherent bureaucracy of organizations and the typically more free-form artistic projects.

For example, the financial and accounting aspects of the organization require
a great deal of control. Rules, regulations, and laws must be obeyed. You can
increase compliance with the rules by making them clear and simple to follow. If, to purchase three yards of fabric for a costume, a staff member must
fill out six forms in triplicate and have them signed by two different people,
the odds are good that people will do whatever they can to avoid using the
"correct" procedures. In this example, the organization would benefit from a
different control system for its purchasing procedures.

MANAGEMENT INFORMATION SYSTEMS

Let's now look at a key supporting system that makes organizational control work effectively. A Management Information System (MIS; Figure 9.3) is formally defined as "a mechanism designed to collect, combine, compare, analyze, and disseminate data in the form of information."[7] For an arts organization, a well-designed MIS should serve as an almost invisible element. The design, implementation, and maintenance of the MIS may not be particularly exciting to people working in the arts. In fact, many organizations never establish a formal MIS; one evolves.

The evolution of the MIS often comes from the crisis management style exercised by many organizations. For example, it is the middle of summer before you discover subscription sales revenue is down 15 percent and your cash has all been spent to meet creditors' bills and last month's payroll. This has never been this big a problem before. What has happened? In this case, maybe the

Figure 9.3

Management Information System (MIS).

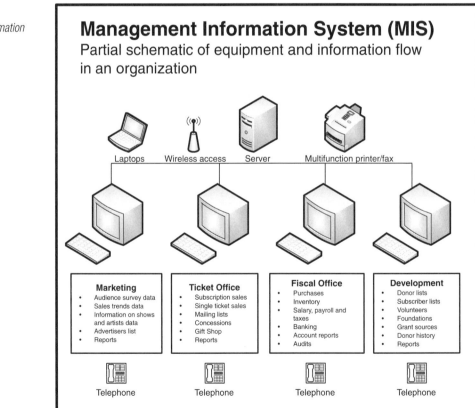

Management Information System (MIS)
Partial schematic of equipment and information flow in an organization

Laptops　　Wireless access　　Server　　Multifunction printer/fax

Marketing
- Audience survey data
- Sales trends data
- Information on shows and artists data
- Advertisers list
- Reports

Ticket Office
- Subscription sales
- Single ticket sales
- Mailing lists
- Concessions
- Gift Shop
- Reports

Fiscal Office
- Purchases
- Inventory
- Salary, payroll and taxes
- Banking
- Account reports
- Audits

Development
- Donor lists
- Subscriber lists
- Volunteers
- Foundations
- Grant sources
- Donor history
- Reports

Telephone　　Telephone　　Telephone　　Telephone

MIS, as it existed, simply did not get financial information about sales and accounts to you quickly enough.

The MIS currently in place may also be too informal. Suppose you are planning a major tour in which your ballet company will perform in five large cities. Two days before the tour starts, you are informed by the management in the first city that only 35 percent of the house has been sold. Whenever you asked about how sales were going, you were told, "Orders are coming in at a steady pace." Because you were led to believe that the sponsor would easily be able to sell 60 percent of capacity, based on previous dance company performances, you signed a contract based on a percentage of the house, not a guaranteed fee. In this example, the lack of hard data delivered in a timely manner could very well mean bankruptcy for the dance company.

Both of these examples demonstrate the importance of a good MIS. A key function of the MIS is to help arts managers make decisions. To make a decision implies you have a choice. To exercise choice means that you select from alternative plans of action. The choices you have may become increasingly limited as time passes. In the case of a subscription campaign, you have to make the sale before the season opens. If you learn early enough that sales are down, you can implement planned courses of action to increase sales. If you learn too late about the shortfall in revenue, all you can do is plan for an operating deficit. Let's examine how to establish an effective MIS so that many of these problems can be avoided.

Data and information

When we defined an MIS, we used the terms *data* and *information*. Each of these terms implies a great deal about the MIS. With the advent of the personal computer, the term *data* has found its way into our daily vocabulary. Data typically comes to us in the form of figures, which we then process to form a meaningful conclusion. The process of making sense of and interpreting the data results in the ability to produce *information* others may use. These data say we sold 500 tickets in a 1000 seat venue. The *information* we distribute to the staff is that we have only sold 50% of the seats. We expected that by this date we should have sold 65%. These data provide the information we need to make a decision about increasing advertising or creating a new element in our sales campaign.

Data and information of course are not neutral terms. Because people process data, certain biases may affect this part of the process. For example, 25 subscriptions sold in one day may seem like a basic piece of data. You might ask how this number compares to the number sold at this time last year or how the number compares to projections of expected sales to date. If, on the other hand, the box office manager only took in revenue from 18 sales and the other 7 sales were phone calls from people who said they would be renewing, these data collected imply something quite different. The ticket office manager may have been telling you what he thought you wanted to hear because he wanted to present as optimistic a sales picture as possible. The point is that the MIS you have in place is meaningless if individuals manipulate the data to present misleading information.

MIS in the arts

In Figure 9.3, a simplified MIS is shown for an arts organization. Ideally, the system would be set up so data and information can be shared. The advances in computing capabilities, the lower costs of the hardware, and the development of low-cost software has greatly aided the low technology budgets found in most arts organizations. Although computerization certainly assists the management decision-making process, simply walking from department to department to gather information is still an option.

There are many routine information systems already in place in arts organizations. For example, daily reports from the stage manager and technical director to the production manager support the design and production information system. Often verbal reports made in weekly staff meetings by the production manager to the managing director complete the cycle of data gathering and distribution.

Most arts organizations start with a small staff of two or three people. The MIS exists as informal communication among people who are often part of a well-established social unit. The group may have morning meetings to review the day's activities, and this meeting becomes the core of the MIS. One person may deal with accounting, finances, and logistics, while someone else covers marketing and fundraising. A personnel system is not even needed. However, as the organization grows, more staff members are added, and specialization and departmentalization occur.

Organizational design has a direct impact on the MIS. For example, the MIS of a regional theater company with three theaters in different locations in the city must take into account the potential problems of decentralization. How will these remote locations operate in relation to the accounting department? How will accounting know about purchases unless the MIS includes the accounting department in the ordering stage? If the information system is required to keep track of and control funds expended, it cannot record purchases based on invoices that may come 15 to 30 days after an item has been purchased.

Computers and the MIS

Computers and management information systems seem to have been made for each other. The computer's ability to store large amounts of data and distribute it through networks within an organization has had a major impact on the business world. The ability to gather, store, and manipulate data is now very cost-effective. The smallest arts organization usually has at least one computer to do the bookkeeping or to manage a mailing list. In fact, many arts organizations now designate an MIS position in the organization structure (e.g., MIS Director in Figure 6.4).

Whatever the scale of operation, careful planning is required if the maximum benefit of computerization is to be realized. The cost of purchasing computer hardware has dropped significantly, which has been of great benefit to resource-starved arts organizations. However, the cost to upgrade software and train staff to make the best use of the software can be problematic for arts groups with minimal budget support. The idea of a replacement cycle for computers in many small arts organizations is just that — an idea. There is usually a mix of old and new computers and some so ancient and slow that one wonders how anyone gets anything done.

An effective MIS

The purpose of any MIS is to facilitate the accomplishment of the organization's objectives through improved problem solving and decision making. In shaping and revising an MIS, three factors must be taken into account: There are uncontrollable, partially controllable, and fully controllable factors that determine how effective the MIS will be.[8]

Uncontrollable factors

Some factors, such as organizational structure and the organization's relationship to its external environments, are beyond the control of the MIS. For example, in a highly decentralized organization in which subgroups have a great deal of autonomy, it may prove difficult to implement an MIS effectively. A regional theater, opera, dance company, or museum may have administrative offices in more than one location, rehearse in two or three different spaces, build sets and props in yet another locale, and perform in two different venues during the year. A museum may have satellite locations in a community or specialized local micro-exhibitions.

This structure would make it more challenging to set up an MIS linked by computers. Yet the flow of information would be possible by using a well-designed Web site and various data transmission formats, such as fax machines and modems hooked up to remote computers that report back to the administrative offices. A computer that functions as a server in the central office may be installed to help manage the data flow and act as a place to share files. Other organizations outsource the server and pay fees to a host company.

An unstable internal or external business environment also has an effect on the MIS. For example, suppose that you are trying to track audience response by collecting data from your mailings. Between the first and second mailings, a fiscal crisis forces the organization to drop two shows from the season. How will you collect meaningful data about the effectiveness of a second mailing if the season package keeps changing?

As noted, many small arts organizations simply do not have the financial resources or expertise to install computer networks. The uncontrollable factor in this case may be that there are five personal computers in the organization, all use different software, and all are isolated from each other. The fundraising staff member uses one type of software to track the donors, and the box office uses a different software to collect sales and subscription information. Data are not shared and information transfer is limited.

Partially controllable factors

It is possible to gain some short-range control over a poorly structured MIS by bringing available resources to bear on the problem. In the previous example, for instance, a managing director might be able to intercede and make sure that the different computer systems use common software. Data files could then be copied from one machine to another, and information could be shared over what is called a *shoe leather network*. For this to succeed, people in the organization must understand the importance of creating a data-gathering and information dissemination system.

Fully controllable factors

The MIS that has fully controllable factors is supported and encouraged by the management of organization. In what may seem like an ideal world for many arts organizations, a staff member is designated to oversee the data and information system. This would be a senior staff position with support staff to assist with system maintenance. The MIS would be fully integrated into the overall organizational operation.

Integrated computer systems with software packages and ongoing operating procedures would support regular data gathering and storage. For example, an effective MIS would allow a marketing staff member to track subscription sales by type of purchaser over the previous five years by accessing a database of subscriber files. When a staff member in the press office needs to look up information about a singer who was in an opera produced by the company three years ago, the information would be available in a database of artist biographies.

Common mistakes

Care must be taken to avoid some common mistakes in establishing a MIS. As noted earlier, many arts organizations evolve and grow without paying much attention to the MIS. Much time is often wasted hunting down information that should be readily available. However, trying to force an MIS on an organization that is not yet ready for it can damage the credibility of the system. Even when the MIS is accepted, there are still pitfalls to avoid. Here are four problems with bringing an MIS into operation.[9]

1. More information is not always better. The issue here is quality, not quantity. Data translated into too much information may turn out to be more of a hindrance than a help. It does not take a great deal of effort to overwhelm people with too much information.

2. Do not assume that people need all the information they think they want. When designing an MIS for an organization, it is important to review with the various staff members exactly what information they need to be more productive. People tend to request more information than they will possibly have time to process and synthesize.

3. Despite receiving more information, decision making might not improve. More information does not translate into more effective management. In some cases, too much information may result in decision paralysis for some managers.

4. Don't assume that computers can solve all of your information management problems. The greatest benefits come when a well-designed software system is carefully integrated with a clear vision of the organization's information management needs. However, organizations tend to forget that time is needed to train people to use a computer-based MIS effectively. A poorly designed and managed MIS will probably be abandoned by the users, and everyone will return to the old procedures.

MIS summary

If you ask a staff member in an arts organization how well the MIS is working you might get a puzzled look. If, on the other hand, you ask him whether the monthly account statements detailing the expenses of their department are informative, the staff person will probably say yes. In this case, the MIS would appear to be working.

The way information and data flow in an organization can be critical to its long-term strength. For example, Figure 9.4 depicts a typical decision support system that most arts groups have in place. Whether they refer to it as an MIS or not, the way information is distributed and then analyzed is instrumental in helping the board and the staff plan for the future.

Figure 9.4
*Decision support
system — data and
information flow.*

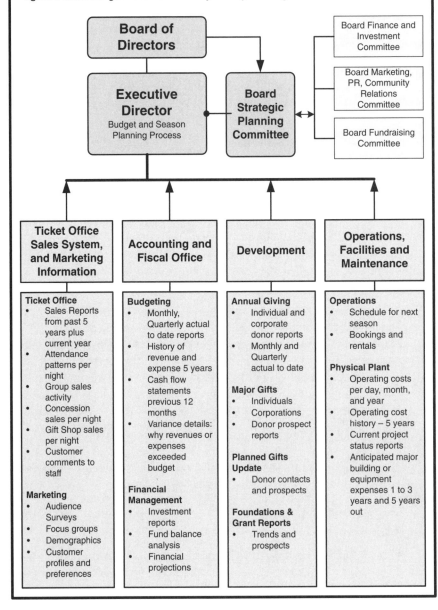

Decision Support System
Data and the Flow of Information

To plan a season of programming and budget for activities facts and
figures must be gathered and analyzed by the organization

Board of Directors

Board Finance and Investment Committee

Board Marketing, PR, Community Relations Committee

Board Fundraising Committee

Executive Director
Budget and Season Planning Process

Board Strategic Planning Committee

Ticket Office Sales System, and Marketing Information

Accounting and Fiscal Office

Development

Operations, Facilities and Maintenance

Ticket Office
- Sales Reports from past 5 years plus current year
- Attendance patterns per night
- Group sales activity
- Concession sales per night
- Gift Shop sales per night
- Customer comments to staff

Marketing
- Audience Surveys
- Focus groups
- Demographics
- Customer profiles and preferences

Budgeting
- Monthly, Quarterly actual to date reports
- History of revenue and expense 5 years
- Cash flow statements previous 12 months
- Variance details: why revenues or expenses exceeded budget

Financial Management
- Investment reports
- Fund balance analysis
- Financial projections

Annual Giving
- Individual and corporate donor reports
- Monthly and Quarterly actual to date

Major Gifts
- Individuals
- Corporations
- Donor prospect reports

Planned Gifts Update
- Donor contacts and prospects

Foundations & Grant Reports
- Trends and prospects

Operations
- Schedule for next season
- Bookings and rentals

Physical Plant
- Operating costs per day, month, and year
- Operating cost history – 5 years
- Current project status reports
- Anticipated major building or equipment expenses 1 to 3 years and 5 years out

The effectiveness of an MIS in an arts organization often boils down to integrating the existing systems shown in Figure 9.4 that produce data and information. The accounting reports of expenses, bills, and payroll, the box office reports of sales, and the fundraising reports of donor amounts may simply need to be pulled together in an overview for the staff and board. Probably the most effective way to quickly pull together an MIS is to ask some very basic questions about what information the organization and the staff need on a daily, weekly, monthly, quarterly, and annual basis. A chart that lists the data, reports, and so on, needed for each time frame can become the foundation for a very simple and effective MIS.

The future

Arts organizations have only begun to tap into the potential of computers as an organizational support and MIS tool. The current application of computers in arts organizations has focused on automating manual procedures. This has resulted in productivity gains in isolated parts of the organization. It may now take minutes to gather the information that used to require days. As lower cost computer networks become more common and computer processing speed increases, the arts manager of the future will need to be creative in extending the effectiveness of the automated MIS beyond record keeping and data management. The new technology is creating systems that will allow the multimedia use of computers. For example, designers, directors, and data managers will be able to update designs, visualize a staging, or manipulate data many times faster than ever imagined. Many arts organizations are using their Web site to post information for external as well as internal use.

Computer Software Packages

In the last 20-years, the development of software for personal computers has made significant strides. The ability of talented high school students and college graduates to develop databases and Web sites has been a great benefit to many small arts organizations. Once these custom applications are developed from off-the-shelf software packages, keeping them working when the designer moves on is a problem the arts manager must face.

Another common circumstance found in small arts organizations is that one of the staff who is particularly adept at working with computers and software becomes by default your in-house IT (Information Technology) person. The advantage of saving money that can be put to other purposes in the organization is hard to resist. Of course, the dependence on this one person and their skills and abilities can lead to its own set of problems.

The alternatives to the do-it-yourself approach have greatly expanded in recent years. For example, paging through the "Resource Directory" in the back of any issue of *The NonProfit Times* provides evidence of many software packages designed to use in not-for-profit organizations. The development of firms who sell integrated accounting and fundraising software offers the arts manager other alternatives to explore. Here is a sampling of Web sites for firms specializing in software for not-for-profit or arts and culture organizations.

http://www.artsman.com/
http://www.blackbaud.com/
http://www.mirasoft-inc.com/
http://www.sagenonprofit.com/
http://www.telosa.com/index.html

In addition, there are numerous arts consulting firms that can advise an organization (for a fee of course) on how best to configure their MIS and establish an effective IT system.

BUDGETS AND THE CONTROL SYSTEM

In this final section on control systems, we look at the important area of budgeting. Budget control and management can very quickly become the major focus of an arts manager's job. To be able to project revenue accurately and to monitor and control expenses is an extremely valuable set of skills to possess. The very survival of an arts organization often depends on the ability to keep current with income and expenses. This is especially important for arts organizations with limited cash reserves. As a control center, budgeting is a key element in the overall MIS of the organization.

What exactly is a budget? One common definition of a *budget* is "a quantitative and financial expression of a plan."[10] A budget therefore represents an allocation of resources in support of the activities of the organization.

If the operational control process is to be effective, the person supervising the use of the funds must be held responsible for the budget. Depending on the organization's culture, the budget development and implementation process may range from highly structured and formal to informal and casual.

Formal budgeting implies a proposal and review process before budget changes are approved. Depending on the structure of the organization, proposing and making changes in the budget could involve very precise procedures. See Figure 9.5 for an overview of a budget development process.

Budgetary centers

Before an arts organization begins the process of trying to fulfill the mission it has established for itself, a budget must be prepared. Even the smallest organization

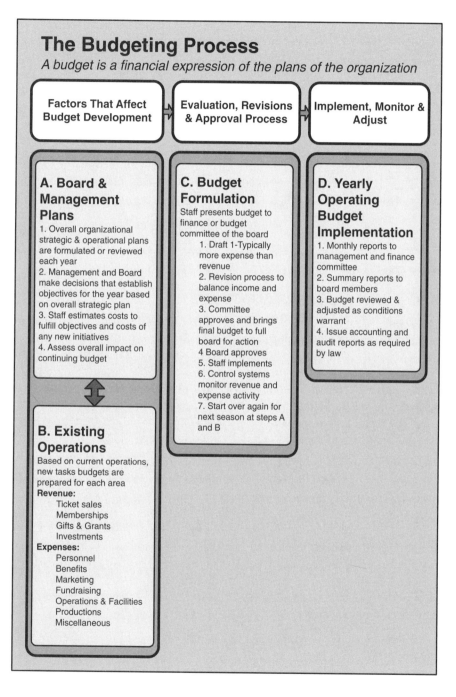

The Budgeting Process

A budget is a financial expression of the plans of the organization

| Factors That Affect Budget Development | Evaluation, Revisions & Approval Process | Implement, Monitor & Adjust |

A. Board & Management Plans

1. Overall organizational strategic & operational plans are formulated or reviewed each year
2. Management and Board make decisions that establish objectives for the year based on overall strategic plan
3. Staff estimates costs to fulfill objectives and costs of any new initiatives
4. Assess overall impact on continuing budget

B. Existing Operations

Based on current operations, new tasks budgets are prepared for each area

Revenue:
Ticket sales
Memberships
Gifts & Grants
Investments

Expenses:
Personnel
Benefits
Marketing
Fundraising
Operations & Facilities
Productions
Miscellaneous

C. Budget Formulation

Staff presents budget to finance or budget committee of the board

1. Draft 1-Typically more expense than revenue
2. Revision process to balance income and expense
3. Committee approves and brings final budget to full board for action
4 Board approves
5. Staff implements
6. Control systems monitor revenue and expense activity
7. Start over again for next season at steps A and B

D. Yearly Operating Budget Implementation

1. Monthly reports to management and finance committee
2. Summary reports to board members
3. Budget reviewed & adjusted as conditions warrant
4. Issue accounting and audit reports as required by law

Figure 9.5
The budgeting process.

will need to look at two key centers: revenue and expenses. The *revenue centers* include income from the sale of tickets or memberships, donations, grants, concessions, program advertising, rentals, and the sale of merchandise. *Expense centers* generally follow the organizational structure that has been established. These two components form the overall operating budget of the organization.

Budgets as preliminary controls

A budget is a preliminary control because it establishes the resources allocated to achieve the objectives outlined in the operational plans for the organization. An opera company that allocates one-third of its production budget to one show of a five-show season would probably be making a statement of artistic priority. The monthly budget reports should give the production manager a clear sense of whether the resources allocated for each show are used as projected. A budget functions as a preliminary control when the production manager tells the designers that they have a specific amount for sets, costumes, and so forth.

Budgets as top secret documents

One would assume that if the budget is such a central part of the control and operational systems of arts organizations, having a copy of the budget available to the staff would be a fairly common occurrence. Sadly, this is often not the case. The culture of many organizations creates barriers for staff attempting to gather budget information. It is not uncommon in arts organizations to find that very few people actually have access to current budget information. The result is that most of the staff operate without any true sense of the budgetary impact of decisions made or contemplated plans.

The secrecy with which budgets are treated more often than not inhibits the exchange of information about the financial status of the organization. The attitude contained in the expression that a staff member may make such as, "the Board doesn't need to know about that" is often at the root of many of the financial problems arts organizations encounter. By the time the budget information is widely distributed it is often too late to address the financial problems facing the organization. The more open the information exchange is about the budgets and the current financial state of the organization, the better equipped the organization is to respond as a team to whatever financial crisis it may be facing.

Let's now review some of the basic types of budgets and the process of creating budgets.

Types of budgets

In a *fixed budget*, allocations are based on the estimated costs from a fixed base of resources. For example, the salary budget is set for the year, and resources are allocated to cover that expense. Typically, the fixed budget becomes the base budget for the work area and is increased or decreased on an incremental basis according to activities and plans proposed each year. For example, some organizations work from incremental increases approved by the board based on the overall consumer price index inflation rate. A budget may therefore be increased a fixed amount of 3 percent, assuming that was the inflation rate.

A *flexible budget* assumes that activity levels will influence resource use. The organization may have a fixed overall budget, but will have a range of revenue or expense projections based on the level of activity. For example, a museum's payroll budget may respond to increased traffic flows due to programming. If the museum has a big exhibit that brings in a larger than average number of paid admissions (increased revenue), it may also have to hire two additional part-time guards to control the crowds (increased expense).

A *zero-based budget* is a planning and objective-setting tool used by some arts organizations. At the end of a fiscal cycle (or end of the fiscal year), all budget lines are zeroed out. Revenues and expenses must be projected and justified in relation to the plans and objectives for the whole organization for the coming year. No budget line item amount carries over from the previous year. Compared to the fixed budget with its yearly incremental increases, the zero-based budget can be an effective tool to help keep an organization from creating budgets filled with underutilized line items.

An *operating budget*, as already noted, is normally a yearly budget created to carry out the organization's operational plans. This budget is typically structured with a revenue or income section, an expenses section, and an indication of the running balance or deficit in the overall budget.

A *project budget* (sometimes called an *opportunity budget*) is typically associated with an event that has a start and end time and is not repeated on an annual basis. A fundraising event, a gala, a benefit concert, or a special production may have a budget specifically set aside for this event. Both revenue and expenses may be kept track of separately from the regular operating budgets. Since arts organizations often do special projects, it can be easier to identify and account for the revenue and expense activity if the budget is kept separate from the normal day-to-day operating budget.

A *capital budget* is typically used for a large-scale or one-time equipment or facility expense. Adding a new wing on a building, replacing the seats in the theater, or buying new equipment that will most likely have a useful life of more than a year are often identified as capital expenses. Organizations usually set a dollar amount for capital expenses and classify items below that amount as regular operating expenses. Setting a threshold such as purchases of $5,000 or above may be appropriate. The amount used will vary from organization to organization.

The budgetary process

As depicted in Figure 9.5, the budgeting process usually begins with a projection of the organization's various sources of revenue. In arts organizations, revenue comes from a variety of sources. The organization's MIS should be able to provide detailed reports of all revenue from the previous year or years. The evaluation of the previous revenue distributions and the comparison with the budget projections for the coming year are the next step. Care must be taken when projecting revenue. A few too many optimistic revenue projections could lead to a midseason budget crisis.

The same type of activity takes place in the organization's various expense centers. Comparing the current year's expense patterns and evaluating the project and programming plans for the next year must be done in the context of the overall revenue for the organization.

The next stage in the process compares and adjusts budgets based on expected revenue. If, after subtracting revenue, expenses still exceed the available resources, a series of revisions are made in the expense budgets.

Arts organizations sometimes find themselves adjusting revenue projections to match expenses. This is a dangerous method of budgeting that usually leads to chronic financial trouble for the organization. For example, unrealistic projections of fundraising or subscription sales revenue may result in a balanced budget to present to the finance committee of the board, but such budget practices are nothing short of fraud.

Budget reality

A manager in an organization soon discovers that the control process in budgeting extends into anticipating behavior patterns by staff members. Staff members may become very territorial about budgets. Some people overestimate needs, while others try to make the budget allocation process a competition for resources within the organization. (One tool for controlling this problem is to work with the previously noted zero-based budgets.) Very few staff members will loudly proclaim, "I don't need this much. Here, take back some of my budget."

Budget controls

Trying to control a budget is usually a full-time activity. Theoretically, the organizational MIS will provide the manager with the required information about revenue and expenses. For budget control to be effective, the manager must have this information as quickly as possible each month. Without computers, this work becomes more time-consuming, but it is not impossible. Simple year-to-date percentage expectations for revenue and expenses can give a manager some element of control over a budget. For example, at the end of a specific period of time (typically by quarters of the year), a specific percentage of the budget should have been expended. The manager's efforts can then be focused on variances from the expected distributions.

Another key element in the budget control process involves the authorization procedures for expending funds. A system of review and approval must exist if the organization is to control its budget effectively.

Finally, the manager must recognize and develop strategies for dealing with the political nature of budgets. Organizational politics play a role in the budget control process. Staff members try to obtain as many resources as possible for their work areas. The information a manager receives may have been filtered by department heads to distort the true budgetary condition of a subunit within the organization.

Budgets in detail

Budgets usually cover what is called a *fiscal year* (FY), which can be any designated 12-month period of expense and revenue activity. Most financial planners suggest that organizations set their FY around the programmatic profile of the organization. The IRS tax year, for example, is January 1 to December 31. However, a performing arts group with an eight-month season of October to May would probably find that a FY of July 1 to June 30 better fits their programming and expense patterns.

The *summary budget* usually works well for smaller operations with a limited number of account lines. Figure 9.6 shows part of a proposed budget for a small theater group. This budget is simplified for the purposes of this presentation format. There might be many more actual expense lines than are shown. In addition, this budget does not show benefits costs (health insurance, retirement, etc.).

In a typical fiscal year, the income and expense lines form the most active part of the budget. However, the budget does not actually reveal whether the organization is financially healthy. It simply tells what is expected in revenue and what is planned in expenses. In this example the theater company has a current year budget that is designed to produce a $40,500 surplus of income over expenses. The budget planning for next year anticipates an even larger surplus, $75,000.

As you review this budget, you will see that certain planning expectations are funded. For example, the company plans to increase its marketing expenses by 20.3 percent, slightly more than the 18.7 percent expected rise in subscription sales. This would indicate some major effort will be undertaken to increase the number of subscribers.

Figure 9.6

Summary budget — theater company.

Summary Budget - Theater Company

INCOME	Current Year Budget	Proposed Budget Next Fiscal Year	$ Change	% Change
Subscription Ticket Sales	817,000	970,000	153,000	18.7%
Single Ticket Sales	602,000	600,000	(2,000)	-0.3%
Group Sales	56,000	60,000	4,000	7.1%
SUBTOTAL Sales	1,475,000	1,630,000	155,000	10.5%
Advertising	77,000	85,000	8,000	10.4%
Concessions	56,000	65,000	9,000	16.1%
Gift Shop Income	15,000	14,000	(1,000)	-6.7%
Interest	16,000	23,000	7,000	43.8%
Costume & Scenery Rentals	3,500	2,500	(1,000)	-28.6%
Space/Equipment Rentals	7,000	5,000	(2,000)	-28.6%
Education	5,200	8,000	2,800	53.8%
Miscellaneous	6,500	5,000	(1,500)	-23.1%
Surcharges on Ticket Sales	17,000	18,000	1,000	5.9%
SUBTOTAL Other Income	203,200	225,500	22,300	11.0%
TOTAL EARNED INCOME	1,678,200	1,855,500	177,300	10.6%
DONATED INCOME	**Current Budget**	**Proposed**	**$ Change**	**% Change**
Individuals	250,000	300,000	50,000	20.0%
Corporations	100,000	125,000	25,000	25.0%
Foundations	100,000	125,000	25,000	25.0%
Co-producers	75,000	100,000	25,000	33.3%
Special Events	205,000	250,000	45,000	22.0%
Matching Contributions	250,000	300,000	50,000	20.0%
TOTAL DONATED INCOME	980,000	1,200,000	220,000	22.4%
GOVERNMENT FUNDING	**Current Budget**	**Proposed**	**$ Change**	**% Change**
State Grants	48,000	45,000	(3,000)	-6.3%
City/County Grants	94,000	100,000	6,000	6.4%
Federal Grants	0	0	0	
TOTAL GOVT FUNDING	142,000	145,000	3,000	2.1%
TOTAL INCOME	2,800,200	3,200,500	400,300	14.3%
EXPENSES	**Current Budget**	**Proposed**	**$ Change**	**% Change**
Artistic Salaries/Fees/Expenses	872,045	1,060,000	187,955	21.6%
Technical Salaries/Fees/Expense	615,907	665,000	49,093	8.0%
Production Cost	139,669	150,000	10,331	7.4%
Administrative Salaries/Fees/Exp	152,409	160,000	7,591	5.0%
Marketing Salaries and Expenses	542,522	652,500	109,978	20.3%
Development Salaries and Expen	162,942	192,500	29,558	18.1%
Special Events & Receptions	128,000	88,000	(40,000)	-31.3%
Concessions	35,858	40,000	4,142	11.6%
Gift Shop Expenses	6,435	6,500	65	1.0%
Occupancy (Utilities, etc.)	70,352	75,000	4,648	6.6%
Contingency	33,561	36,000	2,439	7.3%
TOTAL EXPENSES	2,759,700	3,125,500	365,800	13.3%
VARIANCE - Surplus or (Deficit)	40,500	75,000	34,500	

The detailed budget shown in Figure 9.7 goes into more depth. Account numbers are assigned to the individual line items in the budget. This is a typical component of a budget control system. The account numbering system helps identify the type of transaction that took place, and the system can be further broken down into account subcodes to provide as much detail as possible. For example, under the marketing expense budget (Account number 3000), there is a line item for a season program (3007) and for telemarketing (3008 and 3009).

Figure 9.7 also shows in each line the expenses incurred to date and the percentage of the budget expended. This information is very important to the person responsible for managing the budget. For example, overall the marketing area has used 94.8 percent of its budget to date (see Subtotal Marketing Expenses to Date). The information in the revenue lines shows that the theater company has completed 11 months of the season and is at 97.3 percent of its revenue budget (see Total Ticket Sales). Thus, the marketing department has kept its budget on track in relationship to the season.

A closer look shows that certain expense lines exceeded budget. For example, general advertising (3003), printing (3006), and photography (3011) have all gone over budget. In these examples, the amount of the overage is shown as a positive balance. In line 3005 (Broadcast Advertising), for example, the underage is shown as $2,000 in the Balance column. The marketing director would need to assess why and determine whether adjustments in next year's budget are called for in those lines.

Another way to organize a budget is along project or department lines. A project budget distributes revenue and expense centers across the organization. Figure 9.8 shows one way the theater company could express its budget by using this approach. In this example, the account titles are distributed across five major operational areas: Regular Season, Touring, Educational Programs, Building Fund, and Special Events. This budget format gives much more information about how the organization plans to distribute its income and expenses. For example, it is possible to see that the educational programs are generating more expense than revenue. The variance section of the report at the bottom of the page shows a deficit of $120,700 in the educational programs. In effect, the other activities of the organization are subsidizing this activity. Of course, this may be a management decision, and this deficit may have been anticipated.

The project budget is an excellent way to help with the fundraising needs of the organization. For example, the educational program area could make a case for an additional $120,700 to achieve its objectives. If the $120,700 could be raised from outside sources, funds could be shifted to help pay for other priority projects that the organization has established in its planning process.

Another useful element of the project budget is its ability to show the proposed distribution of resources across the entire organization. The salary lines

Figure 9.7

Detailed budget — theater company.

Detailed Budgets - Theater Company

SAMPLE INCOME ACCOUNT LINES   11 months into Fiscal Year

Acct	Account Title	Budget	To Date	Balance	%
300	Subscription Sales	817,000	775,000	(42,000)	94.9%
321	Single Tickets - Show 1	85,000	84,000	(1,000)	98.8%
322	Single Tickets - Show 2	85,000	82,500	(2,500)	97.1%
323	Single Tickets - Show 3	148,000	152,000	4,000	102.7%
324	Single Tickets - Show 4	85,000	79,000	(6,000)	92.9%
325	Single Tickets - Show 5	85,000	87,000	2,000	102.4%
326	Single Tickets - Show 6	114,000	116,000	2,000	101.8%
	SUBTOTAL Single Tickets	**602,000**	**600,500**	**(1,500)**	**99.8%**
421	Group Sales - Show 1	8,000	7,700	(300)	96.3%
422	Group Sales - Show 2	7,200	6,800	(400)	94.4%
423	Group Sales - Show 3	22,000	24,000	2,000	109.1%
424	Group Sales - Show 4	5,800	6,000	200	103.4%
425	Group Sales - Show 5	5,000	7,200	2,200	144.0%
426	Group Sales - Show 6	8,000	8,500	500	106.3%
	SUBTOTAL Group Sales	**56,000**	**60,200**	**4,200**	**107.5%**
	TOTAL TICKET SALES	**1,475,000**	**1,435,700**	**(39,300)**	**97.3%**

SAMPLE EXPENSE ACCOUNT LINES

Acct	Account Title	Budget	To Date	Balance	%
3000	**MARKETING**				
3001	Salaries	221,000	202,000	19,000	91.4%
3002	Payroll Taxes	20,322	18,600	1,722	91.5%
3003	General Advertising	7,000	7,400	(400)	105.7%
3004	Newspaper Advertising	50,000	47,000	3,000	94.0%
3005	Broadcast Advertising	32,000	30,000	2,000	93.8%
3006	General Printing	30,000	32,000	(2,000)	106.7%
3007	Season Program Printing	53,700	52,223	1,477	97.2%
3008	Telemarketing Expenses	6,325	6,500	(175)	102.8%
3009	Telemarketing Commissions	50,025	48,000	2,025	96.0%
3010	Displays and Signage	6,000	6,200	(200)	103.3%
3011	Photography	13,000	15,000	(2,000)	115.4%
3012	Postage & Distribution	12,000	11,950	50	99.6%
3013	Distribution of Brochures	1,800	1,500	300	83.3%
3014	Program Ad Sales Commission	15,000	14,000	1,000	93.3%
3015	Group Sales	15,000	14,000	1,000	93.3%
3016	Hotel Commissions	3,000	2,800	200	93.3%
3017	Dues/Subscriptions/Clippings	2,000	1,850	150	92.5%
3018	Materials and Supplies	3,500	2,900	600	82.9%
3019	Miscellaneous	850	250	600	29.4%
	SUBTOTAL MARKETING	**542,522**	**514,173**	**28,349**	**94.8%**

(   ) denotes either a revenue shortfall or more expense than budget

Budget Distribution by Projects Current Year

Figure 9.8
Budget distribution — project basis

INCOME	Regular Season	Touring	Education Program	Building Fund	Special Events	TOTAL
Subscription Ticket Sales	653,500	163,500	0	0	0	**817,000**
Single Ticket Sales	481,600	120,400	0	0	0	**602,000**
Group Sales	36,400	11,200	8,400	0	0	**56,000**
Advertising	61,600	15,400	0	0	0	**77,000**
Concessions	47,600	8,400	0	0	0	**56,000**
Gift Shop Income	12,000	3,000	0	0	0	**15,000**
Interest	12,800	3,200	0	0	0	**16,000**
Costume & Scenery Rentals	3,500	0	0	0	0	**3,500**
Space/Equipment Rentals	7,000	0	0	0	0	**7,000**
Education	0	0	5,200	0	0	**5,200**
Miscellaneous	6,500	0	0	0	0	**6,500**
Surcharges on Ticket Sales	12,000	0	0	0	5,000	**17,000**
SUBTOTAL	**1,334,500**	**325,100**	**13,600**	**0**	**5,000**	**1,678,200**
DONATIONS & GOVT FUNDING						
Individuals	100,000	0	0	50,000	100,000	**250,000**
Corporations	45,000	25,000	25,000	5,000	0	**100,000**
Foundations	40,000	10,000	40,000	10,000	0	**100,000**
Co-producers	45,000	15,000	15,000	0	0	**75,000**
Special Events	0	0	0	0	205,000	**205,000**
Matching Contributions	200,000	50,000		0	0	**250,000**
State Grants	0	25,000	23,000	0	0	**48,000**
City/County Grants	29,000	30,000	35,000	0	0	**94,000**
Federal Grants	0	0	0	0	0	**-**
SUBTOTAL	**459,000**	**155,000**	**138,000**	**65,000**	**305,000**	**1,122,000**
TOTAL	**1,793,500**	**480,100**	**151,600**	**65,000**	**310,000**	**2,800,200**

EXPENSE	Regular Season	Touring	Education Program	Building Fund	Special Events	TOTAL
Artistic Salaries/Fees	557,745	175,000	130,800	0	8,500	**872,045**
Technical Salaries/Fees	389,407	125,000	95,000	0	6,500	**615,907**
Production Cost	96,669	28,000	15,000	0	-	**139,669**
Administrative Salaries/Fees	84,059	30,500	15,000	7,600	15,250	**152,409**
Marketing Salaries & Expenses	425,000	102,000	10,000	0	5,522	**542,522**
Development Sal. & Expenses	72,942	10,000	5,000	10,000	65,000	**162,942**
Special Events & Receptions	9,000	0	0	12,000	107,000	**128,000**
Concessions	35,858	0	0	0	0	**35,858**
Gift Shop Expenses	3,735	1,200	0	0	1,500	**6,435**
Occupancy (Utilities, etc.)	70,352	-	-	-	-	**70,352**
Contingency	25,061	3,500	1,500	0	3,500	**33,561**
TOTAL EXPENSES	**1,769,828**	**475,200**	**272,300**	**29,600**	**212,772**	**2,759,700**
VARIANCE - Surplus or (Deficit)	**23,672**	**4,900**	**(120,700)**	**35,400**	**97,228**	**40,500**

Income and expenses are distributed by major areas of activity.

for the artistic, technical, and administrative staff present a clear picture of how much of the budget has been allocated to support the educational outreach program.

FROM THE BUDGET TO CASH FLOW

The budget shows the manager the planned revenues and expenses for the FY. The budgeting process that took us to the point of preparing a detailed budget still does not tell us if we have enough resources to operate the organization during the year. To make the budget work, a cash flow projection must be developed. It will provide a detailed look at the budget before the organization begins to spend money.

Cash flow projections

It is possible to anticipate periods during the FY when the organization may not have enough cash to pay its bills. Figure 9.9 shows the theater company's budget distributed over the current FY that begins in July and ends in June. Performances will take place October through April. The touring activity is scheduled for December and April.

In this example, the variance line of the cash flow statement shows that the company will spend more than it makes in sales and donations for five months out of the year. The actual cash flow projections at the bottom of the page (see Balance) show that four months of the year the company will have a cash flow deficit (February, March, April, May). However, by carefully planning the use of cash reserves, the company should be able to make it through the year.

In this example, if the company starts the year with $154,800 in income in July and $50,085 in expenses, it will have $104,715 left at the end of the month. The balance remains positive until February (see Balance row under Cash Flow Projections). In this month, the theater is short $72,913 at the end of the month. We would describe the organization as "running in the red." It carries that deficit into March. Income exceeds expenses in March, but the theater is carrying a projected deficit of $30,367. The good news is that by June the company has a balance that is positive, or "in the black."

It is easy to see from this simple example how an arts organization can get into financial difficulty. Even though the company is projecting ending the season with a $80,940 surplus (see Balance in the Total column), there might be four months of the season where there is negative cash flow. The financial manager for the theater company would of course take action to prevent this. Funds from reserves could be deposited into the account so it would not be overdrawn. If reserves did not exist in the organization, the possibility of a short-term bank loan might be explored.

Cash Flow Projections - Theater Company

INCOME	July	Aug	Sept	Oct	Nov	Dec	Jan	Feb	Mar	Apr	May	June	TOTAL
Subs Ticket	100,000	175,000	150,000	25,000	0	0	0	0	42,000	75,000	125,000	125,000	817,000
Single Ticket	0	0	7,000	50,000	125,000	150,000	75,000	65,000	60,000	70,000	0	0	602,000
Group Sales	0	10,000	15,000	6,500	7,500	5,000	5,000	2,500	2,000	2,500	0	0	56,000
Advertising	25,000	22,000	22,000	0	0	0	0	0	0	0	1,000	7,000	77,000
Concessions	0	0	0	7,500	8,000	11,000	9,000	8,000	7,500	5,000	0	0	56,000
Gift Shop	0	0	0	1,500	2,500	3,500	2,000	2,000	1,500	2,000	0	0	15,000
Interest	1,300	1,500	1,700	1,200	1,200	1,450	1,400	1,200	1,200	1,300	1,350	1,200	16,000
Set/Cost Rental	0	0	0	0	0	0	3,500	0	0	0	0	0	3,500
Space Rentals	3,500	0	0	0	0	0	0	0	0	0	0	3,500	7,000
Education	0	0	0	0	0	2,500	0	0	0	0	2,700	0	5,200
Miscellaneous	0	0	0	0	0	0	0	0	0	0	3,500	3,000	6,500
Surcharg Tkts	0	0	0	2,100	2,500	2,600	2,500	2,500	2,500	2,300	0	0	17,000
Individual Gifts	8,500	9,500	10,000	10,000	25,000	35,000	30,000	30,000	35,000	30,000	15,000	12,000	250,000
Corporate Support	6,500	7,000	7,500	9,000	15,000	20,000	15,000	8,000	6,500	3,500	1,000	1,000	100,000
Foundations	0	0	25,000	0	0	25,000	0	0	25,000	0	0	25,000	100,000
Co-producers	10,000	10,000	20,000	0	0	30,000	0	0	5,000	0	0	25,000	75,000
Special Events	0	0	0	0	0	0	45,000	55,000	100,000	5,000	0	0	205,000
Matching	0	0	0	100,000	0	10,000	100,000	40,000	0	0	0	0	250,000
State Grants	0	0	0	24,000	0	0	0	0	24,000	0	0	0	48,000
Local Grants	0	0	31,000	0	0	31,000	0	0	0	32,000	0	0	94,000
Federal Grants	0	0	0	0	0	0	0	0	0	0	0	0	-
INCOME	154,800	235,000	289,200	236,800	186,700	327,050	288,400	214,200	312,200	228,600	149,550	177,700	2,800,200

EXPENSES	July	Aug	Sept	Oct	Nov	Dec	Jan	Feb	Mar	Apr	May	June	TOTAL
Artistic Staff	0	0	87,045	110,000	110,000	125,000	110,000	110,000	110,000	110,000	0	0	872,045
Technical Staff	0	61,591	61,591	61,591	61,591	61,591	61,591	61,591	61,591	61,591	61,591	0	615,907
Production	0	38,000	25,000	15,000	10,000	10,000	10,000	10,000	10,000	10,000	1,699	0	139,699
Administrative	12,701	12,701	12,701	12,701	12,701	12,701	12,701	12,701	12,701	12,701	12,701	12,701	152,409
Marketing	18,022	24,500	35,000	100,000	60,000	50,000	5,000	50,000	50,000	50,000	75,000	25,000	542,522
Devel Sal & Exp	13,500	20,000	13,500	13,500	20,000	13,500	13,500	13,500	13,500	13,500	8,000	6,942	162,942
Special Events	0	0	0	0	1,500	1,500	25,000	97,000	1,500	1,500	0	0	128,000
Concessions	0	0	0	4,800	5,000	6,200	5,358	5,500	4,500	4,500	0	0	35,858
Gift Shop	0	3,500	0	0	0	2,935	0	0	0	0	0	0	6,435
Occupancy	5,863	5,863	5,863	5,863	5,863	5,863	5,863	5,863	5,863	5,863	5,863	5,863	70,352
Contingency	0	0	0	15,000	15,000	3,561	0	0	0	0	0	0	33,561
TOTAL EXP	50,085	166,154	240,699	338,454	301,654	292,850	249,012	366,154	269,654	269,654	164,853	50,505	2,759,730
VARIANCE	104,715	68,846	48,501	(101,654)	(114,954)	34,200	39,388	(151,954)	42,546	(41,054)	(15,303)	127,195	40,470

CASH FLOW PROJECTIONS FOR THE FISCAL YEAR ------------>

	July	Aug	Sept	Oct	Nov	Dec	Jan	Feb	Mar	Apr	May	June	TOTAL
RESERVES	0	104,715	173,560	222,061	120,407	5,453	39,653	79,041	(72,913)	(30,367)	(71,421)	(86,725)	$ 40,470
BALANCE	104,715	173,560	222,061	120,407	5,453	39,653	79,041	(72,913)	(30,367)	(71,421)	(86,725)	40,470	$ 80,940

Figure 9.9

Cash flow projections — theater company.

Often an arts organization will not have sufficient reserves to cope with receiving money at times that may not coincide with when it needs to spend money. Once an arts organization begins to find itself in a cycle of borrowing to make up cash flow and paying high short-term interest rates, the erosion of the fiscal foundation of the organization begins. It may take two or three years, but overestimating revenue in combination with overspending and poor cash flow management will eventually lead to a deficit that could bankrupt the organization.

We cover financial management strategies in more detail in Chapter 10, Economics and Financial Management. As you will see, running an arts organization is much the same as running any business. You must make more than you spend. The best way to know if the organization is following this simple rule is to have a good budget reporting system in place. A budget is the key tool to help the manager and the staff stay well informed about the current financial status of the organization.

SUMMARY

Operational control is the process of monitoring performance and making adjustments as required to meet planned objectives. Uncertainty affects all planning. The degree of complexity, human limitations, and centralization also influence how effective an organization's control system will be.

Output and input standards must be clearly established for the organization. Measurement standards must be in place so that a manager can compare what was done with what was expected. A control system requires that there be mechanisms in place for correcting work that does not meet the standard. MBE allows a manager to focus attention on variances in expected performance. MBO encourages the integration of planning objectives and work objectives.

Performance appraisal systems are formal methods for providing feedback to employees on a regular basis. Numerical rating scales, behavioral rating scales, critical incident method, and free-form narratives are techniques used to appraise work output.

Effective control systems depend on data and information gathered from the organization's MIS. The MIS extends into all areas of the organization and is influenced by factors related to the controllability of the information flow through the organization. The organizational design might promote or hinder the effectiveness of the MIS. Some of the possible shortcomings in an MIS include providing too much data, providing irrelevant data, or assuming that computerizing operations will improve the MIS.

Budget control systems are a critical component of an organization. Controlling the distribution of resources and monitoring how effectively the resources are used is a full-time job. Organizations must identify revenue and expense centers and project monetary activity accordingly. A budget can function as a preliminary control on a project by defining the limits on the available resources. Budgets can be fixed, flexible, or zero-based and cover a short- or long-term period. Budget controls concentrate on the timely monitoring of revenue and expenses for all areas of an organization. Budgets may be formatted in a variety of ways to explain how resources are used. Summary, detailed, project, or cash flow budgets may be used in various combinations to provide the information needed to make decisions about the programming for an arts organization.

For additional topics relating to operations and budgeting, please go to www.managementandthearts.com.

Questions

1. What is the relationship of control to the manager's other functions?
2. What are the four steps in the control process? Give a specific example of the control process in an arts setting.
3. Describe the typical steps involved in applying the management by exception process. As a system, how does MBE affect an organization's planning process?
4. From your personal experience, describe a situation in which the control system for an organization did or did not work well. Offer suggestions for appropriate improvements, if applicable.
5. What are the four main appraisal methods used in a control system? Briefly evaluate some of the things you have accomplished in the last year.
6. Define the term *management information system*.
7. What will be some of the future applications of MIS computers in the arts?
8. How is a budget part of the control system?
9. What are the five types of budgets? Which type or types would be most effective in supporting an arts organization?
10. Outline the budget process.

CASE STUDY

Here's an example of an employee who was entrusted as the finance director of an organization losing his way. As often happens when this sort of misuse of resources is discovered, steps are taken to institute a better control system after the fact.

Ex-official of orchestra tells court he's a thief
By John Lynch, Tuesday, Aug. 7, 2007, Arkansas Democrat Gazette
The former finance director of the Arkansas Symphony Orchestra admitted stealing $160,000 from the group Monday,

in exchange for a 10-year prison sentence and paying $24,000 in restitution.

Sentencing is scheduled for January.

Robert David Lee, 48, of Vilonia, wearing the uniform of a Waffle House Manager, pleaded guilty to theft by deception, a Class B felony, after prosecutors agreed to drop five lesser charges of filing fraudulent income tax returns from 2002 to 2006, each a Class D felony.

CASE STUDY (CONTINUED)

Lee, a 14-year symphony employee who earned $42,500 a year, stole the money from July 2001 through September 2005. Deputy prosecuting attorney Suzanne Hixson told Pulaski County Circuit Judge Barry Sims. He used the money for "personal expenses," Hixson told the judge.

Prosecutors are recommending a sentence of 20 years in prison — the maximum — with 10 years suspended and $24,000 in restitution repaid $200 per month upon his release, with a $136,000 civil judgment that will allow the Symphony the option of garnishing his wages. Simms agreed to a request by both sides to delay sentencing until Jan. 14. Lee could be eligible for parole after serving 20 months.

Bill James, Lee's attorney, said Lee is remorseful for the theft, which has embarrassed his family and supporters. He said Lee had been going through "hard financial times." Court records show Lee spent four months in Chapter 7 bankruptcy protection in 1999.

"People sometimes get into these situations, and they get in so deep, they can't get out," James said after the hearing.

He said Lee wanted the sentencing delayed so he could help his daughter finish her high school education.

Lee was placed on unpaid leave in August 2005 when an audit brought on after financial irregularities were discovered revealed about $226,000 in symphony funds had been misspent over the previous four years. Lee, once one of the symphony's highest-paid employees, was arrested in January 2006, accused of embezzling about $160,000. Police and symphony officials said at the time that Lee misused an orchestra credit card, mostly for small household goods and services like car repairs, groceries, and pet supplies. He also got company cellular phones for himself and family members but never reimbursed the symphony, collected a salary advance he never repaid, and used a gasoline card he wasn't entitled to hold.

Gaylen Wixson, who has been the symphony's executive director for about a month, said the symphony has revamped fiscal policies to reduce the opportunities for embezzlement.

"We have taken steps to make sure this could never happen again," he said. "It could happen, but it would be much more difficult."

Lee's thievery, spread over several years, was subtle, Wixson said, and had little impact on the symphony finances.

"The impact on the symphony's bottom line was marginal," he said. "It was not deeply felt."

According to the most recent federal tax filings for the foundation that supports the symphony, representing the nonprofit organization's 2005 fiscal year, the group collected about $3.3 million in total revenue, with about half of that coming from contributions from the public. Concert admissions took in $1.2 million. Total expenses were $3.8 million, and the organization had $2.2 million left over from fiscal 2004.

For more information about the organization got to www.arkansassymphony.org.

Questions

1. What financial controls should have been in place to prevent the finance director from stealing from the symphony?

2. The article notes $226,000 had been misspent in four years, or an average of $56,600 per year. The new executive director notes "The impact on the symphony's bottom line was marginal." Do you reach the same conclusion?

3. The finance director had access to a company credit card, which he used for a variety of household purchases and car repairs. What control system could there have been in place to monitor the use of the credit card?

FYI—Budgeting Information Resources

Two excellent resources on budgeting formation and process are published under the Jossey-Bass Nonprofit and Public Management Series:

> *The Budget-Building Book for Nonprofits*, by Murray Dropkin and Bill LaTouche, 2nd edition (San Francisco: Jossey-Bass, 2007).
>
> *The Cash Flow Management Book for Nonprofits*, by Murray Dropkin and Allyson Hayden (San Francisco: Jossey-Bass, 2001).

REFERENCES

1. John. R. Schermerhorn Jr, *Management for Productivity*, 2nd ed. (New York: John Wiley & Sons, 1986), p. 397.

2. Ibid., p. 397.

3. Ibid., pp. 398–399.

4. Ibid., p. 400.

5. Ibid., pp. 414–416.

6. Ibid., pp. 404–405.

7. Arthur G. Bedeian, *Management* (New York: Dryden Press, CBS College Publishing, 1986), p. 588.

8. Schermerhorn, *Management for Productivity*, p. 447.

9. Ibid., pp. 449–450.

10. Ibid., p. 428.

CHAPTER 10

Economics and Financial Management

Yet no matter how highly we may value them, art and culture are produced by individuals and institutions working within the general economy, and therefore cannot escape the constraints of the material world.

James Heilbrun and Charles M. Gray, *The Economics of Art and Culture*

KEY WORDS

Productivity	FMIS
Inflation	FASB, GAAP
Market and Market Failure	Cash-Based accounting
Multiplier effect	Accrual-Based accounting
TFC, TVC, AFC, AVC, TC, VC, FC	Unrestricted net assets, Temporarily
Law of diminishing returns	restricted net assets,
Economies of Scale	Permanently restricted net
Law of demand	assets
Demand determinants	Liabilities
Law of supply	Assets
Supply determinants	Paper trail
Elasticity, Demand elasticity,	Debits and credits
Supply elasticity	Balance Sheet
Scaling the house	Statement of Activity
Income effect	Ratio Analysis
CFO	CDs and T bills

One of the objectives of this chapter is to help you gain an understanding of the impact of the economy on arts organizations. We also will review some basic concepts in economics, financial management, and accounting as applied to the arts. However, this chapter is not intended as a substitute for course work in economics, finance, or accounting. Undergraduate course work in these subjects will be invaluable to your career in arts management.

Skills and knowledge about managing the basic business affairs of an arts organization can help keep everyone focused on the mission. Without sufficient financial resources your mission statement will be just that — a statement. To put your mission into action you will need cash and credit just like any other business.

THE ECONOMIC BIG PICTURE

The economy has a direct effect on artists and arts organizations every day in the United States. Staying aware of the economic environment allows arts managers the opportunity to prepare plans of action designed to ensure the survival of the organization. Here are some basic questions related to the economy:

1. Will there be a downturn or an upturn in the economy?
2. Will people have more or less disposable income?
3. How will inflation affect our operating costs?
4. How will changes in interest rates affect the budget and the organization's investments?

Ultimately, the answers to these and many other questions remain uncertain because the economic information that a manager needs to make decisions is often contradictory. One report says that the economy is headed for recession, and another says that the growth economy will continue for another year. A mixture of good judgment, diverse sources of information, and a healthy dose of skepticism are necessary ingredients for an arts manager.

THE ECONOMIC PROBLEMS AND ISSUES FACING THE ARTS

A limited number of studies have been done and a few books have been written about the arts and economics. One book that is required reading for all arts managers is William J. Baumol and William G. Bowen's landmark study, *Performing Arts: The Economic Dilemma*,[1] published in 1966. The book was the first detailed analysis of the economic conditions of the arts in the United States and it provides an excellent historical perspective.

A newer source for information about the economy and the arts is James Heilbrun and Charles M. Gray's *The Economics of Art and Culture*, published in 2001. This book provides a comprehensive and updated view on the micro-economics of the arts and public policy in America.

The most recent study of the economic impact of the arts may be found at the Americans for the Arts Web site. *The Arts & Economic Prosperity III* report offers a comprehensive view of the impact of the arts across the United States (see In The News). This report published in June 2007 provides significant data and information about the economic impact of the arts on 156 communities from all 50 states.

In the News

The Americans for the Arts study published in June 2007 titled *Arts & Economic Prosperity III*, was a landmark study of the economic impact of the arts in America. The full study is available at www.artsusa.org/information_services/research/services/economic_impact/default.asp.

The following is an excerpt from the summary report.

Economic Impact of America's Nonprofit Arts & Culture Industry

Nonprofit arts and culture organizations pay their employees, purchase supplies, contract for services, and acquire assets from within their communities. Their audiences generate event-related spending for local merchants such as restaurants, retail stores, hotels, and parking garages. This study sends an important message to community leaders that support for the arts is an investment in economic well-being as well as quality of life.

Nationally, the nonprofit arts and culture industry generates $166.2 billion in economic activity every year — $63.1 billion in spending by organizations and an additional $103.1 billion in event-related spending by their audiences. The impact of this activity is significant, supporting 5.7 million U.S. jobs and generating $29.6 billion in government revenue.

Nonprofit Arts & Culture: A Growth Industry

The nation's nonprofit arts and culture industry has grown steadily since the first analysis in 1992, expanding at a rate greater than inflation. Between 2000 and 2005, spending by organizations and their audiences grew 24 percent, from $134 billion to $166.2 billion. When adjusted for inflation, this represents a healthy 11 percent increase. Gross Domestic Product, by comparison, grew at a slightly faster rate of 12.5 percent (adjusted for inflation).

Spending by nonprofit arts and culture organizations grew 18.6 percent between 2000 and 2005, from $53.2 billion to $63.1 billion (a 4 percent increase when adjusted for inflation). Event-related spending by audiences attending a nonprofit arts and culture event increased 28 percent during the same period, from $80.8 billion to $103.1 billion, or 15 percent when adjusted for inflation. Audience spending was not studied in the 1992 analysis.

Nonprofit Arts & Culture Organizations

Nonprofit arts and culture organizations are active contributors to the business community. They are employers, producers, consumers, and members of chambers of commerce, as well as key partners in the marketing and promotion of their cities and regions. Spending by nonprofit arts and culture organizations nationally was estimated at $63.1 billion in 2005. This output supports 2.6 million U.S. jobs, provides $57.3 billion in household income, and generates $13.2 billion in total government revenue.

Industry Employment Comparisons

Spending by nonprofit arts and culture organizations provides rewarding employment for more than just artists, curators, and musicians. It also directly supports builders, plumbers, accountants, printers, and an array of occupations spanning many industries.

In 2005, nonprofit arts and culture organizations alone supported 2.6 million full-time equivalent jobs. Of this total, 1.3 million jobs were a result of "direct" expenditures by nonprofit arts organizations, representing 1.01 percent of the U.S. workforce. Compared to the size of other sectors of the U.S. workforce, this figure is significant.

Nonprofit arts and culture organizations support more jobs than there are accountants and auditors, public safety officers, even lawyers, and just slightly fewer than elementary school teachers.

It must be noted that the arts and culture jobs represent portions of multiple industry sectors (e.g., musicians, designers, accountants, printers), whereas the comparison groups are single job classifications.

Sources: Americans for the Arts, Washington, DC, 2007 and www.AmericansForThe Arts.org. Used with permission.

The cultural boom from an economic perspective

During the late 1950s and 1960s there was what has been called a "cultural boom" in America. Attendance at arts events was up, the number of performing arts groups was increasing yearly, and regional performing arts centers were built everywhere. One of the interesting facts that Baumol and Bowen found was that, although there was indeed a lot of activity, the actual growth of the arts in relation to all other factors of the economy was very modest. By adjusting and correcting the data for inflation, population increases, and income growth, they found very little change between 1929 and 1963.

Heilbrun and Gray's more recent study came to a more positive conclusion. They noted, "Many of the indicators of real arts activity showed rates of increase during the 1970s that exceeded the growth in real income."[2] They go on to indicate that "The performing arts were gaining faster than the economy as a whole during the 1970s and 1980s."[3] The key measure Heilbrun and Gray examined was spending on the arts as a function of disposable personal income (DPI). "After reaching a level of less than 7 cents per $100 of DPI in the mid-1970s, consumer spending on the performing arts rose to 9.1 cents per $100 in 1980 and 13.4 cents in 1990."[4]

Trend shift in the 1980s

Heilbrun and Gray go on to note that toward the end of the 1980s the number of performances and performing arts organizations began to decline. The DPI increase in spending on the arts noted in the late 1980s and early 1990s therefore seems to be due in part to the price increases for admissions and tickets.[5]

The arts audience

Before Baumol and Bowen's study, there was very little statistical data available about who was attending various theater, dance, opera, and concert performances in the United States. Their landmark study used detailed audience surveys to gather data on income levels, education, age, gender, and preferences.

They found that the "common man" was fairly uncommon among those who attended live professional performances. Audiences were predominantly white-collar with high levels of education and income. Forty-five percent of the audience members were between 35 and 60 years of age. Their research also led them to estimate that in 1966 about 4 percent of the U.S. population over 18 years of age attended some professional arts event. Taken at today's population levels, that would translate to around 12 million people.

Heilbrun and Gray's book updates Baumol and Bowen's study with the assistance of various NEA surveys done in the 1980s. For example, one recent survey of America pointed out that 93 percent watched television and 63 percent attended movies, while only 24.5 percent attended musicals, 15.6 percent classical music concerts, 15.8 percent theater, 5.8 percent ballet, and 4.7 percent attended opera.[6] They found similar results when profiling the participation rates at music concerts, theater, and art museums.

Income also plays a major role in arts participation. For example, participation at the lower income levels for classical music was 6.8 percent. The highest level of incomes recorded participation rates at 35 percent. The same sort of gap seemed to exist for theater (8.2 percent lower income versus 31.9 percent highest income) and for museum attendance (18.8 percent lowest versus 59.6 percent highest).[7]

In the more than 40 years since Baumol and Bowen's study, not a great deal has changed when it comes to audience composition. The audience for "high culture" events such as opera, theater, dance, and museum fine arts exhibits continues to be a defined segment of the population. One trend commented on in *The Economics of Art and Culture* that is of particular concern to arts managers is that, as a percentage, the baby boom generation does not seem to attend arts events to the degree the older pre-WWII generation did. For more details on this trend, please see *Age and Arts Participation*, Research Division Report #34, National Endowment for the Arts, 1996.

Baumol and Bowen's earlier research about the audience profile is further supported by the 2002 NEA Survey of Public Participation in the Arts in America. For example, 26 percent of the 2002 U.S. population were college graduates or had graduate degrees. However, of the survey group, 62.5 percent of the classical music audience had achieved this level of education. When looking at personal income statistics, 61.2 percent of the audiences for the symphony made $50,000 or above.[8]

The NEA report shows many millions of people attending arts events in America. In fact, their study indicated 81 million adults went to at least one arts event in 2001–02. This number represents a much higher percentage than Baumol and Bowen estimated as the participation rate in the 1960s. This difference may in part be due to how the questions were posed in the surveys that were administered.

The productivity issue

Baumol and Bowen's detailed 1966 economic study uncovered data that support the conclusion that the financial difficulties arts groups were experiencing would probably only worsen over time. The basis for their finding was directly related to how the entire economic system has seen slow but steady growth in productivity. *Productivity* in labor, for example, is typically a product of *dividing the hours spent producing an output (a product or service) by the labor it took to produce the output.* In applying this definition, new technologies and processes of production increase the quantity of work output for each employee, that is, worker productivity increases over time. This, in turn, should reduce the cost per unit for production and increase profits. There can be similar gains in a service industry too. As an employee becomes more familiar with a process (selling a ticket), the employee should be able to process more orders per hour up to a point.

To stay ahead of *inflation*, which is the *constant increase in the price levels of everything*, a business must find ways to more productively use the labor force and any other inputs needed to produce the product or service. Without productivity gains, the producer would have to raise the price higher and higher to cover the increasing input costs. If other companies that make a similar product are able to increase productivity, the prices they charge could be kept lower. This would cause consumers to buy the less costly product and would eventually put the less productive company out of business.

Baumol and Bowen applied the result of inflation and the challenge of productivity to arts organizations and found the basis for an ongoing gap between income and expenses. The authors argued that the process of presenting an arts event was subject to limited increases in productivity. The time it takes to rehearse and perform a play, opera, dance, or symphony was not subject to increases in productivity. In addition, the supply of the product was limited. A live performance can only be repeated a certain number of times in a day. Over time, if you increase the wages of the employees (e.g., the orchestra musicians) but it still takes them the same amount of time to prepare and present the product (the concert), you will experience a decline in productivity as economists view it.

The application of technology to almost all phases of American business has also helped increase productivity. Technology in the offices or production areas of arts organizations has helped make people more productive. However, no amount of technology will have a significant impact on shortening the time spent on rehearsing a scene, repeating a musical passage until it is perfect, or hanging an exhibit.

From that conclusion, and from the data collected on the gap between the income generated and the expenses incurred presenting productions and concerts over a 15–year period, Baumol and Bowen predicted that arts productivity would decline over time as other segments of the economy became more productive. The long-term effect of this is an ever-increasing cost that would have to be met by raising ticket prices and increasing donated income. Baumol and Bowen also projected cost increases caused by inflation coupled with limited productivity and higher labor costs would further increase the shortfall of revenue to expenses in the arts.

In most cases, salaries and the costs of benefits, utilities, supplies, and so forth, are increasing each year. The base inflation often cited in the press and in reports from government agencies is between 2 to 3 percent per year. Therefore, unless ticket prices are increased by that amount, more performances are scheduled, or more funds are raised, arts organizations will be facing an ever-increasing income gap.

Any arts group that attempts to ignore the implications of the income gap in its strategic planning, marketing, or fundraising efforts will eventually find itself going into a deficit unless it cuts expenses. However, there was some good news to report by Heilbrun and Gray in their 2001 book. They made the important finding that increased revenue from higher ticket and admission prices had in fact mitigated the severity of the productivity issue and the projected income versus expense gap. They noted that many arts organizations had increased the prices of their services above the rate of inflation.

What do Baumol and Bowen's and Heilbrun and Gray's studies lead us to conclude thus far? The optimist might conclude that the economic system has worked well enough to get us to the point where a substantial number of arts organizations are operating in a wider geographical distribution than ever before. Personal discretionary income keeps increasing at a fast enough rate that consumers have money to spend on tickets and to make gifts for arts organizations after paying all their other living costs. On the other hand, a pessimist might conclude that arts organizations have expanded too much in relation to the real market demand for their products. Because of this overexpansion, there may be too many arts groups chasing too few dollars. Over the long run, arts organizations will need to contract their size and scope to match the ability of audiences and donors to support their activities and programming.

THE ECONOMIC ENVIRONMENT AND THE ARTS

It has been pointed out that our culture as a country is expressed in part through its artistic creations and activity. Our society seems willing to continue to invest its resources in the arts because enough people want and need what the arts provide. The satisfaction gained from creating and consuming the arts ensures their place in the overall economic system. However, if the system is to work for the benefit of everyone, the artists and the arts organizations must take an active role in shaping public policy about the place of the arts in society.

Arts managers need to understand basic principles of economics when contemplating how best to support and sustain an organization in today's business world. What we call "economics," at its most basic level, is a study of how people use the financial resources they possess. How do they use the money they have? After paying for the basics such as food, housing, and clothing, what do people buy or consume that is not essential to survival?

As an arts manager you are especially interested in how consumers behave with these discretionary monies relative to your products. Buying tickets to a show or an admission to a museum, or becoming a subscriber, member, or donor, is something consumers have the choice to do. They may decide to buy something else to achieve whatever entertainment needs they have.

There is stiff competition directed at influencing which arts and entertainment products people use. It is important for an arts manager to develop an understanding of the demand for their arts product relative to the supply, how much people are willing to spend on consuming it, and what the long-term potential is for support through donations or gifts from their supporters.

Another basic economic issue to consider is that for any business to sustain itself in our economy it must bring in as much or more income than it spends to deliver its goods (things) or services (e.g., the experience of attending a show). If you are in the for-profit business of providing an entertainment experience such as a Broadway show, then you must charge enough for the tickets to pay all the costs of doing the show day after day. You must also eventually pay back the investors a profit for the risk they took with their money in the first place. For example, in the twenty-first century, it is common for tickets to Broadway shows to cost in excess of $80 to $100 per seat. In some cases, the price may be even higher. The reason for these high-cost tickets is directly related to the cost to produce the show and sustain its operation week to week. With production costs in the millions, the expectation of making back a significant profit is often low. While there is an incentive for the investor that maybe someday they will make back their investment plus a profit, many of them invest out of a love for the theater as an art form. (See the section Other Resources on Arts Economics and Finance at the end of this chapter for books pertaining to Broadway and Broadway producing.)

Arts managers need to watch several long-term trends relative to the economic health of their organizations. One of the trends relates the exposure to the arts provided through the education system. Early exposure to and involvement in the arts seems to result in later patterns of arts attendance. Education, for example, tends to correlate strongly with arts consumption. There may very well be a drop in future generations of audiences if the education system cannot promote an active learning environment in the arts.

Another trend that will have an economic impact is the demographic shift of the baby boom generation that fueled much of the growth in arts audiences in the second half of the twentieth century. The graying audiences also present an opportunity to share their wealth through legacy gifts. There is a significant demographic shift in America, which involves changes in the ethnic and racial distribution of people. There are economic impacts that need to be anticipated in the shifting demographics. For example, the 2002 NEA survey of public participation in the arts demonstrated that Hispanics and African Americas participated at significantly lower percentages than the White population.[9]

Market failure and the arts

Another core economic concept to remember is that our society supports activities that do not necessarily pay for themselves through sales. For example, government is a sector of the economy that is not driven solely by the profit motive. Some of the basic services provided by government are not designed to generate a profit. They exist as a benefit for us all. Police and fire protection in your community are not operated for a profit, but rather from a motive of providing us with security and peace of mind.

The sector of the economy that many nonprofit arts organizations operate in is also driven, to a large extent, by this motive of providing benefit to society. Our government tax system sanctions a special status to nongovernmental agencies to provide goods and services that the profit sector cannot efficiently deliver. Over the last 100 years, the nonprofit sector became the main force behind the delivery of the fine and performing arts in America. Why? Some economists might say that this is due in part to a *market failure*. This simply means that the supply and demand for the fine and performing arts are not in balance, and some intervention is needed in this market to ensure its continuance. (A *market* is defined as a *designated interaction of buyers and sellers for a product or service*.)

The profit sector, with the exception of Broadway shows, is not in the "business" of delivering the fine and performing arts to its market due to the simple fact that it cannot make a profit doing so. To address this failure of the marketplace the nonprofit tax-exempt organizations arose to solve this economic problem. Although this is a complex subject, the central idea is that the combination of the revenue from discounted admission or membership fees (or ticket prices) plus the resources raised through government support and donations of money and volunteer time cover operating costs for an arts service that the normal market cannot sustain.

THE ECONOMICS OF SPENDING MORE THAN YOU MAKE

From an economic perspective, many arts organizations operate in a marketplace in which they cannot make enough money to sustain themselves from the revenues collected solely from admissions to performances, services, or exhibitions. Arts organizations often deliberately under-price their product with the rationale that they are making what they do more widely available to people in the community. The motive is often stated that nonprofit arts groups are in "business" to deliver their experience to the greatest number of people by keeping the price as low as possible.

The common understanding underlying the not-for-profit sector is that in exchange for doing these performances or exhibitions, the government will grant an exemption from paying taxes on the income from sales, and it will further allow organizations to solicit funds from individuals, foundations, and corporations. In addition, any surplus revenue above operating expenses will be used to support the mission of the organization and not individual "shareholders," or in this case, the board members. Federal, state, and local governments also agree to allow people who wish to donate money or property to the organization to accomplish these good things. The tax system allows people to deduct a percentage of their support of not-for-profit organizations from their personal income taxes.

Ticket Prices and Revenue Generation

As an exercise, take the total operating budget for a performing arts organization in your community and divide it by the total number of seats they have to sell in a season. The resulting number will give you an idea how much each seat must sell for if the organization was to make budget. Further refine this number by developing the average percentage of total tickets sold by the organization in a season and divide that number by the operating budget (assuming the organization will share this information with you). For example, if the organization has a $100,000 budget and 6,000 seats to sell, then each seat would have to sell for $16.67 if the organization was to balance its budget without gifts or grants. If they only sold 60% of their tickets, then they would have to charge $27.78 per ticket to balance the budget. Compare the actual prices of tickets compared to your per seat estimate.

THE MULTIPLIER EFFECT AND THE ARTS

As noted early in this chapter, one key area that arts managers have stressed to their communities in the last few years is the positive economic impact of the organization. Arts organizations expend funds; pay salaries, wages, taxes, and benefits; and purchase goods and services in the community. They also help stimulate the local economy through the multiplier effect of money. The *multiplier effect* describes a process whereby money expended for one purpose (paying a salary) has an impact beyond that single use. For example, the salary paid to a staff member is used to buy groceries and make a rent payment, as well as pay for other goods and services in the community.

The impact of the basic operation of the arts organization extends into other areas of the community. As noted, the salaries paid to staff members are used to pay for goods and services such as car loans, rent, or a mortgage. The money is also then used by the property owner, bank, or store to purchase things or to make loans. In effect, the money that the arts organization puts into the local economy ripples throughout the region and state. In addition, when consumers buy tickets and make the journey to the performance, they may pay for a babysitter, gas for the car, a meal at a restaurant, and parking, and they may make a purchase at the arts center's gift shop. The $50 paid for the ticket may generate four or five times that amount in other goods and services. As noted in the Americans for the Arts economic impact study, the arts generated $166.2 billion in economic activity in 2005.[10]

APPLYING BASIC ECONOMIC PRINCIPLES TO THE ARTS

Let's now look at several terms and concepts from economics and relate them to how an arts organization operates. For example, calculating the impact of such things as *total fixed cost, total variable costs, average fixed* and *average variable costs,* and *marginal costs* helps the organization with financial and operational planning. The ideas related to the *law of diminishing returns*, long-term operational costs, and *economies of scale* have some application to the arts. Let's take a brief look at some of these principles from economics.

Fixed, variable, and marginal costs

All organizations must identify the fixed costs of operation to form the base operating budget. Total fixed costs (TFC) typically include expenses for such things as renting or leasing space, paying salaries, permanent equipment, and repaying loans. The important consideration in assessing your fixed costs is that these costs will not change whether you do any performances or if the museum is open to the public that day or not. TFC are just that, fixed and they have no bearing on your programming. For example, the salaries for a core administrative staff and the various benefits paid to them represent the largest fixed cost of an arts organization.

When performers, designers, technicians, and other specialized staff are hired for a given production, project, or event (assuming a season of several shows or exhibitions), these expenses are usually considered as part of your *total variable costs* (TVC). The variability lies in the fact that you control these costs by selecting the scope and scale of the production. If you decide to do Beethoven's Ninth Symphony you are going to need to add more musicians and chorus members to the budget. If you opt for a chamber orchestra program your variable costs would likely be less. In addition, materials purchased for the scenery and costumes, phone calls, blueprints, paint, and labor to produce the show are all part of the TVC. The *total cost* (TC) represents the total of the fixed and variable costs (TC = TFC + TVC).

Another key indicator of costs is the *marginal cost* (MC), which is defined as *the cost of producing one more of the product or service.* In the performing arts, the most obvious output increase would be the number of performances scheduled. For example, when you plan for an evening concert performance, you can estimate the TVC and TFC associated with that concert. Typically, the MC of doing another performance that afternoon should be less than the marginal cost of scheduling another performance for the next day. One reason why the MC might be lower is that the rental of the performance space may be based on a daily rate of eight hours. If you use the space for only four hours in the evening, you still pay for the time you do not use the space. The matinee performance would not add to the variable costs of the hall. Your payroll and production costs also would rise with the extra performance.

These additional costs would offset the gains from the decreased hall rental and would allow the organization to gain firsthand experience with the *law of diminishing returns*. The law states that *"as more and more of a variable factor of production, or input (e.g., labor) is used together with a fixed factor of production, beyond some point the additional, or marginal, output attributable to the variable factor begins to fall."*[11] To put it simply, at some point the costs rise enough to reduce the marginal gain from scheduling the additional performance.

A similar scenario may be developed for an exhibition. Adding to the time an exhibit is opened to the public may bring increased marginal costs and gains to the organization. The marginal costs of being opened more hours or to run the exhibit longer would need to be calculated to see if indeed the organization was reaping some benefit for the extra expenses. If the costs to pay the gallery monitors continually exceed the admission revenue gained by the extra hours the manager would need to decide if they want to keep sustaining the loss.

Profit-making arts ventures must constantly watch all the direct costs related to making, selling, distributing, and advertising the product as well as the marginal costs. Otherwise, there will be no money left to call a profit. Nonprofit organizations are not in business to generate revenue above costs for the owners or investor. That said, they must also carefully control fixed, variable, and marginal costs. In fact, a nonprofit organization may generate a surplus of revenue as part of its overall budget plan. To generate a surplus or to break even, the arts manager must draw on a great deal of skill in controlling costs, setting prices, and estimating demand. In other words, operating a nonprofit arts organization requires as much financial skill as operating for-profit ventures.

Putting Fixed, Variable, and Marginal Costs to Work

Let's put these concepts of fixed, variable, and marginal costs into perspective. The first important point to consider is that for arts organizations most costs are really fixed costs (FC). Over time, the organization develops a pattern of events that becomes predictable. You open your season in October and end it in May, or your exhibitions change every 16 or 18 weeks. Therefore, in many arts organizations the variable costs (VC) would only surface if you decided to extend the run of the show or the exhibition.

Figure 10.1 is an example of a performing arts group charging $14 a ticket to an event in a 500-seat theater that sells an average of 60 percent of its

Figure 10.1

Production profit versus loss.

Production Profit and Loss

(Assumes $14/ tkt)

Output - # Perfs	Fixed Costs (FC)	Variable Costs (VC)	Total Costs (TC) = (FC)+(VC)	Avg Cost (AC) = (TC)/Output	Total Rev @60% cap of 500 seats	Profit or (Loss)
1	$ 25,000	$ 500	$25,500	$25,500	$ 4,200	$ (21,300)
2	$ 25,000	$ 750	$25,750	$12,875	$ 8,400	$ (17,350)
3	$ 25,000	$ 1,250	$26,250	$8,750	$ 12,600	$ (13,650)
4	$ 25,000	$ 2,000	$27,000	$6,750	$ 16,800	$ (10,200)
5	$ 25,000	$ 3,000	$28,000	$5,600	$ 21,000	$ (7,000)
6	$ 25,000	$ 4,250	$29,250	$4,875	$ 25,200	$ (4,050)
7	$ 25,000	$ 5,750	$30,750	$4,393	$ 29,400	$ (1,350)
Profit point begins at the eighth performance						
8	$ 25,000	$ 6,500	$31,500	$3,938	$ 33,600	$ 2,100
9	$ 25,000	$ 7,500	$32,500	$3,611	$ 37,800	$ 5,300
10	$ 25,000	$ 8,800	$33,800	$3,380	$ 42,000	$ 8,200
11	$ 25,000	$ 10,000	$35,000	$3,182	$ 46,200	$ 11,200
12	$ 25,000	$ 11,500	$36,500	$3,042	$ 50,400	$ 13,900
13	$ 25,000	$ 13,000	$38,000	$2,923	$ 54,600	$ 16,600
14	$ 25,000	$ 14,500	$39,500	$2,821	$ 58,800	$ 19,300
15	$ 25,000	$ 14,500	$39,500	$2,633	$ 63,000	$ 23,500
16	$ 25,000	$ 14,500	$39,500	$2,469	$ 67,200	$ 27,700
17	$ 25,000	$ 14,500	$39,500	$2,324	$ 71,400	$ 31,900
18	$ 25,000	$ 14,500	$39,500	$2,194	$ 75,600	$ 36,100
19	$ 25,000	$ 14,500	$39,500	$2,079	$ 79,800	$ 40,300
20	$ 25,000	$ 14,500	$39,500	$1,975	$ 84,000	$ 44,500

Note: Variable costs are hypothetical

seating capacity. After eight performances, the group begins to make more money than it costs to produce each performance of the event. If the group schedules 16 performances, it begins to make more money than the original investment of $25,000 in fixed costs and $500 in variable costs. Average costs (AC) go down significantly as the number of performances go up (AC = TC/ Number of Performances).

NOTE: The numbers used in Figure 10.1 are fictitious and are not intended to depict any specific arts organization. In the "real world," the FC would be made up of the materials and labor expenses required to produce the event. The VC in this example could be attributed to extra box office staff, house management staff, or run crew hired to work only the performances of the show. The assumption is that the actor and designer fees or salaries are part of the FC.

Economies of scale

Another issue related to overall cost is how economies of scale operate in an organization. The technical definition of *economies of scale* is "a decrease in the long-run average total costs (ATC) of production that occur when larger facilities are available for manufacturing a product."[12] These economies are achieved because the business is able to specialize production techniques, its labor force becomes more expert, volume discounts are available for materials used to produce the product, or the by-products of manufacturing reach a large enough quantity to become salable.

There are limited applications of economies of scale in aspects of the production process and in operating an arts organization. For example, instead of setting up and equipping its own scenery and costume production shop, an organization could develop a central production center used by all of the major arts organizations in the region. This production center could achieve cost savings from scale through construction techniques and bulk purchases as well as by covering shop personnel costs. By scheduling various construction projects and buying in quantity, several organizations may be able to achieve a large enough scale of operation to reduce overall costs.

Another example of economies of scale is a performing arts center with multiple spaces. The assumption is that it is less costly to run three theaters under one roof than three theaters under three roofs. However, *diseconomies of scale* can also affect such centralized operations if management is not careful to control growth as the organization matures. A diseconomy of scale might be achieved by having to hire extra people and buy extra tools to take on the increased scale of production. This would increase the average total costs to produce the sets in the central shop. The savings realized by the scale of the operation would be quickly negated.

Demand, supply, and elasticity

Trying to identify the demand for a particular show or exhibition requires that a manager weigh numerous factors that influence the behavior of consumers. The well-known factors of supply and demand can be directly translated into activities at the core of an arts group's economic operations. Let's begin by looking at the area of demand.

Law of demand

The *law of demand* describes the relationship between the amount of a good or service that a buyer both desires and is able to purchase, and the price charged for the good or service. The law states that the lower the price charged for a good or service, the larger the expected quantity demanded. Conversely, the higher the price, the lower the quantity demanded. This law of demand is based on an important assumption: *only the price change affects the quantity demanded*. Other factors that can influence the ticket buyer are called *demand determinants* and include such things as the prices of other goods and services, income levels, and individual tastes.

Price of other goods

Substitute goods or services may cause a shift in the demand if their prices change. To understand how these factors work, suppose that another group is presenting a classical music concert featuring the same Mozart symphony on the same night in your community. Because the other group is charging $5 less per ticket, the demand for your concert might decline, meaning that the overall demand will go down. Likewise, if the other group is charging $5 more than your group, the demand for your concert may increase.

The demand will also change if a *complementary good* is introduced into the business interaction. A complementary good, which is defined *as a good or service that is used jointly with the original good*, can cause the demand to change depending on whether the price of a complementary good goes up or down. For example, if a large increase in parking fees occurs or the price of gasoline skyrockets, some consumers may be discouraged from purchasing tickets.

Income

Another factor that could affect demand is individual income. If income increases, the law states demand for normal goods and services will also increase. Conversely, if income levels decrease, the demand for normal goods and services will decrease. Normal goods and services are defined as those things that people want as their income increases. Inferior goods or services are defined as those things that people will choose when their income decreases. For example, if there is a significant drop in income levels due to an economic recession, people might choose less expensive forms of entertainment. Instead of buying a $300 season subscription or single tickets to the symphony or theater, people may shift their spending to a less expensive community orchestra or theater series. The community orchestra and theater may not perceive themselves as an "inferior good or service," but in economic theory, the definition can be applied.

Expectations

Demand is affected by individual expectations about the overall economic situation. If consumers think that the price may go up for a good or service, they may make the purchase immediately. This expectation would increase demand. On the other hand, if consumers thought that the price was going to drop, they may delay making the purchase. If enough people share this expectation, overall demand would go down. An arts manager might take advantage of this phenomenon by stressing in a subscription renewal campaign that prices will go up next season but that subscribers who renew by a certain date can save money. This tactic would probably help increase the renewal rate and the demand for tickets.

Tastes

Personal consumer tastes also cause demand to change. If a significant number of people shift their interests away from classical music toward bluegrass, the demand for one will go down while the other increases. An increase in demand also might result from a popular soloist being added to a concert performance.

Market demand and the arts

Do these concepts have any place in the day-to-day planning activities of an arts manager? They can, but remember isolating the variable of the effect of consumer behavior is challenging. For example, a dance group with the mission of bringing "cutting edge" dance to its community would be wise to start with the expectation that there will be limited demand for the product. Although the community may regularly support dance performances by the regional ballet company — indicating a market for the entertainment service of dance — there is no guarantee that this market will also support an experimental dance troupe.

How can this organization affect demand for its concerts? Advertising is one way obvious way to affect the demand for a particular product within an overall market. However, reaching individual consumers with the message about a particular dance organization and the ability to make a sale are two different matters. To understand the entire relationship of the arts organization to the economic environment, we must also look at the supply of the product or service.

Law of supply

We have seen that there is a relationship between price and quantity demanded for a product or service. Now let's look at the supply side laws. The application of these concepts to the operation of an arts organization requires some explanation.

The relationship between the quantity to offer of a product and its price is at the center of the *law of supply*, which states that "suppliers will supply larger quantities of a good at higher prices than at lower prices."[13] For example, if you are the supplier of symphony orchestra performances and your players are all under contract, it is to your benefit to offer this service as many times as possible. Your incentive as a supplier is to offer this product at the highest price you think you can obtain in that market. However, since the product we offer in the arts has a fixed supply (e.g., a concert season of X number of performances with Y number of seats), it is much more difficult to apply the law of supply to what we do. As in the case of demand, there are also other variables that affect the supply of arts events. These variables are called *supply determinants* and include the price of resources, the number of suppliers, and suppliers' expectations.

Price of resources

If the price of resources used in creating the good or service rises or falls, the supply will change. The term *factors of production* is used to describe the "inputs of labor services, raw materials, and other resources" used to create the final product or service.[14] For suppliers, a drop in the factors of production translates into greater profits. Therefore, suppliers have the incentive to supply more because they can make more profit. Conversely, if the factors of production go up, suppliers have an incentive to supply less because their profit margin goes down. Hence, suppliers reduce output to bring production costs into line with the quantity supplied.

However, arts organizations usually have very limited control over the price of resources and even less control over the production costs. For example, a season is selected and the supply of concert performances is set with players paid a pre-arranged fee or salary. The arts manager has little or no ability to intercede by changing the program to reduce the number of players required for a concert.

In the case of arts organizations, we seldom see the behavior exhibited by the theoretical supplier of concert tickets. The law of supply, as applied to this example, does not translate into the ticket supplier reducing the quantity of performances supplied. The idea of creating a shortage of supply is usually not a problem. In fact, if costs increase, the typical concert ticket seller would simply pass the cost along to the consumer in the form of a price increase. The other alternative is to go into debt by not charging enough to cover the costs of production. Ironically, this is what many nonprofit arts organizations do.

Number of suppliers

The entertainment industry, taken as a whole, generally has a great many suppliers at various prices. The supplier of classical music concerts might be able to increase prices if a great number of alternative forms of entertainment disappeared. Or, if you have the only performance available of a specific work with a special performer, you may be able to raise the price despite the number of suppliers in the entertainment industry. A "star" entertainer is a limited supply product that allows the arts organization to increase its price. A star and a single performance become a supply situation that may motivate the supplier to increase the price. It is not unheard of for producers of a special show featuring a star to sell tickets at $500 per seat.

Suppliers' expectations

When establishing the quantity to produce, suppliers consider many different factors. For example, the concert supplier may expect that this will be the final performance before the famous soloist retires and thus increases the number of concert performances and the ticket price.

Elasticity

Let's now turn to the important concept of elasticity. Economists define *elasticity* as the "responsiveness of one variable to the change in another, both changes expressed in percentages."[15] *Demand elasticity* is the responsiveness to changes in the quantity demanded to a change in the price. *Supply elasticity* is the responsiveness to changes in the quantity supplied to a change in price.[16] We will focus on the demand elasticity since that will likely be a more realistic issue an arts manager will face.

Economists say *demand is elastic* when a percentage change in the price produces an even greater percentage change in demand. You might see this happen if you drop your ticket price from $50 to $45 and instead of selling 10 tickets at $50, you sell 13 tickets at $45. We say that *demand is inelastic* if the percentage change in price produces a small or no percentage change in demand. Using the same price change of $50 to $45 may produce no more new sales. *Unitary elastic demand* means the percentage change in price is matched by the same percentage change in demand. In this example, the $50 reduction to $45 produces one more sale. (The formula used for elasticity percentage changes is arrived at by subtracting the change in quantity and dividing it by the sum averaged of the two quantities. The percentage of change in price is determined in the same way. Please see the formula to see how this is expressed.)

ELASTICITY CHANGE FORMULA

Percentage Change in Quantity Demanded

Where $Q1$ = New Quantity and Qo = Original Quantity
$$\%change = Q1 - Qo/(Q1 + Qo)/2$$

Percentage Change in Price

Where $P1$ = New Price and Po = Original Price
$$\%change = P1 - Po/(Pq + Po)/2$$

Price-inelastic ticket sales

Heilbrun and Gray note that studies show that most arts ticket sales seem to be price-inelastic.[17] By that they mean, *changes in ticket prices don't produce significant changes in demand*. If people want to see your production of *Tosca*, and your ticket is $50, that is the price they will pay. If your ticket is $60, they will still buy it because there are no other *Tosca* productions playing in town. The same applies if your ticket is $40. The implication is, if demand is price-inelastic, arts organization could probably charge more for their tickets.[18] In many cases arts promoters do not list ticket prices in their advertising. The assumption is the consumer is not entirely influenced by the price of the ticket. You have probably seen this behavior when a specific touring production or group is performing in your community. Ticket prices might be quite high, but because people want to see the show of the performer they buy tickets anyway.

Supply, demand, elasticity, and revenue maximization

One of your goals as an arts manager may be to maximize revenue from your limited number of events often with a fixed number of seats. You need to consider how much to charge for the event based on what you think your community is willing to pay. You also need to know how price effects demand.

Your first source of information for price points can be found in the other arts groups in your community. A little time spent analyzing the "competition" before setting your prices can help you find the right combination of prices for your arts offering. However, keep in mind that your competition may be under-pricing their product. You must also consider all the other entertainment offerings in your community in your pricing strategies, including theme parks, festivals, first-run films, and so forth.

In Figure 10.2 you will see that if you set your price too high ($50 per ticket) or too low ($10 per ticket) you run the risk of making less revenue. Although revenue maximization is not typically the stated purpose of nonprofit arts organizations, the reality is there are people in the community who are willing to pay $50 for the ticket and others who are willing to pay only $10. In the example given in Figure 10.2, the optimum price to charge is $22 per ticket based on selling 600 tickets. In this example, the estimated demand for tickets has been arbitrarily determined.

The reader may wonder what options they have in making their own estimates for ticket demand. One approach is by comparing your organization's ticket or admission sales history. At what price point do you seem to sell the most tickets? Lacking any historical data, you can try to apply the demand equation demonstrated in Heilbrun and Gray's book The *Economics of Art and Culture*.[19] The challenge with applying the formula is several key variables

Price and Revenue Matrix

Figure 10.2

Price and revenue matrix.

Ticket Price	Estimated Demand with 900 seat capacity	Revenue	Comments
$50	200	$10,000	
$46	225	$10,350	
$42	250	$10,500	
$38	300	$11,400	
$34	350	$11,900	
$30	400	$12,000	
$26	500	$13,000	Range where
$22	600	$13,200	ticket prices and demand
$18	700	$12,600	generate maximum revenue.
$14	800	$11,200	
$10	900	$9,000	

need to be calculated first. For example, you would need to know average annual per capita income in your area, weighted averages for price substitutes (movies, concerts, sporting events, and so forth), and a composite price of complementary goods (gasoline, dinner out, babysitter, and so forth).

Using the information provided in Heilbrun and Gray's formula, you can make a few educated guesses with data you may already have at your disposal. For example, what will be the influence on ticket demand based on per capita income and the cost of substitutes in your region? The per capita income, which will most likely be below the median income in your area, and other key economic indicators are usually available from the local chamber of commerce, the Census Bureau, or from Web sites like www.zipskinny.com.

You also probably know what the substitute costs are for other entertainment options in your community such as movies, DVD rentals, sporting events, and other performing arts groups. The information about complementary goods is also at your disposal. Gasoline prices and the price range of menu items at restaurants that your patrons frequent before or after the show are readily available. After looking at what your audiences may be spending for other related expenses connected to attending your event, you may discover the $22 ticket price in Figure 10.2 is too low.

Looking at Figure 10.2 you can see what happens if you sell 900 tickets at $22 — you generate $19,800 in revenue, which one assumes is a good thing.

However, based on our very rudimentary discussion of demand, supply, and elasticity, it would make more sense to provide $50 tickets to the audience members willing to pay $50 and $10 to the people interested in the less costly tickets. Demand-based pricing is common in the arts, and while more complicated to maintain, it can bring in significantly more revenue per performance.

Scaling the house

Figure 10.3 shows how you can scale ticket prices to match the supply of tickets at certain prices with the demand for those tickets. This example illustrates demand-based pricing or, as it is often called, *scaling the house* using a 900–seat venue. If you were producing an event that was relatively inexpensive, you might be able to charge $14 and $22. Based on your estimated demand you might be able to generate $14,200 in gross sales. On the other hand, this

Figure 10.3

Scaling ticket prices.

Scaling Ticket Prices

Revenue maximization using principles of supply and demand

Assumes 900 seat capacity

Ticket Prices	Quantity to Sell (Supply)	Revenue if sold	Comment
$50	100	$5,000	Pricing based on $4 increments and
$42	150	$6,300	placing a premium on location.
$38	300	$11,400	Assumes a demand for more & less
$34	350	$11,900	expensive seats for the event.
TOTAL	900	$34,600	
OR			
$46	200	$9,200	Pricing based on $4 difference at top
$38	300	$11,400	prices and $8 difference with the
$30	400	$12,000	lowest price ticket.
TOTAL	900	$32,600	
OR			
$38	300	$11,400	Pricing based on $16 difference
$22	600	$13,200	between low and high price.
TOTAL	900	$24,600	
OR			
$22	200	$4,400	Pricing based on customers looking
$14	700	$9,800	for a bargain. Assumes event costs
TOTAL	900	$14,200	are low.

same 900–seat venue could produce almost three times more revenue by pricing your tickets with four levels.

The assumption is that there are a number of people who will want to see the event and are willing to pay $50 to sit in what they perceive is a good location. There is also an assumption that a larger number of people are willing to pay only $34 to see the same artists. Similar price differentials are used in the arts by increasing admissions on the weekends or discounting the admission on weekdays. For example, a museum may charge less Tuesday through Friday and more on the weekends. Depending on your project goals or the cost to produce the event, either pricing approach may be appropriate.

The price scaling of the house may also become a demand-increasing tactic that could have long-term benefits to an organization trying to build an audience. Economists refer to this as the *income effect*. In other words, a price reduction gives people more money to spend. When faced with a choice of paying a minimum ticket price of $34 or $50 for the same event, most people would rather make their dollar go further. However, taking into account your audience members trying to maximize their income by buying lower cost tickets, arts managers will tell you the first seats to generally sell out in a scaled house are the most expensive tickets. The implication of course is then not enough seats were put on sale at the higher price.

Pricing summary

Although this is a simplification of the entire ticket-pricing process, it is a reminder that understanding fundamental concepts in economics is part of an arts manager's job. Most arts organizations base their prices on a complex mix of financial need and educated guesses about what the market will bear. Arts organizations are often stuck with a price set months before the event. For example, if you price tickets at $20 for an event and you sell it out in the first day, you obviously underpriced the tickets. You may think you have just had a big success, when in fact you have in one respect failed by under-pricing your product. You may also be making the error of not supplying enough of the arts product to satisfy demand. Conversely, if you priced the tickets at $50 and sold only 100 of 900 after six weeks, you overpriced the event. Either pricing decision creates problems for the organization.

Summary of basic arts economics

The basic economic principles and laws discussed thus far in this chapter have a clear application to the arts. The relationship of the organization to the macroeconomic environment (the whole economy) and the conditions in the microeconomic environment (the markets) in which the organization operates should have an influence on your planning. Paying close attention to how the overall economy is functioning can help an arts manager develop scenarios for the organization to pursue if the economy in their area begins to falter, flatten, or is booming.

Understanding the demand, supply, and elasticity issues facing the organization is critical. Unless you are fortunate to sell out every performance in a season, the odds are you are going to be grappling with too much supply (seats) and not enough demand. The value a patron places on a seat is relative. If they really want to see your production of *Tosca*, the price is not going to be a big concern.

The ability to predict and control fixed and variable costs, and the ability to calculate marginal costs and gains can help keep the organization from falling into financial trouble. Finally, it is important for nonprofit organizations to accept that the income gap is a factor in doing business. Strict cost-control strategies and plans can be adopted to minimize the negative consequences of this underlying problem. Arts organizations that closely monitor their costs seem better prepared to cope with tougher economic times.

Now let's move on to the important business of managing the funds you do generate from sales, donations, and grants.

OVERVIEW OF FINANCIAL MANAGEMENT

We have seen thus far, to manage an arts organization successfully one must understand something about economics. The financial management of the arts organization is the practice of applying many of the principles of economics to the day-to-day operation of the organization. The financial management, budgeting, and accounting system in an arts organization is in a sense the bridge between the economic environment and the operating budget.

In *Managing a Nonprofit Organization*, Thomas Wolf notes, "financial management is, for many, one of the most forbidding aspects of the administration of nonprofit organizations."[20] This is due in part to phobias about anything related to quantitative thinking. When faced with reviewing a budget or balance sheet, board members may develop a glazed look in their eyes and suddenly lose the ability to reason. Even worse, they may approve budgets and accept financial statements without fully understanding the numbers. Unfortunately, comprehension usually comes to the board of directors when it is too late to correct a financial problem that has been staring them in the face for months.

In this section we first develop an overview of financial management in profit and nonprofit organizations and then move on to the financial management information system. We integrate the whole system into the balance sheet and statement of account activity. Lastly, we develop a basic structure for the business management of the arts organization.

The role of the business manager

In many arts organizations, the responsibility for financial records, budgets, payroll, and money management falls to a business manager who works under the supervision of a general manager, executive director, or managing director. In a smaller organization, an office manager who also acts as an accountant or bookkeeper, may do the business management and the processing and record keeping. This person reports to the artistic director and the chair of the board of directors. In larger organizations you may find a staff listing for the Chief Financial Officer (CFO).

As we saw in Chapter 9, Operations and Budgeting, many arts organizations do not start with a management information system (MIS). Instead, a system evolves as the organization grows. The same is true for the financial management of the organization. If it is to be effective, a *financial management information system* (FMIS) must be a comprehensive reporting, control, and processing system that helps managers realize the financial objectives of the organization. The financial management of the organization is one of the manager's most important responsibilities. The long-term health of the enterprise depends on the arts manager's vigilance in monitoring the revenue, expenses, and investments of the organization.

NONPROFIT FINANCIAL MANAGEMENT

Because the primary objective of most nonprofit arts organizations is not focused on increasing the wealth of the owners or stockholders, the financial manager's job is somewhat different from what it is in the profit sector. A nonprofit organization is still a business and it must collect as much or more revenue than it expends, or it will go out of business.

The business or financial manager's job in a nonprofit organization is critical to planning and using the limited resources available. For example, if the artistic director wants to add another show to the season, do a world premiere, or take a production on tour, how will the organization pay for this activity? Understanding the cash flow, current debt load, assets, and so on, is the first step in analyzing what can and cannot be done.

An effective financial manager maximizes the use of the available resources. For example, revenue raised through ticket sales or cash donations should be invested to generate further revenue. If an organization collects $200,000 from subscription sales for next season's shows, that money should be invested in interest-earning accounts before it is needed for the new season's operating budget. A financial manager also actively seeks out ways to minimize costs for insurance (health and life) and to reduce other operating costs.

FMIS

In Chapter 9, Organizing and Budgeting, we learned that the MIS is responsible for gathering data, formulating information, and distributing it throughout the organization. The FMIS is a key part of the overall MIS. Figure 10.4 shows a schematic drawing of an FMIS.

The FMIS must ultimately provide the board of directors and management with accurate, timely, and relevant information based on the data that the system has gathered. Without this information, making decisions, and planning will not work effectively. The questions are usually very simple: Did we spend more than we budgeted? Why? Did we raise less than we budgeted? Why? Did we increase or decrease our debt? Will we have sufficient resources to continue operating? Can we make the payroll this month?

If the system is working properly, the answers to these questions pose no problem for management. For the system to work properly, the operating system visualized in Figure 10.4 must accurately gather the data needed to process the records. These data become the information used in reports and in the analysis of the current financial health of the organization. At the same time, the organization has specific legal responsibilities to report on its financial activities to various state and federal agencies. The FMIS must be capable of gathering and reporting this information if the organization is to retain its nonprofit legal status.

The FMIS serves two important purposes. It provides information about the fiscal health of the organization to people inside the organization, and it reports to external agencies, such as the IRS, and to granting agencies, such as the NEA and state and local arts councils.

Developing an FMIS

The FMIS illustrated in Figure 10.4 requires that data from the operating system be transmitted to the records system. These data are then drawn from various reports used by the different departments in the operation. To report accurately on the fiscal activity of the organization, an accounting and record-keeping system must be in place. Figure 10.5 shows one version of an accounting system. In this case, the flow is from the top to the bottom of the page.

The personal computer and inexpensive accounting software have had a tremendous positive impact on arts organizations. Inexpensive systems are available to help small organizations quickly enter data and print reports. However, due to the nature of nonprofit businesses, different reporting formats are required when discussing how much the "business" is worth and how it is using its assets.

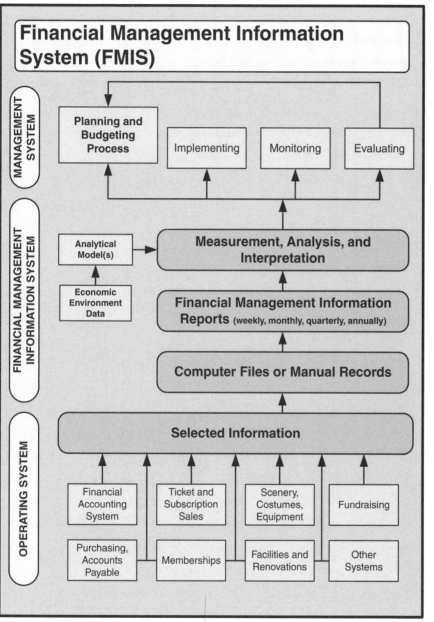

Figure 10.4
Financial management information system (FMIS).

Figure 10.5
Accounting system overview.

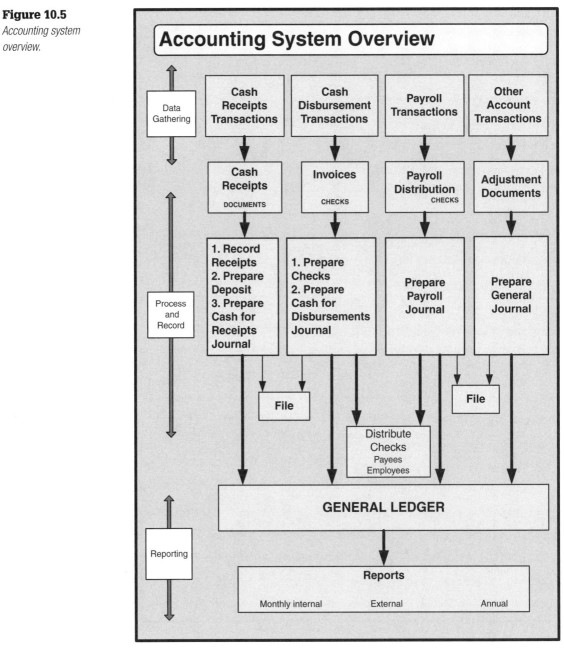

SOURCE: Frederick J. Turk and Robert P. Gallo, *Financial Management Strategies for Arts Organizations,* (New York: American Council for the Arts, 1984). Copyright © 1984 by the American Council for the Arts. Used with permission.

ACCOUNTING AND BOOKKEEPING

Accounting is usually defined as identifying, collecting, analyzing, recording, and summarizing business transactions and their effects on a business. A *transaction*, which is a key element in this definition, is an exchange of property or services. *Bookkeeping* involves the clerical work of recording the transaction. In a sense, the accountant begins where the bookkeeper leaves off by summarizing and interpreting the records or books. In many cases, bookkeeping and accounting are done by the same person.

The Financial Accounting Standards Board (FASB) oversees the practices of the profession and regularly updates what is referred to as the Generally Accepted Accounting Principles (GAAP). Accounting has evolved its own specialized language to describe transaction activity. Let's look at a few key terms.

Cash-based accounting

A personal checking account is one example of a cash-based accounting system. You make a deposit, you write checks, and at the end of the month, you have a positive or negative balance. The major problem with the cash-based system is that it gives you no information about how much you are worth, how much you owe, or how much is owed by others to you. However, it is simple to keep this account, and many small organizations keep cash accounts to record their business activities.

Accrual-based accounting

The accrual system recognizes expenses when they are incurred and income when it is committed. The primary advantage of this system is that it shows future commitments and how much money you owe. When you charge something to a credit card, for example, you are using an accrual system. You will have to make a future payment to an ongoing account in your name.

An organization typically opens charge accounts with several different local vendors. Office, lumber, and paint supplies are purchased with the understanding that the organization will pay for the materials when they are billed. For example, when $250 worth of office supplies are purchased from a local supplier, the $250 becomes a *payable*, and when the bill is paid, it becomes an *expense* item in the budget.

A foundation grant for $5,000 awarded to the organization is called a *receivable*. When the check arrives and is deposited, it becomes *revenue*. The accounting system deducts the payables, adds the receivables, and arrives at the balance with which the organization will operate.

Accounting and budgets

Because nonprofit organizations receive money from grants and gifts, the FASB has a special set of standards for nonprofit organizations to use to report the overall account activity. The net assets, which are the equivalent of the "owners' equity" in a for profit business, in a not-for-profit corporation are divided into three areas: *unrestricted net assets, temporarily restricted net assets*, or *permanently restricted net assets*.[21]

Since nonprofit organizations are allowed to accept various types of gifts from donors, there is an expectation that the reporting and stewardship of these funds will be clearly communicated in the financial reporting of the organization. For example, *unrestricted net assets* would be gifts from donors with no restrictions attached. The arts organization could use the funds to cover daily operating costs, hold the funds in a cash reserve, or use the funds to buy equipment. Temporarily restricted funds carry with them donor stipulations that have a short-term duration attached to them. For example, a donor may indicate their gift of $100,000 is for a new lighting control system for the theater. The other major temporary funds include "contracts, grant agreements, or other written oral statements."[22]

The *permanently restricted* funds carry with them donor limitations the organization is expected to honor. For example, a donor may give an opera company $5 million to set up an endowment for the education department. A percentage of the income earned from this endowment gift can only be used to support activities related to the education department.

In Figure 9.8, for example, the theater company's activities related to the regular season, touring, education, and the building fund could all be established as temporarily or permanently restricted fund accounts depending on donors requests or board actions. A board might decide that funds given to the organization that were originally unrestricted would best be designated as temporarily restricted for a project or special activity.

Figure 10.6 shows a theater company balance sheet with two temporarily restricted fund accounts — one for a building and one for an endowment account. Having too many permanently restricted fund accounts in an arts organization can of course be limiting. The board and the management of the arts organization need to develop policies about how much of the net assets of the organization will be restricted. The assumption is that at some point in the future the organization may have a financial emergency and too many permanently restricted assets might hinder addressing the problems at hand.

The accounting system overview

To extract the information required for an effective FMIS, the accounting input must be as detailed as possible. Figure 10.5 showed how a typical system takes the input of cash receipts, invoices, payroll, and other documentation and processes the data to produce monthly external and annual reports.

When an organization establishes its accounting system, specific account numbers and designated subcodes are used to identify *liabilities* (money owed or funds committed) and *assets* (property or resources owned by the organization). When expenses are incurred, they are recorded as liabilities that reduce the organization's overall worth. When money is received in the form of revenues or gifts, it is classified as an asset that adds to the organization's overall worth.

The accounting system shown in Figure 10.5 identifies a data-gathering area where cash is received, checks are written (disbursement transactions), payroll is processed, and all other account activity takes place. A general ledger processes the four other journals (receipts, disbursements, payroll, and general journal) and allows reports to be assembled that provide the information required by management and the board.

Computer software has automated the bookkeeping to the point that the journal and ledgers are modules within the software. However, all accounting systems still generate a tremendous amount of paperwork. Check stubs, invoices, receipts, purchase orders, requisitions, credit card slips, and so forth, can quickly overwhelm an organization. Organizations are required to keep all of this documentation — it is sometimes called a *paper trail* — to complete an audit or a simple review by an outside accounting firm. Since most not-for-profit organizations file a Form 990 tax return with the IRS (required if you have an operating budget over $25,000) it is a good idea to review the categories of assets and liabilities used by the IRS when establishing your account system reports (IRS Web site: www.irs.gov/charities/article/0,,id=96103,00.html). If nothing else, it will make it easier to transfer data when filing taxes each year.

Accounting formula

The record-keeping system used in accounting is based on the simple formula reflected in the financial statements that assets (A) must equal the liabilities (L) plus the net assets (NE) ($A + L = NE$), and the net assets must equal the assets minus the liabilities ($NE = A - L$). For example, an arts organization starts with $5,000 in cash. The accounting formula expresses this relationship as $5,000(A) = \$0(L) + \$5,000(NE)$. The assets total $5,000, and because no debts have been incurred, there is $0 in liabilities and $5,000 in net assets. (In the profit sector, the net asset would be called equity, and the formula would read $A = L + E$.)

The organization then buys a computer system for $2,000. The business takes on a liability it must pay to a vendor. The cash assets are reduced by $2,000 and the liabilities are increased by $2,000. To recalculate the net assets of the business, we apply the formula. In this case, we find a net asset balance of $3,000 by subtracting liabilities from assets (NE = A − L or $3000 = $5000 − $2000).

Accounting and bookkeeping systems use the often confusing terminology of *debits* and *credits*. The accounting software used today tends to minimize the confusion through easy-to-use data entry screens that in a sense hide the debit and credit postings. In the accounting process, the "T Account," as it is called, is used to track how credits and debits are applied to assets, liabilities, and the equity of the organization. One way to think about the debit and credit activity is to visualize the letter T with debits on the left side of the T and credits on the right side of the T. The bullet list below summarizes how debits and credits are applied to the Balance Sheet and the Statement of Activity.

Balance sheet accounts[23]

Assets
- Debit postings increase an asset
- Credit postings decrease an asset

Liabilities
- Debit postings decrease liabilities
- Credit postings increase liabilities

Net Equity
- Debit postings decrease the organization's equity
- Credit postings increase the organization's equity

Income statement accounts

Revenue
- Debit postings decrease revenue accounts
- Credit postings increase revenue accounts

Expenses
- Debit postings increase expense accounts
- Credit postings decrease expense accounts

Net Income (Revenue minus Expense)
- Debit postings decrease net income
- Credit postings increase net income

If you find this confusing, you are not alone. Many students who have taken an accounting class find the only way to keep this straight is to memorize the debit and credit changes.

You may wonder if you will ever make use of this debit/credit information. As noted above and in the next section, the end result of all these different posting rules does have a direct impact on the balance sheet and income statement of the arts organization. The ability to understand the fiscal health of an organization and the ability to read and understand these two universal financial reports are essential skills of an arts manager and board member.

Financial statements

So far, we have been looking at accounting documentation from the FMIS that was designed for internal use by the staff and the board. These various budget reports do not tell us about the overall fiscal health of the organization. Does the organization have any money in reserves? How much does it owe in short- or long-term debt? To locate this information, we need to review two standard reporting formats in the accounting system: the balance sheet and the statement of activity.

The example used in Figures 10.6 and 10.7 depicts a theater company that is in fairly good financial condition. As you will see, it has an excess of revenue over income and has funds to see it through tough times.

Theater Company Balance Sheet

Balance Sheet as of June 30   **ASSETS = LIABILITIES + NET ASSETS**

Assets	Unrestricted Funds		Temporarily Restricted Funds			
	Operating Fund	Gala Fund	Building Fund	21st Century Fund	Current Year TOTAL	Last Year TOTAL
Cash	$70,812	$106,000	$100,000	$50,000	**$326,812**	$144,000
Accounts receivable	2,800	19,626	15,000	-	**37,426**	12,000
Shop Equipment	25,000	0	0	0	**25,000**	22,000
less depreciation	(9,000)	0	0	0	**(9,000)**	(3,000)
Office equipment	25,000	0	0	0	**25,000**	20,000
less depreciation	(12,568)	0	0	0	**(12,568)**	(4,000)
Scenery & Costume Inventory	35,000	0	0	0	**35,000**	40,000
TOTAL ASSETS	$137,044	$125,626	$115,000	$50,000	**$427,670**	$231,000
Liabilities						
Accounts payable	$47,299	$2,500	$0	$0	**$49,799**	$18,000
Accrued payroll and taxes	18,933	0	0	0	**18,933**	6,000
Bank notes payable	25,000	0	0	0	**25,000**	24,000
TOTAL LIABILITIES	$91,232	$2,500	$0	$0	**$93,732**	$48,000
Net Assets						
Unrestricted net assets	$45,812	$123,126	$0	$0	**$168,938**	33,000
Temporally restricted net assets	$0	$0	$115,000	$50,000	**$165,000**	150,000
TOTAL NET ASSETS	$ 45,812	$ 123,126	$ 115,000	$ 50,000	**$333,938**	$183,000
Total Liabilities & Net Assets	$137,044	$125,626	$115,000	$50,000	**$427,670**	$231,000

NOTE: Assets increased, Liabilities increased, and Net Assets increased. The "Total Net Assets" shown above come from the "Statement of Activity" (Fig. 10-7) bottom line and are listed as "Net Assets - End of Year."

Figure 10.6

Theater company balance sheet.

Figure 10.7

Statement of activity and changes in net assets — theater company.

Statement of Activity and Changes in Net Assets - Theater Company

Revenue	Unrestricted Funds — Operating Fund	Gala Fund	Temporarily Restricted Funds — Building Fund	Temporarily Restricted Funds — 21st Century Fund	As of June 30 — Current Year TOTAL	Last Year TOTAL
Ticket Sales	1,475,000	0	0	0	$1,475,000	$1,425,826
Other Income	198,200	5,000	0	0	$203,200	$198,522
Fundraising	567,000	305,000	65,000	43,000	$980,000	$895,636
Grants	142,000	0	0	0	$142,000	$125,000
Total Revenue	**$ 2,382,200**	**$ 310,000**	**$ 65,000**	**$ 43,000**	**$2,800,200**	**$2,644,984**

Expenses	Operating Fund	Gala Fund	Building Fund	21st Century Fund	Current Year TOTAL	Last Year TOTAL
Staff Salaries	1,602,511	30,250	7,600	0	$1,640,361	$1,510,963
Productions	139,669	0	0	0	$139,669	$142,895
Marketing	537,000	5,522	0	0	$542,522	$535,892
Development	87,942	65,000	10,000	0	$162,942	$154,258
Special Events	9,000	107,000	12,000	0	$128,000	$135,259
Concessions	35,858	0	0	0	$35,858	$27,891
Gift Shop	4,935	1,500	0	0	$6,435	$7,259
Occupancy	70,352	0	0	0	$70,352	$64,895
Contingency	30,061	3,500	0	0	$33,561	$28,569
Total Expense	**$ 2,517,328**	**$ 212,772**	**$ 29,600**	**0**	**$2,759,700**	**$2,607,881**

Changes in Net Assets						
	$ (135,128)	$97,228	$35,400	$43,000	$40,500	$37,103
Net Assets - Beginning of Year						
	$80,940	$125,898	$79,600	$7,000	$293,438	$145,897
Board Designated Fund Transfers						
	$ 100,000	$ (100,000)	0	0	$0	$0
Net Assets - End of Year						
	$45,812	$123,126	$115,000	$50,000	$333,938	$183,000

NOTE: The Board approves a transfer of $100,000 from the Gala Fund to the Operating Fund to cover the deficit of $ (135,128). See Figure 9.6 as the source for the Statement of Activity numbers. The "Current Year Total" in Figure 10-7 equals the "Current Year Budget" numbers in Figure 9-6. The numbers on the bottom line or the "Net Assets - End of Year" appear in Fig 10-6, Balance Sheet, on the line "Total Net Assets."

Balance sheet

The accounting profession typically talks about the balance sheet as a "financial snapshot." This means that on the date the report was issued (typically June 30 or December 31), the balance sheet shows how much money the organization had and how much it was "worth" on that date.

The balance sheet shown in Figure 10.6 is an example of the A = L + NE formula. The top half of the balance sheet details the current and previous years' total assets as of June 30. The bottom half of the sheet shows the organization's liabilities and net assets (hence the term "balance sheet"). On this day, June 30 of the current fiscal year, the organization had $326,812 in cash, $37,426 in accounts receivable, and so forth. In comparison to the previous year ("Last Year TOTAL" in the far right column) the organization had $144,000 in cash and $12,000 in accounts receivable. The total assets for the current year were $427,670 and $231,000 the previous year. Therefore, the organization increased its assets in the current year.

The liabilities that the organization incurred also increased. The company has higher liability for the accounts it owes (accounts payable) and it owes $25,000 for a bank note (a loan) it took out during the year. The company has good news in its various net assets or fund balances accounts. All the funds (Operating, Gala, Building, and 21st Century) were positive at the end of the current year. Overall, the total net assets increased from $183,000 to $333,938.

Statement of activity

The second of the financial reports is the statement of activity and changes in net assets on June 30. The example shown in Figure 10.7 makes it clear where the operating fund deficit came from and what changes took place in the net assets or fund balances. This sheet has a more direct connection to the budget and depicts the annual revenue and expenses for the organization. The breakdown of revenue and expenses allows the reader to see how the organization arrived at its financial condition at the end of its fiscal year and to compare these figures to the previous year.

The revenue section tells us how much money came in to the organization from various sources. In comparison to last year, the overall revenue rose by $155,216 (total of $2,800,200), and expenses increased by $151,819 (total of $2,759,700). Upon closer examination, you can see that the operating fund ended the year with a $135,128 deficit. In other words, the expenses exceeded the revenues attributed to the operating fund. The other funds ended with a positive balance (expenses minus revenues, or Changes in Net Assets). The operating fund ended the year with a positive balance of $45,812 due to a transfer of $100,000 from the Gala Fund. Internal transfers of this type are typically done with the approval of the board and the accountants.

The overall good news for the theater company is that it ended the year with net assets of $333,938, up from $183,000 the previous year. Although the company does not have an endowment account, it has a building fund and what has been designated a 21st Century Fund. Both of the funds are modest (they total $165,000: $115,000 in the Building Fund and $50,000 in the 21st Century Fund), but they represent a little insurance for the organization. However, if a serious financial situation arose (a significant drop in single ticket and subscriptions sales), these net assets accounts would represent a small percentage of the overall operating budget and would be enough to ensure the long-term viability of the organization.

Ratio analysis

Ratio analysis is a quick way of examining the organization's balance sheet and statement of activity. For demonstration purposes two ratios have been selected. Figure 10.8 compares two key indicators of the theater company's fiscal health. In our example, the *ratio of expendable assets to total liabilities* has declined in the current season. Turk and Gallo recommend that organizations have at least a 1:1 ratio of assets to liabilities. The balance sheet for the theater company

Figure 10.8
Ratio analysis — theater company.

Ratio Analysis - Theater Company

1. Ratio of Expendable Assets to Total Liabilities

Expendable Assets
   Total Liabilities

Current Year			Last Year		
Cash $	326,812		Cash $	144,000	
Accts Receivable $	37,426		Accts Receivable $	12,000	
Assets $	364,238	= 3.89	Assets $	156,000	= 3.25
Liabilities $	93,732		Liabilities $	48,000	

Comment: In the current year the organization had fewer liabilities in relation to its assets. The ratio of expendable assets to total liabilities is slightly higher.

2. Ratio of Expendable Net Assets to Total Expenses

Expendable Net Assets
   Total Expenses

Current Year			Last Year		
Net Assets $	333,938	= 0.121	Net Assets $	183,000	= 0.070
Expenses	$2,759,700		Expenses	$2,607,881	

Comment: In the current year the organization increased its net assets in a higher ratio to expenses than in the previous year.

NOTE: Refer to Fig. 10-6 and 10-7 for numbers used in the above ratios.

shows that assets exceed liabilities by a good margin in the current year (3.89:1 versus 3.25:1). In this example, the increase in the ratio from 3.25 tells a manager and board member that they are doing well managing their liabilities. The example shows that liabilities increased from $48,000 the previous year to $93,732 this year. However, the cash on hand also increased significantly, and the manager and board maintained a healthy ratio of debt to assets.

The *ratio of expendable net assets* to total expenses for the current year is 0.121, up from 0.070 the year before. This ratio is a measure of how well the organization is doing at building its financial base. Turk and Gallo suggest that this ratio should be closer to 0.3:1. For the theater company to achieve that ratio it would have to increase its net assets to over $800,000 in relation to its expenses in the current year. In this case, the organization could do better building its cash reserves.

There are dozens of other ratios an arts organization may apply to its operations to measure key financial issues. For example, by monitoring the ratio of personnel expenses to the overall operating budget over time the organization would be able to see if there was an increasing or decreasing amount of the budget going to this one area. The same kind of ratio could be monitored in the benefits section of the budget. The whole point of having a few key ratios to monitor is that it allows the management of the organization to anticipate future problems and avoid conversations with the board finance committee such as "What do you mean we are now paying over 30% of our budget to employee benefits?"

Problem areas

If, as a member of the board of directors of the theater company you read the Chapter 9 cash flow projections (Figure 9.9), balance sheet, and statement of activity, what would be your reaction? A board member might want to ask about the increasing accounts payable (Figure 10.6). The reports also show that operating expenses exceed revenue (Figure 10.7). The total net assets of the organization increased by $150,938 (Figure 10.8, $333, 938 − $183, 000 = $150,938), but the net assets are still a smaller ratio of expenses than is desirable.

The immediate problems facing the theater company include balancing the operating budget and better controlling its cash flow (see Figure. 9.9). Continued overexpenditures in the operating fund will only erode the financial health of the organization. It will be very difficult to build an endowment if funds have to be constantly transferred to the operating fund to offset deficits. As a board member or a manager for this organization, it is important to solve these problems, because in the long run the ability of the organization to attempt new programs or enhance existing operations will be hampered by these financial problems.

Investment

One of the most important responsibilities of a financial manager in a non-profit arts organization is to work with the board of directors to develop investment strategies that will help ensure the survival of the enterprise. The fiduciary responsibility, or trusteeship, of the organization's resources is the fundamental role of the board of directors. To exercise this fiduciary responsibility, the board must have accurate information about the assets and liabilities of the organization. At the same time, a finance committee should work with the financial manager to seek out ways to maximize the assets available. The management of the various net assets of the organization must be monitored closely by the board.

In *Financial Management Strategies for Arts Organizations*, Turk and Gallo detailed the best way to approach the asset management of the organization.[24] Their suggestions include developing a system for managing the cash available to the organization. Cash control can be realized through limiting access to cash accounts, timing the payment of bills, and closely monitoring the organization's accounts receivable. They recommend that the organization invest in a mix of short-term interest-earning instruments, such as certificates of deposits (CDs), Treasury bills (T bills), and money market funds. The objective of short-term investment is to maximize the interest-rate return while maintaining quick access to the funds should an emergency arise.

The board of directors also needs a long-term investment policy. One strategy is to take a conservative approach and invest in a variety of well-known stocks and bonds. Higher risk investments will usually provide greater returns, but board guidance is necessary to ensure that the financial manager invests the organization's assets safely.

Finally, Turk and Gallo urge managers to monitor the fixed assets of the organization, including inventories and expensive capital equipment and property. Maintaining sufficient insurance for equipment, inventories, and buildings helps minimize the financial risk to the organization if a disaster strikes.

Summary of financial management

It is important to remember that the FMIS is a tool designed to help the organization fulfill its mission. Maximizing revenue, building the endowment, controlling cash flow, and conducting ratio analyses are important, but these activities should not be the organization's controlling force. The primary objective of the FMIS is to support the organization in achieving its mission and goals. If the FMIS is working effectively, it should help, not hinder, goal achievement. It should also be remembered that the system is only as good as the people who use it. Inexperienced or poor management, not the FMIS, usually leads an organization into a financial crisis.

For example, if the artistic director insists that the only way to attain a high level of production quality is to build the costumes and sets in the company's own shops, it is the financial manager's responsibility to explain how much this will cost. If it can be done with the resources available in the short and long run and the board approves the idea, then it should be done. If the organization cannot afford to build its own costumes and sets, the financial manager has an obligation to say so. Unfortunately, this scenario is not always followed. Instead, either the manager cannot stand up to the artistic director, or the cost analysis is done without a real understanding of the organization's fixed and variable costs. When poor management is combined with a lack of understanding about the fiscal health of the organization, even the most sophisticated FMIS will not help.

MANAGING FINANCES AND THE ECONOMIC DILEMMA

Without cash coming in, there is little chance that the show will go on or that the exhibit will open. The artists and staff can come to the rescue by working for free or for half pay once in a while, but in the long run, trying to operate an arts organization by using a crisis financial management technique will spell doom. Limited productivity and ever-increasing labor costs mean that all arts organizations must adapt a flexible plan to keep up with the income gap. For example, if we take our hypothetical theater company's budget for $2,800,200 and project the budget for five years with a 3 percent per year increase to allow for inflation, the budget will grow to $3,246,200 (compounding the 3 percent increase). Finding the additional $446,000 in revenue to offset expenses will be daunting, especially if ticket prices are not raised each year. In reality, the cost increases that the company will face will probably exceed 3 percent per year. Salaries, artist fees, construction materials, rents, and so on, will all increase at rates that are very difficult to project accurately.

Without careful planning, the organization will be susceptible to this familiar cycle: a growing deficit leads to a budget crisis, followed by a high-visibility fundraising campaign and a last-minute rescue by a group of donors. These realities make it all the more important for arts organizations to have a five-year plan that establishes expense and revenue projections. Longer range plans make sense for organizations with very high fixed costs, such as museums.

Changing economic conditions require that arts managers and board members revise the financial plans at least every year. In times of recession or when inflation rates begin to exceed 6 percent per year, organizations may need to revise the long-term plans every quarter.

Reserve funds

The question of how much should be set aside for reserves is not easy to answer. As we have seen, most arts organizations operate with a very thin margin between the cash coming in and the expenses going out. As you will also see in Chapter 12, Fundraising, donors prefer giving to financially healthy organizations. A donor does not want to see her money used to support an organization that does not know how to manage its resources. However, since most arts organizations start out undercapitalized (i.e., with insufficient startup funds) the cycle of cash flow shortages usually plagues many arts groups. Controlling costs and not being overly optimistic about ticket sales still remain the best strategies for cash-poor organizations. However, also setting a goal to have "rainy day" funds — that will allow the organization to remain solvent if there were a 25 percent drop in revenue in two consecutive years — would be prudent. For example, the sample theater company used in this chapter should have about $1.4 million in net assets (unrestricted fund balances) to see it through two seasons of poor sales and weak fundraising.

LOOKING AHEAD

In the next two chapters, we study various approaches to maximizing the financial resources needed to realize the organization's goals and objectives through marketing and fundraising. We will look at how the key areas of marketing and fundraising relate to the FMIS of the organization.

For additional topics relating to arts economics and financial management, please go to www.managementandthearts.com.

Questions

1. Summarize the key findings in the Baumol and Bowen study of the economics of the arts.
2. Give two examples of other economies of scale that could be applied to an arts organization's daily operation.
3. List three reasons why an arts organization may not price the admission fees high enough to cover costs.
4. What are the key components of an FMIS?
5. What are the three major responsibilities of a financial manager in a for-profit business?
6. Why is it better for organizations to have unrestricted, rather than restricted, net assets?
7. What is the accounting formula, and what does it reveal about an organization's fiscal health?
8 Using the formula in Figure 10.8, solve for the ratio of expendable assets to total liabilities, and expendable fund balances to total expense and explain whether

the organization has a financial problem or not. The organization has $250,000 in expendable assets, $125,000 in total liabilities, $1.25 million in expendable net assets, and $225,000 in total expenses at the end of a fiscal year.

CREATING A FINANCIAL REPORT

To better understand how a financial report is developed please read the following description and respond to the five questions immediately following.

Dance company financial report

The Wing and a Prayer Dance Company just finished its third season of operation. The company performs four weekends, distributed across one weekend each in October, December, February, and April. They perform from Thursday to Saturday in a 1,000–seat theater. The single ticket prices are $10 and $16, and the series subscription prices to the four weekends are $32 and $52. During this last season, 60 percent of the subscriptions were sold at $52. The single ticket revenue was distributed through sales of 55 percent for the $16 tickets and 45 percent for the $10 tickets.

Statement of activity and changes in net assets

Revenue — This year, the company was able to generate $99,950 in revenue. They sold $30,000 in single tickets and $39,855 in subscriptions. They received a grant from the state arts council for $10,000 and donations of $13,545. They raised $6,550 from a benefit dinner. All these funds were designated as "unrestricted" by the board.

Expenses — The expenses for the year totaled $96,450. The total was distributed in the following manner: $25,500 for salaries and benefits, $30,000 for guest artist fees, $2,400 for the office, $6,450 for travel, $7,800 for marketing, $15,000 for productions, $1,800 for utilities, $6,500 in mortgage payments, and $1,000 for miscellaneous expenses.

Net Assets — They had net assets of $11,500 in their operating fund at the beginning of the year, and $1,500 in a restricted endowment fund.

Balance sheet

Assets — According to the bookkeeper for the company, the year ended with $79,400 in total liabilities and net assets. The unrestricted assets were made up of the following: $13,800 in cash, $1,200 in accounts receivable, $2,500 in prepaid expenses (deposits they made), a $13,000 inventory of scenery and costumes. Their temporarily restricted assets included $1,500 in an endowment fund, and $47,400 in an account for land and a building.

Liabilities — The unrestricted liabilities were listed as $500 in accounts payable, $15,000 in a loan due to the bank, and the $23,000 in temporarily restricted liabilities from the balance due on the mortgage. The total liability was $38,500.

Questions

1. Prepare an annual financial report for the dance company, showing the information above in the standard form of a Balance Sheet and a Statement of Activity (Figures 10.6 and 10.7).
2. Based on the balance sheet you created, what is the change in the dance company's net assets? Did net assets increase or decrease this year?
3. Assuming that cash, accounts receivable, and prepaid expenses are totaled to make expendable assets, what is the ratio of assets to total liabilities? What does this figure tell you about the company's financial condition? (See Figure 10.8 for ratios.)
4. Based on a venue with total of 12,000 seats to sell (a 1,000–seat theater times four weekends times three performances per weekend), what was the *average number of tickets sold per performance* by the dance company? (**Note**: To answer this question you will need to work from the prices given above and the total sales from subscription and single tickets. The calculations assume a subscriber order includes all four shows.)
5. What is the percentage of total income earned through sales versus the total amount from donations, grants, and other sources?

WEB SOURCE FOR FINANCIAL STATEMENTS

An excellent source for financial information about arts organizations, including Form 990 tax reports on file for an arts organization, is www.Guidestar. com. This Web site presents information in an easy-to-use format. When you arrive at the Web site, enter the arts organization name in the Quick Search box and select Go. Typically, the search will bring up data with several options to select about financial information on the organization.

OTHER RESOURCES ON ARTS ECONOMICS AND FINANCE

Steven Adler, *On Broadway — Art and Commerce on the Great White Way*, Southern Illinois University Press, Carbondale, IL, 2004.

Barbara Isenberg, *Making it Big — The diary of a broadway musical*, Limelight Editions, New York, 1996.

REFERENCES

1. J. William, Baumol, and G. William, Bowen, *Performing Arts: The Economic Dilemma* (Cambridge, MA: MIT Press, 1966).

2. James Heilbrun, and M. Charles, Gray, *The Economics of Art and Culture*, 2nd ed. (Cambridge, England: Cambridge University Press, 2001), p. 18.

3. Ibid., p. 20.

4. Ibid., p. 20.

5. Ibid., p. 21.

6. Ibid., p. 43.

7. Ibid., p. 47.

8. *2002 Survey of Public Participation in the Arts*, National Endowment for the Arts, p. 28–29.

9. Ibid., p. 28–29.

10. *Arts & Economic Prosperity III* Summary Report, Americans for the Arts, Washington, DC, 2006, p. 3.

11. Roger N. Waud, *Economics*, 3rd ed. (New York: Harper and Row, 1986), p. 503.

12. Ibid., p. 514.

13. Ibid., p. 70.

14. Ibid., p. 72.

15. Walter J. Wessels, *Economics*, 4th edition, (Hauppauge, NY: Barron's Educational Series 2006), p. 305.

16. Ibid., p. 305.

17. Heilbrun and Gray, *The Economics of Art and Culture*, p. 102.

18. Ibid., p. 103.

19. Ibid., pp. 76–80.

20. Thomas Wolf, *Managing a Nonprofit Organization* (Englewood Cliffs, N.J: Prentice-Hall, 1999), p. 139.

21. Murray Dropkin, James Halpin, *Bookkeeping for Nonprofits* (San Francisco, CA: Jossey-Bass, 2005), p. 132.

22. Ibid., p. 132.

23. Robert Rachlin, Allen Sweeny, *Accounting and Financial Fundamentals for NonFinancial Executives* (New York: AMACOM, 1996), p. 66.

24. Frederick J. Turk, Robert P. Gallo, *Financial Management Strategies for Arts Organizations* (New York: American Council for the Arts, 1984), p. 102.

CHAPTER 11

Marketing and the Arts

The behavior of arts audiences is changing dramatically. Although some performing arts organizations have successfully retained and even grown their subscriber base in recent years, since the mid-nineties many organizations have been losing ground in their efforts to both attract and retain subscribers.

Joanne Scheff Bernstein, *Arts Marketing Insights*

KEY WORDS

Marketing

Needs and wants

Functional satisfaction

Psychological satisfaction

Exchange

Form, time, place, and possession
  utilities

Production, sales, and marketing eras

Product, sales, and customer
  orientations

The four Ps: product, price, place,
  and promotion

Marketing mix

Market segments

Target marketing

Demographic profile

Psychographic profile

Focus groups

Strategic marketing plans

Marketing audit

Niche strategy

Differentiation strategy

Market share strategy

Marketing data system (MDS)

These next two chapters introduce the all-important topics of marketing and fundraising. We will review many of the basic concepts that underpin the activity of promoting the arts and building what we hope are life-long relationships with our audiences and donors. We will also discuss what effective marketing really is (it is not just about posters and press releases). We will review how to develop a marketing plan (see Figure 11.1), develop a better understanding of audience research techniques, and how to assess the effectiveness of marketing and public relations plans.

An arts manager must plan, organize, implement, and evaluate various marketing and fundraising strategies in an effort to maximize revenue to meet the organization's established objectives. There can be enormous satisfaction in seeing a full house, a packed museum, or the groundbreaking for the building made possible by the efforts of well-designed marketing and fundraising campaigns. However, we will also see that no amount of managerial brilliance or sophisticated marketing effort will amount to much if the basic product does not meet the needs of the consumers for whom it is intended.

It is important to remember that, like a management information system or a computer, marketing and fundraising activities are nothing more than tools for an arts manager to use. Marketing and fundraising cannot make a bad script good or a weak performance strong. At best, marketing and fundraising can help support a long-lasting relationship between the individual consumer and the organization. If properly managed, this relationship can evolve, and the consumer can transition from a single-ticket buyer to a subscriber or member, to an annual supporter, and eventually to a major contributor. Unfortunately, this objective is much easier said than done.

THE MARKETING LANDSCAPE

In the world today, it is almost impossible to avoid the efforts of someone trying to sell you something. We are bombarded with thousands of messages every week in the form of television commercials, newspaper and magazine advertisements, flyers and letters in the mail, junk e-mail, banner ads on Web sites, text messages, or phone calls from total strangers. Thousands of new consumer products are released in the market every year. Billions of dollars and millions of hours of labor are expended on product research, design, and distribution.

Promotional activities related to the for-profit-sector of the entertainment industry relentlessly let us know that a new film is opening, the season premiere of a television show starts next week, a new book is coming out, the ice show is in town, or a new ride is opening at the local theme park. The escalating mixture of media blitz, promotional hype, and advertising competitiveness used to get the consumer's attention does not leave a great deal of room for low-budget local arts organizations to make an impact or be heard. For example, it is not unusual for a movie studio to spend more money advertising one new film than a major arts organization as its operating budget for an entire year.

As we have seen, the economic environment in which arts organizations must function requires constant effort to find the resources to survive from year to year. The need to retain and increase the number of subscribers, ticket buyers, members, or donors also places an enormous amount of pressure on the arts manager. Arts managers with expertise and a successful record of managing marketing and fundraising campaigns are very much in demand. However, because organizations depend so heavily on revenues generated from sales, a decline in income may cause a once-successful manager to find herself suddenly unemployed.

Today's arts marketer works with an expanded set of choices that includes a significant diversity of communication channels with consumers. Arts organizations lacking MySpace or Facebook Web pages or video clips featured on YouTube run the risk of dropping even further out of the public eye. However, tapping into the most up-to-date Web sites will not necessarily translate into filling empty seats at a concert. Understanding the concept that the arts are an acquired taste is critical to the development of successful marketing plans (see Marketing and the Acquired Taste For The Arts later). An e-mail or brochure you send someone who seldom, if ever, goes to art events is not suddenly going to turn them into arts consumers.

Let's take a look at some of the challenges you will face in marketing the arts.

THE SEARCH FOR THE AUDIENCE

No matter how lofty the aesthetic aims of an organization, without the regular support of an audience, patrons, or members, there will not be enough money coming in to keep the enterprise alive. In other words, there must be enough demand for the product, or the enterprise will be out of business.

Before the advent of "marketing," arts organizations had a fairly standard set of activities that they undertook in an effort to create enough demand for a show or an exhibit. A press release announcing the upcoming event was sent to the local papers (a photo or two may have accompanied the release) and posters were put up wherever they were allowed. Flyers were sometimes distributed, a few very small advertisements were placed in the paper, and a low-cost brochure was mailed out to names on the mailing list. If the organization was lucky, a preview article might appear in the arts section of the local paper. Organizations with larger budgets placed bigger ads in the paper, and they sometimes ran a few radio or television commercials.

Some managers and board members wondered why, after the term *marketing* came into vogue, their arts organization continued to do the same things but spent twice as much money to get the same audience. What happened was that organizations began to realize that they were really not engaged in marketing. They were still trying to sell events in a scattershot method to an ill-defined public. As a result, they wasted a great deal of money trying to convince people to buy their product without really knowing to whom they were selling. Spending more on advertising, in this case, was wasted money and effort.

As you see in this chapter, marketing requires that the organization adapt and change its fundamental perceptions about its relationship to consumers. Marketing requires the adoption of a customer-orientated perspective that is often unfortunately perceived as incompatible with the fundamental mission of arts organizations. Selling, on the other hand, which is what most organizations do, means that the organization tries to get the consumer to buy the product because it believes the product is inherently good and would be beneficial to the consumer.

A means to an end

No matter what term is applied to the energy and resources used to find, develop, and keep an audience or membership base, these activities are still only a means to an end. Philip Kotler and Joanne Scheff noted in their definitive text, *Standing Room Only*, that we must view marketing as "a *means* for achieving the organization's goals, and using marketing and being customer-centered should never be thought of as the goal in itself."[1]

Let's now look more closely at the definition of marketing and many of the key concepts inherent in this vital area of study.

MARKETING PRINCIPLES AND TERMS

A key part of any arts organization's strategic plan is how it plans to market itself. The marketing plan normally forms a major section in the foundation of an organization's strategic approach to its long-term growth. We will see how the term *marketing* is often used incorrectly to describe various promotional activities that organizations undertake.

The American Marketing Association's definition of marketing "is the activity, set of instructions, and processes for creating, communicating, delivering, and exchanging offerings that have value for customers, clients, partners, and society at large."[2] From the arts manager's perspective, a key phrase in this definition is "value for customers." The experience of being an audience member is at the core of what our customers value. The job of the arts marketer, based on this definition, is to have an effective process in place to communicate and deliver to the arts consumer the value to be found in the experience offered in the music, opera, theater, or dance production or the visual arts experience.

Needs and wants

The marketer strives to achieve a match between human wants and needs and the products and services that can satisfy them. In theory, the better the match of wants and needs to the product or service, the greater the satisfaction. Marketers define a *need* as "something lacking that is necessary for a person's physical, psychological, or social well-being."[3] Psychological needs (such as knowledge, achievement, and stability) and social needs (such as esteem, status, or power) are shaped by the overall value system of the culture.

A *want* is defined as "something that is lacking that is desirable or useful."[4] Wants are intrinsic to an individual's personality, experience, and culture. You may have a need for knowledge, but you want to pursue an idea from a specific book. You need to eat, but you want a particular brand of pizza.

When you have needs and wants to satisfy, two other marketing principles come into play: *functional satisfaction* and *psychological satisfaction*. When we purchase an item like a refrigerator, we achieve a functional satisfaction because of the tangible features of the product. When we purchase a car, we may satisfy a functional need, but a particular make and model may provide an intangible psychological satisfaction for recognition or esteem.

Discussion Point: Marketing and the Acquired Taste for the Arts

Obviously, functional satisfaction and psychological satisfaction are not neutral terms. Americans have attitudes and beliefs about products that have been shaped by advertisements in print and electronic media. Accordingly, the "goal of (the) marketers (is) to gain a competitive edge by providing greater satisfaction."[5]

Unfortunately, for many consumers, the idea that a fine arts event could provide a degree of satisfaction is foreign. This is due in large part to the fact many more people than we care to realize have not been to an arts event in years, or in many cases, ever. After all, there is no shortage of opportunities to be entertained though the mass media. As noted in the previous chapter, the NEA public participation research indicated 17.1 percent went to musical theater productions.[6] If that is the case, then we might assume that 82.9 percent of the adult population did not go to musical theater productions. Opera, which by many accounts is enjoying solid attendance numbers around the nation, had 3.2 percent[7] of the adult population attending, meaning that 96.8 percent of the adult population did not go to the show.

Arts organizations typically do not see their role as appealing to the mass audience, nor do they have the financial resources to do so. In fact, as Heilbrun and Gray point out in their book *The Economics of Art and Culture*, "Art is said to be an acquired 'taste', in the sense that you have to be exposed to it in order to develop the taste."[8]

This observation leaves us with the interesting conundrum. Can marketing the arts experience really help people acquire the behavior pattern of going to the arts? If someone has never been to the opera, are they likely to attend based solely on the ad in the newspaper or the brochure you mailed them? For someone who already has the acquired taste for opera, the ad in the newspaper is a reminder to buy their ticket if they have not. For the rest of the newspaper readers, the ad probably was not even noticed. The humorous phrase often heard among marketers is that "50% of all our advertising expenditures are wasted. The problem is we don't know which 50%."

Exchange process and utilities

Wants and needs are satisfied through the process of *exchange*, which occurs when "two or more individuals, groups, or organizations give to each other something of value to receive something of value. Each party must want to exchange, believe that what is received is more valuable than what is given up, and be able to communicate with the other parties."[9]

For example, suppose that you want to hear a piano recital, and there is a pianist who wants to perform. You make the decision that the time you are spending listening to the artist and the money you give up for the ticket are worth the exchange. The pianist believes that the fee she is paid and the satisfaction derived from playing will be rewarding. The performance and the recognition of applause by the audience complete the exchange process. Performers sometimes forget just how important this final communication really is for the audience. The level of satisfaction felt is greatly diminished when the performer walks off the stage without acknowledging the audience.

The exchange process depends on four utilities that marketers have identified as *form, time, place, and possession*. The utilities interact as part of the exchange process in ways that promote or hinder the final exchange or transaction.

The *form utility* simply means the "satisfaction a buyer receives from the physical characteristics of the product."[10] Attributes such as style, color, shape, and function affect the exchange. Arts organizations that have gift shops must be very sensitive to this utility because the customers usually have fairly sophisticated tastes, and filling the shop with cheap plastic products will do more harm than good for the organization. Unique, high-quality items may provide the organization with a chance to build a strong bond with the discriminating buyer.

Except for the printed program, a performance does not offer any form of utility. The live performance is, as we all know, an intangible experience. However, the psychological satisfaction gained from the event can form a powerful bond between the audience and the organization. The memories that trigger emotional and intellectual responses in relation to a particular performance or exhibit can help build a lifelong relationship between the arts organization and the consumer. In fact, reminding patrons of that experience is an important part of the marketing communications plan of an arts organization.

The *time and place utilities*, which involve "being able to make the products or services available when and where the consumer wants them,"[11] have a direct impact on arts organizations. Arts organizations usually have little flexibility when it comes to time and place. The customer has the choice of either coming to the performance at a specific time and a specific place or not seeing it at all. Experimenting with different performance schedules or locations or different exhibit hours may offer arts organizations occasional opportunities to increase consumer access to their products. However, the live performing arts, by their very nature, will continue to face limitations when it comes to time and place utilities. Television and home recording equipment offers a way of partially overcoming the inherent limitations of the live performance. *Live from the Met* radio broadcasts, for example, have provided a way for opera to reach audiences that would never be able to attend a production in New York City. Now that the Metropolitan Opera has begun to do live High Definition (HD) transmission to movie theaters, it has greatly expanded its audience base. Art museums also have experimented with different programming and exhibit schedules, as well as using other technology (cellular telephones and iPods) to enhance the attendance experience.

In the News

During Intermission, Cell Phones Are Brandished in a Promotion
By Andrew Adam Newman

Typically you are told to turn off your cell phone before a performance. But at a recent Saturday matinee of "Spring Awakening," the Broadway musical that garnered eight Tony Awards last week, the audience was told not to do just that.

"Win Your Chance to Come backstage!" said a flier inserted into the Playbill, which encouraged theatergoers to send the text message "bdway spring" to a five-digit number before the end of intermission.

Source: The New York Times, June 18, 2007.

The *possession utility*, which refers to "the satisfaction derived from using or owning the product,"[12] has some application in the live performing arts. The tangible items offered by the organization can create a degree of consumer satisfaction in much the same way that the form utility did. For example, long-time subscribers often view the seats they regularly sit in as their possessions. For two or three hours on a given night, they do indeed possess those seats. Allowing subscribers to keep their seats each year can be a powerful tool for maximizing on the possession utility. It is also possible to reinforce the experience of having attended through the secondary means of selling souvenir programs or other related material. And while not the same thing as being there for the live event, many performance groups have started selling DVDs in HD through their gift shops or online.

Strategic marketing and the exchange process

As we have seen, the exchange process for consumers of arts products and services fits within the theoretical framework of basic marketing principles. As part of an arts organization's core strategic planning, it makes sense for the staff and the board to spend time asking very fundamental questions about exactly what they are offering to the public. For example, how does the organization's corporate structure and philosophy affect its relationship with its audience? Do its programs and activities satisfy the wants and needs of the audience? What mechanisms are in place to get feedback from the audiences about the organization's programming?

If the organization is to thrive, it must be able to adapt to and plan for changing conditions in the marketplace. "*Strategic market planning* is a managerial process of developing and implementing a match between market opportunities (i.e., unsatisfied wants and needs) and the resources of the firm."[13] This process is not exclusive to the profit sector. One need only look at the necessary changes that nonprofit hospitals have made in the mix of services they offer in the last decade to see how essential organizational adaptability is.

EVOLUTION OF MODERN MARKETING

Marketing has moved through three eras in its evolution. It is important to note that although these phases represent a progression, many organizations still hold to attitudes and beliefs about their product or service that have not changed much in 75 years. As a result, there are no clean breaks in this evolutionary development.

The first era is tied to the production and manufacturing techniques that began with the industrial revolution in the eighteenth century.[14] The main emphasis up through the beginning of the twentieth century was on fulfilling the basic needs of consumers. Mass production techniques dictated an approach of making assumptions about what the consumer wanted and then manufacturing the product in the most cost-effective way. The theory was that consumers would buy whatever was manufactured.

During the second era, more attention was focused on sales of the mass-produced products. The rise of the salesperson as a dominant figure in a system of getting goods to consumers is a part of the American myth. The period after the Civil War was marked by economic growth and expansion. Masses of immigrants came to the United States, which also fueled rapid growth. Thousands of salespeople spread out over the country trying to sell products to people whether they wanted them or not.

The third marketing era is an outgrowth of the diversification of consumer wants and needs that resulted from the demands of unprecedented growth in the economy after World War II. More companies began to pay attention to what consumers were saying about the available products. The idea of a consumer-driven economy meant that companies needed to consider their basic relationship with the consumer. The research and testing of products and the application of psychological theories about purchase behavior led to a greater emphasis on developing a long-term relationship with the consumer.

Marketer Profile

Danny Newman — Mr. Subscription Ticket Sales

Danny Newman's book *Subscribe Now!* was the source for many arts managers on a quest for how to sell subscriptions (see Additional Resources). Newman worked for the Chicago Lyric Opera since 1954 and helped successfully lead their subscription sales efforts. In 1997 he was nominated for a National Medal of Arts for his efforts as a marketer and consultant. Despite the shift away from enlisting subscribers in favor of more flexible purchasing options, Newman remained firm in his belief that the best way to build a long-term relationship with audiences is through subscription plans. Many performing arts centers, college and university art departments, theaters, opera, dance companies, and music groups copied Mr. Newman's approach to building audiences with much success. Gregory Mosher, a well-known theater director, noted in a September 23, 1997 article in the *The New York Times* ["The Unsung Hero of Nonprofit Theater Is Still Selling"] on Newman that, "He's like Henry Ford...I must have read his book [*Subscribe Now!*] 100 times." Mosher went on to note that the subscription series was the cornerstone of the regional theater boom in the United States. The model was based on "a board of directors, a staff led by an artistic director and a managing director, and a six-play subscription series." The recent trend has been toward letting customers build their own series by mixing and matching a specific number of shows in a season. Exchange privileges become the cornerstone of the "Flex-packs," as they are often called.

Note: Danny Newman passed away in December of 2007. Used with permission.

Modern marketing

By the 1990s, the concepts of marketing had been applied in just about every segment of profit and nonprofit business in the United States, including the use of marketing techniques as a way to help candidates get elected. The use of computers to store massive amounts of information about consumer preferences and to provide almost instant feedback to companies about what is selling has revolutionized the marketing industry. The ability to track sales via *point-of-purchase systems* offers marketers immediate access to information about what people are buying. The ubiquitous bar code now gives the store and the suppliers up-to-the-minute sales information about what people are buying. The use of barcodes on tickets can provide next day information to the arts marketing manager about last nights' audience.

The rapid rise of the Internet in the 1990s expanded the reach of marketers through e-mail and Web sites. Online sales activity including services such as Tickets.Com, Ticketmaster, and many other service providers has revolutionized the process of buying a ticket to an arts event, a museum, a concert, or film.

The proliferation of products designed to satisfy consumer needs and wants has led to an explosion of specialty goods and services. A journey to the supermarket provides evidence of products designed to meet special health and nutritional concerns. In fact, the reality of global marketing has led companies to use satellite communications to monitor worldwide sales and to make adjustments in production much more rapidly.

In the News

Nielsen Brings a New Marketing Strategy to Broadway

By Campbell Robertson

"Wicked" is a show for 14–year-old girls. At least that's what everybody on Broadway was saying. So one of the show's producers, David Stone, decided to hire a relatively new research firm called Live Theatre Events to find out if the assumption was true.

Note: The surveys of the audiences proved this notion of who the audience was for *Wicked* as incorrect. For more information about the survey firm go to www.livetheatricalevents.com.

Source: *The New York Times*, nytimes.com, August 1, 2006.

Marketing approaches

A company attempting to make a profit usually has different objectives and goals than a local nonprofit health care center or symphony, but both rely on establishing a positive relationship with consumers. Both private and public sector companies make plans and state their missions based on satisfying the public's wants and needs. The mission statement is typically the source of the organization's goals and strategic plans. The planning process includes defining the function of marketing in the organization. First, let's look at two approaches to marketing used by a great many arts organizations and then focus on customer-oriented marketing.

Product orientation

Kotler and Scheff characterize the *product orientation* as one in which the organization believes that "consumers will favor those products that offer the most quality, performance, and features."[15] They cite as examples "a chamber music association that calls itself a 'society' performs only traditional music, advertises in only a suburban weekly, and doesn't understand why it doesn't attract a younger audience."[16] Product-oriented arts organizations tend to "have a love affair with their products."[17]

Sales orientation

The organization with a *sales orientation* thinks that "consumers show buying inertia or resistance and have to be coaxed into buying more."[18] Many arts organizations approach marketing from the sales perspective. They think marketing is all about advertising, direct mail, e-mail blasts, or telephone solicitations. These efforts can result in short-term gains in audience. However, because the organization is not communicating from the consumer's perspective, the sales-oriented organization constantly has to replenish a large number of subscribers or members who do not renew.

Customer orientation

All of the marketing texts seem to agree that organizations that have evolved or start with a customer orientation have the best chance of competing in the world market today. An organization with a *customer orientation* must "systematically study customers' needs and wants, perceptions and attitudes, preferences and satisfactions."[19] To further clarify this definition as it applies to the arts, Kotler and Scheff go on to say:

> *This does not mean that artistic directors must compromise their artistic integrity.* Nor does it mean that an organization must cater to every consumer whim and fancy, as many managers fear. Those who warn of such consequences if the devil (marketing) is let in the door simply misunderstand what a customer orientation truly means. To restate: marketing planning must *start* with the customer's perceptions, needs, and wants. Even if an organization ought not, will not, or cannot change the selection of the works it performs or presents, the highest volume of exchange will always be generated if the way the organization's offering is described, priced, packaged, enhanced, and delivered is fully responsive to the customer's needs, preferences, and interests. Furthermore, who the customer will be is largely up to the performing arts organization. Marketing will help maximize exchanges with targeted audiences.[20]

As this quote should make clear, an organization that takes a customer's perspective would, for example, use text to describe an upcoming performance in terms that an audience can respond to rather than in the jargon of the profession. If a potential ticket buyer believes that arts events are only for the wealthy and well-educated, and everything the organization does with its promotional activity (ads, brochures, and so on) only reinforces this image, the arts promoter should not be surprised if the consumer feels reluctant to enter into the exchange process. On the other hand, arts organizations usually believe that they shouldn't have to describe a play like *Hamlet* as a "gut-wrenching tale of a family caught up in an whirlwind of lust and murder" in order to sell tickets. However, to discover the language that makes the most sense to its potential audience, the organization must engage in some basic consumer research. Research may show that a more dramatic description of *Hamlet* would make sense in their market.

An organization's key to successfully adopting a customer orientation resides in the research done on its community. What are people's attitudes and perceptions about the value of the music, opera, theater, dance, and art programs offered in your community? Based on that research, the customer-oriented arts organization would have several different approaches to communicating with the different audiences in the community. In some cases, the promotional campaign might be targeted to educating people about a new work or a new author. In other cases, the organization may focus on the strong emotions that a story or a piece of music conveys. For some potential audiences, *Hamlet* may spark their interest if described in more emotional terms. The arts marketer must of course be careful about crossing a line that distorts or debases the product. On the other hand, the risk of offending the sensibilities of a small number of the old guard patrons may prove worthwhile if it brings in new customers. However, unless the organization has a method for tracking the impact of different advertising tactics, these efforts will be wasted.

The lack of money is the problem that most customer- or audience-oriented arts organizations face when it comes time to communicate effectively about the product. The cost of multiple target promotional campaigns is usually well beyond the reach of most groups. However, a marketer would argue that this is money well spent because the objective is to build up long-term audience support and consumer identification with the product. Unfortunately, many arts organizations take a middle ground and ultimately communicate a bland image by trying to straddle too many marketing perspectives in their brochures and publications.

MARKETING MANAGEMENT

The classic four Ps

Using these principles of marketing now allows us to move into the process of marketing management. To market its products or services effectively, an organization must carefully design its marketing mix. *Marketing mix* is defined as "the combination of activities involving *product, price, place,* and *promotion* that a firm undertakes in order to provide satisfaction to consumers in a given market."[21] Each of these elements will have an effect on the exchange process.

The *four Ps*, as they are often called, can be manipulated as part of the organization's overall strategy. For example, if you have a product with a brand name, such as the Metropolitan Opera, you may be able to manipulate the price based on the customer's perception of quality while stressing the place with its crystal chandeliers and red carpet in your promotional material.

The promotional aspect of the marketing mix is the most visible element, and it is usually divided into a further mix of types of advertising: newspaper, magazine, radio, television, direct mail, e-mail, a Web site, raffles, and other public relations activities (e.g., having a soprano invited onto a local television talk show or radio program).

The overall marketing strategy for the organization may have several different marketing mixes. Depending on the target audience, you may stress price or product. For example, a group sales flyer sent to a retirement center may be accompanied by a letter that stresses price first and then product. The same group flyer when sent to a college or university drama department may be accompanied by a different letter that stresses product first and then price.

With the increasing use of the Internet, marketing strategies can now encompass more targeted communications with potential audiences. In fact, many arts organizations have developed many low cost ways to communicate with people who have agreed to receive e-mails from the organization about upcoming events.

Market segments

The marketing manager or director is expected to have a good grasp of the overall marketplace in their community. As we discussed in Chapter 10, Economics and Financial Management, there are many markets in the system of supply and demand, and within the large markets, there are smaller markets for goods and services. Marketers use the term *market segment* to identify "a group of buyers who have similar wants and needs."[22] Once a market segment has been identified, the marketer begins the process of *target marketing* by "developing a mix of the four Ps aimed at that market."[23]

In planning the marketing mix, information is the key ingredient in designing a successfully targeted campaign. For example, if you buy a mailing list from the state arts council with the names of 10,000 people interested in the arts in the state, you have identified a broad market segment. If this list of names is to be useful to you, it will need further analysis. How many of these people attend particular types of performing arts events? Narrowing the list further, how many of these people are geographically close to your performance or exhibition space? After you finish narrowing down the list to people within a three-hour driving distance, are there enough names left to make it worthwhile trying to target this group?

Mailing lists, which are purchased all the time in profit-sector marketing, may be far too costly for many low-budget arts organizations; for these groups, the existing audience is the best and most cost-effective resource for additional customers. The marketer's assumption is that if you consume the arts product, your friends or colleagues may share similar values. Building e-mailing lists by simply asking for your current patrons e-mail addresses is a low-cost way of expanding your audience base. In fact, many arts organizations are discovering that by establishing a Web presence on social networking sites such as Facebook and MySpace they can effectively connect to people interested in the arts.

Managing your brand

One of the key components in your overall marketing management is your "brand" as an organization. The reputation you establish and the perception of your organization in the community typically falls under this notion of your brand. The American Marketing Association (AMA) defines brand as "A name, term, design, symbol, or any other feature that identifies one seller's good or service as distinct from those of other sellers."[24] There are several well-known arts organizations with strong brand name recognition. The typical list might include organizations like the Cleveland Orchestra, Guthrie Theater, Metropolitan Opera, Royal Shakespeare Company, American Ballet Theatre, Chicago Symphony, and the Smithsonian. Each of these organizations has many of the attributes associated with a strong brand name or image.

However, you do not have to be the Metropolitan opera to have a strong brand associated with your organization. Within your region there are likely to be several arts organizations that may have a strong brand. The brand typically is associated with the perceived quality of work they do as an organization. The arts marketer needs to assess what the brand image of your organization may be in the community. If you are the X or Y theater or dance company, what are the first words that pop up in conversation about your organization? If an organization lacks a strong brand, one way to build it would be through a tag line used in all the marketing materials. For example, American Ballet Theatre calls itself "America's National Ballet Company," and uses the ® trademark after its tag line. Manhattan Theatre Club uses the phrase "New Voices, New Works, New Perspectives," as a tag line for branding its distinctive production approach.[25]

Branding Resource

An excellent resource on branding may be found in DK Holland's book *Branding for Nonprofits: Developing Identity with Integrity*. She offers this observation:

> At its most fundamental level, branding is driven by the human need to distinguish one thing from another. Think of all those old Westerns in which cows wandered onto some other rancher's range, causing all kinds of trouble: It was the rancher's brand that protected his herd — his livelihood! On a more abstract, organizational level, the brand promotes the identity and underlying values of a unique culture by communicating the messages, products, and services created by that culture.

Source: *Branding for Nonprofits: Developing Identity with Integrity* by DK Holland, Allworth Press, New York, NY, 2006, p. 5. Used with permission.

Market research

To engage effectively in various forms of target marketing, much detailed information about the potential arts consumer must be known. Understanding the demographics (age, income, education, gender, race) and having an informed psychographic profile (consumer beliefs, values, attitudes) of the potential consumer is crucial to designing the marketing mix for the target market.

Marketing researchers in the profit sector have been developing various behavioral and psychological models in an attempt to make target marketing as cost-effective as possible. The thrust of this work is to divide consumers into lifestyle segments based on such things as activities, interests, and opinions.

A classic example of the psychographic approach (based on a behavioral profile) to understanding consumer behavior can be found in the pioneering work in the 1980s by Arnold Mitchell in his book *The Nine American Lifestyles*.[26] His research resulted in a more elaborate version of Maslow's hierarchy of needs. Mitchell developed a hierarchy chart representing segments of the population as a way to identify consumer behavior. Mitchell called his chart a Values and Lifestyles Segment or VALS distribution.

The Association of Performing Arts Presenters (APAP) hired Mitchell in 1984 to conduct a study of arts audiences. In his report, *The Professional Performing Arts: Attendance Patterns, Preferences and Motives*,[27] he found that four groups, which at that time made up about 66 million people, were the primary market for arts organizations. He called these groups the Achievers, the Experientials, the Societally Conscious, and the Integrateds. Of these four groups, the Societally Conscious (12 percent of the population) were the best market per capita. Mitchell also found that among these four lifestyles, the most common reason cited for attending an arts event was to see a specific show, performer, or group.

He also found that even among these targeted groups, large percentages admitted that they never attended arts events. For example, an average of 28 percent never attended music concerts, 40 percent never attended theater productions, and 68 percent never attended dance events. His research found that lack of leisure time (30 percent), preferences for other leisure activities (34 percent), and not wanting to commit to season or series purchases (33 percent) were the primary reasons given for not attending. (For an updated report on audience segmentation go to www.wolfbrown.com/index.php?page=mcps.)

Another approach to target marketing — one designed to help businesses connect with the consumer — is detailed in *The Clustered World by* Michael J. Weiss. Weiss's book, published in 2000, examines the work of a market research company. Claritas Corporation (www.claritas.com/claritas) developed a system that uses a vast mix of census data to produce information that marketers buy to locate the people who might be disposed to buy their product. The Potential Rating Index for Zip Markets (PRIZM) system uses a zip code analysis of various neighborhood types. For example, Claritas' research has identified the two clusters for classical music and named them Blue Blood Estates and Executive Suites.[28] Blue Blood Estates represent a small percentage of households with median incomes of $113,000. The Executive Suites were listed with incomes of $58,000 and also liked espresso makers, dry cleaning, and *Cooking Light* magazine.[29]

The objective for an arts marketer using the Claritas system is to develop a database of the zip code distribution of its list of current subscribers and, at the same time, to gather information about the zip code distribution of the single-ticket buyers and to compare the data with the neighborhood types. At this point, the marketer could determine which areas the organization has not reached. Buying a list of labels from the local utility company would allow the organization to send targeted mailings to households in the zip code neighborhoods that the organization has identified as potential customers.

Ultimately, a system such as the one Claritas has developed should allow an arts marketer to target potential audiences by very narrow segments. After all, why should an arts organization waste its limited resources doing mass mailings when carefully targeted mailings to "the right people" will yield much more cost-effective results?

In 1996 NEA published a comprehensive report titled "Age and Arts Participation."[30] The data was gathered as part of a Survey of Public Participation in the Arts (SPPA). The report identified seven age groupings, called cohorts, and analyzed the attendance patterns at classical music, opera, ballet, musicals, jazz, plays, and art museums. The highlights of their research included:

- The generation born 1936 to 1945 had very high attendance percentages at classical music concerts, opera, musicals, and plays.

- Younger cohorts (people born after 1946) had higher attendance percentages at jazz concerts and museums.

- Concerns were raised in the report about the fact that the generations born after World War II, despite better education levels, were not attending arts events to the same degree as the older generation.

- The report indicated that younger cohorts (after 1946) substituted television, cable, and radio broadcasts or videotapes and compact discs for live performing arts events.

Other arts research

The PRIZM approach to market research can be very expensive to purchase and is out of reach for most small arts organizations. Other sources to consider for marketing information include the research division of the National Endowment for the Arts (www.arts.endow.gov/pub) that regularly publishes useful data. The *Journal of Arts Management, Law, and Society* and the *International Journal of Arts Management* also include articles on the latest arts marketing research. (Note: For more information go to www.heldref.org/jamls.php or www.hec.ca/ijam.) Another excellent source for marketing ideas is the comprehensive anthology published in 1995 by ARTS Action Issues titled *Market the Arts!*

Arts organizations should regularly survey people in their community for feedback on new programs and on problems with existing operations. A properly designed survey can give an organization the opportunity to adjust and change its marketing mix.

The use of the Internet and Web sites can be a low-cost way for arts organizations to gain continuing feedback from audiences. Online surveys or e-mail feedback about shows can be a useful way of keeping in touch with customers. Operating a Web blog has become more common as arts organizations adapt to the new technology, and as noted, by setting up Facebook or MySpace accounts.

The use of small *focus groups* is also a low-cost alternative for arts organizations. Focus groups of up to 10 or 12 may provide useful insights about the attitudes and perceptions of your audiences to your image and your advertising. Suggested resources for surveys are noted at the end of this chapter (see Additional Resources).

The New Rules of Marketing

David Meerman Scott's book *The New Rules of Marketing & PR* (John Wiley and Sons, 2007) offers the perspective that the World Wide Web offers organizations direct access to potential buyers that bypasses the media as we know it. He argues that the old style one-way communication methods for marketing and PR are no longer as effective. He points out that many Web sites built by companies, many of them billion-dollar businesses, do not understand that a Web site is much more than a sales tool. He notes that the Web sites that are most effective are the ones that understand the interaction and quest for knowledge is a major force that drives Web site usage. In addition to Web sites, the growth of social networks on the Web such as Facebook and MySpace present new opportunities to bypass the conventional marketing channels. Scott's Web site is www.webinknow.com.

Arts organizations that just try to "sell" their shows are missing a great opportunity to engage their potential audience. For example, the Chicago Symphony Orchestra Web site has a section devoted to "Discover Classical Music." There are links to a "Classical Music Glossary" and an "Ask an Expert" section that allows people to post a question they may have about a wide range of questions relating to music. Another interesting arts organization Web site may be found at the Indianapolis Museum of Art — www.imamuseum.org. This site offers the visitor a large number of choices in exploring the museum, its collection, and its programming.

Marketing ethics

Whatever approach is used in marketing research, the goal is to find out what the consumer thinks about the product or service. Marketers believe that with the right information they can better predict which combination of product, price, place, and promotion is needed to complete the exchange process on a regular basis with consumers. To bridge the information gap, marketers look to even more sophisticated applications of computers in their work. As a result, the line between market research and invading people's privacy has grown very thin. The selling of vast amounts of information about consumers is now a fact of life. Michael Weiss pointed out back in 2000 that "the information gathering business is booming, projected to grow to a $10 billion industry this year."[31] As computers have increased in their data storage capabilities and programmers have become even more sophisticated in programming software, the ability to profile consumers will only continue to intensify.

The arts marketer now has at their disposal a powerful research tool: their organization's Web site. More and more organizations are realizing the potential inherent in a system that is driven by the potential audience member coming to you, rather than you trying to go to them. Taking the customer's perspective about the organization's Web site can have long-term benefits to developing audiences.

Arts organizations, which depend on the sales of tickets and subscriptions for 60 percent or more of their operating budget, face a dilemma. How intrusive should they be when trying to reach potential arts consumers? Arts organizations want to identify and target people who are most likely to be long-term consumers of their product. Techniques such as telemarketing, if handled properly, can lead to direct contact with consumers. On the other hand, people resent phone calls and "sales pitches" that intrude into their private lives. In fact, while nonprofit organizations are given a protected status by the National Do Not Call Registry, consumers have been much more aggressive about blocking phone calls. Online surveys to people who have indicated they wanted to be on your e-mail list are certainly less intrusive and give the patron the chance to participate or not.

Marketers for arts organizations must also face the ethical issue of selling information about their customers to commercial firms. The arts consumer is a prime target for the marketer of upscale goods and services. Research has shown that arts consumers have more than the average amount of discretionary income and are therefore good targets for a wide variety of marketing assaults. Having policies in place that restricts how your data are shared will go a long way toward calming any fears your patrons may have about building a file on them.

There are many sources for what the latest thinking may be about how to best maximize on the evolving technology. One such source is PatronMail®, which publishes an e-newsletter featuring the e-marketer of the month. The free newsletter is available at patronmail@patrontechnology.pmailus.com

STRATEGIC MARKETING PLANS

Now that the basic principles of marketing have been outlined, let's examine in more detail the critical planning process shown in Figure 11.1. As noted earlier in this chapter, if the marketing plan is to be effective, the entire organization must carefully consider how all phases of the operation relate to the dynamics of the marketplace. The simple fact facing all organizations is that new opportunities and new threats arise in the marketplace every day. An organization that can adjust to these changing conditions has the best chance of surviving in the long run.

Some board members may wonder why an organization such as a museum or some other well-established performing arts institution would need to worry about the changing dynamics of the marketplace. After all, won't people always go to the museum or to the symphony? Why should an organization spend time planning, reviewing its mission, devising strategies, and developing objectives when what it does is so obvious? Citing the examples of dance companies that have failed, museums that have had to reduce their hours and staff, and orchestras, theaters, and opera companies that have filed for bankruptcy should be enough to counter any argument that strategic marketing plans are a waste of time.

Figure 11.1

Marketing planning and process.

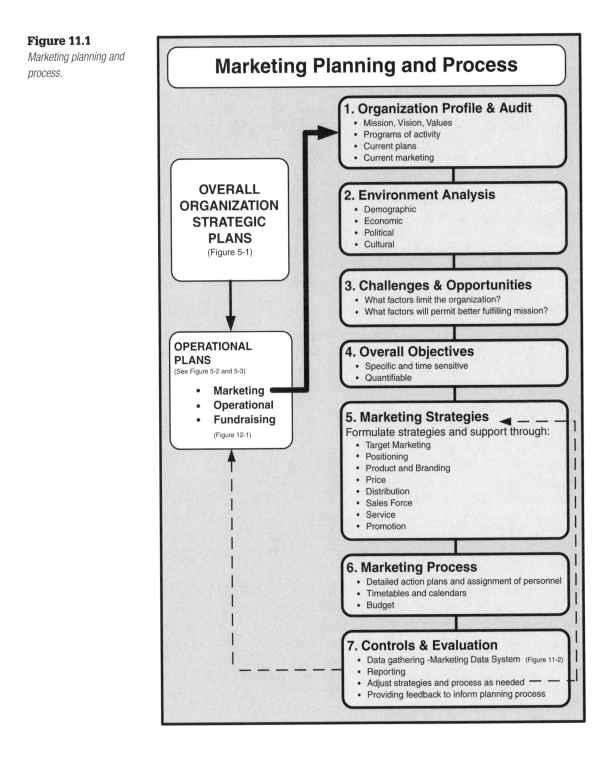

Marketing Initiatives

Here's an example of an initiative sponsored by the Theatre Communications Group (TCG) to help attract new people to theaters across America.

Free night of theater

Free Night of Theater is TCG's annual national audience development program to attract new theatergoers to America's not-for-profit theaters. Since the pilot program debuted in 2005, *Free Night* has increased in scope and participation each year. For more information go to www.freenightoftheater.net.

Planning process

The organization's overall strategic plan (discussed in Chapter 5, Planning and Decision Making) needs to incorporates the marketing plan (see Figure 11.1). The organization's objectives drive the mission, goals, and objectives of its marketing plan. In addition, as noted in Chapter 4, The Adaptive Arts Organization, an analysis of opportunities and threats from the external environments (economic, demographic, political and legal, social and cultural, technological, and educational) is weighed against the organization's strengths and weaknesses.

Once the basic mission and objectives of the organization have been defined in the strategic plan, the core marketing strategy can be developed. The target markets and the proposed marketing mix can be articulated. The process now moves to the final stage by providing the system for carrying out the marketing plan, including what performance criteria will be used to monitor progress. In addition, the specific tactics can be formed. Implementation plans and an evaluation system complete the process. The evaluation process should provide feedback to the core marketing strategy for long-term adjustments and directly back to specific tactics for short-term changes. For example, a short-term change might be to revise an advertisement in the paper when there is poor response to a particular offer. A long-term adjustment might be to evaluate all print media.

Marketing audit

One method that an organization might use to assess its ability to carry out a marketing plan is to do a marketing audit. Essentially, an audit consists of asking and answering a series of questions that explore the organization's markets, customers, objectives, organizational structure, marketing information system, and marketing mix. The Sample Marketing Plan in this chapter gives you a starting place for preparing an audit. The audit gives the staff and the board a common ground on which to build a marketing plan that fits the organization's mission and function.

Sample Marketing Plan

The first step in developing your marketing plan requires you to assess the current status of the organization. Depending on your organization, there may be additional questions you need to pose. Therefore, the items below should be viewed as a guide and not as the only questions you could raise.

1. Organization Profile and Audit
   - Name, type of arts organization, location, brief history, and years in existence
   - Programs and projects currently listed by the organization, or special performance or exhibition activities
   - Mission, goals, and/or objectives statements published? Is it posted on the Web site? Is the mission clear? Are the goals connected to the mission, and do they seem achievable? Are the objectives and priorities clear about who, what, and when?
   - Is the organization operating under a current strategic organizational or marketing plan? If yes, what is its planning and implementation process? Review brochures, flyers, website, and other documents used by the organization in its current marketing activities. Are these pieces effective? Is the Web site updated frequently?
   - Is the organization operating within its budget? Is it a financially healthy organization? Does it have a budget surplus or deficit? Are the board and management functioning effectively?

2. Environment Analysis

   Demographic
   - What major regional and national demographic developments and trends pose opportunities or threats for this organization?
   - What actions, if any, has the organization taken in response to those developments?
   - Economic
   - What major developments and trends in income, prices, savings, and interest rates are affecting the organization?
   - What major changes are taking place in the sources and amounts of contributed income (from individuals, corporations, private and public foundations, and government agencies)?
   - What actions has the organization taken in response to these developments and trends?
   - Political
   - What recent local, state, or national legislation has affected this organization?

- What federal, state, or local agencies should be monitored for future actions relating to the organization?
- What actions has the organization taken in response to these developments?

Cultural

- What changes are occurring in consumer lifestyles, values, and educational opportunities that might affect this organization?
- What actions has the organization taken in response to these developments?

3. Challenges and Opportunities

Challenges: Depending on how you answered the questions above you may have a series of specific challenges facing the organization, such as but not limited to the following:

- Declining subscriber base
- Increased competition from other arts organizations
- Lack of marketing technology
- Lack of single-ticket buyers or members
- Need to diversify audiences
- Poorly focused target marketing
- Lack of commitment to customer orientation by the organization

Opportunities:

- State the opportunities you see that will help meet the challenges facing the organization.
- State these opportunities as facts, not strategies or objectives. For example, you found that a challenge facing the organization was a declining subscriber base. The opportunity is "potential exists to increase subscriber base." Even if your organization is "perfect," you may still have opportunities to venture into new areas such as merchandise or adding an experimental performance series.

4. Objectives

Formulate objectives for the marketing plan based on the factual statements you have made. For example, if you stated "opportunity exists to increase the subscriber base," you could state objectives for each of the areas below. For example:

- Marketing: Objective will be to increase the subscriber base by a net of 5 percent in the next fiscal year.
- Financial: Objective will be to increase earned income from subscriptions by 5 percent above the previous fiscal year.

5. Marketing Strategy
In this section you outline your *game plan* for achieving all the objectives you set for yourself in:

- Target Markets: Who will be targeted?
- Positioning: What will be your positioning statement to sell to these target markets? "We are the only orchestra group performing the work of composer X in the tri-cities area."
- Product: Describe the product in customer terms that your research says these target markets find appealing.
- Price: How will you use price to achieve your objectives?
- Distribution: Will you expand access to tickets by selling through the organization's Web site, Ticketmaster, or Tickets.com?
- Sales Force: Changes needed to achieve objectives? Hire more staff?
- Service: Any changes in how services are delivered? Extra hours? 800 number? New Web site? E-mail enhancements?
- Promotion: All forms of promotion. What specifically do you plan to do? Will you use direct and e-mail or telemarketing, radio ads, PSAs, interactive Web site or what? In other words, what will be your media plan?

6. Marketing Process

Detailed Action Plans
- What will be done?
- Who will do it?
- What will be the benefit?

Timetable
- When will the action plan items be done? (Detail each action plan in a list or on a calendar.)
- Budget
- How much will it cost? (Detail all the costs of the plan: graphics, printing, advertising, Web design, etc.)

7. Controls and Evaluation
How will you monitor your progress? What kind and how frequent will be the reports? Create forms and reports for how you will measure your success in achieving the objectives you set for yourself and the organization.

Consultants

It is usually helpful to get the perspective of outside consultants when formulating any strategic or marketing plan. Someone with expertise in planning can save an organization a great deal of valuable time struggling through the planning process. As noted in Chapter 5, planning is hard work, and because of the pressing daily needs of keeping the organization afloat, managers often assign this essential process a low priority. A consultant, if used effectively, can shake up the status quo and act as a catalyst to put planning at the top of the priority list. You may have a board member who can be particularly helpful with either being a consultant for you, or directing you to a firm that will do some pro bono consulting for your organization. A word of caution, though: Consultants are not infallible, and they have been known to make mistakes. They can give bad advice and make recommendations that make conditions worse, not better. A background check of former clients is a requirement for organizations that want to protect themselves.

Strategies

The profit sector uses terminology borrowed from warfare when developing marketing strategies. Marketers use such terms as *frontal, encirclement, flanking,* and *bypass* attacks to describe marketing plans. Words such as *preemptive, counteroffensive,* and *contraction* are used to describe strategies.[32] Other options for organizations to explore include *market leader, market follower,* and *market niche strategies.* Let's look briefly at the competitive environment facing many arts organizations and discuss strategy options.

The competitive marketplace and core strategies

When a community reaches the point in its growth where it has at least one professional arts organization from each of the major disciplines, the struggle for resources among these organizations will probably intensify. Arts people may carry on a cordial and friendly dialog in public, but competition is tough and there are only so many dollars that people will spend on subscriptions, tickets, memberships, and donations. As we have seen, arts organizations also face competition for the entertainment dollar from DVD rentals, films, television, online games, and amusement parks.

In formulating a plan of attack, an arts organization might consider a *niche strategy.* Such a strategy focuses on the qualities that make a live performance arts event or a trip to the museum a unique activity. The niche strategy can be combined with a *differentiation strategy* in an effort to feature those things that are unique about the product. This strategy combination allows the organization to concentrate on what is special about its product while appealing to a targeted market.

If the organization's planning process leads to a decision to expand its audience base beyond the typical demographic blend, a strategy to increase market share would be appropriate. In this *growth strategy,* the organization takes an aggressive advertising and Web presence approach to reach new audiences. For example, if a theater company wanted to develop its market among African-Americans in the community, an advertising campaign using specific media publications, Web sites, and radio stations with a high ratio of minority consumers would make sense. Also, targeting group sales by using the local network of African-American religious groups might prove successful. However, if the arts organization does not regularly offer a product that has some market appeal to members of various minorities, there is little chance that this strategy will succeed. Another niche strategy may be developed through the organization creating a social networking presence.

Whatever overall marketing strategy an arts organization selects, it is important to remember that it must fit with the mission of the organization. Care must be taken to avoid shifting the organization away from its mission to meet a market strategy. For example, museums are not in the gift shop business, but because these operations can become very healthy sources of cash, it is tempting to overemphasize their importance in marketing the organization.

Project planning and implementation

The details of preparing, budgeting, and implementing the marketing plan require careful attention. Decisions about where to put the usually very limited marketing resources available to the organization can make or break a plan. The work done on researching the community and a detailed cost analysis of various media campaigns will pay off in the project planning stage. Organization and project management skills are required to prepare the overall schedule and budget distribution for the marketing campaign.

Evaluation

After implementing the plan, the organization must carefully evaluate and monitor how well its objectives are being realized. For example, if the costs of implementing the strategy exceed the budget, and the number of new subscribers or members is below the levels established for success, the organization must be able to adjust its tactics or to revise the entire strategy before it is too late. As noted in Chapter 5, Planning and Decision Making, the failure to abandon a plan that is not working can lead to numerous problems.

Marketing data system

Within the organization's overall management information system and financial management information system, you should also establish a marketing data system (MDS). Its purpose is parallel to that of the MIS. The MDS should be designed to gather and analyze data regularly and to issue reports

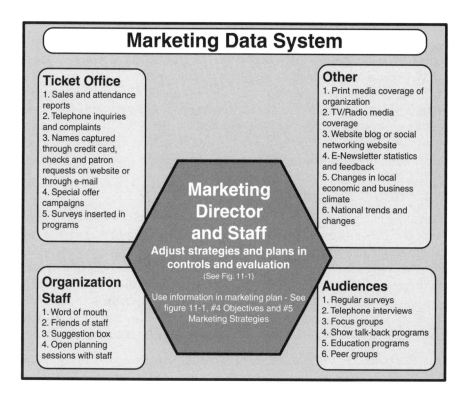

Figure 11.2
Marketing data system.

on the success of current campaigns. Figure 11.2 shows a typical MDS for an arts organization. The four major sources of data are the sales system (box office), audiences, staff, and various external environments. If the system is working properly, the feedback provided to the marketing staff will arrive in time to make corrections and adjustments in the marketing plan. With some sources of information, such as surveys, the data gathered could be translated into information that is useful in planning future seasons or programs.

Computers play a central role in gathering and processing data for the MDS. As we saw in Chapter 9, Operations and Budgeting, the MIS and the FMIS must be linked with the marketing data system if the organization is to monitor its operations effectively. It is essential that the organization have a network of computers that share data among the marketing staff and other members of the management team to enable the marketing plans to be successfully evaluated. The complexity of such a system may require hiring outside consultants to coordinate and advise the marketing manager. Without the ability to track all sales data quickly and accurately, the marketing manager's effectiveness will ultimately be seriously undermined.

CONCLUSION

Marketing can be an effective tool for keeping an organization growing and evolving. However, marketing is also a long-term investment. A well-organized marketing campaign should be integrated with operational and long-term organization plans. It makes no sense to attempt a marketing plan without having first clearly defined the mission and goals of the organization. Like any tool, marketing can be misused. Thousands of dollars can be wasted on advertising campaigns, a new Web site, or printed brochures that have little or no impact on sales.

Don't forget the audience

Ultimately, it is important to recognize how complex the purchase and attendance decision process is for the potential audience members. It can be easy to become enamored of the potential of the Internet and the extended activities now wrapped around the notion of Web 2.0. There is certainly a great many opportunities to take advantage of what the Web offers relative to social networking, Weblogs, wikis, podcasts, and Really Simple Syndication (RSS) capabilities. However, keeping focused on the decision steps required to actually participate as an audience member should never be taken for granted.

First, the potential audience member must achieve awareness of the event, then they have to decide if what you are offering is of interest to them, which takes us back to the important concept of taste. They may go to your Web site for more information about the show or they may ask friends what they thought, but ultimately the decision about taking the next step often does not happen. However, if they remain interested, then they must check their schedules to see if the dates and time you are performing fit in their schedule. Ticket costs are also probably part of the mix in reaching the purchase decision.

Assuming all of those decision points are yes, then they must make contact with your ticket office and engage in the actual purchase process. If the technology you have for processing orders is easy to use, they probably ordered their tickets online. Or, they may want to talk to a ticket sales agent. Did they have to wait for a long time to get through to someone? While they were waiting, did your phone's voice message system offer them more information about your venue or the productions currently playing?

After securing a ticket or making a reservation they need to decide what to wear, make arrangements to travel to your venue, find a place to park, find their way to their seat, and participate as an active audience member by enjoying (or not) your show. Then they have to negotiate the traffic and get back home before they can actually complete the experience.

As you can see, your average frequent attendee must be very well motivated to go through this process. Although people in the performing arts stress what is unique about a "live performance," it is also apparent that it is much easier to rent a DVD, or select a Pay Per View movie, simply watch television, or go online and explore the endless opportunities of the World Wide Web.

Unfortunately, there are no guarantees that your best plans to attract audiences will work. For organizations with limited resources, experimenting with different approaches to marketing may be out of the question. While the Internet has certainly helped level the marketing playing field, a Web site or a blog is not going to be everyone's preferred method of seeking information. In fact, there is bound to be a percentage of your audience who still do not find using a computer a worthwhile activity.

Finding the most cost-effective way to reach audiences across a broad spectrum of age and income demographics can be a challenge when there are limited funds for research. The pressure on the marketing and public relations staff, which may be only one or two people, can become debilitating. It is not surprising to find high turnover in an arts organization's marketing and public relations staff. Impossible goals, limited resources, and poorly conceived plans take their toll on even the most ambitious people. Upper management involvement and commitment to planning and implementation can go a long way toward remedying the problems that arts marketers face.

The most daunting task facing any arts marketer is the development of future audiences. The simple reality of a very limited audience base coupled with the ever-increasing competition from other entertainment options makes for a difficult mix of circumstances. As most arts marketers know, unless you can establish a pattern of arts consumption at an early age, it is both difficult and costly to change people's leisure time behavior later in life. The arts marketing effort will no doubt continue, and wherever appropriate, the arts marketer will borrow from the commercial marketing world those techniques that work.

For students interested in a challenging field of work, arts or nonprofit marketing has a great deal of potential. The use of language and images to express an idea or to convey an organization's mission demands a great deal of skill and creativity. Because this chapter is just a glimpse into the world of marketing, students are urged to explore the readings listed in Additional Resources at the end of this chapter. A college undergraduate course in marketing would also be helpful to the future arts marketer.

SUMMARY

The arts manager must plan, organize, implement, and evaluate marketing strategies to maximize revenue and meet the organization's objectives. Because of the bombardment of marketing efforts by a multitude of businesses and causes, the arts manager must dedicate significant resources to marketing if the organization is to be visible in the highly competitive entertainment marketplace. Marketing is a means to an end, and it should be thought of as one more tool available to the arts manager to be used in realizing the overall goals of the organization.

Contemporary marketing attempts to match the wants and needs of consumers with products and services. Needs are physiological and psychological things that are lacking and are necessary for people's well-being. Wants are things that are lacking and that people find desirable or useful. People can gain functional and psychological satisfaction from tangible and intangible features of products or services.

Marketing activity is designed to facilitate the exchange process. This process involves a transfer of something of value between two or more parties or organizations. The exchange process is successful to the degree that the utilities of form, time, place, and possession can be satisfied through the exchange. The arts exchange usually involves satisfying a psychological want through the intangible features of an experience, which is modified by the inherent constraints placed on the four utilities by the delivery system (the performance or exhibition).

Marketing has seen significant evolution over the last 100 years. The production era, which grew out of the Industrial Revolution, concentrated on satisfying basic needs. It was assumed that people would buy whatever was manufactured. The sales era, which concentrated on increasing demand, began sometime after the Civil War. More emphasis was put on customers' wants, but the manufacturers still dictated what would be available to purchase. The marketing era, which came to the fore after World War II, reversed the relationship between the consumer and the manufacturer. The consumer-driven market relationship starts with what the consumer wants, not the product. The continued development of the Internet has also meant that consumers can do their own research without the marketer's message filters mediating the interaction.

The way an organization markets itself and establishes a brand still depends a great deal on how the marketing is viewed from within the organization. A great deal of the marketing done today is classified along the same historical approaches of product, sales, or customer-oriented marketing. The product-oriented company assumes that its product is inherently good and needs no changes. The sales-oriented company concentrates on trying to increase demand for existing products and services. The customer-oriented company determines the perceptions, needs, and wants of the market and goes about creating a product to fit those needs. Arts organizations can and do use these three orientations. The market-oriented arts organization thrives if it understands the market's perception of its product and describes, prices, packages, and delivers its product to reflect those perceptions. It does not mean that the organization must change the product to attract customers.

Marketing management is based on the organization's manipulation of the four Ps — product, price, place, and promotion — or the market mix. The market mix can be adjusted to suit the target market. Market research has shown that people with various demographic and psychographic profiles react differently to various marketing mixes.

The entire marketing process should be directly related to the organization's strategic plans. The main objectives of the strategic plan are incorporated into the marketing plan. An analysis of external environments and the strengths and weaknesses of the organization are also included. A detailed audit process may be used to assess the organization's capabilities to undertake an effective marketing campaign. From the marketing plan, specific strategies and detailed tactics can be designed to meet the defined objectives. The success of the marketing campaign depends on accurate and timely information gathered by the marketing data system.

Evolving World Wide Web technology offers arts marketing several promising paths to expand the audience base and to communicate directly with audience members without using the traditional media.

For additional topics relating to marketing the arts, please go to www. managementandthearts.com.

Questions

1. Define *marketing*.
2. What are some of the wants and needs satisfied by the following: a brand-name soft drink, a meal at a French restaurant, and a visit to an art museum?
3. Does marketing make you buy things that you do not need? Explain.
4. Give an example of an exchange process in which you recently participated that was not satisfying. What went wrong in the exchange? What would you change to make the exchange satisfying?
5. What suggestions would you offer about form, time, place, and possession utilities to a museum and a children's theater company that are each planning new community outreach programs?
6. When you are considering the purchase of an arts product, which of the four Ps is most important to you? Explain. Do you react differently to various marketing mixes? How?
7. What are some of the different market segments you would identify for theater, dance, opera, symphony, and museum organizations? How much attendance crossover do you think exists among the different segments? For example, do opera audiences go to the theater?

8. Do demographic and psychographic profiles of audiences match your perception of arts consumers? How do you think the profile of the audience will change over the next 20 years? How will changes in demographics affect arts organizations?

9. If you were managing a small modern dance company in a community with a well-established ballet company, what marketing strategy would you adopt to gain a market share? How would you use the Internet to facilitate your dance company's presence?

CASE STUDY

Using the Sample Marketing Plan from this chapter select a local or regional arts organization and apply the criteria and questions in Section 1 and do an organizational profile and audit of their marketing activities. Discuss your findings with the class. Offer recommendations for improving the organization's marketing and public relations efforts.

ADDITIONAL RESOURCES

There is no shortage of information about arts marketing. Resources include sites like www.artsmarketing.org. You can also make a quick trip to a bookstore where you will find numerous titles on marketing and marketing research in general.

Listed below are some additional resources that may prove helpful in your quest to find out more about arts marketing.

Joanne Scheff Bernstein, *Arts Marketing Insights*, San Francisco, CA: Jossey-Bass, 2007.

Albert Blankenship, George Breen, and Alan Dutica, *State of the Arts Marketing Research*, Chicago IL: NTC Books, 1998.

Eugene Carr, *Sign-Up for Culture — The Arts Marketer's Guide to Building an Effective E-mail List*, 2nd edition, New York: Patron Publishing, 2007.

François Colbert with the collaboration of Suzanne Bilodeau, Johanne Brunet, Jacques Natel, and J. Dennis Rich, *Marketing Culture and the Arts*, 3rd edition, Montreal, Canada: HEC, 2007.

Elizabeth Hill, Terry O'Sullivan, and Catherine O'Sullivan, *Creative Arts Marketing*, Oxford, England: Butterworth-Heinemann, 2002.

Finola Kerrigan, Peter Fraser, and Mustafa Ozbilgin, *Arts Marketing*, Burlington, MA: Elsevier Butterworth-Heinemann, 2004.

Neil Kotler and Philip Kotler, *Museum Strategy and Marketing*, San Francisco, CA: Jossey-Bass Publishers, 1998.

Phillip Kotler and Joanne Scheff Bernstein, *Standing Room Only: Strategies for Marketing the Performing Arts*, Cambridge, MA: Harvard Business School Press, 1007.

Bradley G. Morison and Julie Gordon Dalgleish, *Waiting in the Wings*, New York: American Council for the Arts, 1987.

Danny Newman. *Subscribe Now!* New York: Theatre Communications Group, 1977.

Surveying Your Arts Audience, NEA Research Division Manual, Washington, D.C., 1985.

Ruth Rentschler, *Innovative Arts Marketing*, Allen & Unwin Publishers, Sydney, Australia, 2002.

Priscilla Salant and Don A. Dillman, *How to Conduct Your Own Survey*, New York: John Wiley & Sons, 1994.

REFERENCES

1. Philip Kotler, Joanne Scheff, *Standing Room Only* (Boston: Harvard Business School Press, 1997), p. 44.

2. American Marketing Association Web site, June 2008: http://www.marketingpower.com/_layouts/Dictionary.aspx.

3. Charles D. Schewe, *Marketing Principles and Strategies* (New York: Random House, 1987), p. 5.

4. Ibid., p. 5.

5. Ibid., p. 7.

6. 2002 Survey of Public Participation, Tom Bradshaw, Bonnie Nichols, NEA, Washington, D.C., 2004, p. 2.

7. Ibid., p. 2.

8. James Heilbrun, Charles M. Gray, *The Economics of Art and Culture*, 2nd edition. (New York: Cambridge Press, 2001), p 75.

9. Schewe, *Marketing Principles and Strategies*, p. 7.

10. Ibid., p. 7.

11. Ibid., p. 8.

12. bid., p. 10.

13. Ibid., p. 19.

14. Ibid., pp. 14–16.

15. Kotler and Scheff, *Standing Room Only*, p. 33.

16. Ibid., p. 33.

17. Ibid., p. 33.

18. Ibid., p. 33.

19. Ibid., p. 34.

20. Ibid., p. 34.

21. Schewe, *Marketing Principles and Strategies*, p. 33.

22. Ibid., p. 36.

23. Ibid., p. 36.

24. American Marketing Association Web site, December 2007: http://www.marketingpower.com/_layouts/Dictionary.aspx?dLetter=B.

25. Manhattan Theatre Club Web site, December 2007: http://www.mtc-nyc.org

26. Arnold Mitchell, *The Nine American Lifestyles* (New York: Warner Books, 1983), pp. 13–24.

27. Arnold Mitchell, *The Professional Performing Arts: Attendance Patterns, Preferences and Motives* (Washington, D.C.: Association of Performing Arts Presenters, 1984), pp. ES–1 to ES–4, 21–24.

28. Michael J. Weiss, *The Clustered World* (New York: Little, Brown and Company, 2000), p. 79.

29. Ibid., pp. 180, 194.

30. Richard A. Peterson, Darren E. Sherkat, Judith Huggins Balfe, and Rolf Meyersohn; Erin V. Lehman, ed., *Age and Arts Participation*, NEA Research Division Report #34 (Santa Ana, CA: Seven Locks Press, 1996), pp. 1–5.

31. Weiss, *The Clustered World*, p. 39.

32. Schewe, *Marketing Principles and Strategies*, p. 55.

CHAPTER 12

Fundraising

"Successful fundraising is the right person asking the right prospect for the right amount for the right project at the right time in the right way."

Stanley Weinstein, *The Complete Guide to Fundraising Management*, 2nd edition

KEY WORDS

Social exchange model for giving
Funding table
Fundraising audit
Case for support
Fundraising data management
Direct and indirect costs
Comprehensive campaign
Annual campaign
Capital campaign

Restricted and unrestricted gifts
Deferred gift
Bequest
Direct mail promotion
Reciprocity
Strategic fit
Foundations — Private and Corporate

In Chapter 11 we saw how critical it is that arts organizations effectively create marketing and communication systems to build relationships with potential audiences. This chapter takes your through the all important activity of fundraising, which very much complements the marketing function of the organization. In fact, many organizations are realizing that these two functions must be coordinated as part of a larger overall strategic initiative designed to advance and sustain the arts in their communities.

First, we will review the reasons people may or may not give to the arts. Then we will review the techniques employed by arts organizations to attract, maintain, and enhance giving. We will then review the data systems and campaign organization needed to maximize support from a variety of donors. We will also look at the important areas of special events and corporate and foundation support. These three areas play a key part in sustaining arts organizations in the increasingly competitive world of fundraising.

GIVING HISTORY AND TRENDS

The act of giving to good causes is well established in American culture. The charitable system developed by various religious organizations to provide social services in the United States still depends on individual donations of funds, goods, and services. The intervention of direct government support in this system is a fairly recent phenomenon. United States government subsidies only became widely institutionalized after 1933. Today, the United States has a unique mixture of public and private support for health, education, social services, and culture (sometimes referred to as nongovernmental agencies or NGOs). Government support of giving is also reflected in the tax benefits available when a person files a tax form and itemizes expenses.

Organized fundraising by entities other than churches dates back to the nineteenth century. For instance, the International Red Cross operated the first disaster relief fund drives as early as 1859.[1] One source cites Lyman L. Pierce and Charles S. Ward as the fathers of modern fundraising, based on their work for the YMCA in the 1890s. The techniques they developed were used in 1905 to raise money for a new building in Washington, D.C., and these techniques made them pioneers of the major capital campaign. In fact, they may have been the first fundraising consultants, judging by the work they did assisting the U.S. government to sell war bonds to help finance World War I.[2]

From these humble beginnings has risen a multibillion-dollar philanthropy industry. In 2006, for example, *Giving USA 2007* reported an estimated $295 billion was given to nonprofit and charity organizations by individuals, corporations, and foundations. This represented a 1 percent increase (adjusted for inflation) from 2005. The report goes on to note, "In 2006, giving to arts, culture, and humanities organizations reached an estimated $12.51 billion, an increase of 9.9 percent (6.5 percent adjusted for inflation) from the revised estimate of $11.38 billion for 2005."[3] The arts, culture, and humanities accounted for 4.2 percent of the total contributions in 2006 according to *Giving USA 2007*.

WHY DO PEOPLE GIVE?

The act of giving is a particular behavior that is motivated by a complex set of reasons and emotions. Although the giving process mirrors the exchange concept we discussed in Chapter 11, Marketing and the Arts, there is another layer of behavior reflected in the exchange with a donor. The personal satisfaction people derive from giving is difficult to quantify, but fundraisers must carefully consider this factor in how they formulate their approach to seeking support in the community. People give to particular causes or organizations because they believe they are helping society in some way. Joseph R. Mixer's book *Principles of Professional Fundraising*[4] cites numerous surveys and theories about giving behavior. Mixer focuses on the "Social Exchange Model for Giving"[5] to detail the individual giving process. He goes on to say:

> The charitable organization or agency presents client needs and services to a prospect along with a request for funds. If the request is favorably received, the prospect responds with a donation of funds and possibly time. To continue the relationship, the recipient provides some form of satisfaction to the donor.

The essence of what is returned to the donor is not a commodity or service that can be used profitably by the giver, but an intangible, psychic satisfaction that relates to the donor's personal motivations. An enhanced degree of self-esteem, a feeling of achievement, a new status, and a sense of belonging are among the most powerful rewards donors can receive. Giving satisfies donors' fundamental human needs and desires.[6]

A Donor Bill of Rights

Philanthropy is based on voluntary action for the common good. It is a tradition of giving and sharing that is primary to the quality of life. To assure that philanthropy merits the respect and trust of the general public, and that donors and prospective donors can have full confidence in the not-for-profit organizations and causes they are asked to support, we declare that all donors have these rights:

I. To be informed of the organization's mission, of the way the organization intends to use donated resources, and of its capacity to use donations effectively for their intended purposes.

II. To be informed of the identity of those serving on the organization's governing board, and to expect the board to exercise prudent judgment in its stewardship responsibilities.

III. To have access to the organization's most recent financial statements.

IV. To be assured their gifts will be used for the purposes for which they were given.

V. To receive appropriate acknowledgement and recognition.

VI. To be assured that information about their donations is handled with respect and with confidentiality to the extent provided by law.

VII. To expect that all relationships with individuals representing organizations of interest to the donor will be professional in nature.

VIII. To be informed whether those seeking donations are volunteers, employees of the organization or hired solicitors.

IX. To have the opportunity for their names to be deleted from mailing lists that an organization may intend to share.

X. To feel free to ask questions when making a donation and to receive prompt, truthful and forthright answers.

Developed by:

Association of Fundraising Professionals (AFP)
Association for Healthcare Philanthropy (AHP)
Council for Advancement and Support of Education (CASE)
Giving Institute: Leading Consultants to Non-Profits

Endorsed by:

Independent Sector
National Catholic Development Conference (NCDC)
National Committee on Planned Giving (NCPG)
Council for Resource Development (CRD)
United Way of America

Source: Association of Fundraising Professionals at http://www.afpnet.org/. Used with permission.

FUNDRAISING AND THE ARTS

Fundraising is an everyday activity for an arts organization. Whether it is called fundraising, development, or advancement, the basic objective is the same: increase the capability of the organization to fulfill its mission through contributed income. The quest to build, maintain, and enlarge an organization's base of donors who routinely support and believe in your organization is a full-time challenge. Perhaps no area of managing an arts organization comes under closer scrutiny or is subject to more pressure than fundraising. For many organizations, 40 percent or more of the yearly operating budget may come from gifts by individuals and grants from foundations, arts councils, and corporations. If there is a decline in gifts from any of these sources, arts organizations with little or no cash reserves often find themselves in serious financial difficulty. This "unearned income," as it is sometimes called, is very much earned through the hard work of the staff and the board of directors.

As we have discussed, the changing external environments (economic, political and legal, cultural and social, demographic, technological, and educational) create opportunities and pose threats for arts organizations. Each of these environments may have an impact on the organization's fundraising efforts. For example, an economic recession will probably signal a slowdown in giving because people feel they need to retain more of their discretionary income. In an election year, major donors may give more to candidates and less to cultural organizations. Changes in the tax laws also affect giving. In the United States people who itemize their taxes expect they will see some benefit if they make a donation to an arts and culture organization because their overall tax liability will be lowered.

Direct government support of the arts in the United States still represents a relatively small commitment of resources even after 50 years since the establishment of the National Endowment for the Arts. Probably the biggest direct subsidy for the arts in America goes to the military in the form of the support given to various bands, orchestras, and choirs. Other major arts institutions receiving significant direct government support include the Smithsonian, Corporation for Public Broadcasting, and the Institute of Museum and Library Services. For example, in the 2006 Federal budget these three organizations received over $1,244 billion in support.[7]

While direct government subsidies of the arts in many parts of the world are many times greater per capita than in the United States, other countries do not forgo the significant level of revenue allowed through the U.S. tax system. The unique partnership in the U.S. of government, individual, foundation, and corporate support for the arts defines the conditions in which all fundraisers must work. (For more information on how the arts are funded in the U.S. download the report from the NEA Web site at www.nea.gov/pub/how.pdf.)

Fundraising plans

Because fundraising is so closely linked to the overall fiscal health of the organization, management of fundraising activities must be thoroughly integrated into the strategic and operational planning process. In fact, many arts organizations place marketing and fundraising under the control of a chief development director (CDO). This person hires specialists in each area of development to realize the objectives formulated in the short- and long-term organizational plans.

In organizations with inadequate staffing (which describes many arts organizations), one person may try to manage and implement an annual giving program, develop major gifts or a capital campaign (e.g., for a new building), cultivate foundation contacts, and engage in grant writing to local, state, and federal agencies. It becomes very difficult for one person to meet these diverse fundraising objectives. As we have seen in the chapters on planning, organizing, and operations, a manager needs adequate resources to carry out the organization's overall objectives. Because each of these fundraising areas requires a working knowledge of a vast amount of detail, it is unrealistic to expect one person to keep up with this impossible workload. Of course a supportive and active board of directors can be of assistance in the effort. However, the staff person usually ends up as the one everyone looks to when the fundraising goals are not achieved.

As we will see in this chapter, much of the work involved in fundraising is centered on research and writing. As the quote at the beginning of this chapter points out, work needs to be done in advance to carefully cultivate a match between the organization and the donor. A great deal of fundraising also involves social interaction with donors and potential donors. Without the time and help to research, cultivate, and communicate with donors, the fundraiser's success rate will be very limited. Seldom are the benefits immediate to the organization. Years may go by before an individual finally makes a major gift to the organization. People who seek a quick payoff for their effort will probably find development a very frustrating area in which to work.

On the whole, fundraising seems to be a growth industry. There is a constant high demand for people who can organize and effectively manage the fundraising activities of a nonprofit corporation. Generally, salaries can be higher for development staff. The downside of this high demand is the often unrealistic expectations about how much money can actually be raised. The tendency to overestimate gift income can lead an organization into a deficit operating mode. The net result of all this pressure to produce is often a high level of turnover in the development area in the nonprofit sector.

In this chapter, we explore the requirements an organization must meet before it tries to raise money. We also discuss strategies to use in approaching different target donors and organizations that specialize in giving to the arts.

Preparing fundraising plans

James Gregory Lord, a recognized expert in the field of fundraising, notes that "people give to people." He goes on to say, "People don't give to an institution. They give to the person who asks them. Often, a contribution is made because of how one person feels about another. The institution may be almost incidental. People also give for people — not for endowments or swimming pools."[8]

If fundraising managers keep this fundamental fact in the forefront of all planning and solicitation efforts, they will probably be successful in establishing relationships with donors who have a lifelong pattern of giving. No matter what strategy an organization plans to adopt in its fundraising efforts, the bottom line depends on regular gifts. Without the regular support of individuals, corporations, foundations, and government, most organizations would not be able to survive. Let's examine in more detail how to go about establishing a pattern of regular giving.

Association of Fundraising Professionals Code of Ethical Principles and Standards

Ethical principles — Adopted 1964; amended Sept. 2007

The Association of Fundraising Professionals (AFP) exists to foster the development and growth of fundraising professionals and the profession, to promote high ethical behavior in the fundraising profession, and to preserve and enhance philanthropy and volunteerism. Members of AFP are motivated by an inner drive to improve the quality of life through the causes they serve. They serve the ideal of philanthropy, are committed to the preservation and enhancement of volunteerism; and hold stewardship of these concepts as the overriding direction of their professional life. They recognize their responsibility to ensure that needed resources are vigorously and ethically sought and that the intent of the donor is honestly fulfilled. To these ends, AFP members, both individual and business, embrace certain values that they strive to uphold in performing their responsibilities for generating philanthropic support. AFP business members strive to promote and protect the work and mission of their client organizations.

AFP members both individual and business aspire to:

- Practice their profession with integrity, honesty, truthfulness and adherence to the absolute obligation to safeguard the public trust
- Act according to the highest goals and visions of their organizations, professions, clients, and consciences
- Put philanthropic mission above personal gain
- Inspire others through their own sense of dedication and high purpose
- Improve their professional knowledge and skills, so that their performance will better serve others
- Demonstrate concern for the interests and well-being of individuals affected by their actions
- Value the privacy, freedom of choice, and interests of all those affected by their actions
- Foster cultural diversity and pluralistic values and treat all people with dignity and respect
- Affirm, through personal giving, a commitment to philanthropy and its role in society
- Adhere to the spirit as well as the letter of all applicable laws and regulations
- Advocate within their organizations adherence to all applicable laws and regulations

- Avoid even the appearance of any criminal offense or professional misconduct
- Bring credit to the fundraising profession by their public demeanor
- Encourage colleagues to embrace and practice these ethical principles and standards
- Be aware of the codes of ethics promulgated by other professional organizations that serve philanthropy

Source: Association of Fundraising Professionals: http://www.afpnet.org/. Used with permission.

Strategic planning and fundraising

As noted, most fundraising activity begins with a great deal of background work. Unless the organization happens to have a wealthy benefactor who hands out money with no questions asked, countless hours must be spent preparing to ask people for their support. The flow chart in Figure 12.1 depicts a typical system for organizing the fundraising for an organization.

An organization's strategic plan normally contains a specific operational plan for the proposed fundraising efforts. In Chapter 5, Planning and Decision Making, the concepts of the overall organizational strategy and the operational strategies for special areas were discussed. In Chapter 11, Marketing and the Arts, we saw how the marketing plan should be integrated with the strategic plan. Now we consider how fundraising needs should be integrated into the overall strategic plans.

The overall strategy the organization adopts will of course affect the development of the organization's profile and audit. Take the example of an organization that adopts a growth strategy. It is safe to assume that the fundraising staff would need to address the issue of finding more new sources of funds for the organization. This requires that time be spent on donor research. On the other hand, if the organization adopts a stability strategy, the fundraisers might concentrate their efforts on the current donor base. As with any planning process, multiple strategies probably should be incorporated into the overall master plan. However, the staff and budget resources required to support multiple approaches can become burdensome.

Profile, self-assessment, and an organizational audit

The fundraising process shown in Figure 12.1 is broken down into five major activity areas. Of course the starting and ending points in any process are not always clear and distinct. Regardless of the starting point, assessment must be taken before anything else.

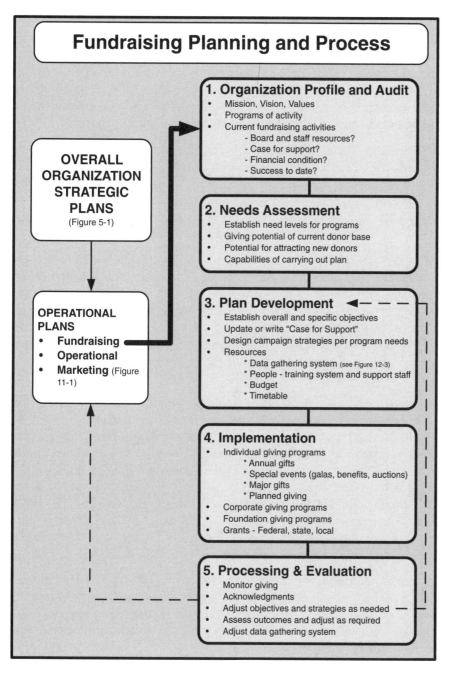

Figure 12.1
Fundraising planning and process.

Fundraising Planning and Process

OVERALL ORGANIZATION STRATEGIC PLANS
(Figure 5-1)

OPERATIONAL PLANS
• **Fundraising**
• **Operational**
• **Marketing** (Figure 11-1)

1. Organization Profile and Audit
• Mission, Vision, Values
• Programs of activity
• Current fundraising activities
    - Board and staff resources?
    - Case for support?
    - Financial condition?
    - Success to date?

2. Needs Assessment
• Establish need levels for programs
• Giving potential of current donor base
• Potential for attracting new donors
• Capabilities of carrying out plan

3. Plan Development
• Establish overall and specific objectives
• Update or write "Case for Support"
• Design campaign strategies per program needs
• Resources
    * Data gathering system (see Figure 12-3)
    * People - training system and support staff
    * Budget
    * Timetable

4. Implementation
• Individual giving programs
    * Annual gifts
    * Special events (galas, benefits, auctions)
    * Major gifts
    * Planned giving
• Corporate giving programs
• Foundation giving programs
• Grants - Federal, state, local

5. Processing & Evaluation
• Monitor giving
• Acknowledgments
• Adjust objectives and strategies as needed
• Assess outcomes and adjust as required
• Adjust data gathering system

The first area to examine is the organization's mission and programs as they are the source for all fundraising activities. These elements are the core from which you build your fundraising goals. The clarity of the mission statement, your fundraising plans, and the organization's programs of activity must be obvious to your potential donors. For example, if one of your programming goals includes bringing opera to schoolchildren in your community, then it will be clear to donors why you need funding for a truck or a van.

You also need to assess your current fundraising activities. The common question that the fundraising staff starts with usually includes, how well are our current fundraising activities working? Is your board capable of giving you the assistance you will need to undertake new fundraising initiatives? Do you have a clear and strong "case for support?" (See Case Statement in the next section.) Is the financial condition of the organization healthy?

The process of self-assessment also can be aided by holding focus group meetings with people from the community. Understanding how people perceive your organization should help you write the case for support. As we noted in Chapter 11, marketing and fundraising are usually less successful when presented in a product- or sales-oriented manner. A general appeal that says, "Give to us because we make great music and we are a world-class organization," will not do much to promote the exchange process between donors and the organization.

The needs assessment step helps determine the various amounts needed to meet your development goal. This step requires a careful analysis of the budget and the fiscal health of the organization. For example, if the strategic plan called for establishing an operating endowment fund to provide an annual income of $60,000, the fundraising goal could be as high as $2 million. This figure assumes that the $2 million would earn a net interest rate of 3 percent, thus yielding $60,000 per year. The net interest figure is as small as it is because there is an assumption that an endowment fund needs to grow each year at a rate above inflation. Taking more than 3 percent could erode the value of the total endowment over time.

The actual campaign planning stage involves formulating written material such as the case statement, creating the graphics and brochures to communicate the projects or programs, planning special fundraising events (e.g., auctions, dinners, and costume balls), and tactics such as telephoning donors to ask for support. The training of staff and volunteers, establishing a detailed timetable, and donor research all must be done before launching a campaign.

The implementation stage typically has several fronts of activity. Gifts from all categories of donors are solicited with the intent of building the long-term relationships necessary for future campaigns. The cycle of preparing, asking, evaluating, and starting to plan all over again is inherent in the fundraising function of an arts organization. There will be several development initiatives happening at the same time. The mix of activities usually includes annual giving, special gifts, major gifts, and planned giving initiatives. For example, your organization may be running a capital campaign during the year.

The *funding table* shown in Figure 12.2 is one approach used to establish how many gifts, at which amount, will be needed to meet a specific goal. A small capital campaign with a goal of $6 million usually concentrates its initial efforts on raising at least half of the money before publicly announcing the campaign effort. A lead gift of $500,000 and gifts down through at least $35,000 are secured before the campaign is announced to build momentum. With at least half of the money raised, fundraisers can tell people, "Here's a project that others are willing to support."

To succeed in building the table from the top down, the fundraisers must do their homework. Identifying possible funding sources, evaluating their giving potential, ranking them within the table, and finding the right contact person could take a year or more. All of this work can amount to nothing if the wrong person asks for the gift. As James Lord says, "People give to people." It is critical that the fundraising staff educate board members and other volunteers about how and when to ask for support. As we will see later in this chapter, the entire fundraising effort is in part a marketing effort. The fundraiser tries to match the wants and needs of the donor with the goods and services of the organization.

Assuming success, the final stage includes processing and evaluation. Monitoring and adjusting the plan is also part of the process. In Figure 12.1 the dotted line going back to Step 3 assumes you are making ongoing adjustments as the year goes on. As with the marketing campaign, evaluation and adjustment go on constantly in an effort to fine-tune and maximize the gift-giving program.

Marketing and the relationship to fundraising

An effective fundraising campaign requires the implementation of a well-organized marketing plan. In the fundraising campaign, the goal is to achieve a close match between the donor and the funding need. In this case, the exchange process should make donors feel that the money, goods, or services they are giving will help solve a specific problem. Finding the right "hot button" for each donor — for example, the young artists' program or the museum arts classes for children — is a way to maximize the satisfaction of giving. The fact is, if the fundraising campaign is not donor-driven in the way it is packaged and presented, it will probably not be as effective or successful. People want to give knowing they are helping to solve problems and making their community a

Figure 12.2

Capital campaign funding table.

Giving Table - Capital Campaign Projections

Number of Gifts	Gift Amount	Total	Cumulative Totals	% of Total
1	$ 500,000	$ 500,000	$ 500,000	8.2%
2	$ 250,000	$ 500,000	$ 1,000,000	8.2%
3	$ 150,000	$ 450,000	$ 1,450,000	7.4%
4	$ 100,000	$ 400,000	$ 1,850,000	6.6%
6	$ 75,000	$ 450,000	$ 2,300,000	7.4%
8	$ 50,000	$ 400,000	$ 2,700,000	6.6%
12	$ 35,000	$ 420,000	$ 3,120,000	6.9%
15	$ 25,000	$ 375,000	$ 3,495,000	6.2%
25	$ 20,000	$ 500,000	$ 3,995,000	8.2%
35	$ 15,000	$ 525,000	$ 4,520,000	8.6%
50	$ 10,000	$ 500,000	$ 5,020,000	8.2%
75	$ 5,000	$ 375,000	$ 5,395,000	6.2%
100	$ 2,000	$ 200,000	$ 5,595,000	3.3%
150	$ 1,000	$ 150,000	$ 5,745,000	2.5%
250	$ 500	$ 125,000	$ 5,870,000	2.1%
500	$ 250	$ 125,000	$ 5,995,000	2.1%
1000	$ 100	$ 100,000	$ 6,095,000	1.6%

Total Gifts 2236   **Goal $ 6,095,000**

Top 10 Donors - Lead Donors $ 1,850,000   30.4% of Total
Top 24 Donors - Major Donors $ 2,700,000   44.3% of Total

Giving Table - Gifts Received and Pledged

Donor Name	Amount Pledged	Amount Received	Total Raised	% of Goal

Totals $ -	$ -	$ -	0%
Amount Pledged	Amount Received	Total Raised	% of Goal

better place to live in. They are not giving just because you say you have a need for support. All organizations have needs for support. The effective fundraiser knows donors want to hear about the effect their giving may have.

MANAGEMENT SKILLS OF THE FUNDRAISER

Fundraising involves the familiar aspects of project management: budgets, schedules, timetables, problem solving, task lists, and group leadership techniques. An individual with excellent group and project management skills is required for a successful campaign. Excellent communication skills are a must for the development personnel. Many of the topics covered in Chapter 8 (Leadership and Group Dynamics) will find an application in the successful development operation of an arts organization. Thousands of details must be coordinated into a unified whole if the organization is to reach its fundraising goals. We begin by examining the background work required for getting ready to ask for support. Then, we review the techniques and tools used to maximize the possibility of support from various funding entities.

THE CASE FOR SUPPORT

What does the organization do?

After completing the fundraising audit and assessment, the process should shift to formulating what the organization can do to address a range of needs in the community. How does the symphony orchestra, museum, or dance, theater, or opera company satisfy the current needs of the community? What needs are not being met? Can the arts organization fulfill any of these needs? In *Managing a Nonprofit Organization in the Twenty-First Century*, Thomas Wolf identifies three important steps in this process, which he calls the case for support:[9]

1. Identify the important problems or needs that the organization intends to address with the help of the contributions.
2. Demonstrate the organization's ability to address these needs.
3. Match the proposed areas of organizational activity with the funder's own philanthropic interests.

The obvious starting point for an organization attempting to identify problems or needs is to address the current programs and projects. For example, the fictitious theater company examined in Chapter 9, Operations and Budgeting, had established a home season, touring operation, education program, and building fund (capital campaign) to meet the various needs of the community. To make its case for support, the theater company would offer proof of how it is uniquely qualified to meet the community's needs through its regular season, which enriches the cultural life of the community by presenting quality productions. The theater could argue that the touring operation provides a service to a wide geographical area and a diverse audience and that the education program offers a school or apprentice program to teach acting skills to young people. The building fund is targeted to provide a permanent home for the theater company so that it may increase its effectiveness in presenting its season and its projects in the community.

Case Statement

Kent A. Dove's book *Conducting a Successful Fundraising Program* lists these "essential elements" for the case statement:

It describes the organization's mission in terms of the human and social issues that are central to the organization. This bullet list offers a more comprehensive view of the case statement.

- It states the organization's objectives in specific, quantifiable terms.
- It describes a set of tasks or strategies for reaching the objectives within a given period of time.
- It reports on the facilities, staff assignments, and budget required to carry out the tasks and strategies, which will include control procedures for continuing evaluation.
- It identifies who will benefit from services offered by the organization.
- It sets forth the reasons why someone should make a contribution to support the organization and thus the cause that it serves.
- It stresses the strengths of the organization. Avoid the trap of publicizing weaknesses or needs; emphasize the positive by selling strengths, successes, and opportunities.[10]

After the theater company outlines what it is doing and how it is effectively addressing the community's needs, the important process of matching activities to funders takes place. Accurate research about potential donors is critical to making the optimal match. For example, a foundation may focus on education, a corporation may support high-visibility activities such as touring, and individual donors may want to be associated with a new facility. A significant amount of time can be wasted if the wrong donor is approached. Even worse, a potential donor may be turned off to your organization because of an inappropriate approach. A closer examination of this matching process is presented later in this chapter when various funding sources are discussed.

Staff and board participation

One of the expectations of any fundraising campaign is that staff and board members will actively participate to help reach the goal. Potential donors may ask how much support staff and board members provide to the organization. Answers about the average contribution per staff or board member must be at hand. The goal typically is to have 100 percent of the board and staff give, even if the amounts per gift are small. After all, why should donors give to an organization that does not have the support of its own people?

When someone is approached to serve on a board of a not-for-profit organization the understanding usually is they are going to be part of the fundraising team. The board members and the board chair need to be part of the fundraising activities for the simple reason that asking for support is rooted in the network of connections the board members have in the community. It is often the case that a member of the development staff will accompany a board member on a meeting with a donor. However, to avoid seeming self-serving, it is the board member who more often than not will be making the request or the "ask," as it is often called.

Many nonprofit organizations expect their board members to contribute a specific amount each year. This could range from a few hundred to many thousands of dollars. The total contribution may include season tickets, a membership, tickets to the gala, and so forth. Other organizations have an expectation that a board member will secure additional funds from their network of contacts. These gifts could be cash donations or services such as free advertising or printing. These two approaches are often called "Give or Get," and are usually published in the board orientation materials.

For some organizations, especially organizations made up of board members selected for their expertise and not for their wealth, there are expectations about contributing specific amounts of time to projects each year. The board focused on providing volunteer services for the organization can help fill critical gaps in the staffing. It is also not unusual to find organizations with two boards — one for the volunteer needs of the organization and the other designated as a fundraising board.

Lastly, some not-for-profit organizations also ask staff members to make an annual gift. The amount is usually significantly smaller on average than the board member's gift, but as noted, the demonstration of strong internal support for the organization is important when talking to outside donors.

DATA MANAGEMENT

A management information system designed to gather data about potential donors is critical if the organization is to organize and implement its fundraising campaigns. Chapters 9 and 11 provide examples of management information systems designed for the overall operation, the financial system, and marketing. In arts organizations, which usually have very limited staff resources, the data gathered about donors should be integrated with the sales and marketing systems. This integration can be achieved if the computer software is designed to capture and store information about sales and giving.

Several companies specialize in fundraising software for nonprofit organizations. Any current issue of the *Chronicle of Philanthropy* will contain advertisements for such systems. A careful analysis of the software's capabilities is required, and the support available from the company after the system is purchased should be explored to ensure that the organization's data management needs will be met in the long-term. For example, the fundraising financial record-keeping system must be able to track revenue through the entire accounting system. As we saw in Chapter 10, Economics and Financial Management, the balance sheet and account statements must reflect changes in the net assets based on these gifts and grants. The donor tracking system must therefore be integrated with the accounting software used by the organization.

Data system needs

An effective data system should allow members of the development staff to be able to sit down at a computer terminal, enter the name of a subscriber, single-ticket buyer, a member, or a donor, and pull up a complete list of all transactions or gifts made by that person. Staff members might also want to do any number of queries such as identifying everyone who donated more than $50 and less than $250 last year. Donor tracking systems usually contain data fields about the estimated personal wealth and giving potential for each subscriber or member. Staff members might also want to know who gave from a particular range of zip codes. The ability to cross-reference donors with sales of subscriptions or memberships is also important. For example, if some patrons only purchased single tickets to the musicals that the theater company performed, this information could be effectively incorporated in a fundraising letter. The letter would mention the individuals' fondness for musicals and suggest that they make a gift to support the production fund so more great shows could be produced for their enjoyment.

Web Resources
The computer software to manage donor data ranges in price from a few hundred dollars to many thousands. Many smaller organizations use software such as Excel or Access or Filemaker Pro to develop their own home-grown donor records system. Some sample Web sites to explore include:

http://www.donorperfect.com/
http://www.blackbaud.com/default.aspx

http://www.linkedsoftware.com/
http://fundtracksoftware.com/
http://www.fundraiser-software.com/

For an overview go to www.techsoup.org/learningcenter/software/page 4829.cfm.

The donor data management system is also critical in developing confidential financial information. For example, if the business section of the local newspaper announces that one of your patrons just received a promotion, this information should find its way into his data file. A promotion probably means a larger paycheck. This information is noted so that the next time a solicitation is made, a higher gift amount might be requested.

A word of caution is in order about confidential information. The tendency to put large amounts of irrelevant personal data in a computer is directly proportional to the ease with which the data can be entered. A clear policy about what information may be kept in the donor file and who may have access to these files is important if the organization is to have any credibility in the community. Policies about the confidentiality of these data gathered by the development staff must also be enforced. Passwords to access the donor data will be meaningless if staff members sit around the lounge discussing how much someone gave to the organization. Any breach in security should be dealt with quickly and visibly.

FUNDRAISING COSTS AND CONTROL

The annual campaign and the various capital fund drives contain a mix of activities designed to reach as many potential donors as the budget will permit. Development managers always seek ways to keep the costs of raising money as low as possible. The impact of these costs cannot be ignored. Potential donors want to know whether the organization is capable of using their gift efficiently. Although fundraising costs may vary with different types of campaigns, if these costs are averaging around 20 percent of the total raised, it probably is time for the organization to reassess its methods. Donors usually view organizations that can keep fundraising costs under 10 percent favorably. Web sites such as Charity Navigator actually provide ratings of the fundraising efficiency of not-for-profit organizations. (Go to www.charitynavigator.org.)

An effective budget control system must be in place before an organization undertakes any fundraising activity. In addition, legal requirements must be met when reporting income raised through donations on federal and state tax forms. Some states require special licenses before any fundraising may begin.

Direct and indirect costs

Arts organizations usually have direct fundraising costs for salaries, wages, and benefits. These costs should be distributed across the budget if several fundraising activities are supervised by one staff. Developing a project budget such as the one shown in Figure 9.8 makes it easier to track costs. Consultant fees could also be listed as a direct cost to the project. Other costs include supplies and services (paper, copying, printing, telephones), equipment (computers), and travel.

Indirect fundraising costs reflect such items as a portion of the rent, lease, or mortgage, utilities, and the maintenance of general office equipment used for fundraising activities. For the purposes of budgeting, the financial manager must calculate the various costs of each area's use of the common resources and formulate a distribution that can be used to prepare fundraising budgets.

When applying for government grants, the organization can be reimbursed for indirect costs if these costs are reflected in the budget. For example, if a museum gets a grant for $1 million to run an educational program, 30 to 50 percent of the budget could be allocated above the grant amount for indirect costs. The organization could therefore expect that an additional $300,000 to $500,000 would be provided above the $1 million to support the costs of supporting the project. Grant applications to foundations and corporations normally show indirect costs as part of the overall project budget. Foundations and corporations may place restrictions on or refuse to support indirect costs. The application guidelines for these granting agencies normally outline the costs they consider to be legitimate.

FUNDRAISING TECHNIQUES AND TOOLS

A successful fundraising campaign never really ends. Most organizations must continually seek donations if they are to survive financially. As soon as the annual campaign has been completed for one fiscal year, it is time to get started on next year's fund drive. The overall goal remains the same each year: to establish a regular pattern of giving to the organization.

Let's examine some of the specific details of the various ongoing campaigns that an organization must maintain. Many organizations are engaged in what is often called a Comprehensive Campaign. This simply means the organization is engaged in a capital or an endowment campaign, special giving programs, the annual campaigns targeted to individuals, and then support from corporations, foundations, and government agencies. These multiple campaigns require constant attention and fine-tuning.

THE COMPREHENSIVE CAMPAIGN

Individual donors

All organizations want to have a substantial number of individual donors who make regular unrestricted gifts to the organization. An unrestricted gift carries no stipulation as to how the funds may be spent. Unrestricted gifts give the organization the flexibility to shift funds to fill the greatest need. Restricted gifts, on the other hand, are given on the assumption that the funds will be used for a specific project or program. The organization has a legal obligation to use restricted funds in the manner designated by the donor. An unrestricted gift might be added to the operating fund balance or be used to cover the expenses of a specific production or project. A restricted gift might be designated only for the building fund endowment. Because solicitations to corporations, foundations, and the government often carry distribution restrictions, the more unrestricted gifts the organization can regularly gather, the better.

The actual percentages of your audience or members who may donate to your organization will vary with how effective you are in making your case. For example, if you have 1,500 regular season subscribers or members you might have between 10 and 30 percent that regularly donate to your annual fund. Obviously the fundraiser's goal is to achieve the highest percentage of donors from the subscriber base as possible. As you see in the following FYI — Giving, the mainstay of support comes from individuals.

FYI — Giving
Giving USA 2007 lists the following estimated distribution of funding sources for the $295.02 billion contributed to charities in 2006:

- Individuals — $222.89 billion or 75.8%
- Foundations — $36.50 billion or 12.4%
- Bequests — $22.91 billion or 7.8%
- Corporations — $12.72 billion or 4.3%

Of the $295.02 billion the top three areas receiving contributions were

Religion — $96.82 billion or 32.8% of the total
Education — $40.98 billion or 13.9% of the total
Human Services — $29.56 billion or 10% of the total
Arts, culture, and humanities — $12.51 billion or 4.2% of the total

Because annual giving is the lifeblood of many organizations, it is fairly common for organizations to maintain a standing committee of board members and staff to coordinate the fundraising activity. Yearly funding goals and objectives are set, a detailed monthly timetable is created, specific details — such as who makes the calls and who signs the letters — are worked out, and assignments are distributed to the board and the staff. This is an example of all of the management theories coming together. The fundraising committee must plan, organize, and lead effectively if the organization is to remain strong.

The techniques for building a large base of individual donors include donor research, offering numerous funding options, personal contact, telephone solicitation, direct mail, and special events.

Donor research

Many of the techniques used to develop an audience are used in donor research. The current subscribers, members, and single-ticket buyers form the core of the active donor base. This core group should be subjected to the most intense research, and as complete a donor file as possible should be compiled on each person (see Figure 12.3).

The next level of research focuses on less active supporters and prospects. Vast amounts of data about prospective donors must be gathered and rated in terms of potential for further use. As Thomas Wolf says, "Only prospectors find gold."[11] The organization must commit personnel to go through lists of former subscribers, patrons of other arts organizations, country club members, and members of social or business organizations. They must also explore Web listings, school phone directories (including college or university phone books), references given by current donors, and published social registers. Sources such as *Who's Who in America*, which publishes regional directories, may also be of use.

Funding options

Fundraisers like to speak of gift giving as an "opportunity" or a chance to make an "investment in the future." In fact, the use of the word donation is often frowned upon. The idea behind using the word "gift" is to stress the one-way nature of the transaction. A gift does not usually carry with it the assumption you will get back something of equal value. Well-organized development managers design several choices for donors using a concept not unlike a menu. For example, gifts can be targeted for the current operating fund for those people who want their gifts to be put to use immediately. Others may want their gift to go to an endowment fund, which is invested, and only a portion of the interest is used to fund operations or special programs. A scholarship fund is a good choice for donors who want their gifts to have maximum longevity. Others may want to offer their funds in the form of a *deferred gift*, that is, a promise to provide funds, property, stocks, bonds, life insurance, property, or jewelry at some future date. Another form of deferred giving is a *bequest*, which is a gift that is distributed through the donor's will. Some donors specify that a portion of their life insurance will be donated to an organization.

Figure 12.4 shows one possible rating system for evaluating major gift prospects. Although there are no hard and fast rules to imply from this table, the

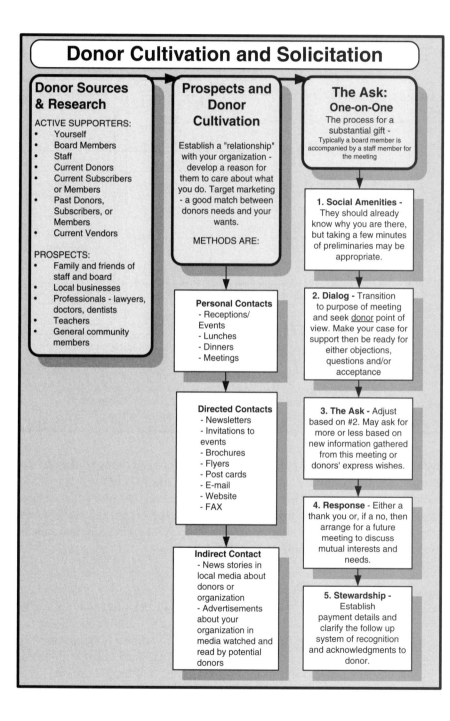

Donor Cultivation and Solicitation

Donor Sources & Research

ACTIVE SUPPORTERS:
- Yourself
- Board Members
- Staff
- Current Donors
- Current Subscribers or Members
- Past Donors, Subscribers, or Members
- Current Vendors

PROSPECTS:
- Family and friends of staff and board
- Local businesses
- Professionals - lawyers, doctors, dentists
- Teachers
- General community members

Prospects and Donor Cultivation

Establish a "relationship" with your organization - develop a reason for them to care about what you do. Target marketing - a good match between donors needs and your wants.

METHODS ARE:

Personal Contacts
- Receptions/Events
- Lunches
- Dinners
- Meetings

Directed Contacts
- Newsletters
- Invitations to events
- Brochures
- Flyers
- Post cards
- E-mail
- Website
- FAX

Indirect Contact
- News stories in local media about donors or organization
- Advertisements about your organization in media watched and read by potential donors

The Ask: One-on-One

The process for a substantial gift - Typically a board member is accompanied by a staff member for the meeting

1. Social Amenities - They should already know why you are there, but taking a few minutes of preliminaries may be appropriate.

2. Dialog - Transition to purpose of meeting and seek <u>donor</u> point of view. Make your case for support then be ready for either objections, questions and/or acceptance

3. The Ask - Adjust based on #2. May ask for more or less based on new information gathered from this meeting or donors' express wishes.

4. Response - Either a thank you or, if a no, then arrange for a future meeting to discuss mutual interests and needs.

5. Stewardship - Establish payment details and clarify the follow up system of recognition and acknowledgments to donor.

Figure 12.3
Donor cultivation and solicitation.

Figure 12.4

Donor rating matrix.

Donor Rating Matrix

Donor Ratings (Sample) When cultivating a long-term donor you will need to establish a target for the maximum you think is achievable over 5 years. The factors that may alter this rating system, which is based on 2% of the income per year or up to as much as 5% of the net worth, include: * Giving history * Timing * Capacity * Interest * Life circumstances	Gift Request if (To be given over 5 years at 2% of income)	Minimum income is .... and	Minimum Net Assets are ...
	$5,000	$50,000	$250,000
	$7,500	$75,000	$375,000
	$10,000	$100,000	$500,000
	$12,500	$125,000	$625,000
	$15,000	$150,000	$750,000
	$20,000	$200,000	$1,000,000
	$25,000	$250,000	$1,250,000
	$50,000	$500,000	$2,500,000
	$100,000	$1,000,000	$5,000,000

For example, a possible ratings could include giving history, interest, and capacity. Donor A on a scale of 1 to 5 might be rated with a 2 for history, 2 for interest, and 5 for capacity for a total of 9. While Donor B might be 3 for history, 4 for interest, and 4 for capacity or a total of 11. The fundraiser would then spend more time cultivating the higher rated donor for a prospective gift.

organization must have a rating system in place for every donor. Without this information, the fundraiser is operating in the dark. Asking for too much or too little money can have equally negative outcomes. Donors who consider a major gift $500 may be frightened away from the organization if you ask them for $5,000. At the same time, donors capable of giving $50,000 may be insulted if you ask them for only $5,000.

As with any menu, it should be possible for the donor to combine several options. For example, an organization with annual donors who make bequests and give regularly to an endowed fund is in a fortunate position. Offering a selection of donor options is taking the principles of being a customer-driven, marketing-oriented organization to its logical conclusion. The donor programs must be designed to provide the maximum social exchange satisfaction for donors who write that check or sign a document giving something to the organization.

Personal contacts

Personal contact is the preferred method for cultivation and for securing larger gifts because fundraising is most effective when people ask other people for their support. The management of public events such as meetings, receptions, lunches, and dinners give the fundraiser the opportunity to keep in direct contact without directly asking for money. Some donors like the social aspects of seeing and being seen at various public functions. Helping them realize their need to be seen will probably pay off later when making the more personal one-on-one solicitation.

Within the comprehensive campaign, a typical major gift or capital campaign operates with the assumption that the organization will be engaged in a long cultivation period with the donor. This process is typically called *donor cultivation*. For example, let's assume that a museum's donor research targets a local business executive for a gift to the building fund. On paper, this person looks like a good candidate, but without an introduction, the organization might get a firm refusal. If the research indicates that a current member of the board knows the executive, then a valuable link exists. If there is no existing contact, an appointment should be made to get the cultivation started. The first meeting will probably be brief and informational (20 to 30 minutes). The board member who knows the executive should attend the meeting to help with the initial contact and communication. A staff member might accompany the board member to be introduced and answer questions, but his or her presence is merely functional. A package of information about the organization and a brief outline of how the current fundraising drive is doing would probably be enough for this first visit.

The key objective in making the first contact is for each party to learn more about the other. The cultivation process would probably include: follow up meetings, invitations to various events sponsored by the organization, a lunch update meeting at a local restaurant, informative personalized notes, and periodic updates by telephone. When the fundraising committee and the staff feel that the time is right, the designated contact makes the request.

As mentioned, the staff member may not be the one actually asking for the gift. For some donors it might appear to be a bit of conflict of interest. After all, the staff fundraiser is getting a paycheck to do fundraising that will in the end help go toward the budget that will support his paycheck. If possible, the board member or a designated volunteer should do the asking. Either way, the organization should have a clear policy about who does the asking. Of course, some board members are better than others when it comes to securing the gift. In this case, the staff member may be acting as the "closer."

The staff and board members need to be sensitive to and aware of the ethical guideless for fundraisers. See the previous section Association of Fundraising Professionals Code of Ethical Principles and Standards for a list of the key concerns of members of the Association of Fundraising Professionals (AF). Their Web site is www.afpnet.org/content_documents/CodeofEthics.pdf.

Communication tools

To keep donors informed and aware of your programs and your case for support a series of carefully planned communications must be part of the cultivation process (see Figure 12.3). For example, newsletters, brochures, flyers, postcards, and even e-mail can prove useful in keeping your current and potential donors informed. The important point is to ask donors how they prefer to hear about your organization. If e-mail is their preferred method of contact then use it. Keeping an up-to-date Web site also helps deliver news to interested parties faster than print media or letters. In addition, the public relations and marketing staff must have a plan to ensure that news stories or advertisements keep the organization visible in the community. Donors like seeing the organization they support being seen by others in the community.

Telephone solicitations

As shown in Figure 12.2, the typical funding table includes many gifts valued at $500 or less. Personal contact is not a cost-effective way to reach all of these donors. However, one of the more cost-effective alternatives to reaching donors in the mid-level gift category is to make phone calls to as many prospects as possible.

Enthusiastic leadership is a must when motivating the board and other volunteers to ask for money over the telephone. This is especially true because the process of asking people for money can be very discouraging. Fundraisers always tell volunteers, "Don't take that 'no' personally!" However, it is only human nature to feel as if your request was rejected because you did not ask in the right way or you were not convincing enough.

The entire process of making solicitations via the telephone is of course much more complicated today. Many people may opt to be listed on the National Do Not Call Registry. And while the Registry still allows nonprofit organizations to make telephone solicitation calls, it is wise to flag donors who do not want to be called at home, on their cell phone, or at the office. Here is where your data management systems can be of assistance. The donor database should list whether the donor or member even accepts phone calls. There is no quicker way to upset a donor than by disregarding what they thought was a clear contact preference.

The process

Small organizations normally schedule a week or two each year for telephone fundraising campaigns to their donor base. Banks of telephones, eager volunteers, and a little training with a well-written and flexible script can translate into thousands of dollars for an organization. Again, solid research can pay off. When a caller begins talking with a prospect, an information card or computer screen should help guide the interaction. Potential donors are initially very hesitant about getting a phone call from a stranger, so the first 20 seconds of the conversation is usually scripted to ask questions designed to get the prospect to respond. Assuming that the information about the potential donors is correct, it should be possible to establish what they thought of the last performance they saw or exhibit they attended. The key is engaging the person and building to the request in a timely manner.

If the caller is able to connect with the prospect, the typical tactic is to ask for a bit more than the donor research indicates. For example, if it is possible that the potential donor might give $150, the caller might be scripted to suggest initially an "investment" of $500. Eventually, an amount with which the donor feels comfortable will be reached, and the "closing" can take place. The logistics of getting the gift information and payment method correct and thanking the donor concludes the process.

Direct mail

Direct mail marketing and fundraising is a big business in the United States. Every day, high-speed computer printers merge-print millions of pieces of what most people affectionately call "junk mail" with names and addresses purchased from list brokers. Many people never open the handiwork of the direct mail marketer, but enough people respond to these offers to convince businesses that the cost is worth incurring.

Arts organizations have used the techniques of the direct mail marketer for years in attempting to build a subscriber or member base. The mailing of a solicitation for funds follows the basic direct mail principles and is traditionally part of the mix of options used by the development staff.

This process can be effective since the potential donor will at least recognize your organizations logo on the outer envelope. The outer envelope represents the critical first contact with potential donors. The envelope must communicate a short, strong, and clear message that something of interest is inside. A popular technique uses the word *free* on the envelope with the assumption that people will be curious to see what the offer is. However, this technique has been so overused that most perceptive donors are not enticed by the word. If the fundraiser can get potential donors to open the envelope, the combination of a well-written letter and an informative brochure will bring readers further into the solicitation. Because most people initially scan the text of the letter and brochure, the copy must be written and laid out in such a way as to get the message across in as few words as possible. The response device (the piece returned to the organization) and the reply envelope should provide a fast and easy way of completing the solicitation.

Tracking responses

Direct mail is a long-term investment. Organizations that expect more than a 1 or 2 percent response rate may be in for a surprise. For example, a 1.5 percent response rate for a 10,000-piece mailing would yield 150 donations. Let's say the average donation is $25. The first mailing thus yields $3,750. First-class postage, letter, brochure, reply device, and reply envelope may cost an average of 90¢ per unit. The first mailing therefore costs $9,000 and only raises $3,750. However, if you view these 150 donors as a long-term investment, the loss will eventually be recouped.

Let's suppose that the arts fundraiser tracks these donors as a target group that responded to a particular campaign. In the next year, a telephone solicitation of these 150 people yields a 40 percent response rate, and the average donation is $75. The organization has gained $4,500 minus the cost of telephone solicitation. Let's say it costs $150 to get this next $4,500. This leaves the organization ahead on its total investment. In the third and fourth years, 50 percent of the remaining donors from the first year's campaign give an average of $125 each. If carefully monitored and tracked, the organization should be able to create an overall system of periodic direct mail solicitations that yield a regular cash flow.

Note that this simplified example of a direct mail cost analysis is used to illustrate a point. Direct mail marketers have very comprehensive formulas for calculating campaign costs. For example, these data in this example do not take into account inflation, which is a cost to the campaign. In addition, the cost of raising money is fairly high in this example. Costs of 20¢ or less per dollar raised would be more appropriate. Of course, if just one of those few donors you recruited five years ago makes a major gift to the organization for $250,000, the direct mail costs can become a minor issue.

E-fundraising

The use of e-mail and the organization Web site to encourage giving can be much less costly. (See Additional Resources, Fundraising Online by Gary M. Grobman.) The effectiveness of these approaches may be questionable to some, but this may be more of a function of technological biases of the fundraisers. At best, the gifts gained via an e-mail solicitation or from the organization Web site represent what may be your very committed supporters. If the solicitation message in the e-mail is compelling, and it is easy to make a gift with a few mouse clicks, why would an organization not want to make use of this approach?

Web sites such as Charity Navigator and GuideStar offer simple ways for people to give to organizations or causes they feel strongly about. Younger donors who have grown up with computers seem to have less trouble with giving online, but that is not a universal rule. Again, the patron preference needs to be taken into account.

Many arts organizations have set up extensive gift shops online to encourage interaction with their audiences and members. In addition, Web sites such as www.shopformuseums.com make it possible for individuals buying a wide variety of consumer items to also make a gift to their organization.

Special events

Arts organizations usually try to hold at least one event a year as a fundraiser. A group of volunteers typically coordinates and produces a costume ball, a silent or live auction, a raffle, or a benefit performance. A well-run and planned special event can be a big money earner for an organization. Of course, the effort and time required to produce a major event can be overwhelming especially if the organization does not have the volunteer resources to make it happen at a high-quality level. The costs of producing an event like a costume ball may run into the tens of thousands of dollars. Careful control of the budget is required or the event may end up costing the organization more than it earns in donations (see the section In The News). However, with a good planning committee and a realistic schedule, it is possible to earn thousands of dollars regularly for the organization and to provide a memorable experience for the donors.

These special events can also provide visibility in the community for the organization. Raffles, for example, can be a way of involving the local business community in the arts by persuading business owners to donate goods and services. State and local governments may place restrictions on certain types of events, so it is always a good idea to consult with a lawyer before proceeding.

In the News

On October 19, 2007, the *Kansas City Star* ran a story with the headline "Jazz Museum Hits Sour Note with its Financial Loss on Fundraiser." The American Jazz Museum posted a loss of $30,000 at its 10th Anniversary fundraising event. The high costs of performers for a concert and a street party contributed to the shortfall. The article also noted "the museum staff and its board of directors failed to keep spending in check."

Source: http://www.kansascity.com. Used with permission.

CORPORATE GIVING

Corporations donated an estimated $12.72 billion to charities in 2006. Although this is a substantial amount, it represents less than 4.3 percent of the $295 billion given by all funders to charities in 2006.[12] The portion of the $12.72 billion that went to arts and culture was approximately 5 percent.[13]

One of the largest gifts to an arts organization in 2006 was made by the Carnival Corporation (the cruise line company). Carnival donated $20 million to the Miami Performing Arts Center Foundation.[14]

Typically, there is also a strong relationship between the economy and corporate giving. Shareholders tend to look less positively on the company management if they are giving away big donations when the company profits are down. In addition, corporations undergo constant changes in ownership as they are bought, sold, and merged. Nonprofit organizations must adapt to the changing business environment if they intend to capitalize on the available funds. In the best of times, arts and cultural organizations are usually not at the top of the corporate funding priority list, but regular support can be found if fundraisers are willing to make the effort to track down the sources.

Corporate support is based in large part on the concept of *reciprocity*: What will the corporation gain by supporting a performance or an exhibition? A company may have motives for funding a specific event because of its public relations value, marketing potential, or benefits to its employees. The fundraiser's research must focus on trying to fit the organization into the corporation's donor strategy. The lack of a good *strategic fit*, as it is called, is the primary reason why support is not given to an organization. Arts organizations must remember that establishing a good strategic match is part of their marketing process. The packaging and emphasis of a proposal may need to be adjusted as the priorities of corporations change.

Corporate support is usually restricted to the immediate community because businesses are concerned about raising their profile in their local market (e.g., Carnival Cruise Lines). Larger corporations sometimes sponsor performances or major exhibits that have a highly visible national tour program. For the most part, a regional arts group has little chance of attracting national corporate support unless there is an active branch of the corporation in the area.

A method used to raise support in some communities follows along the idea of a United Way type fundraising campaign for the arts. This approach allows corporations to decide where they want to target their support (along with individuals). This approach saves corporations from being endlessly approached for gifts by the hundreds of nonprofit organizations in a community. There are several such funding entities around the United States. The United Arts of Central Florida (www.unitedarts.cc) is one example. However, in some cases, nonprofit organizations traded the benefit of a regular funding for a drop in overall corporate giving. Companies no longer had to give as much because they consolidated their giving and reduced their overall commitment of funds. In some cases, corporations saw an opportunity to continue to do good, but for less.

Potential problems

The most problematic issue related to corporate support is the conditions (some direct, some implied) that may be attached to a gift. For example, a performing arts group or museum may find its corporate support quickly withdrawn at the first sign of controversy. Once withdrawn, the chances of getting this support back may be very limited.

There may also be ethical considerations that the organization must take into account before applying for corporate support. For example, seeking funds from companies that produce products thought to be harmful to the environment or to people, or from companies that have holdings in politically repressive countries, could be detrimental to the community perception of the arts organization.

Fundraising process

The overall planning and research process for corporate fundraising is not greatly different from the one used for individuals or foundations. Corporations that make direct grants are listed in publications such as the *National Guide to Funding in Arts and Culture*. The Internet may also prove useful when seeking information about potential corporate donors. Corporations generally establish foundations to distribute their gifts.

One of the most important steps in this process is the direct contact with an individual in the corporation foundation or business. In this simplified model, if there is no existing contact, then a courtship process is undertaken. In many cases, the organization rewrites the proposal before asking for the gift because the initial meeting with the corporate foundation contact made it clear that the original proposal did not address the company's current funding interests. In other cases, contact occurs before the proposal is written.

Whatever the situation, the overall process of corporate fundraising must be integrated within the master plan (see Figure 12.1). The funding manager for a nonprofit organization should read the business section of the daily paper and follow national trends in the business publications in an effort to stay in tune with the opportunities that may arise.

FOUNDATIONS

A foundation is defined as a "nonprofit corporation or charitable trust under state law, with the principle purpose of making grants to unrelated organizations or institutions or to individuals for scientific, educational, cultural, religious, or other charitable purposes."[15] *The Highlights of Foundation Yearbook,*

2007 edition, reports there were 71,095 foundations making grants.[16] The distribution was

Independent foundations: 63,059
Community foundations: 707
Corporate foundations: 2607
Operating foundations: 4722

The Foundation Center is an excellent research source for information about types of grants, amounts granted, purposes, limitations, publications, and application procedures. See their Web site at www.foundationcenter.org. For a monthly fee, grant seekers may explore the extensive directory of grants that are available by specific categories.

As with corporate fundraising, a good match between an organization and foundation must exist. Foundations usually fund specific types of activities. For example, the Shubert Foundation Web site lists the following information:

The *principal goal* of The Shubert Foundation is to support not-for-profit, professional resident theater and dance companies in the United States. The program areas of Arts Related Organizations, Education, and Human Services are smaller than those of Theater and Dance and necessarily limited. The Shubert Foundation awards unrestricted grants for general operating support, rather than funding for specific projects. These grants are awarded exclusively to U.S. organizations, which must have current 501(c)(3) tax-exempt status in order to be eligible for funding.[17]

Among the many grants given in 2005 by the Shubert Foundation were Actors Theater of Louisville ($125,000), Alley Theater in Houston ($80,000), and Jacobs Pillow Dance Festival in Massachusetts ($25,000).[18]

As always, a clear, concise proposal and ability statement is the first step in the application process. Because many small foundations have little or no staffing, the application procedure may be as simple as a cover letter, a one-page proposal, and a budget. A large foundation may require a proposal of eight to ten pages, and a screening committee may review applications before referring them to a grants committee.

Regardless of the length of the proposal, the applicant must state the problem, describe how the organization is qualified to solve the problem, explain the benefits to the community, and outline how the effectiveness of the project will be measured and evaluated.

Fundraising activity remains a person-to-person business, and without the proper introductions, the applying organization is an unknown entity. The greater the depth of involvement of the board in the community, the better the chances that the organization will be able to make itself a part of the grant-making network that exists in foundation funding.

GOVERNMENT FUNDING

It is possible to find funding for the arts at all levels of government in the United States. Local arts agencies usually have limited funds, but if an organization is trying to establish a positive record of effectively using grant money, the local level is a good starting point. For example, local agencies often provide funding for outreach programs into the schools. They may also help sponsor programming, assist with advertising to bring in out of town audiences, or subsidize ticket discounts to students or older audiences. The application procedures are usually simple, and the amount of time and money spent administering the support is minimal.

State arts councils usually have permanent staffs, standard application procedures, formal review panels, and standard evaluation and reporting procedures. They generally offer numerous types of grants, including grants for programming, new works, outreach touring, and individual artists. In many cases, the state agencies parallel the National Endowment for the Arts. Funding research is again required to achieve the best match between the arts organization and the granting agency.

The National Assembly of Local Arts Agencies, located in Washington, D.C., sponsors an annual meeting and offers their members regular workshops on many areas of operation. Because the National Assembly of State Arts Agencies (NASAA; www.nasaa-arts.org) members form the core of agencies that distribute state and federal funds, an arts organization would be wise to cultivate a relationship with these organizations.

The National Endowment for the Arts

As noted in Chapter 4, The Adaptive Arts Organization, the National Endowment for the Arts (NEA) is the major source for funding and recognition in the arts community. The NEA Web site publishes information that gives applicants an overview of the major grant areas. Each program area and division of the NEA publishes detailed guidelines to help applicants through the process.

The 2006 annual report by the NEA indicates that approximately $106 million in grants were awarded.[19] NEA matching grants programs help stimulate an important partnership between arts organizations and donors. Organizations that receive funds from the NEA also benefit from the recognition. Having received a grant adds to the legitimacy of the enterprise and, though the NEA never intended it, creates a "stamp of approval" for the arts group. Donors assume that if a group or an artist had successfully passed through the grant review process, the work must be worthy of merit.

As discussed in Chapter 4, the political turmoil that invaded the NEA's operation in the late 1980s and the 1990s affected the agency's image and its ability to support the arts in America. While the public's attention was focused on a limited number of controversial grants, thousands of grant requests were being reviewed, processed, and funded.

The peer review process

The core of the NEA granting process is the peer review. A panel of experts are assembled at specific times during the year to review applications. Members of the committee are assigned specific grants to study in detail and to discuss at the panel meetings. The time for each presentation is limited, and the competition for support is intense. Each year, the NEA receives thousands of grant applications. The NEA staff reviews the details of the application, but the opening proposal, which is very limited in space, is what is most often read. If the reader's interest is not captured immediately or if the proposal raises more questions than it answers, the request will probably be pushed to the bottom of the stack.

Consulting with the NEA staff may help when researching the kinds of key words, phrases, or concepts that are likely to catch the panelists' attention. At the same time, a brilliant proposal may fail because an organization has no record of accomplishment, meaning that it has no previous history of having effectively used donated funds.

Applying for NEA funding is not very different from the corporate and foundation process. Establishing contacts within the agency and cultivating relationships with key people will help to establish the arts organization as a viable target for funding.

Other government sources

Up to this point, our discussion of grants and the government has focused on the performing arts. The National Endowment for the Humanities also provides grants covering such areas as design, museums, research, music history, and interdisciplinary projects. In fact, thousands of grants are available from the federal government. Many of these grants have criteria that may make it difficult for an arts organization to qualify, but occasionally an opportunity arises that is worth pursuing.

The key to finding government support is research. One helpful source is the *Federal Register*, which is a very thoroughly indexed and cross-referenced publication that lists all federal grant programs. The *Catalog of Federal Domestic Assistance* (http://12.46.245.173/cfd/cfda.html) contains information on government funding programs and is indexed by agency and subject area. The Federal government makes extensive use of its Web sites and the Internet to make much of this information available. Patience is required when wading through the myriad of choices, but vast amounts of information about Federal programs can prove helpful.

CONCLUSION

Arts organizations have come to depend on revenue from a mix of funding sources. Funding levels from individuals, corporations, foundations, and government agencies are subject to changing environments. For example, support for arts and culture changes as the economy improves or declines, as public attitudes about censorship shift, as government support for social services declines, as state arts budgets are slashed or increased, and as companies disappear through corporate mergers. Because the funding arena can be so volatile, arts groups are usually advised to avoid becoming dependent on any one source of funds.

The situation of too many nonprofit groups chasing too few grants by foundations and corporations probably will not improve in the near future. In fact, as the demands for private support increase to cover the budget restrictions on government support for needed social and medical services, the actual amounts available to distribute to arts and culture groups may decline. In fact, the privatization movement in government over the last twenty years has put additional strains on nonprofit organizations as local arts and cultural organizations struggle for attention and resources. Funding cuts for activities that do not directly serve the public with services place a strain on many arts groups. In this situation, the pressure to "downsize" government comes into conflict with the economic benefits that the arts can bring to a community, to say nothing of the improved quality of life. The criteria for what constitutes "public benefit" has been raised, and arts organizations have found it necessary to reframe their message about the benefits they provide to the community.

Individual donors find themselves inundated with direct mail appeals, e-mail in their in-boxes, and telephone solicitations from every conceivable cause. As more organizations learn the tricks of the fundraising trade, individual donors will be asked to support even more groups. The fundraising staffs and the board of directors for many organizations will have to continually reevaluate their fundraising strategies. The trend may be toward more personal appeals in an attempt to form a tighter bond with donors. This has become especially critical as donors have become more assertive about how their funds are used.

The concepts of *venture philanthropy* and donor contracts have found their way into more support exchanges. The venture philanthropist is coming to the funding relationship with the organization from the point of view that her gift is an investment in the organization's future. This type of donor expects results or some kind of definitive measurable outcome.

SUMMARY

Arts organizations in the United States depend heavily on the support of individuals, foundations, corporations, and the government to achieve their objectives. Traditionally, U.S. government involvement in the arts has been minimal.

People give for a variety of reasons based on the concept that they receive intangible benefits in a social exchange with the organization. Giving, which is primarily a person-to-person business, depends on the careful design and integration of the organization's strategic and operational plans. Auditing the organization's readiness to undertake a campaign includes analyzing its mission, objectives, resources, activities, and programs. The fundraising process requires a marketing orientation directed at donors to be effective.

The case for support is a key element in the organization's overall fundraising strategy. Board and staff support are needed to demonstrate to donors the commitment in the organization. An effective data-gathering and management system is also needed. Careful control of the costs of raising money and disbursing funds are required for legal reasons.

Comprehensive campaigns are designed to target funding groups, which include individuals, corporations, foundations, and government agencies. Donor research leads to designing different funding options to fit the needs of different funders. Gift programs are designed to accept current support, deferred giving, and bequests. Personal contact is the most effective way to solicit large gifts from a limited number of wealthy individuals. Telephone, direct mail, and e-mail campaigns are used to reach a wider audience. Donors are also becoming more demanding regarding how their gifts are used.

Corporations and foundations are usually approached based on the strategic fit between the donor's objectives and the organization's needs. Campaigns for government support usually involve meeting program requirements and criteria established by agency staff members.

For additional topics relating to fundraising, please go to www.managementandthearts.com.

Questions

1. What impact do you think will the change in U.S. demographics have on giving over the next 20 years?

2. Do you agree with the concept of expecting staff to donate regularly to the arts organization for which they work? What might be some arguments for not expecting staff to give? Discuss.

3. Do you think it is appropriate for arts organizations to gather personal data on potential donors for future use? What data would be inappropriate to keep? Why?

4. Have you ever been approached to make a gift to an arts organization? What techniques were used to solicit the donation? Did those techniques work? Explain.

5. Should arts organizations reject donations from corporations because of what the company manufactures or the politicians it supports? Explain.

6. If an arts organization unknowingly received donations from an individual later found guilty of defrauding people out of their money, should the organization return the gifts for redistribution back to the people who were defrauded? Defend your position.

ADDITIONAL RESOURCES

Thomas Ahern, *How to Write Fundraising Materials*, Medfield, MA: Emerson & Church, 2007.

Albert Anderson, *Ethics for Fundraisers*, Bloomington, IN: Indiana University Press, 1996.

Ilona Bray, *Effective Fundraising for Nonprofits*, Berkeley, CA: Nolo Press, 2005.

Mim Carlson, *Winning Grants Step by Step*, San Francisco, CA: Jossey-Bass, 1996.

Kent E. Dove, *Conducting a Successful Fundraising Program*, San Francisco, CA: Jossey-Bass, 2001.

Joan Flanagan, *Successful Fundraising*, 2nd ed., Chicago, IL: Contemporary Books, 2000.

Marilyn Fischer, *Ethical Decision Making in Fund Raising*, New York: John Wiley & Sons, 2000.

James M. Greenfield, *Fundraising Fundamentals*, New York: John Wiley & Sons, 1994.

Gary M. Grobman and Gary B. Grant, *Fundraising Online*, Harrisburg, PA: White Hat Communications, 2006.

Mary Hall and Susan Howlett, *Getting Funded — The Complete Guide to Writing Grant Proposals*, 4th edition, Portland State University Continuing Education Press, Portland, OR, 2003.

Dennis P. McIlnay, *How Foundations Work*, San Francisco, CA: Jossey-Bass, 1998.

Henry A. Russo & Associates, and Eugene R. Temple, editor, *Achieving Excellence in Fund Raising*, 2nd edition, San Francisco, CA: Jossey-Bass, 2003.

Mal Warwick, *How to Write Successful Fundraising Letters*, San Francisco, CA: Jossey-Bass, 2001.

Douglas E. White, *The Art of Planned Giving*, New York,: John Wiley & Sons, 1995.

CASE STUDY

The following article from the August 23rd, 2007, *Chronicle of Philanthropy* provides an excellent overview of a wide range of corporate and business sponsorship success stories.

Vying for Corporate Support

Across the country, arts groups turn to sponsorships and other tactics to win donations from companies

By Nicole Lewis

For the same ticket price as a movie, teenagers and their parents can attend a show at Centerstage, in Baltimore, and mingle with the actors over dinner beforehand.

Two years ago, M&T Bank, which has its headquarters in Buffalo, N.Y., but also has branches in Baltimore, doubled its annual contribution to the theater to sponsor a series that encouraged teenagers to bring their parents to the theater. The bank's $40,000 gift last year has contributed to a 70-percent increase in the theater's corporate support over the last five years, to $582,800.

"There's a lot of whining about corporate funding: 'It's going away, it's less, it's over, and it's time to move on to individuals,'" says Michael Ross, the nonprofit theater's managing director. "I don't know if there are huge increases to come, but I'm not giving up yet."

Neither are many of his colleagues around the country. Despite a gloomy report last May from Americans for the Arts, in Washington (*The Chronicle*, May 17), that said corporate giving to arts groups had plummeted 65 percent from 2000 to 2005, many such groups trumpet their success wooing corporate dollars.

However, most assert it takes a lot more effort to get those gifts than it did in the past. And many challenges remain in extracting support from companies, including coping with corporate mergers, shifting priorities in corporate-giving policies, and more competition from an ever-increasing number of nonprofit groups.

"There is only one Fortune 500 company here, and an incredibly large amount of arts groups," says Keith Stava, managing director of the Virginia Stage Company, in Norfolk. "We are all fishing out of the same small pool."

Still, the theater has increased its corporate support by $50,000 this year. "We are having successes because we had room to grow," says Mr. Stava. "The corporate-giving environment is tightening up."

Extra Effort

Other arts leaders say there is money to be had, but the focus needs to shift from asking for philanthropic support to selling the arts group as a place to put marketing dollars.

Five years ago, the Duluth Superior Symphony Orchestra, in Minnesota, switched from what the group's executive director, Andrew Berryhill, calls "mercy philanthropy: Give us your money or something bad will happen to us," to telling companies, "Listen, I have an audience you want, let's talk about your advertising budget."

All the symphony's concerts are now sponsored by businesses, and the group has increased its corporate support fivefold, to more than $100,000, he says.

Still, the new approach has its shortcomings: With each concert spoken for, room to grow is scarce. Mr. Berryhill has pitched some companies on sponsoring preconcert talks, at which several hundred people usually turn up, but says he hasn't "had a bite yet."

CASE STUDY (CONTINUED)

Sponsorships have also helped the Savannah Music Festival, in Georgia, increase its corporate giving by $100,000 in the last year, but the group had to put in extra effort to capture those dollars, says Rob Gibson, the group's artistic and executive director. "If someone sends me a $50,000 check, I send a thank-you note and take them to lunch — it's not that hard," he says.

But following last year's $35,000 donation from a local Mercedes-Benz dealership, officials at the arts group arranged for a Mercedes car to be displayed at the festival, introduced the sponsor at concerts, and organized a raffle with prizes donated by the dealership.

"All that takes work," says Mr. Gibson, who leads a staff of nine people. "If I had my druthers, I would rather not do that, but if that's what it takes to get great music to people, it's a no-brainer."

At the Speed Art Museum, in Louisville, Ky., corporate sponsorships are also on the rise, while gifts to its corporate annual fund, which can be used for any museum expense, have dropped by nearly half in the past five years, to $75,000, says Peter Morrin, the museum's director.

The trend concerns him. "We don't want to build doughnuts," says Mr. Morrin. "We don't want to have terrific funding for shows and then have to close certain galleries during the day because we can't keep them open."

The situation at the museum mirrors what Americans for the Arts found in its May report, which examined studies that showed the amount of general support corporations provide to cultural groups, not money given for sponsorships of particular events.

The move toward sponsorships and away from general support will adversely affect small arts groups, says Gary P. Steuer, vice president of private-sector affairs at Americans for the Arts.

"There's a widening gap between the haves and the have-nots," he says. "Smaller organizations without powerful boards or large professional staffs are finding it harder and harder to successfully operate in this new corporate environment."

Board Recruitment

To compete for dollars, some small arts groups are actively recruiting more people from the business world onto their boards.

Of the 25 board members at the Chicago Sinfonietta, an orchestra that places an emphasis on diversity of its musicians, 17 have connections to a company, up from about a dozen two years ago, says Jim Hirsch, the group's executive director.

The effort has paid off: A board member and senior vice president at Blue Cross Blue Shield of Illinois helped the group secure gifts for each of the past two years and has pledged its support for next year. The company had not previously been a donor to the music group.

At Dallas Black Dance Theatre, any corporation that gives at least $5,000 is offered a spot for one of its employees on the group's 50-person board. "We do not want your money if we do not have your voice," says Zenetta S. Drew, the theater's executive director.

While pursuing corporate dollars has been successful — the dance group receives nearly one-third of its $1.1-million budget from corporations — the group won't take every gift.

"We don't do things that deal with liquor or communicate endorsement of something that would be a detriment to society," says Ms. Drew. "We know how to say no."

Other arts groups have been roundly criticized for how they showed their appreciation to corporations that made big gifts. For example, a critic at *The New York Observer* wrote that the Roundabout Theatre Company, in New York, was "selling out to the highest bidder" after the group named its facility the American Airlines Theatre. The company provided $8.5-million to renovate the space.

The Berkeley Repertory Theatre, in California, is having a more difficult time than officials had anticipated raising money from companies, says Sara Fousekis, the theater's director of development.

Among the challenges: The theater's liaison at Bank of America, who helped secure its $15,000 grant last year, recently moved on, leaving the theater uncertain about future gifts.

CASE STUDY (CONTINUED)

"The contacts are changing for us constantly at corporations," says Ms. Fousekis. "The timeline for developing a relationship with a corporation is anywhere between three months and a year. If someone leaves, you may lose a whole year of funding."

Shifting Priorities

Next year, more arts groups might be searching for support, as a major corporate supporter of the arts, Altria, in New York, shifts its giving approach.

Beginning this year, the company ceded more control over charitable contributions to its operating companies, Philip Morris USA, in Richmond, Va., and Philip Morris International, in Lausanne, Switzerland. Both companies make grants to arts groups, but not with Altria's depth and scope.

Of the arts groups that received Altria support in 2006, only 60 percent will receive a grant in 2007, says Lisa Gonzalez, a company spokeswoman.

Altria informed its grantees about two-and-a-half years ago of the impending changes and has organized several events for grantees, including Harlem Stage and El Museo del Barrio, both in New York, to introduce groups to potential new corporate supporters. In 2006, Altria gave $7.7 million to arts groups.

Altria officials have not yet determined how much the company will give away next year, but already some groups are prepared to weather a change. At the Brooklyn Academy of Music, in New York, $375,000 — its largest corporate grant — came from Altria last year.

"What we have always tried to do is make sure we are putting together the broadest base of support possible, so we can deal with these types of challenges," says Lynn M. Stirrup, the group's vice president of planning and development. "We've had six-figure sponsors drop away before: AT&T used to be in the $250,000 zone."

Last year the phone company donated $10,000 to the academy. "You can't live and die on a single sponsor," she says.

Despite the uncertainty about Altria's support, Ms. Stirrup says she feels "O.K." about the arts group's success in winning corporate support, which increased last year by about $300,000, to $3.5-million. She credits the region's improving economy, as well as several new fundraising efforts.

The academy successfully solicited at least $100,000 last year from a new donor, the credit-card company Visa, to sponsor a patron lounge and the production of *Edward Scissorhands*. (Ms. Stirrup declined to provide the precise sum provided by Visa.)

And the real-estate boom in the Brooklyn Academy's neighborhood prompted it to seek support from building companies that wanted to offer perks to potential home buyers.

The academy encouraged companies to buy memberships that allowed people to get discounted or free tickets to movies at its cinema or a waiver on ticket-handling fees to its performances. One company purchased more than $7,000 in memberships, and the academy plans to approach several others.

"We have high hopes we'll be able to see some good return on this, and make some good connections with new people," says Ms. Stirrup.

American Express

In addition to the giving changes at Altria, in January another longtime corporate supporter of the arts, American Express, in New York, moved its grant-making focus away from general support of the arts to cultural-heritage projects, says Timothy J. McClimon, president of the company's foundation.

Among the new grantees: The Film Foundation, in Los Angeles, received $220,000 this year to screen some of its restored films at festivals in North America over the next two years.

"Some of our old grantees will not find it easy to compete under our new guidelines," Mr. McClimon says. "However, there are an awful lot of other groups who will be in competition."

In 2006, the company made nearly $30-million in grants for cultural-heritage, leadership-development, and community-service projects that involve its employees. Mr. McClimon does not anticipate the amount of such grants to decline.

While many arts groups continue to vie for corporate support — many leaders say the potential for growth is in law and accounting firms, where the arts provide entertainment value for clients — some groups in places with few corporate headquarters are focusing on cultivating individuals.

CASE STUDY (CONTINUED)

After seeing its largest supporter, MBNA Bank, now part of Bank of America, disappear two years ago, officials at the Farnsworth Art Museum, in Rockland, Me., are turning instead to individuals to pick up the pieces.

"Maine is a really hard place to get corporate sponsorship for anything," says David Patrick Stuckey, the group's director of advancement. "There are a lot of generous [individual] donors in Maine. It's a matter of reinvigorating those connections."

At the Syracuse Symphony Orchestra, in New York, gifts from corporations have declined 10 percent, while gifts from individuals have grown by at least the same amount, says Nicki Inman, the group's development director.

Corporations have rearranged their giving priorities, she says.

"The arts might have been number one, and now they are number three," says Ms. Inman. "Our growth potential is purely in individual giving."

Copyright © 2007 The Chronicle of Philanthropy. Used with permission.

http://philanthropy.com/premium/articles/v19/i21/21001401.htm

Questions

1. The article points out the move toward corporate or business sponsorships and away from general support. Has this trend been happening to arts organizations in your community?
2. What might be the positives or negatives of providing board membership for specific sponsorship levels on an arts organization board of directors?

REFERENCES

1. Melissa Mince, "History of Nonprofit Organizations: Summary," in *Nonprofit Corporations, Organizations and Associations*, 5th ed., edited by Howard L. Oleck (Englewood Cliffs, N.J.: Prentice-Hall, 1988), p. 41.

2. Neil Pendleton, *Fundraising* (Englewood Cliffs, N.J.: Prentice-Hall, Spectrum Books, 1981), p. xi.

3. *Giving USA 2007* (Indianapolis, IN: AAFRC Trust for Philanthropy, 2007), pp. 15, 161.

4. Joseph R. Mixer, *Principles of Professional Fundraising* (San Francisco: Jossey-Bass Publishers, 1993).

5. Ibid., p. 10.

6. Ibid., pp. 10–11.

7. *How the United States Funds the Arts*, NEA Office of Research and Analysis, January, 2007, p. 10.

8. James Gregory Lord, *The Raising of Money* (Cleveland, OH: Third Sector Press, 1986), p. 75.

9. Thomas Wolf, *Managing a Nonprofit Organization in The Twenty-First Century* (New York, NY: Fireside Books, 1999), p. 253.

10. Kent A. Dove, *Conducting a Successful Fundraising Program* (San Francisco, CA, Jossey-Bass, 2001), p. 50.

11. Wolf, *Managing a Nonprofit Organization in The Twenty-First Century*, p. 271.

12. *Giving USA 2007*, p. 15.

13. Ibid., p. 85.

14. Ibid. p. 81.

15. Foundation Center Web site, Reference Center, December 2007, http://foundationcenter.org/.

16. Foundation Center, *Foundations Today Series*, p. 4.

17. http://www.shubertfoundation.org/grantprograms.

18. Foundation Center, *Grants for Arts, Culture & Humanities, 2006–07*, p. 245–246.

19. National Endowment for the Arts 2006 Annual Report, p. 142.

20. Ibid., p. 26.

CHAPTER 13

Integrating Management Styles and Theories

Management is about human beings.
Peter Drucker, *The Daily Drucker*, p. 47

Throughout this book, the emphasis has been on applying theory and practice to managing an arts organization. In this chapter, we summarize different approaches and styles of management and various strategies for integrating management systems into the operation of an organization. We also review the specific functions of arts management and see how they can be applied to various management styles and systems. The goal of this chapter is to give the reader a model from which to work while recognizing ultimately, "management is about human beings."

MANAGEMENT STYLES

As discussed in Chapter 8, Leadership and Group Dynamics, management and leadership styles have a profound impact on the way an organization functions. Let's pause for moment to consider the word style itself. When we use the word "style" in this context, what do we think it means? For most of us, we think of style as doing something in a particular way. When we say he has a "hands-on management style," we are describing someone who is very involved in the details and the specific tasks involved in completing a project or activity.

We have also seen that leadership and management are often very different activities. There is clearly a need in the arts for leaders who can manage and managers who can lead. It is equally important for the arts manager to recognize her strengths and weaknesses in her particular position in the organization. Arts managers and leaders have a better opportunity for success if they put together a management team that compliments their strengths and compensates for their weaknesses.

There are as many different ways to run an organization as there are people in this world. Everyone has a slightly different view of what techniques work best in managing an arts organization. In the interest of developing some practical approaches to management, this chapter examines three styles that can be used to lead and manage an arts organization: analytical, system, and organic.

Obviously, many other management styles may be applicable in running an arts organization. Flexibility remains the foundation of any style of management. It is important to develop a repertory of responses from which to choose as situations change. Just as a director or choreographer adjusts their working style based on the talents, skills, and abilities of their actors or dancers, so too must arts managers adjust to their given circumstances.

Before we focus on three management styles, let's visit with an arts manager struggling with a dysfunctional work situation. There is always something to learn — especially in challenging situations.

The dysfunctional arts manager

A model rooted in overextension

Dysfunction has become a very common word in our vocabulary. Often it is used as an excuse or a type of rationalization to explain why an organization or a group of people are not very effective in reaching their goals.

One type of dysfunction may be related to emotional problems and the other may simply mean you are not performing as expected. Often the circumstances may steer you away from being as effective as you could be.

No one starts in management with the goal of becoming a dysfunctional manager. A manager may become dysfunctional as a by-product of an organization with a culture that thrives on disorder as the standard operating mode. Alternatively, an organization may become dysfunctional when an individual with a strong dysfunctional personality is allowed to take control of the management team. Let's examine some of the ways an organization becomes dysfunctional.

Dysfunctional organizations

In Chapter 2, Arts Organization and Arts Management, we saw that when an organization starts up, there is usually a small group of extraordinary people willing to spend 18 hours a day doing everything, including marketing, advertising, contracts, schedules, budgets, and stuffing envelopes. Fayol's organizational *esprit de corps* is seen everywhere. Ambition, optimism, ceaseless energy, and a degree of ignorance about how impossible the job really is — all these elements are mixed together in a flurry of high-speed activity.

The volume of work increases as the number of productions, programs, or exhibits grows each year. Because everyone is so busy working, no one notices the gradual increase in the workload. New tasks and projects are added, and staff members groan but accept the added work. An ongoing adaptation process begins to mask the ever-increasing workload. The promise of more help and more money is held out as a goal to work toward. Planning, if it is done at all, is never for more than a few days or a few weeks at a time. Little crises are put aside until they become big enough to disrupt operations.

Before long, the problems multiply until the small staff spends all of its time solving one organization-threatening crisis after another. For example, one month the funds in the bank suddenly are insufficient to cover the payroll. "How could this happen?" everyone asks. No one is really certain because the payroll always managed to get done. Someone points out that it is not a payroll problem; rather, the issue is cash flow. The investigation into the problem leads to the discovery that everyone was so busy last week dealing with a different crisis that no one deposited the box office receipts in the bank.

This example may seem extreme, but unfortunately it is not. Overextended staff members who sometimes handle three or four major job functions are often the norm in arts organizations. The corporate culture often found might be summed up as follows: "Because you love the arts, you will have the privilege of working long hours at low pay." Arts groups often thrive on having a work force "addicted" to the organization's culture and the constant adrenaline-producing excitement associated with getting the show, special event, or exhibit finished minutes before it opens to the public.

The dysfunctional manager often is a product of this type of organizational system. He may start out with what he feels is a good grasp on what it takes to get the job done. Then the reality of the situation sets in. The stress levels are high, so reason and logic are in short supply. Decisions are made and then quickly reversed because no one thought through the consequences. On any given day, no one knows what is really going on in the organization because of a lack of clear-headed thinking.

One symptom of an organization suffering from a dysfunctional work system might be found in frequent staff turnover. High-energy people burn out quickly in a culture that requires them to sacrifice their personal lives. Workaholic managers often thrive in these dysfunctional situations and they drive their staffs to exhaustion assuming that everyone is capable of matching their own work level. A newly hired employee is expected to adopt the intense work ethic immediately, no matter how unpleasant. Often a beginning level staff person, with no point of comparison, accepts the required work level as the norm. Often, when the realization sets in that this is not a healthy place to work, powerless staff members take the only action they can take — they opt to resign. In this dysfunctional work environment, the employee who resigns is immediately identified by the remaining staff as someone who "just didn't like to work hard," thus carrying on the cultural values of the organization.

An organization may also become dysfunctional when the management team itself is dysfunctional. The cause of this problem is that the person in the role of manager is simply not suited for the job. It is not an exaggeration to say some people were never intended to be managers. Their basic personalities, for a complex set of reasons, are ill-suited to working with people in cooperative employment settings. These individuals may have a whole range of character flaws, including excessive defensiveness, aggressiveness, passivity, verbal abusiveness, and/or they are simply disengaged. Unfortunately, the list could go on.

No one is perfect and everyone has their problems, but the inescapable fact is that the managing process of the organization tends to reflect the personality of the manager. As character flaws become more pronounced and, in some cases, are manifested in severe psychological problems, the workplace becomes more psychologically dysfunctional.

Unfortunately, a new person hired into this situation is usually unaware that there is a problem until a few weeks have passed. After the first few explosions reveal the true personality of the manager and the character of the organization, the new employee has the option of adapting to this dysfunctional culture, trying to change it, or leaving.

One excellent resource for someone new to the management role in the workplace is Loren Belker and Gary Topchik's book *The First-Time Manager*, 5ᵗʰ edition. This book is particularly helpful for the staff member who is promoted to a management position in part because they may be very effective in their specific work area. However, when it comes to playing the role of a manager they are ill-prepared. This book provides the "script" to help someone make the transition from staff member to manager.

The positive profile

How important is it that a manager is able to exhibit a positive personality profile and possess skills and expertise to help further the goals of the organization? *It is central to the success or failure of the entire operation!* No matter how beautifully crafted the mission statement or how detailed and comprehensive the strategic, marketing, or fundraising plans may be, if the individuals hired as managers cannot work with people in a way that promotes commitment, responsibility, and a sense of enjoyment about the work to be done, then the chances of ever achieving anything more than mediocrity are slim.

It is important to remember that an organization is only as good as the people it employs. There is no escaping the fact that organizations can become dysfunctional because of the people who work within them, and not always because of outside forces or the lack of resources.

We now turn to three positive management approaches and contrast them with the dysfunctional manager. One of these three approaches, depending on the situation, may be more appropriate for effective leadership and management. The lines between one style and another are usually blurry, and on any given day, an arts manager may put one or more of these styles to good use. When you are reviewing the information in Figure 13.1, keep in mind that any one or a combination of all three styles may be used on a given day.

The analytical manager: changing the culture

Applying an analytical style of management takes persistence on the part of the manager. The first step in the process is to identify the steps that will be most effective in accelerating change where it is needed most. Analysis needs to precede action. Some parts of the organization will be impossible to change quickly, and others may be ready and willing to assist with making things different.

There are no rules or guidelines that apply universally when trying to change a culture that has grown self-destructive or ineffective. However, one obvious point to keep in mind is that changes are usually a great deal easier to instigate by moving with the flow of the organization rather than against it. This simply means that changing the attitudes and values of people by cooperation rather than coercion will greatly accelerate the acceptance of the analytical manager's point of view.

One strategy to pursue is to enlist the support of the other senior staff and the board to undertake an organizational assessment and audit modeled after the organizational, marketing, and fundraising audits that were outlined in Chapters 1, 11, and 12. The objective is to make board and staff members more aware of how the organization "behaves" and where the values and beliefs need to be changed to make the operation more effective and humane. Making sweeping changes to an organization is a daunting task, especially when it is dysfunctional. It can be done, but it may take longer than anticipated. After all, it usually takes years for an organization to develop a culture of elaborate values and beliefs.

Organizational cultures in conflict have been illustrated in numerous examples in this book. For instance, bringing in new artistic leadership is an opportunity for change, but it can also lead to counterproductive disruption. Analytical managers understand that rapid change in any organizational system leads to a great deal of psychological stress on everyone. The ability to gauge how fast change can be effected is part of the art of managing.

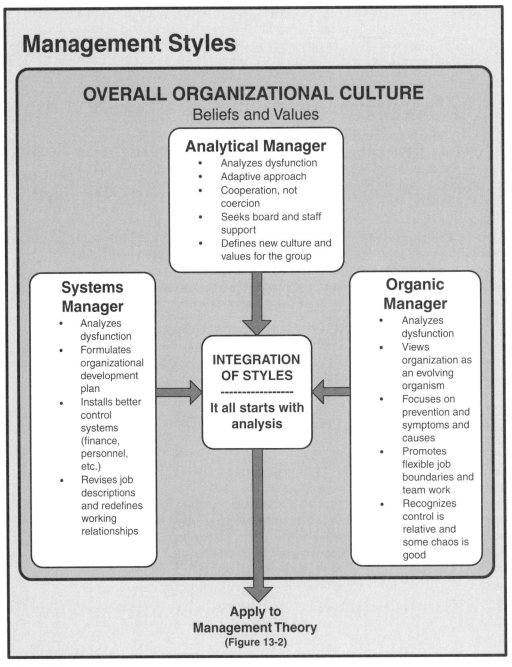

Figure 13.1

Management styles.

Analytical managers believe that organizations and people learn from their experiences and mature over time. A creative artist and a manager (perhaps the same person), working in cooperation with a board of directors, can use the four functions of management to chart a course for the organization that replaces the state of constant crisis and anxiety with controlled growth. Granted, it is not easy to set aside the time for planning and organizing in the midst of the unremitting press of daily business, but once a system is in place, the difficulties every organization expects to go through are smoothed out a bit.

The system manager: structure and control

The system management style emphasizes organizational development techniques and control systems to help reach the stated objectives. Part of the rise of the system manager can be attributed to the change from founder-driven arts groups to board- and staff-driven arts institutions. The museums, performing arts centers, opera, theater, or dance companies that started off with one or two people 30 or 40 years ago may now employ 50 to 100 people and have multimillion-dollar budgets and extensive office, production, and performance facilities.

With this growth and increasing complexity has come the development of the professional arts manager. When a board hires a professional manager, it is usually expected that the organization will adopt a more "businesslike" or corporate structure. The new leadership for the organization might be someone who did not work their way up through the ranks in an arts organization. This person may be a transplant from the for-profit business world. The change to a more businesslike style of operation usually follows a crisis brought about by a financial or personnel problem in the organization.

Not everyone greets what could be called the *managerization* of the arts with enthusiasm. For example, some critics say that adding layers of management produces bureaucratic structures that hinder the accomplishment of artistic goals and objectives and adds to the operating costs. Although unplanned growth can indeed create such situations, the reality is that most arts organizations tend to function with very limited staff resources; therefore, it is a common practice to give people two, three, or four job titles — any one of which could be a full-time job. What is seen by some as too many managers is often the organization's way of finding a reasonable balance between the number of people required to do the tasks and the organization's stated mission, goals, and objectives.

At another level, the role of the system manager has grown in response to the increased pressure to produce a balanced budget and the funding community's desire to see its money used responsibly. To cope with the issues of fiscal accountability and increasing organizational complexity, the two- and three-headed management structures are also finding their way into larger arts organizations.

What was once the vision and passion of one person, and maybe a small circle of friends, is now a multimillion-dollar institution in the community. There is a payroll to make. People are counting on the organization to be a responsibly run business. The time and money given by the board of directors, often the most influential people in the community, can also frequently carry subtle and not so subtle restrictions that can redirect the organization to a safer or less controversial path. The board and the community is looking for leadership of the organization it can trust to operate the organization in a "business-like" manner. Despite this pressure, a vigilant management and artistic team can work with the board to keep passion and the art alive and challenging. From the perspective of the system manager, the organization and control systems they bring to the arts organization can be used to free it from debilitating mismanagement and ineffective business practices.

The organic manager: adjustment and adaptation

The organic management style recognizes that a changing dynamic exists in organizations, and that, like a living organism, the group will grow and change over time. In many ways, the organic manager functions like a doctor who practices preventive medicine. The organic manager works with a dynamic system and focuses on spotting problems that could affect the health of the organization. Intervention is designed to treat the symptoms and the causes. In this case, the tools used to practice this preventive medicine are the theories and practices of management, economics, marketing, and so forth, which have proved to work in given specific circumstances.

Organic managers realize that they are working with very distinct groups, and yet these groups have flexible boundaries of skills and interests that overlap. For example, the marketing staff and the development staff have distinct areas of responsibility, but they also share mutual objectives relating to the fiscal health and well-being of the organization. The ability to give each group a sense of its own importance in the whole, while at the same time promoting communication and understanding, is the most important job facing the organization's leadership.

The organic manager also recognizes that there is an element of chaos in any organizational system. However, chaos does not necessarily mean that the organization is out of control. In the context of an arts enterprise, chaos needs to be recognized as an element of creative unpredictability. No one is ever sure that an arts event or exhibition will really work as planned. The artists need the freedom to experiment. Experiments can succeed or fail. Part of the organic manager's job is to provide an environment where these "experiments" can take place.

The organic manager makes allowances for the different levels of structure required for the various parts of the organization. The accounting department has rules and regulations restricting what must be done, but curators, directors, choreographers, and designers are given more freedom to explore alternative solutions. Recognizing the differences in the way subunits need to operate does not mean abdicating control. The latitude given to creative artists and scholars still fits within the overall control system that everyone agrees is necessary.

One last point to note in all the management style approaches talked about thus far is that you must start with analysis. The key to effectiveness is to spend a little time thinking and assessing. Granted some situations do not require deep analysis. However, when grappling with complex issues such as a declining subscriber base or assessing if you are meeting your artistic goals, quick solutions seldom produce long-term results. It takes hard work and setting aside time for analysis and assessment.

MANAGEMENT MODELS

Having established a management style, which will probably include a combination of analytical, system, and organic techniques, the manager can turn to adapting various management practices to arrive at an overall operating approach to the organization (see Figure 13.2).

Process management model

Many of the fiscal and production aspects of an arts organization can benefit from the application of quantitative procedures and ongoing statistical analysis borrowed from the scientific and process theories of management. There are potential gains in productivity if constant monitoring of routine procedures is a part of the organization's culture. Is there a more effective way to go about the process of constructing, storing, or rigging scenery? Can money be saved if a rehearsal or performance schedule is altered? Is the method used to enter sales data producing the timely information management needs to quickly spot financial problems? Is the procedure for processing an order done with the goal of reducing the number of steps required? For example, nearly all of the tracking of responses to mailings, donation requests, marketing, and sales campaigns relies heavily on techniques related to process management. As we saw in Chapter 9, Operations and Budgeting, and Chapter 10, Economics and Financial Management, an organization's MIS and FMIS require the vigorous application of quantitative systems if the organization is to stay informed about its fiscal health.

One clear signal that it is appropriate to undertake a more process-oriented approach to aspects of the operation is when you hear the phrase: "But we

Figure 13.2

Integration of management styles with operational models.

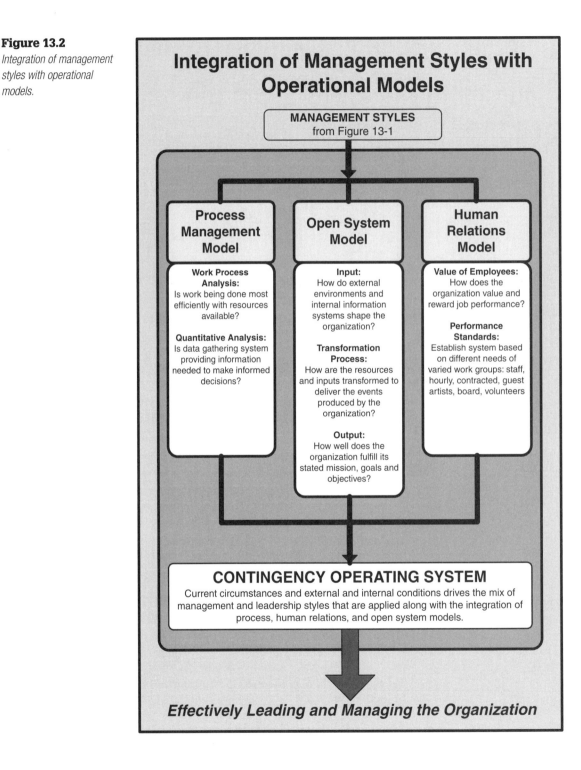

Integration of Management Styles with Operational Models

MANAGEMENT STYLES
from Figure 13-1

Process Management Model

Work Process Analysis:
Is work being done most efficiently with resources available?

Quantitative Analysis:
Is data gathering system providing information needed to make informed decisions?

Open System Model

Input:
How do external environments and internal information systems shape the organization?

Transformation Process:
How are the resources and inputs transformed to deliver the events produced by the organization?

Output:
How well does the organization fulfill its stated mission, goals and objectives?

Human Relations Model

Value of Employees:
How does the organization value and reward job performance?

Performance Standards:
Establish system based on different needs of varied work groups: staff, hourly, contracted, guest artists, board, volunteers

CONTINGENCY OPERATING SYSTEM

Current circumstances and external and internal conditions drives the mix of management and leadership styles that are applied along with the integration of process, human relations, and open system models.

Effectively Leading and Managing the Organization

have always done it that way around here." There may be good reasons why certain procedures are accomplished in specific ways, but nearly everything that is done routinely can usually be done more efficiently if given some thought.

Human relations model

As we saw in Chapter 3, Management History and Trends, and Chapter 8, Leadership and Group Dynamics, the human relations approach to management grew out of McGregor's Theory X and Theory Y, Maslow's hierarchy of needs, behaviorist theory, and other psychological approaches to the workplace. Because the product of a performing arts organization is the work of people, there is a natural fit between human resource management and an arts organization.

The arts manager must realize that each employee group has its own set of behaviors and expectations about the work of the organization. For example, the stagehands working on a show will have a very different perspective about their job and their place in the organization than that of fundraising assistants. Both support jobs are needed to make the organization work, but employees in each category need different types of recognition and rewards for their contributions to the organization.

Developing performance standards and an appraisal system that recognizes the similarities and differences in employee groups while keeping employees focused on the defined objectives requires a significant commitment of the manager's time. Given the dynamics of an arts organization, once-a-year job reviews will simply not monitor adequately the work output of employees. In fact, this approach would amount to "management by neglect" of your employees. Daily, weekly, or monthly reviews, mostly informal in nature, of employee performance may be more appropriate, depending on the type of work done. Paying attention to the contributions employees make to the organization and then publicly recognizing those accomplishments can help create a very positive work environment.

Attention must also be paid to how effectively the organization's communication and management information systems are working. Information is often equated with power. Those who have the information have power over those who do not. However, this is a very destructive approach to information management. As we saw in Chapter 6, Organizing and Organizational Design, all organizations have formal and informal structures and communication systems. If any employee group is excluded from the communication system, the risk of rumors and the harmful distortion of information increases in great leaps. No employee communication system is perfect, but it makes little sense to establish communication approaches guaranteed to alienate people.

THE ORGANIZATION AS AN OPEN SYSTEM

The organizational model of the open system and its ability to adjust to changing circumstances have been stressed in many chapters in this text. Input from clients, audiences, donors, staff, and so on, is combined with input from the external environments — the economic, political and legal, cultural and social, demographic, technological, and educational — to produce an organization that constantly changes and adjusts to the world around it.

The open system approach to management does not mean that the organization's mission undergoes constant change. Rather, the open system allows the organization to capitalize on opportunities that support its mission while minimizing the impact of threats to the enterprise. For example, new digital video and Internet technology may provide additional cash flow opportunities for the arts by opening up new markets for distribution of the product and by creating new viewing audiences. At the same time, an adverse tax ruling by the IRS or a proposed Federal law that affects labor practices can be addressed through active participation in the political system.

THE CONTINGENCY SYSTEM: AN INTEGRATING APPROACH

The approaches and theories reviewed thus far are all directed at finding a way to integrate the various styles and theories of management into a workable system. Combinations of analytical, systems, and organic management techniques applied to theories of process management, human relations, and the open system can help a manager achieve results when carrying out the functions of management.

The model that meshes management styles and operational models is shown in Figure 13.2. The integration of these styles and models into what is called a contingency system holds much promise. The important point to remember with this system is that, depending on the circumstances and the nature of the problem, the manager can select options combining some portion of each approach. Sometimes, it is a human relations problem; at other times, it is a quantitative problem; and on other occasions, the problem relates back to a change in one or more of the environments or input groups. Each individual will feel comfortable with different applications of a contingency system; however, the central point is that a manager must actively choose the particular combination of styles and theories that will best solve the organization's problems.

Let's review the functional areas of management from the perspective of applying this overall contingency system of management.

The management functions

The center of the arts organization's operational system is found in the functions listed in this section. The goal of the entire organization should be to take the contingency system, which integrates management styles and theories, and apply it to the operational areas in ways that achieve the organization's stated goals and objectives.

Planning and development

Looking toward the future is a major responsibility of a manager in any organization. As we saw in Chapter 5, Planning and Decision Making, the ability to plan requires no special genius. However, bringing the same creative energy you would use to envision a production often does not seem to translate to planning. The key ingredients are self-discipline and an established process. Within this framework applying creative problem-solving and imagining different scenarios for success can actual make planning fun. (See the section ?WhatIF! The Innovation Company.)

Of course, the underlying culture of the organization must value looking ahead and should stress the involvement of the board and all levels of staff in the process. Every action that an organization takes should relate to the overall master plan. If it does not, human and other resources will be misdirected and ultimately wasted.

?WhatIF! The Innovation Company

One of the ironies of the planning process in some organizations is that rather than it being a liberating activity, it is seen as something "we have to do." The very creative drive that an artist uses to bring a new work to life often seems to be driven out of the management process. The London-based firm ?WhatIF! was founded in 1992 and employs over 300 people training organizations to tap into their creative reservoirs. The company's client list is worldwide and includes firms such as Audi, Coca-Cola, Thomas Cook, and dozens more. ?WhatIF! is driven by a passion to bring innovation and creativity to the process of running businesses. The company published a fascinating book in 2002 entitled "sticky wisdom" that outlines what is described as "Simple, practical learning about creativity that will stick with you forever." At the core ?WhatIF! is engaged in enabling organizations to tap into the creative ideas and drive of their employees. For more information about ?WhatIF! go to www.whatifinnovation.com.

Types of plans

All managers, including overextended managers, engage in short-term and crisis planning. Problems such as cash flow difficulties, a show that might have to be canceled, a tour cut short because presenters backed out at the last minute, a work of art damaged at an exhibit, and the death of a member of the cast are part of the business. Managers with a methodology in place for quick problem-solving identify the source of the difficulty, generate alternatives, and implement and evaluate decisions before a crisis develops that threatens the operation of the organization. Written outlines and procedures to follow when a crisis does strike can help the organization keep its balance.

Intermediate-range strategic planning (one to three years) is integral to the program development and fundraising activities of an arts group. The key to strategic planning is setting priorities and then pursuing them. For example, launching a fundraising campaign requires coordinated planning to organize resources and people in cost-effective ways. The assumption is fundraising is the highest priority strategic direction to take because the leadership sees this path to financial stability. The case for support must be strong and the reasons for giving must be clear to potential donors. The need for the funds must relate directly to the organization's strategic development.

Long-range planning (four to ten years), although always subject to revision, is also an important process in helping to shape the organization's future. This type of planning is especially important when you are contemplating new facilities or endowment campaigns. Long-term planning is a serious business, but the enjoyable and creative side of the process should not be overlooked. "What if" discussions among the board, the artists, and the staff can lead to new ideas and directions. In fact, planning is a break from the routine of day-to-day work, and it should be a strong selling point for potential board members. After all, would you rather be on a board of directors that was actively engaged in charting the future of the organization, or would you prefer to sit through yet another report detailing fund balance transfers?

Marketing and public relations

As we have seen, arts organizations are businesses that must function in the highly competitive entertainment industry. Effective marketing and positive public relations can help any enterprise target and inform people of goods and services designed to meet their wants and needs. The key to success, especially given the very limited resources that most arts groups have to work with, lies with making sure that you are talking to the right people, at the right time, through the right media.

The universe of goods and services seems to be expanding as thousands of new products come on the market every month, making the task of keeping an arts organization visible even more exacting. Therefore, expanded press and media relations must be a central part of the organization's strategic plan if the organization is to command any attention. As the capabilities and reach of high-speed Internet expand and organization's have become more adept at utilizing their Web site, many new opportunities present themselves to communicate directly to audiences without going through the media. As we have seen, the old rules of media and press relations are being rewritten.

As we saw in Chapter 11, Marketing and the Arts, marketing is an organizational orientation that places the consumer (our audiences) at the beginning of the process. To be truly customer-driven is seen as an ideal in establishing a long-term relationship between product and consumer. However, many arts organizations equate "customer-driven" with lower artistic standards and pandering to the public. They therefore engage in what is more accurately described as a "selling orientation" toward the public. The selling approach assumes that if consumers are made aware of the product, they will buy it. In more extreme cases, organizations adopt a product orientation, which assumes that because the product is so inherently good, people will want to buy it.

Marketing strategies

As was pointed out in Chapter 11, adoption of a marketing orientation for an arts organization requires a careful analysis of the four Ps (product, price, promotion, and place) and, at the same time, an understanding of the limits of marketing. For example, no marketing campaign will suddenly create an arts audience by changing the well-established behavior of masses of people overnight. As we have seen, the audience for high-culture events is a by-product of the education system, especially at the college and university level. Arts marketers interested in building a long-term purchase and donation relationship with consumers would assemble demographic and psychographic profiles of the community, and a distribution of neighborhoods by spending type (e.g., money and furs, pools and patios) in an effort to piece together the most effective campaign that the available resources permit. The objective is to get inside the consumer's head to find out what combination of the four Ps will lead to the exchange process: money in exchange for the arts experience.

Of course, marketing strategies need not be targeted to only a limited segment of the population. Marketing to reach a diverse audience is important and will become critical as the demographic composition of America continues to change. The key to reaching people lies with how and what you communicate about the product to the public. Reaching new audiences, especially the young and minorities, depends on the mix of programs and community outreach, the right price, and access to the facility. Capitalizing on the ever-increasing capabilities of the organization's Web site and the expanding influence of social networking opportunities can assist with expanding the potential audience base.

It must be stressed again that all of the innovative marketing strategies in the world cannot create an arts consumer overnight. Marketing is a long-term investment of the organization's resources. Results designed to educate and develop an audience should be measured over three- to five-year periods of time, not just one season.

Finally, it is also important to remember that marketing and fundraising share the similar goal of establishing an exchange relationship with audiences and donors. The progression from single-ticket buyer to subscriber or member and finally to long-term donor dictates an integrated plan under the general heading of development or organizational advancement.

PERSONNEL MANAGEMENT BOARD, STAFF, LABOR, AND RELATIONS

Even when the manager adopts a human resource management strategy that takes into account the various attitudes and values of the different work groups within the organization, the ability to keep board members and employees happy and productive is still an enormous challenge. Establishing working conditions that support the creative process and encourage the interaction of artists and scholars, the board, and staff members is one of the leader and manager's primary objectives. This would seem to be self-evident, but judging by the stories of dysfunctional or micro-managing boards, or performers, designers, staff, and technicians dealing with the abuses of management — which also includes directors, conductors, curators, and choreographers — it is a miracle that there is not more strife in arts organizations.

Board of directors

Managing relations with the board is just as important to senior and middle-level staff members as is a successful contract negotiation with a union. The board, which could be made up of anywhere from 6 to 60 or more people, has its power blocs, hard workers, and deadwood just like any other organization. A powerful finance committee, for example, could prevent a manager from implementing new programs by not approving a budget. A board personnel committee could hold up a key appointment or lobby for a candidate of the board's choosing. Approval of a season schedule might be held up if the board has doubts about title selection.

For the arts manager, a clear picture of the scope of the board's power and responsibility is of primary importance if the organization is to function effectively. In numerous examples in this book, we have seen board actions both strengthen or undermine arts groups. There never seems to be a shortage of stories about the communication gap between artistic or executive directors and the board. The Case Study in this chapter provides a good example of board staff challenges when a crisis hits.

Unions

The abusive and exploitive past practices of management were a primary reason for the establishment of unions. Although managers and unions may never see eye-to-eye about how the organization operates, the fact remains that it is management's job to establish the criteria for performance. For the arts manager, defining acceptable practices is at the heart of the relationship with the union because, when both sides sit down to negotiate a contract, the odds are very high that labor and management will not agree about levels of compensation, benefits, and work rules.

The arts manager who does not understand how the "backstage" really works in a theater, concert hall, or museum will be at a huge disadvantage when it comes time to evaluate the work rules written into a contract. A lack of understanding of the work environment could cost the organization thousands of dollars every time a show is performed or an event takes place. In addition, an arts manager must remember that a union is also a complex organization and is therefore subject to the same external and internal forces that shape the arts group. Understanding the perspective of union members and the union organization can make the arts manager's job a little easier.

Personnel management

Meanwhile, as organizations mature, issues of salaries, staff training, and renewal will become more important. Finding new challenges, revising job descriptions, reorganizing departments, and combining or separating jobs should all become part of the overall operation of the personnel area.

When adding up all of the work required to manage the personnel functions of an arts organization, an artistic or museum director might wonder when they will have time to direct a production or engage in scholarly research. In reality, there is no time. Upper level managers, like artistic directors who involve themselves in production, find that, more often than not, one or more functional areas in the organization are left unattended.

What options can an artistic director select to resolve this conflict? One obvious approach has been to split the job into different positions based on operations and product development. This explains why more organizations are creating two or three upper level management positions to supervise the fiscal, planning, and operational aspects of the arts enterprise. The tradeoff for some artistic directors is that they must share their power with others. At some future date, should conflict arise with the board, artistic directors might find that one of their operational peers is undermining their credibility and forming a power bloc against them.

FISCAL MANAGEMENT

The area of fiscal planning and control is also at the core of the arts organization. A large portion of a manager's time will probably be spent on this area, often at the expense of such equally important areas as planning, programming, and staff development. Financial management is at the center of so much attention because expectations about the amount of money that can be generated through sales, fundraising, and grants are often unrealistic. At the same time, prices, labor, and operating costs continue to escalate higher than anticipated. The combination of these two elements establishes a perpetual deficit hanging over many organizations.

In *The Quiet Crisis in the Arts*, which was published in the early 1990s, Nello McDaniel and George Thorn noted that arts organizations can find themselves in a state of constant debt crisis, which produces an unbelievable amount of personal stress on the staff.[1] Sadly, the situation has not changed for many arts organizations (e.g., See this chapter's Case Study, Theater Struggles to Go On.). The cycle of overspending followed by painful budget cutting takes its toll on people.

When artistic or executive directors speak of maintaining quality in the face of budget cuts of tens of thousands of dollars, people know that it is simply impossible. If you cut the budget, you usually reduce the quality. The expectation that the performers, designers, technicians, museum staff, and others will somehow be able to create the same quality product with fewer rehearsals, less money for sets or costumes, and so forth, is nonsense. A comment from management like "now we will have to get creative" is insulting to the director and the design team. Maybe a new vision for the show is needed to match the budget resources, but the time to achieve that new vision is often not taken into account.

The assumption some arts managers and boards seem to make is "If we say often enough that we aren't going to lose quality by cutting budgets, then maybe everyone will begin to believe it." Instead, this type of management process leads staff to become very cynical about the leadership of the organization.

Managing and leading by fiscal self-delusion is hardly the most effective way to build board and staff confidence. In fact, a board member asked to go raise yet another million dollars might respond, "Well, if we can do the same quality with a million-dollar budget cut, why did we go a million dollars in debt in the first place?" The answer usually comes back, "Because we are dedicated to pursuing excellence in the arts." The more accurate answer would be "Because we didn't know how to effectively manage the human and production resources we had available to us." Needless to say, the latter reason usually is not a discussion item for staff and board meetings.

Financial strategies

There are a few fiscal management strategies that are likely to keep the organization solvent and the board confident. They include the following:

- Realistic budget planning procedures for revenue first, then expenses
- Organizational attitudes and values that stress that budgets are not to be exceeded
- Very tight control and oversight systems for expenditures
- A clear picture of the cash flow needs of the organization
- A system for accounts payable activity that pays no bill before its time except when there is a discount for early payment
- A very aggressive "asset management program" that involves investment in a wide range of financial instruments

GOVERNMENT RELATIONS

As we learned in Chapter 4, The Adaptive Arts Organization, government relations extend from the federal to the local level. A manager's involvement in the political arena is usually fairly limited. However, as we have seen in the last few years, without the support of the people who make the laws and sit on the appropriations committees, arts organizations will suffer. Arts groups must earn the support of elected officials at all levels of government. Support is not given just because the arts organizations and artists think their enterprise is nobler than other agencies established for a public good.

The first step for successfully interacting with the government system is education. The arts manager must learn how the various local, state, and federal systems work. The second step involves learning about the power brokers and the issues close to them and their constituents. The third step requires the arts manager to visit the various representatives in an effort to become visible. The fourth step involves making the newfound visibility mean something by updating the representatives about the organization's important activities and the positive impact of the arts on the community.

For a weary arts manager trying to cover all of the management functions described in this section, the political system, with its complex subculture, is not always the highest priority. If the arts manager is too busy to have lunch with the local director of cultural affairs or to go to a candidate's fundraising dinner, there should be no surprise when politicians do not spring to the rescue when the arts group has a budget crisis or some other problem.

CONCLUSION

The goal of developing an integrated approach to management styles and theories is to help the organization succeed at whatever it attempts. Figure 13.2 depicts the integration of the differing styles and practices.

As we have seen, managing is an intensely personal process. The theories may provide the overall structure, but the effectiveness of any management system ultimately depends on the people who are doing the managing. The ability to establish an overall work environment where people can express a point of view without fearing for their jobs, or where they can make suggestions that will be heard, is often overlooked when it comes to designing an organization.

Of course, people who work in any organization want to earn enough money to live comfortably, and they want to have the support of health benefits should they have an accident or become ill. However, on a day-to-day basis, people also have an intense desire to believe that their work is making a worthwhile contribution and that their effort is recognized in some way. Therefore, a manager must always remember that it is the people who are important to the organization, not just the product. Treating people with respect and recognizing their daily contribution to the enterprise are key ingredients in successful organizations.

To integrate management styles and practices managers must also know their own strengths and weaknesses. Undertaking a personal inventory helps a manager to see more clearly the things he or she does well and to identify the areas that need improvement. The ability to trust in yourself and to work with what is called a 360-degree review personnel system can pay big dividends later. The advantage of using this approach is that it keeps the manager and the organization renewed. It is also important for the manager to reap a sense of personal satisfaction when it comes time to evaluate how well things are working. Success is a great motivating force, especially when it is widely recognized throughout an organization.

Running an arts organization never was and never will be easy. Although arts organizations can benefit from applying management theory and practice to become better organized and more efficient, there is still no single element that guarantees survival. Getting better at doing well is an ambitious goal that any arts manager should be proud to work toward. To achieve that goal, an arts manager should be prepared to borrow any techniques that work from business, government, educational institutions, or other nonprofit organizations. Successfully integrating these different approaches to effectively manage an organization requires as much creativity as any visual or performing artist. Forging a successful partnership of manager and artist is therefore predicated on each party's recognizing the other's creative contribution to one goal: creating a world in which life is enriched by the accomplishments of both parties.

For additional topics relating to managing the arts organization, please go to www.managementandthearts.com.

Questions

1. Based on your own experiences, can you cite examples of situations in which analytical, systems, or organic management styles were used to solve a problem effectively?

2. With proven approaches to managing, such as scientific and human relations management, and organizational models, such as the open system, to help guide operations, why do so many arts groups have trouble with their management structures?

3. Use any of the case studies in this text to provide examples of the effective use of the following functional areas:
- Planning and development.
- Marketing and public relations.
- Personnel management.
- Fiscal management.
- Government relations.

As this article points out, when a communication gap between the staff and the board reaches a certain point, dire results may ensue.

CASE STUDY

Theater Struggles to Go On
November 28, 2007, Colin Dabkowski, Buffalo News. *Used with permission.*

Nearly a year after midseason financial problems put Studio Arena Theatre in jeopardy, the region's premier theater has again found itself in dire straits [see postscript].

After ticket sales for the first two shows of Studio Arena's 2007–08 season came in far below projections, the theater came to the brink of insolvency.

Two weeks ago, in the face of an unthinkable closure, an emergency fundraising effort managed to pull in about $225,000 from a combination of foundations, theater board members,

and local banks, according to Studio Arena board President Daniel A. Dintino.

That money, according to Dintino and CEO and artistic director Kathleen Gaffney, will ensure that the theater produces at least its next two shows: the family-friendly Christmas play "Indian Blood," which is scheduled to begin in previews Tuesday, and January's "To Kill a Mockingbird." After that, all bets are off. Staffers and board members are hopeful — but can't guarantee — that the theater will be able to produce the season's two remaining shows.

"At this point in time, we're planning on continuing through," Dintino said.

CASE STUDY (CONTINUED)

Meanwhile, ongoing negotiations that came to light in mid-November about a possible merger with Shea's Performing Arts Center are moving ahead, representatives from both organizations said. However, neither side would talk about the issues at hand, what type of merger would be involved, or when a deal can be expected.

Despite deep staffing cuts that went into effect in January, streamlined operations and various other cost-saving measures, Gaffney said that the current model on which the theater operates is unsustainable.

"This kind of operation, even with the cuts that I made throughout last year, having [only] one set designer and so forth, it's still too expensive," she said. "And the audience is just not, they're not coming."

Though Gaffney's contract expires in April, she said she fully intends to stay on and help to pull the theater out of its troubles. But she expressed frustration that her contract has not yet been renewed.

"A new contract, that's what I need," Gaffney said. "It's getting caught up in the middle of all this."

In the midst of disappointing returns, a glimmer of hope for the theater comes from its negotiations with Shea's. The leaders of both organizations said they hope the talks will result, at the very least, in a collaboration that will provide a stable outlook for Studio Arena.

An earlier proposal from Shea's in 2003 to provide certain services and to collaborate was declined by the Studio Arena board for undisclosed reasons, Gaffney said. She added that another potential collaboration between Studio Arena and Artpark had also been discussed in detail over the past two months, but that deal was struck down because of logistical and financial concerns about the organizations' being in two different counties.

Since news of the proposed association with Shea's came out, little has changed. Gaffney said she is 80 percent confident that some type of association will come out of the talks between the two groups, whether it is simply a combination of operational and support services or a more significant merger in the mold of a regional arts facility.

Gaffney pointed to the Denver Center for the Performing Arts, in which one organization runs both the city's producing theater (the equivalent of Studio Arena) and its presenting house (a la Shea's).

"There are some precedents out there," Gaffney said. "They take a little bit of time to analyze and see what things we might be able to do well."

Anthony Conte, Shea's president, confirmed that the two groups were carefully considering a number of models around the country in order to determine the best approach to a possible merger.

"I would think something's going to come out of it. I'm not sure what at this point," Conte said. "We're looking at so many options that, frankly, it gets confusing at times. We're trying to narrow them down a little bit and see what makes the most sense."

As for why the theater's first two shows turned in such disappointing results, Gaffney cited cost-cutting in the marketing department as a major factor. Her projections for the first show, popular playwright Tom Dudzick's "Don't Talk to the Actors," were based on seasons in which a much bigger marketing budget and staff were available.

"We cost-saved our way into a very difficult position," Gaffney said.

The theater's annual fundraising campaign, which by this point in the year would normally be well under way, is also on hold while the theater figures out what kind of organization it's presenting to potential donors.

Asked what individuals can do for the struggling theater, Gaffney made a plea to Western New York's art- and theater-going community. In a nutshell: "They've got to show up for the shows." "We have all of this wonderful stuff," Gaffney said. "I was reading the paper yesterday about the new downtown hotel, and I want to be here for that, but unless the public begins to voice their support and show their support by coming, we won't be around."

Postscript

In January of 2007 *The Buffalo News* published a story by Mark Sommer titled "High Drama." At that time the Studio Arena Theatre had laid off 14 employees and was reported to be $1.4 million in debt. As the November 2007 story indicates the situation is still one of high drama.

Playbill.com published a story on February 26, 2008, noting that the, "Studio Arena Theatre, the 43-year-old Buffalo, NY, not-for-profit that gave life to world premieres and revivals, has shut its doors, canceled the remainder of its season, and laid of 17 staffers, it was announced Feb. 25."

CASE STUDY (CONTINUED)

Questions

1. Gaffney indicates that even after the cuts made in early 2007 "the current model on which the theater operates is unsustainable." She went on to say, "And the audience is just not, they're not coming." What do you think that kind of statement means? For example, does that imply even after the cuts the theater was still spending more than it could make from sales and fundraising? Or, have the shows not been attracting sufficient audiences and that's what is making the operation unsustainable?

2. How do you think a merger with the performing arts center (Shea's) will solve the problem? What advantage would the management of Shea's have by supporting a merger? (For more information about the center go to www.sheas.org.)

3. It would appear from the article that the public is staying away from the theater resulting in the disappointing sales. Gaffney indicates the cost cutting in the marketing budget was why sales were not as projected. It appears from reading the article that the revenue projections were not adjusted downward based on the reduced marketing budget. What might have been a better management strategy to keep sales up in the face of the reduced marketing budget?

4. What strategies can the theater take when it comes to future fundraising? The article indicates that the current fundraising campaign is on hold. What impact could putting a hold on the campaign have on the theater's financial future?

REFERENCE

1. Nello McDaniel, George Thorn, *The Quiet Crisis in the Arts* (New York: ARTS Action Issues, 1991).

CHAPTER 14

Career Options and Preparing for the Job Market

Having studied arts organizations for the last few weeks, you should have a much better understanding of the field itself and the issues that face arts organizations. It is also my hope that your enthusiasm and passion remains high, even as you have discovered how challenging it can be to ensure the stability and sustainability of an arts enterprise.

You should now be fluent in the vocabulary of arts management and you should no longer be unaware of the important business side of the arts. It is equally important for you to have a way to fulfill the passion you have for the arts by using your new-found knowledge, skills, and abilities as a potential manager and leader. Let's look at some of the steps you will need to follow if you are considering a career in arts and culture management.

This chapter is designed to give a few pointers about developing your career as an arts manager. Of course a primary step in the process of developing your career is to create a personal plan. By using some of the same techniques we studied in Chapter 5, you can chart a course for yourself that offers many paths to pursue. This chapter will also look at issues related to compensation, making the transition from a student to a productive employee, and how to go about organizing your job search. We will review some of the essential tools you will need for your job search and hopefully inspire you to become part of the next generation of arts managers.

THE EVOLVING ARTS WORKPLACE

As you have seen, the arts management workplace is undergoing an evolution that parallels the changes occurring in arts organizations, as we discussed in Chapter 1, Management and the Arts, and Chapter 4, The Adaptive Arts Organization; as arts organizations have matured so has the workforce. Many of the senior managers and leaders of today either brought their management training and experience with them from the business sector or they developed as managers through an informal process that is akin to on-the-job training.

Many others in the field started either in the performance, production, operations, or design side of the arts and made a transition into management. You will no doubt find many very smart people working in arts organizations who have figured out how to apply the creative and collaborative process inherent in realizing a production to their work.

Over the last 40 years university programs offering majors or courses in arts management or administration have continued to grow. (The link to the most up-to-date listing of many of these programs may be found at the Association of Arts Administration Educators Web site: www.artsadministration.org/node/9). This growth has had an impact on the quality, qualifications, and quantity of the labor pool. A new generation of university-trained arts managers are finding their way into arts organizations around the world.

WHERE THE JOBS ARE AND WILL BE

As you would expect, the opportunities for employment in the field of arts management are more numerous based on the geographical distribution of arts organizations. The bigger the population base the more likely you will find a wider distribution of all types of arts organizations. This does not mean that there are no arts management jobs in the rural areas. However, common sense dictates that the arts population base will be higher in larger metropolitan areas.

As you know, museums and performing arts organizations are dependent on members, audiences, patrons, and donors to sustain themselves. Not only must the area have the population base to ensure a certain level of support, but as we have seen, there needs to be a sufficient number of people with the educational level, time, and disposable income to form the nucleus audience. Demand for the arts product also requires a sufficient supply of arts consumers. For arts consumers to satisfy their demand for entertainment there must be a sufficient supply of arts organizations.

As we saw in Chapter 10, Economics and Financial Management, the expansion in the number of arts organizations since the 1960s has been supported by the general population growth. There are several trends that will probably continue in the near future. For example, people have migrated from the Northeast to the South and Southwest and this will no doubt translate into more jobs as arts organizations spring up in the new population centers. There also is staff turnover in arts organizations as the founding generation moves on to retirement. There will also probably be many opportunities for recent graduates in arts management especially if you are interested in moving beyond the not-for-profit arts and culture field. The larger marketplace for entertainment and media seems to have a very steady demand for college graduates. Whether you decide to work in the not-for-profit arts and culture side of the industry or the for-profit entertainment and media industry, you will need the same skills to be an effective manager and leader.

PERSONAL CHOICES AND SELECTION CRITERIA

You need to make a number of initial choices as you contemplate your job options. Geography is certainly important, but your selection process will be further narrowed by the criteria you set for yourself, such as the type of arts organization you may want to work for, your range of skills and specialization, and fundamental economic survival issues. For example, you may love dance and your goal is to be a marketing director for a dance company that produces new work. However, the number of jobs in a given area for marketing directors of dance companies may be very limited. Are you willing to do arts marketing for an orchestra, theater company, or museum? Have you prepared yourself for working outside the arts in a related field until that job you really want with the dance company becomes available? Maybe you will take the route of finding a non-arts-related job that provides enough compensation to allow you to volunteer to help the dance company.

So where does this leave you? Do you want to go to larger metropolitan areas such as New York City, San Francisco, Chicago, Los Angles, Seattle, Denver, Atlanta, or Washington, D.C.? Do you feel more comfortable in smaller cities, or perhaps a university arts environment? If the latter appeals to you, then you may want to seek out employment in a university performing arts center or in a fine arts college or school. Perhaps you would prefer going to work for a bigger company in the field of television or a multimedia company. Perhaps you will explore a job with a corporation as an events planner or manager, or move into managing an artist or a touring performing group. Obviously, all of these choices carry pluses and minuses depending on your individual goals.

DEVELOP A PERSONAL PLAN

A student with thousands of dollars of loans to repay has one set of decision-making criteria for employment. An individual who worked for years before going back to school to seek a degree in arts management has a different set of goals and expectations. Some of you may seek more experience and find yourself in circumstances that permit pursuing an internship after you finish school.

Regardless of your situation, the need to establish a plan is important. The process discussed in Chapter 5, Planning and Decision Making, is easily transferred to your own circumstances. You need to use the same five steps we touched on in making a plan:

1. Define your objectives
2. Assess your situation
3. Formulate outcome options
4. Make your choices and implement your plan
5. Continue to evaluate your choices

You need to put your plan in writing and remain flexible as new opportunities arise. If you follow this process you will already be far ahead of many people you will be competing with in the job market. In other words, you need to do your homework.

FROM THE EMPLOYER'S PERSPECTIVE

If you have spent any time around people in the arts you are no doubt aware of how much the process of "networking" is stressed. You may assume that you will be hired for a position entirely on the merits of your application and qualifications, but the fact is that employers are looking for other clues about your potential for success as a future employee. For example, if, all other things being equal, an employer knows of one of the references in your résumé, you have a better chance of getting the follow-up contact on your application.

The process of hiring someone, as pointed out in Chapter 7, Human Resources and the Arts, can be a very complex and often risky activity. The wrong hire can lead to numerous problems for an organization, beyond the obvious one of not getting the work done at the level of quality and quantity expected. Similarly, your career development and reputation may be harmed by accepting a position in which you are not going to be able to succeed. Therefore, employers are usually looking for references to give them information about the quality of your work, your skills and abilities, and how well you work with others — your interpersonal skills. A positive reference from someone the employer knows and trusts can be a critical part of the hiring process.

COMPENSATION ISSUES

One of the key questions you are often told *not* to ask about too early in the process of seeking a job is "How much does the position pay?" A potential employer usually controls the timing of the offering of the compensation and benefits package. Sometimes an employer will list a salary range for a position to clarify for applicants and what they can expect to be paid. However, the trend in recent years has been to not list salary information, which leaves applicants in the dark about how much the position they are seeking will pay. You can list your salary requirements in your cover letter, but then you run the risk of elimination for a job you may really want because the employer cannot meet your salary needs. If you get a follow-up call from an employer, you might then ask about the salary range. The employer might give you some numbers or may simply say the salary is negotiable. This delicate process can be made a little less mysterious if you do a little research.

Salary research

As pointed out in Chapter 2, "Arts Organizations and Arts Management, detailed salary studies in the arts are few and far between. Sources such as *The NonProft Times* can be a place to start gathering information. The *Annual Salary Survey*, which is usually published in early February, provides national and regional average salaries for ten types of positions in the nonprofit sector. The positions profiled are middle- and upper level management positions, however, so the salaries are probably well above the starting salaries one can expect as a recent graduate. (For more information on the survey go to www. nptimes.com.)

The overall operating budget of an organization is a major determining factor of compensation. As you might expect, typically the bigger the overall operating budget, the higher the average salary. However, what about salaries at the entry-level positions? Based on reports from recent graduates of arts administration programs, the salary offers made for new hires are significantly lower than the averages often listed in salary surveys. For example, an entry-level grant-writing position for an organization with a budget under $10 million might range from as little as $18,000 to as much as $30,000.

In the later part of the first decade of the twenty-first century a recent graduate of a master's program might receive salary offers for a position like "development assistant" in the mid- to high 20s in the not-for-profit arts field. Many recently hired arts administration students report getting offers in the mid-20s to mid-30s. A few report starting salaries in the low 40s in larger metropolitan areas.

What about salaries in the arts jobs working at colleges and universities or the for-profit entertainment industry? Little hard evidence exists in the form of higher education arts salary surveys. Often university salaries follow proscribed ranges based on staff classification systems that are not particularly flexible. Probably the most significant advantage university or state jobs offer is the benefits package. Health, dental, and life insurance benefits can be more generous than the norm in not-for profit-organizations.

Other sources for salary information

INTIX (www.intix.org), the association representing the ticketing industry, gives some insight into salaries from the listings on their Web site of job openings (Go to Services/Resources and then to Career Advancement). Many of the INTIX members include large civic centers and sports teams as well as arts organizations and performing arts centers. Starting ticket office salaries in the low to mid-30s to 40s are common.

A helpful tool for determining the adequacy of a salary may be found on the many Web sites that allow you to enter a salary and compare it to the cost of living in various parts of the country (e.g., www.salary.com).

Cost of living and salaries

Common sense should prevail when weighing an offer to take an arts management position for $35,000 in New York City, for example, versus Dallas or Atlanta. The cost of living in New York City makes it an economic fact that a $35,000 salary is not going to allow you to have the same standard of living as other less costly cities.

As you saw in Chapter 7, Human Resources and the Arts, there are more costs related to being hired for a position than the salary. The scope and level of benefits that go along with a position are also a cost to the organization and must be factored into any hiring process. As any business operator will tell you, health insurance is one of the most expensive benefits offered employees. Many small arts organizations either forego this benefit entirely or hold off giving the benefit until you have passed a six-month probationary period. Insurance, if it is offered, is typically a shared cost with the employee. The actual percentages or amounts may vary, but it is not unusual for employees to pay as little as 25 percent up to as much as 75 percent of the cost of their health insurance. Other perks such as dental and vision insurance or retirement benefits, will vary greatly depending on the organization's budget. Paid annual leave and sick leave will also vary widely depending on the financial resources of the organization. From your perspective as a job seeker, many of these benefits will be costs deducted from your gross salary along with a variety of taxes.

Compensation Table

This simple table gives you a quick reference to how an annual salary offer translates to the paycheck you will receive

Per Year	Per Month	Bi-Weekly	Per Week	Per Hour
$20,000	$1666	$766	$385	$9.62
$25,000	$2083	$958	$481	$12.02
$30,000	$2500	$1149	$577	$14.42
$35,000	$2917	$1341	$673	$16.83
$40,000	$3333	$1533	$769	$19.23
$45,000	$3750	$1724	$865	$21.63
$50,000	$4167	$1916	$962	$24.04

All figures are before taxes and deductions and assumes working 40 hours per week at 52 weeks per year, or 2080 hours per year. Calculations are rounded to the nearest dollar.

Doing your payroll math

The Compensation Table in this chapter gives an overview of a set of annual salary totals (before taxes) broken down in to 12 months, and then into 24 bi-weekly, 52 weekly pay periods, and the per hour rate. Most arts management positions will be salaried and are not eligible for overtime. Federal policy guidelines stipulate whether a position is exempt or nonexempt from receiving overtime; for example, one of the conditions includes if the employee is making not less than $455 per week (see Fair Labor Standards Act (FLSA) regulations). There are other key qualifiers about the type of work done that often makes most arts management jobs exempt from overtime payments.

Salary negotiation strategies

The recent graduate seeking employment needs to keep in mind two basic salary negotiating strategies. The first approach is to try to get the highest salary you can walking in the door. This strategy is complicated by the lack of information about the salary. When a position lists the salary is "commensurate with experience," or that it is "competitive," you are at a disadvantage. One employer may see their starting salary of $25,000 as competitive, while another sees you as some who recently graduated from college and your lack of experience translates to the same $25,000 starting salary. An employer may indicate that you will be eligible for a salary increase after a year, but the reality is that most arts organizations struggle to provide a cost of living increase to help keep your salary at the same pace as inflation.

The second option to consider is accepting a low starting salary. It is worth it if it appears the chances for advancement in the organization look good. For example, you are hired as an assistant marketing director at $25,000, which may be below what you really wanted. When you are hired you make it known that if you prove yourself capable, you would like to be the first one considered if there are any internal promotions available in the organization. After three years of hard work, you may have proven yourself to be marketing director material, and when your current boss leaves you are promoted to the position with a $15,000 increase in your salary. Of course, many workplace complications could intervene and sidetrack you from achieving this goal. In any case, you need to reconcile what you feel you should be paid based on your sense of your worth, with what the salary market will bear in the area and, of course, the basic economic facts of life such as the cost of living in the area.

CAREER DEVELOPMENT OPTIONS

Spending time reviewing a few issues of the Theatre Communication Group's (TCG) publication titled ARTSEARCH can be a good way to develop a better sense of what the job market in arts management and administration looks like. The reality is larger organizations can afford to hire assistants or associates in many of the departments. These types of jobs provide an excellent way to get a career established. Smaller organizations are often looking for staff members who will be willing to take on two or more department areas of major functions in the organization. As we have seen in Chapters 4 and 7, arts organizations are typically understaffed, and the culture of the organizations tends to reinforce the expectation that you are not in this for the money. Long hours and low compensation are often a given.

Developing a career requires a willingness to sacrifice something in return for achieving the longer range goals you set for yourself. Therefore, the sacrifices you have to make to be successful in a career in arts management are not any different from any other field. Your success will depend on a mixture of the special skills and talents you possess, interpersonal abilities, your willingness to be adaptable and open to change, and good timing. Opportunities present themselves and your willingness to be open to the unexpected also plays a part in your career development. Your educational background, internships, and life experiences are all factors that help contribute to your potential for success.

How important is it to have a degree in arts management to get a job in the field? That depends to some extent on the hiring philosophy of the organization. First, the organization has the goal of finding someone who can quickly assimilate the requirements of a job and who can be productive as soon as possible. Typically, organizations are looking for people with some experience, usually at least three to five years or more, for positions that involve running a department or an area. Positions with titles like marketing or development director, production manager, or ticket office manager fall into this category. Although the organization looks at what school you went to and what your degree area was, employers are more interested in what your last job was and the scope of your previous duties and responsibilities. The closer the match between what you did before and what the hiring organization wants you to do now, the better the odds that you will make it to the short list. As mentioned, the hiring organization will be more likely to read your application if they are familiar with one or more of your references.

Whatever your educational background has been, making a career shift can be problematic. For example, if you were a marketing director for a large regional opera company and you now want to shift gears and do development for a low budget children's theater company, your application will probably not move to the top of the pile. Like it or not, managers are often typecast in much the same way a performer is. To get back on the top of the pile you could include a reference from a development director where you currently work. This person could speak to your work with them and your keen understanding of how marketing and development work together.

From student to employee

If you are someone who is just entering the field, your degree area takes on a little more significance. You may not have the work experience, but it is assumed that you have learned some skills in school. As we saw in Chapter 2, Arts Organizations and Arts Management, organizations give some indication about the critical management skills they believe are required to work in the arts (see Figure 2.2). However, at the same time, there is an expectation that on-the-job training is still needed.

If you have taken classes in which you produced projects that you can show prospective employers — in areas such as ticketing sales and customer relations, marketing, public relations, fundraising, event planning, budgeting, or grant writing — this will help your application surface for further consideration. The transition from student to staff member is greatly enhanced if you can demonstrate skills and accomplishments that match the needs of the position the organization is trying to fill. Ultimately, employers want to know if you can do the job and are likely to fit in with the mix of people they already have on staff. Employers often do not spend a great deal of time look-ing at your transcript or reviewing what your grades were in your classes.

Internships

One of the proven ways to make the transition from student to staffer of an arts organization is through an internship. If everything works properly, the arrangement is mutually beneficial. You gain valuable experience and expand the scope of your skills and abilities, and the organization gains from your work effort while investing next to nothing in employee overhead.

Publications such as *ARTSEARCH* and arts job placement Web sites often con-tain special sections under the headings "Career Development" or "Internships." Some of these internships offer a small stipend, or living expenses, or in some cases housing. In high-cost metropolitan areas the housing benefit can be a lifesaver for the student on a tight budget. Regardless of the financial consid-erations, students typically look upon an internship as an investment in them-selves and as a good way to further their education.

There are some obvious considerations to make when contemplating the internship option. Beyond your personal costs (getting to the internship site, daily living expenses, the hours you will be expected to work, and insurance and personal liability), you must consider the potential for the internship to further your goal of achieving full-time employment. Unless you are indepen-dently wealthy, internships are obviously a short-term arrangement. The dura-tion can be for a few weeks in the summer to a year that coincides with the organization's program season.

Seeking and flourishing in the internship

The process of securing an internship is not unlike seeking a job. Applications, résumés, cover letters, and samples of your work may be required. Many arts organizations have formal internship programs with staff directors or coordi-nators assigned to manage the activities of a group of interns. Organizations operating at this level will more than likely have a set of expectations, duties, and a job description for the interns. Many have ongoing evaluation systems for interns. As you would expect, the better-organized internship programs are typically found in the larger arts organizations with the budgetary resources to support the program. However, this does not mean that all larger arts organizations have attained a fully functioning intern program. Unfortunately, some of the larger arts organizations have internship programs that are less than effective, and some organizations are not ready for or equipped to effectively manage interns. Word of mouth reports from other students who may have done an internship at the organization can be an invaluable resource.

The skills and abilities required of someone to effectively supervise an intern are not found universally in the workplace. Being relegated to only menial tasks such as making copies, collating mailings, or functioning as the proverbial "go-for" does occur. The reality is someone going on an internship should expect they will be doing low-level tasks. You also have to be prepared to not be accepted by all the staff with open arms. For example, in some workplace situations the student intern may be perceived as a threat to the job security of some of the staff. This kind of environment of course undercuts the whole notion that the intern is there to learn as well as assist.

Many of the potential problems or misunderstandings that can develop when doing an internship can be alleviated with a few basic written documents. When doing any internship it is usually advisable to draw up an agreement with the organization about the basic work conditions and expectations. Having some written goals and objectives for your internship can be very useful and can offer you some protection if the arrangement becomes problematic. Even if it is only a bullet list of goals, it is better than nothing. Of course, the ideal circumstance would be to have an internship that allows the student to experience a range of opportunities working for the arts organization while aiding it in fulfilling its mission.

ORGANIZING YOUR JOB SEARCH

There is no shortage of how-to books when it comes to job seeking, and writing résumés and cover letters. A quick trip to a local bookstore will give you a good idea of just how much is available out there. Web sites have also created more chances to seek out employment opportunities than anyone could have imagined. However, as you will see, your search for a job in the arts management sector narrows your field very quickly. *ARTSEARCH*, the *Chronicle of Philanthropy*, www.artsearch.us, www.artsopportunities.org, and other specialized not-for-profit Web sites and publications are a good place to start. Getting an e-mail list of job openings and making use of your alumni connections through your university can also be of assistance. If there is a particular organization that you are interested in working for, a phone call to whomever handles the hiring is in order. Asking if they are willing to accept your résumé for future reference is a good place to start.

Doing job research about the organization you are interested in applying to has been made easier as arts organization Web sites have begun to post a great deal of information about who they are and what they do. This research can help you further focus on important issues you can address should you be considered for the job.

Analyzing what an organization seems to be seeking through its job postings, and then assessing your match to its needs is an essential first step. I have received a phenomenal number of cover letters and résumés from applicants that prompted me to wonder if they had even read the job advertisement. Tailoring your application to highlight the areas in your résumé and experience that match the employer's needs can often get you called for an interview.

Skills-based résumé

Skills-Based Résumé Structure

The skills-based résumé is created based on the premise that an employer is seeking someone with the capabilities to supervise a functional area and accomplish a set of tasks in support of the organization. If you have a limited work history, the skills-based résumé allows you to focus on what you can do, not how long you worked for your previous employer. A skills-based résumé also helps to minimize the fact that you just graduated, if that is the case. Another assumption in this résumé format is that you would adjust your skills to match the priority or expectations noted in the employment advertisement or job posting. (A chronological résumé mixed with a skills format may be appropriate for someone with more experience in the workplace.)

The following outline is intended to serve as a starting place. The résumé in Figure 14.1 is a simple example of a skills-based résumé.

Skills-based résumé

Title: Arts Manager or Arts Administrator or Production Manager (or whatever title fits what you are)

Contact Information:
Name
Current address
City, State, Zip plus 4
Phone, fax, mobile, and E-mail, and Web site contact information

Objective: (Optional) This can be useful in cases where you can offer some overview of what you are seeking

Major Functional Area 1: (e.g., Marketing and PR, Fundraising, Production Management, Event Planning, etc.)

- Bullet list of your accomplishments using the skills and action verbs (accomplished, achieved, attained, arranged, built, chaired, composed, coordinated, created, devised, demonstrated, etc. For more action verbs go to www.writeexpress.com/action-verbs.html.)

Hopefully Employed

1234 Happy Place Trail, Apt 11c
Anywhere, NY 54321-1234
(212) 555-1212 ** hopeful@urcool.job

Arts Manager

Professional Skills

- Leadership and personnel management
- Project management
- Fundraising
- Marketing and public relations
- Contracts and nonprofit legal issues
- Corporate financial management
- Economic forecasting tools
- Arts event production management
- Website design and development
- Production management

Experience

Business Management & Computer Support

- Create and maintain vendor and invoice database for accounts payable department
- Assist with integration of accounting and reporting software
- Network and email support with Novell and Microsoft systems
- Create and file Articles of Incorporation for nonprofit corporations
- Positions Held
  - Administrative Assistant, No Such Associates, Inc.
  - Research and Computer Support Assistant, Medium Size Arts Org, Inc.

Marketing & Promotion

- Design and graphic layout of Arts Newsletter
- Design and layout newspaper ads for arts series
- Design television ad campaign for PSA on local PBS station
- Compile and update media lists and database
- Positions Held
  - Intern, Really Cool Theatre Company
  - Production Assistant, Vet of Cool Opera Company

Computer Skills

* Ticketing Systems (TicketAgent®, SeatAdvisor™), * Database (Access, FileMaker Pro), * Project Management (MS project), * HTML (Dreamwaver CS3)

Education

- MA, Arts Administration, Pretty Big University
- BS, Business Administration and Communications, Smaller University

Figure 14.1
Skills-based résumé.

Major Functional Area 2, 3, or more:
- Bullet list of accomplishments with action verbs

Special Skills:

Awards:

Education: List schools, degree, major areas. (You are not required to list graduation dates if you do not want to. Employers may remove you from their short list despite your skills if they see you just graduated from college.)

References: List names, phone numbers, and e-mail addresses. (If you say "Furnished Upon Request," you are adding a barrier between you and the potential employer. If someone is interested in your résumé, make it easier, not harder, to consider your application.)

Developing your résumé

Résumés have undergone a significant transformation in the last 25 years as the personal computer has been enlisted to create interesting layouts. The simple chronological résumés that lists jobs or internships you have held has been supplanted by a more skills-based document. As we saw in Chapter 11, Marketing and the Arts, part of effective target marketing for an arts organization consists of trying to reach the right people with the right message. The same holds true in the job search. The more targeted the cover letter and résumé is to the employer and the organization, the better the chance you will attract their attention and interest.

See the previous section Skills-Based Résumé Structure and the sample résumé shown in Figure 14.1 for a place to start when developing your job hunt. Recognizing that your skill sets are transferable to different types of arts organizations is important if you wish to sustain a life in the field of arts management. In fact, it is critical to present your range of skills in such a way that you do not cause potential employers to exclude you from an applicant pool. Like it or not, employers generally make very quick initial judgments about your suitability for the position. If they have to work to see whether what you have listed in your résumé applies to their position, they are much less likely to seek you out.

The simplest adjustment in your résumé can make all the difference. If you are applying for a marketing job, for example, and your current résumé lists development and marketing experience in that order, simply switching the order of these items can make your résumé more effective. Such adjustments are quite easy now with word-processing programs. The advice to heed on this issue is "A résumé without a focus is never as effective as one that relates to a specific job description."[1]

Sample Cover Letter

First Paragraph: Express your interest in the job and where you heard about it.

Second Paragraph: Here is your opportunity to sell yourself. Help the employer find the key points in your résumé that support the position offered and the qualifications sought.

Third Paragraph: Remind the employer that you have many skills by providing a little more background information on yourself.

Fourth Paragraph: Establish that you are ready to take action and that you have even more good skills to show them. Also make it clear that you will respond to a phone call or an e-mail query if they need more information.

Fifth Paragraph: Close with a thank you and express your interest in the job.

Date

Ms. Good Job
First Arts Organization
1234 Nice Street
Good Place, Somewhere Zip code

Dear Ms. Job:

I am interested in the marketing assistant position at the First Choice Arts Organization recently advertised online at Cool Arts Jobs. I have enclosed my résumé and references. Please feel free to contact my references at your convenience.

As you will see in my résumé, I have recently worked on the marketing campaign for the summer arts in the park program. We were able to increase the summer arts sales by 20 percent this year. I believe I can contribute to the marketing efforts of the First Arts Organization through my writing and my extensive graphic design skills. I understand you are also seeking someone to develop a budget system for your marketing office. While I was in graduate school I assisted on revamping our departmental budget system. Please see the attached budget worksheet I designed.

My degree program stressed the importance of fundraising and special event planning in the arts. I feel I am very skilled in these areas. I assisted on several big events held at the summer festival.

I would appreciate the opportunity to meet with you to review my portfolio of recent arts administration projects. Please feel free to call me or send me an e-mail if you need any more information about my previous experience.

Thank you for your time and consideration. I look forward to hearing from you.

Sincerely,

Hopefully Employed

Enclosure: Résumé and budget worksheet

Developing your cover letter

Your cover letter should be an enhancement to your résumé and needs to be directly related to the particular job you are seeking.[2] Sending an employer a generic cover letter of three sentences addressed to "Dear Sir or Madam" is very ineffective as a personal marketing tool. The effective cover letter, which is typically one page for most entry-level and middle-management jobs (longer for more middle- and senior-management positions), should be targeted to the job and should enhance the information in your résumé. It is also a way to begin a conversation with your potential employer.

Assume that you are applying for a grant-writing job and have adjusted your résumé so that your skill sets in grant writing are now at the top of the page. Your cover letter should then take one or more of your grant-writing skills and provide an additional level of detail for the employer. For example, if you indicate that you have successfully written grants for touring performance programs, use the cover letter to let the reader know how successful the program was ("We toured 30 schools during the year and performed for 10,000 students in the district.").

It is equally important to identify the facts of your experience and how your experience relates to this job. (See Sample Cover Letter.) Remember, the employer is typically seeking someone who can do the things they need to have done. It may be wonderful that you were able to secure a grant for a summer workshop in visual arts, but if I already have a successful program in that area, I may not be as interested in you. On the other hand, if you say you were able to add to the curatorial staff of the museum due to your grant and that is what my organization is trying to do, you are much more interesting to me as an employee.

Portfolios and other ways to demonstrate your skills

Let's assume you have been able to attract the employer's interest based on your résumé and cover letter. Now what? You can further help your application for a job if you have examples of your best work. Creating a CD-ROM and a Web site is becoming more common as part of your employment toolkit. Too much information can work against you, but striking the right balance of information by creating a sample of your work electronically could be critical for getting noticed in a crowded field of applicants. If you send samples with your application materials, be sure to keep them to a minimum and highly representative of your skills. If the employer wants more information, you can follow up with details. For example, including the executive summary of a grant application, the summary points of a marketing or fundraising plan, or samples of other graphics or writing projects can serve to move you ahead of the other applicants. The goal, as stated, is to establish the best match between you and the organization.

Interviewing

Seeking out resources about interview techniques also is worth the effort. If you advance from the application stage to the interview, you want to be as effective as possible. Taking the time to read a book such as *Winning Job Interviews*[3] by Paul Powers or to research interview tips on a Web site such as Monster.com can pay off. Chapter 7, Human Resources and the Arts, pointed out the differing styles found in the interview process.

Some organizations are going to have prepared questions they ask all the applicants in a formal setting. Other organizations may have one person conduct the interview, then let others meet you informally for the rest of the process. Since there are no hard and fast rules about how an organization will approach this process, it is incumbent upon you to research the organization and gain as much information as you can about the process the organization plans to use in making its hire.

A follow-up interview may take place if the search is local or regional. Should this be the case, you might have the salary and benefits discussion mentioned earlier in this chapter. Being prepared with the right questions and listening for the details of an offer will save you a great deal of time later. Many people new to the job market do not find out the details of benefits, vacation time, and policies about sick leave and travel until after they are hired. Asking about benefits, for example, may reveal potential problems with taking the job. The organization may not offer health insurance until you have worked there for six months.

Getting hired

Should you be fortunate enough to be hired, the process of making the transition to a new organization, coworkers and supervisors, and adapting to the culture of the organization goes on for some time. Depending on the job, it often takes one full business cycle (or a year) with the organization to become familiar with all of the challenges facing you in the job. As a new employee, you often have a grace period in which to operate with minimal judgments made about you by the people you work with and report to. However, after as little as a week on the job people are forming perceptions about you and your work. It is the nature of the workplace and the acculturation process that you will be judged as a success based on what may seem like rather superficial criteria.

Managing your job and career success remains your responsibility, and the amount of guidance and support you receive will vary with the type of organization. Finding a mentor in the organization can be of great assistance in the early stages of a new job. However, this may not happen, and you will be on your own a great deal. Unlike your teachers and advisors when you were a student, people in the workplace are not necessarily as concerned about how you are doing. That is not to say that the workplace you encounter will be a hostile environment. However, the assumption most people make about you is that you are doing your job unless they hear otherwise. If you are to succeed in your job, your social skills will be as important as your job skills in some circumstances.

BUILDING A CAREER

In the early stages of your career you will discover that ideas you had about what you wanted to do and where you wanted to work will go through several transitions. Most people find new opportunities and experiences in the workplace that lead to new directions or even new jobs. The excitement of learning new skills and successfully meeting important deadlines or completing big projects will create a rewarding cycle of personal development. The normal frustrations of the workplace will be put aside when you see the positive results of your work or the work of a team you led.

Your success will also no doubt lead to you being asked to do more for the organization. Then you will face your first critical career development hurdle. Taking on too many projects or too much work — which is very easy to do in the arts organizations that are strapped for human resources – can undermine your effectiveness and lower the estimates of your capabilities in the eyes of management. The ability to keep enough objective distance between your long-term career goals and the day-to-day challenges of work will become increasingly difficult as you find yourself taking on more responsibility in your job.

How do you stay focused on building a rewarding career for yourself in the arts? Most long-term success lies in applying the same skills you use to be successful in your job to your own personal career plans. As noted, you need to be set goals, develop objectives, implement action plans, and then evaluate the results and adjust for changing circumstances. Taking some time to analyze your own situation and formulate action plans can really pay off when an unexpected opportunity or a crisis arises. As you will soon find out, the career path you take usually does not follow a straight line. For example, internal promotions or lateral moves to other arts organizations in your community may provide you with unexpected opportunities to advance your career. You may also find yourself unemployed when an organization runs into trouble, or worse yet, you may be fired from your job. Being prepared for the worst is very much like having contingency plans in place for an organization, as discussed in Chapter 5, Planning and Decision Making. Recognizing that not all work-related outcomes will be positive, and having a plan in place should an event such as losing your job occur, can actually provide a degree of security.

As you will no doubt discover, many people in the workplace are driven by real or imagined fears that inhibit them from thinking clearly about the situation they may be in and the choices they have. An effective manager realizes, as we discussed in Chapter 8, Leadership and Group Dynamics, that many of the problems and crises one faces in the workplace are part of the context of the work and the working relationships among the staff. Applying situational leadership and management techniques to your own career development can be a very good way to advance yourself to whatever level in the organization you choose.

Career goal

As I noted in the Preface, one of my goals in writing this book was to help develop arts managers who support and collaborate with artists to help fulfill the mission of the organization. Establishing yourself as a leader and manager in the arts will take no less work than it does to become a recognized performer, writer, designer, or scholar in the arts. The discipline and drive needed to excel in the arts are just as important for the staff in the office as they are for the chorus of the opera or the violin section of the orchestra.

Think about your job as an arts manager in the same way you think about what the conductor of an orchestra does. As you work with the staff of an arts organization, try to achieve the exquisite harmony and unity of purpose of a beautifully sounding symphony orchestra. For example, it makes sense to have the customer service aspects of your ticket office working in cooperation with your marketing, public relations, and fundraising functions. You need to have each of these sections of the organization "in tune" with each other. If you agree with this analogy, you can see the necessity for investing a lot of time and energy in your career path. It takes a great deal of hard work to achieve the kind of excellence people have come to expect from the arts and artists in their community. Good luck and best wishes in your choice to make a life in the arts.

CAREER DEVELOPMENT WORK PLAN

1. Create a bullet list of your major employment and career goals for the next two to five years. Indicate the type of organization you would like to work for, the type of job title you are seeking, and any other key factors that describe your employment objectives.

2. Write a draft of a skills-based résumé. Focus on the items noted in the reading and develop your list of action verbs to describe what skills and abilities you possess. Do not become too eager to do the graphic layout for the entire résumé. First work on key phrases to describe what makes you a potential outstanding employee. Write up a skills and abilities inventory. Try to develop a priority ranking of your strengths.

3. Next, using a recent issues of *ARTSEARCH*, a similar publication, or an online resource, analyze the types of job titles, qualifications, duties, and salary information found in the job listings. Look for information in the posting about the size of the organization, its overall operating budget, and the number of staff or season of events performed. Explore the organization's Web site for the facts that may be missing in the job posting. Are there phrases used in the ads such as "an ideal candidate" or "successful candidate"? Develop your own bullet list of key duties in the "responsible for," "oversees," or "experienced in" sections of the ads.

4. Begin putting together several versions of your skills-based résumé that demonstrate how you are that "ideal candidate." Refine and focus the content of the résumé to the major types of positions that interest you. Develop a layout template for the résumé that provides for maximum readability (e.g., leave some white space) with basic graphic design elements (shading, bold type, boxes, frames, or other interesting graphic tools) to create an interesting looking résumé. Proofread your résumé for any errors or typos by reading out loud and be sure to have others proofread it as well.

5. Draft a cover letter of the jobs that interest you the most. Tailor the cover letter to the job ad and provide additional details about the scope and scale of the projects you successfully completed to add to the depth of your application. Again, read it out loud to check for flow and clarity. Have someone else proofread the letter for you.

6. If you are contacted, follow up with the employers immediately. Review sources such as *Winning Job Interviews* by Paul Powers in preparation for a potential phone interview. Often the first approach of interest will come in the form of a telephone interview. If the employer likes what she hears on the phone, it may lead to a face-to-face

interview. Should the employer wish to set up a personal interview, you need to do your research on the organization and brush up on your interview answers to the typical questions employers pose.

For additional topics relating to career options in the arts, please go to www.managementandthearts.com.

REFERENCES

1. Pat Criscito, *Designing the Perfect Résumé*, 3rd edition (Hauppauge, NY: Barron's Educational Series, 2006), p.5.
2. H. Richard, Beatty, *The Perfect Cover Letter*, 3rd edition (New York: John Wiley & Sons, 2004).
3. A. Paul Powers, *Winning Job Interviews* (Franklin Lake, NJ: Career Press, 2005).

Index

Page numbers followed by "f" denote figures.

501 (c) (3) tax exemption, 36–37

A

ABC (antecedent, behavior, consequence) theory, 242
acceptance theory, 69, 70, 228
Access to Artistic Excellence grants, 47
accounting, 328f, 329–332
accounting formula, 331–333
accrual-based accounting, 329
acquired-needs theory, 239
action plans, 138, 139f, 140f
Actors' Equity Association (AEA), 200, 209, 210, 212
Adams, J. Stacy, 230f, 239, 240
adaptations, competitive, 84–86
administrative assistant, 176–177
administrative management (1916 to present), 67–69
administrators, 11
advertising, 317
Age Discrimination Act (1967/1973), 196
agency organizations, 171
aggressiveness, 249
Alderfer, Clayton, 230f, 237, 238
Alliance for NonProfit Management, 133
alternatives and decision theory, 148
American Federation of Musicians (AFM), 209
American Federation of Television and Radio Artists (AFTRA), 210
American Guild of Musical Artists (AGMA), 210
American Guild of Variety Artists (AGVA), 210
American Marketing Association, 348, 358

Americans for the Arts, 95
    Arts & Economic Prosperity III report, 92–93, 303–304, 312
    corporate/business sponsorship, 414, 415
    Web site, 91, 93, 98–99, 303
Americans with Disabilities Act (1990), 196
analytical manager, 423–425
ancient civilizations and arts, 25–26, 62
annual campaigns, 395, 396
applications, for employment, 194, 200–202
apprenticeships, 204
archon eponymous (principal magistrate), 25
art (ability/skill), 60
artifacts, corporate culture, 181
artist-managers, 23–24
arts
    acquired taste for, 349–350
    content sources, 90–91
    economic problems/issues, 302–303
    future of, 5–6, 113–115
    growth of arts/entertainment, 2–5, 105, 303–304
    historical overview, 25–32
    organizing for, 157
    research regarding, 361
    trend shifts in, 305
Arts & Economic Prosperity III report, 92–93, 303–304, 312
Arts Advocacy Day, 99
arts councils, 52, 96–97, 409
arts institutions, 24
arts management. *See* history of arts management; management
arts managers. *See* managers

arts organizations. *See also* organizations
    administrative structure (example), 160f
    bylaws, 36
    common elements in, 11–12
    customer-oriented, 355–356
    division of labor, 11
    education, 37
    environments affecting, 7, 8f, 13f, 158f
    evaluating, 20
    formal/informal structure, 11
    formation of, 34
    for-profit businesses, 35
    growth and change, 87
        opera company (example), 88–89
    hierarchy of authority, 11, 176
    incorporation, 34–35
    information sources, 109–110
    as institutions, 12–15
    legal status and financial statements, 34
    managing change, 86–87
    marketing ethics of, 362–363
    mission/vision/value statements, 13–15, 122
        Seacoast Repertory Theatre (case study), 151–152
    not-for-profit businesses, 35–36
    open systems, 8f, 75, 158f
    outline of bylaws (example), 37–38
    process of organizing, 7–8
    selecting, for class project, 20
    tax exemptions, 36–37
ARTSEARCH, 43, 450, 452, 453, 462
assets, 330, 331, 332–333
Association of Arts Administration Educators (AAAE), 41f, 42, 444

Association of Fundraising
    Professionals (AFP), 382,
    385–386, 401
Association of Performing Arts
    Presenters, 359
audiences, 305–306, 347–348,
    372–373
auditions, 199–200
audits
    fundraising, 386–389
    marketing, 365
    organizational, 423
authority
    acceptance theory of, 69, 70, 228
    coordination of, 176–180
    functional, 179
    hierarchy of, 11, 176
average total cost (ATC), 315

B

Babbage, Charles, 64, 65f
baby boomers, 104–105
balance sheet, 332, 333f, 334–335
Barnard, Chester, 65f, 69
behavior modification, organizational,
    242–243
behavioral approach to management,
    70–71, 231
behavioral decision theory, 148
benefits, employee, 194, 448
bequests, 398
blocking, 249
Board of Directors
    description of, 208–209
    financial problem areas, 337
    fundraising by, 392–393, 400–401
    investment policy, 338
    members as information sources,
        110–111
    in the news, 209
    organizational charts, 163f, 164f,
        165f
    responsibilities/duties, 207–208
    staff interactions with, 251
    working with, 18–19, 251–254, 434
booking agents, 29
bookkeeping, 329
bottom-up planning, 141–142
brands, 358–359
broadcast media, 99–100, 111–112
budgets, 284
    balancing, 337
    budgeting process, 285f, 288
    cash flow projections, 294–296, 295f

centers for, 284–286
compensation amounts and, 447
control system, 288–289
in detail, 289–294
detailed budgets, 292f
opportunity, 287
as preliminary controls, 286
reality, 288
as standing-use plans, 127
summary, 296–297
as top secret documents, 286
types of
    capital, 287
    fixed, 286–287
    flexible, 287
    operating, 287
    project, 287, 291, 293f
    summary, 289, 290f
    zero-based, 287
bureaucracy, 159–161
business manager, 325
business plans, 32–33, 141
bylaws, 36–38

C

capital budgets, 287
capital campaign, 383, 389, 390f
careers. *See also* jobs
    building, 460–461
    development options, 450–453
    goal for, 461
    management, 215
    planning, 462
carrot/stick motivation, 63
case for support, 391
case studies
    Arkansas Symphony Orchestra,
        297–298
    Rhode Island Philharmonic, 260–261
    Seacoast Repertory Theatre, 151–152
    Studio Arena Theatre, 439–441
    Utah Symphony & Opera, 183–185
    vying for corporate support, 414–417
cash flow projections, 294–296, 295f
cash-based accounting, 329
Catholic Church, 25, 26, 62
CDs, 338
censorship, 49, 111–112
    in Renaissance, 28
Census data, 39, 103–104, 112, 321
centralization-decentralization,
    178–179
chain of command, 176–177
Chamber of Commerce, 112, 321

changes
    environment, 86
    growth and, 87–89
    managing, 86–87
charitynavigator.org, 20
Chief Financial Officer (CFO), 325
choices and decision making, 146–148
choregoi (sponsors), 25
Civil Rights Act of 1991, 196
Claritas Corporation, 360
coaching, 203–204
coercive power, 226
cognitive-based motivation theories
    description of, 237
    equity theory, 239–240
    expectancy theory, 240–242
cohesiveness of group, 248
Colorado Council on the Arts, 52
combination strategy, 137
command groups, 246
committees, 247–248
communication, 255
    of data and information, 277–278
    formal/informal, 257
    in informal systems, 170
    lines of, in organization, 169, 429
    marketing, 347
    perception of, 256
    process of, 255–256
    Studio Arena Theatre case study,
        439–441
compensation. *See* salaries
competing, 250
competitive adaptations, 84–86
competitive marketplace, 369, 369–370
complementary good, 316
computer use
    CAD/CAM/CIM, 74
    fundraising data management,
        393–395
    future of, 283
    marketing, 353–354
    marketing data systems, 370–371
    MIS, 276f, 278–279
    paper trail and bookkeeping, 331
    software packages, 280–281,
        283–284, 331, 394–395
consortiums, 110
consultants, 112, 368–369
consumer spending statistics, 4
content analysis, 89–91
contingency leadership, 231–233
contingency planning, 142
contingency system, 430

contingency theory, 74–75
continual evaluation process, 88
contracts
    Actor's Equity Association (example), 210–211
    for designers, 212–213
    for volunteers, 206
control, 265–266, 275. *See also* operational control
coordination, 176–179
    horizontal, 176, 179
    vertical, 176–177
corporate culture, 12, 180–182
corporate giving, 405–407
    case study, 414–417
    potential problems, 407
    process of, 407
cost of living, 448
costs
    average total, 315
    direct mail analysis, 404
    direct/indirect, for fundraising, 395–396
    fixed, variable, and marginal, 312–314
cover letter, 457
Creative Class, 101–103
credits, 332
crisis planning, 142, 432
critical incident appraisal, 274
critical path method (CPM), 73–74
cultural and social environment, 99–103
cultural boom, 304–305
culture wars, 101
customer orientation for marketing, 355–356

D
dance, history of, 27–31
deadlines, 232, 269, 271
debits, 332
decentralization-centralization, 178–179
decision making and planning, 144–148
decision support system, 281, 282f
decision theory, 148–149
decodes messages, 256
deferred gift, 398
delegation, 177–178
demand. *See also* supply
    for arts, 317
    consumer tastes effect on, 317
    determinants, 316
    elasticity, 319
    expectations effect on, 316–317
    income effects, 316, 323

inferior goods or services, 316
    law of, 315–316
    price of other goods effect on, 316
    revenue maximization, 320–322
    scaling the house, 322–323
demographics, 41–42, 103–105
demographics profile, 359
departmentalization, 173–176
departments/work groups, 164–168
determinants
    demand, 316
    supply, 318
development functions of management, 18–19
differentiation strategy, 369
"digital age", 77
"digital divide", 5
diminishing returns, law of, 313
direct mail marketing/fundraising, 403–404
diseconomies of scale, 315
disposable personal income (DPI), 305
disputes, union, 211–212
disrupting meetings, 249–250
distributed leadership, 254
diversity in workplace, 199
division of labor, 11
division of work, 162
divisional structures, 173
domini (Roman managers), 25
donors, fundraising, 392–393
    cultivation/solicitation methods, 399f, 400–405
    Donor Bill of Rights, 381–382
    funding options for, 398–400
    individuals, 397–398
    motivation for giving, 380–381
    ratings matrix, 400f
    research of, 389
    restricted/unrestricted gifts, 397
    tracking systems, 394–395
dysfunctional group activities, 248–249
dysfunctional manager, 420
dysfunctional organization, 420–422

E
economics
    Arts & Economic Prosperity III report, 92–93, 303–304, 312
    basic principles, 312, 323–324
    environment and arts, 92–94, 308–309
    future of arts, concerns about, 5–6
    market failure and arts, 309–310

multiplier effect, 311–312
    perspective on cultural boom, 304–305
    problems/issues facing arts, 302–303
    productivity issues, 306–308
    questions regarding, 302
    spending more than revenues, 310–311
economies of scale, 315
education
    arts organizations, 37
    career development, 451–452
    educational environment, 106–108
Education Act of 1870, 28
effective managers, 61–62
effort-performance expectancy, 240–241
eighteenth century arts, 28–29
elasticity, 319–322
emerging views of management, 75–76
employees. *See* staff
employer's perspective, 446
    career development, 450–451
    geographical considerations, 444
employment. *See* jobs
Employment Retirement Income Security Act (1974), 196
ENCATC (European Network of Cultural Administration Training Centres), 42
encodes messages, 256
entertainment industry, 2–6
environments, 84, 91–92
    changing, 86
    cultural and social, 99–103
    demographic, 103–105
    economic, 92–94, 308–309
    educational, 106–108
    MIS uncontrollable factors, 279
    multiple, and arts organizations, 85f
    open systems, 86
    organizational structure, 172
    organizations, 7, 8f, 13f, 158f
    political and legal, 94–99
    summary, 115–116
    technological, 105–106
Equal Employment Opportunity Act (1972), 196
Equal Employment Opportunity Commission (EEOC), 195
Equal Pay Act (1963), 196
equity theory of motivation, 239–240
ERG (existence, relatedness, and growth) theory, 237
espoused values, corporate culture, 181

ethics
  fundraising, 401
  marketing, 362–363
evaluating arts organizations, 20
evaluation systems, 138, 140f
exceptions, management by, 271–273
exchange process and utilities, 350–352
expectancy theory of motivation, 240–242
expectations, supply/demand, 316–317, 319
expenses, 329
expenses centers, 286
expert power, 227
external controls, 272
extrinsic rewards, 241

F

Facebook, 347, 358, 361, 362
factors of production, 318
Family and Medical Leave Act (1993), 196
FASB (Financial Accounting Standards Board), 329
Fayol, Henri, 65f, 67–68
featherbedding, 212
Federal Register, 410–411
feedback
  communications, 256f
  open systems, 8f, 158f
  on work performance, 274–275
fellowships, NEA, 47
financial management
  business manager's role, 325
  challenges, in Renaissance, 28
  economic dilemma, 339
  investments, 338
  nonprofit, 325
  operational controls, 275
  overview, 324
  problem areas, 337
  reserve funds, 340
  summary of, 338–339
financial management information systems. *See* FMIS
financial plans, 33
financial reports, 341–342
financial statements, 333–334
  balance sheet, 332, 333f, 334–335
  legal status, 34, 38
  profit vs. loss, 314f
  ratio analysis, 336–337
  statement of activity, 334f, 335–336
  Web sources, 342

firing of staff, 204–205
fiscal management, 18–19, 436–437
fiscal year (FY), 289
fixed budget, 286–287
flexible budgets, 287
flexible production technology, 76
FMIS (financial management information system). *See also* MIS
  for corporations, 38
  description of, 325, 326
  development of, 326
  diagram of, 327f
  summary, 338–339
focus groups, 361
Follett, Mary Parker, 65f, 70–71
Ford Foundation, 30, 53, 87
Form 990.. *See* IRS Form 990
form utility, 350
formal communication, 257
formal groups, 245
formal leadership, 223
formal structure of organizations, 11
for-profit arts organizations, 2, 5, 35
foundations, 407–409
four Ps of marketing, 356–357
Fourteen Principles of Management (Fayol), 67–68
  arts application, 69–70
frontline managers, 10
frustration-regression principle, 237
full benefits, 194
functional authority, 179
functional management, 171, 173
functional managers, 10
functional satisfaction, 349
functional structures, 173
fund reserves, 340
fund-based accounting, 330
funding arts, 31–32. *See also* National Endowment for the Art
fundraising
  annual campaign, 395, 396
  arts and, 382–383
  bequest, 398
  Board of Directors participation in, 392–393, 400–401
  capital campaign, 383, 389, 390f
  case for support, 391
  case study of, 414–417
  Comprehensive Campaign, 396–405
  computer use, 393–395
  confidentiality issues, 395
  corporate giving, 405–407

costs and control, 395–396
credibility, 236
data management system, 393–395
deferred gift, 398
direct mail, 403–404
direct/indirect costs, 396
donors. *See* donors, fundraising
e-fundraising, 404–405
ethics, 385–386, 401
foundation sources, 407–409
funding table, 389, 390f
goals for, 388–389, 434
governmental, 409–411
history/trends for giving, 380
loss (In the News), 405
management of, 391
marketing relationship to, 389–391
motivation for giving, 380–381
National Endowment for the Arts, 409–410
organization's role in, 391–392
planning and process, 387f
plans, 140f, 383–385
profile, self-assessment and organizational audit, 386–389
restricted/unrestricted gifts, 397
social exchange model, 381
sources, statistics, 380, 383, 397, 405–406
special events, 405
staff participation in, 384–385, 392–393, 400–401
strategic planning, 386
summary, 411–412
techniques and tools for, 396
telephone solicitations, 402–403
funds
  expending of, 289
  reserve, 340
future of arts, 5–6, 113–115, 117–118

G

Gantt, Henry L., 65f, 67
general managers, 10–11
Generally Accepted Accounting Principles (GAAP), 329
Gilbreth, Frank, 65f, 67
Gilbreth, Lillian, 65f, 67
goals, 124
  in business plans, 32–33
  career, 461
  fundraising, 388–389, 434
  NEA, 46
  planning/plans, 138, 139f, 140f

Seacoast Repertory Theatre (case study), 151–152
government. *See also* National Endowment for the Arts
  funding for arts, 24, 45, 383, 409–411
  as information source, 112
  political and legal environment, 94–99
  regulations on staffing, 195–196
  relations with, 18–19, 437
  visa processing rules, 95
grants, 47, 407–409
Greek civilization and arts, 25
groups/group dynamics, 245–251
  adjourning stage, 248
  cohesiveness, 248
  command groups, 246
  committees, 247–248
  development stages of, 247–248
  disrupting meetings, 249–250
  dysfunctional activities, 248–249
  effectiveness strategies for, 249–251
  formal groups, 245
  forming stage, 247
  informal groups, 246
  interest groups, 246
  leading/managing, 230f
  norming stage of, 247
  norms, 248
  performing stage of, 247
  storming stage, 247
  summary, 258–259
  task groups, 246
  temporary groups, 245
  types of groups, 246–247
groupthink, 248–249
growth
  of arts/entertainment, 2–5, 105, 303–304
  managing, 87–89, 179–180
  strategy for, 137, 369–370
guidestar.org, 20

H
Halo effect, 77–78, 257
hasty decisions, 147–148
Hawthorne effect, 71–72
Hawthorne Wire Works, 71
Hersey, Paul, 230f, 232
Herzberg, Frederick, 230f, 238
hierarchy of authority, 11
hierarchy of needs (Maslow), 71–73, 237–238

hiring employees, 202, 459–460
history of arts management
  ancient civilizations, 25–26, 62
  evolution of management thought, 62–66
  evolution of marketing, 352–353
  human relations management (1927 to present), 70–73
  Industrial Revolution, 63
  international perspective, 31–32
  management timeline, 65f
  management trends to present, 66–70
  Middle Ages, 26–27
  modern management, 73–78
  pioneers, 63–64
  preindustrialization, 62
  Reformation, 62
  Renaissance, 27–28, 62–63
  seventeenth to nineteenth centuries, 28–29
  summary, 52–53, 79–80
  twentieth century, 29–31
  twenty-first century, 31
horizontal coordination, 176
horsing around, 250
House, Robert J., 230f, 233
human relations management (1927 to present), 70–73
  arts applications, 72–73
  behavioral approach, 70–71
  Hawthorne effect, 71, 72
  integrative unity, 70–71
  Maslow's hierarchy of needs, 71–72, 73, 237–238
  McGregor's Theory X and Theory Y, 72–73, 225
human relations model, 429
human resources management
  constraints on staffing
    costs, 195
    government regulations, 195–196
    organized labor, 197
  diversity in workplace, 199
  employee manual (sample), 218
  firing of staff, 204–205
  functions of management, 18–19, 435
  job analysis, 189–191
  job context, 190
  job description and posting, 191–194
  maintaining/developing staff, 214–215

orientation/training, 202–204
overall matrix of jobs, 194–195
performance appraisals, 205
  critical incident appraisal, 274
  and firing, 205
  free-form narrative, 274
  personnel appraisal methods, 274
  systems for, 273–274
  timely feedback, 274–275
planning, 188
recruitment of staff, 197–199
selection process, 199–202
  auditions, 199–200
  formal applications, 194, 200–201
  interviewing, 201
  screening, 201
  testing, reference checking, and hiring, 202
staffing process, 188–189
standards, 190–191
summary, 216
unions, 209–214
volunteers, 206–207
work activities, 190
work tools, 190

I
Immigration Reform and Control Act of 1986, 196
In the News
  Arts & Economic Prosperity III report, 303–304
  audience surveys, 354
  Form 990 changes, 96–97
  fundraising loss, 405
  intermission promotion, 351
  vote to unionize, 209
income
  disposable personal income, 305
  effect on demand, 316, 323
  statements, 332
incorporation, 34–35
individualized entertainment, 6
Industrial Revolution, 63
inelastic ticket prices, 320
inferior goods or services, 316
inflation, 306
informal communication, 257
informal groups, 246
informal leadership, 223
informal organizational structure, 11, 169–170

information sources, 108–113
 audiences, 108–109
 board/staff members, 110–111
 consultants, 112, 368–369
 government/business, 112–113
 media, 111–112
 other arts groups, 109–110
 professional associations, 112
input, open systems, 8f, 158f
input standards for control, 270–271
institutions. *See* arts institutions
integrative unity, 70–71
interest groups, 246
intermediate-range plans, 125, 432
intermezzi, 27
internal controls, 272
international activities of NEA, 46–47
International Alliance of Theatrical
  Stage Employees (IATSE), 210
international perspective on arts, 31–32
Internet, as information source, 111. *See
  also* Web sites
internships, 204, 452–453
interviewing for jobs, 201, 459
intrinsic rewards, 241
inventory of alternatives, 148
investments, 338
IRS Form 990
 changes in, 96–97
 financial statements, 333, 342

J

job analysis
 description of, 189–190
 job context, 190
 personnel qualifications, 191
 standards, 190–191
 step in staffing process, 189f
 work activities, 190
 work tools, 190
job description
 Sample Job Posting, 191–192
 sections of
  application method, 194
  benefits, 194
  compensation, 193–194
  general description, 193
  requirements for employment, 193
  responsibilities, 193
  specific duties, 193
 step in staffing process, 189f
job search
 cover letter, 457
 hiring after, 459–460

interviewing, 459
organizing, 453–454
portfolios, 458–459
résumé, 454–456
jobs
 for art managers, 42–43
 in arts, 4, 217, 304
 ARTSEARCH, 43, 450, 452, 453, 462
 compensation issues, 446–447
 considerations in selecting, 445
 development, 215, 450–451
 employment-at-will, 205
 evolving arts workplace, 443–444
 geographical considerations, 444
 internships, 204, 452–453
 management opportunities, 3f
 matrix of, 194–195
 opportunities in arts management,
  3f, 4–5
 personal plan for, 445–446
 present/future opportunities, 444–445
 from student to employee, 451–452
 training, 39–40, 61, 202–204

K

Kahn's law, 246
Kaizen, 76
Kotler, Philip, 348, 355
KSAs (knowledge, skills, and abilities),
  193

L

labor relations and management,
  18–19. *See also* unions
law of contingent reinforcement, 242
law of demand, 315–316
law of diminishing returns, 313
law of immediate reinforcement, 242
law of supply, 317–318
leadership, 222
 arts applications, 234
 Arts Leader Profile, 235
 case study, 260–261
 central role of leader, 222
 communication and effective,
  254–257
 creative spirit, 234–235
 distributed, 254
 formal, 223
 fundamentals of, 222–223
 future of, 236
 ineffective, 258
 informal, 223
 by management, 17

managerial success and, 223
meetings
 agenda (example), 253–254
 disruptions, 249–250
 rules of order, 252–253
 running, 252–253
 strategies for effective, 249–251
normative model of, 232
planning/plans, 123
power. *See* power
styles of, 224f
summary, 258–259
theories of, 230f
 behavioral approach, 70–71, 231
 contingency approach, 231–233
 Path-Goal Theory, 233
 situational approach, 231–233
 Theory X and Theory Y, 72–73, 225
 trait approach to, 231
 transactional, 233–234
 transformational, 233–234
leadership initiatives, NEA, 47
legal environment. *See* political and
  legal environment
legal status and financial statements, 38
legal status, financial statements, 34
legitimate power, 226
leisure trends, 114
liabilities, 331, 332–333
LLC (limited liability corporation), 35
lobbying for arts, 95
Local Governments Act of 1888, 28
long-range plans, 125, 432
losses, 314f

M

mailing lists, 358
maintenance activities, 250–251
management
 administrative (1916 to present),
  67–69
 arts application, 67, 69–70, 72–73,
  75
 as art/social science, 60–62
 behavioral approach, 70–71
 Board of Directors interactions,
  18–19, 251–254, 434
 career, 215
 challenges, in Renaissance, 28
 changes in America, 64–66
 changing philosophies, 62–63
 classical perspectives, 66–67
 committee-style, 246–247
 contingency approach, 74–75, 430

control functions, 18
definition of (functions), 16, 156
discussion article, 54–56
emerging views, 75–76
evolution of, 62–66
Fayol's Fourteen Principles, 67–70
fiscal, 18–19, 436–437. *See also* financial management
functions of, 6–7
government relations with, 18–19, 437
Halo effect, 77–78, 257
Hawthorne effect, 72
history of. *See* history of arts management
human relations (1927 to present), 70–73
integrative unity, 70–71
leading by, 17
levels of, 8–10, 168
managing change, 86–87
marketing, 356–361
middle, 8–9
models, 428f
    human relations, 429
    open system, 430
    process management, 427–429
modern approaches, 73–78
on-the-job theory of, 61
operational control, 266–267
opportunities in, 3f, 4–5, 444
organizational structure and levels of, 9f
organizing by, 17
participative, 72
personnel/staff. *See* human resources management
pioneers, 63–64
planning/development by, 16–17, 431–432
process, 15–16
production process (In Practice), 18
quantitative approaches, 73–74
scientific, 60, 64, 66, 73–74
shifting paradigms, 76–77
styles of, 419–427, 438
summary, 79–80
systems theory, 74
timeline, 65f
trends to present, 66–70
unions and, 214, 435
management by exception (MBE), 271–273
management by objectives (MBO), 273

management information systems. *See* MIS
managerial level of management, 8–9
managerization, 425
managers, 7, 156. *See also* leadership
    administrators, 11
    analytical, 423–425
    artist-managers, 23–24
    basic functions of, 18–19
    business manager, 325
    combined job titles, 10
    content analysis by, 89–90
    dysfunctional, 420
    effective, 61–62
    first-time, 422
    jobs for, 42–43
    managerial level of management, 8–9
    NEA, 50–51
    organic, 424f, 426–427
    personal mission, 44
    personality of, 422–423
    preparedness, 40f
    professional, 425
    profile of arts manager, 39–40
    salary ranges, 42, 43–44
    skills, 40–41
    standards set by, 190–191
    structure from perspective of, 170–176
    summary, 53
    systems, 424f, 425–426
    training, 39–40, 61
    types of, 10–11
    updating profiles, 40–42
    women as, 41–42
Mandatory Retirement Act, 196
marginal costs (MC), 312–314
market analysis, 33
market research, 359–361
market segments, 357–358
market share strategy, 369–370
marketing, 347–348, 433
    acquired taste for arts, 349–350
    activities, overview of, 346–347
    appealing to audiences, 347–348, 372–373
    approaches, 354–356
    audit, 365
    case study, 376
    Claritas system for, 360
    consultants, 368–369
    customer orientation, 355–356
    direct mail, 403–404
    ethics, 362–363

exchange process and utilities, 350–351
    functional satisfaction, 349
    functions of management, 18–19
    fundraising relationship to, 389–391
    initiatives (examples), 365
    management
        of brands, 358
        four Ps, 356–357
        market research, 359–361
        market segments, 357–358
    Marketer Profile, 353
    as means to an end, 348
    mix, 357
    modern techniques, 353–354
    needs and wants, 349
    new rules of, 361–362
    planning process, 364f, 365
    product orientation, 355
    production, sales, and marketing eras, 352–353
    psychological satisfaction, 349
    sales orientation, 355
    strategic plans, 352, 363–368
    strategies, 369–371, 433–434
    subscription ticket sales, 353
    summary, 373–375
    target, 357
    Web sites, 347, 361–362
marketing data system (MDS), 370–371
marketing plans, 33, 140f, 364f, 365–368
markets, 309–310
Maslow, Abraham, 65f, 71–72, 230f, 237
Maslow's hierarchy of needs, 71–73, 237–238
mass customization, 76
matrix organizations, 173–176
Mayo, Elton, 71
McCallum, Daniel Craig, 64, 65f
McClelland, David C., 230f, 239
McGregor, Douglas, 65f, 72–73
McGregor's Theory X and Theory Y, 72–73, 225
mechanistic organizational design, 158–159
media, as information source, 111–112
meetings
    agenda (example), 253–254
    disruptions, 249–250
    rules of order, 252–253
    running, 252–253
    strategies for effective, 249–251
mentor, 460

mergers (case study), 183–185
Middle Ages, 26–27
middle management, 8–9
MIS (management information
    system), 276
  in art organizations, 278, 283
  computer software packages,
    280–281, 283–284
  computer use, 278–279
  data and information, 277–278
  decision support system, 281, 282f
  effectiveness of, 279
  equipment/information flow, 276f
  factors that affect, 278–280
  finances. *See* FMIS
  fully controllable factors, 280
  for fundraising, 393–395
  future of, 283
  importance of, 276–277
  mistakes associated with, 281
  organizational design effects, 278
  partially controllable factors, 280
  summary, 281, 283
  uncontrollable factors, 279–280
miscommunication, 255
mission, 122
mission analysis, 131–133
mission statements, 133
  in business plans, 32–33
  for NEA, 46
  in planning process, 128–131
  samples, 14–15, 129–131
  Seacoast Repertory Theatre (case
    study), 151–152
Mitchell, Terence R., 230f, 233
modeling/training, 204
Motion Picture Machine Operators, 210
motivation, 236, 258–259
motivation theories
  acquired-needs theory, 239
  cognitive-based, 237, 239–242
  description of, 230f, 237
  equity theory, 239–240
  ERG Theory, 237–238
  expectancy theory, 240–242
  integration of, 244–245
  Maslow's hierarchy of needs, 71–73,
    237–238
  need-based, 237–239
  organizational behavior
    modification, 242–243
  reinforcement-based, 237, 242–243
  social learning theory, 237, 243–244
  two-factor theory, 238

mouseion (museum), 25
multiplier effect, 311–312
museums
  as businesses, 2
  early American, 29
  jobs with, 444
  mouseion and Greek culture, 25
  organizational charts, 166f, 167f
  in twentieth century, 31
music industry, 105–106
MySpace, 347, 358, 361, 362

N

National Assembly of Local Arts
    Agencies, 409
National Assembly of State Arts
    Agencies (NASAA), 51, 409
National Center for Charitable
    Statistics, 4
National Do Not Call Registry, 363,
    402
National Endowment for the Arts
    (NEA), 45–52
  application process, 47
  arts audience statistics, 306
  arts managers, 50–51
  arts research, 361
  book references, 45
  budget battles and censorship,
    48–50, 111–112
  censorship, 49, 111–112
  consumer spending statistics, 4
  creation of, 45
  funding for arts, 24, 45, 47, 49f, 144,
    383, 409–410
  goals, 46
  government support, 47–48
  international activities, 46–47
  leadership initiatives, 47
  national initiatives, 46–47
  new directions, 50
  peer review process, 410
  state agencies, 51–52
  strategic plan, 46
  in twentieth century, 30–31
  vision/mission statements, 46
National Labor Relations Board
    (NLRB), 211–212
National Medal of Arts, 47
National Study of Arts Managers, 42
need-based motivation theories
  acquired-needs theory, 239
  description of, 237
  ERG Theory, 237–238

Maslow's hierarchy of needs, 71–73,
    237–238
  two-factor theory, 238
needs, 349
negative reinforcement, 243
NEH (National Endowment for the
    Humanities), 45, 410
net assets, 330
news aggregators, 91
niche strategy, 369
nineteenth century arts, 28–29
nonprofit arts organizations
  business of arts/entertainment, 2, 5
  creating, 35–36
  IRS filings, 331
  market failure and arts, 309–310
  shareholders, 36
  tax exemptions, 36–37
nonprofit financial management, 325
normative leadership model, 232

O

objectives, 124
  management by, 273
  planning/plans, 138, 139f, 140f
Occupational Safety and Health
    Administration (OSHA), 97
off-Broadway, 30
Older Workers Benefit Protection Act
    (1990), 196
online worlds, 117–118
on-the-job management theory, 61
on-the-job training (OJT), 39–40, 61,
    203
open system model, 7, 430
  environments. *See* environments
  organizations as, 8f, 158f
  systems theory, 74
opera companies
  growth and change example, 88–89
  mergers (case study), 183–185
opera, history of, 27, 30
operant conditioning, 242
operating budgets, 287
operational control, 266
  areas for, 269
  in art organizations, 270–271, 275
  assessment of results, 268–269
  case study, 297–298
  clarity of objectives, 266
  complexity, 267
  corrective actions, 269
  degree of centralization/
    decentralization, 267

elements of, 267–270
financial areas, 275
human limitations, 267
input standards, 270–271
internal/external controls, 272
leadership influences, 269
limitations, 269
management by exception, 271–273
management by objectives, 273
as management function, 266–267
measure/compare performance, 268
output standards, 269
performance appraisal systems, 273–274
performance objectives, 268
process diagram, 268f
steps in, 267–269
summary, 275, 296
uncertainty, 266–267
operational level of management, 8
operational management, 8
operational plans, 33, 126–128, 140f
operations research (OR), 73
opportunity budgets, 287
orchestras, in twentieth century, 31
Oregon Shakespeare Festival Mission, Vision, and Values Statement, 14–15
organic manager, 424f, 426–427
organic organizational design, 158–159
organizational behavior modification (OBM), 242–243
organizational charts, 161–169
departments/work groups, 164–168
division of work, 162
examples, 163f, 164f, 165f, 166f, 167f
lines of communication, 169
management levels, 9f, 168
matrix organization, 175f
work performed, 162
working relationships, 163
organizational culture and management, 423–425
organizational design
approaches, 157–158
bureaucratic, 159–161
impact on MIS, 278
informal, 169–170
mechanistic/organic, 158–159
organizational structure, 161
art manager's perspective, 170–176
in business plans, 33
departmentalization, 173–176

by division, 173
external environment, 172
by function, 173
informal, 169–170
management levels, 9f
matrix organization, 173–176
mergers (case study), 183–185
people, 171
size, 171–172
strategy, 170–171
technology and environment, 172
organizations, 7, 156. See also arts organizations
administrative structure (example), 160f
agency, 171
audit of, 423
dysfunctional, 420–422
fundraising role of, 391–392
growth of, 179–180
life in, 156
structure. See organizational structure
summary, 182
organized labor, 197
organizing, 7, 156
for arts, 157
benefits of, 156–157
coordination, 176–179
by management, 17
process of, 7–8
orientation, 189f, 202–203
output, open systems, 8f, 158f
output standards for control, 269
Owen, Robert, 63, 65f

P
pageant masters, 26–27
paradigms, 76–77
participating style of leadership, 233
participative management, 72
Path-Goal Theory, 233
payables, 329
payroll math, 449
people and organizational structure, 171
performance appraisals
critical incident appraisal, 274
and firing, 205
free-form narrative, 274
personnel appraisal methods, 274
systems for, 273–274
timely feedback, 274–275
performance-outcome expectancy, 241

permanently restricted funds, 330
permanently restricted net assets, 330
personnel. See human resources management; staff
Pew Charitable Trust, 91, 113
pioneers in management, 63–64
place and four Ps of marketing, 356–357
place utility, 350, 351
planning/plans, 124
action plans, 138, 139f, 140f
bottom-up planning, 141–142
budgets, 127
careers, 462
context of, 122
contingency planning, 142
creative approach, 431
crisis planning, 142, 432
decision making, 144–148
developing business plans, 141
difficulty of, 125–126
evaluation systems, 138, 140f
functions of management, 16–17, 19
fundraising plans, 383–385, 387f
goals, 138, 139f, 140f
intermediate-range plans, 125, 432
limits of, 143–144
long-range plans, 125, 432
marketing plan, 33, 140f, 364f, 365–368
necessity of, 123
objectives, 138, 139f, 140f
operational plans, 126–128, 140f
as organization's map/leadership, 123
other approaches, 141
planning document, 139f
process of
formulating strategies, 136–137
mission analysis, 131–133
mission statement, 128–131
resource analysis, 135–136
sample, 144–145
situational analysis, 134–135
vision statement resources, 133–134
production schedules, 127–128
questions answered by, 124
relationship of, to arts, 123
resources, 142
short-range plans, 125, 431–432
single-use plans, 127–128
standing-use plans, 127–128
strategic plans, 126–128, 129f, 140f

planning/plans (*continued*)
  summary, 150–151
  terminology, 124–125
  top-down planning, 141–142
  uncertainty, 266–267
point-of-purchase systems, 354
political and legal environment
  described, 94–96
  government regulations, 195–196
  IRS Form 990 changes, 96–97
  lobbying for arts, 95
  other input sources, 96–99
Poor, Henry Varnum, 64, 65f
portfolios, 458–459
position power, 226
possession utility, 350, 351
Potential Rating Index for Zip Markets
    (PRIZM), 360, 361
power, 222, 225–229
  acceptance theory of, 228
  coercive, 226
  expert, 227
  guidelines for using, 229
  legitimate, 226
  limits to, 227–228
  personal, 226–227
  position, 226
  questions regarding, 226
  reference, 227
  sources of, 226
  zone of indifference, 228–229
Pregnancy Discrimination Act (1978),
    196
preindustrialization, 62
press release, 347
prices
  four Ps of marketing, 356–357
  inelastic, 320
  price/revenue matrix, 321f
  scaling the house, 322–323
  summary, 323
  supply/demand effect on, 316, 318
  ticket revenue, 311
print media, 111–112
Privacy Act (1974), 196
problem solving, 146–148
  alternatives and final choice, 148
  defining problems, 147–148
  expected vs. unexpected problems, 146
  risks, 148
  steps/techniques, 146–147
process management model, 427–429
product and four Ps of marketing,
    356–357

product orientation for marketing, 355
production era of marketing, 352
production schedules, 127–128
productivity, 74, 306
professional associations, as
    information source, 112
professional manager, 425
profits, 2, 5, 37, 314f
programming plans, 140f
project budgets, 287, 291
project organization, 20
projection, 257
promotional activities, 346. *See also*
    marketing
promotions and four Ps of marketing,
    356–357
psychographic profile, 359
psychological satisfaction, 349
public relations, 432–433
  functions of management, 18–19
  media, 111–112

Q
quantitative approaches, 73–74

R
railroads, effect of, 29, 31, 64, 66
RAND research, 4, 5, 91, 106, 113, 114
ratio analysis, 336–337
Reagan administration and NEA, 48
receivables, 329
recessions, 93–94
reciprocity and corporate giving, 406
recognition seeking, 250
recruitment of staff
  difficulties, 198–199
  external, 198
  internal, 197
  philosophies about, 198
  step in staffing process, 189f
  steps in, 197
reference checking, 202
reference power, 227
Reformation, 62
Rehabilitation Act (1973), 196
reinforcement-based motivation
    theories
  description of, 237, 242–243
  organizational behavior
      modification, 242–243
relationship behaviors, 232
Renaissance, 27–28, 62–63
research
  arts, 361

focus groups, 361
market, 359–361
tool for demographics, 104–105
reserve funds, 340
resident theater companies, 30
resource analysis, 135–136
restricted gifts, 397
restricted net assets, 330
résumé
  development of, 456
  skill-based structure, 454–456
retrenchment strategy, 137
revenue centers, 286
revenues
  budgetary process, 288
  fundraising statistics, 380, 383
  income statements, 332
  maximization of, 320–322
  price/revenue matrix, 321f
  spending more than, 310–311
reward power, 226
risks and problem solving, 148
Robert's Rules of Order, 252–253
Roethlisberger, Fritz, 71
Roman civilization and arts, 25–26, 62

S
salaries
  for actors, 212
  arts managers, 42, 43–44
  budget and, 447
  cost of living, 448
  designer's contract, 212–213
  employer's perspective, 446–447
  in job description, 193–194
  negotiation strategies, 449–450
  payroll math, 449
  research, 447–448
sales era of marketing, 352
sales orientation for marketing, 355
scalar principle, 176
scale, economies/diseconomies of,
    315
scaling the house, 322–323
Scheff, Joanne, 348, 355
scientific management, 60, 64, 66,
    73–74
screening applicants, 201
selection process, employee, 189f,
    199–202
selective perception, 257
self-confessing, 249
self-control/self-efficacy, 244
self-fulfilling prophecies, 225

seventeenth to nineteenth century arts, 28–29
shared tacit assumptions, corporate culture, 181
shareholders, 36
shifting paradigms, 76–77
shoe leather network, 280
short-range plans, 125, 431–432
single-use plans, 127–128
situational analysis, 134–135
situational leadership, 231–233
Six Sigma, 76, 77
size of organizations, 171–172
Skinner, B. F., 230f, 242
Smithsonian, 31, 383
social and cultural environment, 99–103
social exchange model for giving, 381
social learning theory, 237, 243–244
social science, management as, 60–62
span of control, 177
special pleading, 250
stability strategy, 136
staff
    administrative titles/organization (example), 160f
    Board of Directors and, 251
    in dysfunctional organizations, 420–422
    employee manual (sample), 218
    employment-at-will, 205
    firing of, 204–205
    fundraising by, 384–385, 392–393, 400–401
    hiring of, 202, 459–460
    as information source, 110–111
    job description, 191–194
    levels of management, 168
    people and organizational structure, 171
    performance standards, 270–271, 429
    recruitment of, 197–199
    "right stuff", 215–216
    salaries/benefits, 193–194
    selection process, 199–202
staffing. See human resources management
standing-use plans, 127–128
state agencies, NEA, 51–52
statement of activity, 334f, 335–336
stereotypes, 256
strategic fit and corporate giving, 406
strategic level of management, 9–10

strategic plans and planning
    described, 126–128
    diagrams of, 129f, 140f
    formulating strategies, 136–137
    fundraising, 386, 387f
    marketing, 352, 363, 364f, 366–368, 433–434
    organizational structure, 170–171
strategies, 136–137
    combination strategy, 137
    growth strategy, 137
    retrenchment strategy, 137
    stability strategy, 136
subscription ticket sales, 353
substitute goods or services, 316
success, calibrating, 149
summary budget, 289, 290f
supply. See also demand
    determinants, 318
    elasticity, 319
    law of, 317–318
    price of resources, 318
    revenue maximization, 320–322
    scaling the house, 322–323
    suppliers, 318–319
Survey of Public Participation in the Arts (SPPA), 360–361
SWOT (strengths, weaknesses, opportunities, threats) analysis, 85, 129f, 134f
symbolic processes, 244
sympathy seeking, 250
symphony orchestra
    mergers (case study), 183–185
    organizational chart, 164f
Synderman, B., 230f, 238
synergy, 74–75, 109
systems manager, 424f, 425–426
systems theory, 74

T
target marketing, 357
task activities, 250–251
task behaviors, 232
task groups, 246
tastes and demand, 317
taxes
    for-profit vs. nonprofit benefits, 2
    generated by arts, 93
    IRS Form 990, 96–97, 331, 342
    tax exemptions, 36–37
    unrelated business income tax, 37
Taylor, Frederick W., 65f, 66
T-bills, 338

TCG (Theatre Communications Group), 43, 208, 251, 365
technology
    concerns about future of arts, 5–6
    environments, 105–106
    growth of arts/entertainment, 2–4
    modern marketing, 353–354
    organizational structure, 172
    shifting paradigms, 76–77
    in twenty-first century, 31
telephone solicitations, 402–403
telling style of leadership, 232–233
temporarily restricted net assets, 330
temporary groups, 245
testing, 161
testing applicants, 202
The Syndicate, 29
Theory X and Theory Y (McGregor), 72–73, 225
Theory Z, 75
ticket prices, 311, 320
time utility, 350, 351
timeline, management, 65f
Title VII Civil Rights Act (1964), 196
top-down planning, 141–142
total fixed cost (TFC), 312–314
total quality management (TQM), 75–76
total variable costs (TVC), 312–314
tracking, for fundraising, 394–395, 404
training
    apprenticeships, 204
    arts managers, 39–40, 61
    coaching, 203–204
    formal training and development, 203
    internships, 204
    job rotation and cross-training, 203
    modeling, 204
    on-the-job, 39–40, 61, 203
    step in staffing process, 189f
trait approach to leadership, 231
transaction, 329
transactional leadership, 233–234
transformational leadership, 233–234
trends
    book sources for, 101–103
    discussion focus, 117–118
    impact on arts, 113–115
turnover, staff, 421–422
twentieth century arts, 29–31
twenty-first century arts, 31
two-factor theory, 238

U

UBIT (unrelated business income tax), 37
unions, 211
  actor salaries, 212
  for artists/employees, 209–210
  constraints on staffing, 197
  designer's contract, 212–213
  disputes, 211–212
  management vs., 214, 435
  sample contract, 210–211
United Scenic Artists (USA), 210
unrestricted gifts, 397
unrestricted net assets, 330

V

valence, 241
value statements
  sample, 13–15
  Seacoast Repertory Theatre (case study), 151–152
values, 122
vertical coordination, 176–179
  centralization-decentralization, 178–179
  chain of command, 176–177
  delegation, 177–178
  scalar principle, 176
  span of control, 177
vicarious learning, 244
virtual worlds, 117–118
visa processing rules, 95
vision, 122
vision statements
  in business plans, 32–33
  NEA, 46
  resources, 133–134
  sample, 13–15
  Seacoast Repertory Theatre (case study), 151–152
Volunteer Lawyers for the Arts, 34, 37
volunteers, 206–207
Vroom, Victor, 230f, 232, 240–241, 259

W

wants, 349
Web blogs, 91, 361, 372, 373
Web sites
  Americans for the Arts, 91, 93, 98f, 303
  e-fundraising, 404–405
  for evaluating arts organizations, 20
  looking for arts content, 90–91
  managementandthearts.com (this book), xix
  for marketing, 347, 361–362
  resources for fundraising MIS, 393–394
  union contracts, 210, 212
withdrawing, 250
Wolf, Thomas, 391, 398
work
  activities performed at, 190
  artists and, 217, 304
  standards for, 190–191
  tools necessary for, 190
work groups/departments, 164–168
Works Progress Administration (WPA), 95–96
wrongful-discharge, 205

Y

Yetton, Phillip, 230f, 232
YouTube, 91, 347

Z

zero-based budgets, 287
zone of indifference, 228–229